TEACHER'S MANUAL

to

STATE AND FEDERAL ADMINISTRATIVE LAW

Third Edition

■ ■ ■

By
Michael Asimow
Professor of Law Emeritus
University of California, Los Angeles
Ronald M. Levin
Henry Hitchcock Professor of Law
Washington University of St. Louis

AMERICAN CASEBOOK SERIES®

WEST®
A Thomson Reuters business

Mat # 40339171

© West, a Thomson business, 1998
© 2009 Thomson Reuters

    610 Opperman Drive
    St. Paul, MN 55123
    1–800–313–9378

Printed in the United States of America

ISBN: 978–0–314–15929–8

PREFACE

This teacher's manual is lengthier than most others of its kind. For each of the principal sections of the casebook, we have provided an overlay of commentary, often including pedagogical suggestions or additional research references. Whenever you find a discussion question in the Notes and Questions in the casebook, you can generally expect to find our answers here. And we have provided detailed analyses of all of the teaching problems. You may disagree with some of our views, but at least you will never be at a loss to figure out what cockeyed notion might have prompted us to include a given case or question in the book. You will always know just what cockeyed notion it was.

We have spelled out the main pedagogical choices that underlie the design of the casebook and manual in an article we published several years ago. Michael Asimow & Ronald M. Levin, "Thoughts and Heresies on Teaching Administrative Law," 38 Brandeis L.J. 259 (2000). This essay may be especially helpful to an instructor who is considering whether to adopt the book, or who is tackling the course for the first time. As we noted in the preface and introduction to the text, the casebook can readily be used to teach an exclusively federal law course, but we believe the state law coverage in the book offers a number of benefits to students. You may well find that the comparisons between federal and state law engage your interest more fully in some contexts than in others.

You will probably not be able to cover the entire book in your course, at least if you teach a standard three-credit course. In the pages following the table of contents, we have provided some sample syllabi as models that you might wish to use as starting points for constructing your own syllabus. As you will see, the two of us have somewhat different approaches to the course, as regards both the topics we cover and the manner in which we teach them. Asimow teaches a four-hour course, with supplementary state-law material included. He focuses primarily on the problems. He starts each class with a problem and uses it as the vehicle for teaching the material in the cases and notes. Levin teaches a three-hour course. He usually concentrates on federal law, although he raises state law issues from time to time. He focuses on cases in some units and on problems in other units, depending on the contents of the individual section.

We hope that the admittedly opinionated comments in this manual will prove useful to you. Any feedback on the book or manual would be most welcome. A number of changes we have made in the third edition are based on suggestions we received from users of the second edition. If you find from time to time that you disagree with our analysis, please consider dropping one of us a line to explain why—perhaps your perspective will show up in a future edition of this manual. Good luck with the course!

Michael Asimow
asimow@law.ucla.edu

Ronald M. Levin
levin@wulaw.wustl.edu

Table of Contents

PART 2. NONJUDICIAL CONTROL OF AGENCY ACTION

PART 3. JUDICIAL REVIEW

[On this syllabus, assignments for each class day are shown in the left column. A plus sign means that material assigned for that day will not be finished until the following day. The syllabus shows assignments for a 39-hour class (52 minutes per class).]

WASHINGTON UNIVERSITY SCHOOL OF LAW

Administrative Law   **Syllabus**
Fall 2009 [projected]   **Professor Ronald Levin**

Texts: Michael Asimow & Ronald M. Levin, <u>State and Federal Administrative Law</u> (3d ed. 2009).

Optional: Ernest Gellhorn & Ronald M. Levin, <u>Administrative Law and Process in a Nutshell</u> (5th ed. 2006).

Many assignments contain references to the federal Administrative Procedure Act (APA) and the 1981 Model State APA (MSAPA). Both acts are reprinted in the appendices. For purposes of class preparation, you are responsible for all sections discussed in assigned text. The final exam will be based primarily on federal law, but you will also be responsible for any state law matters that have been discussed in class.

Many sections of the casebook end with a "Problem" applying the material. We will frequently discuss these problems in class, so please think about them as part of your preparation.

Day

1   <u>I. INTRODUCTION</u>: Chapter 1 (be prepared to discuss the problem in § 1.7).

         <u>II. CONSTITUTIONAL RIGHT TO BE HEARD</u> (Ch. 2)

"   A. Due process hearings, and mass justice: § 2.1.

2+   B. Interests protected by due process: liberty and property: § 2.2.

3   C. Timing of the hearing: § 2.3.

4+   D. Elements of a constitutionally fair hearing: § 2.4.

5   E. Rulemaking versus adjudication: § 2.5.

* * * * * * * *

[This syllabus assumes a four credit course, of which one of the four credits is devoted to teaching California administrative law. If the California materials are removed, the syllabus is suitable for a three-credit course. The CA materials are contained in a separate book referenced below (referred to as A&C). Instructors might wish to teach their own state law if four credits are available.

Note that the assignments are based on 70 minute sessions; the hourly allocations would need to be adjusted for the conventional 50 minute class. |

Mr. Asimow   216 Administrative Law   Fall 2009

ASSIGNMENT SHEET

The required books are Asimow & Levin, *State and Federal Administrative Law* (3d ed. 2009) (hereinafter "A&L"); and Asimow & Cohen, *California Administrative Law* (2002) (hereinafter "A&C). Recommended: ABA Section of Administrative Law and Regulatory Practice, *A Black Letter Statement of Federal Administrative Law* (2004). In each assignment, *concentrate on the problems*, which will usually be discussed in detail.

You are responsible for Federal and California Administrative Procedure Act (FAPA and CA APA) provisions cited in this assignment sheet and in the text. (The APAs are in the back of A&L and A&C.) However, you are *not* responsible for the Model State Administrative Procedure Act of 1981 (MSAPA) provisions, which are frequently cited in A&L, except as otherwise noted.

The following assignments assume a class "hour" of 70 minutes. These time allocations are just estimates and we will often spend more or less time on an assignment than as scheduled below. There will be a system of "assigned experts," meaning you will be assigned to a particular week. Normally I will call only on the assigned experts.

I. INTRODUCTION

1   A&L 1-12; A&C v-vi. Concentrate on the problem, A&L 12.

II. THE CONSTITUTIONAL RIGHT TO A HEARING

2-6   A. Hearing and welfare termination: due process and mass justice. A&L 14-26.

         B. Interests protected by due process: liberty and property. A&L 27-43. A&C 56-58.

C. Timing and elements of trial-type hearings

      1. Timing. A&L 43-53. A&C 61-62 (top).

      2. Elements. A&L 53-61. A&C 58-66 (except 61-62).

D. Rulemaking-adjudication distinction. A&L 62-68. A&C 66-68.

III. ADMINISTRATIVE ADJUDICATION: FUNDAMENTAL PROBLEMS

7-8   A. Statutory rights to a hearing in adjudication. A&L 3-5; 69-84. A&C 55-56, 68-78. Federal   APA (hereinafter "FAPA"): §§551(4) to (9) & 554(a). Calif. APA (hereinafter "CA APA") Gov't Code §§11405.50(a) & 11410.10 (located at A&C p. 241).

B. Limiting issues to which hearing rights apply. A&L 84-91. FAPA §555(e).

9-12   C. The conflict between institutional and judicialized decisionmaking:

      1. Personal responsibility of decisionmakers and exclusive record requirement. A&L 91-98. A&C 90 (bottom)-94, 104-05 (top). FAPA §§556(e), 557(c). CA APA §§11517.

      2. Ex parte contact. A&L 98-107. A&C 115-22. FAPA §§551(14), 557(d), 556(d) (4th sentence). CA APA §§11430.10 to 11430.80.

      3. Legislative pressure. A&L 108-13 (only brief coverage of this subject in class)

      4. Separation of functions and internal agency communications. A&L 113-22, A&C 94-95. FAPA §554(d). CA APA §§11425.30, 11430.30(a).

      5. Bias. A&L 122-28. A&C 100 (bottom)-104. FAPA §556(b). CA APA §11425.40,
          11512(c).

      6. Administrative law judges and decisional independence. A&L 128-37, A&C 78-79 (middle) (very little class time on this material).

IV. THE PROCESS OF ADMINISTRATIVE ADJUDICATION

13-14   A. The pre-hearing phase

     1. Notice and participation. A&L 138-45. FAPA §§554(b), 555(b). CA APA §§11440.50.

     2. Investigation, discovery, & ADR. A&L 145-56. A&C 79-80. CA APA §§11507.5 to 11507.7.

   B. The hearing phase: Evidence and official notice. A&L 156-69. A&C 80-83, 88-89. FAPA §§556(d), (e). CA APA §§11513, 11521, 11515, 11425.50(c).

   C. The decision phase: finding facts and stating reasons. A&L 170-77. A&C 89-90. Only brief discussion of this topic in class). FAPA §557(c). CA APA §11425.50.

V. RULEMAKING PROCEDURES

15-20   A. Introduction and definition of rule, retroactivity: A&L 10-12, 192-211. A&C 32.
     FAPA §§551(4) to (7). CA APA §§ 11342.600, 11405.50(a).

   B. Rulemaking process:

     1. Initiating rulemaking A&L 211-22 (top). A&C 32-37. FAPA §553. Scan quickly the CA APA provisions on rulemaking at A&C 241-263.

     2. Formal v. informal rulemaking. A&L 222-29. FAPA §§553(c), 551(4).

     3. Hybrid rulemaking & judicial discretion. A&L 230-39 (top). A&C 29-32 (top).

     4. Procedural regularity in rulemaking. A&L 239-62.

     5. Findings and reasons; publication. A&L 262-71. FAPA§553(c), (d). CA APA §11346.9.

   C. Regulatory analysis and regulatory negotiation. A&L 280-304. A&C 37-40.

VI. POLICYMAKING ALTERNATIVES

21-24   A. Exemptions from rulemaking procedure

     1. Good cause. A&L 305-12. A&C 48-51. FAPA §§553(b), (d), (e). CA APA §§11346.1 & 11349.6.

     2. Exempted subject matter. A&L 312-15. A&C 40-41. FAPA §553(a).

     3. Procedural rules. A&L 316-19.

     4. Non-legislative rules. A&L 319-42. A&C 42-48. CA APA §11340.5.

  B. Required rulemaking. A&L 342-54. A&C 51 (bottom)-53.

  C. Rulemaking petitions and agency agenda-setting. A&L 354-63.

VII. SEPARATION OF POWERS AND CHECKS AND BALANCES IN ADMINISTRATIVE LAW

25-26   A. Delegation of legislative power. A&L 371-98. A&C 7 (from ¶1.2)-11, 22-26 (to note 4).

  B. Delegation of adjudicative power. A&L 398-406. A&C 12-21, 26 n.4 to 28.

27-29   C. Legislative controls. A&L 406-30. A&C 1-4.

  D. Executive branch controls and removal power. A&L 430-61. A&C 4 (from ¶1.1.3)-7 (to ¶1.2).

  E. Executive oversight. A&L 461-476.

  F. Freedom of information. A&L 477-88. FAPA §552.

VIII. SCOPE OF JUDICIAL REVIEW

30-35   A. Scope of review of agency findings of basic fact. A&L 501-19. A&C 159-61, 172-81. FAPA §706. CA CCP §1094.5 (at A&C 317-19).

  B. Scope of review of issues of legal interpretation. A&L 519-66. A&C 181-90.

C. Judicial review of discretionary determinations

    1. Discretion in adjudication. A&L 566-81.A&C 193-96. FAPA §706(2)(A).

    2. Discretion in rulemaking. A&L 582-601. A&C 196-99.

IX. JUDICIAL REVIEWABILITY OF AGENCY DECISIONS

36-38 A. Judicial remedies. A&L 602-609 (top) (this material will not be discussed in detail but it is essential background). A&C 159-72, 204-05. CA CCP §§1085, 1094.5.

B. Recovery of fees. A&L 615-19. A&C 131-42. CA CCP §1021.5.

C. Preclusion of judicial review. A&L 619-26.

D. Commitment to agency discretion. A&L 626-35

E. Agency inaction and delay. A&L 635-42.

X. STANDING AND TIMING

39-40 A. Standing to seek judicial review.

    1. Constitutional standing doctrine. A&L 643-57. A&C 199-204. FAPA §702.

    2. Standing under the APA. A&L 657-63. A&C 199-204.

41-42 B. Timing of judicial review

    1. Final orders, ripeness, stays. A&L 663-70, 681-91. A&C 212-13. FAPA §§704, 705.

    2. Exhaustion of remedies. A&L 670-81. A&C 205-11. FAPA §704.

    3. Primary jurisdiction. A&L 691-99.

CHAPTER 1: INTRODUCTION

Chapter 1 may be used either as the basis for the first class or as an assignment to be read as background before the first class, so that the first class can begin with § 2.1. The first class can be taught effectively by focusing on the problem in § 1.7 as an introduction to the administrative process and to theories of regulation.

§ 1.3 STATE AND FEDERAL ADMINISTRATIVE LAW

State law matters because students are far more likely to practice state administrative law than federal administrative law. Students (at least those practicing outside the Washington D.C. area) are quite likely to appear before their state medical board or state insurance or securities commissioner, or their local zoning board, but are unlikely ever to see the inside of the Federal Communications Commission. Moreover, state law and federal law differ at many points and the comparison is often instructive.

For a more complete discussion of the reasons for studying state as well as federal administrative law, and the differences between federal and state agencies, see Arthur E. Bonfield, "State Law in the Teaching of Administrative Law: A Critical Analysis of the Status Quo," 61 Tex L.Rev. 95 (1982).

Because they will be relevant throughout the course, it may be helpful during the introductory class to talk about some of the differences between state and federal agencies. In general, state agencies have much smaller staffs and budgets than federal agencies. They are more likely to be headed by part-time heads. State and local agencies tend to deal with less affluent people than federal agencies. People are less likely to be represented by counsel when dealing with state and local agencies.

§ 1.4 ADMINISTRATIVE PROCEDURE ACTS

You may wish to distribute a copy of the APA of the state in which your law school is located or, in the alternative, require students to obtain a copy of the APA of the state where they plan to practice. You might consider holding them responsible for comparing the various provisions of that statute with the federal Act. Many users of this casebook (including one of the authors) teach the administrative law of their state extensively along with the federal provisions.

The 1961 Model State APA (adopted in more than half the states) was quite brief. In contrast, the 1981 Act was lengthy and complex. It contained many cutting-edge provisions. Probably it was over-ambitious, both in its detail and in its prescriptions. For whatever reason, it fared poorly, although major parts of it were adopted in several states such as Utah and Washington. The new Act, under consideration as this book is written, reflects the more modest aspirations of the 1961 Act, but updates that Act in many ways.

The 50th anniversary of the federal APA gave rise to an outpouring of scholarship. In addition to Shepherd's article (which is revisionist in tone), see the symposia in 10 Admin.L.J.Am.U. 1 (1996); 32 Tulsa L.J. 185 (1996); 48 Admin.L.Rev. 307 (1996); and 72 Chi.-Kent L.Rev. 951 (1997).

§ 1.6 AGENCY LEGITIMACY AND ADMINISTRATIVE LAW

This subsection presents one of the major themes for the course, but whether it should be discussed during the first class is debatable. Students may not yet be ready for it. It may be better to refer back to it when you turn to the material on rulemaking or to political control of agencies. The theories of agency legitimacy can be analyzed in class, particularly in connection with the snapshot material in § 1.5 or the biotech problem in § 1.7. Discussion might stress the difficulties in the modern context of ensuring agency legitimacy, the futility of efforts to devise any single theory to justify the legitimacy of the administrative process, and the benefits of seeking legitimacy through procedural regularity and checks and balances.

§ 1.7 PROBLEM

This problem can be used to raise general questions about whether to regulate any presently unregulated sector of the economy. Examples are whether and how to regulate nutritional supplements, cloning, or auto repair. Discussion might focus on emerging technologies such as genetically modified food, genetic testing of human beings, nanotechnology, emission of greenhouse gases, quarantines or other drastic measures to combat a pandemic, control of the internet or other emerging communication technologies, toxic chemicals, DNA registries, or the testing and introduction into the market of new drugs. The basic issue is whether it is better to i) regulate the field, creating an agency with broad power to make rules and engage in law enforcement, licensing, and adjudication, or ii) leave the field unregulated except by market forces and allow the common law of torts, contracts, property or nuisance to handle any resulting problems. Another way to frame the discussion is whether regulation should take the form of cost-benefit analysis and utilitarianism; or whether regulators should pursue the "precautionary principle" and protect the public from risks that are difficult to measure, even if such protection appears not to be cost-effective.

One author uses this problem to teach the entire first class, mostly developing the material in § 1.5—the snapshot of the administrative process—as applied to biotech. The focus is to introduce the administrative sector—a part of government about which students have only vague and uncertain notions but, often, strong political convictions. Students have been nurtured on first-year common law and traditional three-branch civics analysis, and don't comprehend how agencies fit into that scheme. Students also tend to be pretty hostile to government these days, so it's useful to explain why agencies and regulatory schemes exist—and in many cases have to exist. The goal is to convey what agencies actually do, what life would be like without them, and how they impact the private sector and the work of private attorneys. It can also be used to test out legitimacy issues in § 1.6.

a. *General comments on regulation of biotechnology. Foundation on Economic Trends* was a lawsuit brought by an environmental activist to stop an experiment similar to that described in the problem. It's an illustration of how influential courts are in making fundamental political decisions. In most countries, such disputes would be settled politically, not through the courts. In addition, a field like biotechnology might be nationalized, rather than remain in the private sector and be regulated by government.

The experiment would have been the first release of genetically engineered bacteria into the environment. If the technology works, it could save billions of dollars, and it might be among the first of many genetically engineered products of incalculable value. For example, there could be bacteria to eat oil spills or dioxin, nitrogen fixers (that could eliminate the need for nitrogen fertilizer), plants that produce pharmaceuticals or resist weed-killers, cows that produce more milk, bigger transgenic fish, and a range of anti-cancer drugs. We are at the dawn of an emerging technology. The Mandel article, cited in text, gives a complete overview of the whole field of biotech innovation. Many of the possible products are much scarier (but the potential benefits are much greater) than the experiment described in the problem. McGarity's article, which focuses on genetically modified food, is also excellent. Another useful resource is a symposium on the regulation of genetically modified organisms in the U.S. and Europe. 16 Kansas J.L. & Pub.Pol. 257-463 (2007).

But: consider the consequences of the introduction into the ecosystem of a successful new life form, and think about some of the ecological disasters of the past: the kudzu vine, gypsy moth (introduced as substitute for the silkworm), the mongoose in Hawaii (introduced to kill rats that ate sugar cane, but mongooses ate few rats and wiped out numerous Hawaiian birds), chestnut blight (accidental introduction of a virus that wiped out entire species of trees), garden snails in California, or rabbits in Australia. The killing of wolves led to proliferation of deer that destroyed vast areas. Opponents of this experiment fear that the new bacteria will displace the old one and create incalculable harm—for example to insects and vegetables that are already frost resistant. Some people think it could detrimentally affect the entire climate by altering the process of making rain and ice.

Although genetic technology is in its infancy, there has already been a big economic disaster involving the mixing of regular corn seed with genetically engineered Starlink corn. Starlink corn was intended only for animal feed, because it contained a dangerous human allergen, but it turned up in taco shells and many other food products. The Starlink fiasco cost hundreds of millions of dollars to remedy, but it was inevitable that the bio-corn would get mixed up with regular corn. *See* Mandel, 45 Wm. & Mary L. Rev. at 2203-16 (describing Starlink and three other unexpected problems); McGarity, 35 U.Mich.J.L.Ref. at 472-87.

But: all types of science and technology are dangerous, all have risks. Every new chemical introduced into the environment, every new drug might contain unexpected environmental or health hazards. We have to accept some degree of risk to let technology advance. How to balance the risks and benefits of such innovations, such as genetically engineered products like the virus in the problem, is an enormous challenge. On the benefits and risks of genetically modified life forms, see Mandel, *supra*, at 2179-2202; McGarity, *supra*, at 406-26. A second challenge is to design the optimal regulatory mechanism to protect us from excessive risks without stifling the technology.

b. *Regulation of release of genetically engineered material.* If you want some background on the actual regulation of biotech (although it's not necessary to teach this class), here is a summary. Mandel, *supra*, at 2216-30, explains that the Coordinated Framework for the Regulation of Biotechnology was adopted in 1986. It splits regulation between FDA (food safety issues), EPA (pest-protected plants), and USDA (genetically modified plants). It is unclear whether FDA or USDA would have authority over the freeze-resistant virus.

The idea of the Coordinated Framework was that no new legislation was needed, and that genetically modified life forms are no different or more dangerous than familiar plants and animals that have been modified by selective breeding, as has been done for centuries. This approach has facilitated the rapid penetration of genetically modified (GM) food into the American market (in Europe there is a large political movement against GM food). Mandel and McGarity take vigorous exception to this "substantial equivalence" premise. They believes that genetic manipulation is more dangerous by orders of magnitude than traditional selective breeding. A genetically engineered tomato that resists pesticides is not "substantially equivalent" to a tomato whose size, taste, or color has been modified through traditional methods. They explain in detail the numerous gaps and

4

inconsistencies in biotech regulation and the incompetence and inexperience of many of the officials who are regulating it. Mandel, *supra*, at 2230-42; McGarity, *supra*, at 432-72). None of this detail is necessary to discussion of the problem; it may be simpler to just assume a regulatory vacuum and talk about how a good regulatory system could be constructed and what it should do.

The decision in *Foundation for Economic Trends* blocked the experiment because of failure by the National Institute of Health to issue an environmental impact statement (this is an opportunity to discuss NEPA and the EIS process if you're so inclined). The trial court decision blocked not only the particular release, but also all future releases, until a programmatic EIS was prepared. The appellate court affirmed the decision only as to the particular release. *See* Norman L. Rave, Note, "Interagency Conflict and Administrative Accountability: Regulating the Release of Recombinant Organisms," 77 Geo. L.J. 1787 (1989), for discussion of the case and the bureaucratic infighting that it triggered; Judy J. Kim, Note, "Out of the Lab and into the Field: Harmonization of Deliberate Release Regulations for Genetically Modified Organisms," 16 Fordham Int'l L.J. 1160 (1992-93) (international survey). Our understanding is that the bacterium was successfully tested but that regulatory snarls and opposition by environmental groups caused the manufacturer to give up on the process. Other methods for dealing with the frost problem by manipulating plant genes are currently under development.

A piecemeal local approach is probably the worst possible solution to the problem, although the present federal regulatory hodgepodge invites local regulation. In the absence of comprehensive federal regulation of biotech, state regulation is probably the second-best approach. Such agencies have emerged in twelve states. *See* Christine C. Vito, Comment, "State Biotechnology Oversight: The Juncture of Technology, Law and Public Policy," 45 Maine L.Rev. 329 (1993). Minnesota and North Carolina statutes require experimenters to get permits before releasing genetically engineered material. New York and Maine statutes set up a new agency with rulemaking and adjudicatory power. The Vito Comment finds the Maine agency (Commission on Biotechnology and Genetic Engineering) to have the best approach taken in any state.

c. *An agency to regulate biotech.* We often assume that industry always resists government regulation and prefers market approaches, but often this is not the case. The biotech industry might be begging for regulation. Why? First—it's getting cut up badly at the local level. Each city thinks the experiment should occur somewhere else. Second—concern about tort liability is severe (just imagine what might happen if a catastrophic accident resulted from such an experiment). Third—dissatisfaction with existing piecemeal federal regulation. Fourth—make sure there's orderly approval of experiments, so some irresponsible competitor won't rush ahead with an ill-planned experiment that could trigger a PR disaster and prompt drastic legislation that could kill the industry. Note that industries often favor regulation and mistrust an unregulated environment, either because they dislike the competitive market or because of concerns about irresponsible members of the industry.

Can the legislature regulate genetic engineering without an agency? No. Only an expert and specialized agency can regulate experimentation on a case-by-case basis. But there's another side to this coin. Perhaps a new agency would stifle innovation and regulate the new industry to death. Maybe it would be better to let biotech alone for now and rely on self-regulation. If an experiment causes damage, we could rely on the tort system to deal with it (although the problems of proof of fault, causation, and damages would be extremely difficult). Or perhaps a new agency would be captured by the industry and would authorize dangerous experiments or see its role as promoting genetically modified foods. So the public might receive less protection than it would get from the courts in an unregulated environment.

d. *Regulatory philosophy.* A basic question is whether the agency in its rulemaking and adjudication should be utilitarian and cost-benefit oriented. That would mean that the agency would attempt to quantify in dollar terms, and balance the costs and benefits of, particular forms of regulation. Under that approach, regulation should occur only if the benefits exceed the costs (and the form of regulation chosen should maximize the net benefits). In the biotech area, a regulatory regime that made biotech innovation more difficult would have obvious costs (the loss to society of valuable new technologies, or delays in their introduction; increased costs of development and manufacture). The benefits are harder to measure, because so far, at least, biotech hasn't had any serious known human health effects or caused significant environmental harm (but there are ominous signs—see the discussion of Starlink above). Thus, possible health or environmental effects must be heavily discounted and also are very difficult to quantify (what is a life worth? What is the loss of a species worth?) Consequently, a cost-benefit, utilitarian scheme of regulation will tend to be fairly permissive and probably could justify allowing the experiment to proceed and other genetically modified life forms to go on the market.

However, some schemes of health, safety, and environmental regulation do not weigh costs and benefits. Instead, agencies are instructed to regulate in a way that produces the fewest possible number of deaths or injuries regardless of costs. This is true of dangerous chemicals in the work place, cancer-causing elements in food, and certain forms of air pollution control. In Europe, particularly, regulators are instructed to adhere to the *precautionary principle*, under which technological uncertainty is resolved by minimizing risks even though they are unquantifiable. See McGarity, *supra*, at 491-94. These questions of whether to pursue a utilitarian or non-utilitarian approach should be resolved by the legislature when it sets up the regulatory scheme—but often the legislature ducks them and leaves them to the agency to consider.

e. *The administrative process.* Suppose the legislature passes a statute creating a new state agency to deal with the environmental release of genetically engineered products: the Biotechnology Agency (BTA). Issues: Should it be state or federal? Have one director, or should there be multiple agency heads? What would it do? This question can take you through the entire administrative process as well as allowing you to raise issues of legitimacy and checks and balances. The following discussion follows the approach of § 1.5 (the snapshot of the administrative process) by illustrating each of the agency functions in the biotech setting.

i. *Grant-making, research, and promotion.* BTA could help to articulate where the industry is going, what sort of regulation is needed, what are the risks and benefits of biotechnology, what sort of funding is required. The agency can fund research itself and can serve as a clearing-house for information. It should cooperate closely with agricultural and environmental agencies.

ii. *Rulemaking.* BTA will adopt general rules on who can do this sort of research, what sorts of experimentation are permissible, what kinds of containment facilities must be employed for various classes of dangerous research, what kinds of documents must be filed to get permission to do a release, how genetically modified foods should be labeled. (Be sure to mention that the terms "rule" and "regulation" are synonymous and used interchangeably in the course.) Assuming they are consistent with the statute and meet an easily-satisfied reasonableness test, such rules are law and have the same legal effect as a statute (often a shocking notion to students). Introduce the notice and comment procedure for rulemaking here. It's very significant that the public participates in the rulemaking process, because notice and comment is a form of direct democracy. In addition, rulemaking is a surrogate for the political process that should have occurred in the legislature.

You might touch on the legitimacy materials in § 1.6. What is this law-making, law-enforcing, law-adjudicating creature anyway? How can it be constitutionally legitimate? None of the theories works very well. The combination of procedures that require public involvement and agency explanation, plus legislative, judicial and executive checks and balances, tends to produce politically and technologically appropriate results. Some observers think that this combination legitimates the administrative process. Others think that it ossifies the administrative process by making agencies too timid and by making rulemaking too slow and costly.

iii. *Licensing of labs.* What kinds of financial backing or personnel should be required to get a license? What insurance must the company carry? Raise the issue about whether licensing schemes are good or bad for consumers.

iv. *Inspection and enforcement.* BTA will inspect the experimental facilities of its licensees to make sure that guidelines are complied with. It is a law-enforcement agency (in addition to a law-creating and law-adjudicating agency).

v. *Permit system.* BTA might be empowered to pre-approve experiments (or any other release of genetically altered material into the environment) or the introduction of new GM foods into the market. Ex ante permit systems are fairly common in connection with particularly dangerous private activity. Obvious examples are the need to get a permit before introducing a new drug, building a nuclear power plant, polluting the water, filling a wetland, or making health claims for food. While often necessary, permitting is costly and bureaucratic. It is vulnerable to delaying tactics by opponents of the action. Regulators tend to be conservative in granting approval, not wanting to make a mistake. Permit schemes give great power to an agency, especially to staff members. As a practical matter, courts have little ability to interfere with arbitrary agency decisions under permit or pre-clearance systems; regulated parties must do what the agency wants them to do in order to get the permit and move ahead with the business plan. The Bhagwat article cited in text (§ 1.5) is a good run-down on the advantages and disadvantages of ex ante regulatory systems.

Perhaps a clearance system might be less cumbersome. The experimenter would file documents before starting but can go ahead unless the agency disapproves. Compare SEC regulation of new stock sales (seller must file prospectus before selling stock); or the environmental impact statement process (agency must analyze environmental costs and benefits before taking action); or the Hart-Scott-Rodino pre-notification procedure for mergers.

vi. *Adjudication.* If BTA revokes or denies a license or denies a permit, it must provide a hearing process. Introduce formal administrative adjudication procedure. Note that agencies do far more adjudicating than courts do—another shocking notion to students.

vii. *Ratemaking.* Not applicable here.

viii. *Compensation.* BTA might administer a compensation scheme for people injured by biotech experiments. It could run like workers' compensation—no fault, easy to prove injury, but amount is capped. That would be an alternative to reliance on the tort system and private insurance. Probably we don't yet understand the problems well enough to install such a system. But the industry is definitely going to be looking for protection against unlimited tort recoveries (rightly fearing litigation monstrosities like asbestos, tobacco, breast implants, or IUDs). This could be a good spot to talk about the use of agencies to supplant courts in handling mass tort situations.

f. *Controls over the BTA:*

i. *Judicial review.* Judicial review of agency action is pervasive in American law—probably more so than in any other country. Courts scrutinize compliance with procedural norms, errors of law, abuse of discretion, evidentiary sufficiency. BTA's rules and orders will undoubtedly be subject to review, either at behest of the industry or environmentalists. Courts have enormous power to make political decisions in the course of conducting such review.

ii. *Legislative oversight.* There is likely to be oversight as the legislature approves the appointments of the head or heads of BTA, approves its budget, and considers statutory amendments. The legislature can hold oversight hearings. Many states have a rules review process, and a few have legislative vetoes. Either the industry or environmentalists who are unhappy with the agency will alert the legislature to the problem.

iii. *Executive control.* The governor appoints agency members and makes budget requests. The executive may also have a rules-review process. The agency head or heads should not be independent of executive control. Instead, it is more important to retain the governor's support and patronage, and BTA should reflect the governor's political program. Obviously these basic issues can only be hinted at in the first class.

CHAPTER 2: THE CONSTITUTIONAL RIGHT TO A HEARING

§ 2.1 HEARINGS AND WELFARE TERMINATION: DUE PROCESS AND MASS JUSTICE

Note: The casebook gives little attention to procedural due process prior to *Goldberg*. You may want to mention *Joint Anti-Fascist Refugee League v. McGrath,* 341 U.S. 123 (1951), especially Frankfurter's concurring opinion: "[N]o better instrument has been devised for arriving at truth than to give a person in jeopardy of serious loss notice of the claim against him and an opportunity to meet it. Nor has a better way been found for generating the feeling, so important to a popular government, that justice has been done." Another important pre-*Goldberg* case is *Cafeteria Workers v. McElroy,* 367 U.S. 886 (1961) (weighing of interests to determine if due process applies in the context of government employment).

Goldberg was a turning point—a commitment to the use of adversarial trial-type hearings to protect welfare beneficiaries—and is the departure point for modern due process analysis. For a detailed account of the story of *Goldberg,* including details about the plaintiffs and the legal strategies of the lawyers who ultimately won the case, see Judith Resnik, "The Story of *Goldberg:* Why This Case is Our Shorthand," in CIVIL PROCEDURE STORIES 455 (Kevin M. Clermont ed.2004).

For flavor, here is Professor Joel Handler's sketch of the welfare system. He describes the system as it existed under AFDC, but the description continues to apply to TANF.

> Volume [of recipients] is a brutal fact of the welfare state . . . vast numbers of people in our society, as presently organized, will need financial and other assistance. This is especially true for the client group on which we focus: female-headed households. Volume is the cardinal enemy of discretion, professional judgment, individualization; heavy caseloads force routinization. . . .

> Values and attitudes toward the poor are varied, long-standing, and greatly affect how the poor are treated. Society has always distinguished between the deserving and undeserving poor, those whose poverty is blameless and those who are blameworthy. In a prior age, the blind, the halt, and the lame were in the former category; those who could work but failed were in the latter. Today, the aged and the disabled have joined the former, but the nonaged—the childless adults, and the female-headed households—are still the undeserving. It is not only the failure of work that draws the community's hostility; fueling the furies are race, sex, and various forms of deviant behavior and life style. . . .

10

Programs for the undeserving are very different [from Social Security]. They are state and local, discretionary, decentralized, and subject to a great many moralistic and punitive practices. . . . The final cause of the ills of public assistance programs is the distribution of wealth and power. One can never forget that the people we are talking about are extremely dependent. They are ill-prepared to effectively participate in public programs, and, in particular, to understand the procedural systems designed to secure benefits and rights for them. The bureaucracy has control over the information, the resources, the staying power, the power of retaliation; workers, even if well-meaning, are pressed for time, short of money, and, in all honesty, feel that they know what is best for the clients. . . .

Two additional comments: the utter chaos that one witnesses in the public assistance offices—the crowds, the waiting, the shouting, the maze of cubicles, the forms, the fear and resignation of the applicants, and the anger and frustration of the workers; second, that by forcing public assistance recipients to supplement their welfare grants by resorting to General Assistance and private charity—where available—the recipients are now confronting the most discretionary, moralistic public and private programs, in which there are virtually no legal protections.

"Discretion in Social Welfare: The Uneasy Position of the Rule of Law," 92 Yale L.J. 1270, 1271-74 (1983).

GOLDBERG v. KELLY

Notes and Questions

1. *The Goldberg decision.* The class should consider the three separate holdings in *Goldberg* because the balance of the chapter involves a retreat from them.

i. Under *Goldberg*, whether due process applies to the deprivation of a particular interest "depends on whether the recipient's interest in avoiding that loss outweighs the governmental interest in summary adjudication. . . . [C]onsideration of what procedures due process may require under any given set of circumstances must begin with a determination of the precise nature of the government function involved as well as of the private interest that has been affected by government action." In other words, whether an interest gets due process protection depends on a balancing of governmental and private interests.

Brennan made no particular point of whether the individual's interest in a continued flow of benefits was liberty or property, largely because the government conceded that the interest in question was protected by due process. In footnote 8, Brennan found it "realistic to regard welfare entitlements as more like 'property' than a 'gratuity.'" Instead, the key to the decision is the balance of individual against government interest (an approach consistent with prior law such as *Cafeteria Workers*.) *Roth* (§ 2.2.1) rejected *Goldberg*'s approach to identifying a protectable interest. Under *Roth*, whether an interest is "property" depends on whether it is an entitlement, regardless of how compelling the private interest may be. Under *Roth* a balancing process is used to determine *what kind* of process is due and *when* it is due (§§ 2.3, 2.4), but *only after* the interest involved is determined to be liberty or property.

Note that Brennan did not include as a factor in the *Goldberg* balancing analysis the likelihood of error or the likelihood that the procedural right in question would protect the private interest at stake. Yet the lower court *did* include this factor in its balancing test—which Brennan quoted but with an ellipsis for the probability factor. Later, in *Mathews,* the probability factor was reincorporated into the balancing test.

ii. A pre-termination hearing was required because of the desperate need of the family, which is deprived of the very means to live while waiting for a post-termination hearing. This outweighs the government's fiscal imperatives. It distinguishes welfare from the decisions in which a post-termination hearing is sufficient (footnote 10). *Mathews v. Eldridge* (§ 2.3) severely limits *Goldberg* on this issue without overruling it.

iii. The last paragraph of the opinion provides a laundry list of required ingredients for the pre-termination hearing. It is hard to see what else might be required in the supposedly more formal post-termination hearing. The elements are timely and adequate notice of the reasons for a proposed termination, confrontation and cross-examination of adverse witnesses, oral presentation of argument and evidence, the right to be represented by counsel (though not to have counsel appointed), a requirement that the decision rest solely on legal rules and evidence adduced at the hearing, a required statement of reasons for the determination and the evidence that decision-maker relied on, and an impartial decisionmaker.

The list was too inflexible to fit all situations and later "variable due process" cases require much less (§ 2.4). Henry Friendly contended that the Court would have done as well to simply provide for an oral hearing and an impartial decision-maker. "Some Kind of Hearing," 123 U.Pa.L.Rev. 1267, 1279 (1975).

2. *The purposes of due process.* This list of rationales for due process can be used to evaluate each of the fundamental issues in this chapter: Is an interest protected by due process, when must a hearing be provided, what kind of process is due, and what procedure, if any, is required in non-individualized determinations?

    i. *Dignitary function.* Some writers consider the positivist liberty-property scheme of *Roth* and the instrumental calculations of *Mathews* myopic. They stress the fact that the right to a hearing treats an individual with appropriate dignity apart from the outcome. Jerry Mashaw: "[T]here seems to be something to the intuition that process itself matters. We do distinguish between losing and being treated unfairly. And, however fuzzy our articulation of the process characteristics that yield a sense of unfairness, it is commonplace for us to describe process affronts as somehow related to disrespect for our individuality, to our not being taken seriously as persons." "Administrative Due Process: The Quest for a Dignitary Theory," 61 B.U.L.Rev. 885, 888 (1981).

    "No other procedure [than an oral hearing] so effectively fosters a belief that one has been dealt with fairly, even if there remains a disagreement with the result. . . . In a society like ours, which operates on the assumption of and relies for its continued stability on respect for our institutions and voluntary compliance with the dictates of the law, it is crucial that its members perceive that their rights and interests are taken seriously and thoughtfully by the individuals who are deciding their claims. During an oral hearing, the `Government' loses its nameless, faceless quality and comes into focus as another human being with whom the citizen can speak, present his or her case, and look for a responsible decision." *Gray Panthers v. Schweiker,* 652 F.2d 146, 162-63 (D.C.Cir.1980).

    But see Peter Simon, "Liberty and Property in the Supreme Court: A Defense of *Roth* and *Perry*," 71 Cal.L.Rev. 146, 187-90 (1983) (attacking dignitary theory).

    It could be argued that welfare hearings really do not serve a dignitary function. Fair hearings in New York are conducted in "a kind of police court environment; a sense of hurry pervades the hearings. Claimants certainly are not made to feel that an informal process has been designed to provide for a full relaxed opportunity to present their case." Daniel Jay Baum, THE WELFARE FAMILY AND MASS ADMINISTRATIVE JUSTICE 39 (1974).

    Lucie White points out that a welfare fair hearing is anything but dignity-enhancing. Mrs. G's voice was devalued because of intimidation (Mrs. G knew she must not displease her superiors), humiliation (her language as a woman of color would not be considered legitimate), and objectification (inability of hearing officer to deal with her real feelings). Lucie E. White, "Subordination, Rhetorical Survival Skills and Sunday Shoes: Notes on the Hearing of Mrs. G.," 38 Buff.L.Rev. 1, 32-44 (1990). *See also* Lucie E. White, "*Goldberg v. Kelly* on the Paradox of Lawyering for the Poor," 56 Brook.L.Rev. 861, 867-68, 875 (1990) (arguing that *Goldberg* has not compelled government to treat welfare recipients with dignity and may have worked in the opposite direction).

ii. *Empowerment.* A right to a hearing empowers a welfare claimant, especially if she is represented by a skilled advocate, because the demand for a hearing forces the bureaucracy to deal with the claimant's issues, rather than brushing them aside. From a practical point of view, this may be the most significant function of the due process right to a prior hearing in welfare termination cases. *See* White, *supra,* 56 Brook.L.Rev. at 869-71. *See also Gray Panthers v. Schweiker, supra,* 652 F.2d at 162:

> An oral hearing requirement thus serves to ensure that decisionmakers recognize that their decisions affect the lives of human beings, a fact that is often obscured by a jumble of papers and depersonalized identification numbers. We can well believe it is easy for an employee processing an application for a small amount of Medicare benefits to shrug his or her shoulders and conclude that benefits should be denied or reduced, without stopping to gather the information necessary to reach that decision accurately. The situation could well be different if the employee knew that the claimant would have the opportunity personally to challenge that determination and seek an explanation. . . . [H]uman nature frequently leads to careless and arbitrary action when the decisionmaker can retreat behind a screen of paper and anonymity. The principle that those who govern must be accountable to those whose lives they affect informs not only our representative system of government, but on a broader scale, forms the very essence of what we expect from the Government in its dealings with us.

Vicki Lens writes:

> For the marginalized and the powerless, "standing against the law" is a way to overcome its power, if even just a bit [citing Patricia Ewick & Susan S. Silbey, THE COMMON PLACE OF LAW: STORIES FROM EVERYDAY LIFE 165 (1998)]. As Ewick and Sibley describe, while this sometimes may mean laying low, and trying to avoid the law's grasp, it often means engaging and subverting the bureaucratic structures in which public power is ensconced. It is an unscripted resistance that takes advantage of leaks in the organizational structure. It employs its tools against it, for example exposing the bureaucracy's failure to follow its own

rules or looking for cracks within the rules. Sometimes the resistance can take on a decidedly overt tone. Instead of avoiding conflict, resisters may generate complaints, "leapfrogging over layers of the bureaucratic hierarchy" so as to subvert that hierarchy, "converting [complaints] from an individual into an organizational problem"

Vicki Lens, "In the Fair Hearing Room: Resistance and Confrontation in the Welfare Bureaucracy," 32 Law & Social Inquiry 309, 312 (2007).

iii. *Acceptability.* It seems questionable whether losing parties are more likely to accept a decision cutting off their welfare benefits just because they've been given a brief hearing on the issues. For most people, it's the result that counts, not the procedure.

iv. *Accuracy.* Since only a tiny percentage of caseworker determinations are appealed, a system of hearings cannot assure accurate results; the caseworker's initial determination is vastly more important. Still, at least in some states, a high percentage of hearings result in reversal of the initial decision. This suggests that accuracy is promoted by the existence of pre-termination process (but not necessarily an adversary hearing). In addition to the Lens article cited in text N.3 (claiming a 50% success rate), *see* Laura Cooper, "*Goldberg's* Forgotten Footnote," 64 Minn.L.Rev. 1107, 1168-71 (1980) (claimants won 60% of cases in Minnesota, not counting cases in which they made only futile complaints about agency policy; rates didn't vary much whether or not they were represented by counsel).

In *Goldberg*, Brennan asserts that an exchange of documents is less likely to produce an accurate result than a trial-type hearing in welfare cases. *See also Gray Panthers v. Schweiker, supra,* 652 F.2d at 161-62: "Even if credibility is not likely to be directly in issue, personal, oral hearings are an effective way to eliminate misunderstandings and focus issues. Ambiguities which are not readily apparent on the face of a document can be disclosed and clarified with a few moments of oral exchange between the individual and the decisionmaker." However, later cases have held that a paper hearing can often meet due process requirements when credibility isn't in issue. *See* § 2.4 N.7.

v. *Consistency.* A system of trial-type hearings is an ineffective way to achieve consistent decisions in welfare cases, because only a tiny percentage of welfare denials are appealed. Welfare adjudicators make a vast number of quick decisions, which are not published and are only haphazardly conveyed back to caseworkers. There is no system of precedents. Only a better system of management quality control can produce consistent decisions. *See* ¶ viii below.

vi. *Serious and reflective decisions.* In the pell-mell of a mass justice system, such as the welfare fair hearings, a serious and reflective decision is unlikely. Administrative judges must rush through their heavy daily calendar.

vii. · *Improve the exercise of discretion.* It seems likely that one consequence of *Goldberg* was to induce welfare departments to radically reduce the amount of discretion available to the front-line welfare workers. This would reduce the number of disputes that could trigger hearings. See further discussion below. Under TANF, however, there are many disputes about whether the claimant has met work requirements and these decisions entail a considerable amount of bureaucratic discretion.

For an argument that trial-type procedure is most needed when an agency exercises broad discretion, *see* Tim Searchinger, Note, "The Procedural Due Process Right Approach to Administrative Discretion: The Court's Inverted Analysis," 95 Yale L.J. 1017 (1986). Of course, *Roth*, § 2.2.1, cuts in exactly the opposite direction; it held that a professor has no property interest since the university had discretion whether or not to extend his contract.

Handler, in the article cited in N.5, argues that as a program becomes more discretion-oriented, adversary procedures become less appropriate. Highly discretionary programs (like designing an appropriate environment for a handicapped child) involve continuing relationships between government and citizen, resistance to hearings by the professional bureaucracy, indeterminacy of the proper result, apathetic or intimidated parents, and futility of trying to defeat a well-prepared and determined bureaucracy. Handler argues for a largely consultative process, stressing regular and frequent communication, discussion of problems, negotiation, flexibility on both sides, and compromise. If that does not work, there should be third-party mediation. Only then should there be resort to adversary procedures as a last resort.

viii. *Promote purposes of program.* In *Goldberg*, Brennan linked required hearings to the purposes of welfare. Welfare allows the poor to subsist decently, gives them an opportunities to participate in community life, and guards against societal malaise. A right to uninterrupted provision of benefits, secured by pre-termination hearings, *serves the same interests.*

However, Brennan's analysis seems to beg the question: A system of pre-termination hearings promotes the purposes of a welfare program if hearings are a good idea for other reasons. If mandatory hearings are not a good idea, they don't promote the purposes of the program. Compare *Ingraham v. Wright*, 430 U.S. 651 (1977), § 2.4, which held that school officials need not provide a hearing before paddling students: "Hearings—even informal hearings—require time, personnel, and a diversion of attention from normal school pursuits. School authorities may well choose to abandon corporal punishment rather than incur the burdens of complying with the procedural requirements. . . . The effect of interposing prior procedural safeguards may well be to make the punishment more severe by increasing the anxiety of the child."

ix. *Identify recurring problems.* A system of welfare hearings may improve the quality of administration. *See* Cesar A. Perales, "The Fair Hearings Process: Guardian of the Social Service System," 56 Brook.L.Rev. 889, 895-96 (1990) ("barometer" function of fair hearings—information gleaned from hearings process permits Department to make improvements that reduce the need for hearings or to provide additional training).

On the other hand, Jerry Mashaw observes that hearings provide no quality check, because only 2% of all negative decisions are appealed (and more than half of those were in California, New York, and Texas). These few cases do not provide a revealing window on how the bureaucracy is functioning. Instead, better quality control is more likely to produce an improvement in the way the system functions. Mashaw, "The Management Side of Due Process," 59 Cornell L.Q. 772, 784-87, 808-10, 815-23 (1974); Mashaw, BUREAUCRATIC JUSTICE ch. 2, 9, 10, 11 (1983); William H. Simon, "Legality, Bureaucracy and Class in the Welfare System," 92 Yale L.J. 1198 (1983).

x. *Improve judicial review.* So few cases are brought to court in mass justice situations that this is not a persuasive rationale for trial-type hearings. In welfare cases, judicial review may be virtually unavailable, since very few appellants can afford lawyers and there are very few pro bono or legal service lawyers. Moreover, those who cannot pay a filing fee are often excluded. *Ortwein v. Schwab,* 410 U.S. 656 (1973). Obviously, the rationale relating to judicial review argument is more persuasive where a substantial number of cases wind up in court (such as in professional licensing or Social Security disability).

3. *In the wake of Goldberg.* The figures confirm the dissenters' predictions. There was a massive increase in the number of requested

hearings after *Goldberg*. The cost of coping with all these hearings has been a major financial burden for welfare programs. And *Goldberg* clearly resulted in both an objectification of welfare standards and a considerable toughening of application decisions, since it is easier to keep someone off the rolls in the first place than to get them off later.

4. *Consequences of Goldberg.* The primary beneficiaries of *Goldberg* might be the newly employed hearing officers and others needed to carry out all the additional hearings.

Although some recipients certainly gained by the decision (either in obtaining delay of a cutoff of benefits or in preventing an erroneous cutoff), others undoubtedly suffered, in that more money went into administration rather than benefits, and more money went to people who should have been cut off but postponed it by demanding a hearing. Others suffered because it became harder to get on the rolls or because newly objectified standards prevented social workers from exercising discretion in their favor.

Goldberg induced welfare administrators to cut down the amount of discretion exercised by front-line welfare workers, so as to reduce the number of cases in which hearings could be triggered. The budget used to fund recipients' special needs was cashed out and divided among all recipients. And this made it possible to get rid of highly trained social work professionals and hire lower-paid eligibility technicians. Jerry Mashaw, "Organizing Adjudication: Reflections on the Prospect for Artisans in the Age of Robots," 39 UCLA L.Rev. 1055, 1063-64 (1992). Mashaw wisely cautions that every improvement in adjudicatory procedure will be accompanied by tradeoffs in which bureaucratic managers seek to offset the extra costs and loss of control entailed by adjudication.

Of course, it's human nature to empathize with the real people who use the system to prevent a wrongful cutoff of benefits, rather than the anonymous group who are harmed by it. This is reflected in a famous speech given by Justice Brennan about *Goldberg* in which he stressed the human stories involved. Brennan described the case as "an expression of the importance of passion in governmental conduct, in the sense of attention to the concrete human realities at stake. From this perspective, *Goldberg* can be seen as injecting passion into a system whose abstract rationality had led it astray." William Brennan, "Reason, Passion and the 'Progress of the Law,'" 10 Cardozo L.Rev. 3, 20 (1988). Oddly, however, Brennan did not include anything about these stories in the *Goldberg* decision itself, perhaps out of concern with Black's criticisms that Brennan was legislating rather than engaging in constitutional adjudication.

In appraising the decision one must take account of the fact that resources are scarce and limited; welfare department budgets may be a zero sum game, so that money diverted to administration comes out of the grants. Therefore, it may make sense to be at least somewhat deferential to the views of the bureaucracy about how to allocate those resources. *Goldberg* was indifferent to those views, even thought New York had just upgraded significantly the quality of the hearing process it provided. As the rest of this Chapter will show, the Court was never again so indifferent to these concerns.

5. *Adversariness and mass justice.* Brodoff's article observes that in Washington state, of 11,722 hearing requests in public assistance cases, only 112 had attorney representation; of 1735 hearings actually held, only 286 had representation.

There is much to be said for Handler's view that formal adversary hearings in the welfare context are an expensive irrelevance, if the goal is to protect the rights of the vast bulk of recipients or to improve the system. A simple system of face-to-face meetings with an uninvolved mediator or ombudsman would protect far more people at much less cost.

The article by Lens cited in N.2 ¶ ii above is an empirical study of clients who had experienced welfare fair hearings. They indicated their extreme frustration with the system, their inability to deal with paperwork, and their distrust of the administrative judge. She writes (at 329):

> Our political and legal culture celebrates notions such as due process and procedural justice. The "opportunity to be heard" has an almost sacrosanct and hallowed timbre; it implies all have an opportunity to participate in the legal and political institutions that govern our lives. For the welfare poor, the Supreme Court decision in *Kelly* and its requirement of pre-termination hearings was supposed to ensure their participation in the welfare bureaucracy, arguably the most significant government institution in their lives.

> As this research demonstrates, the procedures spawned by *Kelly* are often an ill-fitting vessel for many welfare recipients. While standards of proof are technically the same for both agency and clients, clients are often presumed less credible. Most welfare recipients do not have the power to command the proof they need. They are often outmatched by their opponents, who, by the force and velocity of their questions, can quickly transform the hearing into an interrogation. The stories clients want to tell are not the ones hearing officers want to hear. The language clients speak is at odds with the language of law.

§ 2.2 INTERESTS PROTECTED BY DUE PROCESS: LIBERTY AND PROPERTY

§2.2.1 "Liberty" and "property" as defined in *Roth*

For incisive critiques of the entitlement approach taken by *Roth* and subsequent cases, *see* Sidney A. Shapiro & Richard E. Levy, "Government Benefits and the Rule of Law: Toward a Standards-Based Theory of Due Process," 57 Admin.L.Rev. 107, 119-26 (2005); Cynthia Farina, "Conceiving Due Process," 3 Yale J.L. & Fem. 189 (1991).

BOARD OF REGENTS v. ROTH

Notes and Questions

1. *The right-privilege doctrine.* Under the right-privilege doctrine, due process applied to the deprivation only of traditional forms of property, such as land, cars, money, etc. These are things the government can't take away without paying for them. All other government benefits, such as welfare, contract rights, or employment, which government can abolish legislatively, would be privileges and would not receive any protection. In light of the difficulties of the positivist definition of property that we'll be discussing, it may be attractive to return to the right-privilege distinction. You could deal with cases like *Bailey v. Richardson* by expanding the definition of liberty to cover stigmatic government action without treating government jobs, welfare, etc. as property.

Traces of the right-privilege distinction can be gleaned from the post-*Roth* positivist decisions involving both liberty and property. They indicate that what the state gives, the state can take away on its own terms, by depriving a particular status of its character as an entitlement (for example, the state can convert a tenured job to an untenured job and thus strip away its procedural protection).

The right-privilege doctrine still applies to exclusion of aliens outside the U.S. trying to get in (or paroled after an exclusion decision). *U.S. ex rel. Knauff v. Shaughnessy*, 345 U.S. 206 (1953) (whatever process aliens receive is all that they are due). *But see Jean v. Nelson*, 472 U.S. 846 (1985) (construing regulations to prevent ethnic discrimination in alien parole decisions—dissent argues *Knauff* should be overruled).

2. *New property.* A tenured government job (like welfare or other entitlements) lacks many of the elements ordinarily associated with "property." It cannot be sold, given away, bequeathed, or subdivided by the holder; it cannot be "possessed" in any ordinary sense of the word; it cannot be used or controlled in any manner the holder wishes; it can be destroyed

by the state without compensation (i.e. by abolishing the employing college, converting a tenured job to non-tenured, or abolishing welfare). These don't feel like the things we study in first year Property courses. In short, it is difficult to say that anyone "owns" welfare, public education, or a government job.

Instead, entitlements like welfare or tenured jobs are really more like contractual claims to money and status than "property" as we traditionally use that term. However, the Court chose to describe entitlements as property to engage the benefits with due process, thus providing a set of politically desirable protections for them. Entitlements are property because they *should* have the same procedural protections old property has. *See* Timothy Terrell, "Property, Due Process, and the Distinction Between Definition and Theory in Legal Analysis," 70 Geo.L.J. 861, 865-878 (1982); Shapiro & Levy, *supra*, at 131-34 (explaining the *Roth* methodology as a way to grant due process in welfare without constitutionalizing a right to receive welfare).

For an excellent discussion of the Court's inconsistent approach to defining property under procedural due process, substantive due process, and the takings clause, see Thomas W. Merrill, "The Landscape of Constitutional Property," 86 Va.L.Rev. 885 (2000). Merrill argues that the Court should adopt a "patterning" approach, deciding first whether a particular type of interest merits federal constitutional protection, then looking to non-constitutional sources of law to decide whether such interest exists. He suggests that the court should ask "whether nonconstitutional sources of law confer on the claimant an entitlement *having a monetary value* that can be terminated only upon a finding that some specific condition has been satisfied." *Id.* at 961-68. Merrill's formulation was cited in *Castle Rock* (*see* § 2.2.2 N.4), which said that the wife's rights under a domestic violence restraining order were not "property" because, inter alia, they had no monetary value. 545 U.S. at 766.

Whether the Wisconsin approach to dispensing with pre-termination hearings will work is still undetermined. *See West Virginia ex rel. K. M. v. West Virginia Dep't of HHR*, 575 S.E.2d 393 (W.Va. 2002) (*Goldberg* no longer controlling authority); *Weston v. Cassata*, 37 P.2d 469 (Colo.App. 2002) (Colorado state law created entitlement to welfare).

3. *Stigma as deprivation of liberty.* *Roth* defined "liberty" in a natural law rather than a positive law mode. It relied on the venerable *Meyer* case, which made clear that liberty is something we are born with, not something we get from the state. Thus *Roth's* approach to liberty is dramatically different from its approach to property. Probably the reason for the dichotomy is that the Court was determined to provide procedural protection against stigmatic discharge from government jobs, such as those

that occurred during the McCarthy era. But to keep the doctrine somewhat under control, it had to treat Roth's discharge as non-stigmatic, even though it was academically catastrophic. For a general discussion of the many different definitions of "liberty" that the Supreme Court has employed, see Deana Pollard Sacks, "Elements of Liberty," 61 SMU L.Rev. 1557 (2008).

An excellent and witty discussion of the difference between procedural and substantive due process is Judge Richard Posner's opinion in *Swank v. Smart*, 898 F.2d 1247, 1250-53 (7th Cir.1990), holding that the discharge of a cop for chatting up a teenage girl and taking her for a spin on his motorcycle did not violate substantive due process, since it was rational (barely). Nor did it violate rights of free speech, privacy, or locomotion. However, his hearing failed to measure up to due process requirements, so he was denied procedural due process.

Cases that impose any constitutional scrutiny at all in the economic area are rare, but the Court sometimes invalidates such statutes as irrational, perhaps because it objects to them on some other ground. *See, e.g. City of Cleburne v. Cleburne Living Center*, 473 U.S. 432 (1985). In the *Cleburne* case, a city denied a zoning permit for operation of a group home for the mentally retarded. Its primary reason was that the neighbors did not want the group home there. The Court held that the mentally retarded were not entitled to any special protection under the equal protection clause, but it invalidated the city's action just the same, because the home did not threaten *any* legitimate interest. Other group homes (like fraternities) had received permits, and an irrational prejudice against retarded people was not a sufficient reason to single them out for special treatment.

4. *Free speech rights.* The Court evidently believed that First Amendment rights can be more securely guarded by courts than by agencies—especially state or local agencies like school boards. State employees alleging infringement of First Amendment rights therefore proceed by § 1983 actions in federal court, where a de novo trial is provided. If this issue were relegated to an administrative hearing, the rules of deference would drastic limit the ability of a reviewing court to question an agency's fact findings (such as the difficult question of whether a teacher's purported discharge for poor teaching was a pretext for punishing the teacher for speech). And the administrative decision would probably be res judicata of a new § 1983 case in court. *See* § 4.4.1.

This paragraph is an excursion into the limited First Amendment rights of teachers or other public employees, in case you want to follow that tangent in class. Teachers do not have the right to teach whatever they like nor to engage in speech that is disruptive of the institution. A court must seek "a balance between the interests of the [employee], as a citizen, in commenting upon matters of public concern and the interest of the State, as an employer, in promoting the efficiency of the public services it performs through its employees." *Pickering v. Bd. of Educ.*, 391 U.S. 563, 568 (1968) (protecting teacher's criticism of school board's funding allocations). However, the First Amendment rights of public employees have been progressively narrowed. See *Connick v. Myers*, 461 U.S. 138 (1983) (circulation of questionnaire about office politics is unprotected because not a matter of public concern; question about whether employees were pressured to work on political campaigns was a matter of public concern, but discharge upheld because questionnaire interfered with working relationships in DA's office); *Garcetti v. Ceballos*, 547 U.S. 410 (2006) (statements made in the course of carrying out district attorney's official duties are not protected).

5. *Discretion and due process.* Justice Marshall's dissent in *Roth* argued that denial of any government job is a deprivation of property and that liberty includes the right to work. Much scholarship expresses support for Marshall's position. *See, e.g.,* John Hart Ely, DEMOCRACY AND DISTRUST: A THEORY OF JUDICIAL REVIEW 19 (1980) (if government seriously hurts you, it must provide due process); Richard B. Saphire, "Specifying Due Process Values: Toward a More Responsive Approach to Procedural Protection," 127 U.Pa.L.Rev. 111 (1978) (protection of dignitary values); Edward L. Rubin, "Due Process and the Administrative State," 72 Cal.L.Rev. 1044 (1984) (due process means that government cannot adjudicate the interests of an individual without minimal procedure); Henry Monaghan, "Of 'Liberty' and 'Property,'" 62 Cornell L.Rev. 405, 409 (1977) (life, liberty and property mean all interests valued by sensible men); Tim Searchinger, Note, "The Procedural Due Process Approach to Administrative Discretion: The Court's Inverted Analysis," 95 Yale L.J. 1017 (1986) (need for hearings to control abuse of discretion). As the latter note argues, there is a greater potential for arbitrary decisionmaking when government exercises discretion than when it deprives someone of an entitlement that is protected by a well-defined standard.

According to Rubin, for example, due process means that government should follow its own rules and provide an impartial decision-maker and a statement of reasons before it makes a decision seriously and negatively impacting an individual. In many cases, consultative procedure, as in *Goss v. Lopez*, § 2.4 N.1, would be sufficient. The rationale is that fair procedure is the only protection against personalized tyranny when government deals with the individual one-on-one.

Peter Simon defends the *Roth-Perry* view of property on utilitarian grounds. "Liberty and Property in the Supreme Court: A Defense of *Roth* and *Perry*," 71 Cal.L.Rev. 146, 156-71 (1983). He thinks that a contrary approach would destroy vast areas of administrative discretion. Even a judicially enforceable requirement that government provide a statement of reasons before discharging an untenured employee would ultimately mean that government could not fire anyone without a large expenditure of resources. Therefore, government would have to assemble a thorough dossier before it can discharge or refuse to rehire anyone. Simon points out that civil service laws at the federal level virtually prevent any discharges for cause (only one federal civil service employee out of 5000 was terminated for cause in a 3-year period). Anyone concerned with the cumbersomeness and cost of government must hesitate before requiring due process every time government makes a discretionary individualized decision.

6. *State constitutional law. Saleeby* relied on an earlier decision that expresses strong disagreement with the federal approach to due process. *People v. Ramirez,* 599 P.2d 622 (Cal.1979). The California approach merges the question of whether an interest is protected by due process with the question of what process is due (in comparison to the federal approach that sharply separates these two questions). Thus it closely resembles *Goldberg v. Kelly,* which appeared to use interest balancing to answer both questions.

In California, the same four-factor balancing test is used to answer both the question of whether due process applies and what process is due. The balancing test uses the same three factors as *Mathews v. Eldridge* with the addition of a fourth factor relating to the claimant's dignitary interest.

Unsurprisingly, California courts have encountered difficulty in applying *Ramirez* and *Saleeby,* because they are unsure what a dignitary interest is and how to balance it against the other three factors. Presumably, only people have dignity, not businesses, but what about a personal business (like a professional license)? Some decisions ignore the separate California approach entirely and apply federal law (possibly because counsel have overlooked the issue of whether California provides more protection than federal). Others suggest that they are mystified by the emphasis on dignity and conclude that the result should be the same under both approaches. And a few cases take the California approach seriously and impose due process protection under state law where the federal approach would deny protection. *See* Michael Asimow, "Toward a New California Administrative Procedure Act: Adjudication Fundamentals," 39 UCLA L.Rev. 1067, 1084-89, especially n.66 (1992).

One author of this book believes that the California Supreme Court should overrule cases like *Saleeby*. Michael Asimow, "Administrative Law and the California Constitution," in Bruce E. Cain & Roger G. Noll, eds. CONSTITUTIONAL REFORM IN CALIFORNIA: MAKING STATE GOVERNMENT MORE EFFECTIVE AND RESPONSIVE (Berkeley, Inst. of Gov't Studies Press 1995). He argues that the California approach is too indeterminate for courts to apply (as the confusing maze of case law mentioned in the previous paragraph attests). Moreover, the chapter argues, when the dignitary approach is taken seriously, the result can be over-proceduralization of administrative adjudication.

7. *De facto tenure.* The scope of *Perry* was clarified by *Leis v. Flynt,* 439 U.S. 438, 444 n.5 (1979), which held that an attorney's admission to practice in Ohio pro hac vice was not a property interest, because it was discretionary under state law. The Court rejected the dissent's argument that Ohio's practice of routine admission created reliance and expectation interests. The majority stated that since admission was explicitly discretionary under state law, a contrary practice couldn't turn it into property. This holding is a reminder that the "expectancy" protected by *Perry* depends on legally enforceable rights. If Ohio grants pro hac vice admission to almost every applicant, Larry Flynt's counsel's expectation that the state will do the same for him might be "reasonable" as a matter of factual probabilities, but this is not the same as a "legitimate claim of *entitlement.*"

8. *Deprivation.* There is a common-sense difference between the rejection of an application and termination of an existing status. We are more outraged when we *lose* a job for unjust reasons than when we are *not hired* for unjust reasons. Similarly, our life is probably more disrupted when we lose a license than when our license application is rejected. *See* Henry Friendly, "Some Kind of Hearing," 123 U. Pa. L. Rev. 1267, 1295-96 (1975). Theoreticians refer to this psychological reality as the "endowment effect."

Note that hiring decisions are typically discretionary, so that a refusal to hire someone wouldn't be treated as a deprivation of property under *Roth.* However, welfare is usually not discretionary—even after the enactment of TANF, an applicant for welfare or disability benefits is entitled to the benefit if he or she meets the qualifications. Consequently, under the logic of *Roth,* a denied welfare application should trigger due process. Indeed, the case law does not distinguish between welfare applications and terminations but applies due process to both. *See Kapps v. Wing,* 404 F.3d 105, 115-17 (2d Cir.2005) (application for home heating assistance), which cites numerous cases on the issue and declares that every circuit has found that an applicant for non-discretionary benefits is protected by procedural due process. *See generally* Virginia T. Vance, Note, "Applications for Benefits: Due Process, Equal Protection, and the Right to be Free from Arbitrary Procedures," 61 Wash. & Lee L.Rev. 883, 889-97 (2004) (this student note also discusses the California decisions covered in N.6 of the text).

Nevertheless, the Supreme Court has maintained a coy silence on the issue. In *Walters v. Radiation Survivors,* § 2.4 N.4, the Court noted that the issue is undecided. *American Manufacturers Mutual* seems to signal that the Court will find due process inapplicable to denial of an application once the issue is squarely presented.

§ 2.2.2 Refining the *Roth* approach to property and liberty

CLEVELAND BOARD OF EDUCATION v. LOUDERMILL

Notes and Questions

1. *The bitter with the sweet.* *Loudermill* buried the idea that the state could create an entitlement on the one hand and abolish it on the other by defining a set of unprotective procedures. Arguments for *Loudermill*: *Arnett* (by which we mean the Rehnquist opinion, although he did not carry a majority) provided a perverse incentive for the states to go through their statute books and craft abbreviated procedures for deprivation of statutory entitlements. Moreover, *Arnett* trivialized due process. The judiciary seems best qualified to assess the level of minimum procedure necessary to meet constitutional standards. *See* John Hart Ely, DEMOCRACY AND DISTRUST 102 (1983). The judiciary has always assumed responsibility to determine minimal procedure to protect traditional forms of property. *See, e.g., Mullane v. Central Hanover Bank*, 339 U.S. 306 (1950) (giving notice by publication did not meet due process). "New" property should receive comparable protection.

Arguments against *Loudermill*: *Arnett* was consistent with *Roth*; if the state can make entitlements disappear by dispensing with standards and making a status discretionary, it should be able to do the same thing by providing an entitlement but defining away the procedure for protecting it. *Arnett* is consistent with one reading of the history of due process: that it is a "principle of legality, that every person is entitled to have her case decided in accordance with the procedural law of the land." Thomas W. Merrill, "The Landscape of Constitutional Property," 86 Va.L.Rev. 885, 924 (2000), meaning the procedural law of the statute creating the entitlement.

In addition, *Arnett* simplified the task of deciding what interests are protected by due process as well as deciding what procedure is due and when it is due. By defining procedures in a statute, the state would make it unnecessary to go through a liberty-property analysis. Moreover, it could short-circuit the result-oriented and unpredictable ad hoc balancing test (§§ 2.3, 2.4) by which appropriate procedure and timing is determined. Civil rights cases consume a large proportion of the resources of the federal court system. *See* Christina Whitman, "Constitutional Torts," 79 Mich. L. Rev. 5, 6 (1980) (almost one out of three private federal question suits in federal courts is a civil rights action). Thus *Arnett* promoted predictability and the conservation of judicial resources.

Because *Loudermill* endorsed truncated pre-termination procedure, the majority approach probably picked up some votes that would have been lacking if the Court had equated due process with full-fledged pre-termination hearings as in *Goldberg.* (*See Arnett,* in which White and Blackmun argued that due process rights of public employees are federally defined but do not include a trial-type hearing prior to termination.)

2. *Consequences of Loudermill.* Government functions more efficiently if it can discharge employees at will. Procedural requirements deter managers from trying to fire employees who they perceive are not doing a good job. Rigorous procedure at the time of a discharge also provide an incentive to scrutinize a job application very carefully, which may keep people with questionable records from getting a tryout. Procedural hurdles also encourage government managers to terminate marginal employees at the end of their probationary period, since it will be so difficult to terminate them once they get job security. *See* Peter Simon's article cited in Manual § 2.2.1 N.5. Government might well decide to contract out certain chores because of the private sector's efficiency advantage (although more significant factors that encourage outsourcing of jobs may be that private employees make less than government employees and are less likely to be unionized).

However, this argument can be overstated. Collective bargaining agreements virtually always give employees a form of tenure—a right not to be discharged except for cause and a grievance and arbitral remedy to enforce it. Probably it is no more difficult to discharge a government employee who claims due process protection than to fire a unionized employee for cause. Moreover, the sort of protection provided by *Loudermill* falls far short of a formal tenure system enjoyed by college professors. It should not be all that difficult to discharge someone under *Loudermill* procedure.

Perhaps the key point is that *Loudermill's* written pre-termination procedure is cheap and easy to comply with. By the time a post-termination hearing rolls around, the employee may have another job. Meanwhile, the employer will have gotten the employee out of the workplace and filled the job with someone else. Of course, if an employee wins the post-termination hearing, he or she will be entitled to reinstatement and back pay.

3. *Jobs and licenses as property. Bishop* is puzzling because the Court accepted an interpretation of municipal law that seems at odds with its plain meaning. The language of the ordinance seemed to say that a policeman could be fired only for cause, but the Court deferred to the contrary reading of the trial judge and concluded that the plaintiff was an at-will employee.

Perhaps the *Bishop* approach is simply wrong: federal courts should steer away from this kind of hair-splitting in the interest of simplifying due process adjudication concerning government jobs (the cases are incessant, as a glance at your current Federal Reporter advance sheets will probably confirm). Thus, one might argue, when a statute or contract creates a job and declares it is "permanent," or states that the jobholder can be discharged only for stated causes, the job should be treated as "property" for due process purposes. The court should disregard actual state practice or precedent suggesting that the stated causes are merely advisory. The burden should be on the drafters of contracts or statutes to make clear that a termination decision is purely discretionary, if that's what the state or city wants.

However, the Court could respond that cases like *Bishop* follow from *Roth,* which rests on the premise that the question of whether the plaintiff has been deprived of "property" depends on positive law—here, state law. It is certainly conceivable that a state court would construe an ordinance in a manner that differs from its apparent plain meaning. Therefore, a governmental defendant should be free to argue to a federal court that the "real" law of the state is less favorable to the plaintiff than it appears to be. The due process clause protects against deprivations of "property," not of interests that a claimant reasonably but mistakenly believes are property.

Is access to a public park a "property" right? No, according to *Brown v. Michigan City,* 462 F.3d 720, 728-29 (7th Cir.2006). The city barred Brown, a convicted child molester, from entering a city park that is open to the city residents free of charge. Spending time in the park was Brown's sole pleasure in life. Since there was no state law or city ordinance guaranteeing public access to the park, the court held that the Parks Department had discretion whether and under what conditions members of the public could enter the park. Yet apparently nobody had ever been banned from a city park before. Surely there is an understanding that every resident has a right to enter a park, in the same sense that it's understood everyone has access to utility service or public education or to walk on the sidewalk. If this is not established by statute, surely it is established by implied contract as in *Perry v. Sindermann* or by custom immemorial. As a result of its decision, the court did not have to decide whether due process was in fact provided or whether entry to the park was unworthy of protection since it was *de minimis. Brown* might make a good teaching problem if an instructor doesn't like the tennis coach or hotline problems, particularly because it contains an equally dubious holding on liberty issues. See discussion in N. 7 below.

4. *Standards plus discretion.* The problem of statutes that contain both standards and discretion is pervasive. Local land use planning ordinances, for example, always reserve plenty of discretion to the decisionmaker. Whether such ordinances create entitlements and thus due process "property" is the subject of a vast amount of conflicting law. Shapiro

and Levy argue that due process should apply whenever government refuses to grant (or terminates) a benefit pursuant to a statute that contains a legal standard, regardless of whether the statute also contains a discretionary element. Sidney A. Shapiro & Richard E. Levy, "Government Benefits and the Rule of Law: Toward a Standards-Based Theory of Due Process," 57 Admin. L. Rev. 107, 134-42 (2005).

In *Castle Rock,* it is difficult to envisage just what kind of procedures could protect Jessica's interest in enforcing the DVRO (assuming that the Court had determined that she had an entitlement to such enforcement). Could the police hold a hearing in which Jessica and Simon would argue about whether the police should arrest Simon? If cities were liable for damages in civil rights actions for failing to provide procedural protections when the police fail to enforce a DVRO as aggressively as they might have, all such statutes would swiftly be changed to make enforcement discretionary. In this sense, the Court's holding, which preserves a system in which enforcement is "mandated" by state law but is not considered an individual "entitlement," may well serve the long-run interests of potential victims of domestic violence.

The *Castle Rock* majority articulated an alternative ground for its decision: The harm to Jessica (the wife who received the DVRO) was "indirect" because the DVRO restrained Simon (the husband) and authorized the police to arrest him. Thus the failure to arrest Simon imposed an "indirect" burden on Jessica. This direct/indirect dichotomy was based on the earlier case of *O'Bannon v. Town Court Nursing Center,* 447 U.S. 773 (1980). In *O'Bannon,* the government decertified a nursing home. This action compelled its residents (who were receiving Medicaid assistance) to move. The Court said that the nursing home was entitled to a hearing but not the residents, because the harm to the residents was indirect (that is, derivative from the harm imposed on the nursing home). In *Castle Rock,* Scalia wrote: "An indirect and incidental result of the Government's enforcement action . . . does not amount to a deprivation of any interest in life, liberty, or property. In this case, as in *O'Bannon,* the simple distinction between government action that directly affects a citizen's legal rights . . . and action that is directed against a third party and affects the citizen only indirectly or incidentally, provides a sufficient answer to respondent's reliance on cases that found government-provided services to be entitlements. The *O'Bannon* Court expressly noted that the distinction between direct and indirect benefits distinguished *Memphis Light, Gas & Water Div. v. Craft,* 436 U.S. 1 (1978), one of the government-services cases on which the dissent relies." 545 U.S. at 767-68 (citations and internal quotation marks omitted).

However, the majority's reliance on *O'Bannon* seems questionable. In that case, the interests of the nursing home and the residents were aligned. Both had an interest in keeping the nursing home certified to receive government benefits. However, this is not the case in *Castle Rock*. Simon's interest in not having the DVRO enforced against him is diametrically opposed to Jessica's interest in having the DVRO enforced.

6. *De minimis deprivations.* The *de minimis* issue is raised and discussed in the Problem, N.9. Surely there is some point at which a deprivation would be *de minimis*, such as a trip to the principal's office as a punishment or being made to stay after school. *See Hassan v. Lubbock Indep. School Dist.*, 55 F.3d 1075 (5th Cir.1995) (brief detention of student during field trip is *de minimis*). See also *Ryan v. CIF-SDS*, 114 Cal. Rptr.2d 798, 804-14 (Ct.App.2001), ruling that a high school athlete who has been denied eligibility to play on a team has not suffered a deprivation of liberty or property. *Ryan* cites many state and federal cases in support of its conclusion. It distinguishes *Goss* by stating that there is no property interest in each individual piece of the educational experience, such as sports, drama, or the debate team.

In *Perry v McDonald*, 280 F.3d 159 (2d Cir. 2001), the state deprived a car owner of vanity plates saying SHTHPNS, because the letters were considered offensive. The court assumed that the driver's interest in the particular plates was "property," but said it was pretty trivial. As a result, the "private interest" factor in a *Mathews* balancing was very slight. The court held that post-deprivation process was sufficient. This might be a better way to decide cases like *Swick* or *Hassan*, because it is rather difficult at the margin to decide what is and isn't too trivial to bother with. The interest is "property" but whatever minimal procedures the state is using to avoid errors is all the process that's due.

7. *Stigma as a deprivation of liberty.* When the state imposes a stigma, a state-court defamation suit is a poor substitute for a name-clearing hearing. Damages are extremely difficult to prove, there are numerous procedural obstacles in defamation cases, government officials may be immune from suit, and nothing the court could do will repair the injury to reputation that occurs by reason of the defamation. The tort-due process interface is considered further in § 2.4. In many cases involving random and unauthorized torts by government employees, a prior hearing is not feasible—but it is quite possible to provide a prior hearing in the *Paul* situation.

As discussed in § 2.4 N.2, however, Justice Stevens has suggested that the availability of a state-court defamation action might have been constitutionally adequate to cure the stigma in *Paul*. Even if that is so, surely the majority in *Paul* went astray in holding that Davis was not deprived of liberty in the first place.

After *Paul*, government must still supply a name-clearing hearing before it stigmatically discharges a person from a government job in which the holder has no property interest. *See Doe v. Dept. of Justice*, 753 F.2d 1092 (D.C.Cir.1985) (government attorney discharged for arguing with other government attorneys while taking deposition and for drinking on job); *Campanelli v. Bockrath*, 100 F.3d 1476 (9th Cir.1996) (firing basketball coach for abusing players is stigmatic). But discharge for poor job performance is not stigmatic. *Harrison v. Bowen*, 815 F.2d 1505 (D.C.Cir.1987).

A name-clearing hearing requires notice of the charges and an opportunity to refute, by cross-examination or independent evidence, the allegations giving rise to the reputational injury. Moreover, if the damage to the individual would not be alleviated by the hearing, it is possible to get damages in addition to the hearing. *Lyons v. Barrett*, 851 F.2d 406 (D.C.Cir.1988).

In *Bishop v. Wood*, 426 U.S. 341 (1976), a policeman was fired for reasons that he alleged were both false and professionally harmful. However, the discharge did not deprive him of "liberty" because the city manager did not disclose them to anyone except the policeman himself. The problem is that these reasons will probably be disclosed in the future when the employee seeks another job. Nevertheless, no name-clearing hearing is required either at the time of discharge or at the time of subsequent disclosure.

See Olivieri v. Rodriguez, 122 F.3d 406 (7th Cir.1997), which also involved discharge of a probationary policeman for a stigmatic reason (sexual harassment of female officers). Posner's opinion in *Olivieri* points out that the information may never be disclosed (some former employers refuse to disclose any information to subsequent employers). And even if it is disclosed, this would occur as the result of action taken by plaintiff (applying for new job). A contrary view would encourage him to apply to every police force in the nation in order to magnify his damages. One reading of *Siegert* supports this argument.

Siegert illustrates that a majority of the Court is anxious to avoid allowing due process to serve as a font of tort law, opening government employees to damage actions under § 1983 (in the case of state government) or *Bivens* (in the case of the federal government). It is unclear from the decision whether the reason Siegert failed to meet stigma-plus was that he quit (rather than being fired, even though he quit under threat of being fired) or that the information was disclosed (on Siegert's request) several weeks after the resignation. The Court wrote that the "alleged defamation was not uttered incident to the termination of Siegert's employment by the hospital, since he voluntarily resigned from his position at the hospital, and the letter was written several weeks later."

Brown v. Michigan City, 462 F.3d 720, 729-32 (7th Cir.2006), also discussed in N.3 above, is a startling application of stigma-plus. The city banned Brown, a convicted child molester, from a public park. At the board meeting of the parks department, city officials made derogatory statements about him, which the court assumed were false and stigmatic. However, Brown failed to meet the "plus" part of the test, even though there had been a change in his legal status (he was banned from entering the park that he had been visiting for years). As pointed out above, the court decided that Brown had never had a right to enter the park; entrance had always been discretionary with the city. Consequently, the court appears to be holding that stigma-plus cannot be satisfied unless the court has taken away a non-discretionary property interest. This approach collapses liberty and property. It seems contrary to Roth, which assumed that a stigmatized non-tenured teacher (i.e. one with no property right in his job) would be entitled to a name clearing hearing when his contract was non-renewed. Because Brown contains interesting and dubious holdings on both liberty and property, it would make a good problem for this section.

8. *Prisoners' rights as liberty.* *Hewitt* provided for hearings if the statute or prison regulations appeared to create some sort of entitlement (such as a for-cause requirement) as opposed to a discretionary standard. The reasons for dispensing with the *Hewitt* standard were persuasive. That case forced courts to draw absurd distinctions as to whether a standard in statute or regulation was mandatory or discretionary. Lots of weight was placed on the fortuitous choice of words like "shall" or "may." Typical is the language in *Sandin* itself—it required the committee to find guilt where "the charge is supported by substantial evidence." This attempt in the Hawaii prison regulations to give some procedural protection to prisoners and some guidance to the committee was found by the lower court to constrain the discretion of decisionmakers and hence create a liberty interest under the positivist approach of *Hewitt*.

The Court argues persuasively that *Hewitt* created an incentive for prison managers to delete mandatory language from their regulations in order to avoid due process. Krent provides documentation of this claim, pointing to six jurisdictions that dispensed with mandatory language in regulations to avoid *Hewitt* and related cases. *See* Harold J. Krent, "Reviewing Agency Action for Inconsistency With Prior Rules and Regulations," 72 Chi.-Kent L.Rev. 1187, 1216-18 (1997).

If states turned mandatory standards in prison or parole regulations into discretionary standards, this could be an unfortunate result. There are good reasons to constrain the discretion of front-line prison decisionmakers, such as helping to assure fair procedure and uniformity of decisions. Justice Ginsburg's dissenting opinion in *Sandin* argues that states that do nothing to control behavior of prison workers should not have lesser procedural responsibilities than states that do cabin the workers' discretion.

The unworkability of *Hewitt's* positivist approach to defining liberty suggests arguments against the positivist approach to property articulated in *Roth*. As *Bishop v. Wood* shows, the *Roth* approach drags courts into a morass of sentence-parsing to find out whether the state's discretion is constrained. It encourages states to dispense with discretion-confining language which, in itself, may be a bad result. And it has overloaded federal courts with a vast array of state personnel cases, with questionable benefit to the individuals adversely affected by those personnel decisions. So *Sandin* may be a good occasion to take another look at *Roth*.

Many will disagree with the Court's decision that imposing discipline on prisoners does not infringe a non-positivist aspect of liberty. *See, e.g.*, Susan N. Herman, "The New Liberty: The Procedural Due Process Rights of Prisoners and Others under the Burger Court," 59 NYU L.Rev. 482, 528-43 (1984). She argues that providing hearings in prison discipline or parole denial cases serves important dignitary and rehabilitative interests. Any unduly intrusive effect on prison administration can be avoided through designing an appropriate process. Ginsburg, J., dissenting in *Sandin*, argues strongly for a non-positivist liberty interest in prison discipline cases. In all such cases, she argues, there should be notice, an unbiased tribunal, and a chance to present reasons why the actions should not be taken.

What's left after *Sandin*? If the discipline will "inevitably affect the duration of the sentence," it entails a deprivation of liberty. Even though it's quite possible, even likely, that the discipline imposed on a prisoner would defer his parole date (since the parole board would certainly take a record of prison discipline into account), that's not enough, because the sentence-lengthening effect is not "inevitable." In *Wolff*, the discipline reduced good time credits and thus automatically lengthened the sentence.

Vitek involves transfer to a mental institution and *Washington* involves involuntary administration of behavior-modifying drugs. These are seen as "atypical and significant hardship on the inmate in relation to the ordinary incidents of prison life." *Wilkinson v. Austin* stressed the extraordinarily harsh conditions in the super-max prison in providing that transfer to such an institution was a deprivation of liberty. It's unclear why *Vitek*, *Washington*, and *Wilkinson* are seen as deprivations of liberty when assignment to solitary confinement as discipline for misconduct is not a deprivation of liberty. As Justice Breyer points out in his *Sandin* dissent,

33

the punishment reduced Conner from 8 hours to 30 minutes a day outside his cell, imposed total isolation, and required the wearing of leg irons and waist chains. But at least the Court has fewer cases to overrule through this approach.

Note 11 of *Sandin* reminds us that prisoners retain first and eighth amendments rights, rights to equal protection, and state-law rights under internal prison grievance procedures.

9. *Problem—property* . If Rex's decision deprived Doris of property, there must be "some kind of hearing." Under *Loudermill* the state cannot prescribe procedures that fall below due process minima. This problem presents all of the issues arising out of the *Roth* approach and thus is an excellent review of this important material.

a) Neither statute nor regulation constrains the principal's discretion (at least the problem does not mention any language that would do so). However, the *contract* requires renewal in case of "satisfactory" service. That could be de facto tenure under *Perry v. Sindermann* (discussed in § 2.2.1, N.7), holding that contract rights enforceable under state law create an entitlement. But is "satisfactory" work a sufficient constraint on discretion? *Bishop* counsels deference to prior interpretations by the school board or state courts—if there are any. The standard of "satisfactory" work might be so empty of content that it is the equivalent of pure discretion. The word "satisfactory" probably means "reasonably satisfactory" (as it would in the law of contracts). Thus the term has content (would a reasonable person find the service satisfactory?) and the contract therefore provides for an entitlement rather than merely for a discretionary standard. Reasonable satisfaction with the coach's job is about as constraining as the normal "cause" or "good cause" standard provided by civil service laws as in *Loudermill.*

b) Could this job fall below some *de minimis* level and thus not be protectable? The property interest here is more important than those involved in *Swick, Hassan,* or *Ryan* (see Manual N.6). Doris is, after all, losing her job, with the various career implications that always entails, and $1600. She's not just being denied the right to carry a gun or go on a field trip. Losing a four-month job seems more significant than a ten-day school suspension as in *Goss.*

c) Contract rights as property: In *Vail,* a football coach was hired for one year with assurances that the contract would be renewed for a second year. The coach's contract was not renewed for a second year, but he received no hearing or statement of reasons. The majority affirmed a district court decision awarding him damages. However, Posner's dissent argues that there is a distinction between contract and property rights, and that *Perry v. Sindermann* was a case relating to tenure, not to a mere contract right of renewal. This anticipates the question discussed in § 2.4 N.3 about breach of contract as a deprivation of property. It may be a deprivation of property, but under *Lujan v. G&G Fire Sprinklers,* the remedy is a state-court contract action, not a due process hearing.

You might want to defer discussion of this issue until you reach § 2.4; or you can discuss whether a breach of contract by the government should be treated as a deprivation of property at all. In other words, was *Perry* right in equating breach of an implied contract with a statutory tenure provision? Should we really constitutionalize all government contract law? Especially if the remedy is the same remedy you'd have for non-constitutional breach—a contract case in court—not a prior hearing. The court isn't going to mandate a prior hearing for breach of contract because that would prevent government from engaging in efficient breach.

d) Note that Rex violated the contract by failing to give a written statement of reasons. Numerous cases (including *Bishop v. Wood*) make clear that a state's violation of a *procedural* norm does not trigger a constitutional right to hearing. If a *federal* agency were involved, the courts would require the agency to follow its own rules (even though there is no constitutional requirement that it adopt those rules). *See Wojciechowicz v. Dept. of Army,* 763 F.2d 149 (3d Cir.1985).

e) An issue that is not raised by the problem, but interesting nevertheless, is whether Doris would be entitled to a hearing if she was not rehired because the principal decided to abolish girls' tennis, so that a coach was no longer "needed." This decision would be treated as rulemaking rather than adjudication because it has general rather than particular applicability. *See* the discussion of the rulemaking-adjudication distinction in § 2.5.

f) The discharge was not stigmatic, so it is not a deprivation of liberty as that term is defined in *Roth.* Suppose that Rex accompanied his discharge decision with a press release stating that Doris was an incompetent tennis coach. Under *Harrison v. Bowen,* Manual N.7, calling someone incompetent may not be considered stigmatic. However, suppose Rex announced that Doris had been let go because she had sexually harassed team members. That would be stigmatic by any standard and would require the school to provide for a name-clearing hearing. *But see Brown v. Michigan City,* 462 F.3d 720, 729-32 (7th Cir. 2006), also discussed in Manual N.7 above, holding that a stigmatic decision to bar a convicted child molester from a city park did not deprive him of liberty because his ability to enter the park was always discretionary, not an entitlement. *Brown* would suggest that Rex's statement was not a deprivation of liberty if Doris' job status was discretionary. This really sounds wrong and totally inconsistent with the treatment of stigma as deprivation of liberty in *Roth.*

In *Campanelli v. Bockrath,* 100 F.3d 1476 (9th Cir.1996), the athletic director at the University of California fired a basketball coach, then issued damaging statements to the media which foreclosed the coach from getting another college coaching job. These statements indicated that the coach inflicted psychological damage on the players, not just by the usual yelling and cursing, but by abusing them through incessant, malicious attacks. The court held that the coach stated a *Roth* liberty claim. It also indicated that *Roth* applied even though the press publicity occurred a week after the coach was fired. Presumably, this case remains good law despite *Siegert v. Gilley,* 500 U.S. 226 (1991) (text N.7) since the disclosure occurred on the employer's initiative after discharging the employee.

g) This problem illustrates the importance of a right to a hearing. It at least hints that the discharge was for an improper reason (animosity between coach and principal's kid) and is thus arbitrary. This job may be critical to Doris' career (a stepping-stone to a permanent coaching job or a way to get private students). Provision of some modest procedure (perhaps a face-to-face discussion with someone above the principal's level and a written explanation) would be a significant protection, although hardly foolproof. The contrary view, well expressed by Posner's dissent in *Vail,* is that disputes of this kind do not belong in federal court. Moreover, constitutionalizing this sort of action would impose considerable costs on government and would rigidify the personnel process. You can have an excellent debate about this in class.

10. *Problem—liberty.* The problem simplifies the facts of *Valmonte* but leaves the basic issue intact. In *Valmonte* the court held that placement on the list deprives Anna of a liberty interest, thus triggering due process protections. *Paul v. Davis* holds that governmental defamation isn't a deprivation of liberty; it must be *stigma plus.* Generally a stigmatic discharge from the job is required. But consistent with the positivist approach of *Paul* (especially its treatment of *Constantineau*), stigmatic government action *plus* any change in a person's *legal status* would be a deprivation of liberty.

Valmonte observes that governmental defamation producing "deleterious effects which flow directly from a sullied reputation" would normally be insufficient to trigger due process protection. Such effects would include the impact that defamation might have on job prospects, "or, for that matter, romantic aspirations, friendships, self-esteem, or any other typical consequence of a bad reputation." 18 F.3d at 1001. Similarly, see *Behrens v. Regier,* 422 F.3d 1255 (11th Cir. 2005)—placement of name on list of "verified child abusers" would probably have negative impact on ability to adopt a child, but there is no legal right to adopt a child. Adoption decisions depend entirely on a discretionary "best interests of the child" standard. Consequently, placement on the list does not satisfy the "plus" requirement.

But Anna's case is different, because being listed on the registry places a tangible *legal* burden on Anna's future employment prospects (as opposed to a mere *practical* burden). By operation of law, potential employers will be informed about her inclusion on the registry. Either they won't hire her or are *legally* required to explain in writing why they are hiring her. It's unlikely that many employers would want to go on record explaining why they are hiring a child abuser listed on the registry. This is like *Constantineau*—being placed on the public drunkard list had a *legal* consequence: he couldn't buy alcoholic beverages. *But see Brown v. Michigan City*, 462 F.3d 720, 729-32 (7th Cir.2006), discussed above. *Brown* questionably holds that derogatory statements made in process of banning a convicted child molester from a city park do not meet the "plus" test because he never had a right to enter the park in the first place.

Siegert v. Gilley, discussed above, seems distinguishable. In *Siegert* the employee voluntarily quit his job, then several weeks later asked the former employer to communicate with a new employer. In *Valmonte*, however, Anna did not do anything voluntarily. The legal consequences attach immediately upon listing of one's name in the registry. Consequently, *Siegert* seems inapplicable unless it is read to limit liberty interests exclusively to those who are defamed while in the course of being terminated from government employment.

In *Humphries v. County of Los Angeles*, 547 F.3d 1117 (9th Cir. 2008), the court carried *Valmonte* a long step further. Humphries was placed on the California Child Abuse Registry after his stepdaughter complained he had abused her. The charge was conclusively shown to be false; criminal proceedings were dismissed and Humphries obtained a court order finding him "factually innocent" of the charge. Nevertheless, he was placed on the Registry and there is no procedure for getting off.

California law provides that various agencies need to check the Child Abuse Registry before issuing various licenses, such as for a day care center. If a person is listed on the registry, the agency must investigate further. The court held that this required checking and investigation function met the stigma-plus test, because it imposed a tangible burden on an individual's ability to obtain a status recognized by state law.

The court then took another big leap: Other agencies (such as those granting licenses to work in child care or granting adoptions) have access to the registry but are not required to check it. Nevertheless, said the court, the existence of the registry meets the stigma-plus requirement even without any legal requirement that the agencies check the list. It is sufficient that they "reflexively" check it (as they obviously should do). Despite the court's efforts to distinguish *Paul v. Davis,* the decision (especially the second holding) appears directly contrary to *Paul,* since the bottom line was that the stigmatic listing did practical harm to Humphries but had no legal consequences. Nevertheless, in light of the facts of the case, the decision is wholly understandable.

Assuming Anna has been deprived of liberty, she is entitled to a name-clearing hearing to get her name off the list. The opportunity to complain in writing won't do. Presumably she should be able to explain why and how she slapped her child, so that an impartial decisionmaker can decide whether this act fell within legitimate discipline or was child abuse. She should be entitled to cross-examine the neighbor if there is a dispute over what happened. She should be entitled to present witnesses about her child rearing. The decisionmaker should state reasons for the ultimate decision.

In *Valmonte,* there were procedural protections that are left out of the problem, but the court found them inadequate. There was a provision providing for a hearing. However, the listed person stays on the list if there is any "credible evidence" of child abuse. After an employer refuses to hire a listed person, there is a full hearing. This was found inadequate protection in light of the strong private interest involved and the great risk of error from taking information over a hotline. The court engaged in a *Mathews v. Eldridge* balancing, but that's premature at this point. However, you might wish to come back to this problem after you do *Mathews,* asking whether post-deprivation remedies here are sufficient.

2.3 TIMING OF TRIAL-TYPE HEARINGS

In 2007, Social Security proposed regulations that would make significant changes in the procedure for adjudicating disability cases. See 72 Fed.Reg. 61,218 (Oct. 29, 2007). These regulations adopt many of the procedural changes previously introduced experimentally in the Boston region. *See* 71 Fed.Reg. 16,424 (Mar. 31, 2006); Frank Bloch, Jeffrey Lubbers, & Paul Verkuil, "The Social Security Administration's New Disability Adjudication Rules: A Significant and Promising Reform," 92 Cornell L.Rev. 235 (2007). These included changing the Appeals Council to a Review Board that would review ALJ decisions on the petitioner's request but with limited scope of review. The proposed rules provide for closing the record at the time of the ALJ hearing; written materials must be submitted five days before the hearing and cannot be added to the file thereafter without a showing of good cause. The NPRM pointed out that there is now a backlog of 700,000 cases at the ALJ level and it is climbing. The resulting delays cause great injustice to deserving applicants who can't get benefits until they prevail at their ALJ hearing.

MATHEWS v. ELDRIDGE

Notes and Questions

1. *Dispensing with prior hearings in emergencies.* *Goldberg* used a balancing test to decide *whether* an interest is protected—in contrast to the more absolutist approach to defining liberty and property which appears in *Roth*. On the other hand, *Goldberg* declared that a hearing must precede the deprivation and laid out an inflexible list of the elements that a prior hearing must provide.

Mathews introduced a framework for analyzing timing and element issues that restored traditionally flexible due process analysis. Of course, the other side of the flexibility coin is indeterminacy of result, easily manipulated factors, and holdings that mirror the philosophical biases of particular judges. Rigidity provides more predictable results that are harder to manipulate; but these results may seem inappropriate if they over-proceduralize government programs and impose costs that outweigh benefits. Take your choice.

The various grounds on which *Goldberg* allegedly differs from *Mathews* seem to represent a polite way to break away from *Goldberg* without conspicuously overruling it. The factual assumptions about the degree of deprivation, the nature of the issues in disability v. welfare, and costs to the government are mostly unsubstantiated guesses. *See* Laura Cooper, "*Goldberg's* Forgotten Footnote," 64 Minn.L.Rev. 1107, 1146-53 (1980). Consider the three factors in a *Mathews* balance:

a. Interest of the recipient. The issue here is the intensity of need for a *continued flow* of benefits until a hearing occurs. The Court admits that recipients of disability are apt to be desperately needy and will be without benefits for well over a year before they are restored. Of course, some recipients have other resources, but many do not. By definition, people on disability are not working and are generally subject to very serious long-term health problems. Even if the problem has been alleviated, they will have great difficulty rejoining the work force. They usually will not qualify for any welfare program. As a consequence, people cut off from disability benefits may often be quite desperate and sometimes are suicidal.

On the other hand, truly destitute recipients of disability are also entitled to receive Supplemental Security Income (SSI, which is Title XVI

39

of the Social Security Act). Although they would be cut off from SSI at the same time as from disability, they are entitled to a prior hearing before termination from SSI, because it is a need-based program like AFDC.

b. Risk of error and likelihood that prior hearing will diminish the risk. The Court thought that the issues to be determined in disability cases (medical condition, availability of jobs) are more objective than in welfare cases (where credibility is often in issue); therefore it is more likely that the state agency's determination based on written sources will be correct and less likely that a prior oral hearing will be helpful in correcting errors.

Many but by no means all welfare case issues require credibility determinations. *See* Cooper, *supra,* 64 Minn. L. Rev. at 1165 (only 11% of welfare hearings involved factual disputes; an additional 18% involved application of facts to law; 47% were disputes of law; 22% were protests of policy). The issues in disability cases are often equally subjective: is the individual faking a back injury or psychological disability? how much pain does she really have? just what kind of work can she do? how impartial is the claimant's doctor? Social Security's doctor?

The *Mathews* case relies on the multiple levels at which results are checked, but these occur at the state level with only superficial checking by Social Security. In disability as in welfare cases, an exchange of written materials is unlikely to produce a correct result when a system depends on input from an uneducated and confused individual who must fill out periodic questionnaires. The New York regulations invalidated in *Goldberg* also provided a discussion with the caseworker, reviews by a unit supervisor, written notice, opportunity for written response, additional reviews, and a written determination. Arguably this permitted a recipient to "mold" his or her arguments to the precise questions at issue. The written pre-termination procedure ruled unacceptable in *Goldberg* seems to be just as good in detecting errors as the pre-termination disability review machinery found acceptable in *Mathews.*

c. Government's interest in resisting the desired procedure. Here the *Mathews* analysis is directly contrary to that of *Goldberg.* The Court is swayed by the substantial cost to the program of continuing to pay ineligible recipients until they receive hearings, as well as the incentive that a prior-hearing requirement provides for people to appeal. In addition, the Court defers to the judgment of the agency that the procedure it provided is sufficient. The court ignores the public interest in paying eligible recipients. All of this flies in the face of *Goldberg.*

An interesting example of the emergency exception to the requirement of a prior hearing arose in *Catanzaro v. Weiden,* 140 F.3d 91

(2d Cir. 1998). The case would make a good problem if you don't like the one in N.7 about public housing evictions. An ordinance gives the city of Middletown, New York, the power to immediately demolish any building posing imminent danger to the public. The city must provide a hearing to the building owner after the demolition takes place. P owns buildings at 82 and 84 E. Main St. The buildings (which are connected by a common wall) contain shops and apartments and are ugly and outmoded. The tenants are primarily racial minorities.

A car plows into 84. The mayor orders it to be demolished because it is in danger of collapsing into the street, and it is demolished the same day over P's protests. The next day the mayor orders 82 demolished also. He claims that damage to the common wall occurring because of the demolition of 84 rendered 82 in danger of collapse also unless P immediately reconstructed it which he declined to do. During the demolition, the mayor joked that the process was "instant urban renewal."

P sues the mayor and city for damages under 42 U.S.C. § 1983, claiming procedural and substantive due process violations. He argues the city should have provided a prior hearing before tearing down the buildings and that the public safety argument was a pretext for tearing down some ugly buildings in order to make Main Street look better and get rid of minority tenants. The defendants move for summary judgment. Both sides submit affidavits supporting their position. P's experts say there was no risk of injury to the public (especially in regard to 82) while the city's experts say there was such a risk.

The court split 2-1, with the majority holding that P survived the summary judgment motion. P is entitled to a trial on the issue of whether the declaration of an emergency was arbitrary, a determination that could not be made from affidavits on a summary judgment motion. He is also entitled to a trial on his substantive due process argument that the demolition was a pretext for getting rid of ugly buildings and unwanted minority tenants.

The dissent concludes (correctly in our view) that the summary judgment motion should be granted. City officials should not have to worry about being sued for damages when they determine that a building must be immediately demolished to protect the public and should not be required to delay demolition until a hearing has been held. The risk of getting sued might make them too cautious in making the tough decision to protect the public. Whether the officials were right or wrong in a particular case shouldn't be the issue, provided the ordinance describes a situation in which public safety is a concern and provided that the state provides for an adequate post-destruction remedy.

The dissent cites language in *Hodel* (cited in the text): "Discretion of any official may be abused. Yet it is not a requirement of due process that there be a judicial inquiry before discretion may be exercised. It is sufficient, where only property rights are concerned, that there is at some stage an opportunity for a hearing and a judicial determination." 452 U.S. at 303. The dissent stated that summary judgment should be granted when the city could at least come up with affidavits on its side (but should be denied if the city could not produce such affidavits). This should satisfy the standard provided in *Loudermill* that, prior to the deprivation, there should be some sort of probable cause determination that the deprivation is justified.

Thus there are three positions here, each supported by prior authority and decent arguments: i) P is entitled to a trial on whether the demolition order was arbitrary; ii) P is entitled to a trial on this issue only if the city cannot come up with affidavits supporting its position; iii) in no event is P entitled to a trial if the underlying statute is reasonable. However, we should advise city officials not to tell jokes while demolishing buildings under emergency declarations.

2. *Post-termination disability payments?* We were surprised to learn of the regulation that allows a disability recipient to elect to continue receiving payments until an unfavorable ALJ decision. A SSA ALJ told us that most recipients take advantage of the election and that they have never heard of SSA trying to recoup the payments. One would expect that SSA would have embraced *Mathews* for all the reasons given in that opinion. There is a significant dollar cost to continuing payments, given that the hearing system is overloaded and there are long delays. In addition, the continuation option obviously encourages people to demand hearings even though they are pretty sure they will lose. It is puzzling that these regulations have remained in effect, given the financial difficulties of the Social Security system. All administrations have sought ways to limit the cost of entitlement programs like disability, so these regulations would appear to be an easy target.

3. *Timing and employment decisions.* In *McDaniels v. Flick,* 59 F.3d 446 (3d Cir.1995), noted, 41 Villanova L.Rev. 607 (1996), the court considered whether a *Loudermill*-style pre-termination hearing was sufficient in the case of a tenured college professor accused of sexual harassment who had held the job for 20 years. The court pointed out that the college, as much as the professor, had an interest in preserving its reputation and safeguarding students. Reversing a jury verdict, it held that the *Loudermill* standards were satisfied. The professor argued that he was in a state of shock upon learning that he had been charged with harassment, so was unable to meaningfully respond; the court decided that even if this were true, the professor had sufficient additional opportunities to

respond after the pre-termination meeting. Moreover, it held that the decisionmaker at the pre-termination hearing need not meet due process standards for impartiality, so long as these would be satisfied at the post-termination hearing.

4. *How long is too long?* In *City of Los Angeles v. David*, 523 U.S. 715 (2003), the City towed David's car from a no-parking zone and charged him $134.50 in towing fees to get his car back. He redeemed the car and demanded a hearing on his request for a refund of the fees. He complained that trees had obstructed his view of the "no parking" sign. A hearing was provided, but not until 27 days after the car was towed (David lost).

The lower court held that due process required a hearing within five days of the towing, but the Supreme Court reversed. Under *Mathews* factor 1, David's interest in a prompt hearing was purely monetary. It involved only the use of $134.50 during the time he awaited a hearing. Thus it was of less significance than the loss of a job in *Mallen* (see Text N.1) or the loss of the use of the car itself. Under factor 2, a 27-day delay in presenting evidence is unlikely to spawn factual errors. Factor 3 was decisive—there are only so many courtrooms and presiding officers available. There are about one thousand such hearings per year. Police have to be pulled off of other duties to testify at the hearings. Thus delays in holding hearings are acceptable.

5. *Suspension or discharge.* In *Gilbert*, the policeman was first suspended, then demoted to a different job (groundskeeper), which paid less. The Court's unanimous opinion (written by Scalia) noted that it had never decided whether due process applies to employment actions short of termination, but since the parties had not raised the issue, the Court assumed due process applied. This hints that at least some members of the Court would like to limit the scope of *Loudermill*.

Gilbert will probably encourage many public employers to utilize suspensions without pay and without prior hearing in cases involving serious misconduct, instead of providing pre-termination hearings under *Loudermill*. Suppose a university employee has been caught stealing. It would take five days to organize a *Loudermill* pre-termination hearing. A better approach, from the university's point of view, might be to immediately suspend the employee without pay and provide a post-suspension hearing which would also be a full-fledged trial-type termination hearing as quickly as one can be organized.

Prior to *Gilbert*, the assumption was that an employee must be paid during the suspension period. The lower court had imposed a blanket rule that due process required that paychecks continue during suspension. This was based on dictum in *Loudermill*: "in those situations where the employer perceives a significant hazard in keeping the employee on the job, it can avoid the problem by suspending *with pay.*" *Gilbert* holds that this language in *Loudermill* was never intended to preclude an employer from suspending without pay.

The policeman in *Gilbert* was suspended on August 26. Criminal charges were dropped on September 1. No hearing was provided until September 18. "Once the charges were dropped, the risk of erroneous deprivation increased substantially, and, as petitioners conceded at oral argument, there was likely value in holding a prompt hearing." The Court remanded so that lower courts could consider whether the delay was too long.

As to professional license suspensions, under § 14(c) of the 1961 MSAPA (on which most state APAs are based), "If the agency finds that the public health, safety, or welfare imperatively requires emergency action, and incorporates a finding to that effect in its order, summary suspension of a license may be ordered pending proceedings for revocation or other action. These proceedings shall be promptly instituted and determined." *See also* 1981 MSAPA § 4-501 (providing for emergency adjudicative procedures) and federal APA § 558(c). The latter provision requires in many cases that an agency give the licensee an opportunity to achieve compliance before suspending or revoking a license.

6. *Problem.* *Lopez* involved a private company operating a federally assisted housing project, so there was a state action issue (eliminated from this problem). That case held that tenants have a property interest in continued occupancy, because the owner could evict or non-renew only for cause. The redevelopment company refused to renew a lease, but the court found there was a custom of non-renewal of leases only for cause, which was akin to the de facto tenure of *Perry v. Sindermann*. In *One Tract of Real Property*, the court held that there was an insufficient showing of exigent circumstances even though the property owner's sons were accused of dealing drugs on the property. Since they were under arrest, it wasn't clear what purpose was served by forfeiting their mother's interest without a prior hearing.

In *Richmond*, the court invalidated HUD's Forfeiture Policy, which permitted seizure of property and eviction from public housing after an ex parte judicial finding that any of the occupants was engaged in drug dealing. The administrative hearing comes after eviction. The court held that there must be prior notice and hearing except in exigent circumstances; however, it didn't define what it meant by exigent circumstances. "While the level of and type of drug trafficking in a particular location might amount to exigent circumstances warranting a summary eviction, the mere use or possession of narcotics would not in every case constitute an extraordinary situation permitting federal law enforcement officers to summarily remove all persons occupying the housing unit where the activity had occurred." 956 F.2d at 1308.

If all of the factual issues in dispute can be raised in a state court eviction proceeding, the Court may well hold that the state provides adequate remedies and dispense with the need for a pre-eviction administrative hearing. The adequate state remedy approach to due process, which is becoming increasingly prominent, is discussed in § 2.4 NN.2 and 3 and in the Problem in § 2.5.

Leases in federally assisted housing projects must provide that any "drug-related criminal activity on or off such premises, engaged in by a public housing tenant, any member of the tenant's household, or any guest or other person under the tenant's control" is cause for eviction. Anti-Drug Abuse Act of 1988 § 5103, 42 U.S.C. § 11903. This is known as the "one-strike" policy. In *HUD v. Rucker,* 535 U.S. 125 (2002), the Supreme Court upheld evictions under this language, even though the tenant had no knowledge of the offenses. The public housing authorities evicted the tenants under state eviction procedures, apparently without an administrative hearing, but the Supreme Court did not discuss the issue of whether an administrative hearing was necessary. It did hold that state unlawful detainer procedures provided adequate notice. It also said: "Any individual factual disputes about whether the lease provision was actually violated can, of course, be resolved in these [eviction] proceedings." *Id.* at 136. Thus *Rucker* may be read as authority that an administrative hearing can be dispensed with if state eviction procedure provides for notice and hearing of the factual issues.

The FHA regulations currently provide that, in the case of drug offenses or serious criminal activity, the authority can evict tenants through state unlawful detainer procedure. However, in the case of other lease violations, like those involved in the problem, the authority must provide for an informal grievance procedure followed by an administrative hearing. Although the regulations are not explicit on the timing issues, it would appear that the hearing must be provided before eviction. See 24 CFR §966.50 et. seq. Thus the summary eviction involved in the problem would violate these regulations. So it's important to observe that tenants might be able to win such a case under the regulations without resorting to due process. *See* Paul Stinson, "Restoring Justice: How Congress Can Amend the One-Strike Laws in Federally-Subsidized Public Housing to Ensure Due Process, Avoid Inequity, and Combat Crime," 11 Geo.J. On Poverty Law & Pol. 435, 456-57, 463-66 (2002). Stinson argues that administrative remedies should be available even in drug cases because public housing tenants are unable to represent themselves in state eviction proceedings and cannot afford counsel. Moreover, lawyers in legal service programs funded by the Legal Services Corporation are not allowed to represent public housing tenants accused of drug violations. *Id.* at 464.

Assuming due process requires an administrative hearing, what process is due?

a) The notice seems defective. The notice fails to give any details about when the offense occurred or who, if anyone was disturbed, or other important facts. However, notice must be sufficiently specific to allow the tenant to prepare a defense. *Goldberg* held that there must be "timely and adequate notice detailing the reasons for a proposed termination" and *Loudermill* required an explanation of the state's evidence. The notice must explain the procedures for correction of errors. *Memphis Light, Gas, & Water Div. v. Craft*, 436 U.S. 1, 14 (1978). In his famous article, Judge Friendly (who wrote *Lopez*) considered notice as the second most important element of due process (after an impartial decisionmaker). "Some Kind of Hearing," 123 U. Pa. L. Rev. 1267, 1280-81 (1975).

See also *Grayden v. Rhodes*, 345 F.3d 1225 (11th Cir.2003), involving a city's emergency evacuation of tenants from an unsafe apartment building. The court held that the city did not need to conduct a pre-deprivation hearing because the numerous code violations added up to a public health emergency. However, the court required adequate pre-deprivation notice to the tenants of their right to a post-deprivation hearing on the condemnation. Although the tenants would still be evacuated before this hearing occurred, they would at least know that they should not sign leases for a new apartment if they wished to challenge the condemnation. *Grayden* could serve as the basis for a problem for instructors who don't like the public housing problem in the text.

b) Must a hearing be provided *before* eviction? Balancing the *Mathews* factors:

i) The private interest in continued occupancy is very important. The project is throwing a poor family onto the street with only ten days to find substitute housing—a "uniquely final deprivation." *Memphis Light*, 436 U.S. at 20. Unlike federal disability, as described in *Mathews*, there probably will not be a backup support system. Muriel's family may well join the homeless. These issues were dramatized in John Grisham's book *The Street Lawyer*, in which an illegal eviction of a poor family forces them to sleep in their car and leads to death by carbon monoxide poisoning.

ii) Because the issues involved are inherently factual, it is likely that a hearing would indeed contribute to an accurate result. Credibility is likely to be at stake: what happened? What time of day? Who was disturbed? Who reported it and what was their motive? These determinations are wholly unlike the primarily objective matters that must be determined in disability cases from professional reports etc.

Nor is there a substantial system of impersonal bureaucratic checks and cross-checks like those described in *Mathews* that might furnish some guarantee of reliability. There is only a determination of a local project manager that Muriel should leave—but that determination could be based on mistake as well as upon malice, vindictiveness, corruption (wanting the apartment for a friend or relative) or other illicit motive. Moreover, if there were only a single incident of playing loud music, it might be considered within tolerable limits, justifying only a warning rather than eviction. This discretionary issue would also benefit from an impartial reconsideration. It is like the issue of discretion (whether or not to discharge an employee because of misconduct) which White's opinion in *Loudermill* indicated should be ventilated before the termination occurred.

iii) The government's interest in avoiding pre-eviction hearings may not be strong. Here a relevant factor is that the hearing will take place within a week after eviction. The *Loudermill* opinions treat the extent of delay that occurs before a post-termination hearing as relevant. Even Justice Marshall conceded that a post-termination hearing that occurred within days after the event might be constitutionally acceptable. However, the fact that the delay will be brief is no help to Muriel and her family who still need a place to sleep for a week.

Indeed, the fact that the project can put on a hearing within a week (evidently it has no case backlog) suggests that there is no harm in requiring the hearing to take place before eviction. Surely, another week of occupancy won't do much more harm, while any time without housing is catastrophic for a family. Requiring a pre-eviction hearing gives the Project an incentive to provide that hearing as quickly as possible; allowing eviction first provides the opposite incentive since the Project would hope that once a tenant is out she will go elsewhere and will not want to bother with a hearing.

On the other hand, there are powerful arguments suggesting a strong government interest against being required to provide pre-eviction hearings. Anti-social behavior in public housing (especially drug dealing) is a terrible problem. It can set off a cycle that destroys the livability of a project in which hundreds or thousands of people live. Good tenants become demoralized and leave or quit taking care of the place. The *Richmond* case allows summary evictions only in the case of exigent circumstances, but leaves little doubt that serious drug dealing would meet that test. *United States v. One Tract of Land* questions even that premise.

The public interest in avoiding pre-eviction hearings may be much

47

more substantial than suggested in the case law and may go far beyond the problem of exigent circumstances. Substantial scholarship indicates that the case law imposing hearing requirements prior to eviction has had negative effects on public housing. The combination of the prior hearing (with a right to counsel, cross examination etc.), together with the need to resort to state eviction proceedings, plus elaboration of the requirements of good cause for eviction, all make it difficult to evict anyone (or at least anyone who can come up with a legal service lawyer) without a lengthy and costly effort. Consequently, project managers became discouraged and don't even try. (Cases that eliminated project managers' discretion in deciding which tenants to admit to public housing in the first place have worsened the problem.) These authors blame the due process case law as one of the significant reasons for the catastrophic disintegration of large urban public housing projects. *See* Robyn M. Smyers, "High Noon in Public Housing: The Showdown Between Due Process Rights and Good Management Principles in the War on Drugs and Crime," 30 Urban Lwyr. 573, 593-96 (1998); Michael H. Schill, "Distressed Public Housing: Where Do We Go From Here?," 60 U.Chi.L.Rev. 497, 515-17 (1993).

Note that, as pointed out above, the present HUD regulations provide for summary eviction through state court unlawful detainer procedures in the case of drug use or dealing (even for offenses off the property and of which the tenant had no knowledge). Thus the concerns expressed in these articles may now be outdated.

As to whether Elm Grove could avoid the need for due process hearings by refusing to renew an expired lease, see *Mitchell v. HUD,* 569 F. Supp. 701 (1983), holding that non-renewal of public housing leases requires good cause. It is unclear whether *Mitchell* is still good law, since the statute now provides that "during the term of the lease . . . the owner shall not terminate the tenancy except for . . . good cause." 42 U.S.C. §1437f(d)(1)(B)(ii).

§ 2.4 ELEMENTS OF A HEARING

INGRAHAM v. WRIGHT

Note before Ingraham: Very few elements of an ordinary civil trial are missing from *Goldberg's* list. According to Henry J. Friendly, "Some Kind of Hearing," 123 U.Pa. L.Rev. 1267, 1299 (1975), the only omitted items are testimony under oath, preparation of a transcript, and a hearing open to the public—and *Goldberg* concerned only the pre-termination hearing. The post-termination hearing was assumed to be more elaborate. The absence of discovery is, of course, a significant difference between due process hearings and ordinary civil trials.

Notes and Questions

1. *Due process at school.* *Jennings v. Wentzville School Dist.*, 397 F.3d 1118 (8th Cir.2005), applied *Goss* to suspension of cheerleaders for drinking. It refused to disqualify the principal for bias just because he had investigated the matter.

Goss was a 5-4 decision, as was *Ingraham.* Justice Powell, a former chairman of the Richmond School Board, argued in his dissent in *Goss* that the decision would have negative effects on school discipline, would require an undue expenditure of resources, and would transfer discretionary authority from school administrators to federal courts. He also argued that existing state remedies were more effective than the truncated due process hearing required by the court. These remedies included written notice to the parents of a suspended child and to the school board, as well as the ability of the parent (as a constituent) to complain to the board. Powell also asked whether the new rule would not also apply to disputes between school and student about grading, transportation, passing courses, taking certain subjects, exclusion from extracurricular activities, or tracking.

In *Ingraham*, Powell obtained a majority for what had been his earlier dissenting view, even though the cases seem indistinguishable. Justice Stewart switched sides without explanation. Justice Douglas, who had been in the *Goss* majority, retired; he was replaced by Justice Stevens, who dissented in *Ingraham.*

Ingraham's attempts to distinguish *Goss* seem feeble. Consultative procedure seems equally appropriate or inappropriate in each case, depending on your point of view. First, *Ingraham* did not involve a property claim; *Goss* involved both property and liberty. Second, "the low incidence of abuse, and the availability of established judicial remedies in the event of abuse, distinguish this case from" *Goss.* Essentially, the majority in *Ingraham* (unlike the *Goss* majority) wanted to keep the federal courts out of school discipline. The two cases represent a very different weighing in the school context of the third *Mathews* factor—the government's interest. And perhaps the two cases represent a different level of confidence in school disciplinarians.

See Jerry R. Parkinson, "Federal Court Treatment of Corporal Punishment in Public Schools," 39 S.D.L.Rev. 276 (1994), which questions Powell's assertions about the low incidence of abuse and about the utility of state law remedies. It points out that in 1986, corporal punishment was administered more than 1,000,000 times in school. *See also* Carolyn Peri Weiss, Note, "Curbing Violence or Teaching It: Criminal Immunity for Teachers Who Inflict Corporal Punishment," 74 Wash.U.L.Q. 1251 (1996), which points out that only two states had banned corporal punishment in school at the time of *Ingraham*, whereas twenty-seven had banned it by 1994. The Note calls attention to Alabama's recently adopted civil and criminal immunity for teachers who inflict corporal punishment. The abolition of civil and criminal liability for excessive punishment suggests that the due process reasoning of *Ingraham* would be inapplicable in Alabama.

See also Rick Lyman, "In Many Public Schools, The Paddle Is No Relic," N.Y. Times. Sept. 30, 2006. The article points out that corporal punishment is still used extensively in many southern and lower-midwestern states, particularly in rural areas. Even there, however, it remains controversial and there have been heated fights before schools boards. Of the 300,000 students paddled in 2002-03, 70% were in Texas, Mississippi, Tennessee, Alabama, and Arkansas. Dozens of lawsuits have been filed around the country, but thus far the courts have tended to side with school districts that employ corporal punishment. The article focused on a particular principal in Texas who advocates corporal punishment as the fifth rung up the disciplinary ladder (after behavior hasn't been changed by warnings, pushups, detention, and isolation). At rung 5, students can choose between corporal punishment, having their parents shadow them all day at school, or suspension from school (eight out of ten choose the paddle). The decision to paddle a student is made in consultation with both students and parents. This suggests *Ingraham* was wrong in assuming that corporal punishment wouldn't work if the school were required to conduct a *Goss*-type consultation before it was administered.

The existence of state tort or contract remedies might be persuasive evidence of the lack of need for, or the inappropriateness of, a due process hearing. We consider this in the next two notes. However, it is difficult to take seriously the Florida tort remedy for unreasonable corporal punishment. It is simply not an adequate substitute for a *Goss*-type consultative hearing before the punishment takes place. As White pointed out, the tort remedy affords no protection against a mistaken though reasonable decision to impose discipline. Moreover, it cannot remove the pain, injury, and humiliation that occurred at the time of the paddling. And, on a practical level, getting an attorney to sue the teacher or the school board would be possible only if the injuries were exceptionally severe, so that there would be substantial damages. Nobody is going to bring a tort suit for the type of injuries that were involved in *Ingraham* which, while painful, cleared up in a few days.

Goss required an opportunity for an *oral* presentation to the disciplinarian but did not require a right to retain counsel, confrontation or an independent decision-maker. By establishing that due process does not require an adversary trial-type process, *Goss* was a critical breakthrough. As liberty and property came to include less momentous (or less rule-bound) interests than welfare, it became necessary to design more efficient and practical procedures than the clanking machinery blueprinted in *Goldberg*.

How would a *Goldberg*-type hearing look in the context of a proposed five-day suspension from high school of a student who allegedly had been fighting on the playground? The hearing might take place in the auditorium for the benefit of the whole student body (of course, this would not really be required by *Goldberg*). After getting continuances for a month or two, counsel would cross-examine (and try to discredit) all the faculty and student witnesses, and the school board would designate a decision-maker who had no prior involvement with the dispute. It might be entertaining, but it would be ridiculous.

As to timing, the Court in *Goss* noted that ordinarily the hearing should precede suspension, but students who pose a continuing danger to persons or property or an ongoing threat of disrupting the academic process can be immediately removed from the school. In such cases, the necessary notice and rudimentary hearing should follow as soon as practicable. 419 U.S. at 582-83. Similarly, *see Memphis Light, Gas & Water Div. v. Craft,* 436 U.S. 1, 18 (1978) (requiring opportunity for meeting with a responsible employee before utility termination).

2. *Tort remedies as a form of due process. Parratt* and *Hudson* seem to be a defensible method of cutting down the federal court civil rights caseload. It is not feasible to hold a prior hearing before a random and unauthorized property destruction by a prison guard, whether he does it accidentally or on purpose.

Yet the Court is closely divided on this issue. It is difficult to reconcile *Zinermon* with *Parratt* and *Hudson*. In *Zinermon*, institution officials ignored state law by allowing a person incapable of giving informed consent to voluntarily admit himself to the institution. Some officials will always mess up, but it is very difficult to solve the problem through a prior hearing; the officials will mess up the prior hearing too. For a fine example of the puzzlement created by these conflicting cases, see the en banc opinion in *Easter House v. Felder,* 910 F.2d 1387 (7th Cir.1990), which involved an alleged conspiracy by Chicago officials to deprive Easter House of its adoption agency license.

In deciding that a common law tort remedy substituted for a pre-corporal punishment hearing, *Ingraham* seems much less convincing than *Parratt*. No Florida case had ever sought damages for wrongful corporal punishment, so the tort remedy was highly uncertain. Moreover, unlike *Parratt* and *Hudson*, but like *Zinermon*, it is perfectly feasible to require a pre-deprivation hearing in *Ingraham*. About all you can say about the cases in this note is that the law is in flux on the question of when post-

51

deprivation state tort remedies provide all the process that's due.

3. *State contract remedies as due process.* The *G & G* approach could, if broadly applied, swallow up cases like *Loudermill.* After all, a wrongfully discharged tenured government employee would have a breach of contract action also. See *Baird v. Bd. of Educ.,* 389 F.3d 685 (7th Cir. 2004), which distinguishes *Loudermill* situations from *G & G.* The state contended in *Baird* that after it provided the summary pre-termination hearing required by *Loudermill,* it could dispense with the post-termination hearing so long as the employee could sue for breach of contract. The court disagreed. In the case of the loss of a protected job, state breach of contract litigation will not suffice for the post-termination hearing. Remarking that the difference is somewhat "mysterious," it determined that *G & G* seems to apply only to the issue of payment of money from a government contract, while in job cases reinstatement is also at stake. Also the post-termination hearing must be conducted promptly, which wouldn't be typical of state court contract actions.

G & G is defensible, because private parties shouldn't have to be treated better when they contract with government than when they contract with other private parties. In the latter situation, when A terminates a contract and refuses to pay because it believes B is in breach, B has no right to specific performance. B can only sue for damages. If B had the ability to trigger an administrative hearing on whether A must pay B, that would be equivalent to giving B a right to specific performance.

The adequate state remedy approach found in *Ingraham, Parratt, Hudson,* and *G & G* is obviously very appealing to the Supreme Court. It seems quite possible that it would be adopted in the area of public housing evictions (see the problem in §2.4 N.6). State court eviction procedures could substitute for the due process pre-eviction hearing now required by most cases. Similarly, the adequate state remedy approach might be used in cases of state land use planning (compare the problem in §2.5 N.5). Rather than allowing a federal civil rights law suit for deprivation of procedural due process in land use planning cases, the courts might decide that state court judicial review of land use appeals is all the process that's due. That would get rid of a significant number of federal court cases about land use disputes that judges typically find irritating (they don't like sitting as a board of zoning appeals).

4. *The right to counsel in administrative hearings.* The issue of whether a denied application for a government benefit triggers a hearing is unresolved. However the *American Manufacturers Mutual* decision, §2.2.1 N8, hints that the Court might hold due process inapplicable to denied applications.

Although *Walters* purports to distinguish *Goldberg*, the distinction is not very convincing. The "brutal need" of AFDC recipients is relevant to the timing of the hearing, but it does not have much to do with whether they should be entitled to representation. More significant, perhaps, is the fact that welfare hearings are at the state level (state bureaucracies are subject to local political pressures to get cheaters off the rolls and cut costs), whereas VA hearings are conducted by a sympathetic federal agency. However, there may be equal reason to distrust the VA's system, which often implements government policy in denying liability in Agent Orange, Gulf War syndrome, post-traumatic stress syndrome, and nuclear exposure cases.

Another important distinction between *Walters* and *Goldberg* is that VA claimants are given free representation by non-lawyer specialists who seem to fare about as well as lawyers in BVA appeals. In contrast, the vast majority of welfare claimants must represent themselves. Rehnquist's opinion observes that New York and HEW had not explicitly sought to ban lawyers in welfare cases—which suggests that the Court would be sympathetic if they did.

Justice O'Connor's concurring opinion hints that two Justices would accept an "as applied" challenge to the $10 limitation in complex cases like exposure to radiation. Together with the three dissenters, that could make five votes for a "special circumstances" approach. However, an as-applied challenge was rejected in *National Ass'n of Radiation Survivors v. Derwinski*, 994 F.2d 583 (9th Cir.1992). Plaintiffs were veterans who allegedly suffered injury due to exposure to ionizing radiation. The court deferred to congressional findings, made in connection with other recent veterans' legislation, that the existing system of service representatives did an adequate job and that lawyers would destroy the V.A.'s non-adversarial system. Plaintiffs were unable to prove that a significant number of cases would be decided differently if they had been able to retain counsel before the BVA.

While *Walters* concerns only the right to pay counsel, as opposed to the ability to have pro bono counsel, the reasoning of the decision might support a prohibition on any legal representation. A ban on pro bono lawyers would not raise the concern that claimants should not have to split their benefits with lawyers; but it would be supported by the theory that Congress could find that lawyers would complicate, confuse and formalize the non-adversarial proceedings. Agreeing with the dissent, we would find this result objectionable, especially in complex cases.

5. *Academic decisionmaking.* As to student disciplinary hearings, the case law is all over the map on the issue of whether counsel can be excluded (or its role limited). Unsurprisingly universities would prefer to keep these proceedings informal and keep attorneys out. See Mark Blaskey,

"University Students' Right to Retain Counsel at Disciplinary Hearings," 24 Cal.W.L.Rev. 65 (1988). Many cases restrict the right to counsel. *See Flaim v. Medical College of Ohio*, 418 F.3d 629, 640 (6th Cir.2005) (attorney allowed to be present but not participate nor consult with student—procedure upheld—could be different rule in complex case). *Flaim* also held that the school need not allow cross-examination of the officer who arrested the student for possession of illegal drugs, because the student did not deny his criminal conviction; it need not provide formal written findings; and need not provide for any internal appeal from the Dean's decision.

There might well be a complex/non-complex line to be drawn here (of the sort that O'Connor wanted to draw in *Walters*). Most student discipline cases are pretty simple. But an elaborate, complex case, or one involving constitutional issues such as discipline for inciting a riot or violating a campus speech code, might be a different story. Another factor is whether the university presents its case through an attorney.

Blaskey argues that students are likely to be intimidated by the disciplinary apparatus, even if the case may seem simple to an outsider, and the stakes for the student are very high. Once kicked out of college for cheating, a student is going to have a hard time getting back in anywhere. The liberty and property interests here are obviously more compelling than in *Goss*. Unlike *Walters*, student discipline is not a mass justice situation; and the case involves punishment for misconduct, not an application for money. But, like *Walters* (where the American Legion rep does as well if not better than lawyers), it's possible that an attorney who isn't experienced in university discipline can do more harm than good by using overly aggressive tactics.

Another important issue in student disciplinary hearings (involving expulsion or lengthy suspensions of high school students) is whether the student has a right to confront adverse witnesses. Although most cases hold there is a right to confront, one decision holds that there is no such right. *Newsome v. Batavia Local Sch. Dist.*, 842 F.2d 920 (6th Cir.1988). Using a *Mathews* analysis, the *Newsome* court thought cross-examination of adverse witnesses would be too burdensome for school districts, and it also posed problems of safety and security of the witnesses. *See* Brent M. Pattison, "Questioning School Discipline: Due Process, Confrontation, and School Discipline Hearings," 18 Temp.Pol. & Civ.Rts.L.Rev. 49 (2008).

Here is additional background on *Horowitz* (which concerns a university's academic rather than disciplinary judgments): While on academic probation, Horowitz spent time with seven local physicians (two recommended she graduate, two recommended she be dismissed, three recommended further probation). She had numerous conferences with the Dean. Dismissal was recommended by a faculty-student council, reviewed by the faculty Coordinating Committee, and approved by the Dean and the University Provost for Health Sciences. Apparently Horowitz did not have access to the reports of the seven doctors or to the faculty-student council's report. Rehnquist's opinion assumes without deciding that Horowitz had a liberty or property interest, but held that she received more process than was due.

The opinion does not engage in balancing but simply concludes that the only process required in case of an academic dismissal is i) notice of the faculty's dissatisfaction with her progress and the danger this posed to her graduation; ii) the ultimate decision must be careful and deliberate. Since Horowitz received much more than this, there was no due process violation. But why no requirement of an oral hearing and confrontation before an impartial fact-finder? Or at least a give-and-take with the Dean as in *Goss*?

The opinion distinguishes between a *disciplinary* dismissal (where a trial-type hearing is required) and an *academic* dismissal. What is the difference? Disciplinary cases typically involve individualized facts—who did what to whom and why? Academic dismissals typically involve evaluative judgments. Clearly, the majority believed that judicial intrusion into the academic evaluative process would probably be useless and would do more harm than good.

In *Horowitz* the Court refused to remand to the lower court for consideration of whether the student had been dismissed for substantively invalid reasons. She alleged that the dismissal was in fact based on sex discrimination—that she did not shave her legs, was overweight, a hippie, and in the eyes of some had an inappropriate wardrobe. *See* William G. Buss, "Easy Cases Make Bad Law," 65 Iowa L.Rev. 1 (1979).

6. *Confrontation.* Unsurprisingly, *Van Harken* was penned by Richard Posner, who wrote the book (literally) on law and economics and strongly advocates cost-benefit analysis. *Van Harken* arguably takes *Mathews* a step further by reducing the entire balancing act to a monetized cost-benefit analysis in which one individual's relatively trivial loss, discounted by the likelihood that confrontation would make any difference, is weighed against society's cost in providing the protection. Rather than comparing the individual's rather trivial loss to society's costs in providing confrontation, wouldn't it make more sense to compare the aggregate monetary losses of everybody who gets a ticket and requests a hearing to society's aggregate cost?

Posner's conclusion (if not all of his analysis) seems consistent with *Mathews*. It takes account of the individual's private interest, the government's interest in resisting the procedural innovation, and the value of the proposed procedure in preventing error. Obviously, the key is that we're talking only about a $100 maximum penalty and a $55 average penalty. This is a relatively insignificant private interest compared to welfare or a veteran's pension or a professional license. Still, the parking fine may be a great deal more significant to someone living in poverty than to the rest of us. On the other hand, the factual determinations in parking violation cases are likely to be objective—based on expired meters, parking in no-parking zones and the like. Therefore, the credibility of the officer is less likely to be at stake than in cases of moving violations.

Posner points out that the new system may actually be structured in favor of the driver, since the driver is the only one to actually testify live. This is countered, however, by the fact that the hearing officer is instructed to "searchingly" cross-examine the driver. And, of course, the system takes away the driver's traditional advantage that the case is dismissed if the cop fails to show up.

Bernard Schwartz severely criticized *Van Harken* in 11 Pike & Fischer, AdLaw Bulletin 1 (Feb. 18, 1997): "Even if procedural requirements should be flexible, they should not be flaccid. In the Posner approach, an affirmative answer to the question of whether a procedural right has been violated is not enough. Instead CBA must be applied to determine whether the right itself is guaranteed in the particular proceeding. . . . What appears as objective analysis is really Benthamism in a modern dress, and with a subjective vengeance. . . . CBA in the law reduces our rights to the level of the counting house. . . . CBA a la Posner answers the procedural question in a manner that gives a new perspective to the noted Oscar Wilde aphorism on price and value. . ." But is Schwartz really criticizing *Mathews*, rather than just *Van Harken?* For discussion of the Chicago parking ticket experiment, see Lawrence Rosenthal, "Does Due Process have an Original Meaning? On Originalism, Due Process, Procedural Innovation, and Parking Tickets," 60 Okla.L.Rev. 1, 12-22 (2007).

7. *Paper hearings—or no hearings at all.* Once *Goss* broke the logjam by providing for non-trial procedure, the Court had to custom-design process. *Hewitt* represented a typical version—notice and opportunity to make *written* comments soon after administrative segregation is imposed. Thus not even a *conversation* is required. Note that after *Sandin*, there will be many fewer instances in which due process applies to disputes involving prisoners. However, if the result of a sanction is to extend a prisoner's sentence, due process will still apply.

Hewitt might at least have required *Goss*-type consultative process (a conversation) rather than a written presentation, which is likely to be ineffective, given the minimal ability of many prisoners to communicate in writing and the ease with which a paper communication can be ignored. True, the segregation determination has discretionary elements and involves knowledge of the security problem of the entire prison, but this is equally true of a high school suspension. In fact, it seems likely that the *Hewitt* majority wanted to isolate *Goss* (a hotly contested 5-4 decision).

Hewitt might cause one to question *Loudermill's* rejection of *Arnett*—the bitter with the sweet approach. Rather than requiring the courts endlessly to custom-design procedures, why not let states define the procedure along with the substance when they create an entitlement? As Rehnquist argues in his *Loudermill* dissent, "the lack of any principled standards in this area means that these procedural due process cases will recur time and again. Every different set of facts will present a new issue on what process was due and when. One way to avoid this subjective and varying interpretation of the Due Process Clause in cases such as this is to hold that one who avails himself of government entitlements accepts the grant of tenure along with its inherent limitations." In a footnote, Rehnquist pointed out the inconsistency of *Goldberg, Mathews*, and *Loudermill* on the issue of pre-termination hearings and accurately observed that the balancing process "may look as if it were undertaken with a thumb on the scale, depending upon the result the Court desired."

The issue of whether a trial-type hearing (or any procedure at all) is required when the only disputed issue concerns the exercise of discretion is unclear. Recall that *Mathews* indicates that accuracy in fact-finding is the rationale for due process hearings. A hearing to decide how to exercise discretion would not serve this function. *Hewitt* and perhaps *Horowitz* suggest that no oral hearing is required with respect to decisions concerning evaluation, prediction, or intuition.

White's statement in *Loudermill* indicates that there is a right to some kind of process before discretion is exercised, and *Goss* does also. In a footnote to the quoted material in *Loudermill*, White pointed out that a person cannot insist on a hearing in order to argue that the decisionmaker should be lenient and depart from legal requirements. "The point is that where there is an entitlement, a prior hearing facilitates the consideration of whether a permissible course of action is also an appropriate one. . ." 470 U.S. at 543 n.8.

Another example of the principle that no hearing is required if no facts are in dispute is *Wozniak v. Conry*, 236 F.3d 888, 890-91 (7th Cir. 2005). The case concerned a tenured engineering professor who refused to explain his grades and ultimately was stripped of teaching and research responsibilities. The opinion concedes that such a claim could amount to a constructive discharge (and thus a deprivation of property). Judge Easterbrook wrote:

Even for the most important decisions, an evidentiary hearing is required only if there are material factual disputes. District courts regularly grant summary judgment without receiving oral testimony, and they dismiss complaints without receiving evidence, yet no one supposes that the Federal Rules of Civil Procedure violate the Constitution on that account. The due process clause does not require a hearing—in either a court or a university—where there is no disputed issue of material fact to resolve. See *Codd v. Velger*, 429 U.S. 624 (1977) . . .

Here there is no material dispute: Wozniak refused to follow the University's grading rules, and in this suit he trumpets a claim of right to defy them. Why hold a hearing when the insubordination is conceded? Sometimes the Constitution extends an opportunity to tell one's side of the story and thereby inform the decisionmaker's discretion in selecting the appropriate penalty. [See *Loudermill* and *Goss*. . .] The University gave Wozniak that chance at least three times, thus affording all the process that is due. A faculty member is hardly in a position to argue that the opportunity to submit an explanation or statement of position in writing is inadequate; professors make their living by the written word, so illiteracy is not a risk that the decisionmaker must consider when devising procedures for dispute resolution.

8. *Adversary systems.* *Walters* endorses non-adversary decision-making in mass justice dispute settlement. While it is jarring to find a statute that prevents claimants from paying lawyers, there is merit to the notion that some disputes are best settled by informal, claimant-protective, non-adversary procedure. Judge Friendly's famous article, "Some Kind of Hearing," 123 U.Pa.L.Rev. 1267, 1287-90 (1975), argued that the adversary system of trial by lawyers is not well suited to mass justice in the administrative state (or for that matter in resolving the very different kinds of issues that arise in disputes concerning technology or economic regulation). Friendly pointed out that a lawyer's role may be to cause delay and sow confusion, not to ascertain the truth; and if there's counsel for one party, the government will also need counsel or the government's representative will start acting like a lawyer.

Roger Cramton warns that we should be wary of prescribing formalized decisionmaking systems that are pleasing to lawyers, although not necessarily to the people who must contend with bureaucracy. "A Comment on Trial-Type Hearings in Nuclear Power Plant Siting," 58 Va.L. Rev. 585, 593 n.28 (1972).

One may question the argument made by the *Walters* dissent that lawyers can fit comfortably into a non-adversary proceeding. After *Gault* held that juveniles had a right to counsel, the informality of juvenile court proceedings basically passed into history. Prosecutors, rather than probation officers, represented the state, and the juvenile court became indistinguishable from other criminal trials.

The cases on prison discipline, mental health, and education present models of non-adversary decision-making. *See Parham v. J.R.*, 442 U.S. 584 (1979), concerning commitment of minor children to a state mental health facility. *Parham* upholds a Georgia procedure of pre-admission evaluation by a neutral medical professional. This would include a review of all documents and meetings with the child. There must also be periodic post-admission reviews to see whether continued confinement is needed. An important factor in the *Parham* decision is that the child's interest in avoiding confinement must be discounted by the parental interest in making decisions about what is best for the child.

While non-adversary systems may be acceptable in mass justice situations, it is unlikely that they would be acceptable in cases of physician discipline, where adversary methods are deeply entrenched.

9. *Problem.* Internet hearings for minor disputes were recently suggested in a dinner speech to the ABA Administrative Law Section by N. Y. City Corporation Counsel Michael Cardozo. He complained of the immense number of hearings that N.Y. had to conduct. His main concern was with parking and traffic violations, which have been decriminalized and are handled administratively in New York. But it seems like an interesting idea. How about welfare?

Assume some additional details: The regulations might require that all documents plus the social worker's testimony would be posted online on a secure site. The welfare recipient could post questions for the social worker that the social worker would have to answer on the net within ten days. The decisionmaker would then make the decision based on posted materials but would have the option of calling for telephone or even live hearings if necessary to resolve a credibility dispute. Live hearings could be provided for illiterate recipients. If a recipient doesn't have a computer, all libraries in Madison would have terminals for the exclusive use of welfare agencies conducting internet hearings. The proposal should also deal with language difficulties; the agency needs to make interpreters available on-line to help people with language difficulties.

Because this problem arises in the context of proposed regulations, it provides an opportunity to stress the significance of the informal rulemaking process in administrative practice, particularly in establishing administrative procedures. As these are procedural regulations, under federal law notice and comment is not required, but it is often provided as a matter of policy, because agencies appreciate the value of receiving input.

The APAs of most states contain no rulemaking exception for procedural rules. This problem would make a good written assignment.

The comments submitted by our client (a legal services office that assists welfare recipients) should be polite and constructive and should offer alternatives rather than simply opposing the proposal. Perhaps we should argue that internet hearings might be a great idea but are still ahead of their time. Let's try video-conference first. Then the decisionmaker could actually see the witnesses and make better credibility determinations than are possible just by looking at a computer monitor. Perhaps when video is easily available on the computer, we could try to combine the technologies, but this is not easily available now. We might also propose that internet or other electronic hearing methods be used only in cases in which there is no credibility dispute (but only a dispute about interpretation of the rules, law, policy, or discretion) or only in cases in which both sides (recipient and welfare department) agree to an electronic hearing.

At present, the substitution of phone or video for face-to-face hearings is becoming a prominent and controversial subject in administrative law. The problem just takes this trend a step further. One straw in the wind is a recent proposal that HHS Medicare hearings be conducted on video conference rather than face to face. ALJs would be situated at four locations and would not travel to sites where the petitioner is located. A beneficiary who wants to appear in person before a judge would have to show that "special or extraordinary circumstances exist" (and by insisting on a face-to-face hearing, the beneficiary would lose the right to receive a decision within ninety days). See Robert Pear, "Medicare Change Will Limit Access to Claim Hearing," N.Y. Times, April 24, 2005.

The legality and efficacy of this sort of procedure in various contexts is still being determined. In the deportation context, Congress itself has provided for telephone and video conferencing. 8 U.S.C. § 1229(a)(2)(A). The alien's consent is required for a telephone conference, but *not* for video. So far, mandatory video hearings under this provision have been consistently upheld, but a number of courts have given the procedure careful scrutiny under *Mathews v. Eldridge. See Aslam v. Mukasey*, 537 F.3d 110, 114-15 (2d Cir.2008); *Rusu v. INS*, 296 F.3d 316, 321-24 (4th Cir. 2002). *See also* 60 Fed.Reg. 8446 (1995) (adopting telephone and video hearing procedures for Department of Agriculture, with extensive discussion of legal and policy issues in preamble).

The problem allows you to reconsider the issue of whether adversary trial-type procedure in the mass justice context is the best way to resolve disputes. Is *Goldberg's* rhetoric persuasive, or does *Walters* point the way toward the acceptability of less adversary, more informal and user-friendly approaches?

One place to start is whether the various electronic substitutes for a face to face hearing would deny due process as articulated in *Goldberg*. This would be a good argument to make in your comments, as the agency certainly doesn't want to see its system subjected to a successful due process attack after it's implemented. Neither an internet exchange nor a phone call permits the decisionmaker to see the witnesses, and this may impair the decisionmaker's ability to assess credibility (video conference would get around this). Recall that *Mathews* stressed that credibility is more important in welfare disputes than in disability disputes. Nor do electronic or phone hearings allow a decisionmaker to see and sympathize with the plight of real people, as opposed to disembodied voices. This can make a big practical (though perhaps not a legal) difference. Moreover, the function of a hearing may sometimes be to ask for mercy rather than justice.

Note that Madison is proposing the use of internet hearings in pre-reduction hearings as opposed to post-reduction hearings. Cases like *Loudermill* contemplate abbreviated hearings prior to government action if there's a prompt post-government action proceeding. Possibly courts would tolerate some loosening of pre-action procedures in welfare cases if an oral hearing were provided after the action is taken. Note also that the proposal calls for internet proceedings only in cases of *reduction* of benefits, not in case of complete *termination* of benefits. Therefore, the private interest is less compelling than in *Goldberg* which involved complete termination.

In analyzing governmental interest, *Mathews* indicates that cost and efficiency concerns must be taken seriously. Are the savings significant? The state can avoid some travel costs and wasted sitting-around time, but it has additional costs in setting up a website that can handle the problems and getting computers into local libraries. There might be additional complexities and a need to have an oral hearing after all. The convenience factor may be more important than cost savings; people (including busy welfare workers) sometimes must wait for days for their case to be called and the rushed atmosphere resembles a police court. Also, many recipients may live in remote areas, and there may be substantial cost savings in holding internet or phone hearings, particularly during bad weather months. The recipients may find it difficult to arrange transportation or child care; the agency may find it costly to send its staff on circuit.

The constitutional issue also depends on the issues; is credibility at stake? Then face-to-face hearings may be better. But if it's an argument over interpretation of the regulations, or a discretionary issue, electronic hearings seem appropriate. So maybe the answer is a case-by-case determination of when the internet or the phone will work, rather than an across-the-board solution. On the other hand, cases like *Mathews* and *Walters* support the use of shortcuts if they would be fair in the general run of cases even if they might be unfair in unusual cases. But that's only the due process minimum;

a case-by-case approach may make more sense even if not constitutionally required.

Casey v. *O'Bannon*, 536 F.Supp. 350 (E.D.Pa.1982), was an on-the-face attack on regulations that called for phone hearings in welfare application cases. The court sustained the regulations. In addition to sources mentioned in text, see *Gray Panthers v. Schweiker*, 716 F.2d 23, 34-38 (D.C.Cir.1983) (*Gray Panthers II*) (disallowance of Medicare claims under $100—toll-free phone cannot be used for hearing if issues of veracity involved, assuming that such cases are not rare and are reasonably segregable from other cases); Neil Fox, Note, "Telephonic Hearings in Welfare Appeals," 1984 U.Ill.L.Rev. 445; Jerome R. Corsi & Thomas L. Hurley, "Attitudes Toward the Use of the Telephone in Administrative Fair Hearings: The California Experience," 31 Admin.L.Rev. 485 (1979); Allan A. Toubman, et.al., "Due Process Implications of Telephone Hearings: The Case for an Individualized Approach to Scheduling Telephone Hearings," 29 U. Mich.J.L.Ref. 407 (1996) (unemployment claimants do less well in phone hearings than face-to-face—they should be used only in cases of strong geographic convenience, not as a matter of course). The Toubman article summarizes a lot of state law authority pro and con on phone hearings in unemployment and welfare cases.

It is necessary to look beyond the Constitution; the procedure might violate statutes or regulations. *See* 45 C.F.R. § 205.10(a)(1)(ii) (states must observe all *Goldberg* requirements). Prior to the deportation statute cited above, this issue was raised in immigration cases. *Purba v. INS*, 884 F.2d 516 (9th Cir.1989) (phone hearing in deportation case violates statute requiring that hearing be "before" an immigration judge); *contra, Bigby v. INS,* 21 F.3d 1059 (11th Cir.1994). Query whether phone or internet hearings violate the APA provision that requires an ALJ to "preside at the taking of evidence." APA § 556(b).

On a practical level, we should point out in our comments that an internet hearing would be quite difficult for many welfare recipients to handle. Most of them don't have much education and even in today's computer-literate society, many of them would not be at all comfortable with computers. Many are not fluent in English; although the department proposes to have interpreters available on line, it might not work well. Very few recipients are represented by lawyers or even lay welfare advocates. For the reasons discussed in *Goldberg,* they need an opportunity to express their positions orally. A phone call would provide welfare recipients with more opportunity to mold their arguments to those of the state than would be provided by an internet exchange. Indeed, many welfare recipients might have difficulty arguing with a welfare professional over the phone, especially if legal jargon is used. And a telephone trialogue (between recipient, caseworker, and administrative judge), even between persons with an equal ability to communicate, can be difficult if several people speak at once. A recipient may find it difficult to question the caseworker or other witnesses.

Another problem with phone hearings, although hopefully not with the internet, concerns documents; a person on the phone may be relying on a document that other participants can't see or, conversely, be compelled to discuss a document that she can't see. The Toubman article discovered that unemployment claimants do less well in phone hearings than in face-to-face hearings, perhaps because they seem less like real people.

The design of a phone hearing system is critical. For example, if the claimant and the caseworker were in the same room, with the judge at a remote location, the judge could listen to a face-to-face conversation between the disputants. If the judge and caseworker were in the same room, but the claimant was at a remote location, the claimant would be seriously disadvantaged.

§ 2.5 THE RULEMAKING-ADJUDICATION DISTINCTION

Note before *Londoner*: The adjudication/rulemaking dichotomy has its limitations. *See*, in addition to this section, §§ 5.2.1 and 6.2. However, it is the organizing principle for much of this book, since it is so deeply ingrained in statutes and discussions of the subject. Of course, it is necessary to question the distinction at many points. *Londoner* and *Bi-Metallic* form a nice bridge into the adjudication and rulemaking chapters that follow.

LONDONER v. DENVER

BI-METALLIC INVESTMENT CO. v. COLORADO

Notes and Questions

1. *An oral hearing? Londoner* involves a deprivation of traditional property (money) as opposed to "new property" (such as an entitlement). As discussed in N.3 below (and in § 2.4 N.7), a trial-type oral hearing might not be required today in a case like *Londoner*, since the issues are economic and don't involve credibility. *Londoner* itself said that there was a right to support allegations by argument; as to proof, only if "need be." Depending on the precise issue in dispute, therefore, a court might dispense with oral "proof" through presentation of testimony and cross-examination and require only an opportunity for written submissions plus oral "argument."

Under *Mathews*-type balancing, a written procedure might be more appropriate than a trial to prove that Londoner's parcel was over-assessed relative to his neighbors. *See Loudermill* and the material on paper hearings in § 2.4 N.7. *See* also *Califano v. Yamasaki*, 442 U.S. 682, 696 (1979) (written protest constitutionally sufficient to determine whether overpayment of disability benefits occurred; statute construed to require oral process for determining whether recoupment of the overpayment would be inequitable).

2. *Londoner and Bi-Metallic.* The *Londoner/Bi-Metallic* cases laid the groundwork for the adjudication/rulemaking distinction. *Florida East Coast* reaches back to those hoary landmarks to establish that difference. *Londoner* is the foundation of procedural due process: it requires an oral hearing (an opportunity for a written submission was held insufficient).

Londoner seemed to say that a trial-type hearing had to be provided with respect to many or perhaps all of the issues raised by the taxpayer's complaint to the council. He complained of a vast variety of faults in the political process of forming a special district and paving the streets. In this array of meritless objections, his objection to the allocation of the total paving cost was buried in one sentence and lacked supporting detail. Indeed, the council overlooked it, for their ordinance stated that no objection had been filed against the apportionment. Holmes dissented in *Londoner* and was anxious to limit its scope. In *Bi-Metallic*, he did so by isolating that one little part of Londoner's complaint which dealt with apportionment. This was a neat piece of judicial surgery.

It is helpful to spend class time distinguishing the cases.

i. Is it the *number of people involved*? Holmes says that *Londoner* involved "a relatively small number of people," and he declared: "where a rule of conduct applies to more than a few people, it is impracticable that everyone should have a direct voice in its adoption."

This is a fairly satisfying rationale in a case like *Bi-Metallic*, which involves all the taxpayers of Denver. It would be unmanageable to give each of them separate hearings on the same issue. Of course, the Board could have given a hearing to the Denver assessor who was a named party on Bi-Metallic's side, and the assessor could have represented the interests of all Denver taxpayers. That might have solved the problem of an excessive number of hearings.

However, the number of people involved doesn't always do the job. In a case in which the alleged rule is stated in general terms and could theoretically apply to many people but in fact regulates only a single person, as in *Anaconda,* a hearing would be quite feasible (but due process does not require it). See also *Philly's v. Byrne*, 732 F.2d 87 (7th Cir.1984) (referendum in small precinct shutting down all bars in precinct is not adjudicative even if there is only a single bar in the precinct). On the other hand, thousands of people might have lived in the paving district involved in *Londoner,* so that hearings might have been extremely burdensome (but due process does require them). Thus the number of people involved is relevant, but is not the best way to distinguish the cases.

ii. Is it the *nature of the factual question* at issue? Davis argues (N.3 of text) that due process applies only if "adjudicative" rather than "legislative" facts are in issue. The third quoted paragraph of *Florida East Coast* also draws the distinction between the kinds of factual determinations made in rulemaking and in adjudication.

Londoner complains that all parcels were equally assessed, although they benefitted unequally. The relevant evidence concerns Londoner's parcel as compared to those of his neighbors. Perhaps his parcel was irregularly shaped and had less square footage than another one with the same front footage; or perhaps his parcel contained an outhouse while his neighbor's contained an office building. These are "adjudicative" facts—facts about Londoner's property that he is in a good position to prove by testimony. "Legislative" facts, on the other hand, are generalized facts useful to making law and policy.

Davis's analysis is useful. In general, trial-type processes are relatively unhelpful in the exploration of legislative facts, because, among other reasons, the evidence used to resolve those issues is often pervaded with expert judgments and normative assumptions. They cannot really be "proved" one way or the other. See Stephen F. Williams, "'Hybrid Rulemaking' under the Administrative Procedure Act: A Legal and Empirical Analysis," 42 U.Chi.L.Rev. 401, 405-11 (1975).

One problem with the Davis distinction is that the categories of legislative and adjudicative fact don't line up with the number of people involved. Sometimes, as when the number of regulated persons is small, as in *Anaconda,* the facts about those persons ("adjudicative") are directly relevant to policy choices. Similarly, adjudicative facts may arise even in generalized rulemaking. For example, if you are regulating tobacco, the past behavior of specific tobacco companies in marketing cigarettes to children may be quite important.

A practical problem with the Davis approach is that in the early stages of a regulatory action, when the agency is deciding what kind of proceeding to launch, it does not necessarily know what the critical issues will be. The parties' positions may be ill-defined, and they may evolve over time. Until the facts have been gathered, the briefs or comments have been submitted, and the agency has deliberated, one may not know whether a given factual issue will be critically important, marginally important, or totally uncontroversial. Yet an agency must know in advance what sort of procedure is required to find those facts.

We think the legislative/adjudicative fact distinction is more helpful in deciding what *type* of process is due rather than whether due process should apply at all. This point is discussed further below.

iii. Is it the availability of *judicial review*? Note that the ordinance in *Londoner* precluded judicial review. This was apparently not the case in *Bi-Metallic*, since the taxpayer appealed to the Colorado Supreme Court and since the U.S. Supreme Court assumed that the usual system of protest and appeal was open to the taxpayer. If *Londoner* had the right to appeal to a state trial court that could grant a de novo trial-type hearing, that judicial hearing would have provided sufficient due process. *See Phillips v. Commissioner*, 283 U.S. 589 (1931) (upholding a procedure for seizure of property followed by de novo judicial review). Nevertheless, this is not the fundamental difference between the cases. Even if a statute precluded judicial review in *Bi-Metallic*, no administrative hearing would have been required in that case.

iv. Is it that *Londoner* represents individualized government action? That's our explanation. Holmes emphasizes in his closing paragraph in *Londoner* that "a relatively small number of persons were concerned, *who were exceptionally affected, in each case upon individual grounds.*" The key is the individualized determination involved in Londoner—that Mr. Londoner had to pay x dollars because of the benefits his particular parcel received from paving the street. The state treated him differently from others because of the individual characteristics of his property (or it treated him the same but he wanted to be treated differently). That is the difference between rulemaking and adjudication. It does not matter how many people are involved if each of them are treated "upon individual grounds."

This seems to be Rehnquist's point in *Florida East Coast*: "[T]hese decisions [*Londoner* and *Bi-Metallic*] represent a recognized distinction in administrative law between proceedings for the purpose of promulgating policy-type rules or standards, on the one hand, and proceedings designed to *adjudicate disputed facts in particular cases on the other.*" That explanation does not indicate that *Londoner* is restricted to disputed *adjudicative* facts.

What we are driving at is that a rule has "general applicability"—a criterion that is explicit in most state APAs and has been read into the federal APA. *See* § 5.2.1. If the action is directed at a named party or parties, it is adjudication for due process purposes (as well as for APA purposes). If the action is directed at all persons who fit a general description, it is a rule. By hypothesis, such an agency action *cannot* legitimately turn on individualized facts. The "general applicability" test is easy to apply; the agency knows from the outset whether the proposed action is addressed to named parties or has general application.

In *Florida East Coast*, the Court distinguishes *Ohio Bell* and *Louisville & Nashville*—cases of individualized ratemaking. The critical point is not the nature of the disputed facts in those cases (which might have been adjudicative or legislative), it is that individual utilities or railroads were differentially treated by the state. *See also Southern Ry. v. Virginia*, 290 U.S. 190 (1933), in which a railroad was entitled to a hearing before being compelled to build an overpass. It is not clear whether the underlying facts concerning highway safety are adjudicative or legislative, but the state action was individualized.

Compare Bi-Metallic: the factual question is whether Denver is under-assessed relative to the rest of the state. Although the taxpayer's bill is directly affected by the Board's action, the underlying issues apply identically to a generally described class of people. Thus the state's action is not individualized and there is no right to a hearing on the factual issue. Similarly, the regulation in *Florida East Coast* was based on facts about the railway industry—but still the fact-finding was not part of an individualized proceeding.

3. *Legislative and adjudicative facts.* The approach suggested in the previous note differs from that of Davis. If action is individualized and facts are in issue (regardless of what type of facts), due process should require that the agency use an appropriate type of process. If legislative facts are in issue in an individualized proceeding, the *type* of hearing might change. Instead of taking testimony and cross-examining witnesses, written submissions and oral arguments could be sufficient. Perhaps oral argument could be dispensed with. Note that in *Anaconda* the court provides an alternative holding: even if due process applied to the rulemaking proceeding in issue, the procedure actually provided by EPA satisfied due process.

Many disputed issues of adjudicative fact might be described as "non-percipient," meaning that live witness testimony is unnecessary because the issue does not involve credibility or perception. The disputed fact questions in *Londoner*, for example, are probably non-percipient in nature because they turn on economic analysis of Londoner's parcel vis a vis others on the street. The same is true in *Ohio Bell* and *Louisville & Nashville*. Normally, written submission and oral argument should be adequate for resolving issues of non-percipient adjudicative fact. See, e.g., *Southwest Airlines v. Trans. Sec. Adm'n.*, 554 F.3d 1065, 1075 (D.C.Cir. 2009) (even if due process applied to determination of carrier's past screening costs, the issues could be resolved by written submissions). This discussion, of course, anticipates the balancing equation of *Mathews v. Eldridge* which would suggest that trial-type procedure is unnecessary for determination of legislative facts or non-percipient adjudicative facts even when due process applies because action is individualized.

4. *Rulemaking hearings.* To the extent Holmes is suggesting that political remedies are an effective substitute for hearings, his reasoning doesn't hold up. He argues that in rulemaking, as in the case of legislation (and of state constitutional amendment), people's "rights are protected in the only way that they can be in a complex society, by their power, immediate or remote, over those who make the rule." Even in the case of legislation, political remedies may not be very effective. The targets of a statute or constitutional amendment may be few in number, or disorganized, or lacking in resources, or lacking in as much political strength as people on the other side of the issue.

Furthermore, unelected rulemaking bodies may be even less accountable than the legislature. Typically, they operate under broad delegations of power. Moreover, the Board might be an independent agency, so that it is immune from executive control. Even if the Board is part of the executive branch, it is not very accountable. The governor is not likely to exert much supervision over it—and in a case like *Bi-Metallic*, it might be improper for the governor to do so. Therefore, there is a greater need to provide for some form of public participation in the Board's decisionmaking.

Whether due process *should* apply in some form to rulemaking is an interesting issue. *See, e.g.*, Ernest Gellhorn & Glen Robinson, "Rulemaking 'Due Process:' An Inconclusive Dialogue," 48 U.Chi.L.Rev. 201 (1981). At the time of *Bi-Metallic*, due process meant a trial-type hearing—nothing less. Today, we have nonconstitutional models. Both in adjudication (e.g. *Loudermill, Goss*) and through APAs that require notice and comment in rulemaking, we have learned to provide for an effective and efficient form of participation without the specter of thousands of individual oral hearings.

Thus it is no longer necessary to maintain a dichotomous procedure/no procedure approach to the rulemaking/adjudication distinction. It is arguable that meaningful protection in rulemaking can and should be required by due process. This would be particularly important at the local level where there generally is no APA and no statutory requirement for notice and comment rulemaking.

5. *Problem.* This is a complex problem involving a number of threads drawn from the cases in the due process chapter. The problem can serve as the lead-in to § 2.5.

a) Adoption of zoning ordinance. *Bi-Metallic* and *Florida East Coast* make clear that Ben has no right to a hearing, no matter how you distinguish *Londoner* and *Bi-Metallic*. The only facts in issue are clearly legislative, a great many people are involved, and the action of the Council is not individualized. This is a good example of the rulemaking v. adjudication distinction. If you are so inclined, you can attack that distinction here (along the lines suggested in the previous note); now that we have a well developed rulemaking model (notice, comment, statement of reasons), perhaps due process should apply to rulemaking, especially at the local level. See Newman, J., dissenting, in *Horn v. County of Ventura,* 596 P.2d 1134 (Cal.1979) (Holmes' analysis in *Bi-Metallic* is "hackneyed").

This issue gets difficult if the grounds for the action are broadly stated but there are only one or two individuals affected—and everyone knows it. We discuss this issue further under *Anaconda. See Richardson v. Town of Eastover,* 922 F.2d 1152, 1158-59 (4th Cir.1991) (suggesting that when decision to deny permit renewals to "all" nightclubs on Main St. in fact applies only to a small number of entities, its characterization as a "legislative enactment" becomes suspect for due process purposes); *Philly's v. Byrne, supra* (referendum to shut down all bars in precinct is rulemaking even though applicable only to a single bar). although such is not the case with the zoning ordinance in the problem, it would be easy to restate the problem so the "ordinance" applied only to a single square block and the only undeveloped land in the block belonged to Ben.

b) Denial of variance. There are a lot of issues here.

i) The merits: On the merits, Ben has not established "unusual hardship" by showing that he would make less money if denied a variance. *See City of Eastlake v. Forest City Enterprises, Inc.,* 426 U.S. 668, 673-74 (1976) (diminution of market value or interference with property owner's personal plans to use property is insufficient to invalidate a zoning ordinance or entitle him to a variance or rezoning). He can use his land for residential purposes (even though that yields a much smaller profit). Even if he had met his burden of showing that he would suffer "unusual hardship" but the Council turned him down anyway, he could seek to overturn the decision in a state court judicial review proceeding, but the error would not be treated as a due process violation.

ii) Quasi-judicial v. quasi-legislative. Local authorities make a huge array of land use planning decisions. These range all the way from clearly legislative activity, like approval of a general plan, to clearly adjudicatory activity, like ordering a house torn down because it fails to comply with the zoning or building code. Generally, a decision by a local authority denying an application for a variance or a conditional use permit is considered an adjudicatory decision. (See below, however, for discussion of whether the authority's decision to *grant* the application is adjudicatory with respect to neighbors who disagree). In between the clearly legislative and clearly adjudicatory decisions fall an array of more or less individualized,

69

forward-looking decisions, like individualized amendments to the zoning plan, closing a street, or subdivision approval. Countless state and federal court decisions chase a will-o'-the-wisp in trying to figure out whether such decisions are quasi-judicial or quasi-legislative. On that distinction hangs the applicability of procedural due process as well as many other consequences such as the appropriate method of state court judicial review. *See generally* Daniel R. Mandelker, LAND USE LAW §6.26 (5th ed. 2003 and current supp.). You can just assume the variance denial is adjudicative and take it from there.

iii) Deprivation of liberty or property: The right to a trial-type hearing depends on finding a deprivation of liberty or property. The law on this issue is confused and in need of Supreme Court clarification.

(1) Has Ben been deprived of property? Generally land use planning ordinances are loaded with provisions according the land use agency a substantial degree of discretion. If the statute gives the Council *discretion* whether to grant the variance or not, it would not create an entitlement, and thus Ben would not be deprived of "property" under the *Roth* definition. *See, e.g., Gagliardi v. Village of Pawling*, 18 F.3d 188 (2d Cir.1994) (no entitlement created since municipal officials had broad discretion in determining whether to grant or deny building permit).

"Unusual hardship" can be read as creating a non-discretionary standard (like "good cause" for discharging a government employee). *See, e.g., Littlefield v. City of Afton*, 785 F.2d 596 (8th Cir.1986) (owner had nondiscretionary right to a building permit, and so pre-denial hearing was required); *Shelton v. City of College Station*, 780 F.2d 475 (5th Cir.1986) (right to use property for a lawful purpose is sufficiently a property right—owner had a "legitimate claim of entitlement" to zoning variance).

It may be that when one is talking about "old property" like land, even discretionary actions that reduce the value of land or deprive an owner of the ability to use the land are deprivations of property. Perhaps "entitlement" analysis applies only to "new property" like welfare or government jobs. *See City of Eastlake v. Forest City Enterprises, Inc.*, 426 U.S. 668, 683 (1976) (Stevens, J., dissenting) ("the opportunity to apply for [a zoning amendment] is an aspect of property ownership protected by the Due Process Clause of the Fourteenth Amendment"); *River Park, Inc. v. City of Highland Park*, 23 F.3d 164, 166 (7th Cir.1994) (property interest in land sufficient to entitle plaintiff to contend that regulation of land deprived it of property without due process). *See generally* Kenneth B. Bley & Tina R. Axelrad, "The Search for Constitutionally Protected 'Property' in Land-Use Law," 29 Urb.Law. 251 (1997) (strongly arguing that due process applies to discretionary land use decisions).

(2) Deprivation? There is authority that denial of a zoning variance application (or other individualized negative land use decision) is a deprivation of property and both proponents and opponents of the variance are entitled to a hearing before an adverse decision. See, e.g., "Developments in the Law—Zoning," 91 Harv. L. Rev. 1427, 1502-28 (1978). However, there is an unresolved issue of whether due process applies to the rejection of an application—rejection of an application might not be a "deprivation" of property. Arguably, due process only applies to termination of a status the plaintiff already has obtained. *See* §§ 2.2.1 N.8.

iv) Relevance of state remedies: At least three circuits—the First, Fifth, and Seventh—have held that state remedies provide all the process that's due in the land use context, thus barring constitutional claims unless a substantive constitutional protection (like freedom from racial discrimination) is implicated or a state provides no means to challenge arbitrary actions of land use decision-makers.

The First Circuit has held that prompt, informal proceedings offered by local governments, coupled with the judicial review provided by state courts, satisfies the requirements of the due process clause. *Cloutier v. Town of Epping*, 714 F.2d 1184 (1st Cir.1983); *Creative Environments, Inc. v. Estabrook*, 680 F.2d 822 (1st Cir.1982). These cases suggest that disputes between developers and land use boards are too common to rise to the level of constitutional due process violations. "The conventional planning dispute—at least when not tainted with fundamental procedural irregularity, racial animus, or the like—which takes place within the framework of an admittedly valid state subdivision scheme is a matter primarily of concern to the state and does not implicate the Constitution." *Creative Environments*, 680 F.2d at 833.

The Fifth Circuit held that zoning decisions are to be reviewed by federal courts by the same constitutional standards employed to review statutes enacted by state legislatures, i.e., so long as the rationale underlying a denial of a building permit or other zoning decision is fairly debatable, there is no denial of substantive due process as a matter of federal constitutional law. *Shelton v. City of College Station, supra*. The court further reasoned that since the state gave a "right" to seek a variance, which included review of the Zoning Board's decision by a state district court, and the plaintiffs chose to bypass this state-furnished remedy, the state did not deprive them of any property, at least to the extent that the ignored remedy was a part of the protected property interest.

The Seventh Circuit reaches the same conclusion but arrives there in a slightly more structured fashion. See *Coniston Corp. v. Village of Hoffman Estates*, 844 F.2d 461 (7th Cir. 1988) (Posner, J.); *River Park, supra* (Easterbrook, J.). These cases focus on the relationship between takings and substantive and procedural due process in the context of denied or stalled land use applications. They conclude that since the denial of permission to develop land in a particular way is not considered a taking (because not all uses for the land have been wiped out), this denial should not be actionable for substantive or procedural due process purposes either. The cases rely on *City of Eastlake v. Forest City Enterprises, supra,* to conclude that as long as a state makes available a remedy for any failure to observe state law, that remedy is all the process that's due.

These decisions reflect concern that the federal courts not be transformed into a local board of zoning appeals. Their contention that state remedies provide all the process that's due bears a strong relationship to the adequate state ground opinions in *Ingraham v. Wright* (§ 2.4), *Lujan v. G&G Fire Sprinklers,* and *Parratt v. Taylor* (§ 2.4 NN. 2,3). Even if the land use decision effects a deprivation of liberty or property, state judicial review of the local administrative decision may be all the process that is due. A guess: this approach foreshadows what the U.S. Supreme Court is going to do on this issue at some point.

The land use cases that rely on the adequate state remedy theory take account of an obvious fact: zoning decisions are almost exclusively political tests of strength between special interests (developers v. persons opposed to development). These political struggles do not lend themselves to a trial-type hearing like a welfare or employment dispute. Many times, as in the problem, decision-makers are elected officials who have run for office on a platform of halting or promoting a particular development scheme—a scheme they then must apply in individualized proceedings. The decisional process often involves logrolling or vote trading on multi-member bodies, both sides tend to pack the hearing room with supporters and opponents, and the evidence presented is often ignored unless relevant to the political concerns of decision-makers. Ex parte communications are routine and impossible to prevent. It becomes difficult during such political fights to adhere to due process principles. See Michael Asimow, "The Failure of Due Process in Local Land Use Proceedings," 29 Zoning & Planning L.Rep. 2 (January 2006).

v) Appropriate process for determining factual issues in dispute: Assume now that the adequate-state-ground argument is not accepted and that procedural due process applies to an individualized local land use decision such as denial of a variance. Assuming the presence of factual disputes (or, possibly, discretionary issues), there must be a hearing. *Mathews* balancing determines the nature of the hearing. Due process requires at least an impartial decisionmaker, adequate notice of the issues, an exclusive record, a prohibition on ex parte contact, and a statement of findings and reasons.

The facts relating to the profitability of building a shopping center are adjudicative facts. They relate to a specific project proposed by Ben. However, they are non-percipient facts, meaning that credibility or perception is not in issue. The factual issues may be answered by financial statements or economic projections and may boil down to a battle of expert witnesses. Under those circumstances, a right to present written analyses, together with oral argument, should be sufficient. Oral witness testimony and cross examination should not be required.

The questions about neighborhood convenience and ambiance are contested. These seem like legislative facts. But the Board really shouldn't have to decide what kind of facts they are. To the extent they involve objective facts like location, size, and identification of adjacent properties, paper hearings and oral argument should provide sufficient process.

For an excellent discussion that acknowledges all the confusion in the land use area and cites many academic sources, see *High Horizons Dev. Co. v. N.J. Dep't of Transportation*, 575 A.2d 1360, 1367-68 (N.J.1990), involving an application for highway access by a new development, which the agency refused under a discretionary standard. The court held that due process applies but that a paper hearing was sufficient; the use by the agency of undisclosed evidence required reversal for a new proceeding.

c) Granting the amendment: This is the least clear part of the problem. If the Council proposes to grant the amendment, does Mary (a contiguous neighbor) have a right to a hearing? Has she been deprived of liberty or property? Did the land use plan give her a right to continued all-residential surroundings for her house?

The granting of the amendment to Ben has an indirect effect on the value and enjoyment of Mary's property (as well as on everybody's property in the neighborhood). Such indirect effects might not be sufficient to trigger due process rights. See *Town of Castle Rock v. Gonzales,* 545 U.S. 748 (2005), discussed in § 2.2.2 N.4 (wife has no right to hearing with respect to non-enforcement by police of restraining order against husband, because the effect on her is indirect—alternative holding); *O'Bannon v. Town Court Nursing Center*, 447 U.S. 773 (1980) (residents of nursing home have no right to hearing with respect to revocation of the facility's license, since effect on them is indirect).

Moreover, with respect to Mary, the decision is not individualized—it affects numerous contiguous neighbors, and many more non-contiguous neighbors, in the same way. Perhaps, from Mary's point of view, the decision should be treated as rulemaking and thus would fall under *Bi-Metallic*.

Could it be that due process is asymmetric—a decision denying permission might entitle the owner to due process but a decision granting permission might not entitle the numerous neighbors to due process? Blackmun's concurring opinion in *O'Bannon* stated there were 180 residents, all affected the same way; so that the nursing home owners had a right to due process but the patients did not. *See also McGowan v. Lane County Local Government Boundary Comm'n*, 795 P.2d 560 (Or.App.1990) (even if property adjacent to an annexed area would be affected, adjacent owners have no liberty or property interest originating in the due process clause); *BAM Historic Dist. Ass'n v. Koch*, 723 F.2d 233 (2d Cir.1983) (land use adjudications about one parcel generally do not affect the neighbors' constitutionally-based property or liberty interests). *But see People ex rel. Klaeren v. Village of Lisle*, 781 N.E.2d 223 (Ill.2002) (due process requires that landowner whose property abuts a parcel subject to a proposed annexation, special use, and rezoning petition be afforded the right to cross-examine witnesses at a public hearing regarding the petition); *Horn v. County of Ventura*, 596 P.2d 1134 (Cal.1979) (neighbors are entitled to due process with respect to approval of a subdivision map permitting development on contiguous property); *Neuberger v. City of Portland*, 603 P.2d 771 (Or. 1979) (same).

Another example: laws or regulations that reduce a utility's rates probably trigger due process protection for the utility. Does increasing them entitle consumers to due process? This turns out to be a recurring issue that is not clearly resolved in existing case law. *See RR Village Ass'n v. Denver Sewer Corp.*, 826 F.2d 1197, 1204-05 (2d Cir.1987) (homeowners had property right in current rates and thus were entitled to due process by retroactive increase in rates, but had no property right in future rate increases).

Whatever due process doctrine might ultimately require, however, a real-world planning board would routinely give a hearing to someone in Mary's situation. A point that you can make here, which is pertinent to many other topics that you will cover during the semester, is that the administrative law course deals only with legal obligations—the rock-bottom minimum procedures a government must provide. In practice, however, governmental entities often provide much more than the minimum. Letting people be fully heard can add immeasurably to the legitimacy and acceptability of the ultimate decisions, and it can help the decisionmakers avoid unanticipated problems down the road. Astute officials recognize that generosity with procedure is sometimes very much in their institution's interest.

ANACONDA CO. v. RUCKELSHAUS

Notes and Questions

1. *Adjudicative v. legislative fact.* *Anaconda* illustrates the difficulty of relying on the adjudicative v. legislative fact distinction. Many of the facts in issue were specific to Anaconda, so they would appear to be adjudicative in nature. However, these were non-percipient adjudicative facts, as we used that term above, meaning that the facts did not involve credibility or perception. Other facts may have been legislative in nature (such as the harm done to the environment or public health by sulfur oxide or the availability of anti-pollution technology). However, it didn't matter to the court, because the action was generalized, not individualized. Alternatively, even if the action was individualized, the EPA's rulemaking procedure satisfied due process requirements.

2. *Rules applicable to a single party.* Judge Posner wrote a couple of interesting opinions about the power of Chicago voters to shut down bars. In the first case, *Philly's v. Byrne*, 732 F.2d 87 (7th Cir.1984), Posner rather reluctantly upheld the power of voters to adopt a referendum shutting down all the bars in a precinct, even though a precinct might consist of only 400 voters and have only a single liquor licensee. "The voters must shut down all the retail liquor outlets in the precinct in order to shut down one and they must shut them down for four years because a new referendum cannot be held before that period has elapsed. This means not only that the licensee who is disliked is protected to some extent by the licensee who is liked but also the voters cannot impose costs on liquor sellers without imposing costs on themselves—the costs of not being to buy liquor in the precinct. . . . The requirement that the precinct electorate act across the board shows that the judgment the voters are asked to make is legislative rather than adjudicative in character." He relies on *Bi-Metallic* among other cases. *Id.* at 92.

In the second case, however, *Club Misty, Inc. v. Laski,* 208 F.3d 615 (7th Cir.2000), the precinct voters had the power by referendum to shut down a particular licensee. The goal was to give the voters a quicker way to get rid of a bad apple than to await administrative proceedings of the Liquor Commission. This was adjudicative rather than legislative action, because it was aimed at a particular licensee. It was unaccompanied by any procedural safeguards, so it violated due process. *See also Indiana Land Co. v. City of Greenwood*, 378 F.3d 705, 710 (7th Cir.2004), another Posner opinion citing *Club Misty*: "The greater the number of people burdened by a proposed law, the easier it is to mobilize political resistance, and the likelier moreover that the burdened class includes constituents of the legislators proposing to impose the burden. If a legislature can focus burdens laser-like on a hapless individual, he has no political remedy, while if it has to place an equal burden on many others he has a political remedy in concert with the others."

In general, procedural due process should not apply to a rule of general applicability, even though the rule currently regulates only a single entity, if the rule is stated in a way so that others may be covered by it in the future. *Cf.* Ronald M. Levin, "The Case for (Finally) Fixing the APA's Definition of 'Rule,'" 56 Admin.L.Rev. 1077, 1093-95 (2004)(supporting this view in a statutory context). Exceptions to this principle, if any, should be narrow. The Schwartz statement seems unsound if it means that an agency statement of law or policy that purports on its face to be of general applicability should be treated as adjudicatory when only one or a few known persons are affected adversely. In practice, many rules only affect one or a few individuals who may be known to the issuing agency at the time the rule is issued. Rules are often adopted to deal *generally* with a problem currently being caused by a known individual.

Possibly there should be a "sham" exception for situations in which an agency makes an adjudicative determination and disguises it as a rule to avoid hearing obligations. For one possible formulation, see Arthur Earl Bonfield, STATE ADMINISTRATIVE RULE MAKING 85 (1986). But that situation is probably not presented in *Anaconda.*

The deeper problem with cases like *Anaconda* is that the *Bi-Metallic* rationales become less persuasive as the number of persons affected by the rule drops. A trial-type hearing would not be grossly unmanageable; the relevant facts may be adjudicative rather than legislative; and political remedies are not reliable. The tough-minded answer is that the logic behind the rulemaking/adjudication distinction works most of the time, and its unpersuasiveness in this context is just too bad. As the Court said in *Mathews v. Eldridge*, "procedural due process rules are shaped by the risk of error inherent in the truthfinding process in the generality of cases, not the rare exceptions." But it's not surprising that some courts in the *Anaconda* situation resist this "tyranny of labels" and have gone on to consider whether the plaintiff got due process even if the proceeding were deemed adjudicatory.

The dictum (or alternative holding) in *Anaconda* is on the money. Even if due process was applicable, the notice and comment procedure employed by the EPA, coupled with a public hearing, provided all the process that was due. Moreover, rulemaking procedure was better than adjudicatory procedure in the *Anaconda* situation, since it effectively gives notice to and solicits views from the public, other mining companies worried about a bad precedent, public-interest organizations, etc., whereas adjudicatory procedure tends to be limited only to the disputing parties. This is a preview of the rulemaking v. adjudication issue that is discussed in later chapters.

See also *Quivira Mining Co. v. NRC*, 866 F.2d 1246, 1261-62 (10th Cir.1989), which follows *Anaconda* and cites several other similar cases. *Quivira* involved a rule that affected only Kerr McGee, operator of the thorium mill involved in the *West Chicago* case. *See* § 3.1.1 N.2. The court indicated that due process does not apply to generally stated rules that resolve questions of policy, even those applicable only to a single entity. Like *Anaconda*, the court also indicated that if due process did apply, it was satisfied by notice and comment procedure. Moreover, Kerr McGee had failed to raise any procedural objections before the NRC or asked to present oral argument or to cross-examine witnesses. Finally, Kerr McGee would have a chance in a subsequent licensing hearing to raise site-specific concerns that would require deviation from the regulation.

One may wonder, however, whether the Tenth Circuit put too much reliance on the public's interest in participating in the *Anaconda* and *Quivira* cases. If EPA brought an enforcement proceeding to stop Anaconda from violating its pollution regulations, the public's interest in being heard would be about the same as in the real case. But such a proceeding would unquestionably be an adjudication, and members of the public would not have a constitutional right to participate in it.

CHAPTER 3: ADMINISTRATIVE ADJUDICATION: FUNDAMENTAL PROBLEMS

§ 3.1 STATUTORY RIGHTS TO AN ADJUDICATORY HEARING

§ 3.1.1 Federal Law—Right to a Hearing Under the APA

DOMINION ENERGY BRAYTON POINT, LLC v. JOHNSON

Notes and Questions

1. *EPA's reasons.* It might be interesting to ask the class why Dominion cares about whether it gets an APA hearing on its NPDES renewal. Probably for bargaining purposes, not because it truly believes that a formal trial-type hearing before an ALJ would cause the EPA to change its mind about the terms of a revised permit. If Dominion could compel EPA to provide a full-fledged hearing presided over by an ALJ, perhaps EPA would settle the case to avoid the costly hearing. Even better, if Dominion could force invalidation of the EPA procedural regulation that calls for NPDES permit disputes to be resolved via notice and comment, EPA would have to start over, which might give Dominion years of extra time under its prior permit without its having to comply with the terms of a new one.

Often, the party that wants formal proceedings is a large corporation represented by a large law firm, as in the *Dominion* and *Chemical Waste* cases. We wonder whether the attorneys pressing for formal proceedings don't also have their own agenda. Lawyers like formal proceedings, because they are trained as trial lawyers and because such proceedings consume vastly more attorney time and thus generate increased fees. Possibly some clients would prefer the informal approach validated by *Dominion.* Informal hearings take less time for company executives (who would not have to testify) and cost less in terms of attorney fees. And the results are not likely to differ much in the vast majority of cases.

The reasons why EPA wants to use informal procedure to deal with NPDES licensing (or waste disposal issues as in *Chemical Waste*) are fairly obvious. It sees significant economies and efficiencies in avoiding formal APA adjudication and using the much less formal and more flexible rulemaking-type procedure instead. Shortages of staff and funds radically limit EPA's ability to carry out all of the tasks assigned to it. To the extent that it can save time and money on each case, its limited budget will go a lot further.

Agencies have very real incentives to avoid APA formal adjudication because of the numerous constraints on their discretion in making procedural decisions. The most significant is the requirement that the presiding officer be an ALJ. Agencies such as EPA object to using ALJs because of the broad constraints on hiring ALJs (particularly the veterans' preference and the agency's inability to choose judges with the necessary technical proficiency). In addition, agencies dislike using ALJs because they cannot be assigned to other tasks (even when there is not enough work to keep them busy as judges) and the agency is unable to monitor the ALJ's performance (an agency is forbidden to conduct a performance evaluation of its ALJs). In effect, ALJs have a guaranteed, lifetime job and virtually no accountability. The result has been a proliferation of agency adjudication schemes that are not covered by the APA. This issue is discussed further in § 3.4.

2. *Adjudication required by statute.* *West Chicago* involved an application to the NRC by Kerr-McGee to amend a materials handling license so as to permit additional storage of radioactive waste in West Chicago. The City opposed the application and asked the NRC to provide a full APA trial-type hearing. The Seventh Circuit's decision rejected the presumption, articulated in *Seacoast*, that Congress intends formal adjudication under the APA when it calls for a "hearing." Instead, the court reversed the presumption: formal adjudication is not required absent some clear indication of Congressional intent that "hearing" means "hearing on the record" or otherwise intends that the APA apply.

The Seventh Circuit was plainly motivated by efficiency concerns. It worried about over-judicialization of NRC proceedings, which has indeed been a problem. Many NRC hearings have been marathon affairs with large numbers of interveners, endless cross-examination, and vast delay. Indeed, that is what the City of West Chicago was probably trying to achieve. The Seventh Circuit was concerned about forcing the NRC to provide a costly APA evidentiary hearing in the relatively minor Kerr-McGee case, given the NRC's need to deal with much more important cases of nuclear reactor licensing.

Seacoast involved an application to EPA for a permit authorizing a nuclear reactor to discharge heat (a pollutant) into the sea. EPA had to find that the discharge would protect wildlife and that the best available technology was employed. The court noted that EPA had to make specific factual findings about the applicant (although they are of a technical or scientific nature); frequently these issues will be sharply disputed; adversarial hearings would be helpful in guaranteeing reasoned decisionmaking and meaningful judicial review; there is a serious impact on public and private rights. The First Circuit's *Seacoast* opinion said that these are exactly the situations in which Congress wanted formal adjudication, reasoning directly opposed to the *West Chicago* case.

In addition to Howarth's article cited in the text (N.3), see his more extended argument in "Federal Licensing and the APA: When Must Formal Adjudicative Procedures be Used," 37 Admin.L.Rev. 317 (1985). Howarth argues in favor of the *Seacoast* presumption that APA formal adjudication should be the norm unless Congress explicitly says it should not apply. *Florida East Coast* is not in point; everyone understands that formal rulemaking is cumbersome and useless, while informal rulemaking works well. But in adjudication, formal adjudication protects both the parties and the public interest, while informal adjudication provides no protection at all. Even the Attorney General's Manual on the APA (1946), which was not inclined to read the APA broadly, acknowledged this distinction.

Additional arguments in favor of the *Seacoast* approach are that the APA is the keystone statute of federal administrative law. It provides a wide range of protections to persons who have disputes with government. We should avoid balkanized procedure that allows every agency to write its own ticket. In informal adjudication, an agency can cut back procedural protection to the rudimentary levels provided by due process (if due process applies at all). Moreover, the APA provides sufficient shortcuts so that it is not really that onerous for agencies to comply with it.

On the other side, it can be argued that Congress has decided not to require APA adjudication unless it uses the words "on the record," and that position should be respected. There are serious problems with the way ALJs are selected, assigned, and evaluated under existing law; it is justifiable to let agencies avoid these problems. Especially in situations involving disputes about scientific, technical or economic facts, rather than determinations of wrongdoing, there's nothing wrong with dispensing with the APA and all of its baggage of cross-examination and separation of functions. Experience has shown that the presumption in favor of formality is out of date.

If EPA's *regulations* (as opposed to the statute) had required a hearing "on the record," that would not trigger § 554(a), which states that the hearing must be required by a *statute*. This makes good sense; agencies should not be discouraged from adopting rules providing some procedural protection by requiring them to go all the way if they voluntarily have gone only part way. However, as explained in § 3.1.2, the 1961 MSAPA triggers formal adjudication if a hearing is required "by law," which might well include agency rules.

Even if regulations cannot by themselves trigger the APA, it's worth noting another important point: a federal agency must adhere to its own regulations. That means the agency must actually provide whatever procedural protections its regulations call for. The principle that agencies are bound by their own procedural rules that are intended to benefit the public is generally considered to be administrative common law. Thus, if a regulation were interpreted to mean that an agency *intended* to impose on itself all of the constraints of APA formal adjudication (an unusual but not unheard-of situation), it would be required to follow the APA. *See* Thomas W. Merrill, "The Accardi Principle," 74 Geo.Wash.L.Rev. 569 (2006).

3. *Deferring to the agency's choice.* In addition to *Marathon,* the Ninth Circuit has held that the APA applies to statutes (in this case, Agricultural Department hearings) calling for an "evidentiary hearing." These cases arise under the Equal Access to Justice Act, discussed in §10.3. *Aageson Grain & Cattle Co. v. USDA,* 500 F.3d 1038 (9th Cir. 2007). Similarly see *Lane v. USDA,* 120 F.3d 106 (8th Cir. 1997). To recover fees incurred at the agency level, an applicant must establish that the APA applied to the hearing; these cases hold that it did. It is at present unclear whether *Aageson* and *Lane* really meant (or understood) what they seemed to say. If they did, all agency hearings conducted by the USDA must be governed by the APA. That means they must use ALJs. Since they don't, it would appear the hearing scheme is invalid.

Dominion is faithful to *Chevron* methodology, but we question whether *Chevron* should be applied to an agency's determination of whether the keystone procedural statute, the federal APA, should apply to its proceedings. It is certainly arguable whether *Chevron* deference should apply to an agency's reading of a procedural provision that exists for the very purpose of confining the agency's power. Instead, as Howarth argues, the agency's construction of the term "public hearing" has to be informed by an understanding of what APA § 554 means. If § 554 embodies the *Seacoast* presumption that the words "hearing" or "public hearing" trigger the APA, then the EPA's construction of its own statute might fail at *Chevron* step one. For additional criticism of this application of *Chevron,* see Melissa M. Berry, "Beyond *Chevron's* Domain: Agency Interpretation of Statutory Procedural Provisions," 30 Seattle Univ.L.Rev. 541 (2007).

It can also be questioned whether the EPA has delegated legislative power to adopt the regulation in question; if not, *Mead* rather than *Chevron* applies and the EPA's view should receive weak rather than strong deference. *See* John F. Stanley, Note, *The "Magic Words" of § 554: A New Test for Formal Adjudication under the APA,* 56 Hast.L.J. 1067 (2005). Generally agencies have delegated power to adopt procedural rules, and EPA used notice and comment to adopt this one, so it seems likely that *Chevron* rather than *Mead* will apply. If you are teaching the chapters in order, it's premature to get into these issues at this point in the course; but you may want to come back to *Dominion* when you cover *Chevron.* We raise these questions again in § 9.2.3 N.8.

We edited out references in *Dominion* to *National Cable and*

Telecommunications Ass'n v. Brand X Internet Services, 545 U.S. 967 (2005), which requires a court to defer under *Chevron* when an agency reasonably interprets ambiguous statutory language, even if the same court has already adopted a contrary interpretation of that language. *Seacoast* had stated that the key statutory language in the CWA was ambiguous, which opened the way for EPA to reinterpret it. It seemed to us premature to introduce *Brand X* at this early point in the course. We believe that the instructor should simply explain *Chevron* insofar as necessary but omit detailed discussion of that case when discussing *Dominion*. Of course, if you've taken the materials out of order and completed scope of review before tackling Chapter 3, you should discuss *Brand X* when you deal with *Dominion*.

4. *Informal adjudication.* If a statute calls for a "hearing," but neither due process nor the APA formal adjudication provisions are applicable, an agency might conduct a "paper hearing," meaning that it considers only written materials (with or without an oral argument) but no testimony or cross-examination. The proceeding might also permit ex parte communications and lack any internal separation of functions.

As the text indicates, a few old cases breathe life into the word "hearing" in statutes that do not trigger formal adjudication. *United States Lines* decided that *informal* adjudication was appropriate for approval of an application pendente lite. However, it reversed the administrative decision because the agency had relied on ex parte communications. Thus the court put flesh on the bare bones of the word "hearing." In addition to cases in text, *see also Sea-Land Serv. v. United States*, 683 F.2d 491, 496 (D.C.Cir. 1982) (an evidentiary hearing must be conducted when there are disputed issues of material fact; agency must conduct whatever proceedings are necessary to ensure it has sufficient information to permit consideration of relevant factors).

These cases seem inconsistent with *Vermont Yankee* and *PBGC*. They contribute to a proliferation of hearing procedures and create much uncertainty. An agency might feel it has to offer full-fledged formal procedure in every case lest it be reversed on appeal—the core concern of *Vermont Yankee*. That's why the ABA recommendation discussed in the next note is better than either case-by-case tinkering (as in *U.S. Lines*) or leaving informal adjudication procedures entirely to agency discretion or to due process where it's applicable.

You may wish to save the material about administrative common law for a class devoted to *Vermont Yankee*, possibly considering whether a common law power to create procedure should be recognized in adjudication as opposed to rulemaking. As the text notes, there is a major difference between them. In rulemaking, informal rulemaking has a satisfactory procedural structure that applies to most agency adoptions of binding rules. If adjudication isn't covered by due process, procedural rules, or the APA, however, the agency can dispense with virtually all procedure. APA § 555(e) is about the only protection—you are entitled to prompt notice when they say no and you get a brief statement of why not. APA § 558(c) gives some protection in the case of sanctions against licensees. Thus there is a better argument for tinkering with informal adjudication than informal rulemaking procedure.

5. *ABA recommendations.* The first of the two ABA recommendations (prospectively requiring that the APA formal adjudication procedures apply unless Congress specifically provides that they don't) is problematic. Although it would probably sweep a few future regulatory schemes under the APA when Congress overlooked the issue, it is more likely that the proponents of any new scheme will take care to rule this out. Agencies and their Congressional supporters don't want to be bound by APA formal adjudication rules and they definitely don't want to use ALJs. Moreover, what happens if Congress amends an existing regulatory scheme, perhaps adding new responsibilities for the agency, but fails to make clear that it doesn't want the APA formal adjudication provisions to apply. Would that unexpectedly place the whole regulatory scheme under the APA, bringing it to a halt until the agency could hire a staff of ALJs?

Included in this note are some advocacy statements endorsing and opposing the ABA's proposed default rule. You can use these quotes to highlight the policy issues that underlie the entire unit.

The second ABA recommendation uses the term "Type A" to mean existing APA formal adjudication and "Type B" to mean the many evidentiary hearing schemes that are required by federal statute but are not under the APA. The recommendation would create a special system of procedural rules for Type B hearings. These rules would include the more important of the fair hearing provisions of the APA (such as separation of functions). However, Type B hearings would not be presided over by ALJs, because all agree that it would be politically infeasible to require the use of ALJs. As one of the authors of this book was the chief draftsman and proponent of the ABA recommendation, we will refrain from giving a pep talk for it here. The "spreading umbrella" article cited in the text contains a full presentation of the proposal.

6. *Constitutionally required hearings.* This material links up constitutional and statutory hearings. The two are intimately connected, and there is much uncertain law here. Consider the *Dominion* case. Even if EPA must provide due process in renewing NPDES permits (which is questionable given the high degree of discretion EPA enjoys), written process

may have sufficed under *Mathews v. Eldridge*. The private interest at stake (how much the licensee must spend to cool the water before returning it to the river) is significant but really just involves money; the benefits of oral testimony and cross examination etc. are questionable (in light of the technical nature of the disputed issues); and EPA's interest in resisting oral hearings and APA procedural formalities (especially separation of functions and the need to employ ALJs) in the many water pollution permit disputes is persuasive. *See* § 2.4 N.7.

In the article cited in text, Funk argues that *Wong* was a wise decision and is not really out of line with recent administrative law developments. However, we disagree. Now that due process protects a much wider range of interests than in the 1940s, and modern constitutional doctrine emphasizes that the requisites of due process should be determined in a case-specific manner, *Wong Yang Sung* seems anachronistic and ripe for overruling. The APA requirements (particularly the requirement that ALJs conduct the hearings) simply do not fit every federal adjudicatory scheme.

7. *Problem.* You may want to discuss the assumption in the problem that the wetland in question is within the power of the Corps to regulate. Under the CWA, the wetland must be part of the "navigable waters of the United States" or the non-navigable tributaries of such waters. In *Rapanos v. United States,* 547 U.S. 715 (2006), the Supreme Court split sharply in interpreting this phrase. Justice Scalia's 4-justice plurality ruled that the CWA covered only wetlands that constituted a relatively permanent body of water with a continuous surface connection to navigable waters or their tributaries. This approach would place almost all wetlands (including Mel's) outside the CWA. However, Justice Kennedy's concurrence in the judgment was much more generous to regulatory power. He required only that the wetland in question have a significant nexus to navigable waters, meaning a significant effect on the chemical, biological, or physical integrity of such waters. Under Kennedy's view, Mel's wetland is probably covered by CWA. Stevens' dissenting opinion would defer to the Corps regulation and cover wetlands that have any effect on navigable waters, whether or not significant. Thus Kennedy's view is the one that prevails for present purposes.

A person wanting more formal procedure than government proposes to provide must find some legal authority that requires it. This problem explores the possible sources wherein such authority could be found:

a. APA: Under *Dominion,* no formal APA hearing is required because the statute does not call for a "hearing on the record" or give any other affirmative indication that Congress wanted the APA to apply. The Corps' procedural regulations construe the ambiguous words "public hearing" to mean only informal notice and comment-type procedures. The Corps obviously wants to operate efficiently and would see the requirement of an APA trial-type hearing, presided over by an ALJ, as quite inefficient.

. In *Buttrey*, the court affirmed the Corps' denial of the permit, even though the Corps provided only a "paper hearing" and an informal conference. It pointed to legislative history showing that Congress wanted informal procedure in § 404 proceedings, and it disagreed with *Seacoast*. *Seacoast* was a similar case—an application for an initial water-pollution license (to build a nuclear power plant) with strong opposition from environmental groups and various issues that can be resolved only through scientific studies (such as effects on wildlife, flooding etc.)

Also, as in *Seacoast*, there are important policy issues lurking behind the procedural ones—should we save environmentally sensitive wetlands? Should the Corps' discretion be as broad as it is in this statute? Should a property owner be allowed to develop his own property by draining a mosquito-bearing swamp? The jurisdiction of the Corps under *Rapanos* might also be at issue. Realize that if the permit is denied, the land remains a useless swamp, but (at least under present law) this is not a taking and Mel receives no compensation.

The question for the class is whether a full-fledged APA hearing should be provided; or whether the procedures the Corps provided are sufficient for full and fair ventilation of the issues at an acceptable cost. Actually, APA formal adjudication wouldn't be all that costly. The hearing would have to be held before an ALJ (meaning a person hired and assigned to cases in a way the Corps might not like). The Corps doesn't even employ any ALJs now, so it would have to hire some, and there would be a delay in case processing until ALJs were hired. Nevertheless, the ALJ would be employed by the Corps, so the ALJ would specialize and acquire experience in dealing with the issues that arise in dredging permit cases. Separation of functions would not apply because of the initial license exception. APA § 554(d)(A).

Mel would be entitled to cross examine the environmental experts arrayed against him. However, the ALJ might well rule that cross examination could be limited or dispensed with entirely, since cross examination of expert witnesses is time consuming and not particularly helpful in getting at the correct scientific results. Therefore, arguably it is not required for a "full and true disclosure of the facts." APA § 556(d). Ex parte contacts by outsiders (both Mel and the opponents of the project) would be prohibited, § 557(d), but that seems appropriate. If Mel ultimately won, he'd be entitled to attorney's fees under the Equal Access to Justice Act, which also seems fair.

On the other hand, in *Buttrey,* the Corps argued that in the Mobile district alone there are 1200 dredge and fill applications per year. If trial-type hearings were required, the Corps would be unable to carry out its mandate under § 404. 690 F.2d at 1178. But surely this is exaggerated, in light of the shortcuts available for this type of case under the APA. Moreover, most of the disappointed applicants (or the opponents of applications that were granted) would not demand such hearings in light of the expense and delay involved.

You can have a good class discussion and make respectable arguments in favor of the *Dominion* or *Seacoast* approaches. Perhaps formal APA adjudication procedure is needed in light of the great importance of the property issue to Mel and of the environmental issues to the public. However, even under those cases, a court might be heavily influenced by the legislative history cited in *Buttrey* that shows Congress wanted informal procedure in § 404 cases.

b. Due process. Under *Wong Yang Sung,* if due process applies to Mel's application, he's entitled to full APA formal adjudication. That case says that Congress surely would intend at least as much protection for the private interest in a constitutional case as in one where the hearing is provided only by statute. But as we point out in text and manual N.6, *Wong* is not being followed—for good reason. Even without *Wong,* if due process applied, Mel would still get the benefit of a *Mathews* analysis. Obviously, the informal adjudication procedure provided by the Corps could not fall below the level of what due process would require.

Probably due process is inapplicable anyway, because the statute imposes no limits on the Corps' discretion. The lack of entitlement means there's been no deprivation of property under *Roth.* Assuming due process did apply, an interesting issue arises if the Corps planned to grant the permit and denied the environmental groups a hearing. It is unclear whether due process applies when the person seeking a hearing to oppose the granting of an application is part of a large, amorphous group. See ¶ (c) in the problem in § 2.5 N.5 and accompanying discussion in this Manual. Still another unresolved due process issue is whether a rejected applicant has been "deprived" of anything for due process purposes. All of these issues hark back to material in Chapter 2.

Buttrey upheld the Corps' procedure under a *Mathews* analysis. Under the first factor, an applicant for a license has a much less compelling personal interest than a person who loses something he already has. Under the third factor, the government's interest in not holding a trial-type hearing is strong in light of the huge number of permit applications. The decision turned on the second factor. The court held that the purely paper hearing provided by the Corps minimized the risk of an erroneous deprivation.

It was critical in *Buttrey* that the facts in dispute were "legislative" rather than "adjudicative" and that Buttrey was represented by skilled counsel who spared no expense in hiring experts. Of course, it's debatable how due process should be applied to facts specific to an individual, but that don't involve credibility or perception. We refer to these as non-percipient facts in Manual § 2.5 N.2. Whether you want to call these questions of environmental fact legislative, adjudicative, or adjudicative but non-percipient, the court seems correct in stating that cross-examination would do little to clarify the answers. The court says "cross-examination of scientific witnesses in a case of this sort is often, if not always, an exercise in futility." 690 F.2d at 1182.

c. Regulations. Sometimes, an agency's regulations will provide for procedures required neither by statute or due process. Agencies are bound to follow their own rules. Looks like no help here, however.

d. Judicial creativity. As a result of the *PBGC v. LTV* case, courts are disabled from providing any procedural protections beyond due process. However, there is some pre-*PBGC* precedent imposing requirements on the agency either because of the word "hearing" or because of the needs of the court for a better record on judicial review. See text, N. 4.

§ 3.1.2 Rights to a Hearing under State Law

The new MSAPA, which, at the time this book is written, is still under consideration by the Uniform Law Commission (formerly NCCUSL), will return to the 1961 model, rather than follow the 1981 model. A hearing will have to be required by a federal or state constitution or statute in order to trigger the adjudication provisions of the Act. However, unlike the 1961 version, the new MSAPA may contain both formal and informal hearing models. We will provide further information in the supplement to this edition of the casebook when and if a new MSAPA is approved.

GREENWOOD MANOR v. IOWA DEP'T OF PUBLIC HEALTH

METSCH v. UNIVERSITY OF FLORIDA

Notes and Questions

1. *Greenwood Manor.* The term "public hearing" is ambiguous, as *Dominion* pointed out. It could well entail a notice and comment proceeding, or a town-meeting type "hearing" at which anyone could show up, make a statement, and submit a written argument, rather than a trial-type hearing

with presentation of testimony and cross-examination.

It's quite plausible that the Iowa legislature intended that certificate of need disputes be resolved by an exchange of written documents plus a town meeting. The Council's decision on Greenwood's application is more like rulemaking than adjudication. The Council needs to resolve issues of legislative fact that turn on economic and demographic data. It need not make credibility judgments or determinations about past wrongdoing or states of mind. While the legislative facts are probably disputed, it is inefficient to determine them through trial-type procedures. A trial of these issues would be costly and time-consuming for all concerned and could be used by the existing facilities to stall off new competition.

Instead, experts should prepare written studies, and the parties or their lawyers should make oral arguments based on those studies. In addition, it should be simple for competing facilities, or for ordinary people from the community who have opinions about the need for a new facility, to show up and make an informal statement to the decisionmakers. Thus we think the court reached a wise decision about the most appropriate hearing format.

Indeed, the Council's decision seems more like a matter of business management than government regulation. Essentially, the process here duplicates what a business goes through in deciding whether to expand by opening a new facility. The procedures used by business decisionmakers don't involve hearings. Instead, the executive in charge of the decision talks to all the experts (or anybody else who might have something useful to contribute), commissions studies, and then makes the best possible forecast for whether the new facility will be profitable and the best use of scarce resources. Again, the court seems wise not to require a trial-type hearing for this essentially managerial decision.

We do question whether the court gave too much deference to the agency's regulations. Agencies will always seek to avoid procedural formalities and shouldn't have free rein to take themselves out of the APA just by adopting regulations. In *Dominion,* the court was constrained by *Chevron,* but Iowa doesn't follow *Chevron.*

You may want to spend some time talking about the regulatory scheme involved in *Greenwood* and to consider the criteria for whether business in general should be regulated. Certificate of need ("CON") procedures were required as a condition of federal funding of Medicaid and other federal health programs from 1974 to 1981, but are no longer required. Some states, including Iowa, continue to employ them without a federal mandate. For a rundown of experience under the federal program, see

Bonnie Lefkowitz, HEALTH PLANNING: LESSONS FOR THE FUTURE (Aspen Systems Corp. 1983). Whether CON programs were successful in reducing overcapacity and keeping costs down is unclear, but studies indicated that in states with well established and high-functioning regulatory schemes, there were positive outcomes. *Id.* at 37-38.

Arguments in favor of regulation: The regulators sought to prevent duplication of facilities and over-capacity. This could cause cutthroat competition that would lead to the deterioration of services for consumers and possibly bankruptcies. More capacity often means more patient utilization, which increases the costs of funding agencies (because physicians who own interests in the hospitals refer patients to them). Overcapacity causes cost increases for public and private funding sources, because there are simply more fixed costs in the community that have to be covered to keep the various facilities in business. Thus redundant facilities could increase the total amount of medical costs in the community that have to be covered by the funding sources (private insurance, Medicaid, or other health funding programs).

Against regulation: The scheme could be viewed as unnecessary interference with market forces. In general, regulation is not justified unless there is a market failure that needs to be corrected. Those who oppose regulation would argue that excessive competition from overbuilding is not a market failure. Indeed, it should result in price competition that would cut the costs of the public or private funding programs. Funding sources (insurance and government) don't have to cover all the fixed and variable costs of every facility and should allow facilities to go bankrupt if necessary. Increasing capacity could also lead to competition in providing better quality of service that would be beneficial to consumers. In general, opponents would say, state regulators cannot do as well as the market in predicting future trends in medical care, labor availability, etc. Meanwhile, regulation inserts extra transactions costs into business decisions and could cause long delays that could make new construction much more expensive (for example, by requiring the payment of interest costs during the delays while approval is sought and because of increasing construction costs). Such regulation offers lots of opportunities for existing facilities to block new competition, for example by enlisting politically powerful people on their sides. It invites payoffs by the new facility to the old ones to induce them to stop fighting; or by old facilities to new ones to drop the applications. In other words, as economists would say, the program offers opportunities for rent-seeking (and possibly corruption); therefore, it is better to leave the problem to the market.

An interesting hypo that tests out the 1961 Model Act approach (as well as the rulemaking/adjudication distinction) can be derived from *Oregon*

Environmental Council v. Oregon State Bd. of Educ., 761 P.2d 1322 (Ore. 1988). The State Board *approved* a textbook (called *Getting Oreganized*—not a typo) for fourth grade social studies. An environmental group complained that the book was too oriented toward development and against environmental values. The court had to decide whether the approval of a textbook is rulemaking or adjudication; and if adjudication, whether it is a "contested case" (meaning formal adjudication is required and the decision is reviewed by an appellate court) or other than a "contested case" (meaning no adjudicatory procedure is required and the decision is reviewed by a trial court) .

The court decided that the decision was adjudication, not rulemaking, because it involved a specific book (even thought the decision would have an impact on many students); thus the Board was not required to comply with APA rulemaking procedures. Moreover, the decision involved "other than a contested case" because no evidentiary hearing (or any other procedure) was required by statute or constitution. Under the Oregon compromise mentioned before *Greenwood* in the text, if the Board had *rejected* a textbook application, the decision would require "contested case" treatment since it would have denied a license; but *approval* of the publisher's application does not fall within that provision because it does not cover the decision to grant a license.

Moreover, the Oregon statute treats a hearing required by rule as a "contested case," but the rule here required only that opponents of a textbook adoption have an "opportunity to be heard" which the court said meant submission of written views or a public meeting that fell short of the evidentiary hearing required to trigger contested case status.

2. *Due process and the APA.* As discussed above, we think the Iowa court was correct in not triggering the APA in the *Greenwood* case. Rulemaking, not adjudicatory procedure, was appropriate. The court had difficulty, however, in figuring out exactly why due process wouldn't apply.

First the court said due process was inapplicable because the facts at issue were legislative rather than adjudicative. True, but as we discussed in § 2.5, we disagree with this analysis. If the predicates for due process are present (that is, individualized action and a deprivation of liberty or property), due process applies regardless of what type of facts are at issue. However, under *Mathews* balancing, a rulemaking-type procedure is all that's required. So we would articulate the argument that way rather than saying that due process isn't applicable at all.

Second, the court said that due process didn't apply because there were no factual disagreements. But surely that was wrong. The incumbent hospitals and the new applicant had sharp disagreements about the economics of the new competition.

Third, the court held that neither the applicants nor the competitors had a protected liberty or property interest. We agree with this conclusion, but the court failed to make clear why not. The reason is that the certificate of need procedure does not create an entitlement; the Council's determination is discretionary. Under *Roth,* no property interest is created with respect to the applicant. This is even more true of the existing competitors than of the applicant; they certainly have no entitlement to be protected from new competition. In addition, as discussed in § 2.5, it can be argued that the agency action was rulemaking with respect to the competitors (generalized action) but adjudication as to the applicant (individualized action).

3. *Florida's inclusive approach.* If the Florida statute applied in the *Dominion* case, it seems likely that the license amendment would affect Dominion's "substantial interests." Consequently, an APA adjudicatory proceeding would be required even though no external source required a hearing. However, as discussed below, an informal procedure is available under Florida law, so full-fledged trial would not be needed.

As to choosing which model a state should pursue, there are good arguments on both sides. The Oregon compromise seems particularly sensible. One of the authors of this book changed his position on whether the Florida/MSAPA 1981 inclusive approach was a good idea. *Compare* Michael Asimow, "Toward a New California Administrative Procedure Act: Adjudication Fundamentals," 39 UCLA L. Rev. 1067, 1081-94 (1992) (urging California to adopt the 1981 MSAPA-Florida approach to protect private interests in informal adjudication), *with* Michael Asimow, "The Influence of the Federal Administrative Procedure Act on California's New Administrative Procedure Act," 32 Tulsa L. J. 297, 307-312 (1996) (1981 MSAPA approach is over-inclusive).

In proposing revised adjudicatory APA provisions, the California Law Revision Commission ultimately opted for a version of the 1961 MSAPA approach over the 1981 approach, and the legislature agreed. Basically, the concern was that the 1981 approach sweeps in too much and could create confusion and over-proceduralization. In the Tulsa article, Asimow wrote:

> In an early Commission decision, however, the 1981 Model Act approach was rejected in favor of the federal approach. Essentially, the Model Act approach was subjected to death by ridicule. One Commission member asked—would the 1981 MSAPA approach really require application of the APA to the decision by a state high school

to select cheerleaders? Imposition of a library fine? A state forest ranger's decision in allocating campsites? Every decision affecting a state prisoner that the prisoner dislikes? A decision not to hire someone for a low-level state job or to buy a computer from vendor A rather than B?

The answer was—well yes, but hearings in relatively trivial state/private encounters could be provided through an informal summary hearing procedure. But what if the summary hearing procedure statute left out a category of relatively trivial cases? Would some of the categories be mushy? What if the agency neglected to adopt a rule providing for summary procedure for a particular category? And what if even the truncated summary procedure is too much procedure for some relatively trivial encounter? The Commission thought it would be laughed out of town if it proposed a statute to require any sort of procedure in such trivial matters.

I now believe the Commission's decision was right. The 1981 Model Act approach is overambitious. It would be a mistake to attempt to prescribe procedures—any procedures—for the infinite range of relatively trivial interactions between government and the public. . . . In our litigation-oriented society (and perhaps California is even more litigation-crazed than other states), a few people who resent being denied admission to the university or being turned down for a job or a contract or whatever are going to litigate the question of whether the procedure they received met the requirements of the summary procedure statute. And the near certainty of this sort of pointless litigation was enough to persuade the Commission to jettison the all-inclusive MSAPA approach to defining the scope of the Act." 32 U. Tulsa L. J. 297, 309-310 (footnotes omitted).

Metsch illustrates this problem well. The court was really worried about the impact of a decision giving hearing rights to disappointed law school applicants. (See language at end of the opinion.) As a result, it twisted the statute out of shape to avoid that result. This is a fundamental problem with the 1981 Act approach.

4. *The result in Metsch*. The *Metsch* decision is unconvincing. Being turned down for a low-cost legal education at an excellent state law school that you've always dreamed of attending has to involve a "substantial interest." The due process cases are completely inapplicable. *Ramos* says that admission to graduate school is discretionary, hence not an entitlement and thus not property for due process purposes. That's not at all the test under the Florida statute. It doesn't matter whether the agency decision determining a substantial interest is or is not based on a discretionary

standard.

The text edited out a much more defensible alternative ground for the holding that Metsch doesn't get a hearing. An exception to § 120.57(1) was that the section "does not apply to any proceeding in which the substantial interests of a student are determined by the State University System." The court thought that "a student" in this exemption included an applicant for admission as well as an existing student. Surely, as the court says, the legislators would not have wanted to give greater rights to an applicant for admission than to a present student who is being excluded.

5. *Formal hearings for disappointed law school applicants?* A law school application seldom presents a disputed issue of fact. Generally the facts are clear—LSAT score, GPA, legacy status, college activities, ethnicity (if that can be taken into account). The question is how the law school admission process will exercise discretion in comparing this applicant to all others. As a result, Florida's informal procedure seemingly was applicable. And that procedure—which basically allows the applicant to send a letter challenging the grounds on which the school acted, together with a written explanation of the decision—is not onerous. In fact, allowing it seems like common courtesy. If there is a disputed issue of fact (such as possible transcript falsification), the school should provide a formal hearing if one is demanded. Such cases are sufficiently rare that they would not be any great burden.

6. *Problem.* This problem may be used to teach all of § 3.1 as well as to review due process.

i) Local government: Only due process applies. Ralph has a property interest, because he cannot be discharged without cause. This means that the employment rules cannot abridge his rights to notice and hearing. *Loudermill.* Presumably the property right extends to lesser sanctions like suspension and a warning letter as well, although in *Gilbert v. Homar,* discussed in § 2.3 N.6, the Supreme Court hinted that due process might not apply to sanctions short of termination. The triviality of the sanctions here might suggest no deprivation rising to constitutional magnitude. However, *Goss* held that a student subject to a ten-day suspension from school was entitled to minimal due process protection, so perhaps these sanctions are sufficient also to trigger due process.

Even if no property interest exists, there may be a liberty interest. *Paul* indicates that placing derogatory information in a file, together with some impact on employment, is a deprivation of liberty. A warning letter might not suffice if it were not made public. *Bishop.* A suspension might be enough to meet the "stigma plus" standard of *Paul* and *Bishop.* On the other hand, this information might not be stigmatic enough to trigger a liberty interest—it's probably not bad enough to foreclose Ralph from getting another library job.

Ralph and Martha have a factual dispute--did he smoke? But if Ralph admitted he smoked and wanted only to persuade Martha not to discipline him, there may be no right to a hearing, since there is no dispute about material facts. *See Codd v. Velger*, 429 U.S. 624 (1977) (no right to a name-clearing absent a dispute about material facts). *FDIC v. Mallen* also indicated that oral hearings could be dispensed with if they are unnecessary. *Loudermill* dictum suggests that a hearing is appropriate on an issue of how to exercise discretion. So this remains an unresolved issue.

Mathews balancing suggests that due process would be minimal—something of the meet and confer variety described in *Goss*. It might well not include confrontation with the employee who Ralph thinks tattled on him.

ii) State that adopted the 1961 MSAPA: Under §1(2), the gateway provision in the 1961 MSAPA, there is no statutory right to a hearing. However, the term "law" probably includes constitutional law, so if due process applies as discussed above, the APA might be triggered. However, due process probably calls for only a minimal sort of hearing under *Goss,* not a true evidentiary hearing, so the APA would probably not come into play. The APA would require a full fledged trial-type hearing, but since due process would call for much less, a court would probably decline to trigger the APA. This part of the problem illustrates the difficulty with including due process as "law" under the 1961 APA.

iii) State that adopted the Florida statute: Under the inclusive approach taken in Florida, the APA would apply if "the substantial interests of a party are determined by an agency." There is certainly an issue of whether the very minor sanctions involved here are "substantial." If admission to the state law school isn't substantial, as in *Metsch,* a warning letter or a five-day suspension might not be substantial either. It does seem a poor use of resources to require a full-fledged trial-type hearing in the case of such minor sanctions. If there is no disputed issue of material fact, only an issue of sanction, an informal hearing could be used under Florida law.

iv) Federal—because no statute calls for an on-the-record hearing, the APA does not apply. But it might apply under *Wong Yang Sung*, because Library's action infringes a liberty or property interest (discussed above). In that case, *Wong* indicates that a full-fledged APA hearing is required. However, *Wong* is not being followed today and is ripe for being overruled by the Supreme Court. In any event, it seems very unlikely that a court would use *Wong* to trigger an APA hearing before an ALJ in the case of such minor sanctions. Instead, the court would require the agency to do only what due process requires (probably consultative procedure à la *Goss*).

§ 3.2 LIMITING THE ISSUES TO WHICH HEARING RIGHTS APPLY

HECKLER v. CAMPBELL

Notes and Questions

1. *Foreclosure of hearing rights through rulemaking. Campbell* brings home to students the tangible effect of *Bi-Metallic*. In rulemaking, you don't get any constitutionally mandated hearing, and your statutory right to be heard (through notice and comment rulemaking) falls well short of a trial-type hearing. But you will get no other opportunity to be heard at the administrative level on the issues addressed in the rule, because in subsequent agency proceedings the rule will be dispositive of those issues. Obviously, the chance that Ms. Campbell would have participated in the rulemaking proceeding is nil, but that is no different from saying that the property reassessment in *Bi-Metallic* was binding on all Denver property owners. You can refer back to § 2.5 to review the rationales that might justify this result.

Official notice is a handy device for shifting the burden of producing evidence and burden of persuasion where it is unlikely that disproof is possible. The use and abuse of official notice is discussed in § 4.2.2. Generally, however, a party subject to official notice has the right to offer evidence to disprove the officially noticed facts. When the facts are settled through a pre-existing rule, that isn't possible. Yet the rule in *Campbell* did offer applicants the opportunity to show that the grid rule should not apply to them, especially in borderline situations, so this "safety valve" opportunity may be the functional equivalent of an opportunity to rebut officially noticed facts.

2. *Issues suitable for rulemaking.* Congress often confers rulemaking power on an agency and also provides for individualized consideration. In any given situation, one of these statutes must supersede the other. As in *Campbell*, the Supreme Court has been receptive to arguments that rulemaking trumps adjudication.

American Hospital Ass'n v. NLRB, 499 U.S. 606 (1991), concerned the first substantive rule issued by the NLRB since 1935. It defined an employee unit appropriate for collective bargaining in acute care hospitals. Challengers argued that the statute required the Board to make a separate bargaining unit determination "in each case" and therefore prohibits the

Board from using general rules to define bargaining units. The Court relied on *Campbell*, as well as *Storer* and *Texaco,* holding that those cases "confirm that, even if a statutory scheme requires individualized determinations, the decisionmaker has the authority to rely on rulemaking to resolve certain issues of general applicability *unless Congress clearly expresses an intent to withhold that authority." Id.* at 612 (emphasis added).

You can use this question to explore the benefits and costs of foreclosure of adjudication through rulemaking. Powell mentions some of the factors pressing powerfully towards rulemaking in *Campbell*: the need for efficiency in coping with a massive caseload and the desire to achieve greater uniformity of result than through ad hoc reliance on vocational experts. Cutting the other way is the argument that rules of this kind inevitably rest on crude generalizations, and a full hearing would permit a more situation-sensitive judgment to be made. Claimants' dignitary interests and sense of legitimacy might also be more fully served if they could see their fates determined by a real live human being, with whom they could interact, instead of by an impersonal rulemaking process. Social Security ALJs are more likely to sympathize with the claimants before them in a borderline disability case than were the heads of SSA when they adopted the grid system.

You can also use this question to explore some of the other advantages and limitations of rulemaking as a device for resolving legal and policy issues. For example, rules are easier to find and the rulemaking process facilitates broad involvement by political leaders and members of the public in policy disputes; but when rules become obsolete, they may be harder to fix than precedents would be. *See* § 5.1 for a fuller discussion.

On a doctrinal level, *Campbell's* intimation that rulemaking is appropriate only for "certain classes of issues" has not flourished, as *American Hospital Ass'n* shows. The dissent in *Yuckert* and the majority opinion in *Zebley* relied on situation-specific statutory interpretation, not on theoretical arguments that certain kinds of issues *inherently* "require case-by-case determination." You might call attention to the language in *Campbell* in which the Court observes that a regulation could be challenged for exceeding the Secretary's authority or for being arbitrary and capricious. Those are significant constraints on an agency's ability to settle issues through rulemaking. The arbitrary and capricious test requires the court to examine the rulemaking record to see whether the rule is factually supported; therefore Social Security would have to have solid evidence in the record to support the determination in Rule 202.10 that there are a substantial number of jobs for people in Campbell's situation. But if the Court thinks that "certain classes of issues" are not amenable to rulemaking (or that rules pertaining to such issues cannot supersede a statutory right to an evidentiary hearing), it has not told us what those classes are.

3. *Safety valves.* The safeguards mentioned by the Court in *Campbell* are not exactly equivalent to a waiver provision, because the latter, when available, can be invoked by someone to whom a rule is squarely applicable by its terms. The grid regulations did not allow flexibility in that regard. The Court seems to say that a waiver process is a corrective for overbreadth, but isn't necessary in the case of the grid regulations because they are already narrowly drawn. On a more intangible level, one could say that the ALJ's threshold determinations, on which the Court puts emphasis, are similar to a waiver system in that both insure that the decision process is not totally mechanical—an ALJ will still exercise some human judgment. (This was a particular concern of Justices Brennan and Marshall in *Campbell.* They wrote separately to suggest that the ALJ in Campbell's case had done too superficial a job; the majority didn't reach that issue.)

Regarding the general desirability of waivers: Rules are normally written to promote predictability, stability, uniformity of treatment; they can be easily applied and cover the generality of situations. Consequently they tend to give short shrift to the unexpected or atypical case, where there is a strong case for individual judgment. Administrators often fail to anticipate all the ramifications of their rules—the world is too diverse and changes too rapidly. Thus there will always be anomalies, which create a demand for "regulatory equity" through some sort of exceptions process. Yet there are situations in which no waivers should be allowed. For example, there may be no intelligible way to draw exceptions to the rule or a third party may have relied in good faith on the rule from which a waiver is sought. As in *Yetman,* a waiver provision may flood the agency with an unmanageable number of petitions.

Thus, a waiver provision is helpful to the validity of a rule, but not always essential. In *WNCN,* for example, the FCC was trying to streamline the renewal process by eliminating an entire category of challenges. The transaction costs of these generally unsuccessful challenges were high. The Court thought that, given the open-ended nature of the Communications Act, it had no basis for preventing the FCC from making a clean break from the past.

Historically speaking, judicial emphasis on the availability of "safety valves" was an important "comfort factor" in the early years of the growth of rulemaking. Such provisions permitted the consoling belief that the agency's determinations in a rule weren't *really* conclusive, but only provisional. Today, rulemaking is a much more familiar and commonplace tool of policymaking, and it has developed its own set of safeguards. Thus, the necessity for a safety valve is increasingly seen as contingent, depending on the circumstances of a particular rule or program. For fuller discussion, see § 6.4.

4. *No material issue of fact.* The rules that the Court upheld in *Hynson* placed the burden of showing the existence of a genuine issue of fact on the manufacturer, although the FDA was moving for summary judgment. While this allocation of the evidentiary burden may look odd, it is roughly in line with modern summary judgment practice in ordinary civil litigation. The basis for this allocation is that the manufacturer would (by statute) have borne the ultimate burden of persuasion had a hearing been held. *See Hynson,* 412 U.S. at 617. Therefore, under today's civil procedure principles, the adverse party (the FDA) could use a summary judgment motion to find out whether the manufacturer had enough evidence in hand to justify holding the hearing. If proceedings on the motion make clear that the party who has the burden of proof has no chance of carrying it, summary judgment is proper. *See Celotex Corp. v. Catrett,* 477 U.S. 317 (1986). On summary judgment, *see generally* Ernest Gellhorn & William F. Robinson, Jr., "Summary Judgment in Administrative Adjudication," 84 Harv. L. Rev. 612 (1971).

A later case strongly affirming the *Hynson* principle is *Costle v. Pacific Legal Foundation,* 445 U.S. 198, 214 (1980), which involves the system of NPDES regulation discussed in *Dominion,* § 3.1. EPA's regulations allowed the agency to dispense with an adjudicatory hearing if the request for a hearing raised only questions of law rather than material issues of fact. The Court upheld these regulations, stating that it was up to the petitioner, not EPA, to identify disputed issues of material fact by tendering evidence that required a hearing. It relied on *Hynson* among other cases. However, in a number of cases, appellate courts have set aside agency summary judgments because, in the court's view, there were disputed material questions of fact. *See e.g. Crestview Parke Care Center v. Thompson,* 373 F.3d 743 (6th Cir. 2004); *Rogers Corp. v. EPA,* 275 F.3d 1096 (D.C. Cir. 2002).

We think that the *Board of Water* decision is correct. *Campbell* and *Hynson* establish that an agency can dispense with a trial-type hearing in the absence of a material factual dispute. More controversial, perhaps, is the dictum that allows FERC to dispense with an APA hearing even when there *are* disputed factual issues if they can be resolved on a written record. This would ordinarily be true of issues of legislative fact that involve a clash of expert testimony but not issues of credibility or state of mind. It might also be true of adjudicative facts that are non-percipient such as economic facts about a party (like its costs or profits). Cross-examination can be slow and costly when used to resolve factual issues of this type. Yet the APA might be read to require it. *See* APA § 556(d), fifth sentence. An agency should have discretion to dispense with oral testimony and cross-examination when written materials would serve as well. However, many of the other provisions of the APA should remain applicable (e.g. separation of functions, ban on ex parte communication, etc.), even though no trial is held.

Recall the corresponding issue under due process: it remains unclear whether an agency can dispense with a trial-type hearing if the only disputed issues involve discretion, policy, or non-percipient facts. Cases like *Board of Water* are vague about how to determine whether a party has shown enough of a factual issue to justify the hearing. That vagueness may be unavoidable. If this were a civil trial, the operative test would be whether "the evidence is such that a reasonable jury could return a verdict for the [party resisting summary judgment]." *Anderson v. Liberty Lobby, Inc.,* 477 U.S. 242, 248 (1986). But an expert agency is different from a jury, so civil procedure analogies may not get us very far on this point.

5. *Case-by-case discretion.* Do all lawyers need to know a little administrative law? *Levine* shows that even criminal lawyers have to contend with administrative agencies.

The *Levine* dissent relied on *Lopez v. Davis,* 531 U.S. 230 (2001), which upheld a BOP rule that seems quite similar to the one involved in *Levine.* The statute involved in *Lopez* gave BOP discretion to reduce by up to one year the sentence of drug offenders convicted of non-violent crimes who completed a substance abuse program. BOP adopted a rule categorically denying early release to certain prisoners who had completed the substance abuse program if they had certain prior convictions. The Supreme Court said that the statute involved did not require individualized determinations; but even if it did, an agency can rely on rulemaking to avoid having to relitigate issues that may be fairly and efficiently determined in a single rulemaking proceeding. *Lopez* relied on *Heckler v. Campbell* and *American Hosp. Ass'n v. NLRB.* The majority in *Levine* distinguished *Lopez* because it believed that § 3621(b) required consideration of all the statutory factors in every case.

Our view is that the dissent in *Levine* is persuasive, especially in light of the deference required by *Chevron* when an agency construes an ambiguous statute. BOP's rule about halfway houses seems valid under *Lopez* as well as *Campbell* and similar cases. Agencies can avoid case-by-case determinations, including case-by-case applications of a list of factors, through adoption of a rule that indicates how the factors will be balanced in a specific class of cases.

6. *Problem.* This problem is loosely based on a real but unreported case. Rather than making individual licensing determinations about the adequacy of a particular foreign medical school, the Board settled the

question with a single generic rule. The Board likely realized, after years of experience, that it was consistently turning down license requests from graduates of foreign medical schools, other than British or Canadian ones. By codifying that position, it expected to save time on these all-too-predictable cases, as well as to give clear notice to potential applicants about what their chances were. The Board wasn't thinking about an unusual case like Kate's.

Under the APAs of some states, the Board would have an option to hold a conference hearing rather than a trial-type hearing in situations in which there is no disputed issue of material fact, as appears to be the case here. However, all of the other procedural protections of the APA (such as separation of functions) would still apply. Even without the foreign medical student rule, cases like *Board of Water* suggest that the Board need not schedule an APA hearing if no facts are in dispute or if any disputed facts are legislative or non-percipient.

In any event, the basic message of *Heckler v. Campbell* is clear: a legislative rule can settle an issue and prevent it from being actively contested at a hearing. Due process would appear to guarantee Kate nothing more. It is not settled whether due process applies to an initial license, but it very well may, especially if the decision to grant the license is not discretionary. *See* § 2.2.1 N.8. However, if the rule has left no facts in dispute, there is no constitutional right to a hearing. *See, e.g., Dixon v. Love,* 431 U.S. 105 (1977); *Codd v. Velger,* 429 U.S. 624 (1977).

Ultimately, a hearing won't do Kate any good unless she can find a way around the no-foreign-graduates rule. She should request a *waiver* of the rule, because it is logically inapplicable to her case. The rule is designed to weed out people with inferior medical educations; she completed three years at an American school and a fourth year in an American hospital. She had no classes at Caribbean—it only issued her a diploma. If waiver is a possibility, and due process is otherwise applicable (because the license is an entitlement), Kate might have a right to at least an informal opportunity to present her side of the story. *See Cleveland Board of Education v. Loudermill,* § 2.4 N.7.

As *WNCN* and *Yetman* suggest and § 6.4 will develop more fully, not every rule requires a waiver opportunity, but Kate certainly has some strong arguments here. Application of the rule to her is extremely harsh; the rule is illogical in her case; waiving it will not undermine the rule in the generality of cases (which involve people who took classes at foreign schools); a waiver will not upset anyone's reliance interest (and indeed will vindicate Kate's reliance interest, since the rule was adopted after she enrolled at Caribbean).

It is premature to discuss judicial review extensively, but inevitably this problem leads to discussion of the prospects for judicial reversal of the Board's decision to deny a waiver. One issue is whether the decision to grant a waiver is committed to agency discretion. It probably is not. The Board would be required to set forth its reasons for denial of the waiver and the court could decide if they were arbitrary and capricious. *See* § 6.4 N.3.

But judicial review is long and costly and probably useless to someone like Kate, whose medical career may be permanently derailed unless she can immediately secure a waiver and start an internship. If she cannot, she should probably give up and move to another state that has not yet clamped down on foreign medical schools. This is an important cautionary point about the practical utility of judicial review: it may be too expensive or totally useless for many clients.

§ 3.3 THE CONFLICT BETWEEN INSTITUTIONAL AND JUDICIALIZED DECISION-MAKING

§ 3.3.1 Personal Responsibility of Decisionmakers

There is a good discussion of the institutional model and of probing the mind of the administrator in 1 Richard J. Pierce, Jr., ADMINISTRATIVE LAW TREATISE § 8.6 (4th ed.2002). *Morgan I* and *Mazza v. Cavicchia* are good vehicles to introduce the judicial-institutional model dichotomy. The cases sound reasonable: of course a judge should hear the case or at least know what is in the record, and of course the decision must be based exclusively on the record. But an agency is not the same as a court, and a pure judicial model will not work. The Supreme Court's naive acceptance of the judicial model in *Morgan I* has been watered down to near-invisibility.

Morgan I and *II* are frustratingly unclear about whether they articulate constitutional law or only interpret the "full hearing" statute. Because they involve ratemaking for a large class of persons, due process would not require a trial-type hearing. *See Bi-Metallic*, § 2.5. However, the statute calling for "full hearing" apparently made statutory and constitutional requirements synonymous. Today we would describe the result as "formal rulemaking" meaning rulemaking based on a record made at a trial. For an excellent treatment of the *Morgan* cases, see Daniel J. Gifford, "The Morgan Cases: A Retrospective View," 30 Admin.L.Rev. 237 (1978).

Notes and Questions

1. *"The one who decides must hear."* The rationale for the *Morgan I* requirement is based on accountability. The person who is responsible for making the decision must be the one who thought about the record and the

issues and actually made the decision. Otherwise, the decisionmaking function is lost in a faceless bureaucracy and nobody takes responsibility for it.

2. *Getting around Morgan I.* Many regulatory statutes provide for a non-discretionary appeal to the agency heads. It would be more efficient to make review discretionary. APA § 557(b) probably permits discretionary review. Weaver's article, cited in the text, downplays the importance of allowing agency heads to make final decisions in adjudicatory cases. In his view, very few cases actually require policymaking, and these should be dealt with through adoption of rules (indeed, if agency heads are denied the power to make policy through adjudication, they will have a strong incentive to adopt rules). In addition, Weaver contends that litigants have little opportunity to influence agency head decisions, which are perceived as coming from a mysterious black box. This, he thinks, creates a perception of unfairness and is at odds with the elaborate protections created by the APA at the ALJ level.

Moreover, there can be severe problems with agency head decisions during transitional periods when new political appointees have not yet been appointed or confirmed. In fact, Weaver suggests, the policy decisions are more likely to be made by subordinates who review the record than by the political appointee. In short, Weaver favors intermediate review boards and prefers those in which there is no discretionary review power by agency heads.

3. *Intermediate reports.* You may want to work through APA § 557(b), which usually requires an ALJ to prepare a proposed decision, except in cases of rulemaking or initial licensing. In those situations, the heads themselves can first issue a tentative decision, and even that procedure can be omitted in emergencies. It is unlikely that due process requires the preparation of a proposed decision if the parties have received notice of what the government proposes. Apart from due process, however, it is good practice to prepare such a report.

4. *The right to object to a proposed decision.* As *Ballard* shows, it is customary and good practice to furnish the proposed decision to the parties to permit them to file objections. However, *Ballard* is not pitched on constitutional grounds, and it would appear that the Court would have upheld a statute that had kept the STJ's report confidential. Due process, however, is another matter, and we think *Mazza* states dubious constitutional law. Is the hearing officer really a witness "giving his evidence to the judge behind the back of the appellant"? Did the agency procedure in *Mazza* violate the principle that the decision must be based exclusively on the record? If so, is a party constitutionally entitled to see and object to a

memo from a law clerk to a judge that summarizes the record and the applicable law and makes recommendations?

In *Mazza* there was no claim that the Director had not familiarized himself with the record. Indeed, *Morgan I* makes clear that the evidence can be sifted and analyzed by competent subordinates. Nor did the procedure violate the principle of exclusive record, since the examiner is not a witness and did not add any factual material to the record but merely summarized it. Nor does it violate the principle of separation of functions (§ 3.3.4), since the hearing examiner is not an adversary to the licensee. Constitutionally, the report seems no different from a law clerk's memo or oral advice to a judge from agency staff, which are routinely kept confidential. We revisit the issue of whether non-adversary agency staff can furnish ex parte advice to decisionmakers in § 3.3.4.

5. *Proving a violation of Morgan I.* The admonition of *Morgan IV* has generally been respected by both state and federal courts. According to the prevailing test, inquiry into the mental processes of agency decisionmakers must be avoided absent "a strong showing of bad faith or improper behavior." *Citizens to Preserve Overton Park, Inc. v. Volpe,* 401 U.S. 402, 420 (1971). Thus in a case in which petitioners sought to examine the transcript of a closed meeting, the D.C. Circuit wrote:

> Apparently unable to point to any independent evidence of improper conduct by the [Nuclear Regulatory] Commission, petitioners simply assert that the transcripts alone are sufficient to establish the requisite bad faith and improper conduct on the part of the Commission. We reject this approach. Petitioners must make the requisite showing *before* we will look at the transcripts. We will not examine the transcripts to determine if we may examine the transcripts. There may be cases where a court is warranted in examining the deliberative proceedings of the agency. But such cases must be the rare exception if agencies are to engage in uninhibited and frank discussions during their deliberations. Were courts regularly to review the transcripts of agency deliberative proceedings, the discussions would be conducted with judicial scrutiny in mind. Such agency proceedings would then be useless both to the agency and to the courts. We think the analogy to the deliberative processes of a court is an apt one. Without the assurance of secrecy, the court could not fully perform its function.

San Luis Obispo Mothers for Peace v. NRC, 789 F.2d 26, 44-45 (D.C. Cir.1986). As a result, counsel can only rarely raise a plausible *Morgan I* contention. The courts generally rely on the presumption of regularity and take every opportunity to explain how such consideration might have occurred, despite evidence to the contrary.

7. *Problem*. The issue here is *Morgan I*: Is the Board sufficiently familiar with the record? In the time available, how could it have done any more than simply read the review committee's decision? It could not have listened to the tape of the hearing, since that ran three hours and there was no transcript available. Nor did the Board allow any briefing or oral argument by which it could have become familiar with the record.

However, unlike *Morgan I*, the review committee provided a recommendation, although even that was quite brief. Presumably the School Board read it and thus achieved some familiarity with the case. *Bates v. Sponberg* found no *Morgan I* or due process violation when an appellate board decided to fire a professor without reviewing the transcript or allowing oral argument or briefing. It read only a recommendation that summarized the evidence.

In addition, the presumption of regularity suggests, absent other evidence, that the Board members listened to enough of the tape to familiarize themselves with the case. That, plus reading the review committee's recommendation, might furnish sufficient familiarity with the facts. Without some additional reason to question the process, it would be improper to have a trial investigating the Board's decision-making process. *See Henderling v. Carleson*, 111 Cal.Rptr. 612 (Cal.App.1974) (presumption of regularity that decision-maker listened to tape); *Jones v. Morris*, 541 F. Supp. 11 (S.D. Ohio 1981), *aff'd mem.*, 455 U.S. 1009 (1982) (school board can affirm review committee's decision to fire teacher without hearing argument or reading transcript); *Yaretzsky v. Blum*, 629 F.2d 817 (2d Cir.1980) (appellate panel not required to read transcript; citing much federal and New York state authority).

Also relevant is *Mazza*, which holds there is a due process right to examine and make exceptions to the report of the hearing officer. Assuming that case is followed, it probably would not require reversal here. Since the report was favorable to Rex, there would be no prejudice from the failure to allow him to see and object to it.

But there is another level to this problem. On what basis could the Board have reversed the review committee's findings? It is likely that it depended on some sort of extra-record evidence coming from its advisers or from the public. Or perhaps its decision was based on the personal knowledge of the Board members. A decision based on extra-record evidence (such as personal knowledge of events), or based on ex parte contacts, or on conferences with adversary staff, or perhaps tainted by personal animus, raises severe problems, which are discussed in the rest of this chapter.

There is probably no due process right to file briefs or conduct oral argument in connection with an appeal of an initial decision; Rex has had one full hearing already. *See Bates v. Sponberg.* Yet one could argue that, under all the facts here, using *Mathews* balancing, briefing or oral argument should have been permitted. There is a severe danger of error, very great personal harm, and little cost to government of allowing oral argument or written briefs.

Also on judicial review, the court might engage in stricter scrutiny of whether there was substantial evidence in support of the fact findings. As discussed in § 9.1.1 N.5, when agency heads reverse a fact-finder on credibility issues, this detracts from the substantiality of the evidence in support of their decision.

§ 3.3.2 Ex Parte Contacts

PROFESSIONAL AIR TRAFFIC CONTROLLERS ORGANIZATION (PATCO) v. FEDERAL LABOR RELATIONS AUTHORITY (FLRA)

It is important to separate clearly the material on ex parte contacts (which involve communications between persons *outside* the agency and agency decisionmakers) from separation of functions (which, in part, involves communications from agency staff to agency decisionmakers). The two are often confused in practice (both are often referred to as "ex parte rules"), but the policy issues are different. In a purely judicial model, the rules for the two would be about the same—nobody (other than a law clerk) could communicate about a pending adjudicatory matter with a decisionmaker.

In a combination of the institutional and judicial models, such as typically exist in the universe of administrative adjudication, the two are not at all the same. For reasons developed in § 3.3.4, a variety of off-record communications between agency personnel and agency decisionmakers are essential or at least tolerated. As examples of acceptable communications, we tolerate or even encourage discussions between agency decisionmakers and adversarial agency staff members about whether to issue a complaint, as well as technical and legal assistance to decisionmakers from non-adversary staff members, discussions between agency heads and ALJs, discussions between agency heads and staff about non-adjudicatory agency business such as rulemaking or budgets, and (under federal law) discussions related to initial licensing.

The law strikes a much different judicial-institutional balance when considering communications about a pending adjudication (or formal rulemaking) between decisionmakers and persons *outside* the agency (that is, other than agency staff members). Here there is no reason for such communications to occur off-the-record. Still, as the cases and notes show, many questions arise in trying to patrol outsider ex parte communications. For example, the timing of communications, identification of who is an interested person, identification of what communications are "relevant to the merits," oversight by the executive or legislative branches, and whether the prohibition should apply in hybrid adjudication/rulemaking cases, are just some of the subtle issues that arise in discussing outsider ex parte communications..

A good case on the "relevant to the merits" point under § 557(d) is *Louisiana Ass'n of Indep. Producers v. FERC*, 958 F.2d 1101 (D.C.Cir.1992), which refused to overturn a FERC decision licensing a gas pipeline, despite a large number of ex parte contacts by the applicants to the FERC commissioners. Some of the contacts were made to a settlement judge (rather than an adjudicatory decisionmaker), which the court thought was acceptable. Others concerned general problems in the industry, the procedural status of the application, and other cases pending in court. This illustrates that an agency like FERC is heavily engaged with regulating the entire industry at the same time it's conducting adjudicatory proceedings. It can't cut itself off from the industry while the adjudication is pending.

The D. C. Circuit made clear that the ex parte contact ban in § 557(d) is an absolute rule. The agency cannot create an exception to §557(d), no matter how useful that exception might be to the agency's regulatory mission. *Electric Power Supply Ass'n v. Federal Energy Regulatory Comm'n*, 391 F.3d 1255 (D.C.Cir.2004). In that case, FERC adopted rules allowing ex parte contacts between "market monitors" and FERC decisional staff. The market monitors are not FERC staff. They work for regional transmission organizations (RTOs), but the monitors' job is to report information about possible market failures in electricity transmission.

The court held that these communications clearly fall under §557(d), because the monitors are outside the agency, they are "interested persons," and their communications could well be "relevant to the merits" of pending cases. FERC argued that disclosure of the communications would "impede its goal to receive as much timely information as possible from market monitors on the operation of energy markets." The court was unmoved. "[W]hen an agency acts in violation of an express congressional mandate, its motives are irrelevant. . . If as is the case here, a statute of general applicability directs that certain procedures must be followed, an agency cannot modify or balance away what Congress has required of it."

Notes and Questions

1. *Ex parte contacts—source of law.* The ex parte provision in the

1961 MSAPA is defective because it allows outsider comments to decisionmakers that don't concern facts. Communications about law or policy should also be prohibited. The 1961 provision also appears to allow outsider ex parte communications to staff advisers to decisionmakers; the federal APA provision prohibits them.

The *Idaho Preservation* case seems dubious. First, people who want to preserve historic buildings aren't deprived of a liberty or property interest by the decision allowing destruction of such buildings. Even if they are, the statutes give decisionmakers broad discretion, so there is no entitlement. See discussion of due process in land use proceedings in Manual §2.5 N.5. Second, the case fails to engage in a *Mathews* balancing to ascertain whether the particular contacts in question should have been prohibited. In particular, elected officials need to maintain contacts with their constituents, which the case seems to ignore; as the dissent points out there was probably little or no prejudice from the calls. Third, as discussed in N.5 below, the decision vacates the decision below without consideration of whether there was any prejudice from the comments. On the other hand, the decision has merit in creating a bright line test for city councils and other local land use decisionmakers. You must cut off all ex parte contacts—period—or at least disclose the name of the caller and substance of the conversation. This ruling provides cover for members of the council to refuse to take such calls, even from constituents. Anyway the confusing due process decisions show the importance of having a statute like the APA that sets forth clear prohibitions on ex parte contacts. rules.

Prior to enactment of § 557(d), the law on ex parte contact arose out of cases in which competing applicants for FCC or CAB licenses (and their surrogates) wined and dined the commissioners. Here, the agency has to make a tough call between more or less equally qualified licensees. It would be quite appropriate to assess a significant demerit against an applicant who violates the norms of adjudication through making deliberate ex parte contacts. The courts were unclear about the source of their authority to vacate decisions tainted by ex parte contact, but it appears that the decisions are grounded in the supervisory powers of appellate courts over the procedures of the entity being reviewed.

2. *Lewis' call to Frazier*. Note that § 551(14) states that a request for a status report is not an ex parte communication. Moreover, as provided in FLRA's rules, a discussion about settlement is not "relevant to the merits" as required by § 557(d)(1)(A) and (B). However, Lewis' call did not appear to be either a request for a status report or a discussion related to settlement (it concerned settlement of the strike, not of the *PATCO* case before FLRA).

Arguably, a call relating only to procedure would not be "relevant to the merits," but the court's hesitation to draw that conclusion is understandable. The timing of the appeal from the ALJ's decision to the FLRA was critical to the parties. Moreover, Lewis conveyed a message that the case was extremely important to the government; thus he exerted political pressure on the decisionmakers. Note the majority's comment in part C.1.: the legislative history says that even a status inquiry by a member of Congress can be a subtle method of influencing the substantive outcome. If so, the inquiry is a prohibited communication. The same analysis applies to the interpretation of "relevant to the merits," according to the court. Under this reasoning, Lewis' phone call could well be considered unfair to PATCO if it had not been timely disclosed. Status inquiries from members of Congress raise similar issues. *See* § 3.3.3 N.6.

3. *Dinner with Shanker*. Shanker was an "interested person," because his position as a public sector labor union leader made his interest greater than that of a member of the general public. As far as the APA itself goes, it would be permissible for an old friend (with no contacts to unions) to make a similar pitch to Applewhaite, since the friend would not be an "interested person" (i.e., one with some interest greater than that of the general public). But the court states (in dictum) that even if Shanker were not "interested," a communication intended to influence the decision would still have been improper. It would be a "mockery of justice" for anyone to approach a judge while adjudication is pending. This suggests that even a communication from a member of the general public designed to influence the decision, which is not prohibited by § 557(d)(1)(A), should be placed on the record and that Applewhaite should try very hard not to receive it.

Does this make sense? Does it mean that every newspaper editorial that a judge happens to read that urges the judge to decide in a particular way should be placed on the record? (Indeed, for many years Shanker had a weekly column—in paid space—in the Sunday New York Times. He reportedly did discuss the PATCO strike in it.).

It seems quite extreme to suggest that Applewhaite should not have dined with Shanker (an old friend); after all, if a person's friends are all in the labor movement, must he or she abandon all social life when taking a job as agency head? Shanker's views were certainly no surprise to Applewhaite. It seems excessive to suggest that Applewhaite should be removed from office. FLRA agency heads can be removed by the President only after notice and hearing for inefficiency, neglect of duty, or malfeasance in office. 5 U.S.C. § 7104(b). The President would have to argue that the Shanker conversation was "malfeasance." Applewhaite exercised poor judgment in actually discussing the *PATCO* case, but it did no harm and was probably more a matter of courtesy than indicative of any base motive.

4. *The President as an interested person.* Virtually every aspect of the *Portland* case is criticized in an excellent student Note. *See* Michael A. Bosh, Note, "The 'God Squad' Proves Mortal: Ex Parte Contacts and the White House after *Portland Audubon Society*," 51 Wash. & Lee L.Rev. 1029 (1994). A way to view the *Portland* case in big picture terms is that the court opts for the judicial approach (i.e. insulation of the God Squad from political interference and ex parte contact); but the question is whether an institutional method would make more sense for this type of decision. Deciding whether to prefer the interest of the owls over the timber industry is a political decision in which the President should be involved. Although treated as APA adjudication by the statute, the issue was similar to rulemaking in many respects.

Believers in the unitary executive will be troubled by the case, while believers in the idea that Congress can entrust decisions to lower-level executive officials and strip the President of the ability to make the decision may find the decision more agreeable. *See* § 7.6 N.6. As Bosh explains, it's doubtful that Congress actually intended that the God Squad's decisions should be constrained by APA § 557 in the first place. One reason to think it did not is the fact that the committee was composed of high-level executive officials, who naturally would seek to promote administration policy

5. *Remedies for ex parte contact.* As explained in § 557(d)(1)(C), memoranda summarizing each of these violations of the ex parte rules should have been placed on the record, thus permitting any party to rebut the communication. In addition, the agency may "to the extent consistent with the interests of justice and the policy of the underlying statutes, require the party to show cause why his claim or interest in the proceeding should not be dismissed, denied, disregarded, or otherwise adversely affected. . ." §§ 557(d)(1)(D) and 556(d). These provisions, by their terms, apply only to *parties* who *knowingly* commit or instigate violations.

Although agencies may have some inherent power to penalize violations by nonparties, it would seem excessive here for the agency to punish PATCO. If PATCO had arranged for Shanker's comments to Applewhaite, however, it might well be appropriate to treat this as a factor in deciding the severity of the sanction to be meted out. In general, where a case implicates great issues of public policy—like *PATCO*—it would be perverse to significantly alter the result because of prohibited communications. Placing them on the record seems sufficient.

When counsel are responsible for unlawful ex parte contacts, they can be appropriately disciplined by the agency, for example, by suspending their right to appear before the agency. To an attorney conducting a specialized practice, this would be a highly effective, if not devastating sanction.

What should the Court of Appeals have done? In the end, despite much hand wringing, it did nothing, because it could find no prejudice and a remand would be a pure formality (and a windfall for PATCO, the very party for whose sake Shanker had interfered). The hearing before Judge Vittone and the harsh criticism from the court (especially Robinson's opinion, which is not reproduced) might be punishment enough.

Should there be a rule of guaranteed remand for a new hearing in cases of ex parte contacts, even when there is no showing of prejudice to anyone? That's what the Idaho Supreme Court did in the *Idaho Historic Preservation Council* case in N.1. As discussed above, this creates rather costly wheel spinning; but it also creates an effective deterrent. However, it might encourage people who wanted to delay or sidetrack a proceeding to make a communication, thus necessitating a judicial remand.

6. *Who can you talk to?* If Max "is or may reasonably be expected to be involved in the decisional process," the communication would have been improper. The hypo suggests that Lewis should not have expected that Max would be involved in the decisional process, in which case the communication is proper. Relevant factors might be what Lewis knew or should have known about the process in the FLRA case, whether Max had been used an adviser before, etc.

Even if this turns out to be a prohibited communication, Max probably should not be disqualified from serving as an adviser; instead he should put the communication on record and give the needed advice. Disqualification of an adviser would be an excessive reaction, one not called for by the statute and one quite damaging to the goal of making the most accurate and appropriate decision. Nor, in these circumstances, should FAA be penalized in any way. Note that even putting the communication on record would make public an attorney work product or other confidential material.

This hypo illustrates that § 557(d) has real costs; it can inhibit free and appropriate communication between outsiders and agency staff and agency heads. These communications occur by the hundreds every day, since the same outsiders and the same staff members (or the same agency heads) are engaged in many non-adjudicative matters such as rulemaking, research, investigation, negotiation, etc. Yet such communications may arguably be relevant to the merits of a pending adjudication. As *PATCO* shows, courts are harshly intolerant of ex parte communications that others might see as legal or at least borderline.

7. *Problem.*

a. Due process. As in the *Idaho Historic Preservation* case in N.1, an agency might violate due process by receiving critical ex parte contacts that it fails to disclose (although as N.1 above suggests, the due process analysis in that case is dubious). In this case, *Mathews v. Eldridge* analysis might lead to the conclusion that MTC was denied due process. Its interest in a rate hike is quite substantial. It is arguable as to how strong the PUC's interest is in receiving ex parte contacts, since PUC can insist that all such comments be on the record or at least summarized and placed in the record. However, the PUC members may argue that they have a substantial interest in communicating with the people about the issues in its cases. They are unable to read the massive record, and without public contact all of their information is filtered by the staff. This is especially compelling in the case of an elected commission, where the members may feel a need to stay in touch with their constituents. As to the risk-of-error factor, it seems likely that the contacts probably duplicated a lot of material in the record, briefs and oral arguments, so they probably didn't increase the risk of error much. Thus the *Eldridge* balancing is indeterminate.

But does due process apply to individualized ratemaking by state PUCs? *See* Michael Asimow, "Toward a New California Administrative Procedure Act: Adjudication Fundamentals," 39 UCLA L.Rev. 1067, 1130-34 (1992). Some federal cases suggest due process applies, at least when the utility is complaining. See, e.g., *Ohio Bell Tel. Co. v. PUC*, 301 U.S. 292 (1937) (abuse of official notice). But some federal cases say that ratemaking is "legislative," for purposes of deciding such questions as abstention. *NOPSI v. New Orleans*, 491 U.S. 350, 370-72 (1989). More to the point, numerous state cases say that ratemaking is "legislative" and due process does not apply to it.

A recent example is the *Southwestern Bell* case cited in the problem. In that case, an elected member of the Oklahoma Corporations Commission (Anthony) was an FBI informant about possible corruption in the ratemaking process by SW Bell. Allegedly, the company's agents had tried to bribe him and other commissioners. After disclosing all this, he then refused to recuse himself from the SW Bell rate case. The Oklahoma Supreme Court upheld the rates. The case presents an interesting bias issue—can you disqualify a decisionmaker by first trying to corrupt him? No procedural statute was applicable, and the court held that ratemaking was legislative, so due process didn't apply. It relied on *Bi-Metallic*. Alternatively, it held that the rule of necessity applied, even though Anthony was only one of three commissioners.

We think due process applies in individualized ratemaking, at least to the utility. *Florida East Coast Ry.* indicated in dictum that although due process does not apply to generalized ratemaking, "the decisions represent a recognized distinction in administrative law between proceedings for the purpose of promulgating policy-type rules or standards, on the one hand, and proceedings designed to adjudicate disputed facts in particular cases on the other." 410 U.S. 224, 244-45. Just because due process applies does not mean that the PUC has to conduct trial-type proceedings to determine the economic facts specific to the utility. Informal proceedings and written reports of experts are quite sufficient. But an impartial decisionmaker is still essential and, among other things, this means that all inputs to decisionmakers should be on the record.

Historically, rates were set by the legislature itself, but this led to vast corruption. As a result, the process was delegated to PUCs, which invariably set rates through trial-type processes. Ex parte contact makes a mockery of such process. Reams of evidence are taken by the ALJ, who pulls it together in a decision responsive to the testimony, documents, and arguments in the record. But all that counts for little if a few well chosen words in the ears of the commissioners can turn the case around.

An unresolved due process issue is raised by flipping the problem so that the communication is made by the utility to the detriment of the consumers. Now it looks like the case is generalized, not individualized, from the point of view of those complaining. It is possible that due process is asymmetrical—protecting the utility but not protecting consumers. Here *Bi-Metallic* seems much more in point. This issue is discussed in connection with land use disputes in the Manual, § 2.5. *But see Cincinnati v. PUC*, 595 N.E.2d 858 (Ohio 1992) (utility ex parte contact to PUC chair violates rights of city); *Jennings v. Dade County*, 589 So.2d 1337 (Fla. App. 1991) (ex parte contact by zoning variance applicant to elected local officials violates rights of protesting neighbor); *Idaho Historic Preservation, supra.*

b. MSAPA: Under 1961 MSAPA, individualized ratemaking is clearly a "contested case" if (as is true in the problem) a statute requires an evidentiary hearing. MSAPA 1961 § 13 prohibits ex parte communication by outsiders as to "any issue of fact" but accepts such communications (except from the parties) on an "issue of law." Here the consumers' arguments were not factual in nature but strictly concerned regulatory policy—whether stockholders or ratepayers should have to pay for the cost of remedying environmental violations. As a result, they probably do not violate § 13. The *Business and Professionals* case cited in the text involved a PUC commissioner who made literally hundreds of ex parte phone calls to the utility and its lawyers and lobbyists. This not only violated the ex parte provisions of the Illinois APA (similar to 1961 MSAPA) but also evidenced an appearance of bias (*see* § 3.3.5).

c. Federal APA. Individualized ratemaking is defined as rulemaking under the APA. § 551(4), (5). The statute defines rules in § 551(4) to include statements of "particular applicability" and, in fact, also includes specific language extending the definition to treat all ratemaking as rulemaking. See § 5.2.1. Here, however, a statute calls for a hearing on the record, so the ratemaking would be "formal rulemaking." See § 553(c) (last sentence). As a result, § 557(d) would apply. If, however, there were no requirement of an on-the-record hearing in any applicable statute, it would be only "informal rulemaking," to which § 557(d) is inapplicable. In § 5.5.2 we cover ex parte contacts in informal rulemaking; in almost all circumstances they are permitted. The only hope in such a case is to argue that due process applies, so that under *Wong Yang Sung* the APA kicks in, but as discussed in § 3.1.1 N.6, it is unlikely that the Supreme Court would so hold today.

Since this is formal rulemaking, however, § 557(d) *does* apply. The issue is whether the consumers are "interested." They are not "parties." But it seems likely that they are part of an organized consumer group and have been carefully briefed for their visit by staff of the group. Of course, if they merely walked in off the street to talk to Smith after reading about the case in the paper, it can be argued that they are not "interested," just members of the general public. The mere fact that the consumers pay phone bills might not by itself distinguish them from the general public. But if they are activists in a consumers' group, they should be treated as interested parties. The analysis is similar to that in *PATCO* holding Shanker to be an interested person. The legislative history of § 557(d) indicates that "nonprofit or public interest organizations" can be interested persons. The communications here are far more than the "general expression of opinion" from a "member of the public at large" mentioned in the legislative history.

d. Remedy: Assuming the ex parte contact is found illegal under any of the above theories, what now? Arguably the error was harmless, since the material in the ex parte comment probably duplicated lots of material in the record. The party seeking to uphold the decision (the consumers in this case) should have the burden to show the error was harmless. *Martone v. Lensink*, 541 A.2d 488 (Conn.1988) (an interesting state law ex parte contact case). Since the facts are clear, there seems to be no need for a fact-finding hearing on remand.

The contact was made only to a single commissioner, so that commissioner could be recused on the remand and there would still be a quorum. The *Southwestern Bell* case held the rule of necessity applied to prevent disqualification of a single commissioner on a 3-person board, because of the risk of deadlock. The state had a procedure, analogous to that of 1981 MSAPA § 4-202(e), for appointment of a pro tempore substitute by the governor, but the court held (over a dissent) that the procedure was unavailable on the facts presented there.

Here the likelihood of deadlock is great, since without Smith the vote will be 2-2, assuming no changes of mind. In the case of a deadlock, presumably the ALJ decision would stand. Alternatively, the deadlock may mean that MTC's application is rejected and it will have to start over. But there is an argument that the rule of necessity should be applied here to avoid the deadlock.

§ 3.3.3 Agency Adjudication and Legislative Pressure

PILLSBURY CO. v. FEDERAL TRADE COMMISSION

Notes and Questions

1. *The Pillsbury reasoning.* Clearly the *Pillsbury* court was unconcerned with whether the 1955 hearings in fact affected the 1960 decision. Under the court's reasoning, Kintner and Secrest were automatically tainted because they had been sitting in the room; Kern was tainted because his boss had been sitting in the room. This is "appearance of bias" with a vengeance. Probably, the court wanted a strict prophylactic rule—Congressional committees must *never* quiz agency adjudicators about a pending case. Yet the court's indifference to the issue of whether the error was prejudicial is troubling, because it lacks a logical stopping point. Indeed, if the "taint" was as strong as the court suggested, why wouldn't it equally taint the new commissioners deciding the case after the remand who have, no doubt, read and heard all about the Congressional hearing and the Fifth Circuit's decision? Possibly the court believed that there was nothing to lose from remanding the case, because the merits could readily be redecided by an untainted Commission (although hindsight demonstrates that this assumption was wrong).

A more cynical explanation for *Pillsbury* would focus on the fact that the court took more than a year after oral argument to write this fairly simple, one-issue opinion. One might discern at least an "appearance" that, after struggling for a protracted period with the daunting 40,000-page record (the FTC's brief alone was 400 pages long), the court seized on the procedural due process rationale as an easy way to avoid a decision on the merits of the antitrust issues.

A nice due process case that follows *Pillsbury* is *Esso-Standard Oil Co. v. Lopez-Freytes*, 522 F.3d 136, 148 (1st Cir.2008). The Puerto Rico Environmental Quality Board (EQB) levied a $76 million fine against Esso for failing to report a fuel leak at a gas station. This was after the Puerto Rican Senate committee threatened the heads of EQB with criminal prosecution as well as ethics board prosecution for going too slowly in the

Esso case. *Esso-Standard* is further discussed in §3.3.5, *infra*, because it raised several additional bias issues.

2. *Pillsbury and the APA.* This comment suggests that perhaps analysis of Congressional pressure should focus on the APA rather than due process, at least where the APA appears to be applicable. Note that the APA defines "ex parte communication" to mean contacts that are "not on the public record." Thus one might argue that contacts occurring in a Congressional hearing might not be ex parte communications at all, given that the hearing occurred in public and was recorded and transcribed. This seems like the antithesis of an ex parte communication. *See* Levin, 95 Mich. L. Rev. at 41.

Even if the hearing was a prohibited ex parte communication to agency decisionmakers, § 557(d) does not require automatic invalidation. The court is expected to decide the scope of relief "to the extent consistent with the interests of justice and the policy of the underlying statutes." § 557(d)(1)(D). Since the court's order effectively resulted in the demise of the entire *Pillsbury* proceeding, and since it's unlikely that the ex parte contact in fact made any difference (as discussed in N.1), present law suggests that the court should not have vacated the order. Compare *Pillsbury* to *PATCO*, which refused to vacate the administrative decision despite the violation of § 557(d), since the contacts did not influence the decision and no party benefitted from them.

3. *Congressional oversight.* One way to approach the question of the wisdom of the *Pillsbury* rule is to ask whether the exchange between Howrey and Kefauver would have been proper if the senator had simply interrogated the chairman about the FTC's construction of the Clayton Act without mentioning *Pillsbury*. Presumably Congress has a legitimate interest in asking questions about how an agency interprets an important antitrust statute. The need to cooperate with legislative oversight of agency legal interpretation and policymaking is one way that administrative adjudication necessarily diverges from a pure judicial model. Notice, moreover, that the senator's questions had nothing to do with any adjudicative facts (or any facts at all); it is hard to imagine a more purely legal issue than whether or not § 7 called for a per se rule or a rule of reason. (A more serious due process problem would arise if an FTC chair were summoned to an oversight hearing so that legislators could insist that she crack down on charm schools, such as Cinderella, which was the respondent in a pending case—see §3.3.5.)

If the Senate could have asked about the FTC's abstract legal interpretation of § 7 without mentioning Pillsbury, the question is whether the real case was significantly different. Everyone would have known what proceeding was really under discussion. One might argue that Senator

Kefauver should have waited until the *Pillsbury* case ended; but that would take years, which is a long time to wait if the FTC is indeed misconstruing the statute. Moreover, how could the senator assume there would ever be a time when the FTC would have *no* merger case pending?

In any event, later cases refuse to vacate formal adjudications despite Congressional interference. A rule of harmless error has emerged. Indeed, some cases go further and stress the importance of oversight, treating it as another factor that justifies judicial flexibility. See Levin, 95 Mich. L. Rev. at 42-43. There seems to be a well recognized rule of etiquette—avoid referring to individual cases by name and don't discuss the facts of the cases, but only the legal principles announced there. As a practical matter, staff members for the agency and the committee usually agree in advance on the bounds of legitimate inquiry, since neither wants to sabotage the underlying legal proceedings. *See* Peter L. Strauss, "Disqualification of Decisional Officials in Rulemaking," 80 Colum.L.Rev. 990, 1026-27 (1980). This procedure allows nominal compliance with *Pillsbury*, but it actually may constitute a rejection of some of the more stringent implications of that case.

4. *Informal adjudication.* In informal adjudication that does not touch on interests protected by due process, congressional ex parte contacts are not improper as such, but they do not overcome an agency's duty to act only for appropriate reasons. The court's legal analysis in *D.C. Federation* is basically correct. Natcher was an influential member of Congress, but he was not the entire Congress. He did not speak for the Senate, for example. The Secretary was still required to apply the statute as Congress passed it and the Supreme Court construed it. Thus, we disagree with Pierce to the extent he suggests that the Secretary could lawfully have approved the bridge in order to get a subway system. Or at least this is true under the Supreme Court's interpretation of the relevant legislation in *Overton Park*, which the court of appeals was obliged to follow. That interpretation itself may well have been too narrow, however. *See* discussion in Manual § 9.3.

However, Pierce's argument has some force, and there is another way of giving effect to it. The real weak spot in *D.C. Federation* was Judge Bazelon's willingness to assume, on weak evidence, that the agency had in fact been influenced by the representative's pressure. The Secretary's formal decision did not so indicate, and under cases like *Overton Park* and *Camp v. Pitts* that decision was entitled to a presumption of regularity. *See* 459 F.2d at 1256-59 (MacKinnon, J., dissenting). One reason for the presumption is to allow administrators a little space to take account of political realities such as the need to get along with Congress. Compare the more indulgent attitude towards politics in *Sierra Club v. Costle*, § 5.5.2 *infra*.

5. *Preliminary investigations.* The court's statement that the case

would not reach the "quasi-adjudicative" stage until the hearing may arguably be correct under the due process clause, but is incorrect under the APA. Under § 557(d)(1)(E), ex parte prohibitions apply not "later than the time at which a proceeding is noticed for hearing unless the person responsible for the communication has knowledge that it will be noticed, in which case the prohibitions shall apply beginning at the time of his acquisition of such knowledge."

Whether this provision applied to Huckaby's letter in *DCP Farms* is not as clear. At the time of that letter, a county committee had ruled for the farms, and the department's Inspector General had released a report condemning DCP Farms' subsidy as an egregious abuse of the statute. Later a deputy USDA administrator ruled against DCP, at which time DCP appealed and a hearing was scheduled. So Huckaby didn't literally "know" a hearing would be "noticed." Yet, after the IG report, it wouldn't take a genius to foresee that this case was headed for formal adjudicative proceedings. Whether that sort of highly reasonable anticipation should trigger the APA ex parte restrictions is the pivotal issue. Even if it does not, it might well trigger due process constraints.

The authors of this book disagree about *DCP Farms*. Levin thinks that the case was an acceptable example of legislative oversight. He acknowledges that, technically, the possibility of statutory amendment was not relevant to the meaning of current law. Still, he argues, drawing that distinction would be

> excessive hair-splitting. . . . Certainly one would not have wanted an influential member of Congress to commence efforts to change the statute *without* informing the agency and giving it an opportunity to consider whether it wanted to head off possibly unpredictable legislative action by acquiescing in the member's interpretation. The participants' interchange provided an opportunity for the kind of dialogue over legal and policy issues that ought to take place between the lawmaking and law-enforcing branches.

95 Mich. L. Rev. at 58-59. Asimow thinks that Huckaby's explicit reference to the trust gimmick in *DCP Farms* violates existing law and created an extreme appearance problem. It would cause DCP to think that the fix is in and that it could never get a fair hearing. When an influential Congressman picks on you like Huckaby did, how much chance do you have? If the court set aside the USDA proceeding and ordered that the subsidy be paid, Congress would receive a strong signal that it is improper to interfere so blatantly in pending adjudications. Huckaby's letter is a good example of Congressional arrogance. There probably needs to be a case like *Pillsbury* every decade or so to remind Congress members that they must mind their

manners.

Similar to *DCP Farms* is *ATX Inc. v. DOT*, 41 F.3d 1522 (D.C.Cir. 1994), in which the court tolerated Congressional interference in an application by a company owned by the ever-unpopular Frank Lorenzo to operate a new airline. House members introduced legislation to prohibit Lorenzo from reentering the industry and 125 of them wrote the Secretary of Transportation to voice their opposition to the application. One congressman testified at the administrative hearing. All of this was legitimate Congressional activity, the court ruled, although it was especially troubled by the Congressman's testimony at the hearing. After all, "any person" has a right to participate in these hearings. There were no threats in the testimony and the agency decision didn't mention the testimony, which suggested it didn't make any difference.

6. *Legislative casework.* Outside the realm of formal adjudication or formal rulemaking, § 557(d) does not constrain legislative intervention. Similar, *Pillsbury* is inapplicable, as *D.C. Federation* and *DCP Farms* make clear (conceivably a particularly egregious contact harmful to the interest of a party to a pending case could raise a due process issue). Nevertheless, the casework system raises significant policy issues, as detailed in the Levin article. Congressional staff inquiries to agencies can serve some legitimate functions, comparable to the role of the "ombudsman" offices maintained in other countries, and is in fact one of Congress's more popular activities. Every member can tell stories of having rescued a hapless constituent from some instance of bureaucratic rigidity or incompetence. Yet agencies often find that responding to those inquiries is a time consuming nuisance. Furthermore, while ad hoc intervention by a member into an agency's operations may result in relief for the individual constituent, it does not necessarily upgrade the agency's performance as a whole; it may simply mean that other citizens, who have not called their legislator but have cases that are just as meritorious, get moved down on the priority list. So the debate quickly turns into a battle of anecdotes.

Senator Dirksen's defense of casework is disingenuous. Obviously a "status inquiry" is intended to nudge, and sometimes to push, the agency to be more attentive to the constituent's concerns. The fact that members of Congress possess more political leverage than ordinary mortals is precisely what makes the casework system work, for better or worse. On the other hand, according to Levin, 95 Mich. L. Rev. at 48, members generally understand—with some regrettable exceptions—that cases in which formal proceedings are pending are different: court-like norms come into play and the congressional role has to be handled more delicately or simply declined.

7. *Problem.* If you taught *Greenwood Manor* in §3.1.2, you should link

that discussion with this problem. The regulatory scheme is similar and the same economic issues are presented. If you didn't teach *Greenwood,* you might want to consider a discussion here of the economics of this particular breed of regulation. The issues are discussed in the Manual's treatment of *Greenwood. Greenwood* discussed whether an adjudicatory hearing had to be provided for either the applicant or existing facility under the 1961 MSAPA. This problem assumes that a hearing was required and provided and discusses the problems of legislative interference with decisionmaking. Approach this problem under due process, 1961 MSAPA, and federal APA.

Whether due process is applicable depends on i) whether the statute provides for an entitlement, as opposed to a discretionary standard, and ii) whether due process covers applications as opposed to terminations. Both of these issues have been well covered before and we won't extend this answer by repeating them. *Pillsbury* held that due process was violated by Congressional interference into a pending adjudication. If anything, the circumstances of this case are worse than in *Pillsbury,* because the legislators spoke directly to adjudicative facts involved in the case and did not do so in a public arena. Moreover, their intervention is far more likely to have influenced the Director's decision than was the case in *Pillsbury.*

Section 13 of the 1961 MSAPA is applicable, since the hearing is required by statute. Thus the proceeding qualifies as a "contested case." There appears to be a violation of § 13 (§3.3.2 N.1), since the legislators communicated on an issue of fact with an agency decisionmaker. There was no notice to Midway or others interested in the matter and no opportunity for them to participate. It can be argued that the proceeding was not yet a "contested case" because no hearing was scheduled at the time the ex parte communications occurred. Cf. *First Sav. & Loan Ass'n v. Vandygriff,* 617 S.W.2d 669 (Tex. 1981) (§ 13 does not apply after an application for banking license is rejected and before a new application is filed). However, under the Madison statute, Midway's application was pending at the time of the ex parte communication, and a hearing is very likely no matter whether the application is rejected or granted. Consequently, § 13 should be applicable.

Compare federal APA §557(d)(1)(E), which goes into effect when a "proceeding is noticed for hearing unless the person responsible for the communication has knowledge that it will be noticed, in which case the prohibitions shall apply beginning at the time of his acquisition of such knowledge." The legislators must have known that City General would contest the application (presumably City General had a lot to do with the writing of the letter in the first place), and therefore they should have had knowledge that the case would be noticed for a hearing.

The ex parte contact tainted the application process, but whether the courts can give any effective remedy is unclear. Since the director immediately disclosed the ex parte communication as required by APA § 557(d)(1)(C), there appears little likelihood that the decision can be overturned on that ground. APA §557(d)(1)(D) provides that if City General knew about the legislator's communication (which seems likely), the agency can require it to show cause why its interest should not be "adversely affected." Similarly, § 556(d) (fourth sentence) provides that an agency can treat a § 557(d) violation as grounds for a decision adverse to a party. It would be improper for the court to order that the application be granted, since it may well be true that Midway would trigger ruinous competition and thus should not be built. A remand to the Director to reconsider the application with a thumb on the scale against City General might be a good idea. Yet such a hearing could produce the same result as before, assuming the same Director is still in office. The legislators wouldn't have to make a new threat—she will remember the existing one. But then we don't know whether the threat actually motivated the Director's decision; perhaps she was convinced on the merits and might wish to reconsider the decision by penalizing City General for engineering the ex parte communication.

The court could consider the remedy set forth in 1981 MSAPA § 4-202(e), which requires the governor to appoint a substitute for a person who is disqualified because of bias. However, the facts don't clearly show that the Director herself was biased, and the idea of placing the ultimate decision in the hands of someone who has no continuing responsibility for health care regulation is troublesome at best. In any event, it is hardly likely that the substitute would be unaware of the circumstances that had led to the governor's appointment.

Midway may have other types of remedies available, however. If the Director's decision is shaky on the merits, Midway can challenge it on judicial review, and it could certainly allude to the procedural breach in an effort to engage the court's sympathies and induce the judges to take an especially hard look at the support for the Director's decision. Midway can also try to generate unfavorable press coverage of the legislators' interference; that would put pressure on the Director to rule for Midway next time around. Finally, Midway could file a complaint with the ethics authorities in the Madison legislature. Although few legislatures have confronted these issues head-on, a strong argument can be made that the letter in this case may violate legislative ethics principles. *See* Advisory Opinion No. 1 of the House Comm. on Standards of Official Conduct, 116 Cong. Rec. 1077 (1970) ("Direct or implied suggestion of either favoritism or reprisal in advance of, or subsequent to, action taken by the agency contacted is unwarranted abuse of the representative role."); Ky Rev. Stat. Ann. § 6.744(1) (suggesting that casework is permissible "[a]bsent an express or implied threat of legislative reprisal"). Enforcement of these provisions has been weak (to put it mildly), but the controversy could help Midway in its effort to generate favorable publicity.

Quite aside from the due process or APA approaches, there is a question of whether the decision was arbitrary and capricious. Obviously, as in *D.C. Federation*, the legislators' threat was extraneous to the merits of the dispute. Defunding the agency has nothing to do with the merits of Midway's application, just as the bridge and subway in *D.C. Federation* had nothing to do with each other. *DCP Farms* is distinguishable, because the intervention there was at least generally related to a legitimate issue in the proceedings—whether trusts could be used to get around the $50,000 limit. Here the defunding threat is just that—a form of extortion not linked to any plausible reading of the governing statute. *ATX* is also distinguishable, since it didn't involve any threats.

Nevertheless, Midway may have trouble proving, as it must, that the legislative threat actually influenced the Director's decision. Here the Director did everything right: she disclosed the letter to Midway immediately, even though she must have known that its disclosure might make it harder for her to defend an ultimate decision to reject Midway's application. Midway can point to the fact that the Director reversed the staff's decision; whether that argument succeeds may depend on whether or not she normally upholds the staff, as well as whether she offers a cogent explanation for her own position. But, because this case reveals no improper behavior by the agency itself, the court is likely to accord a presumption of validity and reject the substantive challenge to the agency decision.

Change the problem so that there is no threat—just an expression of opinion by ten legislators that the application should be rejected on the merits. It may have been an ex parte contact, but, like Secretary Lewis's contact in *PATCO*, it was placed on the record and thus was at worst a non-prejudicial breach. Moreover, it was relevant to the merits. Thus, it falls under the category of legislative constituent service, which is broadly accepted in American practice. (It does not really fit the legislative oversight model, since the action was not taken by a committee or other duly constituted unit of the legislature.) It would not violate any statute, nor would it taint the proceedings. This revised scenario can lead to a more general discussion of the law and ethics of legislative casework. For example, what if City General had made campaign contributions to the legislators? That twist would make the situation resemble the Keating Five scandal of the early 1990s. Those ethics issues are explored in Levin, 95 Mich. L. Rev. at 67-109. Senate Rule 43 states that a senator's decision to intervene with a regulator on behalf of a citizen may not be based on campaign contributions. Needless to say, this rule is seldom if ever enforced.

DEP'T OF ALCOHOLIC BEVERAGE CONTROL v. ALCOHOLIC BEVERAGE CONTROL APPEALS BOARD (QUINTANAR)

Notes and Questions

1. *Due process and combination of functions.* For discussion of the due process implications of the combination of functions, see Michael Asimow, "When the Curtain Falls: Separation of Functions in the Federal Administrative Agencies," 81 Colum.L.Rev. 759, 779-88 (1981). The final footnote in *Quintanar* points out that the Court avoided the due process issue because the Calif. APA clearly resolved the question. This is a major advantage of APAs, because application of the statutory provision avoids the need for indeterminate *Mathews v. Eldridge* balancing. In fact, the due process status of separation of functions is quite murky and not well developed by case law.

The *Withrow* opinion is mainly dictum. The Board members did not personally engage in investigation and prosecution; staff members did most of the work. The Board members' only significant contact was that they heard evidence at an investigatory hearing—at which Larkin was present—and decided that further action was warranted. As explained below, it is well accepted that decisionmakers can participate in the decision to issue a complaint. The *Withrow* decision goes far beyond its facts and confirms that agency heads can perform every function personally without violating due process (and this often occurs, especially in small state or local agencies). If the agency heads choose to engage in investigation, prosecution, and decision, the principle of necessity indicates that they should not be disqualified from making the final decision, or else nobody could make that decision.

The ex parte advice to the agency head in *Quintanar* might well have violated due process. The situation is distinguishable from *Withrow*, because the prosecutor who advised the agency head was a staff member, not himself an agency head. It was not necessary to use a prosecutor to give advice; a law clerk or previously uninvolved staff member could have done the job. Such a holding would not be disruptive to agencies everywhere (whereas disqualification of the agency heads in *Withrow* would have had a huge disruptive effect on many state and local agencies). Equally so for *Goldberg v. Kelly*—different welfare workers can make the determination and adjudicate the dispute. The law on separation of functions and due process is poorly developed. *Withrow* doesn't decide much and *Goldberg's* prescriptive list of due process procedures is outdated. The problem would have to be approached through a *Mathews* balancing—and we know how indeterminate that is.

For an interesting recent case that illustrates the indeterminacy of the constitutional status of separation of functions, see *White v. Indiana Parole Bd.*, 266 F.3d 759 (7th Cir.2001). *White* involves a prison disciplinary hearing which involved "good time" credits and thus the actual term of imprisonment. As a result, due process applies. *See* § 2.2.2 N.8. At White's hearing, officer Thompson, who had investigated and filed the drug trafficking charge against him, conferred with members of the Conduct Adjustment Board after the close of evidence. The case is thus similar to *Quintanar*. Judge Easterbrook's majority opinion found no due process violation, largely because of the prison disciplinary setting, where relaxed procedures are in order, and because the boards are entitled to receive and act on information that is withheld from the prisoner. As a result, prison officials must be entitled to discuss that evidence off the record with decisionmakers. However, Easterbrook notes, Thompson could not have been a member of the board itself. *Id.* 766-68. Judge Rovner's dissent takes sharp issue with the majority view. Because White had no opportunity to challenge whatever Thompson told the Board, due process was violated. The state offered no justification for this procedure, particularly not for Thompson's presence during the Board's deliberations. *Id.* 768-71.

In *Cherry Communications, Inc. v. Deason,* 652 So. 2d 803 (Fla. 1995), the Florida Supreme Court held that ex parte communications to an agency head from an agency prosecutor in a license revocation case violated due process. Factually, the case is similar to *Quintanar*.

The California Supreme Court confronted an interesting due process separation of functions issue in *Morongo Band of Mission Indians v. State Water Resources Control Bd.*, 199 P.3d 1142 (2009). A was a staff adviser to the agency heads in Case 1. In unrelated Case 2, A served as the prosecutor. The lower court held that A's prior service as adviser would cause the agency heads to unfairly defer to her views as a prosecutor. The Supreme Court rejected this claim which, if accepted, would have had enormous repercussions on the structure of small state and local agencies.

2. *Pennsylvania view.* We come down on the dissenter's side in *Lyness.* The Medical Board's procedure would not violate federal due process (or the federal APA) under *Withrow, Vanelli* or numerous other federal cases. And we think it's a good thing for the agency heads to decide whether to proceed with a prosecution, rather than leaving it to the prosecuting staff. Whether or not to prosecute a physician or other licensee is often the most critical decision in the entire case; if the Board proceeds, the physician can count on huge expense and trauma, bad publicity, and professional

uncertainty even if he wins at the hearing. And of course, he may well lose. But a decision not to prosecute quashes the case at the beginning. Many discretionary elements are involved in the decision to prosecute—how serious is the misconduct relative to other targets, is this a really bad guy or did he just slip up, do we have the staff to do a good job on this case, how much will it cost to prosecute, how strong is our evidence, can we get a good settlement, etc. If the agency heads choose to retain the prosecutorial decision, we think they should be able to play that role effectively.

We also seriously doubt that making a decision to prosecute really taints the agency heads when the case returns to them a year or two later. They may not even remember what they heard when they approved the prosecution. And even if they do, the two functions are completely separable. The decision to prosecute is based on the idea that there is probable cause to suspect a violation. The agency heads didn't perform the investigation or develop a will to win in the case; they merely confirmed that what the investigators told them sounds like a prima facie case. It's no different than a judge deciding to issue a search warrant or a wiretap order, then hearing the criminal case on the merits.

3. *External separation of functions.* The structure involved in California ABC regulation is anomalous. As § 3.4.4 points out, when external separation is used (for example, in respect to OSHA and OSHRC), one agency handles only investigation and prosecution; a second agency handles only adjudication. Here the Department investigates, prosecutes, *and* provides two levels of adjudication; then the Board provides a third level of adjudication. Then you go to court for additional levels of adjudication, all fighting over a 20-day suspension of a liquor license. This is a silly structure and obviously attributable to the political power of the alcoholic beverage industry. It is, however, set forth in the California constitution, so it can't be readily changed. *See* Art. 20, § 22, which was added by an initiative in 1932. California is the home of direct democracy with large numbers of initiative provisions on every ballot. The absurd alcoholic beverage regulatory scheme is a fine example of an ill-informed and damaging initiative.

4. *Separation of functions under the federal APA.* Section 554(d) is complex and you'll need to walk students through it. The problem in N.9 should be helpful in doing so. The underlying theme here is that adversaries in a case (i.e. those engaged in investigation and prosecution) can't be decisionmakers or advisers to decisionmakers in that same case. As *Quintanar* explains, it is doubtful whether adversaries can give neutral advice (they are psychologically predisposed to the position they took as investigators or advocates) and their presence as advice-givers risks violation of the exclusive record rule.

Under the federal and California APAs, staff members who are *not adversaries* in a particular case (but may be in other cases) can give off-the-record advice to decisionmakers. Getting advice from non-adversary staff may not be too important in simple cases and may be objectionable in cases that are highly prosecutorial in nature. But in cases involving difficult economic or scientific issues (say water pollution violations as in *Dominion* or the licensing problem below, or complex securities or accounting cases, or technical engineering problems in telecommunications), it's important to the parties and to the public interest for the agency to get it right. See *Norooz v. Inland Wetlands Agency*, 602 A.2d 613 (Conn.App.1992), which concerned a complex local permitting dispute involving wetlands. The court approved the agency's use of an ex parte report furnished by an outside engineering firm that worked for the agency, so long as its report was confined to an analysis of the material in the record rather than adding new factual material. The court noted: "It is beyond dispute that a municipal administrative agency composed of laymen, is entitled to technical and professional assistance regarding matters beyond its expertise." *Id.* at 616. However, as the discussion in N.7 of the text makes clear, there remains considerable dispute about whether to permit non-adversary staff members to advise agency heads off the record.

In federal practice at least, ALJs do not seek or take advice from anyone (adversary or non-adversary); they regard themselves as like federal district judges. Depending on how you read *Butz v. Economou*, N.5, the APA may preclude them from getting any staff advice. However, insulating ALJs from any advice is not calculated to produce the best initial decisions. See John J. Mathias, "The Use of Legal and Technical Assistants by ALJs in Administrative Proceedings," 1 Admin.L.J. 107 (1987). Mathias, himself an ALJ, contends that ALJs need and should be able to receive legal and technical assistance.

5. *Additional separation of function provisions in the APA.* In focusing on § 554(d)(1), you might discuss ALJs and their central role in adjudication under the APA, particularly if you're planning to skip § 3.4. One important objective of the APA was to raise the status of ALJs and protect them from undue influence by the agencies. Thus § 554(d)(1) insulates ALJs from ex parte contact on factual issues with "a person or party." But it would not appear to cover contacts concerning law or policy as distinguished from facts.

Butz states in dictum that "person or party" means anybody, inside or outside of the agency. In the second edition of his treatise, Kenneth Davis criticized this interpretation, saying that "party" as defined in APA § 551(3) does not include the agency that is conducting the hearing, although it does include *other* agencies that happen to be parties to the case. Thus he argued that § 554(d)(1) does not cover communications with agency staff, only outsiders. 2 ADMINISTRATIVE LAW TREATISE § 17.9 (2d ed. 1980). However, *Butz v. Economou* settled the question for good.

    6. *Exceptions to separation of functions.* Ratemaking for the future is defined as rulemaking under the APA. APA §551(4). No separation of function exception was needed for future-oriented ratemaking, since § 554(d) covers only adjudication, not rulemaking. Even when ratemaking is treated as formal rulemaking because a statute or due process calls for a hearing on the record, only §§ 556-57 apply, not the separation of functions provision in §554(d). However, the exception in § 554(d)(B) covers more than just ratemaking. It covers "proceedings involving the validity or application of rates, facilities, or practices of public utilities or carriers." Thus cases involving the validity of *past* rates are adjudications, but separation of functions doesn't apply.

    Initial licensing and rate disputes don't normally involve allegations of wrongdoing or the necessity for resolving credibility disputes. Instead, they usually involve the use of expertise and economic or scientific data. Thus Congress favored an institutional rather than a judicial method in these cases. As a practical matter, however, most agencies have instituted separation of functions even in cases covered by the (A) and (B) exemptions. *See* Asimow, *supra*, at 804-820.

    The purposes of the agency heads exception in § 554(d)(C) are explained in the quoted material from the Attorney General's Memorandum. The agency heads exception may have been intended to allow the agency heads to supervise other personnel in all phases of a case and perhaps to participate personally in all phases (up to the point at which such participation would be so unfair as to violate due process). *Withrow* is based on the assumption that the members of the Wisconsin Medical Board were participating personally in all phases of the case. *Withrow* specifically referred to the APA's agency head exception as evidence that a combination of functions at the agency head level did not automatically constitute a violation of due process.

    However, we believe that the agency head exemption does not allow adversaries to advise the agency heads, as the second quoted excerpt from the AG's Memo says. Otherwise, the language in § 554(d) about "agency review" would be meaningless and separation of functions would be trivialized (it would not apply when it was most needed). However, there is disagreement about this. Some people believe that the (C) exemption means agency heads can receive ex parte advice from anyone. Judicial clarification would be most welcome.

7. *Separation of functions under the MSAPAs.* The 1961 Act prohibits ex parte communications on issues of fact by any person as well as by any party. Thus it appears to prohibit all ex parte staff contacts to decisionmakers relating to facts. However, as to issues of law, it appears that the decisionmakers can speak to anybody except to a party (or its representative), but a "party" includes the agency and its staff members. (Davis argued under the federal act—see Manual N.5 above— that "party" doesn't include the agency that is conducting the adjudication, only other agencies that happen to become parties).

According to the comment, "no objection is interposed to discussions of the law with other persons, e.g., the attorney general, or an outside expert." Thus § 13 of MSAPA 1961 appears to prohibit *all* ex parte communications by *non-adversary* agency staff members to agency heads in a contested case. The only exception would be where the staff member is an agency member's "personal assistant." It is unclear whether a staff member can be designated as a "personal assistant" for purposes of giving advice in a particular case. Thus the 1961 Act provisions appear quite close to the position taken by the majority of the drafting committee of the new MSAPA as described in the text. Yet it is hard to believe that § 13 of the 1961 Act is really interpreted that way in the many states that have adopted it. We have not found a case that deals squarely with the issue.

Numerous states have explicitly departed from § 13. The New York statute, which is based largely on the 1961 Act, deleted the reference to "personal assistants." Instead, it states that an agency member "may have the aid and advice of agency staff other than staff which has been or is engaged in the investigative or prosecuting functions in connection with the case under consideration or factually related case." SAPA § 307(2)(b). The same is true in Connecticut. Gen. St. Ann. 4-181b. Similarly, the Texas statute allows consultations by decisionmakers with nonadversary staff if "for the purpose of utilizing the special skills or knowledge of the agency employee in order to evaluate the evidence." Tex. Gov't Code § 2001.061(c). This provision was upheld against due process attack in *Smith v. Houston Chemical Services*, 872 S.W.2d 252, 278 (Tex.Ct. App.1994). In *Smith*, the court upheld a decision despite ex parte communications by a commissioner with a staff member regarding a technical issue, because it did not add any facts outside the evidentiary record.

Section 408 of the draft revised MSAPA has been further revised from the version discussed in the text (the number of the section has also changed over time and might change again). As of the time this Manual was prepared, § 408 would allow ex parte advice to agency heads concerning legal issues as well as technical or scientific matters. However, it would prohibit advice relating to the credibility of expert witnesses or any other witnesses.

The provision remains quite controversial and will probably be subject to further compromise before it is submitted to the ULC (the former NCCUSL). The problem is that several members of the drafting committee believe in the judicial rather than the institutional model of adjudication (see text § 3.3 before § 3.3.1). If outsiders can't make ex parte contacts with the agency heads (see § 3.3.2), they contend, staff members should not be permitted to do so either. Their position reflects the views of many private lawyers who litigate against agencies and are deeply suspicious of secret conversations between staff members and agency heads.

Other members and advisers to the drafting committee believe that agencies desperately need confidential staff advice when deciding difficult and complex matters critical to the public interest, such as water pollution permits or other environmental or economic matters. Often state agency heads are part-timers or political appointees and have little background in the matters they must decide. They need staff advice to assist them in understanding the scientific or technical issues presented in complex cases in order to render informed decisions. Staff members are career employees, specialize in particular areas the agency regulates, and often have deep understanding of the problems. As the Supreme Court acknowledged in *Morgan I,* agency heads need staff assistance in dealing with huge records.

In the view of the minority members, staff advice must be ex parte, because staff members will never be candid when their words are on the record. When the public, the press, or the litigants are listening, advisers watch every word and cannot give unvarnished advice. This concern for encouraging candid advice is reflected in other areas of administrative law, such as the pre-decisional memorandum exception in the Freedom of Information Act (*see* § 8.1.1). It seems inherent in *Morgan IV,* § 3.3.1 N.5, in which the Supreme Court prohibited judicial inquiry into the decisional processes of adjudicators in order to foster "uninhibited and frank discussions during their deliberations." Limiting the privilege of ex parte advice giving to "personal staffs" is not adequate. In many small agencies, the agency heads have no personal staff. The total number of staff members is small and each of them have to be prepared to play multiple roles. Even in large agencies where members may have law clerks or a personal staff, in difficult cases the decisionmakers need access to all non-adversary staff expertise, which their "personal staff" or "law clerks" may not have.

It should be obvious that the authors of this book favor allowing ex parte advice from non-adversary staff members when needed by agency heads. Asimow was an adviser to the NCCUSL drafting committee and disagreed vehemently with the view of the private lawyers that all staff advice should be on the record. Levin succeeded Asimow in this role and has taken the same position (perhaps less vehemently). Because this book is written before the final decision of the full Commission on the revised MSAPA, users of this book should consult the final version of the law before teaching this section. We will include the final version in supplements to this book.

8. *The principle of necessity*. The principle of necessity overrides the various rules discussed in this portion of the book—separation of functions, ex parte contacts, bias, exclusive record etc. It's better for a biased judge to make the decision than to let an unqualified doctor keep practicing. This principle seems to underlie *Withrow*: disqualifying the agency heads in that case would disable a great many small state agencies in which the agency heads engage in all the functions including investigation, prosecution, and adjudication.

In contrast, if it's possible to separate functions without disabling the agency, a combination of functions may violate due process. *Goldberg, GM v. Rosa*. The principle of necessity should be limited as far as possible. For example, in the problem that follows, recusing only one of a three-member agency would not disable the agency from deciding the case, since a quorum is still possible. And when a biased judge serves because of the principle of necessity, a reviewing court should exercise greater than normal scrutiny.

In *Lyness*, the court did not discuss the necessity problem. At the time of the adjudicatory decision there were ten members of the agency (apparently there was one vacancy). Of the ten, five were disqualified because of participation in the conference call. At the meeting that took up Lyness' case, only seven were present, of whom three were disqualified (two disqualified members were absent). Presumably a quorum was six, so it would require four affirmative votes to take action. It appears that four members were present who had not taken part in the conference call; consequently, there would have been enough votes from non-tainted members to revoke Lyness' license at the meeting in question. Over the objections of one judge, the court in *Lyness* remanded to the agency for further consideration, apparently without knowing whether there had been additional turnover. This action implies that the court thought there were enough members who were not disqualified to take action; therefore the court did not have to decide whether the principle of necessity overrode its separation of functions decision. A subsequent Pennsylvania decision, in dictum, states that the principle of necessity would override the *Lyness* rule. *Turner v. Penn. PUC*, 683 A.2d 942, 946 n.8 (1996).

The 1981 MSAPA provides a method for avoiding the principle of necessity; if an agency head is disqualified, a replacement can be appointed. Thus the agency isn't disabled. § 4-202(e). In *Nationscapital Mortgage Corp. v. State Dep't of Financial Inst.*, 137 P.3d 78, 95-98 (Wash.App.2006), the court held that a similar provision in the Washington APA is satisfied even though the disqualified agency head names the replacement. It is not necessary that a neutral party name the replacement. The court rejected the argument that this was like allowing one sports team to pick the referee for an upcoming game. Similarly, the appointment of the replacement by the disqualified person did not violate due process. *Id.* at 100.

An interesting twist on the rule of necessity occurred in *Valley v. Rapides Parish School Board,* 118 F.3d 1047 (5th Cir.1997), an employee discharge case. Of the nine members of the school board, six were biased against the employee; the other three favored her retention in the job. If she had disqualified all six biased members, the rule of necessity would have applied because the board would be deprived of a quorum; consequently none of the six biased members would have been disqualified. Instead, she sought to disqualify only four of the six biased members. This left the Board with a quorum able to vote (five out of nine); and since the employee had three votes in her pocket, she would win by a three-two vote. The court held that nothing prohibited her from challenging only some of the biased members rather than all of them!

9. *Problem.* If the problem were asked on an exam, there would be serious *Universal Camera* issues. *See* § 9.1.1. Credibility issues are paramount; the ALJ heard the witnesses but the agency heads did not. In applying the substantial evidence test, the court must give special weight to the ALJ's fact findings. If you have covered scope of review issues before adjudication, this would be a good opportunity to review *Universal Camera.* However, the problem is limited to the question of whether Wanda must disqualify herself because of the ex parte conversations she conducted with Ted and Gloria; therefore it excludes scope of review issues.

You might start your discussion by pointing out that SC combines functions of rulemaking, investigation, prosecution, and adjudication, but this is now well accepted. *Withrow.* It would be possible to split off the adjudicating function, but this leads to other problems discussed in § 3.4.3. You could also make the SC ALJs members of an independent central panel, as occurs in about half the states, and which we consider in § 3.4.2, but that would have made no difference in this case. Instead of focusing on external separation, we now turn to internal separation—that is, whether non-adversary staff members like Gloria or adversary staff members like Ted are prohibited from participating in adjudication (either by serving as adjudicative decisionmakers themselves or by giving ex parte advice to decisionmakers).

Gloria is a nonadversarial staff member in this case. She would not be disqualified by either due process or by the federal APA or by most state

APAs from serving as a hearing officer (if SC used staff members as hearing officers, which it does not), even though she sometimes serves as an investigator or prosecutor in other cases. (In federal agencies, if the APA applies, ALJs cannot do anything except hear cases.) In small agencies, it's inevitable that some staff members will swing from one function to another in various cases in order to properly maximize personnel resources. *See V-1 Oil Co. v. Dep't of Envir. Quality*, 939 P.2d 1192 (Utah 1997) (prosecutor in other cases can serve as hearing officer under due process and state APA). Now as to the advice issue:

i) Due process. If no APA applied, a combination of functions could still violate due process and require Wanda to be disqualified from deciding the case, although the law is poorly developed. *Withrow* establishes that Wanda could personally engage in investigating the case, but it doesn't answer the hard question in this problem about Ted's conversation with Wanda.

Ted's first conversation with Wanda urging her to issue a complaint is probably OK under federal cases like *Vanelli*. However, *Lyness* would require Wanda to be disqualified by reason of participating in the decision to issue the complaint. Here you can have a good pro-and-con discussion of *Lyness*. We incline toward the dissenting views in that case, because we think it is a good thing for agency heads to be involved in the prosecutorial decision. However, such conversations do expose Wanda to a lot of ex parte information about the case, some of which may never be received in evidence, and it is delivered by a person with a will to win who has spent a lot of time investigating the case and doesn't want to admit it was a waste of time. So agencies should consider whether to remove the agency heads from the prosecution decision.

Gloria's conversation with Wanda should be no problem, since she was not involved in the case as an adversary. Allowing non-involved staff members to consult ex parte with agency heads is quite traditional and, as discussed above, especially necessary in difficult or technical cases. A due process holding that questioned such conversations would have enormous practical repercussions, and the courts are unlikely to stir up that kind of trouble.

In *White v. Indiana Parole Bd.*, discussed above in N.1, Easterbrook He points out that staff/decisionmaker conferences (such as FTC agency heads discussing a case with the economic staff) are routine and accepted. "When the Chairman of the FTC has a private meeting with the agency's Chief Economist, does this spoil all cases then under advisement? Hardly. Agencies and courts have different methods of resolving disputes; what is unthinkable for a court may be normal for an agency; and although the FTC must in the end defend its decisions by reference to the administrative record, no rule of law prevents the Commissioners (or, say, Members of the National Labor Relations Board) from discussing pending matters with agency employees." 266 F.3d at 766.

The serious due process issue concerns Ted's ex parte conversation with Wanda about the case after the ALJ hearing. Although Ted does not introduce any new factual information (which would violate the exclusive record principle), he is not a neutral adviser. He has given ex parte advice, despite his commitment to win the case and his disappointment with the ALJ decision. Although *Quintanar* did not reach due process, wisely choosing to decide the case under the California APA (see footnote 13), the court might very well have found a due process violation. The *Nightlife* case (cited in N.1 of text and decided by a lower California court) so held, as did the Florida Supreme Court in *Cherry Communications*.

In *White v. Indiana Parole Board,* discussed above in N.1, the majority found no due process violation from an ex parte communication between the prosecutor and the decisionmakers. The majority relied on the relaxed standards applicable to prison disciplinary board hearings (which allow, for example, the decisionmaker to consider evidence not made available to the prisoner). Rovner's strong dissent in *White* would have invalidated even a prison case because of the ex parte contacts by the prosecutor with the Board.

To discuss the due process issue properly, you need a *Mathews* balancing. However, some people do not agree that *Mathews* balancing is appropriate to decide issues of agency structure, such as separation of functions; these persons prefer bright-line rules permitting or prohibiting specific types of conflict between adversarial and decisional functions. In the *Morongo* case, also discussed above in N.1, the briefs offered a *Mathews* analysis, but the California Supreme Court did not refer to *Mathews* in its decision and did not decide the case through balancing.

Using *Mathews* balancing, Roz's interest in her brokerage license is very significant—her entire ability to function as a professional is at stake; the government interest in a decisionmaker receiving ex parte advice from a prosecutor is slight, given the availability of advice from non-involved staff such as Gloria; and the risk of error from biased advice is quite substantial. Thus we think a due process violation is likely here.

New York seems unduly aggressive in applying due process to combination of functions. Several cases involve investigator/prosecutors who become agency heads but were only marginally involved in the actual case. *Beer Garden, Inc. v. N.Y. State Liquor Auth.*, 590 N.E.2d 1193, 1198-99 (N.Y.

1992). *Beer Garden* disqualified X, an agency lawyer who had not been personally involved in the investigation or even known about the case. However, his stamped signature had appeared on a complaint: "X, Counsel to the Authority." X then became one of the five members of the liquor licensing agency and refused to recuse himself. The New York court held that this violated fundamental fairness because it created an "appearance of partiality." It is unclear whether the decision is based on due process or administrative common law. We think this case is wrong. Actual (rather than purely symbolic) personal involvement should be required in order to disqualify a person as an adjudicator under separation of functions. Similarly, see *General Motors Corp. v. Rosa*, 624 N.E.2d 142 (N.Y.1993) (adjudicator previously was General Counsel, and was noted as such for the record, even though the case was tried by a different lawyer; court fails to inquire whether the GC was actually involved in the case, as opposed to merely having her name appear on a piece of paper).

ii) 1961 MSAPA. Section 13 of the 1961 MSAPA seems rather primitive. It would appear to invalidate all three contacts in the case. Section 13 prohibits agency adjudicators from engaging in ex parte communications with any person or party in a contested case in connection with any issue of fact; it also bans communications concerning law with any party. The only relevant exception is that an agency member can have "aid and advice of one or more personal assistants." Under the facts, neither Ted nor Gloria appears to be a "personal assistant" although possibly Wanda could designate Gloria as a personal assistant for the purpose of the case.

Gloria's advice concerned policy and discretion (the severity of the penalty against Roz) rather than facts or law. It is unclear how § 13 applies to a discussion about policy or discretion. Presumably, the court would hold that the provision in § 13 banning discussions of "issues of law" with "any party or his representative" would cover Gloria's discussion, since the section would otherwise leave a large gap between law and fact. Gloria is probably a "party or his representative" under the 1961 MSAPA's definition of party: "each person or agency named or admitted as a party. . ." §1(5). (However, this is not completely clear; see Davis' point discussed above in N.5.) However, if policy is more like law than fact, Wanda could apparently discuss it with anybody outside the agency, such as the Attorney General.

The 1981 MSAPA would allow all the communications except Ted's meeting with Roz after the ALJ decision. § 4-213(b). We said in N.7 of the casebook that the revised MSAPA may well return to the policies of § 13 of the 1961 MSAPA and prohibit most ex parte staff advice to agency heads. However, as noted in the manual discussion of N.7, the draft has been revised since the text went to press, and in its current form it would permit much more ex parte staff advice than the version discussed in the text.

Nevertheless, the version of the new Model Act discussed in the text raises serious policy issues that might make for a good class discussion.

iii) Federal APA: The federal APA requires the use of ALJs in formal adjudication, as occurred here. The ALJ would work for SC but would have substantial protections concerning hiring, job duties, rotation, and evaluation. Basically, an ALJ can engage only in judging, not other agency functions. Clearly, Gloria's conference with Wanda is acceptable under §554(d), as she was neither a prosecutor nor investigator. Note that this is explicit in the California statute discussed in *Quintanar*. As explained in N.2 of the text, federal cases like *Vanilli* have upheld Ted's pre-complaint conference with Wanda. The rationale is that Ted was not giving advice "in the decision, recommended, decision or agency review" as defined in § 554(d) when he recommended that the agency issue a complaint.

However, Ted's ex parte communication with Wanda after the ALJ decision presents serious issues under the federal APA. *Quintanar* involves such a conference (a prosecutor's memo to agency heads); the Court overturned a decision that might have been influenced by such a memo under the California statute. However, the CA statute has no "agency head" exception, so it is not settled how the conference should be handled under the federal statute which does contain such an exception in § 554(d)(C). We believe that the (C) "agency head" exception would allow Wanda to personally investigate or advocate in the case, but would not allow a staff adversary like Ted to advise agency heads off the record at the time of the agency review. We'd cite the Attorney General's Memorandum discussed in N.6 of the text, which explains that the agency head exception does not permit such contacts. To permit them would trivialize the separation of functions provision in § 554(d), particularly the reference to "agency review."

However, some people read the agency head exception more broadly than does the Attorney General's Memorandum; they believe that the (C) exception does permit agency heads to receive off-record advice from adversaries. Their view is that the agency heads have a complete exemption from separation of functions, both with respect to deciding the case and with respect to the advice they receive. Thus the ban on adversarial advice would cover only communications with decisionmakers below the agency head level.

§ 3.3.5 Bias: Personal Interest, Prejudgment, Personal Animus

CINDERELLA CAREER AND FINISHING SCHOOLS, INC. v. FEDERAL TRADE COMMISSION

Notes and Questions

134

1. *Personal interest. Van Harken v. City of Chicago*, 103 F.3d 1346 (7th Cir. 1997), is the administrative parking ticket case discussed in § 2.4 N.6. Under Chicago's decriminalized system, attorneys served as hearing officers in parking ticket cases. They could be fired at will by the City's Director of Revenue. Plaintiffs tried to apply *Ward v. Village of Monroeville*, arguing that the hearing officers would fear getting fired unless they maximized parking ticket revenues. The court didn't buy it. There was no quota for the hearing officers. If their fear of getting fired for not being tough enough were enough to disqualify them, this theory would disqualify judges in criminal cases who fear they won't be reelected if they aren't tough on crime. The court applied a *Mathews* balance—the fines are low and the City's desire to save money on hearing officers is a valid state interest.

With *Van Harken,* contrast *Haas v. San Bernardino*, 45 P.3d 280 (Cal. 2002). A small county selected a local attorney as a temporary hearing officer to adjudicate a massage parlor license revocation case. She was paid an hourly rate by the county for her work. The California Supreme Court reversed the revocation decision, holding that the temporary officer had an incentive to decide in favor of the county and revoke the license, so that she would have a better chance of being hired to hear future cases. This holding put the county in a bind; either it had to hire a permanent hearing officer (even though there wasn't enough work to support one), or hire a central panel ALJ from the state (which is quite costly), or disqualify any temporary hearing officer from being rehired (despite the limited pool available and willing to work for the modest amount the county was paying). We believe the *Haas* case is wrong. The possibility that a hearing officer might not be rehired if she decided the case against the County is too remote to disqualify her. (For a similar decision, see *Esso Standard,* discussed *infra*—selection process of pro-tem hearing officers suggests that they have to decide cases in agency's favor to get rehired).

Courts generally requires a showing of actual bias rather than the "appearance of bias." (See Manual N.3 and discussion of the problem in N.6) In cases of pecuniary bias, however, it would seem that an "appearance of bias" is all that it takes to disqualify a decisionmaker. It's too difficult to ascertain whether the decisionmaker was or wasn't actually biased by the personal interest. Thus, as in *Haas,* the facts that establish that interest are sufficient to disqualify the decisionmaker without any additional showing. *Friedman v. Rogers*, N.2, however, suggests the contrary.

Possible class hypo: Does an agency have a financial stake in a decision if it keeps the penalties collected to pay for its annual budgetary costs? Or suppose that the agency is empowered to order a disciplined licensee to pay its costs of investigation and prosecution? These cost recoveries enable the agency to cover part or all of its operating budget and thus avoid staff layoffs. These hypos sounds a bit like *Ward v. City of Monroeville* (where the mayor could use traffic fines for the city budget and avoid raising taxes).

Esso-Standard Oil Co. v. Lopez-Freytes, 522 F.3d 136, 146-47 (1st Cir. 2008) is a dramatic example of the first type of case. The Puerto Rico Environmental Quality Board (EQB) levied a $76 million fine against Esso for failing to report a fuel leak at a gas station. EQB gets to keep such fines to finance its operating costs. The fine in this case was twice EQB's annual budget and 5000 times greater than the largest fine it had ever imposed. Even worse, the pro-tem hearing officer could get paid, according to his contract, only out of fines imposed by the agency!

As to recovery of investigation and prosecution costs: Cal.Bus. & Prof. Code § 125.3 authorizes agencies to recover costs in all licensing cases. *Zuckerman v. Bd. of Chiropractic Examiners,* 53 P.2d 119 (Cal.2002), upholds such cost recoveries but requires the agencies to exercise discretion in imposing recoveries, depending on the severity of the offense and the penalty. *But see Trust & Inv. Advisers v. Hogsett,* 43 F.3d 290, 296-97 (7th Cir.1994) (expressing concern about bias, especially if the agency controlled the money and the cost recoveries were a material part of the budget). Where cost recovery statutes are in effect, agency investigators and litigators, including the deputy Attorney Generals who do most of the prosecuting, must keep meticulous time sheets to justify later cost recoveries. This situation is distinguishable from *Marshall v. Jerrico* in the text, because the agency in question in *Jerrico* was solely prosecutorial, not adjudicatory.

An interesting case that combines the different claims of bias—personal interest, prejudgment, and animus—is *Stivers v. Pierce*, 71 F.3d 732 (9th Cir.1995), involving a rejected application by the Nevada State Private Investigators Licensing Board. The court held that a § 1983 suit for damages against the individual members of the Board survived summary judgment.

One member of the Board (Pierce) was already in direct competition with the applicant (Stivers) in Reno. And Pierce had a grudge—Stivers had outbid Pierce for a lucrative security job at Bally's Casino. Such competition does not trigger a per se rule of disqualification (since members of the licensed profession serve on most licensing boards), but the court said that Stivers should be allowed to introduce evidence that in this case the head-to-head competition did create a personal interest.

There were additional facts suggesting personal animus: An affidavit stated that Pierce had made derogatory statements about Stivers. Stivers had been shot by an unknown assailant while investigating a burglary and

Pierce said "everybody knew Marty had shot himself." In addition, there were a series of events suggesting that the Board (led by Pierce) had treated Stivers in an extremely harsh, harassing, and highly irregular manner. These suggested factual prejudgment. For example, the Board disregarded recommendations of its own legal counsel.

An important issue in *Stivers* was whether the Board denied a fair hearing when only one member out of five was biased and the decision was unanimous. As in *Cinderella,* the court ruled that a single person's bias is likely to have a profound impact on the decisionmaking process and was likely to have infected the vote.

2. *Professional bias.* *Gibson* is an example of built-in personal interest affecting an entire board. Under the disqualification standards applicable to federal judges, a judge who was also an independent optometrist and who had to decide whether all corporate optometrists violated professional standards, would be required to disqualify himself. See 28 U.S.C. §455(a) (judge shall disqualify himself in any proceeding in which his impartiality might reasonably be questioned); §455(b)(4) (judge shall disqualify himself where he knows that he has a financial interest in the subject matter in controversy). But a standard that strict would remove a great number of board members who are members of the profession being regulated. Thus judicial disqualification standards may not work very well in the administrative sphere.

Does *Gibson* make sense? The statute required every member of the board to be an independent optometrist. This provided a built-in, guaranteed bias against optometrists who worked for chain stores. See also *American Motors Sales Corp. v. New Motor Vehicle Bd.,* 138 Cal.Rptr. 594 (Cal.App. 1977) (holding invalid a nine-person board, four of whom had to be car dealers but none had to represent manufacturers).

As a prophylactic against a board so heavily stacked, *Gibson* makes sense—even though it prevented the board from acting in a range of cases until restructured by the legislature. But *Friedman* showed that the Court could not live with the rigor of *Gibson*; to invalidate all licensing boards with guaranteed representation for one faction of the industry would sweep too broadly. Thus, *Friedman* held, a facial attack on a stacked board (not arising out of a particular disciplinary action) failed because there had been no particularized showing of unfairness.

Gibson and *Friedman* provide an opportunity to discuss the economics of professional licensing and the conflict of interest between persons in a profession and those trying to cut prices or gain some other market advantage (*e.g.* the conflict between independent and employed optometrists). Another such conflict is between those in the profession and those seeking admission to it (e.g. bar examiners raising standards to make it harder to pass the bar exam; practicing barbers raising the educational requirements for new barbers). In many states, statutes have added public members to licensing boards to decrease this sort of institutional pecuniary interest. Indeed, many people see professional licensing as a shrewd marketing tool by a profession to raise barriers to entry, decrease competition, and raise prices. As a result, policymakers should exercise caution in approving new licensing schemes, *e.g.* of auto mechanics. Just because there are consumer complaints about fraud in auto repairs does not necessarily indicate that mechanics should be licensed. Courts have reason to be wary of occupational licensing boards' decisions also—as we discuss below in connection with the *Connecticut Medical Society* case (§ 9.2.1 N.1 of this manual).

3. *Prejudgment.* For discussion of bias issues, including the difference between prejudgment of adjudicative and legislative fact and the "in role" distinction, see Peter L. Strauss, "Disqualifications of Decisional Officials in Rulemaking," 80 Colum.L.Rev. 990, 1010-27 (1990). A good survey is Judith K. Meierhenry, "The Due Process Right to an Unbiased Adjudicator in Administrative Proceedings," 36 S.D.L.Rev. 551 (1991). For a state case similar to *Cinderella,* see *1616 Second Ave. Restaurant v. NY State Liquor Authority,* 550 N.E.2d 910 (NY 1990) (in 4-3 decision, court finds prejudgment from agency head's statement before legislative oversight committee that agency expects it will soon catch a particular bar for serving minors).

The statements in *Cinderella* and *Texaco* seem to evidence Dixon's prejudgment of adjudicatory facts—facts concerning the specific parties and their conduct—rather than of legislative facts, law and policy. The same is true of *Cyanamid.* In that case Dixon was chief counsel and staff director of the Antitrust and Monopoly Subcommittee of the Senate Judiciary Committee (the Kefauver Committee). In that capacity, he investigated Cyanamid and Pfizer's conduct in getting a patent on tetracycline. The investigation concerned quite specific facts about price fixing and fraud on the patent office, and Dixon's report to Kefauver contained very firm and negative conclusions about the companies.

Another example is *Antoniu v. SEC,* 877 F.2d 72 (8th Cir.1989), in which SEC commissioner Charles Cox gave a speech in which he said that Antoniu would be permanently barred from work as a broker-dealer—while his case was still under consideration by the SEC. The interesting twist in *Antoniu* is that Cox recused himself, but only on the day that the decision was announced. The court could not determine whether his participation tainted the SEC's deliberations, so it nullified all Commission decisions (including rejection of a settlement offer) occurring after Cox's speech. The case is severely criticized in an article written by Cox's former law clerk, who is now a law professor. Douglas C. Mitchell, "'Prejudgment' Rejudgment: The True Story of *Antoniu v. SEC*," 61 Admin.L.Rev. 225 (2009). Mitchell argues that Cox's comment about the permanent disqualification referred to an earlier stage in the litigation, not to the case pending before the SEC.

Cinderella and *Texaco* (as well as *Antoniu* and *1616 Second Ave.*) can be questioned. Essentially, the criticism is that agency heads have to make public appearances, and the use of examples from pending cases to liven up a speech hardly suggests that the heads cannot judge the cases fairly when the cases come before them for decision. Instead, they can easily avoid the problem by just saying "alleged" before stating the facts, but how could the issue depend on whether this word was used? The same is not true of *Cyanamid*; there is nothing necessary about the agency head having previously served as a Congressional investigator of the same conduct now under investigation by the Commission. And the conclusions are much firmer than the loose sort of language involved in Dixon's speeches in *Cinderella* and *Texaco*. In *Cyanamid*, Dixon should have disqualified himself; *Cinderella* and *Texaco* are closer cases.

The statements evidencing prejudgment in *Cinderella, Texaco, Antoniu*, and *American Cyanamid* were made "out of role" (that is, they were not made in connection with the adjudicating function); whereas the statements evidencing prejudgment in *Donnelly Garment* and *Hortonville* were made "in role." This distinction is supported by *Liteky*, N.4 in text, relating to personal animus, indicating that information giving rise to animus by judges (except in extreme cases) must come from extra-judicial sources to require their disqualification. *See also* Strauss, *supra*, at 1019-22; *Boughan v. Bd. of Engineering Examiners*, 611 P.2d 670 (Ore.App.1980) (prior contact with case in non-official capacity—as a successor engineer on a project—disqualifies board member).

With *Cinderella* and related cases, compare *FTC v. Cement Institute*, 333 U.S. 683 (1948), which refused to disqualify the FTC members because they had previously supervised an investigation of the pricing method in question and testified before Congress that it was illegal. *Cement Institute* is distinguishable from *Cinderella* and *Cyanamid* on three grounds: i) the FTC members were in role when they investigated the pricing system; ii) in *Cement Institute* the dispute concerned more questions of law and policy than specific facts about the individual companies; iii) *Cement Institute* triggered the rule of necessity—a contrary holding would have disqualified the whole FTC and prevented it from acting, whereas disqualification of Dixon would not prevent the FTC from acting.

It is important to distinguish an adjudicator's view about policy from prejudgment of adjudicatory facts. If it were otherwise, how many members of the NLRB could sit? Many of them had careers entirely representing unions; others spent their lives fighting unions in company personnel departments. Nobody expects triers of fact to be intellectual eunuchs. See *Pennsylvania v. Local Union 542*, 388 F.Supp. 155 (E.D.Pa.1974). In this civil rights case, Judge Higginbotham, who was black, refused to disqualify himself despite having just given a speech to a group of black historians that heavily criticized recent Supreme Court decisions.

Judge Tamm states several times in *Cinderella* that adjudicators must not only be fair, they must *appear* to be fair. Quoting *Texaco,* he says that a hearing "must be attended, not only with every element of fairness but with the very appearance of complete fairness." The "appearance of fairness" test is also used in the statute relating to disqualification of federal judges: 28 U.S.C. §455(a): A federal judge shall "disqualify himself in any proceeding in which his impartiality might reasonably be questioned." In addition, a federal judge must disqualify himself if he has "personal knowledge of disputed evidentiary facts concerning the proceeding." § 455(b)(1).

However, it is (and should be) harder to disqualify an administrative adjudicator than a judge. In order to disqualify an administrative adjudicator, a litigant should show some specific cause for doing so, such as actual statements evidencing prejudgment or animus, as distinguished from the sort of appearance-type facts that might be sufficient to disqualify a judge. As a general rule, decisionmakers cannot be disqualified for what might be generically referred to as "institutional bias"—that is, a strong predisposition toward effective enforcement of the agency's statute and regulations. Instead, there must be some specific, well-founded basis to believe that an adjudicator cannot judge the case fairly, and that claim must fall into the rather narrowly defined criteria for bias established in administrative cases. *See* Michael Asimow, "Toward a New California Administrative Procedure Act: Adjudication Fundamentals," 39 UCLA L. Rev. 1067, 1145-49 (1992).

The special rules about bias of agency adjudicators are examples of a compromise that leans closer to an institutional approach than a judicial one. The distinctions discussed above in the text—the "in role" rule, the tolerance for prejudgments about law, policy, or legislative fact, the rule of necessity—all seem institutional in nature. They allow agencies to function normally without constantly confronting claims that decisionmakers are disqualified by institutional biases or personal knowledge of facts in the dispute arising out of more or less normal agency activity.

The state of Washington's attempt to apply an amorphous

"appearance of fairness" doctrine to its local land use planning adjudicators illustrates the problem. The trouble is that local zoning administrators are often themselves involved in various phases of land development or have family or personal or political ties to applicants for planning permission. There has been a long string of confusing cases and strong criticism in the literature of the appearance of fairness doctrine. *See* Asimow, *supra*, at 1148 n.285 for citation to Washington authorities.

Colorado adopted the appearance of bias standard. This case would make a good class hypothetical: the Del Norte School Board is considering whether to fire Iris Wells, a sixth grade teacher, for incompetence. There is a hearing before an ALJ. In the midst of a witness's testimony, there's a lunch break. The ALJ takes a seat at a table where the witness and the counsel for the school board are eating. There was no other available seat in the cafeteria. Before sitting down, the ALJ said that the Wells case would not be discussed and it wasn't discussed. However, Wells was also eating in the cafeteria, and she saw the ALJ talking with the witness and the counsel for the school board.

Held: this created an appearance of bias and the case is remanded for a hearing before a different ALJ. The court said that judicial standards applied, and a judge must avoid the appearance of impropriety. *Wells v. Del Norte School District*, 753 P.2d 770 (Colo.Ct.App. 1987). Considering that an ALJ often works for the same agency that is prosecuting a case, it's inevitable that ALJs will have social conversations with persons who have some kind of adversary role in cases. Otherwise they would have to eat lunch in their office. Isn't the *Wells* case pretty silly?

A North Carolina case presents another interesting twist and would make a good class hypo. Hearne was an animal control officer who got entangled in a public debate about euthanizing animals. His superior, Sherman, called and asked him to resign. Whether Hearne's resignation was voluntary or whether Sherman compelled him to resign was the disputed issue in the case. An ALJ ruled that the resignation was coerced (so that Hearne, a civil service employee, gets his job back). Sherman was the agency head and he ruled that his own testimony should be believed rather than Hearne's testimony. This is an extreme form of prejudgment of specific facts! By an equally divided vote, the North Carolina Supreme Court affirmed the decision of the court below that the resignation was voluntary and that Sherman's decision to believe his own testimony rather than Hearne's did not violate due process. The rationale of the judges who wished to affirm was that there were no disputed issues of fact, but the ALJ and the dissenting judges disagreed strongly. *Hearne v. Sherman*, 516 S.E.2d 864 (N.C.1999).

4. *Personal animus.* The most famous example of admitted personal

animus is *Berger v. United States*, 255 U.S. 22 (1921) in which Judge Kenesaw Mountain Landis, presiding over an espionage trial, announced that the hearts of all German-Americans were reeking with disloyalty.

Wang is a good example of the "extreme case" exception to the extrajudicial source rule. There have been quite a few such cases (and even more cases in which judges have harshly criticized the reasoning of IJs who seem to nitpick the cases in an effort to deny the requested relief). *See, e.g., Cham v. Attorney General*, 445 F.3d 683 (3d Cir. 2006); *Iliev v. INS,* 127 F.3d 638 (7th Cir. 1997) (requiring that all litigants including aliens be treated with dignity and respect); *Benslimane v. Gonzales*, 450 F.3d 828 (7th Cir. 2005) (denial of continuance to file a document that the applicant had already filed with INS).

The cases involving personal animus of Immigration Judges reflect deep pathologies in the immigration adjudication system. (As a result of the reorganization resulting from the Homeland Security Act of 2002, immigration adjudication is now conducted by the Executive Office for Immigration Review which is housed in the Justice Department, rather than the Immigration & Naturalization Service which has been abolished). There are immense backlogs and the IJs have to dispose of a large caseload every day. While there is no evidence of any quotas, IJs appear to be under pressure to turn down most asylum applications (as in *Wang)* and to approve deportations. As a practical matter, IJs just have no time to be patient with litigants who are struggling with language difficulties or procedural complexities or consider difficult cases carefully or write reasoned opinions. It may be that the unpleasant working conditions of IJs have resulted in a relatively poor caliber of personnel; in any event, these conditions insure that IJs will be rushed and irritable.

In earlier times, IJ decisions were reviewed by a three-judge panel of the Board of Immigration Appeals (BIA); today BIA review is usually by a single member and is usually a rubber stamp. The effect is to funnel a huge number of cases into the courts of appeals, where the judges have frequently responded by slamming the agency. Immigration cases accounted for 18% of all federal appeals in 2005, up from 3% in 2001. In the Ninth Circuit, immigration appeals made up 41% of the 2005 caseload. For overviews of this major problem in administrative law (including the huge disparities in Immigration Judge decisions), see Edward R. Grant, "Laws of Intended Consequences: IIRIRA and Other Unsung Contributors to the Current State of Immigration Litigation," 55 Cath.U.L.Rev. 923 (2005) (as well as other articles in the immigration symposium in the same issue); Margaret Tebo, "Asylum Ordeals," 92 A.B.A.J. 36 (Nov.2006); Bill Blum, "Crossing to Safety," Cal.Lwyr. 18 (Jan.2007); Andrew Schoenholtz & Jonathan Shrag, "Refugee Roulette: Disparities in Asylum Adjudication," 60 Stan.L.Rev. 295

(2008) (study shows sharp disparities in grant rates in asylum cases as between various IJs).

5. *Agency publicity.* There is a discussion of agency publicity in connection with the problem in § 4.1.2 N.8. The obvious difference between the two *Cinderella* cases is that the press release says only that there is reason to believe that Cinderella had engaged in misleading advertising— not that it had actually done so. Moreover, issuance of a press release is both routine and institutional; they are issued in case of every complaint and aren't the responsibility of any particular Commissioner, whereas the second *Cinderella* case is very personal to Commissioner Dixon. These differences are hardly likely to persuade persons who are the subjects of FTC complaints and the targets of damaging negative publicity that their cases haven't been prejudged by the agency heads. Agencies should consider Gellhorn's recommendations and not routinely issue press releases announcing investigations or prosecutions in the absence of some kind of public harm.

6. *Problem.* There are several arguments for disqualifying Perez. The *Andrews* case rejected all of them.

a) Financial interest: It could be argued that Perez had an indirect financial interest. He represents farm worker unions. If he decided for Smith and against the union, farm worker unions or other Hispanic organizations might steer their cases to some other lawyer. Joseph E. Maloney, "Disqualification of ALJ's in California," 16 U.S.F.L.Rev. 229 (1982), is critical of *Andrews* on this ground. Yet if the Board is going to appoint temporary judges and they have any knowledge of labor law, they'll probably represent clients on either the union or management side, so all of the available pool will have some sort of financial bias.

It is arguable that Perez would be disqualified if the applicable test were the one set forth by 28 U.S.C. § 455(b)(4), (d)(4), relating to federal judges: The judge must disqualify himself if he "knows that he . . . [or a family member] has a financial interest in the subject matter in controversy or a party in the proceeding, *or any other interest that could be substantially affected by the outcome of the proceeding.*" That test is probably too strict to be applied in administrative adjudication, since there are many ways in which an adjudicator could have an "interest that could be substantially affected by the outcome of a proceeding." For example, the agency head might be interested in being appointed to the President's cabinet and might feel that a decision one way or the other would be helpful to him. Or the administrator might hope to get a job as the general counsel of a litigant after resigning from the agency. Absent additional facts showing bias, that probably should not be enough to disqualify him.

b) Prejudgment: The fact that Perez is Hispanic and the farm workers are also Hispanic should not be used as the basis for disqualifying him. Otherwise women judges could not hear cases involving women. The California statute now contains language perhaps inspired by *Andrews*. It provides that a presiding officer (PO) cannot be disqualified on the basis that he or she is or is not a member of a racial, ethnic, religious, sexual, or similar group and the proceeding involves the rights of that group. Or that a PO has experience, technical competence, or specialized knowledge of, or has in any capacity expressed a view on, a legal, factual, or policy issue presented in the proceeding. Or has as a lawyer or public official participated in drafting laws or regulations or in the effort to pass or defeat laws or regulations, the meaning, effect or application of which is in issue. Cal. Gov't Code § 11425.40(b). California did not adopt the provision in 1981 MSAPA § 4-202(a) that calls for disqualification of agency adjudicators for any reason for which a judge may be disqualified. Thus it avoided the "appearance of bias" standard, which applies in many states as well as in federal courts.

Perez's published articles establish that he is philosophically committed to the interest of farm workers and their unionization. That cannot be the basis for disqualifying him. Every judge has political views and prejudgments of issues of law and policy. If that meant the judge couldn't provide a fair trial, as Judge Frank once said, nobody has ever had a fair trial and nobody ever will. *In re J. P. Linahan, Inc.,* 138 F.2d 650, 651-52 (2d Cir.1943).

Suppose Perez said in the article that, in his opinion, a union has no chance of organizing farm workers unless the organizers can actually meet up with the workers, and that farmers often obstruct such meetings, even though they occur after working hours. Such statement would represent prejudgment of legislative facts. Probably prejudgment of legislative fact is not disqualifying (although this is not so well settled and you could have a good discussion about whether it should be). As long as there's no showing he has made up his mind about the particular disputed facts in the Smith case (that is, whether this particular farmer obstructed contact between organizers and workers), he can't be disqualified on the basis of prejudgment. See the California statute quoted above.

c) The underlying problem is that Perez is a judge pro tem, not a regular employee of the agency. That magnifies the problem of financial bias, because he might want to decide the case so as to please his clients to whom he will return after he finishes deciding the case. On the prejudgment side, Perez might reason that he might as well strike a blow for the union while he has the chance; a regular ALJ who hears these cases every day wouldn't think that way. See *Haas v. San Bernardino*, discussed above in N.1, in which the California Supreme Court disqualified a temporary hearing officer in a local licensing case because of concern that she might slant things in the County's favor in order to get appointed again as a temporary judge.

Haas is distinguishable from the problem because the agency isn't one of the parties (in labor cases the agency is supposed to be a neutral arbiter between employer and union). Even so, the same concern might arise in the problem. Perez might want to slant things the union's way to get reappointed by the agency heads (assuming they happen to be strongly pro-union). Although distinguishable, *Haas* points up the fact that the incentives of temporary administrative judges are different from those of permanent judges. In *Andrews,* the California Supreme Court dismissed the arguments about prejudgment and financial bias by saying that you need to show actual bias, not merely the appearance of bias, which seems generally correct. Although *Andrews* said that no special rules applied to temporary judges, courts might decide that stricter bias rules should apply to temporary administrative judges.

§ 3.4 ADMINISTRATIVE LAW JUDGES AND DECISIONAL INDEPENDENCE

The three subdivisions of § 3.4 correspond to the three hypos students are asked to address.

§ 3.4.1 Selection and Appointment of ALJs

We think there should be changes in the ways in which federal ALJs are selected and evaluated. For an excellent historical treatment of ALJs from before the APA to the present, see Daniel J. Gifford, "Federal Administrative Law Judges: The Relevance of Past Choices to Future Directions," 49 Admin.L.Rev. 1, 4-52 (1997). Gifford (along with Verkuil) was one of the team of academics whose study led to ACUS Rec. 92-7.

Federal ALJs are a hybrid—they are part of an agency yet independent of that agency. In addition to the various statutory protections of their independence (OPM's role in hiring, separation of functions within the agency, prohibition on internal communication, the requirement of rotation of cases, OPM's control over compensation and promotion, the ban on agency evaluation of ALJs, and MSPB's control over discharge), there is great de facto independence. Federal ALJs consider themselves judges and act accordingly. The change in title from hearing examiner to ALJ was of enormous symbolic significance, particularly to the ALJs themselves; they reject any notion that they should be viewed as members of the agency team.

Apart from Social Security, most federal administrative judges are not ALJs, and most federal administrative cases are not formal adjudications governed by the APA. AJs preside over a vast number of cases including immigration, veterans' benefits, government contract disputes, security clearances, and numerous others. As ACUS Rec. 92-7 points out, this represents a regrettable movement away from the APA. The reason it occurred is primarily agency resistance to the provisions of the APA relating to the hiring, management, and evaluation of ALJs. Until those provisions are changed, there will be no movement of agency adjudication back toward the APA.

The most important part of Rec. 92-7 is the proposal to get rid of (or at least water down) the veterans' preference which discriminates against women and minorities. It results in the appointment of less qualified veterans over more qualified non-veterans. However, the political prospects for this recommendation are poor. Veterans' groups oppose the recommendation and are highly influential in Congress.

Assuming the veterans' preference stays in place, the key issue is whether agencies can choose qualified non-veterans. At present, OPM certifies only the top three applicants on its list for agencies to choose from. Moreover, agencies cannot pass over a veteran to take a non-veteran among the top three. Thus Rec. 92-7 suggests that agencies be permitted to select anyone among the highest-ranked 50% of those qualified. This recommendation is highly controversial, because many in the private bar oppose "selective certification," meaning they don't want the agencies to select only judges who are former agency staffers. Agencies, on the other hand, naturally want to choose judges who are already expert in the subject matter. If they are sympathetic to the agency's point of view, so much the better.

There was a major disagreement in the ABA Administrative Law Section over this issue. Ultimately, the ABA recommended that agencies be able to choose from the top 10 on the list—slightly more liberal than the present rule of three but much less liberal than the top 50% approach of ACUS Rec. 92-7.

ACUS' comments on evaluation of judges also touches on a sensitive issue. At present, agencies cannot engage in any systematic performance evaluation of their ALJs. This is unique in the federal government and prevents agencies from discovering which of their judges are problematic and building a case against those who are bad apples. Although in theory ALJs can be removed for good cause, only a tiny number have ever been removed against their will. In particular, the MSPB, which adjudicates such cases, refuses to find that low productivity is "good cause." As a result, ALJs have effective life tenure regardless of whether they do much work or maintain proper judicial temperament. And ALJs ardently seek to preserve this status. They feel that any sort of evaluation scheme will be used to compromise their independent status and punish them for deciding cases against the agency. Needless to say, agencies would like to have some ability to weed out ALJs whom they view as performing poorly. There have been major struggles in Social Security over agency efforts to improve the judges' productivity.

The cautiously hedged ACUS recommendation is that agencies should be allowed to introduce a system of performance evaluation run by their chief ALJs. The theory is that the chief ALJ will be a person who is sympathetic to ALJs and unlikely to punish a judge for a decision that the agency power structure dislikes. But ALJs strongly resist this recommendation. Political action by the ALJs triggered by resistance to these recommendations touched off a process of ACUS delegitimation that ultimately led to ACUS being defunded a few years later. Within the ABA the final compromise resolution omitted any reference to ALJ evaluation.

For a pungent assessment of ALJs, *see* Antonin Scalia, "The ALJ Fiasco—A Reprise," 47 U.Chi.L.Rev. 57 (1979). Scalia concludes: "Whatever solution is adopted, surely the current system—hiring 'by the numbers' into an effectively life-tenured job, with no advancement potential, and with no allocation of simpler work to less experienced (and hence lower-paid) individuals—is a horror story of personnel management which should come to an end. It does not even have the dubious merit of providing gold-plated judicial services at an exorbitant cost, but rather prevents intelligent selection and adequate compensation of the finest judges, deters voluntary departure of the worst, and erodes incentives all along the way." *Id.* at 79-80.

§ 3.4.2 ALJs: The Central Panel Issue

Additional sources: Symposia in 19 New Eng. L. Rev. 693-811 (1984); 6 W.New Eng.L.Rev. 587-828 (1984); 65 Judicature 233-277 (1981) (concentrating on state central panel systems); Karen Y. Kauper, Note, "Protecting the Independence of ALJs," 18 U.Mich.J.L.Rev. 537 (1985); Michael Asimow, "Toward a New California Administrative Procedure Act: Adjudication Fundamentals," 39 UCLA L.Rev. 1067, 1181-90 (1992) (California's smoothly functioning central panel should not be expanded to cover additional agencies); Gerard E. Ruth, "Unification of the Administrative Adjudicatory Process: An Emerging Framework to Increase 'Judicialization' in Pennsylvania," 5 Widener J.Pub.L. 297 (1996) (urging a central panel for Pennsylvania). Particularly helpful is Harold Levinson, "The Central Panel System," 65 Judicature 236 (1981), which surveys the central panel states as of the early 1980's.

Many articles about a proposed federal central panel (including the one by Simeone) are written by federal ALJs, most of whom are in favor of the proposal. They feel their status and independence would be enhanced if they worked for a central panel rather than for the agency for which they decide cases. No doubt, the public would be more favorably disposed toward central panel ALJs than toward judges who work for the agency that is prosecuting them. In general, it is fair to say that the central panels in the twenty-five or so states and cities that use them work well and are favorably viewed by counsel who practice before them. They are grudgingly tolerated by the agencies that must use central panel judges. This, at least, is Asimow's anecdotal impression and is based on considerable study of California's central panel.

ALJs at some federal agencies are opposed to a central panel. They do not want to be merged into an agency that would consist mostly of Social Security judges, and they want to continue deciding the cases for which they've been trained—not Social Security cases. *See, e.g.*, Norman Zankel, "A Unified Corps of Federal ALJs is Not Needed," 6 W. New Eng. L. Rev. 723 (1984); Alan W. Heifetz, "The Future of Administrative Adjudication," 1 Widener J.Pub.L. 13 (1992). Surprisingly, a majority of California workers' compensation judges did not favor being transferred to a central panel. Asimow, *supra*, at 1189.

In New York, the legislature repeatedly passed and the governor repeatedly vetoed central panel legislation. *See* Patrick J. Borchers & David L. Markell, NEW YORK STATE ADMINISTRATIVE PROCEDURE AND PRACTICE § 3.19 (2d ed. 1998). However, the City of New York has adopted a central panel.

One major advantage of a federal central panel is that it would help to solve the problems discussed in § 3.4.1. Hiring would be done by the central panel itself, rather than the agencies, so there would be less concern about selective certification. Therefore, the panel could be given greater latitude to choose from all names on the qualified list. And the judges would have less reason to resist evaluation done by the chief judge of the central panel, since, by definition, the evaluation would not be used to punish them for anti-agency decisions.

Transition to a central panel can be painful. If all former hearing officers are grandfathered, some mediocre personnel will find themselves promoted to hear complex cases beyond their level of competence (in accordance with the Peter Principle). If some form of evaluation is performed (thus easing out the less qualified), a major bloodletting is likely. This was the story of the transition to Civil Service Commission management of agency ALJs after the APA was adopted in 1946. *See* Ralph

F. Fuchs, "The Hearing Officer Fiasco under the APA," 63 Harv.L.Rev. 737 (1950).

On the federal level, the central panel approach is debatable. In addition to the dead weight losses arising from the transition to the new system, the advantages of the panel may be exaggerated. Verkuil et al. argue that ALJs are already sufficiently independent under the existing system. Anyone who has dealt with federal regulatory ALJs would probably concur with this evaluation. Simeone's arguments to the contrary are not persuasive.

Simeone's argument that a central panel would promote efficiency is dubious. The argument assumes that there are ALJs sitting around with nothing to do in some agencies while those in other agencies are overworked. But in fact it is likely that all of the ALJs are busy. And a central panel system is inherently inefficient, since it complicates the scheduling of hearings. Agencies have to phone up the central panel and arrange for a judge who may or may not be available when the agency has a need. Similarly, files have to be moved around more than if the judges are located in the same building as the agency.

Moreover, the issue of expertise is serious. SSA or black lung ALJs may not be competent to handle a complex FCC telephone case. Perhaps this can be handled by breaking up the panelists into groups to handle similar cases, but there will still be many cases in which ALJs must be educated about the fundamentals of the matter they are hearing. Although a judge can always be brought up to speed, are the costs and delays of doing so (and the inevitably higher rate of reversals) really worth it? Perhaps SSA (and other benefit-dispensing agencies) could be treated in a special category. Their ALJs could be broken off and employed by a central panel that would decide only SSA cases (and a few other benefit-type cases like black-lung or veterans claims). You can have an interesting discussion about specialist v. generalist administrative judges; the arguments on either side are sketched by Simeone and by Verkuil et al.

At the state level, the argument for central panels (particularly for licensing and other prosecutorial-type agencies) is stronger. In the states, there are many fewer guarantees of ALJ independence. Small licensing agencies may have only one or two part-time ALJs, and the judges may have other duties that conflict with judging. There might be significant efficiency gains from a central panel that could supply the ALJs as needed as well as have its own library, hearing rooms etc. ALJs can be effectively hired and evaluated within the central panel and, if expertise is needed, they can be divided into panels.

You should ask whether judges of the gaming board should be central panelists, assuming the state decides to adopt a panel. To really deal with disputes about cheating in gambling casinos, you have to know what you're doing. Having specialized and experienced judges would be a big help to this fledgling agency. Yet this is an area where the reality and perception of fairness is very important. The Gaming Board might be strengthened in the eyes of its constituents if it used independent ALJs.

One serious problem with the use of central panels concerns agency policies and guidelines that have never been formally adopted or even written down. ALJs attached to the agency know all about these policies; central panelists might not. Thus there might be more initial decisions departing from agency policies that would have to be corrected by the agency on review. For example, the agency may have penalty guidelines to assure consistent penalties for the same type of offenses. Central panel ALJs who do not have guidance will render inconsistent penalty decisions. This is an even more serious problem under the administrative court model, discussed below. The answer is i) adopt the policies as rules, or ii) introduce testimony about them at the hearing, or iii) file briefs setting forth previous decisions which enunciated the policies.

Whether ALJs (central panel or in-house) must follow policies of the agency that have not been embodied in binding rules is a contentious issue. ALJs argue that they should not be required to follow agency guidance documents (or other policies that haven't been written at all), while agencies say that the judges must follow all agency policies regardless of whether they have been formalized. For a decision that falls squarely on the agency side of this argument, see *Asmussen v. Commissioner, Dep't of Safety*, 766 A.2d 678, 692-95 (N.H.2000).

Asmussen held that there was nothing wrong with the agency head's communicating procedural and evidentiary instructions to the agency's judges, because they did not involve specific pending cases. Thus the instructions were not forbidden ex parte contacts and did not create bias through prejudgment. However, the court said that some of the instructions (such as that the hearsay rule should not be followed) were substantive changes binding on persons outside the agency and thus were an invalid attempt to adopt a rule without going through rulemaking proceedings.

§ 3.4.3 ALJs: The Administrative Court Issue

Consideration of central panels leads smoothly into a more radical reform: stripping agencies of adjudicatory power. We do have models: the Tax Court, Occupational Safety & Health Review Commission, and Federal Mine Safety and Health Review Commission at the federal level. At the state level, many agencies are engaged only in adjudication, and several states provide for ALJ finality or limit agency power to overturn ALJ fact findings. The general consensus is that the federal Tax Court (which hears appeals of tax cases from the IRS, which is the enforcement and prosecuting agency) works very well but that other federal schemes that split adjudicatory and enforcement powers have not worked well.

Many scholars do not agree with split-enforcement models. In addition to Verkuil's discussion in the text, see Carl A. Auerbach, "Some Thoughts on the Hector Memorandum," 1960 Wis.L.Rev. 183; Sidney A. Shapiro & Thomas O. McGarity, "Reorienting OSHA: Regulatory Alternatives and Legislative Reform," 6 Yale J. on Reg. 1 (1989); Asimow, *supra*, 39 UCLA L. Rev. 1067, 1152-64 (1992). Asimow observes that in many instances (such as workers' compensation and unemployment benefits) California has already split the adjudication and law enforcement functions into separate agencies. However, the article opposes further external separation of functions, especially in professional licensing. A cockeyed California split-enforcement agency was described in *Quintanar* in § 3.3.4—an Alcoholic Beverage Control Department that is responsible for enforcement and the the initial adjudicatory decision; followed by a specialized administrative court to hear appeals from those decisions; followed by judicial review.

The problems encountered by OSHRC and OSHA, which feuded over policy, seem endemic to a system which splits rulemaking from adjudication. The Supreme Court resolved a big circuit split in *Martin v. OSHRC*, 499 U.S. 144 (1991). In this case, OSHA (the rulemaking and enforcement agency) and OSHRC (an independent court for OSHA cases) disagreed on how to construe language in the regulations. To which entity should the courts give the strong deference accorded to an agency's interpretation of its own rules? The Court decided that OSHA's interpretation would prevail since it made the rules. The deference normally given to an agency when it adjudicates doesn't apply to OSHRC; it isn't like the traditional unitary agency to which Congress delegated law and policy making powers in either its rulemaking or adjudicatory functions.

And consider Missouri: in a case of license discipline, the case is heard by AHC—then reheard by the licensing agency which has to set the level of punishment. This does not make sense. The Project in Mo.L.Rev. also indicates that disagreements between licensing agencies and the AHC were quite common; the agencies find AHC unsympathetic or unqualified in the niceties of professional practices for the various professions that are regulated.

In *State Board of Registration for the Healing Arts v. Finch,* 514

S.W.2d 608 (Mo.Ct.App.1974), a California doctor served ten years in prison for murdering his wife, and then relocated to a town in Missouri. The Board denied his application for a medical license on the ground that it was "not suitable or appropriate to the best interests of the people of the State of Missouri to paradoxically permit an individual who has brutally murdered his wife to reenter the practice of medicine—a profession which peculiarly and uniquely is dedicated to the prolongation of human life." The AHC reversed, finding "overwhelming evidence" of rehabilitation on the basis of a psychiatric report and numerous character testimonials from local residents. A divided court affirmed the AHC. It conceded that evaluation of Dr. Finch's character would have been within the Board's discretion in past years, but the creation of the AHC had changed the situation. Rejecting the argument that the AHC's role was merely to find facts, the court said it was "inconceivable that the legislature intended any separation of the exercise of discretion from the determination of facts which are necessarily preliminary to and decisive of how that discretion is to be exercised." For a favorable evaluation of the AHC, *see* Frederick Davis, "Judicialization of Administrative Law: The Trial-Type Hearing and the Changing Status of the Hearing Officer," 1977 Duke L.J. 389, 402-08. For a historical account, see Eugene G. Bushmann, "The Origin of the Administrative Hearing Commission," J.Mo. Bar (Nov-Dec. 2006).

The Louisiana/South Carolina model giving final decisional power to ALJs may be a trend that will spread to other states. We understand that the South Carolina 1993 reform resulted from the fact that there was great dissatisfaction with agency adjudication and the low quality of decisionmaking by agency heads. However, because the various boards were popular with the governor for patronage reasons, they were not abolished. Instead, they were emasculated. Central panel ALJ's are now the policymakers in South Carolina. Either they make the final decision at the agency level or their proposed order is subject to very limited review at the agency head level—the same scope of review a court would have (i.e., arbitrary and capricious, substantial evidence, etc.). Obviously, there is an enormous incentive for agency heads to adopt rules to avoid turning over the policymaking function to unspecialized, inexpert central panel ALJs. South Carolina takes a different approach in professional licensing cases; there the agency heads make the agency decision and the ALJs serve as an administrative court that reviews those decisions. Evidently, therefore, agency heads can still make policy in licensing cases.

The Gaming Board probably should retain adjudicatory power. Agencies make policy through adjudication as well as rulemaking. A new agency is especially likely to need to do so, because many policy questions must be resolved. Agencies should use rulemaking whenever possible, but it is not always feasible to do so. *See* § 6.2. The Gaming Board cannot be expected to anticipate and solve every problem through a prior rule that would control the adjudicating agency; it should be allowed to muddle its way through to the right approach through case-by-case adjudication. Thus the Louisiana/South Carolina model (stripping agency heads of the power to set policy through adjudication) should not be followed, at least in this instance. A lack of expertise among the administrative court judges would be a concern. The same problem applied to the central panel proposal—but at least errors could be corrected by the agency upon review. That would no longer be possible in the case of an administrative court.

CHAPTER 4: THE PROCESS OF
ADMINISTRATIVE ADJUDICATION

§ 4.1 THE PRE-HEARING PHASE: NOTICE, INVESTIGATION AND DISCOVERY

§ 4.1.1 Notice and Parties to Adjudication

BLOCK v. AMBACH

Harmless error. Cases involving notice issues often must consider whether a defect in giving notice was a harmless error or whether the defect is sufficiently prejudicial so that a reviewing court should vacate the agency decision and require it to start over. See the *University of Wisconsin* case discussed in N.3 of text and manual. In a case decided after the text was completed but before the manual went to press, the Supreme Court clarified the harmless error issue in a case involving defective notice by the VA. *Shinseki v. Sanders*, 129 S.Ct. 1696 (2009). The case arose out of a claim for veterans' benefits. The VA's regulations require elaborate notice after a vet applies for benefits. Among other points, the reg requires that the notice must indicate what additional information is needed and which portion of the information must be provided by the applicant and which portion the VA will attempt to obtain. A statute provides that the Veterans Court shall "take due account of the rule of prejudicial error." 38 U.S.C. § 7261(b)(2).

In the two cases before the Supreme Court in *Sanders*, the VA failed to comply with the notice regulation. The Board of Veterans' Appeals rejected the applications. The Veterans Court held the error was harmless, but the Court of Appeals for the Federal Circuit reversed. Relying on its prior cases, the CAFC held that where the VA notice is deficient in any respect, the Veterans Court should presume the error was prejudicial, unless the VA can show that the error did not affect the essential fairness of the adjudication. The Supreme Court rejected the CAFC formulation, holding that § 7261(b)(2) is equivalent to the APA's harmless error provision. APA § 706 provides: ". . . due account shall be taken of the rule of prejudicial error."

Under both § 706 and § 7261(b)(2), and in civil cases generally, a petitioner (the applicant for benefits here), not the respondent, has the burden of showing that an error was prejudicial. Moreover, the Court held that there is no presumption that any particular type of error is harmful and that the sort of rigid presumptions and rules applied by CAFC in this case are inappropriate.

The Court remarked that the Veterans Court could rely on an empirically based analysis of the "natural effect" of various types of notice errors, but that is up to the Veterans Court, not the CAFC. This conclusion was strengthened by the limited scope of review that CAFC exercises over

Veterans Court decisions. CAFC can review Veterans Court decisions only if an alleged error concerns "the validity of . . . any statute or regulation. . .or any interpretation thereof." But harmless error determinations are highly case specific, and "it is the Veterans Court, not the Federal Circuit, that sees sufficient case-specific raw material in veterans' cases to enable it to make empirically based, nonbinding generalizations about 'natural effects.' And the Veterans Court, which has exclusive jurisdiction over these cases, is likely better able than is the Federal Circuit to exercise an informed judgment as to how often veterans are harmed by which kinds of notice errors."

The three dissenters in *Sanders* said that the VA is different from other agencies in that it is obliged to help the claimant develop his claim and must give the claimant the benefit of the doubt. This thumb-on-the-scale rule suggests that interpretive doubts about the prejudicial error statute must be resolved in the veteran's favor. The dissenters thought that the CAFC formulation did not create a rigid and unworkable system and has the added virtue of giving the VA a strong incentive to comply with the notice obligations.

Notes and Questions

1. *Six years?* It's worth discussing the shocking fact that it took six years to conduct the hearing, not to mention additional years of administrative and judicial review, before Ackerman's license was revoked. Licensing agencies are often terribly under-funded relative to the task of patrolling an entire industry, such as New York medical practice. And the agencies are often quite forgiving. The agency heads are members of the affected industry and sometimes think "there but for the grace of God go I."

Regulated parties have every incentive to drag things out—and are often prepared to pay unlimited counsel fees to do so. While the Board undoubtedly had some kind of interim suspension power, it may well not have utilized it, absent a showing that Ackerman was killing patients. And the courts may well have granted a stay pending at least some of the judicial review stages, out of concern that the revocation order would destroy Ackerman's practice. If he is ultimately vindicated on judicial review, it would be too late to unscramble the omelet. The result is that licensees like Ackerman, who should be removed from practice (assuming the charges against him are true), can drag out the process of license revocation for many long years, during which the public is unprotected.

2. *Statute of limitations.* Charges of sexual misconduct (whether in employment, professional licensing, or family law) are easy to make and hard to disprove. This is especially true if the alleged misconduct occurred many years in the past. Such charges are not always true, but they can

155

destroy the career of the person charged. On the other hand, a short statute of limitations on charges of this sort might prevent the agency from taking action, because the victims are often not anxious to report the charges (which are personally humiliating). Yet the misconduct may have affected many patients over a long period of years, thus invoking powerful public protection arguments. Or the misconduct may well have occurred when the victims were children who might not be able to or know how to report the transgressions. So the question of whether there should be a statute of limitations on this type of case is not a simple one.

The *BP American* case indicates that courts should not reach out to impose a limitations period on administrative action when the legislature has not done so. Under 28 U.S.C. § 2415(a), "Every *action* for money damages brought by the United States or an agency thereof . . . [is subject to a 6-year statute of limitations]." The court said that the term "action" applies to litigation in court, not to administrative litigation designed to recover the same type of royalties that could be recovered in court. It distinguished cases where the statute in question applied to "proceedings." The Court said: "To the extent that any doubts remain regarding the meaning of § 2415(a), they are erased by the rule that statutes of limitations are construed narrowly against the government. . . . This canon is rooted in the traditional rule *quod tertium tempus occurrit regi*—time does not run against the King. . . . A corollary of this rule is that when the sovereign elects to subject itself to a statute of limitations, the sovereign is given the benefit of the doubt if the scope of the statute is ambiguous."

An interesting federal case that seems inconsistent with *BP American* is *3M Co. v. Browner*, 17 F.3d 1453 (D.C.Cir.1994). The Toxic Substances Control Act imposes no statute of limitations on EPA's collection of civil penalties. The court borrowed a 150-year-old statute imposing a five-year limitation period, which was applicable to an "action, suit, or proceeding for the enforcement of any civil fine, penalty, forfeiture. . . " The court held that this statute was applicable to administrative proceedings as well as proceedings in court (because the statute uses the term "proceeding," it is distinguishable from the statute in *BP American*, which uses the word "action"). The D.C. Circuit also refused to toll the statute during the period in which EPA was unaware of the violation. The subtext of the *3M* case is that there should be a statute of limitations on administrative enforcement actions, but *BP American* seems inconsistent with that notion.

Using a laches approach may be better than importing a statute of limitations into administrative enforcement proceedings. Laches requires the agency to move quickly to charge someone once it obtains inculpatory information. If it just sits on the information for years, it may lose the ability to prosecute if the delay has caused prejudice to the licensee.

3. *Notice.* Ackerman used this argument as a tactic; not knowing the actual dates on which misconduct occurred probably did not prejudice him. The dates are of little significance, since it's unlikely that Ackerman would claim to have an alibi for each of the dates in question. But if he did wish to assert an alibi, the dates could be critical. The Board probably did not know the dates, since the victims did not keep a diary. Even if it knew the dates, the Board should not be required to produce a lengthy and complex pleading containing details of each instance of sexual misconduct. The goals of administrative procedure are speed and informality—obviously goals that weren't achieved in this case!

You may wish to contrast cases like *General Electric Co. v. EPA*, 53 F.3d 1324 (D.C.Cir.1995), discussed in § 4.4 N.5. *GE* involved a $25,000 civil penalty imposed by EPA for disposing of PCBs in violation of EPA regulations. The court upheld EPA's interpretation of the regulations. Nevertheless, GE's interpretation was reasonable, too. The court held that the regulations failed to furnish proper notice; consequently, the imposition of a penalty violated due process. The agency has to issue interpretive rules or otherwise bring its interpretation to the company's attention before penalizing the company for a violation. So this is an example of a quasi-criminal law fair notice requirement being imported into administrative law.

Generally, administrative enforcement cases do not have to follow criminal law norms regardless of the severity of the penalty. *See, e.g., Flying Food Group v. NLRB*, 471 F.3d 178 (D.C.Cir.2006) (pleadings in administrative proceedings not judged by the standards of an indictment; it is sufficient if petitioner understood the issue and was afforded the opportunity to justify its conduct during the hearing). In addition to the inapplicability of the criminal law notice standard, the subject of administrative law enforcement has no right to appointed counsel or a jury or to refuse to take the stand (only to refuse to answer incriminating questions) or numerous other criminal law protections. Yet the sanction of license revocation is economic capital punishment—more serious in the long run than even a short jail term. Even though criminal law protections don't apply, courts should assure that basic norms of fair adjudicatory procedure be observed (whether they are derived from statute or due process).

The double jeopardy point is interesting. In a criminal case, you'd need to know the dates, because if you're acquitted, the government couldn't prosecute again for those specific violations. Double jeopardy doesn't apply in administrative cases, but if Ackerman won the first case, the Board would be collaterally estopped to recharge him with those instances. So you'd have to know just what he's been charged with. Arguably, under res judicata, the Board might be barred from charging him with any other similar instances that could have been included in the first case.

The Wisconsin case in the text seems questionable, because what happened seems non-prejudicial. B has already won on the merits of the hostile work environment claim arising out of telling racist jokes. The only issue is the amount of backpay he's owed. Say that as a result of the jokes, he was terminated on January 1, Year 1. He won reinstatement as a result of the State Personnel Commission decision on December 31, Year 4. Thus he would be owed four years of back pay. The employer has learned that B was guilty of a different offense for which it would have fired him on January 1, Year 2. Thus the employer reasons that B is entitled to back pay for only one year instead of four. But this is the equivalent of asserting a new and completely separate offense about which B has not received notice.

The Wisconsin court thought that statutory and constitutional norms applied to the decision to charge B with the new offense (even though it was only for purpose of computing backpay with respect to the first offense, not for actually firing him). The dissent thought B had received ample notice about the issue of taking files home. Perhaps it hadn't occurred to B that the issue would come up in the back pay hearing, but he was well prepared to contest the merits because the parties had already been fighting over the issue and B anticipated that the University would file a separate state court replevin action to recover the files.

One good way to have handled the situation would be to allow the University to amend its pleading to conform to proof and given B additional time, if needed, to respond. Whether or not provided for in APAs, amendment of pleadings is generally permitted in administrative cases. This liberality accords with modern principles of civil procedure. *See* Fed. R. Civ. P. 15(b) (amendments of pleadings to conform to proof should be freely allowed unless opposing party shows that admission of evidence on a new issue would prejudice that party's case; and continuances may be allowed as needed).

A deeper point to make about the case is that it shows the manipulation of procedural rules in order to achieve what a court considers a just result. Perhaps the majority in the Wisconsin case felt that B had been picked on enough for relatively non-serious behavior (telling crude jokes). The dissent, on the other hand, written by a female justice, appeared to believe that the offense (creating a hostile work environment) was quite serious and the rules shouldn't be stretched to give B a break.

The majority distinguished *McKennon v. Nashville Banner Pub. Co.*, 513 U.S. 352 (1995), which allowed introduction of after-acquired evidence of a separate offense to limit a back pay award in a discrimination case. The basis of the distinction was that the employee in question in *McKennon* was an employee at will rather than a civil service employee whose job was protected by due process. The case did not involve the issue of proper notice, just the issue of whether the new evidence could limit back pay. The dissent persuasively argued that *McKennon* should apply to B's case.

4. *Forcing a hearing.* What's being discussed here is often referred to as a "right of initiation." A might very well want to force the Board to hold a hearing against Ackerman, simply to help in her own healing process or out of a sense of personal responsibility toward other innocent victims of Ackerman's gross sexual misconduct.

But A might have an economic incentive also. She might be suing Ackerman in tort. If Ackerman is found to have violated the medical board regulations, this determination could be very helpful in the tort action. A might well have the benefit of affirmative collateral estoppel (discussed in § 4.4.1). She might be able to use the administrative findings against Ackerman as evidence of negligence per se or of violation of relevant medical standards. Ackerman might make crucial admissions during the administrative hearing that could be used against him in the tort case. At the least, the ongoing administrative case would put pressure on Ackerman to settle the tort case.

Obviously, Ackerman would resist a private prosecution. If he has persuaded the Medical Board not to file charges against him, he would bitterly resent being forced into an administrative hearing by A, especially if there's a pending tort case. The Medical Board would also seek to avoid holding a hearing, because A is commandeering its scarce resources for a case that it chose not to bring. If the Board found the evidence was too weak to proceed (or the violation was not serious enough compared to others to justify expending its limited resources), it certainly would resist being forced into a hearing anyway. Generally the same reasons that counsel against private criminal prosecutions should apply in the administrative area as well.

A different result might be appropriate in the case of license applications, as illustrated by the *United Church* and *Envirocare* cases in the next note. For example, members of the public often have a right to force a hearing with respect to applications for liquor licenses; the community may feel there's already an overconcentration of liquor stores or bars. And third parties should have initiation rights in land use cases, especially ones triggering significant environmental consequences.

In 2005 Nevada adopted an interesting statute that probably reflected the political power of organized professional groups that wanted to keep victims from initiating or intervening in license disciplinary proceedings. It provided that no person could be admitted as a party to such a proceeding unless he demonstrated that his financial situation was likely to be *improve* as a direct result of *granting or renewing* the license, or that his financial situation was likely to *deteriorate* as a direct result of the *denial or non-renewal* of the license. Nev.Rev.Stat.Ann. § 233B.127(4) (2005 Cum. Supp). In other words, nobody could either initiate or intervene in a proceeding involving initial licensing or license renewal unless that person's interest was aligned with that of the applicant, as opposed to being adverse to that of the applicant. Evidently the unfairness of this situation became impossible to sustain, however, because the statute was repealed two years later.

5. *Intervention*. A might wish to intervene as a party for the same reasons that she wishes to initiate the hearing—to have some control over what happens and possibly to enhance her chances of using the case as res judicata. She may feel the Board's staff is insufficiently attentive to the interest of victims. She may want to cross-examine Ackerman and the other witnesses herself or bring in additional witnesses or victims that the Board overlooked. Ackerman and the Board would resist intervention, because A's participation would complicate the hearing. Since it took 6 years to finish the process, the last thing the Board wants is further complication.

As to res judicata, see § 4.4.1. If A is a party to the administrative case, the decision will be preclusive of later tort litigation. If the Board finds violations of the Medical Practice Act, the findings should be binding on those issues in the subsequent tort case. And if the Board finds no violations, Ackerman should be able to use these findings preclusively against A.

If A is not a party, however, the collateral estoppel issue is more difficult. There is some authority that permits a non-party consumer to use findings in an administrative case against a licensee in subsequent litigation. See *Imen v. Glassford*, 247 Cal.Rptr. 514 (Cal.App.1988) (real estate broker disciplined for fraud—victim entitled to collateral estoppel with respect to fraud issue in later tort case). See the discussion of non-mutual collateral estoppel in § 4.4.1.

As to the burdens on the agency of intervention, *see generally* Jim Rossi, "Participation Run Amok: The Costs of Mass Participation for Deliberative Agency Decisionmaking," 92 Nw.U.L.Rev. 173 (1997) (discussing the negative effects of excessive public participation on the deliberative function under the civic republican model); Lars Noah, "Sham Petitioning as a Threat to the Integrity of the Regulatory Process," 74 N.C. L.Rev. 1 (1995) (petitioning before the FDA is used as a competitive tool); David L. Shapiro, "Some Thoughts on Intervention Before Courts, Agencies and Arbitrators," 81 Harv.L.Rev. 721 (1968).

You may want to contrast material on agency intervention with Fed. R. Civ. P. 24, with which most students will be familiar. Rule 24 contains provision for both mandatory and permissive intervention and parallels 1981

MSAPA § 4-209(a) and (b). Under Rule 24(a)(2), intervention must be allowed if the applicant "claims an interest relating to the property or transaction that is the subject of the action, and is so situated that disposing of the action may as a practical matter impair or impede the movant's ability to protect its interest, unless existing parties adequately represent that interest." See *San Juan County v. U.S.*, 503 F.3d 1163 (10th Cir.2007), which concerned intervention by an environmental group in a federal lawsuit by which a county sought to quiet title against the federal government to a right-of-way in a national park. The case produced five opinions, but the bottom line was that the federal government (under the George W. Bush administration) adequately protected the interests of the environmental group, so that it could not intervene under Rule 24.

Compare *Coalition of Arizona/New Mexico Counties for Stable Economic Growth v. Dep't of the Interior*, 100 F.3d 837 (10th Cir.1996), with *Solid Waste Agency of Northern Cook County v. U.S. Army Corps of Engineers*, 101 F.3d 503 (7th Cir.1996). Both cases hold that an intervenor in an agency enforcement action in court met the required "interest" test. In *Coalition*, it's a naturalist who specializes in protecting the spotted owl. In *Solid Waste*, it's neighbors concerned about a landfill. But the cases split on whether the "interest is adequately represented by existing parties." In *Coalition*, the court held that the Interior Department did not adequately represent the naturalist's interest because it had been reluctant to protect the owl. In *Solid Waste*, however, the court thought the Corps of Engineers adequately protected the neighbors' interests.

There is an important distinction between the two issues described in NN. 4 and 5 (triggering an adjudication and intervening in ongoing adjudication). An agency is burdened if a third party forces a hearing or agency appeal that otherwise would not have occurred (as in the case of the agency's refusal to prosecute a licensee or in case of an agency decision to grant a license application or renewal). Intervention poses less of a burden, because there is already an ongoing proceeding.

Yet the burden of accommodating intervenors can be substantial. See the USF Comment cited in text for an example in the NRC licensing context. Each new party to the proceeding may introduce new issues, call more witnesses, cross-examine other witnesses, produce more documents, make oral arguments. Each new litigant has a busy schedule into which agency proceedings must be fitted—thus probably requiring continuances. And, as in the NRC context, intervenors (whether environmental or economically motivated) often have a stake in delaying an otherwise inevitable result, so may adopt delaying strategies.

There are several ways for persons to take part in an administrative hearing short of becoming a party through intervention. Especially in land use cases, agencies generally welcome public participation. One could file an amicus brief or simply seek the right to make a statement without becoming a party. Or one could contribute to the attorneys' fees of the parties. APA § 555(b) provides a right to "appear before an agency" to "an interested person" in any sort of agency proceeding, including adjudication, but only "so far as the orderly conduct of public business permits." Cal. Gov't Code § 11440.50(f) allows agencies to adopt regulations allowing participation by a person short of intervention. The *United Church of Christ* case deprecated these techniques of non-party participation, but they may in fact be a cost-effective method of influencing the result.

The *United Church of Christ* case (written by former Chief Justice Warren Burger while he was on the D.C. Circuit) leads into a general discussion of the benefits and costs of public participation in the administrative process. An important theme here is the "interest group" or pluralist political model. See § 1.6, which discusses pluralism as a legitimating model for the administrative process. You can use *United Church of Christ*, intervention in nuclear power plant licensing, and the problem in N.6 about the Coastal Commission as examples of the use of administrative adjudication to vindicate interest group politics. If we assume that agency rulemaking and initial licensing adjudications are inherently political contests, perhaps the agency should be compelled to hear and accommodate all interested groups (as a legislature would). A political, interest-group based approach suggests broad participation by all interest groups. This would include those in the Coastal problem in N.6 who do not live at the beach. Perhaps *Envirocare* reflects current skepticism about the pluralist model.

Envirocare might be used to discuss the zone of interests test under standing doctrine if this makes sense in the organization of your course, but it would be premature if you are following the organization of the casebook. If you skip it now, you could refer back to it when you get to standing. The NRC initially denied Envirocare standing to intervene because it thought the company would have failed the zone test for purposes of standing to seek judicial review. It contended that only persons concerned with safety, not economic competitors, are within the zone of interests test. In a subsequent case, NRC decided that it could deny standing to intervene independent of whether a person had standing to seek judicial review, and the D.C. Circuit upheld this approach.

For a good discussion of *Envirocare, see* Jordan's article cited in the text, 30 E.L.R. 10597 (2000). Jordan contends that the NRC was correct to deny Envirocare standing to intervene even if it had standing to seek judicial review, because the NRC need not consider the economic interest of competitors. In addition, Envirocare's participation threatened negative efficiency consequences. Nevertheless, Jordan objects to the use of *Chevron* analysis in this context, because, as *United Church of Christ* showed, mission-oriented agencies may abuse discretion in excluding appropriate parties such as TV viewers that it would prefer not to be bothered with. *Chevron* deference prevents courts from patrolling this sort of exclusionary decision and thus threatens the legitimacy of agency regulation. Despite ambiguity in the term "interest," Congress could not have intended to delegate this sort of decision to agencies.

On the connection between standing and intervention, see Carl Tobias, "Standing to Intervene," 1991 Wis.L.Rev. 415 (1991) (criticizing cases linking intervention as of right with standing criteria); Patricia A. Dore, "Access to Florida Administrative Proceedings," 13 Fla.St.U.L.Rev. 965 (1986) (criticizing Florida cases that assimilate the issues). Standing to seek judicial review is encumbered with constitutional constraints that have no place in determining party status.

6. *Problem*. The Commission should consider encouraging non-party participation by techniques such as filing an amicus brief or making a statement (oral or written) at an agency public hearing. These methods of non-party participation were deprecated in *United Church of Christ*, but they may be adequate for the purposes of the third party. They allow the participant to avoid shouldering the costs of full-fledged participation as a party in an administrative process that may go on for years.

An agency that wants to limit public participation should explore the adoption of rules that indicate who can be an intervenor and how the agency will select among several competing intervenors. It might want assurances that an intervenor is well financed, so it can see the case through and hire experts, etc. It might ask for a track record to assure that an intervenor will be responsible. A record of non-constructive participation in past proceedings would be a good reason for exclusion. The Commission might wish to limit intervention to organizations, rather than individuals, and only those with a reasonably large and representative membership.

The Commission might want to draw a distinction between intervenors who support and those who oppose an application. Supporters of the application probably will have less to contribute than opponents. It should assess whether the interest which an intervenor seeks to protect is adequately protected by other parties or the staff; what contribution the intervenor can make; and the degree of delay or confusion that its participation might entail.

The agency should also adopt procedural rules that allow a presiding officer to impose conditions on intervenors. For example, if there is more than one intervenor, the presiding officer could require them to combine their presentations or allow only one of them to cross-examine witnesses or make oral arguments. Presentation of repetitious material could be precluded. Intervenors could be limited as to the issues on which they can participate. They could be barred from participating in settlement negotiations. The presiding officer could be empowered to reject requests for continuances from intervenors. Their discovery rights could be limited. *But see Citizens' Utility Ratepayer Bd. (CURB) v. State Corp. Comm'n*, 941 P.2d 424 (Kan.App.1997), finding a restriction on discovery by intervenors to be an abuse of discretion. The case involved determination of a phone company's costs for ratemaking purposes. CURB was allowed to intervene but was denied access to the company's cost data. The court said that there was no indication that allowing access to the data would be unduly burdensome or that denial would serve the purpose of prompt and orderly proceedings. Participation without access to this key data "can hardly be viewed as meaningful."

Agencies often raise floodgate arguments, complaining they will be swamped by intervenors. However, this is unlikely. The costs of participation are so substantial, and funding for public interest intervenors is so scarce, that the Commission probably will not be inundated. On the other hand, this concern cannot be summarily dismissed. Intervention has been a real problem at the Nuclear Regulatory Commission and in some local environmental impact cases, as discussed by Rossi. NRC's concerns in *Envirocare* about delaying tactics by competitors are valid. That's why having an arsenal of measures in place to condition intervention is so important.

The Commission's problem might be more a lack of public participation than the contrary. Members of the public may be able to contribute a perspective that an overworked staff has failed to press. So perhaps you should try to calm down your bosses and tell them that the problem they are worried about isn't so serious and can be readily handled by the sort of procedural rules discussed above. Maybe there will be a problem in a few cases, but it won't happen very often.

§ 4.1.2 Investigation and Discovery: An Agency's Power to Obtain Information

CRAIB v. BULMASH

Craib raises a number of interesting issues.

i) Mosk's dissent focuses on state constitutionalism. The majority opinion in *Scott* (N.5 in text) raises the same point. State courts relying on state constitutions can provide elevated levels of protection beyond those provided by identical provisions of the federal constitution. *See also* § 2.1 N.

6, concerning state constitution due process clauses.

The interesting issue is when and whether state courts *should* do so? In many cases, the state provision will be different or have a different legislative history than the federal provision. California has an explicit constitutional right of privacy that formed the basis for Mosk's argument for departing from *Shapiro*. Or federalism notions may inhibit the U.S. Supreme Court from imposing high uniform standards on every state (for example with respect to school financing); but state courts need not share this concern. In a famous article, Justice Brennan argued that the U.S. Supreme Court's retreat from Warren Court precedents should encourage state courts to step forward and restore the lost protections under state constitutions. "State Constitutions and Protection of Individual Rights," 90 Harv.L.Rev. 489 (1977). Many writers on state constitutions assert that state courts should construe the state constitution first; then look at U. S. Supreme Court precedents second.

We do not believe that state courts should depart from U.S. Supreme Court precedents without a substantial justification—which can include a strong conviction that the U.S. decision is wrong. There is a value in uniformity, and to some degree the U.S. Supreme Court deserves a position of national leadership in construing identical constitutional language; but this merely puts a thumb on the scales. Check the dissent in *Scott*—it's an impassioned and strident attack on the idea of state constitutionalism.

ii) *Craib* is a nice case because it involves facts that students can easily relate to. Here's Bulmash—who is paying for his sister's caregiver and asserts a right of privacy against the intrusive demands by the Labor Commissioner to inspect his payroll records (which may not exist or which may be difficult to locate). Probably he's struggling to care for a disabled sibling; this isn't a big business transaction by any means.

Here's Craib—who suspects that Bulmash hasn't paid minimum wage or overtime or employment taxes (employers of in-home service-providers commonly fail to discharge these responsibilities—as numerous federal appointees to political office have discovered to their sorrow). Craib wants to protect domestic caretakers—a segment of the labor market traditionally helpless to bargain for itself and very subject to exploitation. How can Craib possibly prove that Bulmash failed to pay minimum wage—and thus get the money for the caregiver—unless he can inspect Bulmash's records?

iii) *Craib* shows how very limited are the constitutional protections against administrative investigation. The Fourth Amendment hardly exists—Craib need only show the demanded documents are relevant to a matter he's entitled to investigate. There's no need for a warrant (not even the watered-down variety that applies to administrative physical searches), no showing of probable cause, no factfinding by the court about whether Bulmash or the caregiver is even covered by the law. There is the possibility of getting the judge to scale down the subpoena if it's too burdensome, but that would call for a vastly greater demand than we've got here. The problem in N.8 illustrates a subpoena that might be limited as too burdensome. Some cases suggest that the state may be somewhat more constrained when it demands documents from an individual than from a corporation, but the *Craib* case rejects that possibility out of hand.

The Fifth Amendment is almost never helpful either. As pointed out in n.14 of *Craib* and in text at N.4 ¶ iv, even without the required records exception of *Shapiro*, the Fifth Amendment doesn't apply to the contents of business records (and probably not to personal papers either), only to possible incrimination from producing the records. It is questionable whether there would be any such incrimination from producing the sort of records involved in this case. But we don't even get to that under *Shapiro*. The Fifth Amendment doesn't apply at all, because the records in question are required to be kept. Here you can have a good discussion of whether the Fifth Amendment should apply—covering both the *Doe* rule that the Fifth doesn't apply to the contents of documents and the *Shapiro* rule that says the Fifth doesn't apply to required records.

In discussing *Craib*, the issue should be put into perspective for the class. Realistically, the chance of criminal prosecution is nil. Craib just wants Bulmash to pay wages and overtime plus employment taxes, possibly with some penalties; he's not interested in putting him in jail. Criminal sanctions for minimum wage violations would be reserved only for egregious repeat sweatshop-type offenders—and is really unheard of even there. Therefore, the Fifth Amendment arguments in *Craib* seem attenuated. On the other hand, Craib should be willing to grant Bulmash use immunity if he produces the documents; he really has nothing to lose by making that offer, and doing so would satisfy Justice Mosk.

Notes and Questions

1. *Judicial enforcement.* There is further discussion of judicial enforcement in connection with the problem below. Whether agencies should enjoy the contempt power, or the power to enforce their own subpoenas, is debatable. It would certainly streamline the investigatory process if agencies could enforce their own subpoenas. Investigated parties frequently force agencies to go to court to enforce subpoenas purely for purposes of delay and obstruction. On the other hand, a judicial check on investigation may be worthwhile. As discussed below, in extreme cases courts do restrain overzealous investigating agencies.

It is arguable whether an agency should be allowed to sanction a party that ignores a reporting requirement or a subpoena by holding against the party or denying it the right to introduce evidence. The agency could have gone to court to enforce the subpoena. If it fails to do so, but exacts a penalty for noncompliance, this could be equivalent to giving it the power to enforce its own subpoenas, which *Brimson* held it could not do. On the other hand, perhaps *Brimson* only denies contempt power, allowing an agency to impose less onerous sanctions, such as holding against the party or denying it the right to introduce evidence. This leaves the responsibility on the investigated party to go to court to restrain the investigation. If it fails to do so, and ignores the subpoena, perhaps it is justifiable to allow the agency to hold against the person.

2. *Defenses to subpoena enforcement.* There is additional material on these issues in connection with the problem in N.8 below.

Endicott Johnson Corp. v. Perkins, 317 U.S. 501 (1943), resoundingly echoes the message of *Oklahoma Press* (and the two cases are usually discussed together). *Endicott* makes clear that an agency need not establish probable cause to believe that a violation of law has occurred, nor that the subpoenaed person is subject to its jurisdiction, nor that the information sought would be relevant evidence in some future adjudication. It is sufficient that the information is gathered for a purpose that the agency is entitled to pursue (e.g. investigating to ascertain whether Bulmash paid minimum wage) and is reasonably relevant to that inquiry.

An interesting (and debatable) application of these principles occurred in *EEOC v. Sidley, Austin, Brown & Wood*, 315 F.3d 696 (7th Cir.2002), involving the EEOC's investigation of mega-law firm Sidley's demotion of thirty-two older partners. Whether this was prohibited age discrimination turned in part on whether the partners were "employers" or "employees." (The case was finally settled in 2007 when Sidley capitulated). The EEOC subpoenaed documents related both to coverage (that is, the employee issue) and to discrimination (whether the demotions were based on age or on permissible reasons). Judge Posner's opinion applied *Oklahoma Press* and *Endicott* and enforced the subpoenas relating to coverage, despite Sidley's claim that the issue was "jurisdictional." The agency is entitled to obtain documents that establish whether or not it has jurisdiction. It would only be prohibited from doing so if it were clear from the face of the subpoena that the agency had no jurisdiction because the partners had to be classified as employers—which was anything but clear. (Concurring in result, Judge Easterbrook thought it was clear that the partners were employers, not employees).

However, Posner believed it was "unreasonable" to enforce the subpoena insofar as it sought information about the merits (that is, whether the demotions were based on age discrimination) until the materials on coverage were first produced. If, based on those materials, the district court rules that the partners were not employees, Sidley would not have to comply with the demand for information about the merits.

The latter holding seems wrong in light of *Endicott* and *Oklahoma.* The EEOC, not the district court at the subpoena enforcement stage, should determine whether partners are "employees." Then, if it so determines, the EEOC can file charges and proceed against Sidley in district court. And it should be able to obtain information on the merits as well at the subpoena stage in order to decide whether to file that lawsuit. Posner's opinion allows the district court to shut down the lawsuit at the subpoena enforcement stage by ruling on the tricky issue of whether the partners are employees, but that approach seems contrary to *Endicott* and *Oklahoma Press.* These cases aim to streamline the subpoena stage by postponing all merits issues to a subsequent adjudicatory stage. Does *Sidley* demonstrate that judges offer a little more protection to fellow-lawyers than they would to other demandees?

3. *State law and investigative subpoenas.* In a subsequent case, the Medical Board again subpoenaed Dr. Levin's patient records. The Board made an in camera probable cause showing before the trial judge. It had a confidential informant, and disclosure of his identity would destroy his usefulness. Also premature disclosure might expose complainants to harassment or groundless lawsuits. The Appellate Division held that a "minimum threshold foundation" had been established and that in camera proceedings were appropriate. 492 N.Y.S.2d 749 (1985), *aff'd per curiam,* 499 N.Y.S.2d.680 (Ct.App. 1985), *cert. denied,* 476 U.S. 1171 (1986).

Bottom line: the original subpoena was issued in 1980 and only after cert. was denied in 1986 can the investigation proceed. Levin got six years of delay, during which he probably continued to practice (with potential damage to patients if he is unfit). Thus it can be argued that the New York courts were wrong in interfering with the agency investigation by requiring a showing of probable cause for the investigation. For discussion of *Levin,* see Patrick J. Borchard & David L. Markell, NEW YORK STATE ADMINISTRATIVE PROCEDURE AND PRACTICE § 6.3 (1998).

See also Bearman v. Superior Court, 11 Cal.Rptr.3d 644 (Cal.App. 2004), refusing to enforce a Medical Board subpoena to Dr. Bearman for his records concerning patient Nathan. The Board suspected Dr. Bearman of indiscriminately prescribing marijuana (he had prescribed it to treat Nathan's migraines and A.D.D.). The court held that the Medical Board must demonstrate through competent evidence that the particular records it seeks are relevant and material to its inquiry, so that the trial court can independently make a finding of good cause to order the materials disclosed. In part the decision relies on California's constitutional right to privacy, which can be infringed only to serve a compelling interest. Here the Board alleged no facts to support its contention that Bearman had indiscriminately prescribed marijuana. Mere suspicion that a violation might have occurred is not sufficient. However, decisions like *Levin* and *Bearman* are questionable. Doctors do sometimes prescribe controlled substances indiscriminately, and the Board cannot gather the necessary evidence without examining patient records.

You can have a good discussion about the question posed in the text about whether the older carte-blanche subpoena cases like *Oklahoma Press* are in tune with modern concepts of privacy and concern about intrusive government bureaucracies. We favor the *Oklahoma Press* approach and believe, as the preceding notes suggest, that regulatory agencies should have basically free rein to investigate, notwithstanding potential abuses like overzealous or vengeful bureaucrats. Regulated parties often have virtually unlimited resources to fight subpoenas and have every incentive to delay or obstruct governmental investigations into potential violations of health, safety, financial, tax, environmental, or worker protection laws. Meanwhile, regulatory agencies are often underfunded and overwhelmed with regulatory responsibilities and huge caseloads. It is not in the public interest to increase the agency's costs of handling that caseload. But class discussion will probably turn up students with a philosophical disposition to disagree with our approach.

4. *Privileges.* There is additional discussion of Fourth and Fifth amendment defenses in connection with the problem, N.8 below.

5. *Physical searches.* You might want to refer to some of the language of the New York court in *Scott.* It noted:

> The dissent's reliance on the "staggering" statistics [of] automobile theft in New York and the economic burdens such crime imposes are hardly a persuasive ground for relaxing [the State constitution's] proscription against unreasonable searches and seizures. The alarming increase of unlicensed weapons on our urban streets and the catastrophic rise in the use of crack cocaine and heroin are also matters of pressing social concern, but few would seriously argue that those unfortunate facets of urban life justify routine searches of pedestrians on the street. . . . Indeed the writs of assistance [which were general warrants in colonial times authorizing officials to search any residential or commercial premises and which induced the framers to adopt the Fourth Amendment] were themselves a response of the colonial government to an unprecedented wave of criminal smuggling. . . . Our responsibility in the judicial branch is not to respond to these temporary crises or to shape the law so as to advance the goals of law enforcement, but

rather to stand as a fixed citadel for constitutional rights. . . .

8. *Problem.* This problem is designed to cover all of the material on investigation and discovery.

a. *Background.* As introduction, one could contrast the various remedies that might be available against the practice of refusing to pay justified claims. A bad faith refusal to pay an insurance claim is tortious and in many states can give rise to punitive damages. See John Grisham's *The Rainmaker,* and the subsequent film, which involves a sleazy health insurance company whose policy was to refuse to pay valid claims. After the hero wins a monster judgment against the company, it then files for bankruptcy, so nobody recovers anything.

An administrative remedy is more effective. Tort actions are slow and costly. They overcompensate a few plaintiffs and their attorneys, while doing nothing for other victims. Class actions mostly seem to benefit attorneys rather than victims. The criminal law is ineffective. It is hard to convict a big company (with unlimited resources) of a crime. For example, it is not easy to prove beyond a reasonable doubt that management approved the practice.

No federal agency regulates insurance companies, a historic anomaly that is difficult to change because of the great lobbying power of the industry. State regulation historically has been toothless. Obviously it is difficult for a single state to effectively regulate an insurance company that operates in several states and that invariably has powerful political leverage on the legislatures of each such state. Thus militant enforcement is rare—and it is not surprising that Security is distressed to actually encounter it.

One good way to get aggressive enforcement is to elect the Insurance Commissioner. Crusading against insurance companies is always popular with the voters at election time. However, election of any administrative official creates many problems, particularly if state campaign finance law allows the candidates to raise money from companies that they will regulate. In addition, candidates are likely to make rash promises to the voters, which can result in overly zealous prosecutions after the election.

b. *Publicity.* A press release that MIC is investigating Security for refusing to pay claims could have a devastating economic effect and might trigger a barrage of lawsuits. A later press release announcing that the investigation had not turned up evidence of a violation would not undo the damage. Thus the threat to issue a press release may be a more potent remedy than any that the agency might ultimately order. And its political value to Gloria is obvious. The issue of agency publicity is discussed in §3.5.3 of text and manual. The majority opinion in the first *Cinderella* case upheld

170

an agency's right to publicize the fact that it was issuing a complaint; such publicity is within the agency's authority and is important to protect the public. It does not evidence agency prejudgment of the issues in the case. *See* Ernest Gellhorn, "Adverse Publicity by Administrative Agencies," 86 Harv. L.Rev. 1380, 1398-1419 (1973). Gellhorn discusses the use of publicity as a sanction and its value in building political support for the agency.

Under the majority view in the first *Cinderella* case, it is unlikely that a court would interfere with the issuance of an MIC press release signaling the beginning of an investigation. However, Judge Robinson's cautious concurring opinion in that case might be more promising. It said that the agency must not automatically publicize everything it does—it should do so only upon a calculated weighing of the damage to private industry as against protection of the public. Robinson voted to uphold the release because the FTC had specifically considered whether it should be issued, and it was fair, accurate, and in accordance with a consistent practice. If the FTC had singled out Cinderella for more severe publicity than others, it would have been a much different case.

Under Judge Robinson's approach, it can be argued that MIC should not publicize an *investigation*—even if it can publicize a *complaint*. An investigation is a tentative, early step. It may not turn up sufficient evidence to file a complaint. MIC does not know anything yet—that's why it's investigating. The damage to Security would seem to outweigh the benefit to the public from publicity at this time. A complaint is different—an investigation has turned up enough evidence to proceed; and the complaint itself would ordinarily be a public document. Note that MIC "sometimes" issues press releases about its investigations—thus there is lacking the consistent practice of publicizing every complaint which was relied on in *Cinderella*. As ACUS Rec. 73-1 points out, the real danger is that agencies will use publicity randomly, never having adopted rules or considering when it should be used.

Of course, if Security tries to enjoin the issuance of the press release, the resulting publicity from the litigation would do as much if not more damage than the press release itself.

c. *Judicial enforcement.* Tell Bill that MIC has no contempt power; it must go to court. Or Security could go to court first by moving to quash the subpoena. If Security loses at the trial court level, it could further delay matters by appealing. (*See Levin* in N.3.) Perhaps by the end of the appeal, a new commissioner will have been elected, or MIC will become weary of struggling and will drop the investigation. Or perhaps the Attorney General will disagree with the Insurance Commissioner about the scope of the subpoena sought by Gloria and refuse to seek enforcement.

Although the law is not favorable to resisting demands for documents, a particular trial judge may be sympathetic to a well-prepared defense (see Posner's opinion in *Sidley, Austin* discussed above in N.2), and appellate courts tend to defer to lower court discretion on subpoena enforcement issues. The cost of going to court is that Security will probably lose and perhaps become liable for MIC's attorneys' fees as well as its own, but the client will probably feel that is a small price to pay.

Prevailing law indicates that due process requires judicial enforcement of subpoenas—but query whether *Brimson* would be followed today. It may be a relic of bygone days with little current utility. Even though judicial enforcement is almost automatic, it provides demandees with a way to slow up agency investigations, clog the courts, and preoccupy busy government lawyers (like the staff of MIC and of the Attorney General in this problem). Modern due process analysis under *Mathews*, as well as separation of powers analysis, suggests that *Brimson* might not be followed.

d. *Coverage.* Security asserts that MIC has no power over insurance transactions in other states. MIC says it does have such power because Security's home office is in Madison. Can Security raise the coverage problem at the subpoena enforcement level? Not if it will get the subpoena-enforcing court involved in a factual inquiry. *See Oklahoma Press* and *Endicott-Johnson.* As in the case of exhaustion of remedies (§ 11.2.4), you must litigate the coverage question before the agency prior to obtaining judicial review. However, if the legal question of coverage can be determined from the face of the subpoena, the court may be willing to rule on the question. *See Major League Baseball,* N.2 of text. Compare, however, the questionable analysis in *Sidley, Austin,* N.2 above, which appears to allow the subpoena judge to shut down the case prematurely, if it determines from documents produced at the first stage of document production that the EEOC lacks jurisdiction to proceed any further.

e. *Fifth Amendment.* A corporation has no privilege against self-incrimination through disclosure of its documents. Neither does Bill, insofar as he is a custodian of corporate documents. Although he can claim the privilege in his own compelled oral testimony (unless MIC is empowered to and actually offers him immunity), it is unlikely that an officer of a reputable business would ever claim the privilege. The public associates such claims with criminality, something which no business could afford.

Now change the hypo: suppose Bill is an individual insurance broker suspected of having cheated clients (e.g. by pocketing their insurance checks). Could Bill claim the privilege against disclosing documents such as his financial records? Work through the list of reasons why self-incrimination is not much help in administrative investigations even of an individual.

(i) He cannot refuse to testify—but can claim the Fifth for specific questions put to him. Agency can draw adverse inference against him because of his privilege claim.

(ii) Agency may offer immunity from criminal prosecution and thus force testimony. It can impose administrative sanctions resulting from immunized testimony.

(iii) State can seize papers using a search warrant.

(iv) Under *Doe*, the focus is not on whether papers are incriminating. It is on whether the act of producing them is incriminating (because production admits authenticity, existence, or possession of the documents where such facts are not "foregone conclusions"). The act of producing the documents (as distinguished from the contents of the documents) would seldom be incriminating. However, if Bill kept actual records of how much money he had stolen, those should be protected by the privilege because the act of producing them would admit their existence. It remains unclear whether *Doe* applies to purely private, non-business papers like a diary.

(v) Under *Shapiro*, there is no privilege for papers that the law required Bill to prepare and retain. This would probably cover most of his business records involving the relationship between clients and insurance companies. As *Craib* shows, if the required records doctrine applies, the documents must be produced even if the act of production would be incriminating.

f. *Fourth amendment—probable cause.* *Oklahoma Press* and *Craib* make clear that the Fourth Amendment applies only in very attenuated form to a subpoena duces tecum. Fishing expeditions are acceptable. Conceivably individuals (as opposed to corporations) might have more protection, but *Craib* rejected this idea in California. While *Barlow's* imposes a watered-down warrant requirement for most administrative physical searches, *Craib* makes clear that this rule is inapplicable to a subpoena. Certainly there is no probable cause requirement.

But would Madison take a different view? Consider *Levin* in N.3 (and *Bearman* in N.3 of the manual)—and discuss the merits of the *Levin* opinions (compared with the carte blanche approach taken in federal cases). The *Levin* dissent may be correct that the majority's probable cause requirement would hamper the Board's ability to deal with medical discipline. Although the benefits to individuals of requiring probable cause are obvious, it would permit reluctant demandees to throw roadblocks in the way of investigations, thus delaying the inevitable. If *Levin* and *Bearman* were followed here (and note that, as in those cases, this demand concerns medical rather than business records and thus implicated patient privacy), MIC would have to establish probable cause to believe that the pattern of refusing to pay justified claims actually exists—which might be difficult. Or is *Levin* limited to individual as opposed to corporate demandees, or to professional licensees as opposed to regulated industries? This is possible, since *Oklahoma Press* does appear to draw an individual/corporate distinction.

g. *Fourth amendment—burdensomeness.* Under *Oklahoma Press*, MIC has a proper purpose (investigating claim payment practices). The documents are reasonably relevant to that purpose—because patient files will give information about nonpayment of claims. However, the demand here is highly burdensome, and as *Craib* and many other cases make clear, the trial court has discretion to scale down the demand or make it less onerous. Here, compliance might well disrupt or unduly hinder the normal operations of the business. *See EEOC v. Quad/Graphics, Inc.,* 63 F.3d 642, 648-49 (7th Cir.1995) (demandee must show that compliance would threaten the normal operation of its business). We might ask the court to

i) permit copying at Security's headquarters, so that the MIC rather than Security has to incur the enormous search costs and the documents will not be misplaced or damaged;

ii) require only a sampling of files—for example, consumers whose names start with B and F;

iii) limit the request to persons who made claims that were refused;

iv) limit the demand to Madison residents only;

v) require production of only certain documents, such as claim forms and the company's response, rather than the entire file (although it would be costly for Security to segregate this material);

vi) limit the time span to one year instead of three;

vii) omit materials on microfiche;

viii) give Security more time to make the search.

Here is an alternative strategy: suggest that Security consider complying in full. This would bury MIC under so much paper that it would take them years to go through it—if they really have the staff to do it at all. This strategy is illustrated in the movie *Class Action*.

h. *Judicial discretion—bad faith.* If court finds MIC is in bad faith, it will refuse to enforce the subpoena, because that would abuse the court's process. Any chance we can show harassment or discrimination here because of the hard feelings between Bill and Gloria? Or that Gloria is just out to score political points? *See SEC v. Wheeling Pittsburgh Steel Corp.*, 648 F.2d 118 (3d Cir.1981), criticized in Robert A. Bourque, Comment, 82 Colum.L. Rev. 811 (1982). In this case, the SEC investigated potential securities fraud at the urging of Senator Weicker. The Third Circuit (en banc, 6-4 vote) held that subpoena enforcement would abuse the judicial process if the SEC started a formal investigation in bad faith. For example, the SEC would be in bad faith if it knowingly pursued frivolous allegations or was investigating without having formally evaluated the case. Discovery is appropriate to prove these allegations. The majority stressed that Supreme Court precedents allow continuing evolution of the judicial standards for subpoena enforcement.

    i. *Confidentiality*. This part of the problem anticipates material on the Freedom of Information Act (§ 8.1.2). Could third parties obtain this information from MIC? Potentially yes. Security might fear that MIC will release some of the documents—for example, in connection with consumer lawsuits. These materials involve private data about insured persons. FOIA allows non-disclosure for files that would constitute a clearly unwarranted invasion of personal privacy—but what if MIC chooses to disclose them anyway? Moreover, the files probably contain valuable information about how Security rates insurance applicants. And Security's competitors would love to get a list of its customers to solicit the business. Possibly, the court might impose a protective order. For example, MIC might be required to give ten days notice before it discloses any of the documents to anyone. That would allow Security to litigate any possible disclosure before it occurred.

    j. *Relationship of investigation to adjudication and to criminal enforcement*. Note that if MIC had already begun an adjudication against Security, it would have to meet discovery standards to get this material; probably there would be stricter rules of relevance and burden. An ALJ (or perhaps a judge) would control discovery. *See FTC v. Atlantic Richfield Co.*, 567 F.2d 96 (D.C.Cir.1977) (expressing grave doubt about whether material obtained through investigatory subpoenas can be introduced in evidence without complying with discovery rules).

    How about the risk of criminal enforcement? Gloria might be using this whole matter as a political springboard—and what better platform than a criminal prosecution? Security fears that the documents and testimony obtained in the present investigation will be used against it in a criminal proceeding. However, it seems clear that this is no defense to producing evidence. In tax cases, *United States v. LaSalle National Bank,* 437 U.S. 298 (1978), prohibits the use of a civil subpoena once the IRS has referred a case to the Justice Department for criminal prosecution. Generally, however, courts allow agency investigations to proceed even though a criminal case is pending. *SEC v. Dresser Industries*, 628 F.2d 1368 (D.C. Cir.1980).

Even if the criminal case had begun, *Dresser* and *Keating* (N.4) hold that there is no right to delay the civil proceeding, but a court may exercise discretion to stay civil proceedings or postpone discovery. This is a more serious concern if an individual (rather than a corporation) is involved, since the individual might wish to testify in the civil matter without waiving the right to claim the privilege against self-incrimination in the criminal case. *Keating* has a detailed balancing of all relevant concerns and decides not to postpone an OTS administrative proceeding against Charles Keating (of Lincoln S&L fame) despite the pending criminal case.

k. *The bottom line.* This material crosses over into the next subject on ADR and perhaps should be delayed until you reach it. Indeed, the problem in § 4.1.3 explicitly follows up this problem. But if you want to cover it here:

In light of the above, negotiation is better than confrontation. Security has some cards—it can force MIC to go to court and there will be a long and expensive litigation process. That process might well result in trimming down the request. In the end, however, if MIC sticks to its guns, it will get most of what it wants. By then there may be huge expense and much unfavorable publicity.

Thus, why not try to bargain for i) no press release, ii) much reduced scope of the CID, iii) more time. Surely MIC cannot process all the papers they have asked for anyway. They may well have made unreasonable demands (and threatened publicity) simply as a bargaining chip to force Security to seek a settlement. If bargaining does not work, file a motion with MIC to the same effect.

Also, it's not a bit too early to consider settlement of the entire dispute. Could Security live with a consent order prohibiting it from maintaining any practice of refusing to pay justified claims, without admitting that this has ever occurred? Such consent settlements are quite common. Security could agree to institute various internal checks and balances to make sure that its employees do not refuse to pay justified claims. It could improve training of adjustors to assure this doesn't happen. The consent order would avoid any admission of liability so could not be used as evidence against Security in civil litigation. It would be a "global" settlement, in that it would also negate criminal liability (thus the Attorney General should be a party to negotiations).

It might be wise for Security to accept that kind of settlement rather than endure bad publicity and years of struggle in discovery, trial and appeal—and face the real possibility of ultimately losing the case, which would open the door to tort liability for bad faith refusal to pay claims. And Gloria might well go for the deal—she could boast politically of a settlement that assures protection of insurance consumers without diverting huge agency resources to the case. And, if there are new complaints against Security, she can always reinstate the case, claiming that the consent order was violated.

§ 4.1.3 Alternative Dispute Resolution In Administrative Adjudication

There is a large literature on ADR. You might read: Wallace Warfield, "The Implications of ADR Processes for Decisionmaking in Administrative Disputes," 16 Pepperdine L.Rev. S93 (1989) (obstacles to ADR in government contract disputes); Victor Lawrence, "Adopting ADR for Use in Administrative Proceedings," 13 J. Nat'l Ass'n of ALJs 109 (1993); Alan W. Heifetz, "ALJs, ADR, and ADP: The Future of Administrative Adjudication," 1 Widener J.Pub. L. 13, 27-32 (1992) (ALJs can serve as settlement judges); Frank Grad, "ADR in Environmental Law," 14 Colum.J.Envtl.L. 157 (1989).

The California APA authorizes all forms of ADR in adjudication, but the authors are informed that the provisions for mediation and arbitration are virtually never used. So far, at least, the adversarial culture on both sides seems to preclude ADR. However, there is an extensive system of mediation and arbitration to resolve disputes between licensed building contractors and consumers who complain of various regulatory violations. The regulatory agency has insufficient resources to administer this system on its own.

Problem. There is additional material on this problem in § 4.1.2 N.8 of this manual. It discusses various ways in which the document dispute could be settled and suggests that an overall settlement would be in the interests of both sides. Please refer to that prior discussion if you intend to discuss the ADR problem in class.

ADR seems quite appropriate for the dispute over production of documents. You might try a role play here, in which a class member serves as mediator between the positions of Security and the Commissioner. You can discuss the types of compromises that are listed in the manual (such as sampling documents rather than producing all of them).

It is less clear whether ADR is appropriate for the underlying dispute over failure to pay claims. As the problem text makes clear, litigation of either the documents dispute or the underlying dispute will be very costly, will take many years, create massive uncertainty and bad publicity for the company, encourage tort litigation, tie up Security's executives in working on the litigation instead of doing business, and make large claims on the resources of the Insurance Commissioner and prevent her from undertaking other cases. It will be bitterly adversarial. The attorneys will do well. Everyone else, including consumers, will suffer because of the costs and delays.

As to the underlying dispute: Security has every reason to want to settle it quietly for a promise to sin no more (i.e. a consent decree) and some minor payment of civil penalties. However, it is less clear that the Commissioner should settle it as opposed to litigating it. This is a very important consumer protection case and might be the occasion to get a binding precedent. To achieve this, Gloria might need to litigate it right up through the state supreme court, whereas a settlement would not create a binding precedent. The public interest might require much more onerous remedies than could be obtained through ADR. Also Gloria may want a well publicized fight against Security to promote her political career; a consent decree might not seem aggressive enough in a political campaign.

You can use some of the factors set out in ADRA about when it is inappropriate to use ADR. Under 5 U.S.C. § 572(b), ADR is inappropriate if

(1) a definitive or authoritative resolution of the matter is required for precedential value, and [an ADR] proceeding is not likely to be accepted generally as an authoritative precedent;

(2) the matter involves or may bear upon significant questions of government policy that require additional procedures before a final resolution may be made, and such a proceeding would not likely serve to develop a recommended policy for the agency;

(3) maintaining established policies is of special importance, so that variations among individual decisions are not increased and such a proceeding would not likely reach consistent results among individual decisions;

(4) the matter significantly affects persons or organizations [i.e. insured parties] who are not parties to the proceeding;

(5) a full public record of the proceeding is important, and a dispute resolution proceeding cannot provide such a record.

(6) the agency must maintain continuing jurisdiction over the matter with authority to alter the disposition of the matter in the light of changed circumstances, and a dispute resolution proceeding would interfere with the agency's fulfilling that requirement.

§ 4.2 THE HEARING PHASE

§ 4.2.1 Evidence at the Hearing

REGUERO v. TEACHER STANDARDS AND PRACTICES COMMISSION

This section contains no teaching problem, but the problem at the end of § 4.2.2 contains both evidence and official notice issues.

The Prince William County, Virginia, school board confronted a case similar to *Reguero*. High school teacher David Perino was acquitted by a jury of forcibly sodomizing a student with Down's syndrome. However, he was then fired by the board. The board refused to call the student as a witness, relying entirely on the transcript of her cross-examination at the criminal trial. In addition, pornography was found on Perino's computer, but he denied loading it and said others had access to the computer. You might want to distribute the Washington Post account of the hearing, which raises the question of whether a school board is able to stand up to the school superintendent in personnel cases of this kind. *See* Ian Shapira, "A Differing Definition of Justice," Washington Post, Oct 9, 2005, www.washingtonpost.com/wp-dyn/content/article/2005/10/09/AR20051009011506.html. Perino lost when he challenged the school board's decision in a federal § 1983 action and when he sued the board members for defamation. Ian Shapira, "Fired N. Va. Teacher Loses Legal Bid to Return," Wash. Post, Jan 8, 2006.

Notes and Questions

1. *Admission of evidence.* For discussion of evidence and official notice see Ernest Gellhorn, "Rules of Evidence and Official Notice in Formal Administrative Hearings," 1971 Duke L.J. 1; 1 John Henry Wigmore, LAW OF EVIDENCE § 4a, b, c (Tillers rev. 1983); William H. Kuehnle, "Standards of Evidence in Administrative Proceedings," 49 N.Y.L.Sch.L.Rev. 829 (2004-05).

Under 1961 MSAPA, agencies must follow the rules of evidence (presumably both statutory and common law rules) followed in non-jury civil cases, except that inadmissible evidence can be admitted if "necessary to ascertain facts not reasonably susceptible to proof under these rules. . . " Thus agencies are presumably required to exclude hearsay (unless necessary to ascertain facts that can't be proved by admissible evidence) as well as to observe many other rules of evidence. For example, this provision might require an agency to prohibit non-experts from giving opinions and to follow the so-called best evidence rule (i.e. that the original of a document should be introduced rather than a copy). It must follow state rules excluding certain evidence designed to impeach a witness because of prior criminal convictions. Yet these civil rules seem irrelevant to administrative practice.

The Federal APA contains two limitations on the admission of evidence. First, "the agency as a matter of policy shall provide for the exclusion of irrelevant, immaterial, or unduly repetitious evidence." APA § 556(d), 2d sentence. This provision—which bans useless or irrelevant evidence—isn't likely to produce a judicial reversal on complaint that the ALJ failed to exclude evidence, since the admission of such evidence would be harmless error. The provision does, however, give an ALJ power to exclude useless evidence in order to shorten the hearing and keep the record manageable. *See Underwood v. Elkay Mining, Inc.,* 105 F.3d 946 (4th Cir.1997).

Second, a sanction, rule, or order must be "supported by and in accordance with the reliable, probative, and substantial evidence." APA § 556(d), 3d sentence. This provision applies to the aggregate of the evidence supporting the agency's conclusion, not to the admission of any particular item of evidence. The Fourth Circuit describes this provision as a gate keeping function. "The gate keeping function to evaluate evidence occurs when the evidence is considered in decisionmaking rather than when the evidence is admitted. Even though it arises later in the administrative process than it does in jury trials, the ALJ's duty to screen evidence for reliability, probativeness, and substantiality similarly ensures that final agency decisions will be based on evidence of requisite quality and quantity. . . . [T]o prove by a preponderance of the evidence each element of a claim before an administrative agency, the claimant must present reliable, probative, and substantial evidence of such sufficient quality and quantity that a reasonable ALJ could conclude that the existence of the facts supporting the claim are more probable than their nonexistence." *U.S. Steel Mining Co. v. Director, Office of Workers' Comp. Programs,* 187 F.3d 384, 389 (4th Cir.1999) (reversing decision supported only by a letter from deceased applicant's physician that "it is possible that" death resulted from pneumoconiosis).

The § 556(d), 3d sentence, test looks redundant, because it seems to duplicate the judicial review "substantial evidence" test (APA § 706(2)(E), discussed in §9.1.1), which is basically a "reasonableness" test. Indeed, in a judicial review context the weakness of evidence (such as unreliable hearsay) could certainly undermine the substantiality of evidence supporting the order, as in *Reguero* and as discussed in N.3 of the text. However, the Supreme Court has held that this language in § 556(d) also establishes a standard of proof for the finder of fact, because it says that a finding must be "in accordance with" evidence of the specified quality and quantity. Specifically, the agency must apply a preponderance-of-the-evidence test. *Steadman v. SEC,* 450 U.S. 91 (1981). In other words, the party who has the burden of proof must show that the evidence *does* support the required conclusion, not just that a reasonable decisionmaker *could* have thought it does.

In *Reguero,* if the 1961 MSAPA provision were in effect, the hearsay statements would all be inadmissible and the court would have reversed the decision because they were admitted into evidence. Because Michelle and Leasa could have testified themselves, admission of hearsay was "not necessary to ascertain facts not reasonably susceptible to proof under" the state's usual evidence rules.

In our opinion, the judicial rules limiting admission of evidence—particularly of hearsay but other rules as well—should be presumptively inapplicable in administrative proceedings. These rules were designed to protect juries from unreliable evidence. Expert fact finders need not be protected from hearing or seeing any evidence they consider probative, material to the issues, relevant, and not unduly repetitious. Agency decisions concerning admission or exclusion of evidence should seldom be overturned by reviewing courts. *See Underwood v. Elkay Mining Co., supra* (ALJ allows mining company in black lung case to introduce over 100 exhibits—ALJ did not abuse discretion to exclude additional evidence that is unduly repetitious).

All of us constantly rely on hearsay evidence in the course of our daily affairs. Agencies should be able to do the same. For an argument the other way, see Michael H. Graham, "Application of the Rules of Evidence in Administrative Agency Formal Adversarial Adjudications: A New Approach," 1991 U.Ill.L.F. 353 (urging adoption of Federal Rules of Evidence in administrative proceedings).

Use of the common law evidence rules would require constant objections and evidence hassles in administrative cases and, no doubt, numerous judicial reversals because of evidence errors. Hearsay, in particular, presents many close calls; to use one of the scores of exceptions, it is often necessarily to lay an elaborate foundation. All this takes time and produces disputes about tangential matters.

ACUS Rec. 86-2, 51 Fed. Reg. 25642 (July 16, 1986), counsels against statutes or regulations that compel agencies to follow the Federal Rules of Evidence (FRE). The NLRB's statute is particularly mysterious: what does it mean to follow the FRE "so far as practicable"? *See generally* Richard J. Pierce, Jr., "Use of the Federal Rules of Evidence in Federal Agency Adjudications," 39 Admin.L.Rev. 1 (1987), pointing out that cases concerning NLRB evidence issues are hopelessly confused by the "so far as practicable" standard.

Pierce criticizes the APA § 556(d) standard because it does not give ALJs discretion to exclude material that seems obviously unreliable or because it would be a waste of time to hear it. Pierce recommends that agencies adopt by rule a version of FRE 403 (evidence may be excluded if its probative value is substantially outweighed by dangers of undue delay, waste of time, etc.). See the recently enacted Cal. Gov't Code § 11513(f) (presiding officer has discretion to exclude evidence if its probative value is substantially outweighed by the probability that its admission will necessitate undue consumption of time).

One interesting evidence issue is whether an agency should be required to follow the rules applicable in civil cases that constitute the trial court as the gatekeeper of scientific evidence. *Frye v. United States*, 293 F. 1013 (D.C.Cir.1923), prohibits introduction of scientific evidence unless the scientific technique is generally accepted. The case is still followed in many states. The Supreme Court discarded the *Frye* general-acceptance test under the Federal Rules of Evidence. *See Daubert v. Merrill Dow Pharm.*, 509 U.S. 579 (1993); *Kumho Tire Co. v. Carmichael,* 526 U.S. 137 (1999). These cases hold that a trial court must assess whether the underlying reasoning or methodology offered by an expert witness is reliable in light of such factors as publication or acceptance in the scientific community. If the evidence fails to pass this screen, it must not be admitted and the jury cannot consider it.

Should agencies, as distinguished from courts, be bound by *Daubert* or *Frye*? We think not. Agencies are far more competent than juries to pass on scientific evidence and to assess its value, and the public interest is often critically involved. If an administrative fact-finder believes that expert evidence could have value, regardless of whether it could pass through the *Daubert* screen, the evidence should be admitted. *Seering v. Dept. of Social Serv.*, 239 Cal. Rptr. 422 (Cal. App.1987), was a child molestation case in which the agency sought to prove that molestation occurred by using a test based on the way a child plays with anatomically correct dolls. The court required the evidence to be excluded since, under *Frye*, the test had not achieved general scientific acceptance. Especially in a case where the public interest is as compelling as in *Seering,* we think the evidence should be admitted.

In *Peabody Coal Co. v. McCandless,* 255 F.3d 465 (7th Cir.2001), the court applied *Daubert* by analogy, rejecting a decision in which an ALJ tried to resolve a medical controversy by a rule of thumb that the opinion of the doctor who performed an autopsy prevails over the opinions of the pathologists who examined tissue slides from the decedent. The court denounced the decision as the sort of junk science that *Daubert* and *Kumho* reject. In *Elliott v. CFTC,* 202 F.3d 926 (7th Cir.2000), the court suggested in dictum that it might have applied *Daubert* to invalidate some shoddy statistical analysis if the point had been properly raised. In *Naim v. Ashcroft,*

354 F.3d 652 (7th Cir.2004), Judge Posner said that *Daubert* was not strictly applicable to administrative proceedings but it might apply by analogy.

2. *The residuum rule. Reguero* rejects the residuum rule, but a majority of the states still retain it. Some states take a middle ground, retaining the residuum rule in cases in which an interest protected by due process (such as a claim to unemployment compensation) is asserted. *Trujillo v. Employment Security Comm'n,* 610 P.2d 747 (N.M.1980). The dissenting judge in *Reguero* would retain the residuum rule for cases in which the asserted conduct would constitute a crime, presumably because in such cases the agency should observe higher standards of proof than are normally required.

The residuum rule is probably unwise and should be abolished in all cases. Much hearsay is quite reliable (even though it does not happen to fall within one of the thirty-odd judicial exceptions to the rule), so an otherwise reasonable decision based on it should be upheld. All of us rely unthinkingly on reliable hearsay in our daily affairs. *Richardson v. Perales* is a case of inherently reliable hearsay. The set of consistent doctors' reports, produced routinely by SSA, seems reliable and probative. A requirement that the doctors must testify in every case would be prohibitively expensive. And Perales could have subpoenaed the doctors but failed to do so. *Perales* probably abolished the residuum rule at the federal level even in cases where the declarant could not be subpoenaed, but that issue is not definitively settled.

The residuum rule requires only a smidgeon of non-hearsay evidence. The non-hearsay doesn't need to be substantial evidence on its own. Thus parties who are aware of the residuum rule can usually come up with at least something that supports their position in addition to the hearsay.

There's a practical problem in states with the residuum rule. Under the rule of issue exhaustion, you must raise every issue before the agency that you want to raise on judicial review. Therefore, you must object at the agency level to a finding based on hearsay. Yet you don't know that the residuum rule will even apply until the entire case is concluded. No point in objecting to items of hearsay evidence as they come in—they're admissible. So you have to object right at the end of the hearing (or possibly to the agency heads if you failed to do so at the hearing). Pro se parties (who constitute the vast majority of administrative litigants) would never know enough to make this objection. If they fail to make it, it's gone unless the state allows the objection to be made for the first time in court, contrary to the issue exhaustion rule. *See Sims v. Apfel,* § 11.2.4, which excused the normal rules of issue exhaustion in Social Security appeals. Thus the residuum rule strongly favors litigants who are represented by counsel. *See* Cal. Gov't Code § 11513(d) (litigant must make timely residuum rule objection, meaning before submission of case or on reconsideration or other administrative review of judge's decision).

3. *Hearsay and substantial evidence.* If the particular items of hearsay evidence on which an agency relied are inherently unreliable, the decision should be reversed because the fact findings would not be supported by substantial evidence. *Reguero* is a fine example of this approach. Clearly, the court is treating hearsay evidence as less worthy than other sorts of evidence. But why? If the evidence in question were not hearsay, it would surely be considered substantial enough to support the decision. We have three independent but consistent accounts of what happened, all three reliable witnesses, and all testifying to conversations in which it is likely the girls were telling the truth. This seems like pretty substantial evidence. Why should it be necessary to drag Michelle and Leasa into the hearing to testify and be cross-examined about some very embarrassing and unpleasant events? After all, Reguero could have subpoenaed them if he wanted their testimony. Note 22 seems wrong in placing the burden of calling the girls on the TSPC; why not require Reguero to call them if he's going to rely on their failure to testify?

As noted above, there's hearsay and there's hearsay. Some of it is reliable because it's consistent, the circumstances in which the out of court statement were made suggest the statements were truthful, and the persons testifying to the out of court statements are reliable. Sometimes it's just a bunch of trashy rumor. Both federal and state APA's make this distinction clearly. *See* 1961 MSAPA §10(1) (in cases where evidence is admitted in administrative cases that would not be admitted in court, it must be "of a type commonly relied upon by reasonably prudent men in the conduct of their affairs") and APA § 556(d) (order must be supported by reliable, probative and substantial evidence).

The test in the 1961 MSAPA is drawn from a famous Learned Hand opinion. *NLRB v. Remington Rand, Inc.,* 94 F.2d 862, 873 (2d Cir.1938). Hand recognized that the NLRB was then allowed to admit evidence not admissible in court. He added: "[N]o doubt, that [fact] does not mean that mere rumor will serve to 'support' a finding, but hearsay may do so, at least if more is not conveniently available, and if in the end the finding is supported by the kind of evidence on which responsible persons are accustomed to rely in serious affairs." Perhaps in *Reguero* the hearsay was not sufficient because, in Hand's words, "more [was] conveniently available," in that the Board, not Reguero, was required to subpoena the girls.

4. *Hearsay and confrontation.* Due process wasn't discussed in *Reguero,* perhaps because Reguero could have subpoenaed the girls. This would undercut his due process argument. For a thorough rundown of the due process implications of admission of hearsay, see Kuehnle, *supra,* at

The possible constitutional right to confront accusers in cases like *Reguero* or *Ezeagwuna* derives from the due process clauses of the Fifth and Fourteenth Amendments, not from the Sixth Amendment, which applies only to criminal cases. When applicable, the Sixth Amendment as now construed contains a strong anti-hearsay rule. It bars admission of "testimonial statements of a witness who did not appear at trial, unless he was unavailable to testify *and* the defendant had a prior opportunity for cross-examination." *Crawford v. Washington,* 541 U.S. 36 (2004). "Testimonial evidence" includes police interrogations about past crimes (and presumably would cover the statements involved in *Reguero* which related to investigation of past offenses). But it does not include calls for help by a victim of ongoing domestic violence to 911 if the interrogation by the 911 operator is primarily to enable police assistance to an ongoing emergency. *Davis v. Washington,* 547 U.S. 813 (2006). Under a now-disapproved line of authority, testimonial evidence could be admitted despite the confrontation clause if it "falls under a firmly rooted hearsay exception or bears particularized guarantees of trustworthiness." *Ohio v. Roberts,* 448 U.S. 56 (1980), overruled by *Crawford.*

5. *Burden of proof.* We don't think that the burden of proof should be elevated, even in a case in which sexual misconduct is alleged. Remember, the public interest in getting rid of teachers who engage in misconduct is also involved. It should not be made unduly difficult to discharge teachers (whether for misconduct or incompetence). The teacher already has more than enough protections against error; since these cases often come down to conflicts of testimony, an elevated burden of proof might make it just too difficult for the school district to win.

6. *Responsibility of judge to bring out evidence.* In *Baker v. Employment Appeals Bd.,* 551 N.W.2d 646 (Iowa App.1996), a *pro se* applicant for unemployment benefits mentioned a key letter from his supervisor but didn't introduce it into evidence. The appellate court said:

> An [ALJ] has a duty to develop the record fully and fairly, particularly when the claimant is not represented by counsel. . . . While a mere lack of counsel alone does not deprive a claimant of a fair hearing, it does enhance the [ALJ's] duty to bring out the relevant facts. . . . We find the [ALJ] was under a heightened duty to develop the record since Baker was unrepresented in this case. This duty required the [ALJ] to inquire about and consider the letter from Baker's supervisor . . . While we make no findings regarding the letter, we find it was error for the ALJ to fail to inquire about the letter and to fail to at least consider it in reaching his decision when it was brought to his attention . . .

7. *Closed or open hearing.* The 1981 MSAPA requires open hearings unless a provision of law expressly authorizes closure. § 4-211(6). However, "provision of law" includes regulations, so an agency conducting personnel hearings could adopt rules requiring the hearings be closed. Cases like *Reguero* can justifiably be closed to protect the privacy of the children who were victims of misconduct. *See* Cal. Gov't Code § 11425.20(a)(3), which allows a hearing to be closed to protect a minor witness from intimidation or prevent other harm, taking into account the rights of all persons. There may be many other situations in which an AJ could justifiably close the hearing—for example, to protect confidential business information in a tax case. The Committee on Communications and Media Law of the Association of the Bar of the City of New York severely criticizes the government's position in the Creppy Directive that it can issue a blanket order closing deportation hearings in terrorism cases. *See* 23 Cardozo Arts & Ent. L. J. 21 (2005).

8. *Cross-examination under the APA.* We agree with the *Citizens Awareness* decision. Cross-examination is seldom necessary with respect to proving scientific or technical facts, and it can be enormously time-consuming. Although NRC licensing hearings are governed by the APA, the statute allows the NRC to use judges that are not ALJs. The hearings usually are conducted by panels of NRC staff scientists with one administrative judge—not an ALJ—presiding. That means the decisionmakers on the panel are well qualified technically and don't need cross examination to help them decide about the probative value of direct testimony.

The NRC AJs argue that cross examination is helpful even in nuclear licensing cases, because it can disclose that the experts who furnished direct testimony (especially on behalf of the applicant) were biased or that they committed methodological errors that are not obvious from the face of their oral or written direct testimony. Cross examination also helps citizen-intervenors who can't afford to hire their own experts. Moreover, the judges argue that cross-examination will tend to discourage exaggerated direct testimony. These are good arguments, but we think they are outweighed by efficiency concerns. Cross is a very expensive luxury in hearings that already take a great deal of time and are highly complex. It can take days to cross-examine an expert witness, but all of the points that can be brought out on cross can be introduced as easily through a written rebuttal. Obviously, as the court says, there can be exceptional situations in which credibility is at stake; then cross examination is probably a good idea. But not in the generality of cases.

§ 4.2.2 Official Notice

CIRCU v. GONZALES

Official notice is a time-saver because it dispenses with the need to offer documentary or oral proof of matters that are likely to be non-controversial. However, the implications of taking official notice go well beyond efficiency. By taking official notice of a fact, an agency may shift the burden of coming forward with evidence and satisfy its burden of persuasion. Say that the case involved revocation of a professional license. The agency has the burden to show the licensee committed misconduct. If it can establish a key fact through official notice (such as that it violates local medical standards to sew up a sponge inside a patient), it has both shifted the burden of producing evidence on that point and also satisfied its burden of persuasion. It wouldn't have to call expert witnesses to establish a failure to meet community standards.

As discussed in the problem below, a court might find that an agency cannot rely on official notice to satisfy its burden of showing some particularly critical and disputable fact but must put on testimony instead. See *Burkhart v. Bowen,* 856 F.2d 1335, 1340-41 (9th Cir.1988) (ALJ erred by taking official notice of jobs applicant could do instead of calling vocational expert); *Dayco Corp. v. FTC,* 362 F.2d 180 (6th Cir.1966) (unfair to prove case by taking notice of facts in the record of another case to which respondent was not a party).

Here are some reasons why agencies can notice many more facts than courts.

· Rules of evidence are more liberal in agency proceedings.
· The volume of cases is much greater, resulting in a greater need for efficient hearing processes.
· Agencies are more likely than courts to find legislative as opposed to adjudicative facts.
· Agencies have responsibility to develop the record and should not rely solely on evidence offered by litigants.
· Agencies hear many related cases which raise the same fact questions—this gives them expertise and experience, so it would be wasteful to keep litigating the same issues. This is particularly true of asylum cases like *Circu.*
· ALJs wouldn't pay attention if they had to keep hearing the same evidence over and over.

MSAPAs have consistently limited official notice to "technical or scientific matters." The limitation appears in § 10(4) of the 1961 MSAPA as well as the § 4-212(f) of the 1981 MSAPA, and apparently will be replicated in the 2010 MSAPA. But the Federal APA is not limited to technical or scientific matters. This provision thus allowed official notice of the proposition involved in *Circu*, which seems neither technical nor scientific.

This might be a good opportunity to talk about the decisionmaking process in deportation cases (including asylum cases) if you didn't do so earlier. (See Manual § 3.3.5 N.4) The agency (presently the Executive Office for Immigration Review housed within the U.S. Justice Department) employs about 200 IJs. They hear more than 250,000 cases each year including about 25,000 asylum petitions. About 40,000 cases are appealed to the BIA and 12,000 to the federal courts of appeal. Because of the heavy caseload and staggering backlogs, efficient decisionmaking is essential. Therefore, the IJs must use official notice to deal with recurring issues, as they did in *Circu* as well as in the earlier cases cited such as *Getachew*.

As pointed out in § 3.3.5 N.4 of the text and manual, the quality of decisionmaking in immigration cases has been poor and has been repeatedly chastised by appellate courts. Among numerous other grounds for criticism, some IJs appeared to be biased and the quality of findings and reasoning has been poor. Findings that applicants lack credibility are based on nitpicking. *See, e.g., San Kai Kwok v. Gonzales*, 455 F.3d 766 (7th Cir.2006). There is incredible disparity in results between different immigration judges. See Lindsey R. Vaala, Note, "Bias on the Bench: Raising the Bar for U.S. Immigration Judges to Ensure Equality for Asylum Seekers," 49 Wm. & Mary L.Rev. 1011 (2007).

The abuse that occurred in *Circu* is just one more example of sloppy and rushed decisionmaking. To deal with the overwhelming backlog, the appellate function of the Board of Immigration Appeals has been streamlined. Instead of three-judge review of IJ decisions as in the past, there is only single-judge BIA review. The vast majority of these are rubber stamp affirmances, as in *Circu*. Therefore, there is little accountability for IJ decisionmaking. The result is a huge increase in the number of cases appealed to the federal courts of appeal and, in some circuits, a serious workload problem for federal judges. See Manual §3.3.5 N.4; Symposium, 55 Cath.Univ.L.Rev. 905-1058 (2006); Margaret Tebo, "Asylum Ordeals," 92 A.B.A.J. 36 (Nov.2006); Bill Blum, "Crossing to Safety," Cal.Lwyr. 18 (Jan.2007). The Ninth Circuit judges are obviously aware that BIA review of IJ decisions is pretty much a sham, which may explain why countering the noticed facts at the BIA level was not an adequate rebuttal opportunity.

We include the following discussion contrasting judicial notice under Federal Rule of Evidence (FRE) 201 and official notice under the various APAs because the issue is confusing and students may raise questions about it. If they don't raise questions, you should probably leave it alone in class, unless you want to let yourself in for a lengthy and obscure discussion. FRE

201(a) limits federal courts in taking judicial notice of "adjudicative facts." Under rule 201(b), judicially noticed facts must be indisputable (that is, capable of accurate and ready determination by resort to sources whose accuracy cannot reasonably be questioned—like determining the phases of the moon from an almanac). Even as to these, a party is entitled to be heard on the propriety of taking judicial notice and the tenor of the matter noticed. Rule 201(e). But to administrative law readers, the question that jumps out at you is—what about legislative facts? Can they really be noticed without giving the opposing party notice and an opportunity to rebut? Or does FRE 201 imply that legislative facts cannot be officially noticed? The latter reading would be especially provocative, because, in practice, official notice almost never applies to adjudicative facts—meaning those specific to a party to the case—but almost always to legislative facts (meaning those that are not specific to parties).

The perplexing wording of Rule 201 suggests that its drafters may have seized on Davis' adjudicative/legislative fact distinction without fully understanding it. Administrative lawyers would treat the question of whether the moon was full on Aug. 1 as legislative and indisputable because it isn't specific to the parties. They would also treat as legislative the question of whether Pentecostals can worship freely in Romania (the noticed fact in *Circu*), though this one is disputable. In the judicial realm, however, Rule 201 cannot apply to either of these questions unless they are treated as involving adjudicative fact. Under that somewhat odd reading, the first one would be considered appropriately the source of judicial notice because indisputable; the second one would be inappropriate for judicial notice because it is disputable.

By limiting Rule 201's coverage to adjudicative fact, the drafters meant to exclude from Rule 201 (and its response opportunity) broad questions of policy-making fact such as whether marriage would collapse if the spousal privilege were abolished or whether segregation imbues black children with a feeling of inferiority. Courts rely on such broad factual propositions all the time and are not obliged to give the parties prior notice and an opportunity to rebut. Similarly, the drafters did not intend to include in Rule 201 heuristics for evaluating evidence or other common-sense propositions (e.g., people who are late for appointments tend to speed). But the upshot is that the domain of official notice is different under FRE 201 than it is in administrative law.

Perhaps the clearest reconciliation of these concerns was that of Davis himself. In his view, Rule 201 deals only with official notice of adjudicative facts and, therefore, leaves the subject of official notice of legislative facts to case law development. 3 Kenneth Culp Davis, ADMINISTRATIVE LAW TREATISE § 15:6 (2d ed.1980). Under this reading, the rule doesn't *prohibit* official notice of legislative facts, nor does it *authorize* such notice without a rebuttal opportunity. It is simply silent on the subject. As a matter of common law development, courts (and by extension agencies) are free to allow official notice of legislative facts without a rebuttal in some situations (as in the lunar example) and to allow it only *with* a rebuttal opportunity in other situations (as in the religious freedom example). So construed, Rule 201 isn't helpful with respect to legislative facts, but it needn't be mischievous either.

Notes and Questions

1. *Rebuttal opportunity. Circu* talks about the distinction between legislative and adjudicative facts and the distinction between controversial (or disputable) and indisputable facts. Normally, an agency takes official notice of legislative rather than adjudicative facts. As administrative lawyers use the term, adjudicative facts are those specific to the parties (such as whether Circu's family was previously persecuted for being Pentecostalists). These facts ordinarily must be proved, not officially noticed. Generally, legislative facts are those that are not specific to the parties (like whether there is freedom of worship in Romania)—although, as we said above, it's not clear that the FRE contemplates the same understanding.

The APA and due process generally require an opportunity to respond to an agency's decision to take official notice and the nature of the noticed fact, as in *Ohio Bell* or *Circu*. However, a court is unlikely to reverse an agency for failing to give a response opportunity for an indisputable fact (like water runs downhill or the Communist government of Romania has been overthrown). The failure to give notice and an opportunity to rebut in such a case is not prejudicial. This explains *Market St. Railway*: it hardly seems disputable to conclude that lowering transit fares will increase ridership. Similarly, if the noticed fact is not central or critical to the case, a court may find the decision not to give warning and a rebuttal opportunity to be non-prejudicial. *See* Peggy C. Davis, "'There is a Book Out. . . ': An Analysis of Judicial Absorption of Legislative Facts," 100 Harv.L.Rev. 1539, 1593-1604 (1987) (cautioning against hasty judicial findings of legislative fact).

Sometimes, the act of taking official notice occurs in the proposed decision of a hearing officer. In such cases, the rebuttal opportunity can be provided as part of a rehearing or reconsideration of that proposed decision. Circu's appeal to the BIA did not provide her with a proper opportunity to rebut the officially noticed fact that Pentecostals could worship freely in Romania. The BIA does not take new evidence; it considers only the evidence of record and the IJ's report. Therefore, the BIA should have remanded the case to the IJ to take additional evidence. In addition, as discussed above in the manual, BIA review consists of a decision by a single judge and almost always involves rubber-stamp approval. Even if in theory the BIA could have taken additional evidence, it refused to provide any such opportunity and merely rubber stamped the IJ's decision. *See also Burger v. Gonzales,* 498 F.3d 131 (2d Cir. 2007) (BIA failed to give prior notice that it intended to take official notice of a critical and disputable fact and the procedure of a motion to reopen the BIA's decision is inadequate).

2. *Official notice or evaluation of the evidence?* It is often hard to say whether an agency is taking official notice or just evaluating evidence—the difference is a matter of degree. *See* Ernest Gellhorn, "Rules of Evidence and Official Notice in Formal Administrative Hearings," 1971 Duke L.J. 1, 43-44; J. A. Millie, "The Problem of Official Notice: Reliance by Administrative Tribunals on the Personal Knowledge of their Members," [1975] Public L. 64 (adjudicator should furnish chance for rebuttal of facts on which he proposes to rely if they are capable of being attributed to specific identifiable sources).

Judges as well as agencies are expected to use their background knowledge and experience in evaluating testimony. A court need not allow an opportunity for rebuttal when it decides that the testimony of a witness is inherently implausible or that a witness with a conflict of interest is unreliable or that a witness who fidgets or fails to maintain eye contact is lying (though such rules of thumb are notoriously unreliable). Agency fact finders are no less able to make use of their common sense, experience and knowledge in evaluating testimony.

However, because the concepts of evaluation of evidence and official notice shade into each other, an agency should be careful about invoking the concept of "evaluation of evidence" in order to deny a litigant the opportunity to rebut the agency's position. Thus, even if the *Cohen* case involves evaluation of evidence in some sense, the results are sound. The decision requires the agency to inform the licensees of their evaluation of the evidence so that they might offer additional evidence to rebut that evaluation. In effect, *Cohen* seems to unify the subjects of official notice and evaluation of the evidence—requiring the agency to give appropriate warning in both situations when there is risk of prejudicial error.

In analyzing the IJ's treatment of the expert in the hypo in text N.2, a good authority is *Miles v. Chater,* 84 F.3d 1397 (11th Cir.1996). *Miles* was a social security disability case with conflicting expert testimony about whether Miles suffered from major depression or was just faking it. The ALJ rejected the evaluations of one of the applicant's physicians because his examinations "almost invariably conclude that the person being examined is totally disabled." The court reversed because the ALJ was biased against the expert witness (which also appears to be the case in the hypo). Another way to have decided the case was that the ALJ failed to give timely notice about why he was rejecting particular expert testimony. Normally one would think that assessing the credibility of a witness falls squarely within the concept of evaluation of evidence. But in this particular case, the ALJ's evaluation rested on a specific factual premise about the witness's track record. That premise is readily susceptible of exploration through evidence. If Miles wants to dispute the ALJ's assertion, the conclusory label "evaluation of evidence" shouldn't stand in the way.

Some students may raise the First Amendment issue about *Cohen*: truthful advertising by professionals is a form of constitutionally protected commercial speech. *Virginia Pharmacy Bd. v. Virginia Consumer Council*, 425 U.S. 748 (1976). The court in *Cohen* did not reach the constitutional issue. But the case seems an obvious example of established chiropractors trying to punish an upstart who is expanding her market share through shrewd advertising and thus a good case to question professional licensing schemes in general.

Questions about the scope of an agency's competence to evaluate evidence often arise in connection with rejection of the testimony of experts. Within limits, agencies are permitted to draw upon their own expertise in analyzing the record, even though this entails the rejection of expert testimony. *McCarthy v. Industrial Commission.* Today, however, prevailing opinion is skeptical about claims of expertise. We are less certain than was the *McCarthy* court that agency factfinders (ALJs or board members) possess the expertise that they claim to have. Indeed, we might suspect that an agency has been captured by a regulated group or that a licensing agency is engaged in protectionism.

In the hypo in N.2, the IJ probably committed reversible error in rejecting the expert testimony, at least without further explanation of why he disbelieved the expert. Just because the IJ has heard a lot of asylum cases, even a lot of Romanian cases, he does not have the type of technical expertise in evaluating testimony that is assumed by decisions like *McCarthy*. Nor, without a great deal more backup, should the court accept the IJ's conclusion that the expert is basically a prostitute who will say anything he's paid to say.

Cases like *Davis* suggest a disinclination to uphold findings that are based only on claims of expertise and that reject apparently well-considered views of qualified experts. *Davis* requires a court to decide whether it actually owes deference to the agency's expertise, and it strongly encourages the agency to indicate its objections to the expert's testimony at the hearing, so that the expert can address them. *See also* Ronald M. Levin, "Scope-of-Review Doctrine Restated: An Administrative Law Section Report," 38 Admin.L.Rev. 239, 281 (1986) (suggesting that "official notice without documentation can provide only fragile support for an agency fact finding").

At the margin, it is impossible to say whether an agency has taken official notice (meaning it must give prior notice) or whether it has merely relied on factual predicates in evaluating evidence (in which case it need not give prior notice). *Cohen* and *Davis* help avoid having to draw that distinction by requiring the agency, in many cases, to give notice of its evaluation or to develop its objections to expert testimony in time to permit additional rebuttal.

3. *Problem.*

a. *Hearsay issue.* As the proponent, Red has the burden of proof to establish by a preponderance of the evidence his right to an increase; but the Board should have the burden to establish that rents should be decreased. APA § 556(d).

As in *Reguero,* the Board's decision on the issue of Red's investment is entirely based on hearsay. Although Red's statement to Gloria would be an admission against interest (and thus within a hearsay exception), Gloria's statement to Max does not come under any exception and would not admissible in court. The problem asks the student for analysis under both the federal APA and the 1961 MSAPA.

As to the federal APA § 556(d) (2d sentence), hearsay evidence is freely admissible (unless irrelevant, immaterial, or unduly repetitious). However, it can be argued that under §556(d) (3d sentence) the finding is not supported by "reliable, probative, and substantial evidence." This argument is further discussed just below (under the "commonly relied upon by reasonably prudent men" standard of the 1961 MSAPA).

Under 1961 MSAPA §10(1), the agency is required to follow the state's evidence rules and exclude the hearsay evidence unless it is "necessary to ascertain facts not reasonably susceptible of proof under" the usual rules. It is unclear whether the question of whether Red cooked his books is "reasonably susceptible of proof" under normal evidence rules. It would seem that the Board could easily have established this point without using hearsay by calling Gloria as a witness; if so, the decision should be set aside on the ground that the evidence was inadmissible. If Gloria was unavailable (or if the Board had no subpoena power), it could be argued that the fact could only be proved by hearsay.

Even if it's found that the question of fraudulent records is not "reasonably susceptible of proof" under normal evidence rules, the hearsay evidence must meet the standard of being "commonly relied upon by reasonably prudent men in the conduct of their affairs." 1961 MSAPA § 10(1) (3d sentence). Red testified that he had a $2,000,000 investment and introduced apparently correct records to prove it. How credible is Max's wholly uncorroborated evidence to the contrary? As a tenant, Max is hardly disinterested. His double hearsay testimony does not have the ring of truth.

Would Red's mother really have made such a statement to Max? This doesn't seem credible and it's not the sort of thing that reasonably prudent people would rely on in the conduct of their affairs. Unlike *Perales*, the hearsay was anything but a routinely prepared report. There are no "circumstantial guarantees of trustworthiness." FRE 803(24). The hearsay is much less reliable than that in *Reguero*, where it came from three reliable, unbiased officials who had interviewed the girls. (The same arguments would establish, under the federal APA, that the finding on the value of the building is not supported by "reliable, probative, and substantial evidence" under §556 (d) (3d sentence).

Putting aside the issue of admissibility of the evidence, if the state follows the residuum rule, the decision should be reversed because the finding on the value of the building is supported exclusively by hearsay. There is not a scintilla of non-hearsay evidence supporting it. However, the residuum rule is not followed under federal law. *Reguero* rejected the residuum rule under Oregon law.

If the residuum rule doesn't apply, the next issue, as in *Reguero*, is whether there is substantial evidence to support the finding (*see* § 9.1.1). This point will require you to introduce the substantial evidence test if you haven't done so earlier. Essentially it is a reasonableness test. A court must affirm a reasonable agency fact finding even if the court disagrees with it. This problem shows that you cannot generalize about hearsay support for findings—some of it is highly unreliable, some the opposite. For the reasons discussed above, this evidence seems quite unreliable and should flunk the substantial evidence test. *Reguero* makes things tougher for the agency when it relies exclusively on hearsay than if there is some non-hearsay evidence in support of the finding. *See* E. Gellhorn, *supra* at 18-22. (The substantial evidence issue could be framed under APA §556(d) (third sentence): is the finding based on "reliable, probative, and substantial evidence?—this seems to duplicate the judicial review substantial evidence test).

Another issue here is whether the use of the hearsay evidence violated due process because it denied Red the ability to confront and cross-examine Gloria. However, this seems unlikely, given that Gloria is Red's mother and he certainly could have produced her to testify (assuming the Board would have granted a continuance so that he could do so) but chose not to. As in *Perales*, the failure to produce an available declarant is damaging. Also Red could have produced additional evidence to show that his books were not cooked (original purchase documents, etc.) which again suggests that due process was not violated.

b. *Rate of return issue*: It can be argued that the Board has established the rate of return by taking official notice of what is a reasonable rate of return on a real estate investment. Arguably, the rate of return is a "technical" issue so that official notice is permissible under the 1961 MSAPA, though the word "technical" seems to refer more to engineering-type technicalities than economic conclusions. However, because the Board did not notify Red that it planned to take official notice on that issue, it failed to offer a proper rebuttal opportunity as required by *Circu* as well as APA § 556(d) and 1961 MSAPA § 10(4). The conclusion about reasonable rate of return concerns legislative fact and is both critical and highly disputable.

It could be argued that it is unfair for the Board to establish the critical point about rate of return by taking official notice. Instead, it might be required to establish the point by putting on witnesses who could be cross examined. Especially with respect to reducing rents (as opposed to refusing to permit an increase where Red has the burden of proof), it seems unfair for the Board to shift the burden of proof by using official notice. See the cases cited in the Manual at the beginning of § 4.2.2 (*Dayco* and *Burkhart*); *Cohen v. Ambach*; *Chase v. Dept. of Prof. Reg.*, 609 N.E.2d 769 (Ill. App.1993) (Board must put on expert testimony to revoke architect's license, not just rely on its own expertise).

The Board would argue that its conclusion involved the use of expertise in evaluating the evidence before it, not the taking of official notice. In its decision to reject Beth's expert testimony, it would rely on 1961 MSAPA §10(4): "The agency's experience, technical competence, and specialized knowledge may be utilized in the evaluation of evidence." Even if you assume the Board has expertise and specialized knowledge about rent control (which is debatable at best), *Davis* suggests that the Board would still be reversed because it did not develop its objections to Beth's testimony at the hearing and thus failed to give Red the chance to rebut them. Under *Davis,* the Board's rejection of unopposed expert testimony is proper only when the court can be sure that the Board would not have been affected by anything the expert said in rebuttal AND where the court should affirm despite the expert's hypothetical rebuttal out of deference for the agency's judgment on so technical a matter. Similarly, *Cohen* would be a strong authority that the Board could not rely on its expertise to avoid submitting evidence.

Just because 9% has been used in other rent control cases does not establish that the Board can rely on it without further proof. If the rate were established by statute or a valid legislative rule, it could then be relied on in every adjudication (although perhaps only if there was an opportunity to seek a waiver because of unusual facts). *See Heckler v. Campbell*, §3.2 (agency can preclude adjudication, and can avoid the procedural rules of official notice, by adopting guidelines setting forth whether jobs exist for persons with various degrees of education, disability etc.). But Red cannot be bound by a factual conclusion reached in other cases.

Finally, apart from all this, there is serious doubt about whether the Board's decision on rate of return can pass the judicial review substantial evidence test, given Beth's unopposed testimony. A court could easily find that the conclusion about rate of return was simply not reasonable. It is unreasonable to compare the risks of owning real property to a risk-free bank account and reliance on the fact that the Board has used 9% in other cases is just bootstrapping. A court might well be influenced by the fact that the Board is elected and perhaps captured by tenant interests, as is often the case. On the other hand, the court might sympathize with the Board's problems— it has to deal with a huge caseload and a short meeting time. It has to take some shortcuts to get through its agenda.

§ 4.3 THE DECISION PHASE: FINDING FACTS AND STATING REASONS

SHIP CREEK HYDRAULIC SYNDICATE v. STATE

The *Ship Creek* decision (together with the earlier *SEACC* case) commits Alaska state (and presumably local) government to a requirement of preparing a decisional document for important discretionary management-type decisions, such as a major timber cutting contract or a condemnation of property for building a highway. The document must contain a statement of the grounds of the decision, the essential facts on which it is based, and a response to objections that have been made. Thus the decisional document resembles the "concise general statement of [a rule's] basis and purpose" required by APA § 553(c) in connection with rulemaking. As we'll see in discussing this rulemaking requirement, the so-called concise statements may exceed 100 pages in length and the requirement of preparing them is quite onerous, since agencies feel they must respond to all objections raised during rulemaking and anticipate all objections to the rule that could be made in court.

SEACC contains approving cites to the Davis treatise's critical comments about the federal *Overton Park* decision (which refused to imply a findings requirement into the statute relating to federal funding for interstate highways and its limitation on building roads through parks). Thus *SEACC* and *Ship Creek* represent a major and serious resource commitment, given that most such decisions are never challenged in court. As discussed below, these cases also appear to assume that a court will provide "hard look" judicial review of important discretionary decisions. As discussed in §§ 9.3 and 9.4, our confidence in the efficacy of hard look judicial review has waned since its heyday in the 1970's.

You may want to discuss the final portion of the opinion in which the court decides to make its decision about mandatory decisional documents prospective only. This was reasonable; the court did not want to overturn dozens or hundreds of quick-take decisions occurring before the date of its opinion. However, the result seems pretty harsh as applied to Ship Creek: it wins the battle but loses the war since the new requirement is not applied to its case. It persuaded the court of its position, but got nothing for it and wasted all the resources it spent on the litigation. It might have seemed fairer if the court had applied the decision to Ship Creek (and remanded for preparation of a decisional document) but not applied it to any other quick-take decisions that occurred before the date of the decision. Courts do have the ability to make new decisions prospective only when they upset serious reliance interests, but it is questionable whether agencies can do so. See discussion of *Wyman-Gordon* in § 6.2.

Notes and Questions

1. *Legal authority.* Due process generally includes a requirement that the agency state findings and reasons, and the case involves a deprivation of old property (real estate being condemned for a highway). However, the quick-take procedure allows de novo judicial consideration of whether the conditions of a quick-take were complied with (exactly this occurred in *Ship Creek*—there was a four-day trial on the merits of the engineering decisions entailed in the choice of highway routes). This judicial remedy provides all the process that is due, so the requirement of preparing a decisional document couldn't be based on due process. All APAs contain a findings requirement (and some contain a reasons requirement also), but there is no statutory right to an agency hearing in connection with the quick-take decision, so the APA doesn't seem applicable.

While the decisional-document requirement is being read into statutes (and obviously could be reversed by a legislative determination that no decisional document should be required in a particular statutory context), the court does not pretend that it is engaged in interpretation of particular statutes. Instead, the overarching decisional document requirement apparently applies to all contexts in which important governmental discretionary decisions are made and statutes impose some judicially-reviewable substantive constraints on those decisions. Alaska thus rejects the holding in *Overton Park* that such decisions are not constrained by a findings/reasons requirement absent some explicit statute requiring them.

There are, however, many examples of a court reading a particular statute to require the agency to explain its decision. *Dunlop v. Bachowski,* 421 U.S. 560 (1975), is a leading example. *Dunlop* involved a statute allowing the Secretary of Labor to sue in district court to set aside a union election tainted by fraud. The Secretary refused to bring suit to set aside a particular election. The Court held his action judicially reviewable and interpreted the underlying statute to require the Secretary to state reasons for his refusal and the essential facts on which the decision was based. Such a statement would permit intelligent judicial review, would inform a complaining union member why his request had been denied, and would promote careful consideration. The Secretary had furnished a brief letter to the complainant. The Court stated that the letter might satisfy APA § 555(e), but not the more exacting requirement of explanation that it had discovered in the statute.

The decisional document requirement in *Ship Creek* is primarily based on the needs of a reviewing court for a set of findings/reasons, so that the court can decide whether agency discretionary action was arbitrary and capricious. In addition, it is based on common-law type rationales for requiring findings, including the instrumental one of producing better agency decisions and the non-instrumental one of respect for individual autonomy, derived from Rabin's article . Thus Shapiro & Levy are correct in treating the findings/reasons requirement as basically a common law innovation that has multiple purposes beyond facilitating judicial review.

SEACC contains language approving an article by Judge Leventhal in favor of hard look review of discretionary action. You may decide that it's premature to discuss hard look here (*see* §§ 9.3, 9.4). But if a court is going to engage in hard look review of discretionary action (as opposed to highly deferential rational basis review), an adequate agency statement of findings and reasons is obviously essential.

The court appears suspicious about the quality and fairness of the sorts of discretionary decisions involved in *SEACC* and *Ship Creek*. Decisions by timber officials to allow private companies to cut down trees in state forests are suspect. The official may well be a former timber company executive, or interested in getting such a job after leaving government service. Often the official is more interested in facilitating maximum timber harvest at least cost (which would please the companies and generate additional state revenue in the short run) and are less interested in long-term sustained yield or in competing forest uses such as recreation, fishing, or protection of the habitat of endangered species that are not as able to lobby the official. Highway departments want to build the road as cheaply and quickly as possible. They are committed to the route they have decided upon, and are not really interested in reconsidering the optimum route to minimize private injury. Thus a findings requirement makes sense, given that decisions of this sort may well be a little fishy. It's a way the court can send a message to the agency that they need to watch out, that they can be held accountable. This notion (the connection of a findings requirement with possible fishiness of the decision) is further pursued in connection with the problem below.

Even if the decision is purely common law, it would not run afoul of *Vermont Yankee*. The Supreme Court made this clear in *LTV*. *See* § 5.4.3

N.4 and accompanying manual discussion. Although *Vermont Yankee* counsels against implying procedures to enhance judicial review, a findings requirement is distinguishable, because a court cannot meaningfully review a decision that has not been explained. Indeed, numerous post-*Vermont Yankee* cases have reversed and remanded because an agency decision has not been sufficiently explained.

2. *Construing statutes to require findings.* The *Virginia Beach* and *Winston-Salem* cases involving local government decisions about cellular transmission towers correct the possible misimpression from *Ship Creek* that courts always force agencies to produce better findings.

Here, given an obvious opportunity to construe a specific statute to require an explanation (after all, a decision "in writing" should require something more than a rubber-stamped "denied"), the court passes. The idea that a court can perform responsible substantial-evidence or arbitrary-capricious review without an explanation of the decision is a myth. You can't review a decision for arbitrariness unless you know what the decision was and how the decisionmakers weighed the many bits of evidence in the record. A simple "denied," accompanied by minutes of a hearing summarizing the views of the people who spoke up is just not adequate. Those minutes will, no doubt, articulate a whole variety of reasons for and against (technical, economic, esthetic, health-related, or just the usual NIMBY). There's no way to evaluate the decision without knowing exactly what it was based on and why.

However, the *Winston-Salem* case gives a clue to the court's thinking. There's a federalism issue. A federal court is reviewing the decisions of local zoning boards. The federal court is reluctant to interfere with the routine of the local boards (normally review of their decisions would be in state, not federal courts, but review of these decisions about cell phone towers is in federal court under the Telecommunications Act). In general, federal courts dislike being treated as a board of zoning appeals, and their unwillingness to prescribe procedures for local decisionmaking is understandable.

In addition, the federal courts are understandably reluctant to impose specific duties on zoning boards. Those boards are politically responsible, often consisting of elected officials, who have a great many other things to do besides hearing zoning cases. In smaller cities, zoning boards typically involve part-time decisionmakers who meet in the evening after doing some other kind of day job. The agencies have inadequate staff if they have any at all. Yet such boards often have a heavy caseload, consisting of all of the land use decisions for the town (including whether Aunt Nellie can build a bedroom over her garage). The boards may not be required to furnish explanations of all these other decisions (although perhaps they should be so required), so are not really set up to explain their decisions about cell towers. Anyway, these practical and prudential reasons may explain the otherwise puzzling reluctance of the courts in these cases to require explanations in cell phone tower cases.

3. *Overton Park.* The Court's decision in *Overton Park* that there must be a judicial trial to determine the reasons why the Secretary approved the route through the park was poorly considered and has been politely overruled by subsequent cases. The *Overton Park* approach caused a lengthy 27-day trial in district court, seeking to reconstruct what the Secretary knew or should have known on the questions relating to the park route, based on a enormous set of documents and a long history of struggle over the route. This is a poor use of the resources of courts. Subjecting the Secretary to this sort of inquisition is contrary to *Morgan IV* which prohibits scrutiny of an administrator's decision-making process. *See* § 3.3.1. Far better to remand to the administrator to supply the missing explanation and take it from there.

4. *Link between facts and law.* Even in a typical and routine administrative adjudication like *Adams*, the findings requirement is critical. Here the emphasis is on connecting up the evidence with the final conclusion, so the rationality of the decision can be assessed. Otherwise, the agency can lazily decide what it wants to do without really engaging in the necessary analysis. (The same is true of the cell phone tower cases discussed in N.2.) A well-known California decision that requires local zoning boards to explain decisions granting variances makes the same point.

> Implicit [in the judicial review statute] is a requirement that the agency which renders the challenged decision must set forth findings to bridge the analytic gap between the raw evidence and ultimate decision or order. . . . By focusing . . . upon the relationship between evidence and findings and between findings and ultimate action, the Legislature sought to direct the reviewing court's attention to the analytic route the administrative agency traveled from evidence to action. . . .

> Absent such roadsigns, a reviewing court would be forced into unguided and resource-consuming explorations; it would have to grope through the record to determine whether some combination of credible evidentiary items which supported some line of factual and legal conclusions supported the ultimate order or decision of the agency. Moreover, properly constituted findings enable the parties to the agency proceeding to determine whether and on what basis they should seek review. They also serve a public relations function by helping to persuade the parties that administrative decision-making is careful, reasoned, and equitable.

Topanga Ass'n for a Scenic Community v. County of Los Angeles, 522 P.2d 12 (Cal.1974).

5. *Explanations by agency staff or lawyers.* Remand to the agency heads to make fresh findings or state adequate reasons when these were lacking in the original decision is not a meaningless ritual. For further discussion, see the answer to the problem, N.7 below. The parties deserve an opportunity to persuade the agency heads to adopt different findings, reasons, or legal interpretations. This opportunity can be secured only by a remand. In addition, the appellate counsel's interpretation may not reflect the views of the agency heads (particularly when the rationalization is supplied by the Solicitor General or a state Attorney General or some other lawyer who is not part of the agency's staff). Finally, a position taken in litigation documents may have been developed hastily or under pressure and not as the result of the agency's deliberative processes. *National Wildlife Federation v. Browner*, 126 F.3d 1126 (D.C.Cir.1997); *FLRA v. Dep't of Treasury*, 884 F.2d 1446, 1445 (D.C.Cir.1989). In an understandable desire to secure a judicial affirmance of a flawed decision, the agency heads and staff may have expediently adopted findings or reasons that they would not have adopted in the first place.

In some cases, courts have considered post-hoc rationalizations that were approved by the responsible agency officials, rather than remand the case back to the agency for additional consideration. See *Bagdonas v. Dep't of Treasury,* 93 F.3d 422 (7th Cir.1996) (court accepts the explanatory affidavit of official who was responsible for an earlier unexplained decision); *Population Institute v. McPherson,* 797 F.2d 1062 (D.C.Cir.1986) (after court indicated disagreement with agency's original rationale, administrator issued revised rationale which court sustained). *Bagdonas* is an unusual case but understandable in light of the agency's overwhelming backlog. (It had to approve applications for persons convicted of gun crimes to possess firearms.) However, *Bagdonas* pretty much guts the post-hoc rationalization rule; an agency could dispense with findings in every case and then supply them by post-hoc affidavits in the few cases that go up on appeal.

We would opt for Judge Wald's dissent in *Saratoga*. Allowing the staff report to serve as an agency explanation, when the agency heads did not specifically state they were adopting the staff report, seems irresponsible and a serious departure from the teachings of *Chenery*. The agency heads and nobody else must take responsibility for the decision. For an insightful treatment of numerous aspects of the *Chenery* doctrine, see Kevin Stack, "The Constitutional Foundations of *Chenery,*" 116 Yale L.J. 101 (2007).

6. *Findings at every level?* *Guentchev* is an easy case. If an administrative judge has written a satisfactory opinion, why shouldn't the agency heads be allowed to adopt that opinion as their own? Appellate

courts do this with trial court opinions all the time.

In the *Guentchev* situation, if a reviewing court is dubious about the substance of an agency's findings, its readiness to intervene may be influenced by the care with which the agency apparently acted. If the agency heads merely adopted the administrative judge's opinion, that fact could make the court less willing to defer (especially if the administrative judge's opinion also looks cursory).

7. *Problem.* The instructor may want to discuss substantive constitutional objections to the statute. *Spilotro* upheld it against a facial attack, but that case involved a mobster, not a mobster's friend. The statute is not void for vagueness, since one cannot violate it until after an order is entered. The Nevada court held that the statute did not punish someone for his associations and was not cruel and unusual punishment, because it was regulatory and did not impose punishment. The court also held that the statute did not violate equal protection or substantive due process (it had a rational basis) nor the First Amendment, even though it interfered with certain forms of speech and association. All of these conclusions are debatable.

The concurring opinion indicated that the statute could not be applied in ways that would violate the First Amendment, such as barring someone from attending a political rally that takes place in a casino. All of the majority's points are less persuasive when the statute is applied to a *friend* of a mobster, rather than the mobster himself. For discussion of constitutional issues, see Michael Bowers, "Nevada's Black Book: The Constitutionality of Exclusion Lists in Casino Gaming Regulation," 9 Whittier L. Rev. 313 (1987).

Quite apart from a requirement of explanation, you can discuss this as a judicial review problem. Given the record, there may be no substantial evidence for the finding that Sally has an unsavory reputation and the discretionary decision to exclude her might be found arbitrary and capricious. These matters are covered in detail in §§ 9.1.1 and 9.3.

The Board made findings in the language of the statute (i.e. "ultimate" facts). This may be a good opportunity to introduce the distinction between findings of basic fact, applications of law to fact (which include "ultimate facts"), interpretations of law, and discretion. These distinctions are also covered in § 9.2.1 N.3. As *Adams* (quoted in N.4) explains, conclusory findings of ultimate fact are inadequate to expose the agency's reasoning process, to establish what Sally's reputation is and why that reputation would impair public confidence in the industry. Nor do such findings explain why the Board exercised its discretion to exclude her.

On the other hand, it is fairly obvious what the detailed findings and reasons would have been if the Board had made them. Thus the basic issue is whether a court should remand to the agency to make more detailed findings—and what the utility of such a court order would be. *If* it is obvious what the agency will do, why waste everyone's time? Why not just accept the post-hoc rationalizations of counsel as to the agency's explanation? Or an affidavit by the Board members themselves, as in *Bagdonas*, N.5 above.

The court should not order a de novo judicial trial, as in *Overton Park,* at which the Board members would be witnesses and would testify as to their reasons. As explained above, the *Overton* dissenters are right that such trials are a bad idea. Under the *Morgan IV* analysis, it is unseemly that the decisional processes of any judge or administrator be put on trial. *Camp v. Pitts* and many other cases have rejected this approach. Instead, if findings or reasons are lacking, the correct step is to remand to the agency for further proceedings. Whether to vacate the original decision, or remand without vacation, is a separate and sometimes difficult issue discussed in § 9.4 N.4.

The Board's action just does not feel right. It seems a little fishy. It is one thing to exclude Max, but quite another thing to exclude his friend, who, according to the record, has not done anything very serious and does not have a bad reputation. It seems like the Board may be trying to acquire a tough-guy reputation by picking unfairly on Sally. Maybe there is a good reason for this—but it calls for some explanation.

A findings requirement can force the Board to address squarely these submerged issues. It can explain why discretion was exercised this way; do you really want to exclude all the close friends of mobsters? Have they done this consistently? There may be no way for the Board to state a convincing rationale for excluding Sally, consistent with the evidence in the record. A findings requirement thus serves the purposes spelled out in *Ship Creek*. It respects Sally's autonomy; it forces an agency to engage in better decisionmaking; it informs the parties why they lost; and it enables better judicial review. Imposing an explanation requirement is often a surrogate for reversing on the merits; a remand for additional findings and reasons often sends the message that the reviewing court is uncomfortable with the substantive result and wishes the agency to reconsider it. Thus remand for additional explanation is not a meaningless ritual.

a) If no APA applies: Due process may apply, and due process requires a statement of findings and reasons under *Goldberg*. Entering casinos may be a property right; it's an entitlement that can be abridged only for specific statutory reasons. *But see* the dubious decision in *Brown v. Michigan City*, 462 F.3d 720, 728-29 (7th Cir.2006), discussed in Manual § 2.2.2 N.3, which holds that admission to a city park is not a property right, since no statute specifically gives the public the right to enter the park.

Similarly, it would appear that Sally has been deprived of liberty, in that she is precluded from walking into a building that is open to the general public. Beyond that, the exclusion is stigmatic (she has been officially denounced as having an unsavory reputation) and the defamation is accompanied by a legal exclusion order; therefore it meets the stigma-plus requirement of *Paul v. Davis*. Here it would matter whether the order was public or secret. *See Kraft v. Jacka*, which held that no liberty interest was invaded when gambling license applications were rejected because of associations with organized crime, because the Board did not publicize the reasons for its denial of a license.

Kraft also involved denial of a license application because the applicant cohabited with persons the Board thought were undesirable. Even if interference with a cohabitational relationship was an invasion of her liberty, the court thought the governmental interests in gambling regulation outweighed the effect on her relationship. The circumstances indicated that the man would continue to run things through the woman, his cohabitant, who was more of a front.

If the basis for applying due process is the stigmatic effect of the order, Sally is entitled to a name-clearing hearing in which she can show she doesn't have an unsavory reputation. If she wins that, presumably the Gaming Board would have to rescind its order; it would be arbitrary to exclude her after she has re-established her good name.

If *Goldberg* is followed, the failure to state reasons and indicate the evidence relied on would violate due process. However, federal law no longer subscribes to the one-size-its-all list of procedures spelled out in *Goldberg*. Instead, such issues must be resolved by *Mathews* balancing. The balance might go something like this: Exclusion from casinos that one likes to patronize is a significant (but hardly life-and-death) interest. However, avoiding the stigma associated with being labeled "unsavory" would be even more important. The Gaming Board has little interest in resisting a requirement that it state specific findings and reasons (they don't have a massive caseload and don't need to dispose of their cases in a quick and summary manner). As discussed above, a findings requirement would have utility in a case like this in both instrumental terms (forcing better reasoning) and non-instrumental terms (protection of dignity). Consequently, the balance tips in favor of requiring findings and reasons.

Apart from due process, it would be possible to imply a requirement of findings and reasons from the underlying statute or impose it as a matter of common law. *Ship Creek* is an excellent example. Even if *Vermont Yankee* would inhibit that in a federal court, which we doubt (see discussion above), a state court would not be required to follow that case. *Topanga* endorses a findings requirement to enable the court to exercise judicial review. It holds that an agency cannot simply state the basic facts and declare that they fit or don't fit the statutory standard. Instead, the agency must connect the basic facts to the ultimate conclusion.

b) and c). Both § 12 of the 1961 MSAPA and § 557(c) of the Federal APA require that an agency state findings. Section 12 explicitly requires a statement of the underlying facts supporting a finding that is couched in statutory language. However, § 12 does not mention a requirement of stating reasons for discretionary decisions. Federal APA §557(c)(A) requires a statement of both findings and reasons for discretionary action.

§ 4.4 EFFECT OF DECISION: RES JUDICATA, STARE DECISIS, EQUITABLE ESTOPPEL

§ 4.4.1 Res Judicata and Collateral Estoppel

J. S. v. BETHLEHEM AREA SCHOOL DISTRICT

Notes and Questions

The leading modern federal case on collateral estoppel is *University of Tennessee v. Elliott*, 478 U.S. 788 (1986). *Elliott* involved a black employee who was fired for misconduct but who contended that the discharge was racially motivated. The discharge was upheld by an administrative hearing, which lasted five months. The ALJ rejected the claim that the discharge was racially motivated. Elliott did not seek judicial review but filed a separate action for damages in federal court under both Title VII of the Civil Rights Act of 1964 and 42 U.S.C. § 1983. The Supreme Court held that collateral estoppel applied to the § 1983 claim but not to the Title VII claim. Federal courts should apply doctrines of claim and issue preclusion to the same degree that the relevant state would enforce them.

In *Elliott*, the Court found evidence in Title VII and its legislative history that Congress did not want findings in judicially unreviewed state administrative proceedings to collaterally estop discrimination claims under Title VII. Clearly there is a subtext here of judicial distrust of determinations by state agencies as to whether discrimination occurred. Yet the Court is oddly more protective of Title VII claims than of § 1983 claims. Perhaps because it has never been clear just why these two overlapping remedies are needed and how they relate to each other, the Court doesn't mind getting rid of some § 1983 cases.

The Court followed the Title VII part of *Elliott* under the Age Discrimination Act. *Astoria Federal S&L Ass'n v. Solimino*, 501 U.S. 104 (1991) (no preclusion of federal court action from judicially unreviewed state administrative findings).

The hints drawn from Title VII and its legislative history are far from conclusive. Perhaps collateral estoppel should apply to Title VII cases that were fully and fairly litigated before a state agency. The purposes of res judicata and collateral estoppel—minimizing the burdens of multiple litigation on courts and litigants, avoiding inconsistent decisions—favor preclusion under Title VII as well as § 1983. If the state administrative hearing procedure fully and fairly adjudicated Elliott's claim, does it really need to be tried afresh in federal court? Moreover, it seems anomalous to treat the two civil rights statutes differently.

For a thorough discussion of res judicata and collateral estoppel in administrative law, see Richard J. Pierce, Jr., ADMINISTRATIVE LAW TREATISE §§ 13.3 and 13.4 (4th ed. 2002).

If anyone asks, the Commonwealth Court, involved in the *J.S.* case, is a Pennsylvania appellate court that specializes in reviewing administrative law cases decided by state or local agencies. Thus its judges acquire a great deal of expertise in administrative law matters.

1. *Constitutional issues and collateral estoppel.* We cannot expect sophisticated constitutional analysis from agencies such as school boards (given that its members need not be lawyers, students are often not represented by counsel at school board hearings, and the lawyers who do participate in such hearings aren't likely to be constitutional law specialists). However, the student has the ability to appeal and raise the constitutional issues through several levels of courts, as J.S. in fact did. See the Pennsylvania Supreme Court decision, 807 A.2d 847, 853-69 (2002), exhaustively discussing and rejecting J.S.'s constitutional claims because the website materially and substantially interfered with the educational process. Thus it is not unreasonable to apply collateral estoppel from an administrative to a judicial forum, even though the administrative hearing resolved constitutional questions.

The *Patsy* case, discussed in the chapter on exhaustion of remedies (§ 11.2.3 N.8), would allow J.S. to concede his expulsion (after all, he had already been admitted to an out-of-state middle school), skip the school board hearing, and go straight to a § 1983 damages action. Thus he could avoid the collateral estoppel problem. *Patsy* might be viewed as a question of primary jurisdiction rather than exhaustion of remedies since § 1983 provides trial court (not appellate court) jurisdiction over the same constitutional claim that can be raised in the school board hearing. See § 11.2.5. Under primary jurisdiction analysis, it would appear appropriate to allow a § 1983 action; the court should not send the case to the school board to make the initial decision. There is no need for uniform results and the school board has little or no expertise in constitutional decisionmaking. In addition, the school board cannot supply a damages remedy. Applying primary jurisdiction and requiring that the issue be resolved in the agency would complicate the case and delay its resolution; the parties (both the student and a small school district) would often have difficulty paying the extra costs and legal fees from protracting the dispute.

2. *Collateral estoppel in unemployment cases.* It is justifiable to treat unemployment compensation and student expulsion differently, because unemployment hearings are usually brief and informal affairs designed to get money to an unemployed person quickly. Because the stakes are small, neither party is likely to invest substantial effort and resources in the unemployment hearing.

Cases like *Ryan* sharply raise the stakes in unemployment hearings. Since the findings will determine the outcome of future tort or contract litigation, such as wrongful termination actions, both sides (especially the employer) must invest much greater resources in the administrative hearing. That could strain the resources of the unemployment adjudicating agency which is geared for quick and informal resolution of unemployment claims. In Missouri, a decision similar to *Ryan* triggered legislation prohibiting any collateral estoppel effect from an unemployment proceeding. *See* Merry Evans, Comment, "Collateral Estoppel and the Administrative Process," 53 Mo. L. Rev. 779 (1988), discussing *Bresnahan v. May Dep't Stores Co.*, 726 S.W.2d 327 (Mo.1987) and its legislative sequel.

3. *Criminal cases.* If recipient is convicted in a criminal case that precedes a civil matter, she should be estopped in the civil case to relitigate any issues determined in the criminal case—such as the entitlement question. *Armstrong v. United States*, 354 F.2d 274, 290 (Ct.Cl.1965) (criminal tax evasion—civil tax fraud). However, an acquittal is not preclusive of the administrative case, because of the different burdens of proof. The state may have failed to prove guilt beyond a reasonable doubt but may be able to prove welfare fraud in the administrative case by a preponderance of the evidence (or even by clear and convincing evidence if that is the standard).

The issue of whether a win by the recipient in the prior administrative case precludes the government from bringing a criminal case is controversial. *Payne* is pretty convincing. If the administrative decision wipes out a subsequent criminal prosecution, the government would have to either i) wait to bring the agency case until the criminal case is concluded, ii) omit the agency case entirely, or iii) put much greater resources into the administrative case than it would normally. *See* Thomas F. Crosby, "Administrative Collateral Estoppel in California: A Critical Evaluation of *People v. Sims*," 40 Hastings L J. 907 (1989).

If the individual loses the earlier administrative case, that clearly should not preclude the issues in the criminal case—both because this would undermine the protections accorded in the criminal justice system and because the criminal burden of proof is greater.

4. *Preclusion against the government* on issues of law. The arguments made in *Mendoza* against automatic application of non-mutual claim preclusion against the United States from an unreviewed trial court decision seem persuasive. *See* Pierce, *supra*, § 13.5. However, the Harvard Note takes the contrary position.

5. *Non-acquiescence.* The second *Lopez* case states that *Mendoza* is distinguishable because plaintiff's theory was not based on offensive non-mutual collateral estoppel but on constitutional grounds. HHS's non-acquiescence in Ninth Circuit precedent violated separation of powers—it thwarted the constitutional judicial review power under *Marbury*. In addition it violated due process because it denied plaintiffs a meaningful opportunity to be heard. These are dubious conclusions. *See* Estreicher & Revesz, 98 Yale L.J. at 718-35.

The cases are distinguishable on a different and perhaps more persuasive ground: *Mendoza* involves an *unappealed* trial court decision, while *Lopez* involves a government decision to ignore a court of appeals decision in the same circuit. This seems like a sounder way to distinguish *Mendoza* than the constitutional arguments mentioned in the preceding paragraph. The arguments made in *Mendoza* against non-mutual collateral estoppel are much less persuasive when applied to a government decision to relitigate an issue settled by an appellate decision that will be appealed to the same circuit.

Estreicher & Revesz, *id.* at 753-58, would allow intra-circuit nonacquiescence where i) an agency has responsibility for securing a nationally uniform policy on the issue (as in the case of air pollution standards or labor law), ii) the agency is reasonably seeking vindication of its position before the circuit and before the Supreme Court (and candidly explains the grounds of its disagreement), iii) there is a justifiable basis for belief that the agency's position is legally sustainable.

In many situations, an agency cannot predict which circuit a decision will be appealed to. A party can appeal in any circuit where it transacts business and large corporations do business in every circuit. Suppose, for example, that the Second Circuit has previously reversed the agency on a certain point. The agency need not change its position, even though a respondent can choose any circuit to appeal to, including the Second. Otherwise, an adverse decision in any one circuit would become the law everywhere. However, the agency is expected to deal forthrightly with the conflict between its view and the Second Circuit's view, not sweep it under the rug. *Nielsen Lithographing Co. v. NLRB*, 854 F.2d 1063 (7th Cir.1988).

6. *Problem.* If Jed loses before MCC, its findings may be binding, through offensive, non-mutual collateral estoppel in litigation brought by private plaintiffs. Although *Mendoza* held that non-mutual collateral estoppel does not lie against the government (at least not from an unappealed trial court decision), it is often permitted against a private party. *Parklane Hosiery Co. v. Shore*, 439 U.S. 322 (1979), is the leading federal case on this issue. The Court endorsed offensive non-mutual collateral estoppel from one litigated case (brought by the SEC in district court) to another (a private damage action). Should the same result follow if the first case were administrative? Offensive non-mutual collateral estoppel may seem unfair—if Jed wins before MCC, its findings would not be binding on the private plaintiffs, but if he loses, he is estopped to relitigate the issues. As *Parklane* points out, offensive collateral estoppel gives a potential plaintiff an incentive to wait until someone else litigates—and discourages him from intervening in the first action.

Imen v. Glassford, 247 Cal.Rptr. 514 (Cal.App.1988) is an example of non-mutual collateral estoppel. In case A (administrative), I loses his real estate license for fraud; in case B (tort action in court), victims of the fraud can rely on offensive collateral estoppel to resolve the fraud issue. However, there is a spirited dissent in *Imen,* and it certainly can be argued that the decision is wrong.

Parklane points out that offensive collateral estoppel is discretionary. It should not apply if defendant in the first case is sued for small or nominal damages, as he would have little incentive to defend vigorously (that is not helpful here—Jed is likely to fight vigorously before MCC). Also, it would be unfair if the judgment relied on is inconsistent with previous judgments, or if the second action affords defendant procedural opportunities that were unavailable in the first action and that could readily cause a different result.

Here, if Jed decides to fight MCC and loses, he might argue that MCC denied him procedural opportunities available in court—better discovery, higher burden of proof, narrower rules of evidence, etc. (This is a good opportunity to review these issues, which have been covered in prior chapters.) But cases like *J.S.* suggest that normal administrative hearings trigger collateral estoppel (although that case doesn't involve non-mutual collateral estoppel). And *Parklane* held that the absence of a jury in the first case (which was an action for injunctive relief) was not the kind of procedural limitation that would prevent preclusion.

Jed could also argue that the legal or factual issues determined by MCC are not the same as those that must be established in the private litigation. We would need to know more about the precise statutes and rules involved in both proceedings before we could evaluate this. Kerr & Stillman make some arguments in favor of this approach.

On the other hand, if Jed takes MCC's deal, there would be no prior adjudication that would be issue-preclusive in the later case. See *Halyalkar v. Bd. of Regents*, 527 N.E.2d 1222 (N.Y.1988) (no collateral estoppel from administrative consent decree). *Halyalkar* distinguishes cases holding that a guilty plea in a criminal case is collateral estoppel, because a consent judgment in an administrative case is surrounded by fewer procedural protections.

It might be argued that the consent decree should have collateral estoppel effect, since Jed had a full and fair opportunity to litigate and declined to take it. But that would be incorrect, because collateral estoppel requires not only that the precluded party had an adequate opportunity to litigate, but also that the proposition in question was actually litigated and decided in the earlier case. Generally, therefore, a consent decree does not have preclusive effect (unless the agreement itself provides otherwise). *See* Restatement of Judgments 2d § 27, comment e. Indeed, the Restatement goes on to say that a guilty plea doesn't result in issue preclusion either, although the plea might create an estoppel under the law of evidence. *Id.* § 85 comment b. (Presumably that is a reference to the doctrine of judicial estoppel—courts don't let you deny in one case something that you formally asserted in a previous case.)

The MCC's deal also means Jed avoids the risk of a permanent license revocation; but, of course, he would be out of business for a year—which could be career-ending.

§ 4.4.2 CONSISTENCY OF DECISIONS AND STARE DECISIS

UNITED AUTOMOBILE WORKERS v. NLRB

In *FCC v. Fox Television Stations, Inc.*, 129 S.Ct. 1800 (2009), the U.S. Supreme Court rendered a major decision on the agency's obligation to articulate and justify changes in position. This opinion was handed down too late to incorporate into the text. We summarize some highlights here and also, in the context of arbitrary/capricious review, in § 9.4 NN.1 & 3.

Fox TV involves the federal statute that bans broadcasting of "any indecent language" on radio or TV between 6 AM and 10 PM. and allows the FCC to impose heavy penalties for violation of the statute. 18 U.S.C. § 1464. In this case the FCC changed its policy involving the use of bad words (including those the Court describes as the F-word and the S-word). Under the prior policy, *fleeting* (rather than repetitious) use of the words as *expletives* (as opposed to vulgar descriptions of sexual or excretory functions) were not considered violations of §1464. In 2004, however, the FCC changed course by declaring that even fleeting use of the words as expletives could be treated as violations, depending on the context. Thus the fleeting use of the F-word and the S-word (mostly as expletives) by Bono, Cher and Nicole Ritchie while receiving music awards (in television shows that were watched by children) were violations of § 1464, especially because Fox had apparently encouraged them. However, the FCC assessed no penalties because Fox might have relied on prior law.

In a 5-4 decision, the Supreme Court upheld this change in position under the APA (but did not reach the First Amendment issues). The 5-4 split seems to accurately mirror the Justices' political preferences about issues such as whether to prohibit the use of bad words on television.

The FCC did not conceal its change in position but explicitly acknowledged that it had occurred. Justice Scalia's majority opinion stated the established principle that an agency must articulate a satisfactory basis for its decision in order to enable a court to engage in arbitrary and capricious review under the APA. Also it must display awareness that it is changing position. However, the burden of explanation and justification is no greater when the agency changes its position than when it adopts a position for the first time.

The lower court required the agency to explain why the original reasons for adopting the displaced policy are no longer dispositive as well as to explain why the new policy effectuates the statute as well as or better than the old rule. The Supreme Court rejected that formulation. Perhaps there is a greater burden of justification for a change in policy as compared to a *failure to act in the first instance*; but there is no greater burden of explanation when an agency in case 2 changes the policy it stated in case 1.

Scalia wrote: "It suffices that the new policy is permissible under the statute, that there are good reasons for it, and that the agency *believes* it to be better. . .This means that the agency need not always provide a more detailed justification than what would suffice for a new policy created on a blank slate." However, there might be a greater burden of explanation when the "new policy rests on factual findings that contradict those which underlay its prior policy; or when the prior policy has engendered serious reliance interests. . ."

The Court found the new policy was not arbitrary and capricious, despite the existence of strong First Amendment implications, and despite the fact that the FCC had no empirical evidence that its new policy would better protect children than the old policy or that the old policy would encourage fleeting use of bad words. The abandonment of the distinction between expletive and literal meanings of bad words was also rational.

There are several concurring and dissenting opinions in *Fox TV* and this brief summary cannot do justice to them. Most centrally, Breyer's dissent (in which the other three dissenters joined) found the switch in position arbitrary and capricious. He felt that the fact that the FCC is an independent agency (and thus free of executive control) enhanced the judicial responsibility for review and requires the agency to furnish a more complete explanation for a switch in position than for adoption of a new position. Agencies must do more than simply say that they prefer the new position to the old. He followed language in *State Farm* and *Overton Park* that require agencies to justify switches in position. (Scalia rejected the idea that judicial review differed as between independent and non-independent agencies.) The switch was arbitrary because the FCC failed to explain why it was rejecting the prior policy's concern about the First Amendment implications of government censorship and because it failed to consider the impact of its policy on local broadcasters that lack "bleeping" technology.

Notes and Questions

The requirement of consistency (or at least articulation that the agency is changing course and why it is doing so) reflects relatively recent changes in the relationship between courts and agencies. During the New Deal, people believed that problems could be solved by agency expertise. If an agency wanted to change direction, fine—it should be able to respond to new problems with new solutions; it should experiment and discard failed initiatives. So long as a new approach was legally supportable (and courts were deferential in substantive judicial review), it should be upheld.

Within recent years, however, confidence in agency expertise has waned, and suspicion of the administrative discretion has become widespread. Judicial scrutiny of substance (e.g. hard-look review) and procedure is now more intense. There are many manifestations of this throughout the course. The requirement of justification of a change in position is consistent with this changed way of viewing administrative agencies. *See* Richard J. Pierce, Jr., ADMINISTRATIVE LAW TREATISE § 11.5 (4th ed.2002).

As Judge Leventhal said in his pioneering opinion in *Greater Boston TV Corp. v. FCC*, 444 F.2d 841, 850-53 (D.C.Cir.1970): "[A]n agency changing its course must supply a reasoned analysis indicating that prior policies and standards are being deliberately changed, not casually ignored, and if an agency glosses over or swerves from prior precedents without discussion it may cross the line from the tolerably terse to the intolerably mute."

1. *UAW and waiver.* The political background of NLRB decision-making is important here. The Board tends to change policy with each new administration. The *UAW* decision came from the Reagan Board, which was trying to avoid precedents dating back to earlier, more pro-union Boards. This seems to be the normal, expected course of behavior at the Board. And this observation supplies useful background for important NLRB cases which follow—like *Bell Aerospace* and *Wyman-Gordon* (*see* § 6.2).

Like courts, the Board is reluctant to come right out and say that it is overruling prior precedents. This draws attention to the shift and to the overtly political dimension of NLRB decisionmaking. It prefers to get rid of undesirable precedents by ignoring them or distinguishing them on spurious grounds. This may well explain the Board's reluctance to make rules; the case law method for changing course is more discreet (it's also quicker than rulemaking and consumes less staff time). On the other hand, by keeping the prior precedents alive, the Board makes it easy for a later (more pro-union) Board to rehabilitate them.

This technique of lawmaking fails to give fair warning to the public that a change has occurred. Only labor law experts may be aware of the change and even they may overlook it if the ruling is buried in a long decision. They may be unsure whether the change was inadvertent.

The source of the consistency requirement is not really clear. It could be considered administrative common law (and thus might be vulnerable to an attack under *Vermont Yankee* and *PBGC*). However, the consistency rule can be plausibly tied to the requirement of findings and reasons, APA § 557(c), and to the power of courts to set aside agency decisions that are arbitrary or capricious. APA § 706(2)(A). For how can a court decide whether a change in position was reasoned, accidental, or capricious unless the agency explains why it occurred?

For these reasons, it is not a waste of time to reverse an agency decision so that it can provide an explanation of inconsistent conduct. The change might not withstand careful analysis at the agency level. In multi-member boards, members who oppose the change might have overlooked the development. They will be able to focus on it and try to persuade their colleagues or at least write a dissent. All of this will enable a reviewing court to make a better assessment of the correctness of the decision when it is again reviewed. Moreover, a careful explanation will give people fair warning that a change in the law has occurred.

The requirement that an agency identify a change in position is probably more important in adjudication than in rulemaking. A newly adopted rule is expected to signal a change in position, or else why bother to adopt one? The notice and comment procedures (including the requirement of furnishing an explanation of the rule) are well adapted to focus attention and criticism on any such change. However, for the reasons discussed above, an unexplained change in position in adjudication may go unnoticed and may be very confusing to persons who try to follow the law. The parties might not even have anticipated that the agency was considering a change in the law so may not have briefed the issue. Adjudication relies on established precedents and adjudication is seldom used to articulate new law; when it is used for that purpose, the agency should be required to make clear that it has done so. In rulemaking, on the other hand, the main purpose of the consistency requirement is to upgrade the quality of the agency's reasoning, and as we see from comparing *State Farm* and *Fox TV*, that rationale will get a court only so far. *See* § 9.4.

2. *Refusal to depart from precedent. NLRB v. St. Francis Hospital*, 601 F.2d 404, 414-17 (9th Cir.1979), discussed in § 6.2 N.3, is similar to *Flagstaff:* an agency must give a party an opportunity to argue that a prior precedent should be overruled.

The *Flagstaff* case is better understood in light of a previous case, *Bechtel v. FCC*, 957 F.2d 873 (D.C.Cir.1992), in which the court had ordered the FCC to reconsider the integration policy. The FCC brushed this mandate aside, in the first and in the remanded *Bechtel* opinions and again in *Flagstaff*. Unsurprisingly, the court found this quite irritating.

The FCC claimed that "requiring the agency to explain its decision to adhere to established policy in cases such as this would severely compromise the ability of the Commission to bring lengthy and litigious comparative licensing proceedings to a close." But the court was not impressed. The obligation to explain why the agency adhered to established policy arose only in case of a supported challenge to the policy. Flagstaff

> repeatedly asserted throughout the proceedings that its proposal would further the Commission's policy objectives. All the Commission had to do was give a reason—any rational reason—why it did not. If the Commission had ever reviewed its policy, this probably would have been a simple task.

> Undoubtedly, there are cases in which this Court is faced with a genuine risk of burdening the Commission by requiring lengthy defenses of established policy; this case does not present that danger, however. In this case, as well as in *Bechtel*, we simply reiterated the well-settled proposition that an agency must be able to explain its reasons for continuing to adhere to a particular policy when properly challenged in a specific case. Since the Commission failed to give a single reason for applying its integration policy, or its refusal to hear evidence regarding an alternative means of furthering the policy,

there is little reason to distinguish this case from *Bechtel*.

Thus, the obligation to explain adherence to precedent arises when the existing policy is "properly challenged." But if the court doesn't think the plaintiff has presented a seemingly credible argument against the agency's current approach, it is likely to allow the agency to just cite quickly to precedent and move on. To this extent, some of the language quoted from *Flagstaff* in the casebook seems overbroad. We return to this distinction later in the course, in relation to both administrative case precedents, § 6.2.N.3, and agency policy statements, § 6.1.4b N.5.

§ 4.4.3 Estoppel

FOOTE'S DIXIE DANDY, INC. v. McHENRY

Notes and Questions

1. *Federal law of estoppel. Richmond* was the first equitable estoppel case in which the Appropriations Clause played a prominent role. Historically, common law precedents and policy arguments have been more important in the development of estoppel doctrine. In *Richmond,* two concurring Justices (White and Blackmun) joined the Court's opinion but suggested that estoppel might lie to prevent the government from unfairly "exercising its lawful discretionary authority in a particular case," as opposed to compelling the government to violate a statute. White and Blackmun relied on *U.S. v. Pennsylvania Industrial Chemical Corp.,* summarized in N.5.

An interesting lower court application of equitable estoppel to the government is *Watkins v. U.S. Army,* 875 F.2d 699 (9th Cir.1989) (en banc). In this case, the Army was estopped to refuse Watkins's reenlistment. He was a homosexual and the Army's regulations then required discharge and precluded reenlistment by homosexuals. However, the Army had known of Watkins's sexual preference ever since his original induction. He had never hidden it. The Army had repeatedly investigated it, and had always cleared him and given him glowing performance ratings. Thus he invested fourteen years in the Army and refrained from entering the civilian sector or accruing pension rights there. In addition to all the usual elements of estoppel, the court found that "affirmative misconduct" had occurred, and also that the damage to Watkins far outweighed the damage to the public interest from applying estoppel. Although this is an appealing case on the facts, it seems unlikely that the U.S. Supreme Court would agree with *Watkins*. This is especially so today, because the "don't ask-don't tell" policy is now codified in statutes rather than Army regulations.

2. *Rationale for federal no-estoppel rule.* One traditional reason for

the no-estoppel and no-apparent-authority rules is sovereign immunity: the government can do no wrong and cannot be sued without its consent. But sovereign immunity has increasingly been discredited or abolished. Thus the foundation of the no-estoppel principle has been undercut, as *Foote's* points out.

Some cases distinguish governmental and proprietary functions. Under this approach, sovereign immunity would not apply (and estoppel is possible) if the government engages in the fields of insurance, contracting, or other routine private sector functions, while sovereign immunity is more compelling in areas like tax, immigration, or regulation that lack private sector counterparts. The same distinction is important in considering governmental liability in tort. *See* § 10.2.1. *Foote's* arises out of taxation and therefore cannot rely on that distinction.

The Supreme Court is obviously concerned about the possible consequences of abolishing the no-estoppel and no-apparent-authority rules. It fears that there would be a rush of litigation by disgruntled citizens who claim to have been misled by some bureaucrat. There might be collusion between a taxpayer and a clerk who could be paid to give erroneous advice (or to testify later that he had given it). Or the result of an estoppel could be a massive loss of revenues, a whole new class of people entitled to immigrate or become citizens, or a highly destructive effect on a government program.

One can agree that the government and private litigants should not be treated alike. There are many circumstances in which government should not be estopped (or bound by apparent authority) even when a private litigant would be. For example, suppose a clerk told an oil company that it could obtain drilling rights on a piece of public land. The company then spends $1,000,000 in exploration and development. However, in fact the rights were owned by an Indian tribe and are worth $100,000,000. If estoppel or apparent authority applied, the clerk's advice would destroy the rights of the tribe.

But such horribles are no excuse for maintaining a rule that causes so much personal misfortune, and state courts seem to have comprehended this, even if the Supreme Court has not. Cases like *OPM v. Richmond* (and such earlier Supreme Court no-estoppel cases as *FCIC v. Merrill*, 332 U.S. 380 (1947), and *Schweiker v. Hansen*, 450 U.S. 785 (1981)), involve modest amounts of government money and individualized harm. The loss from paying benefits to the victim of the wrong advice can be easily absorbed by the program. Indeed, the policy of most agencies is to avoid changing position retroactively and to rectify the harm to individuals who rely on erroneous advice. *See* Asimow, cited in text, at 30-31.

We think that a court should have the power to estop the government, or to hold that its employees have apparent authority, if the plaintiff's case is sufficiently compelling and the harm to the individual from denying protection outweighs the harm to the government from granting protection. The indeterminate "affirmative misconduct" standard should be abandoned. A statute that would set forth the ground rules would be highly constructive. For example, see Frank Newman, "Should Official Advice be Reliable?," 53 Colum.L.Rev. 374 (1953); Asimow, *supra,* at 63-67. Numerous specific statutes have been enacted protecting reliance interests in particular situations.

3. *Prerequisites for estoppel.* According to *CHS*, any estoppel claim against the government must *at least* rest on a showing that the citizen's reliance on government advice was reasonable. (In this respect, the *CHS* criteria are plainly stingier than those of *Gestuvo,* which requires reliance, not "reasonable" reliance.) Furthermore, the "injury" resulting from that reliance must be one that actually made the citizen worse off; any hardship that would result from correcting the error now may not count if that correction merely offsets an undeserved benefit the citizen received earlier. *Foote's* allowed reliance on oral advice; *CHS* says that is automatically unreasonable.

The Court's application of estoppel principles in *CHS* may seem strict, but notice that even the Court's most liberal Justices joined it. Apparently the Court fears that lower courts will get too generous with the government's money unless the elements of an estoppel are applied in a toughminded way. Or maybe the liberals thought that this restrictive approach to the elements of reasonable reliance and detrimental change of position was a price they would have to pay, as a tradeoff for the opinion's dicta implying that there might be circumstances in which the Court *would* uphold an estoppel claim. Those dicta were, in fact, the most progressive comments about estoppel that have appeared in any Supreme Court majority opinion in many years. (Burger and Rehnquist declined to join the majority opinion, because they thought the Court might be leaving *too much* room for estoppel in some future case.)

Anyway, *Foote's* is distinguishable on its facts from *CHS*. Unlike the clinic in *CHS,* the CPA for Foote's relied on a state official, not a government contractor. One might still argue that he had to "get it in writing," but for a small-time operation like Foote's such an expectation may be excessive. Furthermore, the court says the lower tax rate is the one that the stores really deserved—indeed, they would have received it without question if the paperwork had been completed correctly. Thus, estopping the state would not result in a windfall for Foote's. The CPA's reliance on Yates did cause Foote's to forfeit a legal right.

4. *Advice-giving.* It is unlikely that a cautious policy of estoppel

would deter agencies from giving advice. They give advice because it serves their interests to do so—it improves compliance and minimizes violations of the law. It is politically difficult (and contrary to human nature) to refuse to give advice to people who need guidance. Besides, as a practical matter, agencies do usually respect reliance interests that their employees have created, at least by written advice. For example, the IRS guarantees recipients of private letter rulings that they can rely on the ruling; it informs the entire public that it can rely on public revenue rulings. Any changes are prospective only. For the contrary view, see 2 Richard J. Pierce, Jr., ADMINISTRATIVE LAW TREATISE § 13.1 (4th ed.2002) (17-page discussion of estoppel, arguing that application of the doctrine would dry up government advice giving).

5. *By any other name. . . .* Cases like *GE* are burgeoning rapidly; this trend is worth watching. In addition to cases in text, see *United States v. AMC Entertainment, Inc.,* 549 F.3d 760 (9th Cir.2008) (enforcement of ADA requirements to require retrofitting existing theaters would violate due process, because government never made its position on viewing angles available to theaters).

These cases are not functionally equivalent to a federal estoppel doctrine. The cases in the *GE* line of authority involve attempts to penalize a private party for breaching a norm that did not exist at the time of the relevant conduct, or that was at best ambiguous. In contrast, the estoppel cases involve efforts by the government to enforce a clear requirement that legal research would have uncovered at the time of the citizen's conduct—but neither the citizen nor the government agent who gave the advice was aware of that requirement. The logic of *GE* does not apply in the latter situation. Furthermore, the cases discussed in this note arise in an enforcement context, in which a private party wants to use the government's bad advice as a shield. They don't offer much comfort to individuals who have missed out on government benefits because of bad advice.

Chrysler seems questionable. The *GE* line of cases is persuasive insofar as it protects the private party from various forms of sanctions (usually monetary or otherwise punitive), but it should not be invoked in ways that might harm the public. Equitable balancing would have been a more appropriate vehicle for the *Chrysler* holding. If the recall would have been expensive and the safety benefits low, a court could legitimately hold that the retroactive impact of the agency's order was an abuse of discretion. *See* § 6.2 N.4. (The court hinted that this was indeed the situation, because it noted that NHTSA had not actually found the cars to be "defective.") But the *GE* analysis doesn't directly bring the public interest into the equation. If the cars are dangerously unsafe and could be fixed cheaply, due process should not prevent the government from ordering Chrysler to recall them.

6. *Declaratory orders.* Unlike agency advice-giving, a declaratory ruling is the product of an agency adjudicatory process. Like any agency order, it is binding on the parties, has res judicata effect, and is subject to immediate judicial review. It differs from ordinary agency adjudication in that it clears up uncertainty rather than settling a ripened dispute. Declaratory orders arise from stipulated facts (as opposed to most adjudications that require the facts to be found). Thus agencies can issue them without a time-consuming trial.

Clients might seek a declaratory order when they need absolutely reliable guidance on how a particular regulatory scheme would be applied. If you're going to underwrite a public stock or bond offering, or merge two railroads, and it is unclear how a statute or regulation would impact the transaction, you need this kind of guidance. An advisory letter may not be sufficient. Similarly, the client might believe that an agency's negative advice is wrong. Rather than defy the agency by acting contrary to its position and risking sanctions, the client might seek a declaratory order. The order will probably be contrary to the client's position, but it could seek immediate judicial review. *See* Burnele V. Powell, "Regular Appellate Review, Direct Judicial Review, and the Role of the Declaratory Order: Three Roads to Judicial Review," 40 Admin.L.Rev. 451, 453-54, 490-501 (1988), suggesting use of the declaratory order by broadcasting licensee threatened by FCC sanctions for indecent speech; the declaratory order provides a speedy avenue to judicial review. Lubbers & Morant provide numerous additional examples of uses of declaratory orders to expeditiously clear up various sorts of jurisdictional problems without trials.

An agency might want to issue a declaratory order to articulate new law and policy without going through the expense and bother of rulemaking. It might also want to stimulate immediate judicial review of its position, thus clearing up uncertainty about the legality of its position. The order would compel affected parties to go to court immediately; if they don't, the agency precedent stands as authority. And in many situations, judicial review of a declaratory order takes place in an appellate court (whereas direct judicial review of unapplied agency rules usually occurs in a trial court). *See* Powell, *supra*, at 474-479, 483-90.

The federal act leaves the decision to issue a declaratory order to the agency's discretion. According to Lubbers & Morant (following the earlier work of Powell), the useful declaratory order procedure is drastically underutilized in practice. Neither agencies nor private parties seem to understand its benefits or to consider it as a strategic alternative. Of course, an agency might have many reasons to decline a request to produce a declaratory order other than misunderstanding the utility of the procedure. For example, it might be too busy settling real disputes to use its resources to clear up uncertainty. Or an agency might need more experience in administering a particular regulatory statute before it is in a position to bind itself to one interpretation of that statute. Or the particular request might be politically too hot to handle.

The placement of § 554(e) might suggest that an agency is authorized to issue declaratory orders only in circumstances in which the APA adjudication provisions otherwise apply (that is, the gatekeeper provision in § 554(a) is applicable). However, that interpretation seems wrong. Any agency that has power to adjudicate (whether or not under the APA) should be deemed to have the authority to issue a declaratory order. By the same token, the agency should not be required to comply with APA adjudication procedural requirements (such as the ban on ex parte contacts or separation of functions) unless the agency's statute satisfies the § 554(a) gatekeeper requirements (i.e. the statute requires a hearing on the record). See *American Airlines, Inc. v. DOT*, 202 F.3d 788 (5th Cir. 2000) (declaratory order can be issued as part of informal adjudication and ex parte communications are permitted because APA does not apply). If Congress ever overhauls the APA's adjudication provisions, it might consider an independent statutory provision on declaratory orders (giving much more guidance than the existing skeletal provision and emphasizing the utility of declaratory orders). At a minimum, Congress should consider moving the declaratory order provision out of § 554 and placing it in § 555 (so that it would clearly cover informal adjudication).

For discussion of cases arising under the 1961 MSAPA provision, see Arthur Earl Bonfield, "The Iowa Administrative Procedure Act," 60 Iowa L.Rev. 731, 805–23 (1975).

7. *Problem.* This problem presents an opportunity to contrast the state and federal views about equitable estoppel. Under the federal view, the Department cannot be estopped. According to *CHS*, reliance on oral advice is per se unreasonable. *Richmond* says there can be no estoppel when the result is to require payment of money from the Treasury contrary to statute (in this case the payment is contrary to regulations, but they are as binding as statutes.) Here the government is seeking recoupment of illegal payments (as in *CHS*), whereas in *Richmond* plaintiff sought payments from the government. That factual distinction probably means that the government cannot use the *Richmond* Appropriations Clause argument, but it does not dispose of the broader concerns motivating the Court to refuse to allow estoppel.

Beyond the money aspect, federal courts reject estoppel because it contravenes sovereign immunity; the government did not consent to be sued. There is also great concern about collusion; Ann and the friendly social worker might get together and concoct this story of erroneous advice. There is concern about a rush of litigation, as disgruntled citizens claim they were misled by bureaucrats and the courts have to decide difficult factual questions concerning whether advice was given and relied on. Finally, if estoppel applies, the welfare department might have to institute a more elaborate system of checks and balances to prevent advice-giving errors from being made. This would be costly and would diminish the amount available for welfare benefits. And if it discouraged the agency from advising welfare recipients about the complex provisions of the law and regulations, that would be an unfortunate result.

Like many states, Arkansas in *Foote's* holds that estoppel against the government is often appropriate. *Lentz* unanimously held that estoppel can apply in welfare cases. There are good arguments for applying estoppel here. Ann told Courtney the correct facts and Courtney gave wrong advice; Courtney intended her advice be acted on; Ann reasonably relied; Ann suffers injury. Balancing harm to the individual against harm to the government, estoppel costs the state $14,000 (which it might never collect anyway); it does not threaten to disrupt a major program or harm the public interest. Ann should have been given the choice of applying for welfare and naming the father or not applying. By taking the money in violation of the regulations, she has seriously jeopardized her financial future. In that sense, we have a solid case of detrimental reliance.

One can argue that Ann should have gotten the advice in writing, but this seems unrealistic in the context of a welfare applicant and a social worker who is supposed to be an expert in welfare. As a practical matter, Ann's going to have to prove that Courtney gave her wrong advice; Courtney may well deny it and claim that Ann said she didn't know who the father was. After all, Courtney may be blamed for giving wrong advice and lose her job.

Lentz comes out in favor of equitable estoppel in welfare cases, but only where the error is procedural. If a recipient was substantively ineligible for welfare, dictum suggests that estoppel should not apply (or that the case would have to be much more compelling for it to apply). Like the taxpayer in *Foote's*, the recipients in *Lentz* made procedural errors (like failing to provide proper documentation when the documentation could have been provided if they had been correctly advised). It is not so clear whether Ann's case involves a procedural or a substantive defect. It can be argued that the problem is procedural—failure to furnish data. But the defect may be substantive—if the Department had the father's name, he might have been tracked down and made to pay, and the county would not have had to pay Ann the $14,000. *Lentz* cites a couple of Oregon cases that also make the procedural/substantive distinction in welfare estoppel cases.

Lentz goes on to discuss a further interesting issue: could the Welfare Department choose to apply estoppel principles in its fair hearings, or is this something only courts can do? Note that the overpayment claim would normally come up first in an administrative hearing. The court said that the statute permits consideration of all equitable factors in welfare fair hearings, and administrative consideration of estoppel issues is not an invasion of the judicial power of the courts. There is nothing unusual in allowing agencies to exercise equitable remedies or powers.

CHAPTER 5

RULEMAKING PROCEDURES

§ 5.1 INTRODUCTION: THE IMPORTANCE OF RULEMAKING

1. *Rulemaking "ossification."* This section's catalog of advantages that rulemaking offers to the administrative process invites the conclusion that ossification is a bad thing. Some people would disagree. After all, as the Pierce quotation suggests, the external review processes that McGarity describes impinge most heavily on high-stakes environmental, health, and safety regulations. These measures can be deeply controversial, and many observers believe that the high costs of these regulations are too often out of proportion to their benefits. So why shouldn't regulators be forced to do their work carefully?

A counterargument is that even if one believes that society is overregulated, tighter external review of agency rules may not be the best solution. Relief from overregulation, if that is what one wants, might be better pursued by sustained efforts to amend the underlying substantive laws, or by electing administrations that are committed to implementing those laws less aggressively. Moreover, as later materials in this book will develop, regulation is itself a political process that should be, and usually is, at least somewhat responsive to arguments based on the burdens of compliance. In other words, it may be a mistake to impose procedural complexity when what is really desired is substantive reform (although the former may often be politically easier to achieve than the latter). More than a few thoughtful administrative lawyers with politically conservative leanings have argued in this vein. For a brief, characteristically pungent statement of this viewpoint, see Richard J. Pierce, Jr., "The APA and Regulatory Reform," 10 Admin.L.Rev.Am.U. 81 (1996).

2. *Rulemaking authority.* If you decide to devote class time to the contrarian analysis offered by Merrill and Watts, you may want to steer away from getting bogged down in the historical issue of whether the "original convention" ever reflected the shared thinking of the administrative law community. It is not easy to see how one can say that a drafting convention existed, in a legally authoritative sense, if it was known only to staffers and not to members of Congress themselves. On the other hand, Merrill and Watts are surely correct in their premise that the authors of the FTC Act, the FDA Act, and other legislation of similar vintage did not think that agencies would use the general rulemaking clauses for important policymaking. Until the Supreme Court's expansive interpretations of rulemaking power in cases like *Storer* and *Texaco* (discussed in *Campbell*, § 3.2), the prevailing assumption in the administrative law community was that important agency business would

be handled through formal proceedings.

The basic question for class discussion, therefore, is whether the inherent benefits of rulemaking are substantial enough to justify the somewhat revisionist interpretive approach found in modern judicial opinions. We certainly think so, but the question obviously implicates jurisprudential assumptions about "originalism" versus "activism" on which students will probably have diverse opinions. It is too early in the course to consider on a doctrinal level the "nondelegation principle" that underlies Merrill and Watts' normative argument, but the basic policy question is not particularly esoteric: is agency rulemaking an inherently dangerous activity, or a perfectly normal administrative function? As we will see later in the course, the idea that Congress should be presumed not to have delegated authority to an agency *in certain sensitive subject areas* has significant case law and scholarly support, but the Merrill-Watts thesis extends the "nondelegation canons" reasoning a good deal further.

3. *Scope of rulemaking power.* As the text notes, discussions in administrative law about the breadth of an agency's rulemaking authority are usually couched in terms of judicial deference. See John F. Duffy, "Administrative Common Law in Judicial Review," 77 Tex.L.Rev. 113, 200-02 (1998) (suggesting that, conversely, most *Chevron* analysis could be reconceived in the mold of *Mourning* and like cases). The theoretical reason for treating the topic in this chapter is that, in principle, the legislation defines the agencies' power rather than the courts' power. As a practical matter, however, judicial review is usually the main constraint on agencies' misapplications of their rulemaking authority, and most of the relevant case law reflects that focus. Accordingly, we deal with the issue primarily in § 9.2, and only briefly here.

If you do decide to explore the issues, the Florida developments reviewed in this note may provide a useful pathway into the discussion. Rossi's article, cited in the note, makes some thoughtful and measured arguments against the Florida experiment. Although the legislative desire to curb overly ambitious regulation is understandable in the abstract, he says, this sort of vague, across-the-board mandate leads to uncertainty and inconsistent judicial enforcement. It also invites courts to venture into the inherently political process of policymaking, which is not among their principal areas of competence. And the abstractness of the statutory command avoids any real legislative accountability for tradeoffs and is no substitute for legislative consideration (concentrated in the respective committees of specialization) of the possible need for changes in the agency's enabling legislation. 8 Widener J.Pub.L. at 317-18, 343. To this critique you can add the practical costs from the agency's standpoint: A narrow-construction policy impairs the agency's ability to take advantage of the pragmatic benefits of rulemaking that are outlined in the main text of this section of the casebook, such as broadly participatory decisionmaking, a clear legal standard that promotes consistent adjudication in individual cases over time, compilation of a record that could facilitate judicial review, etc. Conversely, the expansive "necessary and proper" approach to rulemaking clauses in federal law allows agencies broader leeway to reap those benefits.

The poker case discussed in the note highlights the mischief that a statute like § 120.536 can bring about. Nothing about the department's actions smacks of an abuse of the rulemaking power. The kennel club is obviously trying to circumvent the limitations of the Cardroom Act. The proposed rule's definition seems well tailored to advance the goals of the regulatory scheme, by taking care of a situation that the legislature did not precisely foresee. So what purpose is served by an insistence that the legislature must previously have authorized rulemaking in the "specific" context of defining poker? Here, the Florida APA provision seems to be obstructing an efficient and fair administrative procedure for no good reason—a lesson underscored by the fact that the agency was later permitted to reach the same result without a rulemaking step. (For more details on the underlying fact situation, see the ALJ's decision below, at 1997 Fla. Div. Adm. Hear. Lexis 5595.)

4. *Problem.* If the Commission is certain it wants to reform the industry's practices in regard to ZIP Code pricing, and that it can ultimately get its way, rulemaking is probably the most effective and efficient method of achieving that end. All other things being equal, a single rulemaking proceeding is probably cheaper than multiple adjudicative proceedings. Rulemaking would allow the agency to give notice of that proceeding in an inexpensive manner to the whole industry and interested members of the public; to gather easily, efficiently, and inexpensively, from all of them, whatever information it considers relevant to its determination of the question; to ascertain accurately the political acceptability of the various policy alternatives facing it; and to settle in one proceeding many issues relating to this question that may not be adequately presented by the case at hand (i.e., other insurers may be committing abuses that are similar but not identical to those of Ranchers).

Of course, practical considerations might make the choice to proceed by adjudication more desirable from the agency's point of view. If you are convinced that the political muscle of the insurance industry is sufficient to frustrate highly visible agency action to outlaw the rating of customers by ZIP Code, you might suggest that the agency proceed by lower visibility adjudication, which is also more insulated from political pressures than is rulemaking. After all, the political muscle of the insurance industry might enable it to stop the adoption of a rule, but might not be strong enough to enable the industry to secure passage of a statute overcoming a series of specific agency decisions in particular cases, which would accomplish the same result on a precedential basis. Similarly, if there is a formal scheme for legislative and gubernatorial review of agency rules in your jurisdiction, and you believe that either the legislature or governor would be opposed to rules on this subject, you might propose that the agency proceed by adjudication to avoid direct legislative or gubernatorial review of such rules.

Note, in this connection, that some of the "advantages" of rulemaking discussed in this section are desirable from society's point of view, but not necessarily from the agency's. One persistent criticism of lawmaking by adjudication is that an agency may pick on a single member of an industry for engaging in conduct that is actually industry-wide. The agency will probably get away with this, because courts are reluctant to interfere with such prosecutorial choices. *FTC v. Universal-Rundle Corp.*, 387 U.S. 244 (1967). Nevertheless, it can be unfair to subject one company to restrictions that put it at a competitive disadvantage with a rival that is no less culpable. Rulemaking avoids that situation. For an agency planner, however, "divide and conquer" may be a quite inviting strategy.

There may also be "merits" reasons to proceed by adjudication rather than rulemaking. The staff apparently has enough evidence to proceed against Ranchers, but it may not have the same evidence about the other insurers. Perhaps they aren't using ZIP Code pricing in a legally "unfair" manner at all. Or, if they are, the staff might have trouble proving it. Uncertainty of this kind would support the more cautious "test case" strategy.

Furthermore, you might recommend that the agency proceed by adjudication if you are convinced that the agency is not ready to settle this issue now in any general way—whether because of rapidly changing conditions in the industry, or because of apprehensions about the actual effects of agency action on this subject, or because of a currently irreconcilable division of opinion within the agency, or because there are so many factors to consider and deal with that they could not easily be captured in rules. Acting through rulemaking would give the agency less leeway to limit its action, temporize, or decide ad hoc.

A point to consider on a totally different level is that if the Commission feels morally outraged by the industry's past conduct and wants to make use of its power to order companies to issue refunds, it will probably have to proceed by adjudication, at least if the state follows the principle of *Bowen v. Georgetown University Hospital*, § 5.2.2. The general principle that agencies cannot impose retroactive liability through rulemaking without explicit legislative authorization is discussed in this section as an "advantage" of rulemaking, but the Commission is more likely to view this restriction as an impediment to its ability to fulfill its mission.

Finally, you can use the Problem to explore the issue of the existence and scope of the Commission's legislative rulemaking authority. The language of the provision is taken from the Communications Act, 47 U.S.C. § 201. You might ask students whether, in light of the words "necessary" and "in the public interest" in the provision, the insurance commission's rulemaking powers should be read more narrowly than cases such as *Mourning* would contemplate. The policy considerations reviewed in this section would be relevant to that discussion. Actually, however, no such restrictive gloss has been placed on the FCC's authority, at least as a general proposition. *See, e.g., AT&T Corp. v. Iowa Utilities Board*, 525 U.S. 366, 380-81 (1999).

On the other hand, one could certainly doubt whether the insurance commission's general rulemaking clause authorizes it to establish a private cause of action for damages, as the co-clerk in the Problem recommends. In one sense, such a cause of action could be considered helpful, even important, to the fulfillment of the commission's statutory mission. Still, judges are often reluctant to conclude that the legislature would want an administrative agency to have a say in adjusting rights to bring civil actions. That is seen as a judicial prerogative. *Alexander v. Sandoval*, 532 U.S. 275 (2001); *Adams Fruit Co. v. Barrett*, 494 U.S. 638 (1990), discussed in § 9.2.3 N.6. *But see Global Crossing Telecomms., Inc. v. Metrophones Telecomms., Inc.*,550 U.S. 45 (2007) (allowing such an extension in a Communications Act context). In each of these cases, Congress had already created an express private cause of action (or an implied one had already been found to exist), and the agency was merely seeking to define its scope. Creation of an entirely new right of action would, presumably, be a harder sell.

For a more factually apposite case, see *NAACP v. American Family Mutual Insurance Co.*, 978 F.2d 287 (7th Cir.1992), in which Judge Easterbrook refused to assume that Wisconsin courts would read a private remedy for residential redlining into the state insurance code. He relied on past state-court case law holding "that enforcement of administrative rules defining unfair practices is for administrative officials, which can revoke an insurer's license or impose other penalties." The lesson in brief is that, while most courts are basically receptive to rulemaking power, they don't give out many blank checks.

§ 5.2 DEFINITION OF "RULE"

§ 5.2.1 Generality and Particularity

1. *The "or particular" language.* Even when one knows the history of the "or particular" language, it seems to be a blunder. The last clause of

§ 551(4) expressly defines ratemaking as rulemaking; the drafters didn't need to tinker with the opening clause to achieve that result. More fundamentally, the definition of rulemaking as a proceeding of "general or particular applicability" is profoundly at odds with the customary understanding of a rule. An amendment to the APA to cure this gaffe is long overdue. For full discussion, see Ronald M. Levin, "The Case for (Finally) Fixing the APA's Definition of 'Rule,'" 56 Admin.L.Rev. 1077 (2004).

The note asks whether due process would permit individualized ratemaking for a telephone company or a cable television franchise without an opportunity for a hearing. We think not, because, despite its historical origins, an individualized ratemaking case is functionally an adjudication. It is expressly directed at a single company and, in *Bi-Metallic* terms, would probably turn on "individual grounds." As to whether a *trial-type* hearing is required, the answer may turn on precisely what issues are in controversy. Even the APA formal adjudication procedures allow an agency to avoid an oral proceeding in certain circumstances in which written ones will do. *See* 5 U.S.C. § 556(d), last sentence; Text § 3.2 N.4. So perhaps the answer is that the telephone or cable company does have a due process right to a decision reached through evidentiary proceedings—but the ground rules for such proceedings incorporate built-in limitations that sometimes prevent the holding of an actual trial.

2. *State law definitions.* As must be apparent by now, we think the 1961 and 1981 MSAPAs were on the right track in dropping the words "or particular" from the federal model. The federal government could learn from their example. The MSAPA's abandonment of "rulemaking" status for individualized ratemaking is of course a different kind of question, as it involves a genuine dissimilarity in procedure, not just a drafting question. However, the 1970 ABA recommendations for amendment of the APA would have followed the states' lead on this issue as well. 24 Admin.L.Rev. 389 (1972).

The alternative approach to drafting a definition of "rule," exemplified by Washington's APA, seems questionable. Some of the fault may rest with the courts. Apparently the purpose of the list of agency statements in the Washington statute was simply to ensure that there *would* be coverage of the items mentioned, not to exclude other statements that would meet the ordinary definition of a rule. *See* William R. Andersen, "The 1988 Washington Administrative Procedure Act—An Introduction," 64 Wash.L.Rev. 781, 790 (1989).

3. *Other criteria.* This and the next note provide an opportunity for review of the criteria used to apply the rulemaking/adjudication distinction in due process case law. That problem largely if not entirely parallels the APA issue. The last criterion mentioned in the note--whether rulemaking

or adjudication procedures appear in fact to be the most expeditious, effective, and fair means of resolving the dispute--has a pragmatic flavor that many judges will surely prefer to the somewhat conceptual approaches competing with it.

One could argue, however, that there are reasons to be wary of ad hoc judicial judgments about whether rulemaking or adjudication procedure is more appropriate or fair in the circumstances. Courts may not be as expert as agencies about whether a particular procedure was effective or fair. Moreover, result-oriented decisionmaking could be quite unpredictable and lead to judicial decisions that unexpectedly and disruptively set aside agency decisions. In addition, the prospect that such decisions could occur might cause the agency to provide more formal procedures than are really needed or legally required. These arguments foreshadow *Vermont Yankee*, § 5.4.3.

4. *Consequences of rulemaking label.* The *Yesler* opinion is unpersuasive insofar as it says that the HUD action had "no immediate, concrete effect on anyone." It did have such an effect on the public housing authorities; it authorized them to engage in summary eviction of suspected drug dealers. Anyway, the idea that a rule differs from an order because it has no "definitive effect" on individuals until it is applied is troublesome. Members of the public often obey or acquiesce in a rule as soon as it is promulgated; they may not await further proceedings. Conversely, some orders lack any immediate binding effect. (For example, an NLRB order is not binding in its own right; to force an individual to comply, the Board has to seek a judicial enforcement order.) The court's generalization is correct, however, if it is read to mean simply that a rule *speaks to* an unnamed class, while an order speaks to identifiable individuals.

In any event, the holding in *Yesler* seems correct. The analogy in the note to *Overton Park*, designed to test the students' understanding of the APA definition, is not valid, because in *Yesler* HUD was not addressing the state as a single entity; the immediate addressees of HUD's determination were a generally described class of public housing authorities.

5. *Critiques of the rulemaking-adjudication dichotomy.* We agree with the commentators mentioned in the note that the distinction between rules and orders is not a panacea. Society places many conflicting demands on its administrative processes, only some of which are captured in the typical descriptions of agency action as "quasi-legislative" and "quasi-adjudicative." Because of the imperfections in those two metaphors, the law has to make careful choices as it designs specific doctrinal principles for rulemaking and adjudication; it also has to leave room for flexibility in the implementation of each model.

The question posed at the end of this note provides an opportunity to review methods by which an agency engaged in adjudication can resolve factual disputes, especially regarding legislative facts, without having to resort to a full trial-type hearing. Devices such as official notice, summary judgment, and the use of legislative rules to narrow the issues in dispute may be covered. The converse question of whether an agency should be required to use trial-type devices in rulemaking is premature at this point in the course. Later sections of this chapter will show that the revolution wrought by *Florida East Coast* and *Vermont Yankee* has made this question almost obsolete, at least as a matter of judicially-enforceable obligation (it may still be relevant as a matter that the legislature should consider when adopting new administrative schemes). Despite the manifest social interest in promoting careful investigation of factual issues in rulemaking, the law has moved strongly away from the idea that courtroom methods are an effective means of eliciting the desired care, or at least that courts are in a good position to decide when agencies should employ those methods.

6. *Lesser pronouncements.* There are valid arguments against reviewability in *Independent Equipment Dealers*, but Roberts's analysis of the definition of "rule" is unpersuasive. A letter that reaffirms an extant enforcement policy can easily be described as "implementing" law or policy, and there does not seem to be any good reason to shun that description. Whether the letter articulates the policy for the first time should be irrelevant. Indeed, the whole point about an advice letter or other interpretive statement is that it *doesn't* change the law; that is what distinguishes it from a ruling that has the force of law. Moreover, under the court's reasoning, an agency might be able to evade judicial review of an advice letter by simply declaring that it had taken the same position in some earlier pronouncement (which the plaintiff may not even have seen). The court's unwillingness to treat the letter as reviewable agency action may have been motivated by a fear that disgruntled trade groups might flood its docket with petitions to review agency policies that they don't like but that are still in an early stage of development. Perhaps, however, that fear could be best addressed through application of the (admittedly subjective) ripeness doctrine, rather than through the more heavyhanded barrier to review that the court seems to erect. We return to this issue in § 11.2.4.

Industrial Safety is a more thoughtful opinion. In considering whether to characterize the guide as a rule, and therefore a reviewable action, the court focused on the need "to accommodate two separate goals of a fair administrative process: protecting parties from false or unauthorized agency news releases and promoting Congress' clear mandate that government information, particularly from consumer-oriented agencies, reach the public." Under the particular circumstances of this case, the court held that the guide was not subject to the APA, but it suggested that it might have decided differently if the agencies had appeared to be trying to punish the manufacturers of "air purifying" respirators, or if those companies had claimed that statements in the guide were false. For a recent opinion in which the court adhered to this measured approach to review of agency publicity, see *Trudeau v. FTC*, 456 F.3d 178 (D.C.Cir.2006). See also *Flue-Cured Tobacco Coop. Stabilization Corp. v. USEPA*, 313 F.3d 852 (4th Cir.2002), holding that an EPA report on the health effects of second-hand tobacco smoke was not subject to judicial review. Instead of resting on a limiting gloss on the APA's definitional provisions, the court relied exclusively on "final agency action" precedents. *See* § 11.2.2 for coverage of that issue.

7. *Unwritten rules.* Ordinarily one would not think of unwritten policies as the kind of "rules" that are governed by a state's APA. The holdings of the Utah and Florida cases can be explained by the fact that those states, unlike almost all others, have laws on the books that broadly *require* agencies to codify their policies using the rulemaking process. *See* § 6.2. We can understand how those state's courts might conclude that an agency that refuses to commit its policies to writing is evading this requirement. (Florida did not adopt its required rulemaking provision until 1991, however, so the *Schluter* court probably read too much into the comments that the APA reporter had written to accompany the original Act in 1974.) The concept of applying an APA to an unwritten "rule" seems decidedly unwieldy, and we would not expect it to be followed in jurisdictions that give agencies more discretion to decide whether or not to resort to rulemaking.

8. *Problem.* The court in *Faulkner* decided that a resolution approving the sale of bonds for a bridge was not a regulation. Therefore it did not have to be published in the state administrative code along with other regulations, nor was rulemaking procedure required. That conclusion seems correct and is consistent with *Overton Park*, discussed in N.4. The resolution pertained to only one bridge and was not of "general application," even though the community at large would be affected by the bridge. However, as Bonfield notes in the cited passage of his treatise, a weight limit for that same bridge would likely be considered a rule, because it would directly constrain the behavior of all members of an open class of persons, i.e., all operators of heavy trucks.

The latter determination would surely meet the test of "generality," but, on the facts of this Problem, it may be too inchoate to qualify as a rule. It might be regarded as just an expression of opinion, or as part of the department's planning process, rather than as the "implementation" of any policy. From this standpoint, it would be comparable to the non-rules involved in *Independent Dealers Ass'n* and *Industrial Safety*. After all, the bridge hasn't even been built yet. On the other hand, if the determination that the department makes now is going to remain on the books and, without further action, operate as an outright prohibition, enforceable with criminal penalties, the "rule" designation seems fine. (That is the situation Bonfield contemplated.)

On a question like this, it may be helpful to move beyond conceptual conundrums about generality and particularity, in favor of more functional thinking. The students haven't yet studied APA rulemaking requirements, but you can easily mention a few consequences that could follow from a finding that the ten-ton weight determination is a rule: publication obligations, notice and comment procedure, judicial review. Would it make sense to apply any of these to the weight determination? Is anyone going to rely on the department's announcement? Will the ten-ton figure have to be revisited before the department actually starts posting signs on the highway and notifying the highway patrol to begin enforcing the limit?

§ 5.2.2 Prospectivity and Retroactivity

BOWEN v. GEORGETOWN UNIVERSITY HOSPITAL

Notes and Questions

1. *Literalism.* At first blush, Justice Scalia seems to be correct in his textual analysis. If one interprets the words "future effect" in § 551(4) to mean nothing more than that a rule is to be applied in the future, regardless of whether or not it attaches new legal consequences to events that occurred in the past, the phrase would appear to be entirely superfluous. (For an argument defending such an interpretation, however, see Frederick Schauer, "A Brief Note on the Logic of Rules, with Special Reference to *Bowen v. Georgetown University Hospital*," 42 Admin.L.Rev. 447 (1990).)

But the more important question is the extent to which the wording of § 551(4) counts at all. Back in 1978, as our cross-reference shows, Scalia was much more willing to take liberties with that wording. To be sure, he could argue that his earlier statement was only meant to lampoon the words "or particular" in § 551(4), and that this acknowledgement doesn't prove that the words "future effect" should likewise be ignored. Even that acknowledgement, however, does seem to undermine the Justice's claim that prospectivity is the only basis on which one can distinguish a rule from an order. "General applicability" is the principal criterion that separates rulemaking from adjudication, even though the words of § 551(4) appear to say otherwise.

The absence of the words "future effect" from the MSAPA definitions of "rule" offers another hint that Justice Scalia may be misinterpreting the federal provision. It is unlikely that the APA and MSAPA could rest upon fundamentally different conceptions of (in his words) "the entire dichotomy upon which the most significant portions of the APA are based."

2. *Consequences of the Scalia view.* An even more telling reason to question Justice Scalia's interpretation of § 551(4) emerges from reading that provision in the context of the entire APA. Per § 551(6), an agency action that is not a rule is an "order." Yet the latter seems a deeply counterintuitive label to affix to the Secretary's Medicare reimbursement regulation. Moreover, calling the action an "order" would seem to mean that the Secretary could issue the regulation *without notice and comment procedure.* Something must be wrong with a construction of the APA that allows agencies to issue retroactive rules with fewer procedural safeguards than would be required for other rules.

What Justice Scalia (and Judge Edwards in the court below) seemingly overlooked is that § 551(4) is not designed to tell agencies what actions they can and cannot take. Agencies don't get their power to issue rules from that provision, nor from any other section of the APA; they get it from their respective organic statutes. Therefore, to say that an action falls outside § 551(4) doesn't mean that the agency can't take that action. Section 551(4) is merely a definitional provision. Its purpose is to identify which actions are subject to APA rulemaking procedures. Maybe a mandate not to issue retroactive rules (absent express authorization) could be ascribed to § 551(4) through judicial creativity, but to reach that result in the name of *literalism* is indeed perverse.

Still another strong argument against the Scalia position is that interpretive rules are rules under the APA, but they are frequently allowed to be retroactive. Nothing prevents an agency from applying an interpretive rule in an adjudication to events that occurred before the interpretive rule was adopted. And courts do the same thing, as the example of *Meritor* illustrates.

In *Health Insurance Ass'n,* however, Judge Williams argued that, because interpretive rules receive judicial deference (he assumed it would be *Chevron* deference but added that any other level of deference would raise similar concerns), they alter the legal landscape. When deference is accorded, therefore, an individual whose actions predated the issuance of the rule suffers the same kind of unfair surprise that the *Georgetown* presumption is intended to prevent. (Williams acknowledged that an agency should be able to apply an interpretive rule retroactively within *administrative adjudication,* because the agency could have reached the same retroactive result in the adjudication even if it had not issued the rule, and one doesn't want to deter agencies from spelling out their interpretations in guidance documents. In the *Health Insurance* case, however, that problem didn't arise, because the agency was bringing an enforcement action directly in court.) We think that, although Williams's argument seems logical in the abstract, it could lead to practical problems. It suggests, in effect, that a court might construe a statute or regulation one way in a case in which the interpretive rule would operate retroactively, and a different way in another case in which it would not. Or else the agency could get stuck with an adverse precedent indefinitely, simply because of circumstances that would be unique to the litigant involved in the first case to present the interpretive issue. A better solution, we think, would be for courts to declare that all interpretive rules fall outside the domain of *Georgetown* and *Landgraf,* and to use reasonableness review to curb particular injustices if they arise.

3. *The majority's canons.* Justice Kennedy's position is more attractive than Scalia's. Retroactive liability can be troublesome, for the reasons articulated in *Landgraf.* The problem is that the *Georgetown* presumption sweeps more broadly than necessary to assuage those concerns.

a. In *Combs,* SSA clearly stated that it would apply the revised guidelines to pending cases that had not yet been adjudicated. However, the Fourth Circuit assumed that SSA had no power to issue retroactive rules. Thus, under the second *Georgetown* canon, the case turned on whether SSA's intentions would result in "retroactivity," a question that the court addressed using *Landgraf* criteria. The en banc court was deeply divided, upholding the agency by a vote of 7-6. The four judges who wrote in the case consumed thirty-six pages debating it. Here is a brief recap of the competing arguments:

The plurality (per Judge Rogers) argued that the amendment to the guidelines (deleting listing 9.09) should apply to Combs' case and didn't implicate *Landgraf* concerns, because it was procedural rather than substantive. The underlying statutory criteria were unchanged, and the purpose of the guidelines was to streamline the adjudicative process. Indeed, he continued, the rule was not retroactive at all, because what it regulated was the agency's adjudicative conduct, which occurred *after* the amendment. Moreover, he saw no reason to believe that Combs had relied on the old rule when she became obese, nor when she filed her claim with SSA.

As the dissents by Judges Clay and Griffin pointed out, however, the plurality's position that the amendment made only a procedural change was tenuous. Shifts in a burden of proof are usually considered substantive. Here, if Combs could not make use of listing 9.09, she would have more to prove and less chance of recovering. That's pretty substantive, isn't it? Clay also suggested that Combs might have relied on the earlier, relatively liberal disability rule in her financial planning decisions. The two dissenting opinions had different bottom lines, however. Clay would have given Combs the benefit of the presumption for the entire period since 1996, but Griffin would have done so only with respect to the 1996-99 period. He probably had the better of that disagreement. Once the new guidelines had been promulgated, their adverse effect on Combs would probably constitute, at worst, secondary retroactivity. *Cf. Martin v. Hadix*, 527 U.S. 343 (1999) (congressionally mandated cap on reimbursement of attorney fees incurred in pending prisoners' rights cases was inapplicable to fees for work done before the cap went into effect, but enforceable with respect to work done afterwards).

Another interesting analysis was that of Judge Gilman. Although he admitted that the deletion of listing 9.09 was more substantive than procedural, he concurred in the plurality's result because he thought that, generally speaking, the unfairness against which *Landgraf* is directed is after-the-fact imposition of liability, rather than after-the-fact revocation of the right to receive benefits. For example, he argued, Combs's act of filing an application in 1996 did not give rise to the expectations of stability that underlie the retroactivity doctrine. Except when those particular concerns are implicated, he concluded, courts should adhere to their usual practice of applying the law that is in place at the time of their decisions. Gilman's distinction seems helpful, although it might be considered too facile. After all, *Georgetown* itself involved a claim by hospitals for "new property" benefits. But in that case the hospitals' reliance on prior law was obvious and substantial, so retroactivity concerns were sharply implicated.

b. In *Bernklau*, the Federal Circuit cited *Landgraf* and declined to apply § 3(a) to the claimant's case. As the court recognized, however, appellate tribunals often do remand a case for reconsideration in light of an intervening change in the law. Notice, moreover, that the usual *Landgraf* concerns about reliance, fair notice, etc., are completely inapposite to this situation, because § 3(a) would, if anything, make Bernklau better off, not worse off. So the reason to deny him and similarly situated claimants the benefits of the statute must be administrative convenience, i.e., the disruptive effect of having to reopen numerous cases that the department has already finished handling. From that standpoint, the decision seems reasonable. *See Landgraf*, 511 U.S. at 275 n.29, 281 n.34. (suggesting that a court need not apply a new procedural rule to a pending case if it has already completed the stage of litigation to which the new rule is relevant).

c. In *Figueroa*, the majority ruled for the claimant, declining to follow the Massachusetts counterpart of the first *Georgetown* presumption against retroactivity. It relied in part on case law indicating that "curative" changes in the law, designed to "remedy mistakes and defects," can be applied retroactively. That line of argument was not very persuasive, because, as the dissent pointed out, the new regulation was basically a liberalization of the substantive criteria, not a correction of a "mistake" in the old one. The presumption against retroactivity could not very well survive if courts were to choose to override it whenever an agency replaces one regulation with another that it thinks will better serve statutory policies. However, the majority also had a stronger point: On the facts of this case, the policy arguments underlying the presumption were scarcely, if at all, implicated in the first place. Here (as in *Bernklau*), the new regulation would make nobody worse off except the government, so retroactivity would not threaten private reliance interests at all. Nor did administrative convenience militate against giving the claimant the benefit of the new rule. To this extent, the majority's willingness to engage in ad hoc pragmatism seems more appealing.

4. *Reasonableness limitations.* Presumably the reason the Court didn't rest on a *Retail Clerks* rationale is that it had strong feelings against retroactive liability and believed that case-by-case balancing would give reviewing courts too much latitude to pursue competing agendas. The rationale that the Court did use provides a clear and predictable decisional principle. However, we believe, as does Luneburg, 1991 Duke L.J. at 140-41, that the virtues of a bright line principle are outweighed, in this instance, by the overbreadth of the Court's presumption. It's also worth noticing that the result in *Georgetown* may, in practice, ensure that agency policymaking with retroactive effects will be implemented through ad hoc adjudication rather than through rules, because the latter must be prospective only, according to that case. For reasons indicated in § 5.1, this appears to be an undesirable result.

5. *Problem.* (a) First, is Directive 14-1 a rule? You can use this Problem to review the issues raised in § 5.2.1, or in lieu of the Problem at the end of that unit. If Madison has adopted the 1961 or 1981 MSAPA, "general applicability" is explicitly required by the state's definition of "rule." As explained in the preceding section of this Manual, we also believe that, despite the literal language of 5 U.S.C. § 551(4), "generality" is an integral element of a "rule" as that term is used in federal law.

In this instance, the directive arguably lacks sufficient "generality" to be a rule, because it applies to only three companies, and the department has relied on facts pertaining to Colossal in deciding to adopt the directive. (It's hard to say whether those facts are "adjudicative" or "legislative," because they are relevant to a particular party's circumstances *and also* to the desirability of the rule.) The issues in *Bi-Metallic* and *Anaconda* can be reviewed in this connection. In our view, the directive is a rule. The critical fact is that the directive is framed in general terms, applying in principle to an unlimited number of companies.

Another reason why the directive might not be considered a rule is that it seems explicitly retroactive. Justice Scalia argues that the federal APA forbids retroactive rules. For reasons discussed in this section, however, we believe that Scalia has read too much into the "future effect" language of APA § 551(4). Anyway, if Madison has adopted the 1961 or 1981 MSAPA, Scalia's analysis is entirely beside the point, because the definition of "rule" in each of those Acts does not contain the "future effect" language in the first place.

(b) Assuming the directive is a rule, is it fatally retroactive under the *Georgetown* test? At first glance, one would think so, because the directive applies to past violations, and the Mining Control Act does not confer express authority to issue retroactive rules. In *National Mining Ass'n,* which arose under the Surface Mining Control and Reclamation Act of 1977, the D.C. Circuit reached essentially that conclusion, although the situation was somewhat more complicated. (The rule dealt with acquisition of one mining company by another. All permits sought by the acquiring company were to be blocked due to environmental violations committed by the acquired company, even though both the violations and the acquisition had occurred before the agency issued the rule.)

However, the department has two possible counter-arguments. First, Directive 14-1 might be a mere interpretive rule. The *Georgetown* opinion refers to grants of "legislative rulemaking authority." Thus, it can be read as making its holding inapplicable to interpretive rules. Here, DNR can argue that the Directive merely articulates a position that could have been inferred from § 22 of the Mining Act. Because § 22 has been on the books since 1980, there is no retroactivity.

Second, even if we assume that Directive 14-1 is a legislative rule, it may not be retroactive in the relevant sense. It might simply be an example of what Scalia calls "secondary retroactivity," like increasing the tax rates for a pre-existing trust. DNR can say that it is merely redefining the conditions under which it will issue permits in the future. If Colossal wants a new permit, the company should cure its continuing violation.

In exploring the critical question of whether Directive 14-1 is "retroactive" at all, you can direct attention to the language of *Landgraf* (as quoted in N.3). The required inquiry goes to "whether the new provision attaches new legal consequences to events completed before its enactment" and is influenced by "familiar considerations of fair notice, reasonable reliance, and settled expectations." There is room to debate what "conduct" or "event" DNR is trying to regulate. Is it the *creation* of damage to the environment? If so, the penalty for committing such a violation should not be augmented ex post facto. Or is the relevant conduct the *inaction* of failing to rectify the damage? If so, that nonfeasance is still occurring, and the permit-blocking that aims to overcome it is not a retroactive measure. On the facts of this Problem, the failure-to-restore violation might be described either way.

Even if the rule is deemed to be an example of secondary retroactivity, it would have to survive reasonableness review under *Retail Union*. The court would have to weigh competing equities of the government and the private entity. Colossal would probably argue that it made its decisions about environmentally risky conduct in reliance on the law as it stood before September, and it is unfair to replace that law with a more stringent one after the fact. The government, however, can argue that this fairness interest is outweighed by the public interest in giving companies a broadly applicable incentive to come into compliance with environmental requirements. Both arguments are plausible, so the court's reaction would be hard to predict. But the importance of *Georgetown* and *Landgraf* is that they do not contemplate such a subjective balancing of equities. If the regulation is viewed as increasing the penalty for past violations, and DNR has no specific statutory authority for retroactive rulemaking, retroactive application is categorically forbidden.

§ 5.3 INITIATING RULEMAKING PROCEEDINGS

CHOCOLATE MANUFACTURERS ASS'N v. BLOCK

Notes and Questions

2. *Detail required.* The *Richard* holding is certainly questionable, because the welfare department's notice contained no substantive information at all. The state can argue that everyone who was really interested (e.g., a legal aid office) would have asked for a copy of the proposed rules; Ms. Richard probably wouldn't have commented regardless of whether the details had been published. But that argument may miss the point. Forcing an agency to publicize its intentions in a widely distributed publication, like the *Federal Register*, enhances the likelihood that any questionable changes will come to the attention of people who might object to them. It's not unreasonable to give Richard standing, as a private attorney general, to enforce the state's obligation. The Abbott article cited in the note is a good compilation of authorities on this issue. Probably, this sort of problem will rarely arise in the future, because agencies will tend to post proposed rules on the Internet, making them readily accessible to all.

The MSAPA approach of requiring publication of the text of the proposed rule (with narrow exceptions, none applicable in *Richard*) will probably lead to good results most of the time, and it certainly avoids the problem in this case. Most federal rulemaking notices do contain a proposed text, although the law does not require this. A possible argument against making this step mandatory is that an agency might want to commence a rulemaking proceeding for the purpose of obtaining input, without a clear sense of where it wants to end up. It may be wasteful to force officials to declare a tentative position on all unresolved matters (some of which may be quite controversial) when no one expects the proposal to survive in anything like this form anyway. In reply, however, it can be argued that the agency should use an "advance" notice of proposed rulemaking for this purpose, followed by a notice that does contain a proposed text.

3. *The logical outgrowth test.* It's no wonder that "logical outgrowth" issues are a constant subject of litigation in challenges to agency rules. The operative test is unavoidably subjective. Obviously, rules do change between the proposal and final stages, and challengers often have good reason to think that a sympathetic court might agree that the agency could have signaled its ultimate destination on a more specific level than it did.

The government can argue in all of these cases that an overly stringent application of the right to notice would deter agencies from making changes in the proposed rule in response to constructive comments—or, by forcing them to hold new comment periods, protract rulemaking proceedings unduly. There's also the possible disruption of a remand, which may be especially threatening when the court is wielding an issue that's as subjective as "logical outgrowth." Offsetting these interests is the private party's claim, which may be stronger or weaker in various cases, to have been deprived of fair notice. Beermann & Lawson's article, excerpted in the text, makes a forceful case for the government side of this balance, but we think it gives too little weight to the private side. The benefits of the notice and comment process itself—including the agency's opportunity to learn from the comments, the public's interest in having its views considered, the resulting legitimacy that attaches to the adopted rule, and the creation of a record that facilitates judicial review—all hinge on adequate notice of what matters the agency will address in the proceeding.

The *Chocolate Mfrs.* case makes for a wonderful class discussion, because the facts are accessible and the issue is very close. Without question, the court's analysis is plausible, but there are also strong counterarguments. In class, you'll want to bring the discussion around quickly to the question of whether CMA had reason to know that USDA was considering a change affecting chocolate milk. That question is much easier to argue about on a practical level than abstract concepts like "logical outgrowth" and "substantially departs."

a. Part of the Fourth Circuit's argument is that flavored milk had long been accepted in the WIC program—an explicit warning was necessary if USDA proposed to change that state of affairs. To be sure, as we discuss in the next note, a broad reading of *Long Island Care* could lead to the conclusion that the agency actually *did* give an adequate warning by mentioning flavored milk in one of the food packages proposed in the rulemaking notice. But even if one disagrees with the premise that the specific mention provided fair notice, the court's argument is open to question, because the 1978 legislation directly advised the agency to start paying more attention to fat and sugar content of foods. The statutory mandate implies a need for change. When the Secretary raises that issue, chocolate milk would seem to be a pretty obvious target.

Defenders of the court's holding can respond, however, that the private sector shouldn't be forced to generate comments addressed to every issue that an agency has some *bare possibility* of reaching. Nor does an enlightened agency really want such a deluge of paper. The whole process works more smoothly when the rulemaking notice raises issues with specificity and outsiders submit comments that are directly relevant to those issues. We think that Beermann & Lawson go astray on this point, because they seem to imply that *every* manufacturer of foods that USDA said it was planning to retain in the WIC program should have been expected to file comments detailing the reasons why such continued inclusion would be a good idea. We seriously doubt that § 553 should be construed to invite that result. Thus, if the rulemaking notice put CMA on notice that its products might be dropped, the reason is not that *all* foods were placed in controversy by being listed in the notice, but rather that the nature of the proceeding would naturally raise questions about the suitability of chocolate milk for the program.

b. Of special interest is what might be called the court's "expressio unius" argument: by listing certain foods as possible targets, the agency implied that the status of chocolate milk was secure. The point is somewhat undercut by the agency's invitation to the public to "make recommendations for alternatives not considered in the proposed regulations." More fundamentally, doesn't the court's reasoning give an agency a perverse incentive to leave details out, defeating the basic goals of § 553(b)? You can ask whether USDA would have won if it hadn't mentioned any foods on the hit list, and whether such a notice would have been more in the public interest.

c. The court's opinion doesn't mention anything that CMA claims it would have said if it had been given a chance to comment. Should a litigant be able to get a rule set aside without any showing that it was prejudiced by the lack of notice that a particular issue was in play? You can raise the issues in N.9 in this connection.

In the *Chocolate Mfrs.* case, CMA's prospects of success were evidently not bad, for on remand the department restored flavored milk to the approved list. The reasons weren't really spelled out, but the agency hinted at a possibility that lactose intolerant individuals might be better able to tolerate flavored milk. 51 Fed.Reg. 13,207 (1986).

4. *U-turns.* The reasoning of *Long Island Care* seems correct to the extent it means that, when an agency gives clear notice that an issue is under examination, people who agree with the agency's tentative view cannot complain about lack of fair notice if the agency, after receiving comments, reverses its position. *See American Medical Ass'n v. United States*, 887 F.2d 760 (7th Cir.1989). The possibility that this might occur is inherent in the comment process. Typically, people who disagree with the proposed policy or interpretation file comments criticizing it; people who agree with it file comments supporting it; and the agency chooses whether or not to revise its tentative position. (Thus, we disagree with the quoted language from *Environmental Integrity Project v. EPA*, 425 F.3d 992, 998 (D.C.Cir.2005), a case in which the parties knew exactly what problem the agency would address, even though the agency's solution turned out to be surprising.)

The facts of *Long Island Care* fit fairly easily into this analysis. A new statute had gone into effect, and interested parties could easily have foreseen that the Labor Department's task of writing implementing regulations would implicate the question of whether the preexisting obligations of third-party employers would survive. Indeed, the department's proposed rules contained a paragraph dealing with that very question. These circumstances suggest that the Court was correct in finding the logical outgrowth test satisfied. (The analysis is complicated, however, by the fact that the agency characterized that paragraph as an interpretive rule, a circumstance that might have led some people to doubt that the agency was soliciting comment on it.)

We do not think that reasoning is dispositive of the problem in *Chocolate Mfrs.*, however. We distinguish between a challenger's ability to foresee what position the agency will ultimately adopt (not needed) and the challenger's ability to foresee that an issue will be considered by the agency at all (generally necessary). *Long Island Care* would be in point if the preamble to USDA's proposed rule had expressly stated that the department anticipated that flavored milk would remain eligible under the WIC program, notwithstanding the congressional mandate to promote healthier diets. The problem is that, in the real case, the crucial issue was not flagged as conspicuously as that. There was a preexisting program, and CMA might reasonably have thought that the department was simply taking the eligibility of flavored milk for granted. The department's fleeting references to flavored milk on the proposed menus did not clearly signal otherwise. In other words, considering the multitude of ways in which USDA might potentially have altered the program, we do not think the Fourth Circuit was unreasonable in putting a burden on the department to let food producers know which specific foods might lose their eligibility. (As we said above, however, the elimination of chocolate milk from the program may nevertheless have been a logical outgrowth of the notice, by virtue of the

241

general thrust of the proposed policy change.)

5. *Logical outgrowth of what?* Ordinarily, public comments are kept in an open file, and private interests who are concerned with a proposed rule, at least the better financed ones, will frequently visit the agency's reading room to see what the various commenters have to say. Nevertheless, as a general rule, we don't think that comments themselves put the public on notice of a contemplated change in a proposed rule. (Despite the phrasing of its opinion, the Fourth Circuit probably didn't think so, either, as it gave no evident weight to the 78 comments that had favored removal of chocolate milk from the WIC program.) The rulemaking process is different from court litigation; it's designed to be *broadly* participatory. Thus, a small company that's located thousands of miles from Washington, or in a county far removed from the state capitol, might well wish to comment, but can't be expected to monitor what comments are being filed by others.

That concern may become increasingly irrelevant as more and more rulemaking agencies post comments on the Internet for all to see. Even if one interest group becomes aware of a suggestion that another interest group is making, however, it may not be fair to expect the former to file a response if it has seen no indication that the agency might go along. Nevertheless, in some cases, the concerned groups are few in number and well known to each other, and it would be artificial for one of them to claim that it was unaware of the existence and importance of what others are seeking. *See Common Carrier Conference—Irregular Route v. United States,* 534 F.2d 981 (D.C.Cir.1976). Also, in a close case, the fact that some members of the public commented on an issue could at least be probative of whether the rulemaking notice actually raised that issue. *Union Pacific Resources Co. v. FERC,* 936 F.2d 1310 (D.C.Cir.1991). But these are exceptional cases, and we think the *Horsehead* case cited in the text represents the preferable view.

6. *State variations.* Possibly the wording of the "substantially different" test in the MSAPA provision invites somewhat closer judicial scrutiny than the logical outgrowth test. Under federal law a rule might well differ in many respects ("substantially") from the proposed rule, yet be upheld on the ground that it is a logical outgrowth of the proposal. However, the MSAPA provision has been authoritatively explained as focusing on the extent to which parties affected by the final rule had received fair notice of its likely contents from the published text of the proposed rule on which it is based, so that they had a fair opportunity to present their views on that rule prior to its adoption. *See* MSAPA § 3-107, Comment. Since this is also the standard explanation of the purpose behind the federal "logical outgrowth" test, the two standards could well tend to converge in practice. The Indiana experience discussed by Oddi may be an

isolated phenomenon. Incidentally, after Oddi's article was published, the Indiana legislature revised the statute. It now allows an agency to adopt a rule that substantially differs from the proposed rule if it is "a logical outgrowth of [the] proposed rule *as supported by any written comments submitted*" (emphasis added). This is not exactly the federal test, but as yet no Indiana cases shed light on how the new language will be construed.

We would have thought that a system like Maryland's, in which an agency is required to publish a new notice of proposed rulemaking whenever it makes a "substantive" change in the text of a proposed rule, would prove impractical. One could expect it to result in an endless series of rulemaking proceedings and an unwillingness of agencies to make desirable changes in proposed rules, thus frustrating the very purpose of APA rulemaking procedures.

Nevertheless, Professor Tomlinson reports that the Maryland system of strict limits on an agency's ability to revise a rulemaking proposal without inviting further comment works acceptably (although he would like the legislature to consider relaxing those limits). Edward A. Tomlinson, "The Maryland Administrative Procedure Act: Forty Years Old in 1997," 56 Md.L.Rev. 196, 204-05, 272 (1997). Part of the reason may be that the state attorney general has construed the provision leniently and the courts have not overridden that interpretation. Moreover, according to Tomlinson, rulemaking in Maryland is not at all ossified. The agency does not need to explain the basis and purpose of a rule, nor is there judicial review of the rule's rationality. *Id.* at 205, 208, 210. Presumably, the easier it is for an agency to issue a rule, the less one needs to worry about forcing it to run through the process twice.

We think the *Brocal* case really missed the boat. The court doesn't seem to have grasped that the purpose of variance restrictions is to ensure that the public is on notice of important changes in a proposed rule. In many cases, including *Brocal* itself, the ultimate goal of a proposed regulation may be utterly noncontroversial; the only hard questions concern the means that the agency will use to fulfill that goal. In such cases, the court's reasoning gives the agency carte blanche to propose one rule and adopt a vastly different one. True, the Pennsylvania statute was poorly drafted; but the court, starting from the known fact that the act was based on the federal APA, could surely have construed the statute in a manner that would have been more in tune with modern administrative law thinking. It might have interpreted "enlarge the original purpose" to mean "significantly alter the thrust," or something like that. Such an interpretation would have required no more creativity than other courts have displayed in reading a "logical outgrowth" interpretation into their rulemaking statutes.

7. *Information that forms basis of rule.* It is difficult, to put it mildly, to find in § 553(b) of the federal APA a requirement that an agency disclose all of the specific information on which it relies when it files a notice of proposed rulemaking. Section 553(b)(3) calls for disclosure of "either the terms or substance of the proposed rule *or* a description of the subjects and issues involved" (emphasis added). As a purely textual matter, the "subjects and issues involved" could perhaps be deemed to encompass the technical data underlying a rule, but an agency that discloses the "terms or substance of the proposed rule" (as most do) wouldn't have to worry about that language. And as *Vermont Yankee*, § 5.4.3, indicates, courts ordinarily may not impose procedural requirements in informal rulemaking in addition to those required by § 553 of the APA. (With respect to an alternative theory under which *Portland Cement* can be justified on the basis of § 553(c), see the following note in this manual.)

Nevertheless, the emergence of the *Portland Cement* doctrine is not difficult to explain. As Pierce discusses in the article cited in the text, the doctrine illustrates how rulemaking has evolved into a mechanism that allows members of the public to probe an agency's factual assumptions for weaknesses and to build a factual record with which to contest the agency's view. For this model to work, a mere description of the studies on which the agency means to rely can't be sufficient; the challenger has to be able to review the actual studies in order to see whether they stand up to scrutiny. In major rulemaking proceedings, in which the impact of an agency's discretionary judgments can run well into the millions of dollars, courts have understandably put a high premium on procedures that are designed to ensure that the agency gets its science right. The courts' bold interpretation of the APA is a direct response to those pressures.

Moreover, a member of the public could ordinarily obtain all of the studies in the agency's possession relevant to a proposed rule by making a demand for them under the Freedom of Information Act (discussed in § 8.1). If there were no *Portland Cement* doctrine, well-financed commenters would routinely request all such materials. Thus the effect of *Portland Cement* is to make disclosure of the documents automatic.

On the other hand, the *Portland Cement* line of cases poses significant litigation risks for the agency. It is all too easy for a challenger to advance a colorable contention in court, with the benefit of hindsight, that it would have made a more powerful case to the agency if it had received earlier disclosure of some of the information that ultimately finds its way into the rulemaking record. Courts have to analyze such contentions without any clear guideposts to tell it how "critical" a given study or methodology really was to the rulemaking proceeding. Whether the courts have the technical competence to oversee the scientific dialogue in this manner is also open to debate. But the federal courts' response to these risks has been to apply the doctrine restrictively in many cases, as in *Mortgage Investors* and *Time Warner*, rather than to abandon it entirely. Although Judge Kavanaugh, in his *American Radio* dissent cited in the text, does express interest in reopening this settled doctrine, basically on *Vermont Yankee* grounds, we would be astounded to see the courts accept his invitation.

8. *Subsequent additions to the record.* We don't recommend classroom discussion of the subject matter of this note (or at least the interpretive question that it presents), because that legal issue forms part of the basis for our *Vermont Yankee* teaching problem in § 5.4.3 N.6. There are plenty of other issues to cover in this section. Teachers who do wish to discuss the issue in this section, however, can consult our analysis in the manual's discussion of that problem.

9. *Prejudicial impact.* The argument for requiring challengers to explain why their lack of access to a scientific study was prejudicial is compelling. Agencies may generate reams of paper (or zillions of bytes of data) during a rulemaking proceeding, and an obligation to disclose this stuff would become completely unworkable without a materiality limitation. Perhaps a similar showing should be demanded of a plaintiff who complains of inadequate notice of the terms of the rule that an agency contemplates adopting. A court might at least ask the challenger to indicate what sort of arguments he would have advanced if he had been given a chance. Intuitively, however, a breach of the "logical outgrowth" doctrine (or one of its state law counterparts) seems more fundamental than a failure to disclose data. A member of the public should at least know *what* is proposed, even if she isn't given all the reasons *why* it is proposed. Moreover, a requirement that a challenger show prejudice would overlook the fact that "fair notice" of an agency's intentions can serve purposes other than giving members of the public an opportunity to present arguments that the agency would find intrinsically persuasive. It might also mean an opportunity to enlist support from legislators who can lean on the agency.

10. *Problem.* This problem raises two issues: first, whether the final rule was valid in light of the difference between it and the proposed rule contained in the notice of proposed rulemaking on which it was based; and second, whether the Board was required to disclose the second group of articles in a manner that would enable persons interested in the proposed rule to comment on them.

a. *Notice.* Resolution of the first issue requires an application to these facts of the "logical outgrowth" test under the federal APA and the § 3-107 "substantially different" test under the 1981 MSAPA. In the *Psychiatric Health* case, Judge Kessler held that the one-hour rule was a logical outgrowth of the proposed rule. That conclusion seems at least reasonable, because the one-hour requirement is at least in the ballpark of the measures proposed in the rulemaking notice.

However, the hospitals also have some good arguments on their side. Although they knew generally that controls on physical and chemical restraints would be considered in this proceeding, they apparently had no warning that this particular measure would be considered. Surely one could not expect them to "reasonably anticipate," and file comments on, *every* possible restriction the Board might devise.

Moreover, as spelled out in the problem, the hospitals seem to have identified some reasonable arguments that they could have raised against this particular measure (had they known about it) but would not have been likely to mention otherwise. In *Psychiatric Health*, the plaintiffs made these same points in the context of claiming that the HHS rule was arbitrary and capricious. The court replied by deferring to the Secretary, noting that the issues involved technical or scientific judgment. For purposes of substantive review, that response may have been correct. Even so, however, the hospitals in our problem can say that they should have had a realistic opportunity to make those points to the Board itself, so that it could reach its expert judgment in light of them. Finally, the fact that the one-hour requirement is stricter than the hospitals' accreditation standards might strengthen the argument that the hospitals could not "reasonably anticipate" that the Board would impose it.

On the other hand, the Board may be able to convince the court that it became thoroughly familiar with behavior-controlling restraints through the comment process and its own research, so that the plaintiffs' objections to the one-hour requirement result from a difference of opinion about its merits, rather than from a breakdown in the deliberative process.

Policy arguments favoring the Board would probably be pitched at a more general level. The agency has a strong interest in being able to promulgate rules without too much second-guessing by the court. More specifically, it ought to be able to revise its proposed rule on the basis of newly acquired suggestions and information without having to start the rulemaking process over again. This type of reasoning may have been in the background of *Psychiatric Health*. The tone of the opinion suggests that the court thought that the Secretary had written a basically sound rule that would address a genuine problem; therefore, the rule should not be set aside because of a relatively small divergence from the proposed rule. (The court does not necessarily face an all-or-nothing choice, however. It would seem that, if the hospitals were to prevail, the court could sever the one-hour rule and remand it for further consideration while leaving the rest of the rule in place. On severability in the administrative context, see Ronald M. Levin, "'Vacation' at Sea: Judicial Remedies and Equitable Discretion in

b. *Disclosure.* With respect to the federal APA, *Portland Cement* and *Connecticut Light* suggest that the agency should have disclosed at an earlier time that it planned to consider the second group of professional articles, so that the hospitals would be able to comment on them. The facts are ambiguous as to whether those articles added much to the research findings contained in the articles that the rulemaking notice did mention. If they did not, possibly the agency can sustain the rule by showing that the articles were merely "supplementary" and that the hospitals had an adequate opportunity to articulate their positions on the factual issues raised by the medical literature.

Section 3-103 of the 1981 MSAPA does not appear to require an agency to include in its required notice of proposed rulemaking the information on which it based a proposed rule. Possibly such a requirement could be implied by reading that provision together with § 3-104(a), which guarantees persons "the opportunity to submit in writing, argument, data, and views on the proposed rule." Of course, it is clear that such a result was not intended by the drafters of the MSAPA (any more than it was intended by the drafters of the federal APA), so this requirement would have to depend heavily on the policy considerations mentioned above.

Note that if the agency failed to place its new analyses in the public rulemaking record required by § 3-112, interested persons would have a ground for seeking reversal of the agency's action. Section 3-112(b)(3) appears to require *all* "written materials considered by the agency in connection with the formulation of the rule" to be placed in the public rulemaking record. But it does not say *when* the items must be placed there. If interested persons did not know prior to the end of the comment period that these analyses had been placed in that record, it still would not have helped them.

§ 5.4 PUBLIC PARTICIPATION

§ 5.4.1 Informal Rulemaking

Notes and Questions

2. *E-rulemaking structures.* As the note mentions, the development of e-rulemaking has been gradual. The challenges are remarkably complicated. Commentators have been particularly frustrated about the limitations of the Regulations.gov site, which lacks many of the user-friendly features found on the sites of the most forward-looking individual agencies. For a brief but pungent example of this critique, see Richard W. Parker,

"The Next Generation of E-Rulemaking: A User's Perspective," in ERULEMAKING AT THE CROSSROADS 15 (2006), available at *erulemaking. ucsur.pitt.edu/doc/Crossroads.pdf.* Recurring criticisms of the central site and individual agency sites have included the following: that comments are not posted promptly enough to permit timely responses; that too few electronic dockets include supporting documents and links to background regulatory actions for each pending rule; and that search engines should facilitate a wider range of searches. The designers of Regulations.gov have argued in their own defense that it isn't easy to secure the cooperation of officials from agencies throughout the government.

We have dealt only cursorily with these management challenges in the text, because we think they don't readily lend themselves to classroom discussion, but they are undoubtedly important. A recent report by a blue-ribbon ABA committee examines these issues carefully and in detail. *See* ABA Committee on the Status and Future of Federal e-Rulemaking, ACHIEVING THE POTENTIAL: THE FUTURE OF FEDERAL E-RULEMAKING (2008), available at *http://resource.org/change.gov/ceri-report-web-version.fixed.pdf.*

3.   *E-rulemaking in practice.*   The widespread enthusiasm for expansion of e-government is entirely understandable, for a variety of reasons. First, on a mundane and uncontroversial level, online submission of comments is convenient for both commenters and recipients, and the easy availability of documents that will comprise the rulemaking record is conducive to an informed exchange of views. Second, the promise of broader participation stemming from electronic rulemaking resonates with good-government values such as openness and political responsiveness. Agencies want to be seen as receptive to the views of the public. Politically accountable officials, too, naturally tend to endorse reforms that are intended to render bureaucratic decisionmaking more transparent and thus more legitimate in the eyes of the electorate.

Third, particularly in academic commentary, e-rulemaking enthusiasts discern a large upside potential for deliberative democracy and dialogue. They argue that technological innovations might allow members of the public who have been underrepresented in traditional rulemaking procedures to make their voices heard. (Note that these new participants would not necessarily be more "representative" of public opinion than current participants are. Even if they are not, however, broader participation might ensure that non-elite perspectives would play a larger role in the conversation, ameliorating the current dominance of "insiders.")

All of these arguments are straightforward and reasonable, but the note attempts to inject some cautionary considerations into the discussion. The first issue is whether e-rulemaking can ultimately be expected to elicit comments from ordinary citizens in a wider range of rulemaking proceedings. The prevalent criticisms of existing websites, as summarized in N.2, imply that technological improvements may have this effect. However, Coglianese contends in the cited article that technology cannot eliminate other factors that dampen public participation in rulemaking. In his view (which we somewhat oversimplify here), average citizens know little about regulatory agencies and their missions. Moreover, even when they do find out about a pending rulemaking, they also have other claims on their attention. Usually, therefore, they will decide to free-ride on the efforts of organized interest groups, instead of taking time to learn about the issues in a particular rulemaking proceeding and to submit comments about it. 55 Duke L.J. at 964-67. This critique may prove correct—but perhaps it is never wise to bet against the transformative power of the Internet.

Given that a minority of rulemaking proceedings do attract huge numbers of e-mailed comments from ordinary citizens, the note asks whether such mass participation should be welcomed. Shulman's article presents a pessimistic view in forceful terms. He believes that an interest group is more likely to get results by dispatching knowledgeable, thoughtful experts for dialogue with the agency than by unleashing a flood of comments from their membership. However, this issue is not beyond debate. You might ask: If EPA is poised to issue a rule on mercury emissions that a half million citizens find objectionable, shouldn't the agency hear that message, even if the comments are not particularly articulate or original?

A difficulty that arises in this connection is that comments from the general public may be barely, if at all, relevant to the issues that the agency, under the governing statute, has been instructed to consider. (For what it is worth, the mercury rule mentioned in the text was eventually struck down, but the court relied on technical statutory interpretation grounds that surely did not loom large in comments from the general public. *New Jersey v. EPA*, 517 F.3d 574 (D.C.Cir.2008).) As one court said long before the electronic revolution, "The substantial-evidence standard has never been taken to mean that an agency rule-making is a democratic process by which the majority of commenters prevail by sheer weight of numbers." *NRDC v. EPA*, 822 F.2d 104, 122 n.17 (D.C.Cir.1987). To be sure, rulemaking proceedings are often both technocratic and political at the same time (not always in the same proportions in every context). It follows that citizen input is, and should be, neither entirely irrelevant nor entirely determinative. In the article cited above (at 17), Parker writes:

> [Duplicative emails] constitute public opinion which may not matter much on technical issues, but is quite relevant to the disposition of both normative issues and factual issues that turn on public perception or behavior. Ideally, such emails would be identified, sequestered, tallied, and then, in appropriate cases, *probed* to

identify where possible the solicitation message which triggered the mass mailing, the veracity of that message, and (possibly) the response of mass e-mailers to a computer-generated reply message which offers a corrected version of the facts.

In short, teachers can, if they wish, use a discussion of e-rulemaking to preview the theme of technocracy versus politics, which becomes more prominent later in the course in connection with cases such as *Sierra Club v. Costle*, § 5.5.2, and *State Farm*, § 9.4.

Whatever its contributions to enlightened governance, mass participation in rulemaking leaves an agency with formidable management challenges. Some agencies have hired consultants to sort through the deluge of comments on controversial rulemaking proceedings. Efforts are also under way to develop software that can sort through the duplicative messages and thereby reduce the amount of human time needed to react to them. Remember that agencies are expected to "consider" all comments, but some concessions to reality have to be made. For an overview of other management challenges that have loomed on the horizon, see Jeffrey S. Lubbers, A GUIDE TO FEDERAL AGENCY RULEMAKING 223-36 (4th ed. 2006)

4. *Written or oral comment.* The text mentions some of the attractions of oral hearings in rulemaking. These points are, of course, similar to the factors that led courts to insist on a *right* to an oral hearing in cases such as *Goldberg v. Kelly*, § 2.1, and *Londoner v. Denver*, § 2.5.

But, of course, that is a far cry from saying that oral hearings should ever be mandatory in rulemaking. See ACUS Recommendation 72-5, 38 Fed. Reg. 19,782 (1973) (Congress should not require procedures beyond notice and comment unless it has "special reasons" for doing so). Here are some of the countervailing considerations: In *most* situations, written submissions will be effective to communicate to the agency necessary information and argument, and will provide a relatively efficient and inexpensive method by which the agency may review and digest the material. Oral proceedings can tie up some agency staff members for substantial periods of time and can impose other financial burdens on the agency, such as the cost of transcribing oral proceedings so that the final decisionmakers can review them. Oral submissions are also not always effective, especially when they are repetitious or polemical.

Moreover, the opportunity to furnish oral comments may not enhance public satisfaction with the process if the staff member who conducts the proceeding fails to engage in any interchange with commenters, but merely listens passively or in fact zones out from sheer boredom. All of these points support the prevailing view that an agency should have discretion not to hold an oral hearing in any given case.

§ 5.4.2 Formal Rulemaking

UNITED STATES v. FLORIDA EAST COAST RAILWAY CO.

Notes and Questions

1. *The trigger for formal rulemaking.* The *Florida East Coast* case does not say that a statute triggering formal rulemaking must actually repeat the exact words--"on the record after opportunity for an agency hearing." But it does indicate that the statutory language will have to make clear that Congress intended for the formal procedures of the APA to apply to that rulemaking. It can be strongly argued that the framers of the APA did expect that ratesetting proceedings of the ICC would be conducted through formal ruleamking, and that the Court's interpretation ignores this historical context. *See* Nathaniel L. Nathanson, "Probing the Mind of the Administrator: Hearing Variations and Standards of Judicial Review Under the Administrative Procedure Act and Other Federal Statutes," 75 Colum.L.Rev. 721, 732–33 (1975). The *Florida East Coast* holding should be seen as resting primarily on the Court's belief that trial-type proceedings are not ordinarily appropriate for rulemaking of general applicability.

As a practical matter, a strong presumption against reading the statutory term "hearing" as mandating formal rulemaking (*Florida East Coast*) will lead to the same outcomes as a policy of giving *Chevron* deference to an agency's interpretation of "hearing" (*Dominion Energy*). Of course, in the unlikely event that an agency were to decide to utilize formal rulemaking even without a statutory requirement of that procedure, a court that followed the *Dominion Energy* logic would find itself "deferring" to an choice that the statutory presumption does not address. But that wouldn't actually be deference in the *Chevron* sense. The APA would no longer be relevant, because an agency always has discretion to engage in more procedures than the APA minimum.

In pre-*Dominion Energy* days, it was not difficult to reconcile the *Florida East Coast* presumption with the pro-hearing presumption applied in the *Seacoast Anti-Pollution League* case, which *Dominion Energy* abandoned. The contrasting presumptions could be rationalized on the basis of the same arguments that are used to distinguish *Londoner* from *Bi-Metallic*: In rulemaking cases, the number of parties affected tends to be large, making hearings less feasible; the critical facts tend to be generalized and policy-laden, and thus not conducive to being settled through trial-type methods; affected interests are more likely to be able to resort to political remedies than the target of an adjudication could. *Florida East Coast* contains language that seems to invite such a distinction. Now that *Dominion Energy* dominates the adjudication landscape, however, that analysis would seem to be beside the point.

On the other hand, notice that the Supreme Court did not arrive at its holding in *Florida East Coast* on the basis of deference. In fact, it suggested that deference was inappropriate in that situation because the APA "is not legislation that the Interstate Commerce Commission, or any other single agency, has primary responsibility for administering. An agency interpretation involving, at least in part, the provisions of that Act does not carry the weight, in ascertaining the intent of Congress, that an interpretation by an agency 'charged with the responsibility' of administering a particular statute does." *Florida East Coast*, 410 U.S. at 236 n.6. We agree with the Supreme Court's reasoning on this score. As we explained in the manual's notes accompanying § 3.1.1, we think *Dominion Energy* gave too much weight to deference principles in the context of a statutory requirement that is designed to serve as a check on agency power. In our view, the persuasive aspect of *Florida East Coast* is that it adopts a desirable reading *of the APA* in the rulemaking context, namely that the § 553(c) "trigger" should not be easy to pull. For reasons suggested just above, and also in § 3.1.1, there is more room for debate about the merits of a similar presumption in the context of the § 554(a) trigger in adjudication cases. That is why *Dominion Energy* remains a less convincing decision.

2. *Statutory "hearing" rights in rulemaking.* Both *Florida East Coast* and the *Morgan* cases involved ratemaking of general applicability—true rulemaking. Consequently, the only arguable justification for the Court's conclusion that trial-type procedures were required in the *Morgan* cases but not in the *Florida East Coast* case appears to be the different language in the respective enabling acts involved—a "full hearing" being required in the former and only a "hearing" being required in the latter. The Court went out of its way in *Morgan* to indicate that "the requirement of a 'full hearing' has obvious reference to the tradition of judicial proceedings in which evidence is received and weighed by the trier of fact." But this is a weak distinction, as even Justice Rehnquist seemed to recognize (410 U.S. at 242-43). Given the traditions of ICC practice at the time of the 1966 legislation, Congress probably expected that the word "hearing" would be construed to mean exactly what the Court had said "full hearing" meant in the *Morgan* cases.

Fundamentally, therefore, *Florida East Coast* seems inconsistent with the *Morgan* cases. The *Morgan* cases were decided in the 1930's, when the federal judiciary was suspicious of the administrative process and hostile to government regulation in general. Therefore, it was likely to sympathize with claims that rulemaking procedure was unfair to regulated parties. Moreover, the Court then had little practical experience with the administrative process. It was natural for judges of that time to prefer the familiar judicialized procedure over unfamiliar institutional methods of decisionmaking. Moreover, the judges lacked experience with the bad consequences of formal rulemaking spelled out in this chapter. By the time of *Florida East Coast Ry.*, all this had changed. Rehnquist was certainly well aware of the highly adverse consequences of requiring trial-type procedure in cases of industry-wide rulemaking.

3. *The merits of mandatory trial-type rulemaking proceedings.* This note summarizes the factors that have led to a general repudiation of formal rulemaking in federal administrative law (except in individualized ratemaking, which is really a misnamed variety of adjudication, and in a few other unreformed areas). In *most* rulemaking proceedings, trial-type hearings with rights of confrontation, cross-examination, rebuttal, etc., will not be particularly helpful, and are likely to serve only to discourage, delay, or obstruct agency action. To be sure, an agency may have good reasons for deciding in a particular rulemaking situation that the truth-seeking benefits of oral testimony and cross-examination might justify the time and energy they consume. Therefore, trial-type methods should not be totally purged from rulemaking. Nevertheless, because those circumstances are rare and almost impossible to define intelligibly, it may be best to make an agency's decisions on this issue totally unreviewable. That is roughly the position that the Supreme Court adopted in *Vermont Yankee*, as will be seen in the next section.

4. *Fadeout.* The discussion in this note about the near demise of formal rulemaking is addressed to rulemaking of *general applicability*. It is less clear that federal agencies have abandoned formal rulemaking in the context of rulemaking of *particular* applicability, such as ratesetting for a specific company. Proceedings in this category are considered "rulemaking" by virtue of the clause at the end of 5 U.S.C. § 551(4). Although these proceedings are not subjct to separation of functions restrictions (because §§ 556 and 557 apply, but § 554 does not), they are functionally quite similar to adjudication. As such, they have not been subjected to the same criticism as true rulemaking. For example, the condemnatory language in the ACUS recommendation cited in the text expressly excludes them. Individualized rulemaking is discussed in § 5.2.1 N.1 and in the problem in this section.

The incorrect usage described in this note usually occurs in the context of scope of review. It is a direct byproduct of the *Christensen* and *Mead* cases discussed in § 9.2.4. A court may say that a guidance document is merely entitled to *Skidmore* deference, but would have been entitled to *Chevron* deference if the agency had taken the trouble to promulgate it through "formal rulemaking." The fact is that, as a simple computer search would confirm, *most* references to "formal rulemaking" in the case law of the past decade have been to what administrative lawyers grew up calling "informal rulemaking." If you choose to highlight this development in class, be sure to stay extra precise in your terminology.

5. *Presidential oversight.* Of course, agencies have always had authority to use formal rulemaking as a matter of discretion, so the amendment adopted by President Bush did not give them powers they had previously lacked. Presumably the amendment was intended as a mild nudge encouraging agencies to use, or at least consider using, formal rulemaking. Yet, in light of the widespread criticism of that process, this nudge is certainly puzzling. Many critics of the Bush administration assumed the worst, fearing that its purpose was to bring about delay in the development of important regulations. We think it more likely that the author of this language in the order was simply uninformed about the poor reputation that formal rulemaking enjoys in administrative law circles and assumed that the language was innocuous.

In any event, the administration, after hearing withering criticism of the language, did not seriously defend it. Instead, in a memorandum advising agencies about implementation of the order, the Office of Management and Budget (OIRA's parent agency) explained: "This [sentence] is a reminder to agencies of an authority that they have long had, and that remains available to them, under the APA. Some agencies have utilized this authority and may want to consider doing so in the future, and other agencies may identify situations in which it could be beneficial." OMB Memorandum M-07-13 (April 25, 2007), *http://www.whitehouse.gov/omb/ memoranda/fy2007/m07-13.pdf*. To us, this tepid explanation sounds like a tacit acknowledgement that the order's invitation to agencies to "consider" formal rulemaking was a misstep (i.e., an "oversight" in the not-so-complimentary sense of the word).

6. *State law.* Federal and state law have more or less converged on the matter of formal rulemaking. After *Florida East Coast*, trial-type procedure in rulemaking exists only where Congress has called for it in very clear terms. This seems equivalent to 1981 MSAPA 3-104, which invokes such procedures in rulemaking only when "another statute expressly requires" them. Note, however, that federal and state law may diverge in the case of *individualized* rulemaking. The analysis supporting this conclusion is spelled out in N. 7 below.

7. *Problem.* The problem is easy insofar as it involves the proposal to adopt a rule to govern the conversion of non-profit hospital corporations in general. First, *Florida East Coast* would undoubtedly call only for procedures of informal rulemaking rather than formal rulemaking. As that case makes clear, the reference to a "fair hearing" would not be considered equivalent to a requirement that the hearing be "on the record," as required under the APA to convert rulemaking from informal to formal. Second,

under the 1981 MSAPA, only the informal notice and comment rulemaking procedures of Article 3 would apply. Section 4-101(b) of that Act makes clear that the "fair hearing" language would not be sufficient to turn such a rulemaking into a judicial-style proceeding in which a right to cross-examination was required. That provision states that formal adjudication provisions are applicable to rulemaking "only to the extent that another statute *expressly* so provides." And finally, under due process, Mercy won't fare any better, thanks to *Bi-Metallic*.

The problem gets trickier insofar as it involves Mercy's application for conversion to nonprofit status.

a) *Federal APA.* Under § 551(4) of the federal APA, as the text points out, this proceeding is technically rulemaking even though it is of particular applicability. If this is "formal rulemaking," Mercy would have a right to various trial formalities, including cross-examination.

Or would it? APA § 557(d) provides for "such cross examination as may be required for a full and true disclosure of the facts." Thus the question is, what does Mercy seek to accomplish through cross-examination? It's hard to see what cross-examination could really accomplish here. Whether Mercy wants to argue that it is worth much less than $50,000,000, or whether it wants to argue that it should be allowed to convert to profit status without making any such contribution (regardless of its value), the issues do not involve credibility or perception. This sort of factual issue can be handled efficiently through submission of written expert reports. Discretionary issues can be argued through briefs.

Anyway, is this APA formal rulemaking? *Florida East Coast* is arguably inapplicable here, because it involved only ratemaking of general applicability--true rulemaking. This case involves particular applicability. In *Florida East Coast* the Court dropped a few hints that it would be receptive to drawing that distinction, including the "host of meanings" passage included in our excerpt in this section, as well as the due process analysis quoted in § 2.5. Nevertheless, if that case does not apply, *Dominion Energy* apparently does. Under *Chevron* principles, DOC would prevail if the "fair hearing" language in its governing statute is deemed unclear (as it seems to be) and its interpretation is deemed reasonable. Here, the denial of cross-examination seems reasonable on the grounds just stated. If an issue in a conversion case were to involve a serious credibility issue, however, the agency would be well advised to allow some sort of adversarial process. Otherwise it would be at risk of having a court find its choice "unreasonable," even under the *Chevron* standard of review.

This analysis points towards a general conclusion about agency actions that look adjudicative but nevertheless are classified as rulemaking because they fall within the proviso to § 551(4)—including, most notably, individualized ratemaking: Assuming that the *Dominion Energy* approach will remain dominant, such actions may still be subject to formal rulemaking, but only if the applicable statute uses the magic words "on the record" or something very close to that.

b) *1981 MSAPA*. Under the 1981 MSAPA, DOC's decision on Mercy's application wouldn't be a rule at all. Under § 1-102(5), it would be considered an order (and it would also appear to be a "license" under § 1-102(4)). Section 4-101(a) requires the agency to conduct this proceeding as an adjudicative proceeding. In such a proceeding § 4-211(2) would give Mercy a right to cross-examine Jay. However, the latter section also requires trial procedure "to the extent necessary for disclosure of all relevant facts and issues." As discussed above, cross-examination seems of little utility in this situation. Moreover, if no issue of fact is in dispute (i.e. the only issue concerns how Rhoda should exercise discretion), a conference hearing would be especially appropriate (assuming DOC has provided for one by rule, which it should do). § 4-401. In a conference hearing, § 4-211 is inapplicable.

c) *No APA*. Finally, if no APA applies, Mercy would have to rely on due process, but it may have an uphill climb. The standard that Rhoda will apply seems to involve pure discretion. Mercy has no legitimate claim of entitlement to approval of the conversion—a necessity under *Roth* for "new property." Moreover, even if the statute does create an entitlement, Mercy must get past the case law that suggests that the denial of an application for status—as distinguished from termination of an existing status—isn't a "deprivation" for due process purposes. *See* § 2.2.1 N.8. On the other hand, Mercy may be able to avoid these obstacles by arguing that this case involves "old property" as opposed to a *Roth*-type entitlement. Mercy would say that it owns an asset—a hospital that is capable of earning substantial profits— and if Rhoda wants to interfere with its use of this "property," she must first afford due process.

If due process does apply, a *Mathews v. Eldridge* balancing might well lead a court to conclude that cross-examination is not required. While Mercy's interest is very substantial, cross-examination would have little utility, and turning this complex matter into a trial would be costly and inefficient.

§ 5.4.3 Hybrid Rulemaking and the Limits on Judicial Supervision of Administrative Procedure

VERMONT YANKEE NUCLEAR POWER CORP. v. NRDC

Notes and Questions

1. *Responses to Vermont Yankee.* We believe *Vermont Yankee* was fundamentally a sound decision. The Court's strongest point is that judicial review would be very unpredictable if, in each case of rulemaking, courts could determine in an ad hoc manner whether the prescribed notice and comment procedures were fair and, if not, what additional procedures were necessary. That would either induce agencies, in order to protect themselves, to use trial-type procedures in all cases, a bad result, or induce them, whenever possible, to do their lawmaking in individual adjudications rather than rulemaking, another bad result.

Despite Davis' argument, § 559 seems inconclusive on the question of administrative common law. It could easily be read to refer to such sources of law as the Constitution or an agency's own regulations. A broad statute such as the APA is naturally worded in open-ended terms, but we do not think it purports to settle the issue of administrative common law one way or the other. Indeed, the Court has elsewhere suggested that the savings clause of § 559 should be applied with restraint, in order to avoid frustrating the APA's purpose "to bring uniformity to a field full of variation and diversity." *Dickinson v. Zurko*, 527 U.S. 150, 155 (1999).

On the other hand, we would question Byse's position to the extent it militates against all of the innovations that courts have read into § 553 over the years. A fifty-year-old foundation statute for administrative law has to be reinterpreted to keep up with modern realities, just as a 200-plus-year-old Constitution must be. Today's notions of what a rulemaking notice must contain, or what a statement of basis and purpose must say, *see* § 5.6, are not what Congress envisioned in 1946. But agencies have adapted to the new understandings with a fair degree of success. In this sense, although *Vermont Yankee* is a desirable reaction against totally unconstrained judicial supervision of agency procedure, it should not be read as totally negating a judicial role in the continuing development of administrative law. Nor has it been, as we shall see.

2. *Hybrid rulemaking after Vermont Yankee.* The disappearance of interest in trial-type procedure in rulemaking (leaving aside "rules" of particular applicability in the ratemaking context) is striking. A notable sign of the new consensus occurred during the national debate over regulatory reform in 1995. That initiative was led by business interests, which had previously been among the strongest proponents of hybrid

rulemaking. The sponsors of the leading bill, S. 343 (which in a number of ways would have imposed very burdensome obligations on the rulemaking process), not only refrained from proposing trial-type formalities in rulemaking—they actually sought, at one point, to codify the *Vermont Yankee* principle. One provision in the Senate Judiciary Committee's draft of the bill would have amended § 553 to state that agencies should consider using procedural devices in addition to notice-and-comment to illuminate the issues; but the provision would also have stated that agencies' decisions about whether to use such devices *would not be subject to judicial review.* *See* S.Rep.No. 104-90, at 3, 51-52 (1995).

The Boyer and Williams studies are excellent demonstrations of some of the practical objections to hybrid rulemaking. (Incidentally, you may have noticed that the title of the Williams article, "Hybrid Rulemaking under the Administrative Procedure Act," is actually a misnomer; by definition, hybrid rulemaking obligations go beyond what the APA requires. In Judge Williams' defense, however, let it be noted that he did not actually write that title. Rather, it was written by a poorly informed student editor—who is now one of the authors of the present casebook.)

3. *Vermont Yankee and interpretations of § 553.* The *Vermont Yankee* case prohibits courts from requiring agencies to observe rulemaking procedures *in addition to* those imposed by Congress in § 553; it does not prohibit courts from enforcing the procedures of § 553 itself. Thus, *Chocolate Manufacturers* causes no tension with *Vermont Yankee* at all, because the logical outgrowth test is a straightforward, and not particularly surprising, gloss on the meaning of § 553(b).

Much more interesting is the survival of *Portland Cement*—and it certainly has survived, at least until the Supreme Court says otherwise. As is discussed in this manual's notes to § 5.3 N.7, one cannot readily find in the language, structure, and legislative history of § 553 much support for a duty to disclose scientific data underlying a proposed rule. After *Vermont Yankee*, therefore, one might have foreseen at least some possibility that the courts would abandon *Portland Cement*, deeming it to be a judicial imposition of an additional requirement on agency rulemaking, as opposed to judicial implementation of a requirement impliedly imposed by Congress.

The survival of *Portland Cement* demonstrates that courts do not believe that *Vermont Yankee* contains an implicit mandate to construe the APA restrictively. Indeed, in a way the Supreme Court's opinion itself tends to undercut such an implication. If you have already covered the scope of review chapter (or wish to anticipate a point that will be made there), you can note here that *Vermont Yankee* itself endorses at least one creative judicial gloss on the APA. The Court says that on remand the court of appeals must review the NRC's rule on the basis of the "administrative record." Justice Rehnquist must have been aware that the idea of confining judicial review to an exclusive record in informal rulemaking is a pure judicial invention, not contemplated by the framers of the APA. *See* § 9.3 N.6.

Moreover, exchanges of information in rulemaking have proven to be *effective* in a manner that trial-type formalities have not. *See* Williams, 42 U.Chi.L.Rev. at 448-56. In the policy analysis that dominates so many of today's rulemaking proceedings, competing teams of experts join issue over highly esoteric and technical matters that do not lend themselves well to exploration through oral testimony and cross-examination. "Paper hearings" establish a dialogue between agencies and the private sector that does promote accuracy in decisionmaking. Or, at least, a belief in the utility of this device is prevalent and probably helps to account for the continued enforcement of the *Portland Cement* doctrine.

4. *Substantive review after Vermont Yankee.* We include this note to draw attention to the interaction between substance and procedure in judicial review; the court's ability to oversee the former must inevitably result in at least some influence over the latter. Unless you have already covered the scope of review chapter, you probably will not be able to develop this point very fully, but students should be able to see that there is less to *Vermont Yankee* than meets the eye.

The difference between what *Vermont Yankee* does and does not establish seems to come down to this: The Court evidently continues to desire that administrative rulemaking should be subject to significant checks. Thus, it has not (or at least has not consistently) discouraged the reviewing courts from demanding that the agencies write explanations and compile records that demonstrate the rationality of their decisionmaking. What *Vermont Yankee* does say is that the agency has wide discretion to decide the *manner* in which it will generate that record. The agency can build its case through internal staff work, successive rounds of notice and comment, oral proceedings, or any other procedural mechanisms, unless statutes circumscribe these options. Fairly read, *LTV* and *National Lime* are consistent with this analysis.

Seen in this light, the protection from judicial reversal that *Vermont Yankee* gives to the agencies is not meaningless, but it is limited. Judges do comply with the precise holding of that case, but there is still a risk that they will use substantive review to engage in obstructionism or result-oriented decisionmaking, contrary to the larger concerns expressed in the Supreme Court's opinion. To that extent, some of the Court's underlying objectives remain unfulfilled.

5. *Vermont Yankee in adjudication.* The Court's extension of *Vermont*

Yankee principles to informal adjudication deserved more of a defense than the Court gave it (i.e., none at all). APA § 555 merely deals with a handful of "Ancillary Matters" (which is what it is called) that might arise in various contexts, including informal adjudication. It cannot reasonably be deemed equivalent to the template for informal rulemaking codified in § 553. Thus, the Court's surprising assertion that § 555 contains "the minimal requirements" for informal adjudication is unpersuasive. Previously the generally accepted understanding had been that the APA does not purport to standardize the manner in which agencies adjudicate cases, except in "formal" proceedings. *See* § 3.1.1. In this light, it is difficult to think of § 555 as "a formula upon which opposing social and political forces have come to rest" (to use the language from *Wong Yang Sung* that Justice Rehnquist quotes twice in *Vermont Yankee*). One doubts that these "opposing forces" "came to rest" on an agreement that parties to informal adjudication should have virtually no protection at all.

Still, some of the policy arguments underlying *Vermont Yankee* do have force in the adjudication context, such as the argument that unconstrained procedural second-guessing by courts gives agencies an incentive to overproceduralize their decisions. Further, one can argue that *Vermont Yankee* principles aren't really very constraining anyhow, in light of the courts' continuing power to conduct substantive review and to interpret existing procedural statutes creatively. In addition, in the adjudication context (unlike that of rulemaking), the due process clause is generally available as a fallback line of defense against truly unfair procedural lapses. Considering the huge sums at issue, LTV might well have had respectable grounds for a constitutional challenge to the procedures used in this very case.

6. *Problem.* The first part of the problem is simple and is intended to provide a vehicle by which the teacher can elicit the core reasoning of *Vermont Yankee*. If Madison courts follow the principles of that case, they surely can't require the agency to hold a second round of notice and comment. True, successive comment periods can be helpful in the development of a complex rule. *See* ACUS Recommendation 76-3, 41 Fed. Reg. 29,654 (1976). Moreover, comment periods are the *kind* of procedure specified in the APA, which is not true of cross-examination, at least in informal rulemaking. Nevertheless, the APA requires *one* round of notice and comment. If *Vermont Yankee* is good law, the decision about whether to hold a second one rests with the agency, not the reviewing court. *See Texas Office of Public Utility Counsel v. FCC*, 265 F.3d 313, 326 (5th Cir. 2001).

John may be able to convince the court that the agency's "superficial" explanation is in fact so flawed as to render the rule arbitrary and capricious. But the gap between "unpersuasive" and "arbitrary" is sizable, and that's where the principle of *Vermont Yankee* has its bite.

The second issue essentially raises the question of whether *Vermont Yankee* undermines the *Portland Cement* doctrine, and specifically the application of that doctrine to materials that the agency created or received during the comment period. We discussed in this manual's analysis of § 5.3 N.7 the difficulty of finding support in the language of § 553(b) for a requirement that an agency must disclose technical data that forms the basis for its proposed rule. You can cover that material here if you have not already done so.

But the language of the APA arguably provides even *less* support for a requirement of an opportunity to comment on subsequent additions to the rulemaking record. Section 553(b), the provision invoked in *Mortgage Investors* and many other cases that follow *Portland Cement*, sets forth the matters that the agency must include *in its notice of proposed rulemaking.* Obviously, the rulemaking notice cannot contain information that the agency did not possess, or had no expectation of consulting, until afterwards. Under the 1981 MSAPA, the language of § 3-103(a) presents the same problem.

In functional terms, however, it would make no sense to exclude studies developed after the commencement of the rulemaking from the scope of the *Portland Cement* doctrine. An agency's study of the subject matter of a rule normally continues into the period during which its proposal is pending (that's why we have comment periods). Naturally, therefore, new information will be developed during that period. The same policy arguments that support disclosure of "critical" technical material that was in the agency's possession at the beginning of the proceeding also support an agency obligation to permit members of the public to comment on "critical" material developed later in the proceeding. These policy arguments are spelled out in N.3 above. Notice that the second paragraph of the excerpt from *Portland Cement* quoted in § 5.3 N.7 clearly contemplates such post hoc disclosures.

Chamber of Commerce v. SEC (discussed at § 5.3 N.8) and other cases have responded to this difficulty by invoking APA § 553(c) to provide at least part of the foundation for the obligation to disclose technical data in a rulemaking. That analysis can be traced back to a footnote in *Portland Cement* itself in which Judge Leventhal explained how EPA had responded to an interlocutory order of the court: "Written comments were submitted as requested, and as required by the APA § 4(c), 5 U.S.C. § 553(c). Obviously a prerequisite to the ability to make meaningful comment is to know the basis upon which the rule is proposed." 486 F.2d at 393 n.67. In other words, the agency's obligation to make timely disclosure of technical data may be inferred from the § 553(c) duty to "give interested persons an opportunity to participate" (or from the parallel language of 1981 MSAPA § 3-104(a)).

This is not only a stretch on its own terms, but also a rather revisionist reading of Leventhal's opinion, because his footnote reads as though it was almost a throwaway remark. In calling for disclosure of technical data, he put more emphasis on the idea that the "opportunity to make further comments [was] necessary to sound execution of our judicial review function." *Id.* at 393. However, *Vermont Yankee* has forced the courts to justify their rulemaking requirements in APA terms. This textually based reinterpretation of *Portland Cement* was pioneered, not surprisingly, by Judge Scalia. *See Ass'n of Data Processing Serv. Orgs., v. Board of Governors,* 745 F.2d 677, 684-85 (D.C.Cir.1984).

In the *Industrial Liaison* case, from which the problem is drawn, the New York Court of Appeals refused to require disclosure of studies on which the agency had relied during the rulemaking proceeding. In doing so, the court pointed out that the agency had held public hearings, workshops, and seminars, extended the length of the original comment period, distributed "fact sheets" describing the research behind the rule, etc. If you find that students are generally sympathetic to applying *Portland Cement* in this situation, you might ask them whether, if the Department had taken similar steps in the problem, the court would nevertheless be justified in reversing the agency. Arguably, when an agency has made ample disclosure, the court is in a poor position to evaluate how much more disclosure is needed. Moreover, the practical problem raised in the *Vermont Yankee* opinion may apply here: if the court is going to second-guess the agency's judgment call on that issue, the agency will have no choice but to make disclosures of critical background studies in every case.

Experience at the federal level seems to show, however, that the *Vermont Yankee* objection, whatever its abstract appeal, has not proved insurmountable in practice. Agencies now know that they have to comply with *Portland Cement* during the entire period of a rule's development, they generally do so, and the sky hasn't fallen. At the same time, the affirmative benefits of that requirement are evident. In our problem, Martha's report implicates the core issues of the rulemaking, and John has a clear interest in being able to comment on it at the agency level.

In any event, the New York legislature was apparently not satisfied with the gap that the *Industrial Liaison* case had left. Within a few years, it effectively overruled the case by adding the following new sentence to the New York statute prescribing a regulatory impact statement (applicable to most rulemakings): "Where one or more scientific or statistical studies, reports or analyses has served as the basis for the rule, the statement shall contain a citation to each such study, report or analysis and shall indicate how it was used to determine the necessity for or the benefits to be derived from the rule." 1992 N.Y. Laws ch. 520, § 1. In 2000 the legislature expanded this obligation by also requiring an agency to publish a summary of the cited study and the name of the person who had prepared it. *See* N.Y. A.P.A. § 202-a (current version). *See generally* Patrick J. Borchers & David L. Markell, NEW YORK STATE ADMINISTRATIVE PROCEDURE AND PRACTICE § 4.7 (1995). In short, the court's decision may have comported with the spirit of *Vermont Yankee*, and may have been defensible in terms of deference to the political branches, but it was on the wrong side of history.

§ 5.5 PROCEDURAL REGULARITY IN RULEMAKING

There are two reasons why the principles applied in adjudication concerning ex parte communications, bias, and personal involvement should not be applied with full force to informal rulemaking. First, the elements of the judicial model are specially calculated to ensure accurate and acceptable decisionmaking with respect to the particular types of issues predominant in adjudication—principally specific fact-finding about identified persons. The elements of that model are not specially calculated to ensure the best resolution of the particular types of issues predominant in rulemaking— principally the making of general law or policy. Second, judicial style procedural requirements are, to a large extent, inconsistent with the successful accomplishment of legislative type functions. The latter functions require more continuous and intimate contact with the ongoing political processes of the community, and less detachment from the matters at stake, than the performance of judicial type functions. However, there may be specific situations in which some elements of the judicial model would be appropriate in the rulemaking context. In those situations the courts, the legislature, or the agency should selectively impose them.

§ 5.5.1 Role of Agency Heads

The text notes that agency heads are required to consider written and oral submissions received in rulemaking proceedings, but that agency heads need not personally preside at oral proceedings nor personally read all written submissions. To the extent feasible and practical, it may be desirable for agency heads to perform these functions. However, the arguments for enforcing the *Morgan IV* restrictions on inquiry into an agency decisionmaker's mental processes would appear to apply with full force in the informal rulemaking context. The right to examine an agency head's knowledge of the record in an informal rulemaking proceeding would be just as detrimental to the agency's rulemaking process as an examination of an agency head's knowledge in a particular case would be detrimental to the agency's adjudicative process. Were such a right recognized, it would be exercised in every instance in which a controversial rule was adopted,

263

thereby imposing great burdens on agencies. Such an examination of agency heads on a routine basis would also fly in the face of the usual presumption of regularity that attaches to agency action.

Problem. The facts of this problem come straight out of the real *Nutritional Foods* case. The presumption of regularity is the first difficulty confronting the dietary foods manufacturers. The authoritative gloss on *Morgan IV* in *Overton Park* requires them to make a "strong showing of bad faith or improper behavior" before the court will conduct any further inquiry into the bona fides of the Commissioner's decision. The petitioners' circumstantial evidence probably does not meet that test.

In class, after making that point and exploring the reasons for the presumption, you can go on to ask what the court should have done if the new Commissioner had admitted that he had merely "considered the summaries of the objections and of the answers contained in the [preambles to the dietary foods regulations] and conferred with his staff about them." In *National Nutritional Foods,* Judge Friendly said emphatically that such conduct would have sufficed. 491 F.2d at 1146. "With the enormous increase in delegation of lawmaking power which Congress has been obliged to make to agencies, . . . and in the complexity of life, government would become impossible if courts were to insist on" the Commissioner's personal familiarity with the enormous record. *Id.* The petitioners thought that the volume of business the Commissioner had transacted during those initial two weeks (not to mention meetings, speeches, testimony, and maybe even thinking about major policy questions) was circumstantial evidence of misconduct. It seems more realistic to argue that these competing obligations are dramatic proof that the "consideration" required by *Morgan I* has to be defined quite leniently.

One of the authors would go still further. In his view, it might be a good idea to deem *Morgan I* completely inapplicable in the rulemaking context. (Even in adjudication, he notes, the arguments for *Morgan I* are pretty shaky in this era of monster dockets and underfunded agencies.) In other words, suppose the new Commissioner conceded that he never looked at the rulemaking materials concerning dietary foods at all; he merely signed his name where the staff told him to sign. So what?

Perhaps, this author thinks, the requirement in state and federal APAs that "the agency" consider public submissions mean the agency in an institutional sense, not the agency heads. We don't expect legislators to know what they're voting on; often they simply vote as their staff (or their party leader) tells them. The check on legislators is purely political--they have to take the heat for their votes. It's the same for agency heads--whether they are familiar or not with what they promulgate, they get the blame or credit for what the agency has done. Considering the size and complexity of rulemaking records, and the enormous number of tasks and responsibilities imposed on agency heads, it seems naive to imagine that they will pay attention to any except the most politically contentious or most economically significant rulemaking proceedings. So, this author concludes, why have a doctrine (usually unenforceable because of *Morgan IV*) that purports to require them to do so?

The other author wouldn't go that far. He thinks that the principle of *Morgan I,* properly diluted to fit the realities of bureaucratic life, should apply to rulemaking proceedings. An agency head ought to feel some degree of personal responsibility for regulations she signs, even if courts will virtually never police this obligation. The signature is a representation that says, "I supervised this as much as one could reasonably expect, although, realistically speaking, there's only so much I can do." An agency may well produce a more disciplined work product if it internalizes the notion that somebody (not just the department as a whole) should be personally accountable for the quality of the rules it issues. Accountability should not be defined solely in terms of the threat of political reprisal, because some rulemaking proceedings have such low visibility that the agency doesn't risk much political damage no matter what choice it makes. Maybe in the biggest and busiest agencies those proceedings won't get—or deserve—much attention from the top leadership, but can you say the same about smaller agencies with fewer responsibilities overall?

§ 5.5.2 Ex Parte Communications and Political Influence in Rulemaking

We have combined our notes for *Home Box Office* and *Sierra Club*, on the assumption that they should be taught as a single unit. *Home Box Office* has been so thoroughly abandoned in the case law that a focus on that case alone seems artificial. Some instructors might decide not to teach it at all. We think, however, that it can serve as a valuable foil to *Sierra Club*. Decided almost on the eve of *Vermont Yankee*, it can be viewed as the high-water mark of the courts' efforts in the 1970's to superimpose judicial norms onto the informal rulemaking process. The contrast between Judge Wright's apprehensiveness about the contaminating potential of backroom dealings with interest groups, on the one hand, and Judge Wald's frank openness to the political elements of policymaking, on the other, shows students a great deal about the inevitable tradeoff between procedural regularity and political responsiveness in rulemaking.

Notes and Questions

1. *Contrasting views.* Even apart from the argument that ex parte contacts have affirmative value (about which more later), one can question

the arguments that *Home Box Office* cited to justify its ban on ex parte contacts. In the first place, we doubt the validity of Judge Wright's claim that ex parte contacts frustrate effective judicial review. In *Sierra Club*, Judge Wald accurately states the meaning of the federal courts' policy of reviewing rules on an exclusive administrative record, which is explicitly required in the Clean Air Act and implied from the abuse of discretion test in § 553 rulemaking. (Note that not all state courts subscribe to this policy in the first place. *See* § 9.4.) That policy means that the agency "must justify its rulemaking solely on the basis of the record it compiles and makes public." It has not generally been understood to mean, however, that the court has to measure the rule against every bit of information that the agency may have received concerning the rule.

Second, the *Home Box Office* court's concerns about ulterior motives seem misplaced. To be sure, the Nathanson quotation in the text is somewhat overstated. There is more reason to worry about an agency's improper motives than a legislature's, because an agency normally acts under a bounded statutory mandate, and, therefore, some motives could not lawfully form a basis for its action. Nevertheless, Nathanson's analysis appears to be correct insofar as it rests on the notion that agency action should generally be presumed valid by the courts. An endless inquiry into the real reasons for agency action would be inconsistent with the duty of the courts to afford at least some deference to the decisions of a co-equal branch of government. Indeed, theoretically the risk of ulterior motives exists in every administrative proceeding, not just those proceedings in which ex parte contacts occurred; but the courts normally are willing to live with that risk. Under the *Morgan IV* principle, as explicated in *Overton Park*, the agency's explanation for its action should be taken at face value absent a "strong showing of bad faith or improper behavior." Nothing like that has been shown here; one can't say that ex parte contacts are evidence of improper behavior without assuming the very proposition that Judge Wright is trying to establish.

The fairness issue raised by Judge Wright does seem more substantial, at least in the abstract. When a decisionmaker meets with one side of a dispute behind closed doors, the party on the other side naturally feels aggrieved by the inequity. You can use this point as an entree into the policy issues raised in the following note. Nevertheless, whatever one thinks about the inherent fairness of ex parte contacts, the judiciary's institutional competence to solve that problem looks highly dubious in light of (a) *Vermont Yankee*, decided the year after *Home Box Office*, and (b) the fact, mentioned by Judge Wald, that Congress had very recently examined the issue of ex parte contacts in the Sunshine Act and had elected to curb them only in formal proceedings.

2. *Political rulemaking.* Justice Scalia's argument for a political

model of rulemaking has force, but it seems overstated, or at least incomplete, for reasons suggested in the quoted comments of Glen Robinson. A democratic government ought to be responsive to the wishes of the public, and open communication with groups that would be most immediately affected by a proposed regulation can facilitate that objective. Private discussions may be the most effective medium for ascertaining what solutions along a spectrum of possibilities are most acceptable to these groups. Yet, contrary to Scalia's starkly pluralist analysis, our society does not want rulemaking to be *purely* political. Otherwise, as Robinson explains, it would not typically impose legal constraints on agencies' discretion, nor would it devise procedural norms that promote rational deliberation and accountability. A credible resolution of the ex parte contacts problem has to acknowledge a role for politics as well as a role for bureaucratic rationality in the rulemaking process.

The *Sierra Club* opinion properly acknowledges both. Judge Wald ably articulates the importance of political discussion to the legitimacy and effectiveness of agency policymaking. Yet one certainly cannot read her opinion as intimating that the ideal way for an agency to conduct a rulemaking proceeding is merely to acquiesce passively in power politics. The quoted excerpts from *Sierra Club* make clear that the court will expect EPA to justify its decision against a rulemaking record. Our passing reference, in the statement of facts, to the court's *sixty pages* of analysis of the merits of the sulphur dioxide regulations is intended to bring home to students the significance of this judicial check. Indeed, you might want to quote from the famous lament with which Judge Wald concluded her *Sierra Club* opinion (657 F.2d at 410):

> We reach our decision after interminable record searching (and considerable soul searching). We have read the record with as hard a look as mortal judges can probably give its thousands of pages. We have adopted a simple and straight-forward standard of review, probed the agency's rationale, studied its references (and those of appellants), endeavored to understand them where they were intelligible (parts were simply impenetrable), and on close questions given the agency the benefit of the doubt out of deference for the terrible complexity of its job. We are not engineers, computer modelers, economists or statisticians, although many of the documents in this record require such expertise—and more.

Whatever its faults, hard look review by the judiciary responds to Robinson's concerns by serving to maintain the rule of law as well as a high degree of rigor in agency policymaking; political choice can occur only within the boundaries that these constraints set.

3. *Switching off Home Box Office.* Although *Home Box Office*

appears to have been abandoned, *Sangamon* is probably still good law. Not only does *Sierra Club* reaffirm it, but there is language in *Vermont Yankee* that can be read to accommodate it: "In prior opinions we have intimated that even in a rulemaking proceeding when an agency is making a `quasi-judicial' determination by which a very small number of persons are `exceptionally affected, in each case upon individual grounds,' in some circumstances additional procedures may be required in order to afford the aggrieved individuals due process." Just how far this exception extends is a puzzle, however, as the Problem in this section is intended to illustrate.

4. *Written summary of ex parte communications.* Presumably, in the absence of a statute like the Clean Air Act, a court could not impose the *Sierra Club* docketing obligation on its own authority (and the *University of Washington* case refused to do so). *Vermont Yankee* would seem to be dispositive on that point. But this does not dispose of the policy question of whether statutes or regulations should require such docketing.

In the passage cited in text, Bonfield defends the MSAPA's failure to require that the agency rulemaking record contain summaries of relevant factual material expressed through oral ex parte contacts. He argues that the category of "factual" material, as distinguished from opinion or political argument, is elusive, yet the legal obligation to disclose it would invite much unproductive litigation. However, the regulations of EPA, FEMA, and other agencies mentioned in the ACUS rulemaking guide do not seem to have generated many practical problems, or lawsuits, over time. Thus, experience does not (yet) confirm Bonfield's stated concerns. The relative lack of controversy concerning these rules may reflect a high degree of compliance with them; or it may reflect the difficulty under *Morgan IV* of proving a violation.

Yet, if there is no strong evidence indicating that these federal procedures are too strict, it is far from certain that the more lenient approach exemplified by the MSAPA was a mistake, either. In a sense, one could say that state law (as represented by the 1981 MSAPA) is basically the same as federal law in this area. It may have been wise for the drafters of the MSAPA to avoid imposing a docketing obligation government-wide; individual state agencies are free to impose such obligations on themselves if they wish. That is the same situation in which federal agencies have found themselves since the decline of *Home Box Office.*

Ultimately, the narrow question of whether agencies should be required to disclose "significant" *factual* information that comes out during oral ex parte communications may not be very important. For one thing, as Bonfield also suggests, situations in which persons outside the agency convey such information orally, without putting the information in writing, are probably rare. Furthermore, when an agency does find itself in that situation, it has a strong incentive to memorialize the information in the record even in the absence of a docketing requirement. That incentive stems from the agency's interest in being able to rely on the information during any court challenge to the merits of the rule. (Even in a state that does not confine judicial review to the contemporaneous administrative record, the agency would likely recognize its interest in disclosing the information at some point.)

5. *Executive branch intervention in rulemaking.* The extent to which *Sierra Club* made special accommodations to the President is difficult to gauge. One reading of the opinion is that the court's remarks about presidential prerogatives were all dicta, because the court did not treat the meeting with the President any more leniently than it would have treated a meeting with anyone else. The ground rules for "anyone else" were that the meeting should be summarized for the record if the Administrator determined, in his discretion, that it was of "central relevance" to the rulemaking. Perhaps the court's position is simply that EDF hasn't shown that the failure to docket this meeting was an abuse of discretion, especially since no new facts or information emerged at that time. The opposite reading would be that, in the court's view, this meeting *was* of "central relevance" (perhaps because it *did* involve the President), but the lack of disclosure is not fatal to the regulations because of the special status of intra-executive communications.

However that may be, the court does seem willing in a proper case to apply a looser standard to presidential communications than to others' communications. As long as the President does not present new factual information, he can express forceful policy positions to the agency, and no one needs to know about them. Basically, this is the same as the ACUS Recommendation 80-6 position. Supporting this position are the court's various arguments for allowing presidential communications at all: the chief executive's constitutional prerogatives as head of the executive branch, and the policy interest in central coordination of national policy. A President can perform these leadership functions more forcefully if he does not have to worry about how his conversations will look in public. The basic counterargument is that White House leadership can itself be abused, and disclosure is the key to accountability. This argument may have greater force when the White House contacts come not from the President but from an unelected bureaucrat at OIRA. We explore the OIRA-agency relationship more fully in § 7.6.

6. *Congressional intervention in rulemaking.* In a regime in which ex parte contacts in rulemaking are generally disclosed, the case for an exemption for Congress is weaker than for the executive branch. A close reading of *Sierra Club* supports that distinction: the court treats presidential communications as *desirable,* congressional input as merely

legitimate. The comments of individual members of Congress do not necessarily promote coherence in governmental policymaking—quite the contrary. For example, Senator Byrd was (very legitimately) making sure that EPA took account of West Virginia's perspective on coal priorities, but that perspective might or might not coincide with the overall national interest. On the other hand, if the rulemaking agency is an "independent" agency, the distinction may be less sharp, because such entities are, at least in conventional understanding, supposed to operate unfettered by presidential control. (ACUS Recommendation 80-6 took no position regarding independent agencies. For general treatment of independent agencies, see § 7.5.2..

To be sure, one can make a strong case that congressional oversight is a vital part of the checks and balances system of the government, helping to keep the executive branch in line. But that analysis would not seem to justify an agency's giving members of Congress more latitude to make comments in secret than it would give to private parties, whose input in rulemaking proceedings keeps agencies accountable in a similar fashion.

Even if the SALT treaty story had been totally undisputed, it would not have justified setting aside the rule, because the court could not assume that the EPA had been influenced by what the senator had said. The second step in the court's two-part test would not necessarily be fulfilled. Indeed, *Morgan IV* would seem to require the court to presume that the EPA's technocratic explanation for its decision was sincere. To be sure, in the *D.C. Federation* case, § 3.3.3 N.4, Judge Bazelon made a rather adventurous assumption that congressional pressure had, in fact, influenced the Secretary of Transportation, but the other judges on the panel declined to join in that assumption. And the *D.C. Federation* case does make the key point that, outside the realm of formal proceedings, a legislator's leaning on an agency to act for ultra vires reasons does not itself make the agency action illegal. What would be illegal would be the agency's capitulation to such pressure.

7. *Problem.* This problem is intended to resemble the facts of *Sangamon*, but not so completely as to make that case directly controlling. The facts here are more difficult to characterize as "quasi-adjudication." Many people will be personally affected by the department's choice: not only individuals associated with Tyler and Fillmore, but also the homeowners and business owners mentioned in the problem, as well as anyone else who lives within walking distance of either proposed station location. (On the other hand, the court in *Sangamon* chose to overlook the fact that the FCC's decision in that case would affect third parties such as television viewers in St. Louis and Springfield.) Application of *Sangamon* would be plausible but not inevitable; thus, we hope, students will find it necessary to examine policy considerations ventilated in this unit in order to decide whether the

court should rely on that precedent.

The circumstances here appear to present a relatively weak case for allowing ex parte contacts. The ex parte contacts involved factual material—Tyler's expansion plans—rather than policy arguments. There is a strong argument for requiring factual material to be docketed so that Fillmore could respond to it. Fillmore can argue that Tyler's supposed expansion plans may never come to pass; had this issue been broached in public in a timely way, the university could at least have raised hard questions about the reliability of these projections. (Some of the facts about Tyler's plans might be legitimately kept out of the public record, as confidential commercial information; the agency or a court has some flexibility to determine, under privilege doctrines, how much must be revealed. *See Izaak Walton League of America v. Marsh*, 655 F.2d 346, 370 (D.C.Cir.1981).)

Moreover, the department has to make a rather simple bilateral choice. Sometimes, when an agency is designing a complex regulatory regime, it needs to stay in constant touch with affected interests in order to refine details of the regulations as the program takes shape, but that situation doesn't appear to be presented here. The basic issues of competing uses, ridership, and cost can be effectively expressed through the usual channels (written comments and the public hearing).

On the other hand, a court that is sympathetic to the department's interests may be reluctant to extend *Sangamon* beyond its facts. Presumably, most route decisions the department makes are pure rulemaking; they implicate numerous citizens' interests, and the "quasi-adjudication" label would be wholly inapt. Must the department adopt across-the-board regulations on ex parte contacts just to accommodate unusual situations like the present case, in which there happen to be two principal contending parties? Or must the department ban, or force disclosure of, ex parte contacts solely in such situations? Working guidelines that would implement such a distinction would be hard to write. Perhaps, therefore, this problem falls within the rationale of *Vermont Yankee*; the court should be reluctant to override the agency's discretionary decision about whether or not to regulate ex parte contacts.

Suppose MTD were subject to a provision like that in the Clean Air Act, requiring the docketing of documents submitted after the close of the comment period, provided that the agency determined the documents were of central relevance to the decision. *Sierra Club* applied that provision to oral ex parte comments of central relevance to the decision. Under that approach, Tyler's submission would have to be summarized by agency staff and that summary inserted into the rulemaking record so that others would have an opportunity to comment. Under the circumstances, this seems like an appropriate result in this case, although the burden on agency staff to write up and summarize an extensive presentation is substantial. We can expect that the staff summaries will be rather skeletal summaries of what might have been very lengthy ex parte presentations. In addition, there is an obvious problem with leaving it to the agency to decide what communications are and aren't of central relevance. Similar issues arise if the agency by rule (like EPA or FEMA) has required the disclosure of ex parte contacts.

Note that the problem does not appear to present a *D.C. Federation* issue, because the substance of Tyler's reported private communications would presumably be very relevant to the route decision. If Tyler is going to expand, more customers for the subway can be anticipated. If the lobbyists had come around primarily to remind the department about how helpful Tyler had been in the governor's last election campaign, the case would be different.

§ 5.5.3 Bias and Prejudgment

ASSOCIATION OF NATIONAL ADVERTISERS, INC.
v. FEDERAL TRADE COMMISSION

Notes and Questions

1. *The "unalterably closed mind" standard.* The standard announced in *ANA* appears to be basically sound. Rulemaking is quasi-legislative in nature, focusing on the determination of issues of general law or policy. Determinations of this kind require decisionmakers to be at least generally familiar with the issues of public policy involved in the matters they must decide. That being the case, they will inevitably have some opinions on the subject. Any effort to ensure that rulemakers be absolutely neutral about proposed rules is unlikely to be successful and would necessarily disqualify the most able and informed persons in a field from being agency decisionmakers in rulemaking.

It may be argued that, while decisionmakers may possess opinions about proposed rules, they should discreetly keep those opinions to themselves during the rulemaking proceeding. Yet, as the court explains, the policymaking process requires agency heads to consult actively with interested persons and groups, which necessarily entails a two-way dialogue.

The dissent in *ANA* concedes that FTC commissioners must discuss proposed rules with the public, but asserts that they should be disqualified if they slip from discussion into sustained, vigorous advocacy for a cause. Even that proposition seems too constraining, however. Administrators are commonly appointed to pursue a policy agenda. (Note the Pederson quote in footnote 38 of *ANA*.) Pertschuk, for example, was a well-known consumer advocate (as chief counsel to the Senate Commerce Committee) before his appointment, and his views must have been a factor in his selection. Getting things done in a complex government environment normally does require promotional activity, including the use of speeches, articles, and the like to mobilize public support for an initiative. This is not to say that all agency heads will, or must, try to be leaders; some might choose to be relatively passive facilitators, melding the views of the regulated or beneficiary community without promoting their own agendas. But surely the law of disqualification should not make efforts to display leadership impossible.

One might then ask whether there should be any disqualification standard at all in rulemaking. The court in *ANA* says that there should, although its articulation of the standard may leave something to be desired. (What would an "alterably closed mind" be?)

The views of the authors of this book diverge slightly on this point. One author considers the "unalterably closed mind standard" at least somewhat reasonable. He posits that one way to think about the bare minimum degree of required impartiality is to recognize that a rulemaking proceeding usually does not result in total victory or total defeat for anyone. A responsible agency can normally manage to write a rule that takes into account the concerns of both (or many) sides in a dispute. In the "kid-vid" case, as the *ANA* rulemaking proceeding was popularly known, there must have been dozens of ways in which the FTC might have structured its ultimate rule. Even if the industry knows it is going to take a hit, it could reasonably expect a commissioner to listen and deal constructively *at the margins* with its concerns. Even a Pertschuk should appreciate that industry may be able to shed light on whether one option is more workable than another, or on whether a certain option should be abandoned because its likely benefits are slim and its costs are heavy. But a zealot who won't even pay attention to his "enemies" may lack the detachment that we have a right to expect from decisionmakers, regardless of the merits of their cause.

Seen from this vantage point, the critical issue may have more to do with temperament than with "prejudgment" of factual propositions. In the particular circumstances of *ANA*, the industry never really made a case that Pertschuk could not be openminded on the details, although he certainly knew where he wanted to go in general. But Stofferahn, the South Dakota commissioner in the problem case discussed in N.6, may have been properly disqualified under this test.

In the opinion of the other author, however, since courts are not equipped to make distinctions relating to temperament, courts should impose no bias standard at all with respect to rulemaking. Little will be gained by asking courts to distinguish unalterably closed minds from alterably closed minds, but the standard encourages litigation and might tempt judges like MacKinnon to overturn regulations from time to time because of imprudent speeches or articles by agency decisionmakers.

2. *Judicial authority.* Under *Bi-Metallic*, the courts could not rely on due process as the basis for a disqualification standard for rulemakers. Presumably the standard would have to rest upon the obligation in § 553(c)—or a state provision such as 1981 MSAPA § 3-106(c)—to "consider" comments submitted in the proceeding. Arguably, this reasoning crosses the *Vermont Yankee* line that divides permissible interpretation of the APA from forbidden judicial creation of new duties. This interpretation move may seem particularly dubious when disqualification is sought at an early stage of the proceeding. The agency head can argue that he or she cannot be thought to have violated the obligation to consider the rulemaking comments, because those comments have not even been submitted yet, and the thrust of the motion is to prevent the official from even having the *opportunity* to consider them.

However, the duty to be prepared to address the issues without an "unalterably closed mind," when regarded as a principle that enforces § 553(c) prophylactically, does not seem any more remote from the text of the APA than other well-established duties that have been read into that Act. Moreover, we do not agree with the article cited in text that a judicially defined disqualification standard "is likely to render the APA highly unpredictable and encourage overproceduralization." Beermann & Lawson, 75 Geo.Wash.L.Rev. at 890. The practical problem on which *Vermont Yankee* focuses is the tendency of risk-averse officials to take excessive precautions in order to avoid reversal. We do not think a rulemaking official would win much sympathy by arguing to a court that "if you make me be openminded in this case, pretty soon I'll have to be openminded in *every* case!"

3. *Formalized rulemaking.* The reasoning of the D.C. Circuit's opinion implies that the court would apply the *ANA* test even in formal rulemaking. The court argues that Magnuson-Moss did not create a hybrid between adjudication and rulemaking at all, but only a hybrid between formal and informal rulemaking, and the *Cinderella* test applies to neither. In other words, the court thinks that, no matter how many procedural formalities the legislature may impose, rulemaking involves policy judgments and closely related legislative fact determinations that will inevitably, and properly, be influenced by the administrator's value system and political worldview. (Put aside situations such as individualized ratemaking, which do involve adjudicative facts even though they are artificially labeled rulemaking.) Running through the opinion is the

implication that Congress was naive in supposing that it could force agency decisionmakers to purge from their minds the sort of factual assumptions that are an integral part of their regulatory philosophy.

4. *ANA and adjudication.* This question points up a shaky aspect of the reasoning of *ANA.* The court seemingly assumed that rulemaking and adjudication cases can be cleanly distinguished because of the importance of legislative facts in the former. But in the hypothetical (as in many agency adjudications), no adjudicative facts are, or are likely to be, in controversy. The real factual disputes will deal with legislative facts. One would need only a small extension of the logic of *ANA* to conclude that in this situation a prejudgment such as Pertschuk's would be legitimate and perhaps unavoidable. The D.C. Circuit could again argue that Pertschuk would not be required in any event to decide legislative fact issues solely on the basis of the trial record, that his factual assumptions are inseparable from the policy positions he intends to pursue, and that he ought to discuss those policies with members of the public. (He should not, of course, engage in public discussions of circumstances pertaining specifically to Kellogg; but he doesn't really need to mention Tony the Tiger in order to make his general points about the effects of television advertising.)

Nevertheless, we know of no trend towards applying the *ANA* test to allegedly prejudged legislative facts in adjudication, and even the secondary literature seems to envision that *Cinderella* will apply (*see* Gellhorn & Robinson, 48 U.Chi.L.Rev. at 230-31). Are there sound reasons for the courts to adhere to *Cinderella* in this situation, even if they were to agree that some of the rationales of *ANA* are implicated? One reason might be a belief that it is easier to apply a single disqualification test in adjudication than a test that turns on whether the prejudged facts are legislative or adjudicative. But this may not be so, because to pursue the issue of disqualification at all, one has to identify what particular factual propositions were allegedly prejudged, and there will surely be some such propositions that are unambiguously legislative in nature.

It could be argued that prejudgments of policy or of indisputably legislative facts arising in adjudication should not be disqualifying. Similar distinctions appear in the law relating to official notice. *See* § 4.2.2. If Pertschuk had unalterably made up his mind that tooth decay among small children had been increasing at the rate of 10% per year, and that this is a serious public health problem, it's hard to see a court reversing an order against Kellogg on that basis alone.

It could also be argued that the strict disqualification test in adjudication will serve as a desirable incentive to induce the agency to resolve the policy issue through rulemaking rather than adjudication. Yet, even if that argument would in principle be a valid reason to adhere to an otherwise overbroad disqualification standard, FTC practice is a poor context in which to advance the argument, because of the wide agreement that the Magnuson-Moss Act scheme for hybrid rulemaking is seriously flawed (*see* § 5.4.3 N.2).

5. *State cases. Mahoney* is a different kind of case from *ANA*, because the agency not only "made up its mind" before the end of the rulemaking proceeding, but also *implemented* the change. Notifying the Social Security Administration of the offset actually set into motion the reduction of benefits to SSP recipients, a result highlighted by the federal agency's letters to recipients announcing this development. *Mahoney* can be read as holding, quite sensibly, that DSHS can't subvert the rulemaking process by taking official action before the notice and comment process has run its course; else comments received after such action will be moot and cannot possibly receive due "consideration." (Section 3-106(a) of the 1981 MSAPA expressly forbids adopting a rule before the end of the comment period.) This holding doesn't force the court to speculate about the agency's motives or mental state; rather, it regulates the agency's behavior.

On the other hand, *Mahoney* can also be read more broadly. Perhaps the court did not assume that the DSHS letter had operative effect, but merely treated it as revealing something about the agency officials' mental state. So interpreted, the case probably is not reconcilable with *ANA*. Although it is true (as the court noted) that the agency could have used a phrase such as "the state *may* revise the SSP," the fleeting phrase in the actual letter is surely not evidence of a closed mind, let alone "clear and convincing" evidence of one. This analysis of the court's line of reasoning would also cast doubt on its interpretation of the state APA. If one takes seriously *ANA*'s teachings about the inevitability of policy goals and agendas among agency officials, then the "consideration" demanded by statutory rulemaking provisions has to be defined in a manner that harmonizes with those teachings. It can scarcely mean much more than a willingness on the official's part to read the submitted material and reflect at least passingly on whether her extant views may need some adjustments at the margins.

An analogous case is *Radaszewski v. Garner*, 805 N.E.2d 620 (Ill.App.2003). This was another case in which a state public assistance department jumped the gun by notifying HHS of a policy change before the new policy had actually been adopted. In fact, the department, after receiving federal regulatory approval of the new policy, persuaded a federal court to dismiss, on mootness grounds, a lawsuit that had been brought to challenge the prior policy. *Then* the department commenced the rulemaking process to go through the motions of "considering" whether to adopt the new policy. The court thought that this allegation of "fait accompli rulemaking" was serious enough to survive a motion to dismiss. But it distinguished the objection from an allegation of *bias*, which it said would be governed by

ANA.

6. *Problem.* The facts of this problem are drawn from the *Stofferahn* case, in which the South Dakota court disqualified a commissioner from proceeding in a deregulation docket involving a telephone company that he had excoriated in campaign statements. The Court used the *ANA* test. (Even if you don't teach the Problem, you may want to call this holding to students' attention, in order to show that the *ANA* standard is not necessarily impossible to satisfy. The colorful rhetoric in our problem comes straight out of the opinion.)

But was the court right? To the extent that Henry simply voiced strenuous objections to deregulation, it would seem that he was merely doing what Pertschuk did, and that *ANA* is not distinguishable. However, his comments about Sludge in particular may be enough to trigger the "animus" branch of disqualification law. *See* § 3.3.5 N.4. Even in proceedings that are technically rulemaking, a major pipeline company will obviously be a major participant in quite a few proceedings, and if Henry is hostile to that company in and of itself, some of the case law developed in the adjudication context may well be apposite.

One complicating factor here, however, is that Henry is an *elected* official. If a state is going to elect its public utility commissioners, shouldn't it expect that it will sometimes wind up with commissioners who have campaigned and won on a platform of socking it to the pipelines? Colorful, simplistic rhetoric, including analogies to Jesse James, would seem to go with the territory. It is a bit surprising, therefore, to see a supreme court prohibit a commissioner from promoting the very views that the electorate presumably chose him to pursue. Compare *City of Fairfield v. Superior Court*, 537 P.2d 375, 381-82 (Cal.1975), refusing to disqualify a city councilman from deciding a zoning proceeding. The councilman had made strong statements during an election campaign against the very development which he was called upon to approve in an adjudicatory proceeding. The court said: "A councilman has not only a right but an obligation to discuss issues of vital concern with his constituents and to state his views on matters of public importance. . ."

There are very interesting issues here about the extent to which a political system should be committed to democratic or popular government, on the one hand, and deliberative ideals, on the other. Compare the "civic republicanism" material in § 1.6. You also can allude to Judge MacKinnon's dissent in *ANA*, in which he wanted to hold administrators to a higher standard than legislators because, inter alia, the former are *not elected*.

On the question of remedy, the South Dakota Supreme Court chose option (a) from our problem: it upheld Stofferahn's disqualification with respect to the four pending deregulation proceedings, but not with respect to any future case:

> The trial court was correct in the factual findings relating to Stofferahn's unalterably closed mind, bias and prejudice and the judgment declaring that Stofferahn should be disqualified in cases pending at the time of the entry of the declaratory judgment. This does not mean, however, that Stofferahn cannot or will not adopt a different attitude at some time in the future. . . . That determination, however, should be for the trial court to decide at the appropriate time.

> USWC argues that to compel it to attempt to disqualify Stofferahn in future cases will create an undue hardship and burden. Although we recognize that USWC may suffer a hardship as a result, we do not find such an increased burden sufficient to justify the forever condemnation of an elected public official from participating in any future adjudicatory or rule-making case where USWC may be a party without a proper due process showing that he should be disqualified under the standards above set out.

On a purely logical level, the South Dakota court's analysis seems unconvincing. If the court in our problem has found "clear and convincing" evidence that Henry's mind is "unalterably" closed, then by hypothesis he is unlikely to alter it. Yet, if the court does not believe the existing factual record would justify barring Henry from future deregulation rulemakings, it's going to be very hard for Sludge to make the requisite showing in the future, at least absent fresh provocations on the commissioner's part. Sludge's right to a fairminded decisionmaker thus seems to be at serious risk.

> On a pragmatic level, however, the South Dakota court's disposition may have been about right. Since the court felt it could not justify permanently barring a duly elected official from participation in a large chunk of the PUC's caseload, it imposed a mild sanction, together with an unmistakable warning that the commissioner had better watch his mouth from now on if he wants to avoid any reprises of this lawsuit down the road. To some extent, the law of disqualification is intended to keep up appearances, and a mild sanction now will probably deter similar gaffes in the future.

§ 5.6 FINDINGS AND REASONS

The subject matter of § 5.6 has more than a little overlap with that of other sections of the casebook. By and large, the pros and cons of reasons requirements in the rulemaking context are similar to the arguments that we canvassed in § 4.3 in the context of adjudication—although this section tries to bring out the differences, to the extent they exist. Moreover, most cases discuss the sufficiency of statements of basis and purpose in the course of conducting review of the merits, rather than treating that issue as a question of compliance with rulemaking procedure as such. Our treatment of that doctrinal material appears in § 9.4. Teachers who plan to cover those sections and are pressed for time might reasonably decide not to assign this section.

NATIONAL ASS'N OF INDEPENDENT INSURERS V. TEXAS DEP'T OF INSURANCE

Notes and Questions

1. *Merits of a reasons requirement.* In general, we think, the case for a reasons requirement is powerful in the rulemaking context, just as it is in the adjudication context (*see* § 4.3). The *Independent Insurers* opinion makes this case, at least in general terms. A required statement of reasons in rulemaking facilitates judicial review; helps to ensure that the rules issued are within the scope of the agency's authority; helps to reduce the likelihood of arbitrary, abusive, or unreasonable rules; helps adversely affected persons to plan their strategy and future course of conduct; and enhances the likelihood that agencies will perform their duty to consider carefully the submissions in that proceeding. In addition, such a statement helps the public to understand the precise scope of a rule, and how it will be applied in particular cases.

How do Frohnmayer's observations stack up against these considerations? His most persuasive point may be the time—and therefore the staff resources—that an agency has to expend in order to comply with a reasons requirement. We discuss these costs later in this section. When the issue is whether an agency should have to explain itself at all, we believe that these costs are well worth paying, for the reasons stated in the preceding paragraph. But, as we will develop, concerns about resources should at least be taken into account in the decision about how strict a reasons requirement to impose.

Frohnmayer's other arguments strike us as much weaker. The obligation to state reasons may indeed draw upon the agency's reserve of "political courage," but we have serious doubts about his implicit preference for the kind of "courage" an agency is willing to display only if it doesn't need to explain its actions.

Frohnmayer's suggestion that it is impossible to report all the reasons for a collective decision seems to rest on a misconception of the purpose of the explanatory statement. The purpose is to articulate a justification for the rule that meets certain standards of rationality and contains a line of argument for which the agency is willing to be accountable. Of course it can't recite every reason that motivates everyone who participates in the decision, but so what? Surely a judicial opinion does not have to meet that test. An "opinion of the Supreme Court" articulates a collective rationale—a majority of Justices are willing to sign off on it, be accountable for it, and live with it, even though individual members of the Court might well have preferred different analyses of the legal issue involved. The process of opinion-writing is not designed to *compile* these views but to *synthesize* them into a common position. Much the same can be said about the agency's statement of reasons. Thus, we would not, as Frohnmayer does, denigrate an explanatory statement for being based on the "lowest common policy denominator." To the contrary, we see the forging of consensus as desirable.

2. *Independent Insurers.* The court's unanimity in striking down Rule 1003 is not surprising, because the Board's explanation basically says nothing. Vague references to fairness and greater availability of insurance don't clarify why the Board adopted this particular rule. You can use this branch of the case to explore the general pros and cons of a reasons requirement.

Rule 1000 presents a more debatable situation. In addition to writing some unhelpful boilerplate, the Board did identify "blacklisting" as the problem it was trying to solve. As the dissent argues, the agency's point is fairly straightforward. If Company A's refusal to insure an applicant is going to trigger similar rejections from Companies B, C, D, and so forth, that applicant is going to have difficulty getting insurance, or may be shut out of the market entirely. Thus, the theory goes, insurers should not be able to decline an application for that reason. Moreover, as the dissent also recognizes, the rule does allow an insurer to ask whether another company has previously declined to insure the applicant, although the insurer must base its ultimate decision on its normal underwriting criteria, independently of that information.

On the other hand, the majority has understandable reasons for deeming the Board's reasoning to be superficial. The court obviously thinks that an applicant's history of being rejected by another company is a legitimate indication that the applicant may present a higher than normal risk. Yet Rule 1000 may well serve, as a practical matter, to deter or prevent insurers from taking account of that factor in their underwriting decisions. How easily could an insurer carry the burden of proving to some regulator that the information about an applicant's history with other insurers had no impact on its decision? Perhaps not very easily. The result may be that some insurers will simply take the path of least resistance by not asking for the information. The majority thus seems to be on defensible ground in arguing that the agency needs to provide a more careful analysis of the rule's effects on insurers (and ultimately on other policyholders whose premiums could be affected).

Even if one considers the result in *Independent Insurers* defensible, however, this case provides little support for the court's claim that the function of judicial review is to police the agency's "process," as distinct from the substance of its decision. The disagreement between the majority and the dissent appears to have as much to do with the judges' respective attitudes toward insurance regulation as with their views about the role of reason-giving in the administrative process. You may have noticed that the author of the majority opinion was Justice John Cornyn, who is now a U.S. Senator and well known as a staunch conservative. (In case you were wondering, however, the junior dissenter in the case was *not* Alberto Gonzales, the future U.S. Attorney General, but rather his immediate precessor on the Texas Supreme Court, Raul Gonzalez.) As Mashaw writes in the fine article from which we have repeatedly quoted in this section, "The demand for reasons and yet more reasons, *at least rhetorically*, keeps the court within its appropriate domain. . . . That this 'restrained' judicial posture may in fact disable or seriously impede regulatory activity is merely an ironic, unintended consequence. . . ." Mashaw, 76 Geo.Wash.L.Rev. at 111 (emphasis added).

The Texas legislature's revision of the reasons requirement is reminiscent of Justice Frankfurter's statement in *Universal Camera*, § 9.1, that Congress "expressed a mood" in favor of relatively searching judicial review when it enacted the "substantial evidence" test in the Taft-Hartley Act. In that instance the "mood" favored relatively searching judicial review of agency action, but the signals in the Texas example favored greater deference. We doubt, however, that the Texas legislature's small adjustments in the verbal formulas for judicial review will have any actual impact on the highly subjective judgment calls built into the reasons requirement. Indeed, another appellate panel subsequently concluded that the legislature "did not intend to effectuate a material change" in the law. *Reliant Energy, Inc. v. Public Utility Comm'n,* 62 S.W.3d 833, 840 (Tex.App. 2001). Our main reason for mentioning these legislative developments in the text is to demonstrate that the court's analysis, which may seem self-evidently correct to lawyers steeped in federal case law, met with a decidedly unwelcome reception on the home scene.

3. *Federal law.* In federal law, and that of many states, the role of a statement of basis and purpose has evolved dramatically to meet a changing conception of judicial review. As students will see in § 9.4 N.1, administrative rules were originally challenged in court in the same manner as statutes are. The court looked at whether a rational argument *could* be made in support of the rule, without regard to whether the agency actually had acted for that reason. This traditional model still prevails in some states. (Frohnmayer's analysis, of course, presupposes the traditional model of substantive judicial review. 3 BYU J.Pub.L. at 11.) But the federal courts, as well as certain states such as California, have adopted a model in which the quality of the agency's reasoning is crucial. This system cannot function unless agencies generate explanations for their rules. And, as rulemaking has come to be used for many of society's most complex decisions, those explanations have had to become quite detailed (as our *Sierra Club* example illustrates).

Accordingly, we fully agree with the linkage in the *Auto Parts* opinion between the "realities of judicial scrutiny," as currently practiced in the federal courts, and the interpretation of § 553(c). Major developments in the legal system pull strongly away from the words and original intent of the APA. At this point in the course, you cannot do justice to the question of whether hard look review itself is a good or bad idea. That question will have to await the scope of review chapter. The point to make here is simply that the evolving construction of § 553(c) accommodates the inherent needs of such review.

The *Vermont Yankee* questions raised in this note have fairly clearcut answers, at least as a doctrinal matter. *Auto Parts* does not violate the letter of the Supreme Court's decision, because for better or worse it rests on a construction of the APA, not on freefloating judicial notions of fair play. Moreover, in its remand instructions to the D.C. Circuit in *Vermont Yankee*, the Court itself emphasized that "when there is a contemporaneous explanation of the agency decision, the validity of that action must `stand or fall on the propriety of that finding . . . .'" Any lingering belief that the federal courts' demands for explanation of agency decisions are contrary to *Vermont Yankee* would seem to have been put to rest in *PBGC v. LTV*, discussed in § 5.4.3 N.4.

4. *"Major issues of policy."* This note alludes in passing to the developing literature on "ossification" of the rulemaking process. We cover this topic in depth in § 9.4 N.2 (having previewed it in § 5.1 N.1), but this may be an appropriate place to mention some of the practical burdens of compliance with the "reasons" requirement in particular. Drafting a coherent account of one's reasoning process can take a lot of thought (again, compare this task with the process of drafting a judicial opinion). When an agency has to go public with a stated rationale, it has to make sure it can

substantiate its claims; it has to work out answers to interested parties' comments; it has to ask whether its arguments are politically acceptable. Moreover, in doing this the agency has to reach some degree of internal consensus on a single statement of reasons. Often officials agree on what steps the agency should take, but not on the reasons why. Indeed, a given solution may be a compromise among different individuals, none of whom wholeheartedly supports it. The challenges may increase geometrically as the number of people and the complexity of issues involved grows. (This is most obviously a concern in a multi-member agency. Even in an agency headed by a single administrator, however, the agency head is likely to give a lot of weight to staff views, because of their subject-matter expertise, not to mention the need to maintain office morale.)

In a system like the federal one, in which the reasons requirement is driven primarily by the imperatives of judicial review, the only variable that could really affect the burdens of writing statements of basis and purpose would be a change in the scope of (or possibly the availability of) judicial review. Where judicial review is less of a factor, however, the phrasing of the statutory reasons requirement could become important—which takes us to the subjects of the next two notes.

5. *Responses to comments.* In the passage cited in text, then-Judge Breyer argues emphatically that the courts' practices in adjudication are a poor model for delimiting the scope of an agency's duty to respond to comments in rulemaking: "[D]istrict courts, unlike agencies dealing with policy change, do not face, say, 10,000 comments challenging different aspects of complex policies. And, when appellate courts 'answer' an argument they write a few words or paragraphs, perhaps citing a case or two. A satisfactory answer in the agency context may mean factfinding, empirical research, detailed investigation." Breyer thinks that reviewing courts overlook these differences and that their demands for responses to "important" comments contribute mightily to the ossification problem.

To the extent that Breyer is calling for a rollback of *Rodway* itself, however, we would not agree. His concerns can be seen as part and parcel of the larger dilemma that the debate over ossification has brought to light. The experience of recent decades is that society has been willing to accept a degree of ossification as the price of the benefits that a vigorously enforced reason-giving obligation entails. Indeed, what would be the point of mandating disclosures of data and methodology under the *Portland Cement* doctrine, which we've extensively explored in §§ 5.3 and 5.4.3, if the agency weren't ultimately expected to respond to technical comments in detail, with judicial review available in the background to enforce this expectation?

6. *Explanations on request.* The fundamental problem with § 3(a)(2), and state provisions based on it, is that an APA should require a rulemaking

agency to issue an explanatory statement in *all* cases (unless some exemption applies), not just on request. Although this approach puts a greater burden on agency resources, we believe the burden is outweighed by its advantages, as described in *Independent Insurers* and in N.1 above. Furthermore, the "on request" approach unfairly prejudices persons who may not have been in a position to demand such an explanatory statement prior to or immediately after the adoption of the rule. Many affected persons might not have realized, at the time a rule was proposed or adopted, that their interests would be affected by it, and so would have been unable to make a timely demand for a statement of reasons.

7. *Post hoc rationalizations.* This note recalls, but does not entirely overlap, the treatment of *Chenery* at § 4.3 N.5. There, the focus was on the question of who speaks for the agency. This note addresses the kinds of issues to which *Chenery* applies in the first place. It is clear that in a controversy over whether an agency complied with the APA, the court can take suggestions from counsel and reach its own conclusion without necessarily getting the view of the agency head, because the APA has not been entrusted to the discretion of any particular agency. *See* Stack, 116 Yale L.J. at 966.

However, the matter is more complicated when interpretation of the agency's organic statute is involved, because under *Chevron* the court and the agency share responsibility for such interpretation. To the extent that the court considers the statute unambiguous, it is likely to rely on its own interpretation regardless of whether the agency heads ever addressed that point. The *Bank of America* case cited in this note is a good exposition of this reasoning. If the agency's lawyers can persuade the court to adopt such an interpretation that favors their cause, so much the better for them. On the other hand, if the court does consider the statute ambiguous in relation to the point in dispute, *Chevron* would require substantial deference to the agency's interpretation, and thus the court needs to get the reasoning of the agency head (or, at the very least, someone who can credibly expound the agency head's view). Thus, as Stack argues persuasively, *Chenery*—and thus the judicial resistance to post hoc rationalizations—should apply at step two of the *Chevron* analysis, but not at step one. 116 Yale L.J. at 1008-10. That distinction may be too difficult to be covered directly at this stage of the course, but the problem in N.8 can be used to open up some of these issues.

8. *Problem.* In *Texas Hospital Ass'n*, the case from which the problem is drawn, the court set aside the reimbursement rule. This was another of the judicial decisions that apparently led the Texas legislature to amend the state APA to counteract what it perceived as excessive judicial meddling with agency rulemaking (or so says the court in *Lower Laguna*). See N.2 of the text. Yet few lawyers who are accustomed to a federal-law

perspective would consider the court's action surprising. The explanation by the Texas commission, which was substantively not much more detailed than the one in the problem, was quite thin. *See* 17 Tex.Reg. 4949 (1992). (The real Texas agency apparently did do a conscientious job of responding to each and every rulemaking comment. The problem is that none of these responses was more than a few lines long.)

The Board's explanation isn't horrible. It does convey a general notion as to the Board's reasons for changing its reimbursement system. It might well have been considered adequate under the original conception of § 553(c) of the federal APA. Under today's federal law, however, it probably wouldn't pass muster, because it doesn't quantify, or otherwise try to prove, any of its assertions. It recites the appropriate abstract factors, but unless the Board spells out the details of its analysis, the public has no assurance that its positions were taken seriously, and a court cannot engage in searching judicial review.

One might argue that the general statements in the Board's explanatory statement are good enough, because counsel can elaborate on the details in the agency's briefs during judicial review if any is sought. But that line of argument would raise serious problems under the *Chenery* doctrine. It would mean that agency counsel are doing the analytical work that we expect from the duly appointed agency heads (or at least the heads must supervise and sign off on that work as part of the normal bureaucratic routine).

If Madison follows the 1981 MSAPA, the same analysis probably applies, except that the operative provision, § 3-110(a)(1), has no established judicial gloss. It says that the agency's concise explanatory statement must contain "its reasons for adopting the rule," but this could logically be read as endorsing either the original interpretation of § 553(c), or the current interpretation, or something in between. This branch of the problem, therefore, brings students face to face with the question of what the better interpretation is. (Actually, the reporter's note to § 3-110(a) said that paragraph (1) "forces an agency to clearly articulate all of its factual, legal, and policy reasons for adopting the rule." One can presume that the courts would adhere to that interpretation, but it's not certain.)

Another interesting feature of § 3-110 is that it doesn't explicitly require an agency to respond to rulemaking comments. That omission is potentially relevant to the problem, because the Board's statement responds only obliquely to MHO's critique. In practice, however, a court that subscribes to hard look principles would probably read the generalized reason-giving obligation as incorporating a duty to reply to comments, as N.5 shows has occurred at the federal level.

If Madison follows 1961 MSAPA § 3(a)(2), some of the above uncertainties would be dispelled, because that provision expressly requires the Board to discuss the "principal arguments for and against [the rule's] adoption," as well as "its reasons for overruling the considerations urged against its adoption." (This assumes, however, that somebody *requested* a statement of reasons from the Board. In the highly unlikely event that nobody asked for an explanation, arguably no one should be able to complain about any deficiencies in the explanation the Board gave.)

Finally, if the state's APA does not explicitly call for a statement explaining the rule at all, MHO may be out of luck. The court might demand a better explanation in order to perform its judicial review function in this case, as *PBGC v. LTV* allows. It might even decide, in the exercise of its common law powers, that the imperatives of substantive judicial review impel it to impose a duty of explanation in *all* rulemaking cases. Although *PBGC* appears to say the latter is impermissible, a state might take a broader view of its common law powers than federal precedent would allow. Indeed, one state (prior to *PBGC*) appears to have done just that. *See Tri-State Generation & Transmission Ass'n v. Environmental Quality Council,* 590 P.2d 1324 (Wyo.1979). Nevertheless, a state like Utah that doesn't require explanatory statements might very well take a restrictive view of the courts' substantive review authority, too. (As a matter of fact, Frohnmayer reports that the Utah legislature was so determined to preserve judicial deference in review of agency rules that it even deleted from its APA the requirement that an agency must *consider* rulemaking comments! 3 BYU J.Pub.L. at 12.)

The statutory deadline aspect of the problem raises a question about the scope of the *Chenery* doctrine. At first glance, the issue appears to fall outside the scope of the doctrine. If the legislature prescribed a deadline, and the agency had no discretion to ignore it, the Board's failure to respond to MHO's argument in favor of a postponement makes no difference. (Notice that a literal reading of the relevant provision of the 1981 MSAPA, § 3-110(b), would forbid counsel from making the argument that they made in the problem. We assume, however, that the provision would be read as declaratory of the case law, which does recognize this *Chenery* exception.)

However, as students will see in § 6.3, courts do not always strictly enforce statutory deadlines, because they recognize that legislatures are often unrealistic about agency workloads. If the deadline in the Workers' Compensation Act is considered to be only presumptive, the agency's reasons for deciding to adhere to it would be important, and the absence of any discussion of this point in the statement of basis and purpose could be a problem that a post hoc rationalization could not rectify.

As a fallback position, Board counsel might argue that even if the agency had the option not to comply with the statutory deadline, its willingness to obey the legislature's command cannot possibly be considered an abuse of discretion. That is a fair point in isolation, but perhaps not in the context of the Board's weak performance in this rulemaking. If the court thinks that the Board 's analysis of the reimbursement guidelines on the merits was truly slapdash, it would want to hear from the agency itself about, for example, the kinds of problems that it would have faced if it had failed to meet the deadline. The Board would have been on safer ground if it had explained its reactions to the deadline argument in its written statement (as did the Texas agency in the real case, albeit briefly).

§ 5.7 ISSUANCE AND PUBLICATION

POWDERLY v. SCHWEIKER

Notes and Questions

2. *Publication of guidance documents.* The problem of distinguishing between the relative domains of § 552(a)(1)(D) and § 552(a)(2)(B) is solvable as a textual matter (all rules of *general* applicability have to be published, and by negative implication rules of *particular* applicability need not be), but this straightforward reading leads to a very burdensome result, as commentators such as Davis have uniformly recognized. Thus courts have tried in various ways to read clause (a)(1)(D) narrowly. Cases like *Powderly*, for example, make "general applicability" mean "affecting substantive rights," which is a strained reading of the text. In the ordinary sense of the words, the claims manual obviously was "generally applicable," because it applied to all forgers, not just to Powderly. *See* § 5.2.1.

On the other hand, the outcome in *Powderly* seems correct, because even if the agency did err, its error was harmless. The court obviously disagrees with plaintiff's interpretation on the merits. In that sense the agency's claims manual did not affect her rights at all. To allow her to keep the money that she wrongfully acquired because of the agency's failure to publish the manual would be to give her a windfall.

The Federal Circuit's analysis in *Cathedral Candle* is puzzling. The opinion observes, reasonably enough, that if a court believes that the interpretation in an agency letter is *correct*, the agency's failure to publish the letter is unimportant. Or, more precisely, the agency *should* have published it (since the agency could not know in advance that the court would agree with it), but the failure to publish could be considered a harmless error. As we just said, the outcome in *Powderly* can be rationalized on this basis. But in *Cathedral Candle* the court made abundantly clear that it was deferring to the agency's view. That fact should have made a considerable difference. Perhaps, if the ITC had disclosed its interpretation to the challenging parties in a timely fashion, they could have persuaded the agency to adopt a different interpretation that would have been more favorable to their interests. Certainly one cannot be sure that this would *not* have happened, so the failure to publish cannot be dismissed as harmless.

Why, then, did the court in *Cathedral Candle* recoil from enforcing § 552(a)(1)? Apparently because it believed, on the basis of Supreme Court case law, that an unpublished guidance document can be entitled to deference (in this instance *Skidmore* deference). Although that certainly is true, it does not justify the court's conclusion. The issue of whether a document must be published (and what should be the consequences of not publishing it) is quite distinct from the issue of whether deference should be afforded to it.

3. *Consequences of failure to publish.* Several aspects of the *Nguyen* analysis are attractive. The court is decidedly more respectful of the language of FOIA than *Powderly* was. A test that turns on the impact of a nonlegislative rule on substantive rights can be extracted much more easily from the FOIA phrase "adversely affected" than from the phrase "of general applicability." Moreover, the *Nguyen* analysis has an intelligible policy basis. If an agency is stretching its statute by "interpretation," or using a policy statement coercively, arguably the targets of its action *should* be able to use the sanction provision of § 552(a)(1) as a shield. This will give agencies an incentive not to misuse guidance documents by treating them like legislative rules. The court's mode of analysis thus brings the pressure of § 552(a)(1) to bear in the very circumstances in which the use of nonlegislative rules is most troubling.

On the other hand, the *Nguyen* solution isn't entirely satisfactory, either. The court's interpretation gives agencies less relief from the compliance burdens of a literal interpretation of § 552(a)(1)(D) than *Powderly* does. They are still *legally obligated* to publish all guidance documents of "general applicability." Yet, at the same time, it doesn't do much to assist private persons. Arguably the *Nguyen* analysis makes the § 552(a)(1) sanction largely superfluous in cases involving interpretive rules and policy statements. If the criteria in the court's test are met, the challenging party will usually be able to prevail anyway on the ground that the rule was adopted without notice and comment. Students haven't studied the rulemaking exemptions in depth yet, but they should be able to see readily enough that in *Powderly* the court's analysis of "substantive rights" was basically the same for purposes of § 553 and § 552.

Furthermore, the implication of *Nguyen*'s narrow construction of "adversely affected" is that agencies will rarely suffer any accountability in court for failing to publish interpretive rules or policy statements in the *Federal Register*. This seems to subvert the intentions of FOIA, because § 552(a)(1)(D) does specify that guidance documents of "general applicability," *in addition to* "substantive rules of general applicability adopted as authorized by law," should be published. *Nguyen* seems to mean that this obligation will usually be unenforceable. The agency merely has to give the targeted party "actual notice" of the document at the time of the dispute and allow him to argue back against the agency's position.

A broader lesson that apparently emerges from this entire series of cases is that courts agree with Davis that FOIA's requirements for *Federal Register* publication of guidance documents are too onerous, and they have worked assiduously to weaken them.

4. *Filing of rules.* Section 3-114(a) of the 1981 MSAPA is intended to ensure that all rules are in fact accessible to the public, and that agencies do not establish secret law. To this end, the original copy of all rules must be deposited in one central depository that is open to the public and that is fully reliable as the final and unimpeachable official source for all agency rules. In *Cull*, the court reasoned that, without such a requirement, "a failure to file, though it would not leave a motorist in ignorance of a posted speed restriction, would prevent him—for instance, following a charge—from examining the contents of the rule establishing such limitation in order to determine its legality, effectiveness or accuracy." 176 N.E.2d at 498. The story of the *Panama Refining* case, in the introduction to this section, highlights what can happen without such a requirement. (The FRA also requires filing as a condition of effectiveness, 44 U.S.C. § 1507, but this point rarely gets any attention, because filing with OFR goes hand in hand with *Federal Register* publication.)

An opposing view would be that publication of a rule nearly always provides all the official notification that citizens need or want. Individuals rarely have any reason to consult, and rarely do consult, the official, original text of an administrative rule. Although the official text occasionally has legal significance, such as where there is some question about whether it was signed, or was accurately transcribed in the published version, the chances of this being true in a given situation are remote. Thus, whatever small costs may be suffered by persons who wish to examine the official text in the central depository, but cannot do so, are outweighed by the benefits that society realizes from letting an otherwise legitimate rule go into effect after it has been published (or, in a case like *Cull*, publicized through signs on the highway). But this view seems not to have prevailed; the law insists on a minimum degree of formality in this realm, as it does in many others, ranging from filing of a will to entry of a court judgment.

Section 3-115(a) of the 1981 MSAPA provides that the delayed effective date begins to toll only after a specified number of days subsequent to filing *and* indexing *and* publication. The premise of this provision is that mere filing and publication alone will not give the affected public adequate or fair notice of the precise contents of a new rule; only after a rule is filed, indexed, and published for a reasonable length of time is it fair to assume that adequate notice has been given and that the public has had a fair opportunity to ascertain the law. Again, however, one might question this tradeoff on pragmatic grounds. The case for insisting on indexing as a precondition to the effectiveness of a rule seems weaker than in the case of the other preconditions.

5. *Delayed effectiveness.* The *Rowell* majority's construction of § 553(d) is far preferable to that of the dissent. The purpose of the statute is to give regulated interests time to *prepare* for the new regime. Rational people who see a new regulation coming will make some advance preparations, but normally the serious preparations occur only after the rule has been issued in final form. Only then, after all, do they know what the rule is going to say. In *Rowell* it turned out that the final rule was identical to the proposed rule, but regulated entities can't necessarily count on that eventuality. Besides, if they want to petition for rehearing, or to appeal, they should have time to prepare for that course of action before the rule actually goes into effect.

To be sure, the facts of the *Rowell* case are compatible with the dissent's point to a much greater extent than usual. The agency's decision simply instituted a price increase. One might argue that leaseholders don't need to make elaborate preparations to comply. They just have to pay more money, and probably they started budgeting for this expenditure long ago, at least on a contingent basis. (Moreover, these particular plaintiffs are lease *applicants* whose real goal in this litigation is to force the department to act on their applications before the new rate goes into effect, so that the lower rate will be locked in. In that sense, they aren't "preparing" to comply at all, because the initiative rests with the agency.) Normally, businesses have a much more tangible need for at least thirty days' preparation time before a regulation goes into effect. They need that time in order to make plans for compliance with the new regime, rewrite their forms, train employees, explain their new policies to customers, and so forth.

Even on the *Rowell* facts, however, some lease applicants may well need the thirty days in order to reassess whether they might wish to withdraw or revise their applications in light of the higher charges. More broadly, the court in *Rowell* was on sound ground in sticking with a simple construction of § 553(d) that in most cases serves a very useful purpose. Indeed, that construction doesn't cause big problems for the agencies, because a good cause exemption is available for urgent regulations, and the remedy for a breach of § 553(d) is quite mild anyway, as the next note explains.

6. *Remedy*. As in *Rowell*, most courts have declined to throw out a rule because of a § 553(d) violation, but have merely extended the time before the rule becomes enforceable. *Prows v. Department of Justice,* 938 F.2d 274, 276 (D.C.Cir.1991) (citing cases). We agree with them. Such a violation casts no doubt on the intrinsic soundness of the regulation, and the extension gives the individual precisely the protection that § 553(d) contemplates. After the required thirty days are up, *subsequent* violators have little reason to complain that the rule went into effect too early. Wouldn't it be inequitable, after all, to let a regulated party off the hook for his breach of a rule in 2009, on the ground that the rule had an effective date of April 2001 when the APA said it had to be May 2001? True, this line of cases weakens an agency's incentive to comply with the APA, but the cases appear to reflect a sense that a § 553(d) violation, although preferably avoided, is a relatively minor sin.

8. *Midnight regulations.* The transition from Bush to Obama has reinvigorated debate about midnight regulations, and various proposals to curb them have been made.

One suggestion has been that an outgoing administration should be prohibited from adopting any rules in its final months (except in emergency situations). This proposal, however, would seem to be overkill. Although controversies over midnight rules typically bring partisan disagreements out into the open, some of the reasons why an administration may issue more rules at the very end of a presidential term than at other times are surely legitimate, or at least tolerable. Some delays may simply be attributable to procrastination The human tendency to put off making difficult decisions is universal. Moreover, circumstances that are beyond the agency's control, such as lawsuits or congressional constraints, may have prevented earlier action. In practice, the motives that lie behind the timing of various midnight regulations are often mixed, and it may be hard to decide whether the agency's delay in a given situation was justifiable. Anyway, some post-election rules are routine and not particularly politically charged.

In addition, it has been argued that the entrenching effect of a midnight regulation has a salutary effect on public dialogue in some situations. The outgoing administration's rule can serve as a benchmark by which the new administration will have to justify its revised policy to the public. *See* Mendelson, 78 NYU L.Rev. at 629-31.

A more promising approach would be to expand the options available to the incoming President to intercept rules adopted by his predecessor. A relatively modest step would be for Congress to expressly authorize the incoming administration to postpone the effective date of a recently adopted regulation, so that it can be reviewed. Both Republican and Democratic administrations have in fact asserted that they can do this, but, in light of cases such as *NRDC v. EPA*, a statutory confirmation of this power would be desirable.

But what kind of action should the new administration be able to take against those rules that it decides it does not support? Should it be empowered to modify or revoke such rules without a notice and comment period? Conferral of such power would respond to the argument that a just-elected President has a particularly strong claim to democratic legitimacy—in a sense, more than the President whose administration is on the way out. Moreover, after the election the outgoing administration has temptations to overreach or abuse its power, because the new regulation can no longer be used as a campaign issue against the party's nominee. Although the legislature could, in theory, use the Congressional Review Act to counteract midnight rules, in practice the CRA is almost never invoked, because of the difficulty of getting Congress to agree on any legislative action, not to mention the competing claims on its time at the beginning of a new session. *See* § 7.4.1 N.7.

However, there are also significant objections to any plan that would give the new President a summary revocation power. Even if the motives behind a particular midnight regulation are questionable, at least the outgoing administration will normally have issued it subject to the structural checks that are built into the rulemaking process. In most cases, the rules will have been developing over a considerable period of time, in a process that is at least conducive to thoughtful refinement of the issues. In contrast, the leaders of the incoming administration will by hypothesis be new to the job. Their desire to invalidate a rule may well rest on a quick, visceral reaction, detached from the responsibilities of managing the agency as a whole. This reasoning suggests that, even where officials in the incoming administration have good reasons to want to undo the previous administration's handiwork, they should not be authorized to do so without conducting a rulemaking proceeding of their own.

If you don't mind making a brief digression into material that will be covered in the next chapter, you might mention that, even without new statutory authority, the "good cause" exemption in § 553(b)(B) gives agencies a degree of latitude to reexamine certain midnight regulations when a new administration takes power. In some cases, for example, an agency might find that immediate suspension of the scheduled effective date of a midnight regulation is urgent (i.e., full rulemaking proceedings would be "impracticable" or "contrary to the public interest"), because the affected industry would suffer disruptive consequences if it were obliged to comply in the short run with a regulation that is very likely to be rescinded in the foreseeable future anyway. Or the agency might conclude that a sixty-day suspension of a particular rule would have so trivial an impact on private interests that notice and comment proceedings would be "unnecessary." *See* § 6.1.1.

However, we do not agree with the suggestion in Beermann, 83 B.U. L. Rev. at 983 & n.120, that the desire of an incoming administration to reexamine the policy choice recently made by its predecessor would *ipso facto* constitute "good cause" to suspend the effective date of a midnight regulation. That suggestion strikes us as difficult to reconcile with the courts' tradition of construing the exemption narrowly. *See* William M. Jack, Comment, "Taking Care that Presidential Oversight of the Regulatory Process is Faithfully Executed: A Review of Rule Withdrawals and Rule Suspensions under the Bush Administration's Card Memorandum," 54 Admin.L.Rev. 1479, 1508-11 (2002). This student comment is an excellent analysis of the doctrinal legal issues presented by midnight regulations.

Beermann has recently published a brief followup essay on midnight regulations. It has only limited overlap with his article cited in the text, and we recommend it. *See* Jack M. Beermann, "Combating Midnight Regulations," 103 Nw.U.L.Rev. Colloquy 352 (2009). In addition to exploring various potential legislative responses to concerns about midnight regulations, he contended that the Supreme Court should reevaluate its doctrinal principles that make it especially hard for agencies to revoke a prior administration's rules. Since then, the Court has already indeed action that comports with Beermann's recommendation. In *FCC v. Fox Television Stations, Inc.*, 129 S.Ct. 1800 (2009) (which is not limited to midnight rule situations), the Court said that when an agency alters its position, its burden of explanation is normally no more demanding than if it were writing on a clean slate. The case is discussed in this manual at §§ 4.4.2 and 9.4.

9. *Problem.* In the *D & W Food Centers* case, the fact situation was quite similar to the one sketched in the problem. The agency involved was the U.S. Department of Agriculture, and the statute was the Federal Meat Inspection Act, 21 U.S.C. § 606, which was originally adopted in 1907 in direct response to Upton Sinclair's muckraking novel *The Jungle*. The Sixth Circuit held in *D & W Food Centers* that the grocery chain's pizza kitchen was outside the scope of the Act. The court went on to say that it did not need to consider the possibility of deferring to the government, because the interpretation had never been published pursuant to § 552(a)(1).

a. *Publication issue.* The question of whether Alvin is immune from sanction for the period predating the promulgation of Regulation 36 turns, initially, on whether the bulletin had to be published at all. If the court gives § 552(a)(1)(D) a literal reading, the issue is whether the bulletin has "general applicability." An affirmative answer is not inevitable, because the bulletin seems to have been written with Alvin's situation in mind, and possibly no other grocery chains have comparable facilities. But even if Alvin's pizza kitchen actually is unique in the state (which seems unlikely), students saw in § 2.5 and § 5.2.1 that the usual test of "generality" is whether a rule is *written* in general terms, regardless of how many entities actually fall within its terms.

However, the practical burdens of a literal interpretation of § 552(a)(1)(D) have troubled a number of courts, so the inquiry cannot end there. On the surface, the facts of this case are like those of *Powderly*, because the agency bulletin purports to be interpreting an existing mandate rather than making new law. Students should readily see, however, that this argument may prove too much. The department's position on the merits is tenuous at best. Alvin's operation is scarcely "similar" to a packinghouse. Indeed, the remaining terms in the statute—slaughtering, rendering, packing—connote a workplace of a quite different character. (This point could be more formally expressed with reference to the statutory construction maxim known as *ejusdem generis*—general catchall terms in a statute are construed in light of the specific terms accompanying them.) And the purposes of the statute do not seem sharply implicated, because Alvin's kitchen facility bears little resemblance to the horrific slaughterhouses and packinghouses that the Act was enacted to regulate. In reality, therefore, the department is using the bulletin to deploy a new interpretation and redefine Alvin's substantive rights.

Perhaps the court would be willing to stretch a point if it were presented with a strong record that Alvin's facility, or others like it, are prone to unsanitary conditions. By any reckoning, however, the argument for MDH jurisdiction does not flow easily from the "plain language" of the statute. The agency has to hope that the court will defer to administrative judgment. But if the agency's interpretation does matter to the outcome, Alvin has a clear interest in being given a chance to try to persuade the agency to alter its interpretation, and the agency's failure to publish or otherwise make him aware of the bulletin hampered his ability to do so. The *Cathedral Candle* case can be brought into the discussion at this point. As stated above, we believe the court in that case gave the role of deference too little weight.

Even if the department did have an obligation to publish Bulletin 260, the *Nguyen* case highlights the additional issue of whether the agency's breach of that obligation "adversely affected" Alvin. The government can argue here that the bulletin as such had no effect, because Alvin was still able to be heard before the agency. On the facts of the problem as stated, however, this proposition seems incorrect. The department apparently relied squarely on the bulletin, treating it as conclusive rather than as a guideline. Moreover, Alvin had no access to its reasoning and thus no ability to rebut that reasoning at the agency level.

Because students have not yet encountered the intricacies of the issue of how to distinguish guidance documents from legislative rules, our problem is designed to present a relatively simple and clear-cut situation. If you wish to anticipate some of those complications, you can easily posit variations on the facts as stated in the problem. What if the department purported to entertain Alvin's argument that his stores' pizza-making occurs at the "retail" level, but it actually gave his arguments a cursory brushoff? Or what if the frontline officers with whom Alvin dealt at the local level simply assumed that the bulletin should be followed and gave the interpretive question no consideration, but he could have obtained meaningful consideration at a higher level of the bureaucracy? (This question would also raise an issue of exhaustion if Alvin did not pursue that appeal, but under *Darby v. Cisneros*, § 11.2.3 N.4, exhaustion may not be required.) Under either of these circumstances, the *Nguyen* issue would be closer. These are murky waters, however, perhaps best postponed until you reach § 6.1.4.

The federal case law is at least suggestive as to interpretation of the 1981 MSAPA. Under § 3-115, an interpretive rule is treated in the same way as a legislative rule: it cannot be "effective" until it is filed, published, and indexed. Therefore it could not have been used against Alvin during the period before the rule went into effect. (Indeed, the facts don't say that Regulation 36 has yet been filed or indexed, so it may not be effective yet at all. You may want to make that point, then posit for the sake of discussion that those events occurred in the regular fashion.) The agency could try to argue that it didn't need for the bulletin to be "effective": Alvin's actions violated the Madison Meat Inspection Act, and its enforcement actions rested on the statute rather than the bulletin. But that argument is unlikely to succeed in light of the events outlined, which clearly suggest that the agency treated the bulletin as determinative. In fact, the MSAPA doesn't even exempt interpretive rules from notice and comment except in limited circumstances not presented here (see § 3-109), so an MSAPA jurisdiction is unlikely to take a very tolerant attitude toward an agency's abuse of such rules.

b. *Effective date issue.* Per our analysis above at N.4, the agency's failure to allow 30 days' preparation time before the regulation became effective plainly violated § 553(d). Indeed, the equities are clearer here than in *Rowell*. Alvin needs time to make the structural changes in his kitchen facility, train employees in the newly instituted requirements, etc. Also note here that MDH cannot claim an exemption from § 553(d). It cannot rely on the "good cause" exemption, because it did not make a contemporaneous finding that good cause existed.

Although the § 553(d) violation is clear, the most that Alvin can expect by way of a remedy is an extension of the effective date of the regulation until thirty days after the rule was published. Total invalidation of the rule is unlikely for the reasons discussed above in N.5. Deferment of the rule until thirty days after the court has ruled on its legality is a more tenable possibility, and we know of one case that has given this sort of relief, *see Ngou v. Schweiker*, 535 F.Supp. 1214 (D.D.C.1982), but the general practice is simply to give the plaintiff the month's time that the APA says should have been given initially. Section 553(d) has a limited purpose, and the latter remedy is regarded as adequate to vindicate that purpose.

Alvin's request for a postponement of the rule until the court challenge is over is more properly analyzed as a request for a judicial *stay*. *See* APA § 705. We discuss stays at § 11.2.4 N.5. The basis for such relief is a balancing test that weighs public and private interests. The problem thus points up the contrast between two types of postponement. Regulated parties have a statutory right to thirty days' preparation time automatically (although in narrow circumstances the agency can invoke the good cause exemption to shorten or waive this presumptive right). If a party wants more of a postponement than that, it will have to appeal to the discretion of the agency or court.

Under the 1981 MSAPA, the effective date issues would turn on § 3-115(a) (and for judicial stays, see § 5-111). We perceive no specific reason to expect a state court to disagree with federal law on these issues.

§ 5.8 REGULATORY ANALYSIS

This section treats regulatory analysis as a step in the rulemaking process, but it also exposes students to a taste of substantive regulatory policy. Much, much more could be said about the analytical refinements that have been brought to bear on the science—or art—of risk assessment and cost-benefit analysis. These refinements are important to the regulatory enterprise, but a detailed examination of them would go well beyond the natural bounds of a basic administrative law course. Entire courses can be, and sometimes are, devoted to these topics. Our treatment is necessarily limited, but students should find it interesting, because it has a strong ideological dimension. The trend toward cost-benefit analysis and related modes of policy analysis has alarmed and offended many supporters of strong health and safety regulation, and the passions that the debate has elicited are clearly visible in much of the scholarship in this area.

CORROSION PROOF FITTINGS v. EPA

We have presented here a severely truncated version of the Fifth Circuit's thirty-page opinion. Indeed, the legal analysis section alone (from which our excerpt is drawn) extends over eight pages and addresses quite a few legal issues that our edited version omits. Because our visit to this domain is necessarily fleeting, our excerpt focuses on a handful of recurrent problems with cost-benefit analysis in rulemaking.

TSCA aftermath. In *Corrosion Proof Fittings*, the court surely reads the statute more restrictively than it need have. The language says that both costs and benefits must be considered, but it does not overtly mandate a rigorous, quantified cost-benefit analysis. One can argue that EPA brought this misfortune on itself by adopting an exceptionally stringent rule. That argument rests on debatable premises about valuation, as we discuss in N.5. More fundamentally, even if the particular regulation being reviewed was too ambitious or weakly supported, it would seem that the court overreacted by prescribing too much intensive analysis for future cases.

More particularly, notice the passage in which the Fifth Circuit discusses unquantified benefits that EPA said would be realized after 2000. Here, the court basically takes the position that *all* of the major elements of the agency's assessment of costs and benefits must be quantified. Even supporters of CBA such as Sunstein and Weidenbaum would agree that this premise is extravagant—many of the variables that a rulemaking authority must consider cannot be quantified. One can understand the judges' feeling that the EPA in this case was out of control, and that the court could not effectively review the rule without objective points of reference. Again, however, even if the court's view of this particular rule is right (and, as we say, that is debatable), the cure may have turned out to be worse than the disease, because hindsight suggests that the effect of the tight leash has been that EPA can barely make use of TSCA § 6 at all As the GAO study documents, rulemaking under that provision can be viewed as a quintessential case of "paralysis by analysis." The agency's procedural burdens, as construed, turn out to be in severe tension with its substantive mandate.

For Heinzerling's detailed critique of *Corrosion Proof Fittings*, see her testimony before the House Energy and Commerce Committee on July 13, 2004, which is available at *http://energycommerce.house.gov/reparchives/108/Hearings/07132004hearing1345/Heinzerling2191.htm.*

CASS R. SUNSTEIN, THE COST-BENEFIT STATE: THE FUTURE OF REGULATORY PROTECTION

LISA HEINZERLING & FRANK ACKERMAN,
PRICING THE PRICELESS:
COST-BENEFIT ANALYSIS OF ENVIRONMENTAL PROTECTION

1. *Cost-benefit analysis mandates.* In practice, according to the GAO, the CBA provision in the Unfunded Mandates Reform Act has turned out to be ineffectual. "Unfunded Mandates: Analysis of Reform Act's Coverage and Views on Possible Next Steps," GAO-05-533T (2005), at 8-10. This track record obviously dovetails with experience under other schemes in which lack of judicial review has led to weak compliance, as discussed below in NN. 9-13. Congress, of course, anticipated this result; that's why legislators moved on to the stronger bills discussed below.

2. *Cost-benefit decisional criteria.* The questions posed in this note provide an opportunity to explore the theoretical perspectives suggested in the Sunstein and Heinzerling/Ackerman readings. Clearly there are strong arguments against the notion that rulemaking decisions should depend directly on the results of a formal cost-benefit study. Regulatory analyses are not models of scientific precision; they are often based upon dubious assumptions and unreliable data, and come to conclusions that are, at best, educated guesses at approximations. They also do not solve the problem of comparing incomparables in order to determine whether costs outweigh benefits. Furthermore, requiring agencies to follow the results of cost-benefit analyses exalts technocratic processes over political processes, suggesting that in public policymaking expert opinion should prevail, on a wholesale basis, over the political judgment of the community.

One might, however, argue that agencies should be directed to do their best to adopt rules that are cost-justified, even if those determinations can't be made with precision and have to be made by politically responsible leaders rather than technocratic experts. This is a more understandable proposition, but Sunstein seems to concede that it is still overbroad. Undoubtedly some administrative decisions can and should be resolved on the basis of at least a crude comparison of costs and benefits. In other situations, however, cost-benefit criteria are simply meaningless or out of place, as the government's decisions will inevitably turn on noneconomic criteria such as distributive equity. Of course, Heinzerling and Ackerman offer a more fundamental critique of the CBA enterprise as a whole.

5. *Valuation problems.* We come down on Sunstein's side on the broad question of whether cost-benefit analysis can properly entail assigning a number to the value of lives saved. To put it differently, we would not abandon the entire enterprise simply because it unavoidably entails such an assignment. Some such exercise seems essential if agencies are to engage in meaningful comparisons between alternative courses of action.

On the other hand, it is worth emphasizing that any value-of-life figure has to be used cautiously. It can facilitate intelligent discussion about the pros and cons of a proposed policy, but in any ultimate decision about a policy, nonquantified considerations will have to be part of the mix. The calculations employed along the way should not be embraced too mechanically or uncritically. By that same token, one of the best arguments *against* cost-benefit analysis as a tool for making decisions about lifesaving or health-promoting measures is that, in practice, decisionmakers will indeed take the numbers too seriously and rely on them as a substitute for a wider and more thoughtful inquiry into the merits.

The numbers generated by CBA also become important to the agency when it makes its public defense of its decision. That is one reason why EPA's downward adjustment in its baseline figure for the value of a statistical life is significant. Usually, such figures have been raised, not lowered, and so the EPA decision raises questions about the political perspectives of the agency as of that time.

The question raised in this note about *Corrosion Proof Fittings* comes down to whether the costs of the rule should be measured in the aggregate (in which case the price tag of between $2.4 million and $5.2 million per life saved is well within normal ranges, if not *less* expensive than many comparable rules) or on a product-by-product basis (in which case certain elements of the rule, including the bans on asbestos pipe and asbestos shingles, are much more expensive than usual). In the abstract, either of these perspectives seems tenable. The costs of rules of this sort are frequently discussed on an aggregated basis, and EPA could reasonably have expected to get the benefit of that practice. Yet, if a ban on pipes or shingles is phenomenally expensive when considered on its own terms, manufacturers of those products could understandably feel aggrieved about those applications.

One potential answer to this conundrum is that, given a choice between two reasonable alternatives, the court should defer to the agency. This is essentially McGarity's argument in the *Texas Law Review* article cited in this section, and it is at least a reasonable approach. By this point in the course, students will have at least a general awareness of the rationales for deference, such as expertise and political accountability. But not everyone will find this answer satisfactory. After all, deference can cut either in favor of regulation or against it, depending on what sort of administration is in power at a given time. Moreover, it is not clear who deserves the deference. Arguably, the "expert" on cost-benefit methodology is OMB, which has a clear policy favoring separate analysis of the benefits and costs of different regulatory provisions. OMB Circular A-4 at 17 (Sept. 17, 2003), available at *http://www.whitehouse.gov/omb/circulars/a004/a-4.pdf.*

You may want to mention to the class that EPA calculated these unflattering disaggregated figures in direct response to a request from OMB. Lisa Heinzerling, "Regulatory Costs of Mythic Proportions," 107 Yale L.J. 1981, 2006 (1998). One lesson that this episode teaches, therefore, is that the process of regulatory analysis can serve as a significant brake on regulation—not only because the agency will have to expend significant resources in order to generate the analysis, but also because the analysis itself may generate information that can be used to contest the agency's position on the merits.

6. *Discounting.* If cost-benefit analysis is to be pursued, discounting fits logically into it, for reasons expressed in the Revesz quote, but the practice does give rise to a number of problems. Revesz himself argues that discounting of benefits that will accrue to future generations is unethical. The "present value" of these benefits may look small as a mathematical matter, he says, but in this context discounting essentially subordinates the interests of future generations to our own. This aspect of the discounting issue has become increasingly important as awareness of the challenges of climate change has spread. (However, most of the articles in the Chicago symposium cited in the note take a more sympathetic view of the utility of discounting in the intergenerational context.) Revesz does not object in principle to discounting of benefits that people who are alive now will realize in the long run rather than the short run. He maintains, however, that such discounting requires adjustments from customary practice if it is not to prove misleading.

Heinzerling and Ackerman's objections rest largely on an apprehension that discounting will be used by opponents of regulation to minimize the benefits that a proposed standard would bestow. If the stated dollar value of the rule is a lower number, the benefits of adopting it look smaller. In theory such a distortion should not occur, because costs should also be discounted, but the fear may be realistic as a practical matter. Indeed, the rhetorical strategy of *Corrosion Proof Fittings* seems to support this apprehension. Furthermore, assuming that discounting will be pursued, the analyst's choice of a discount *rate* makes a tremendous difference in the estimate of benefits, yet there is no consensus as to what the rate should be. For these and other reasons, we think that the cautionary sentiments we expressed in the previous note, as regards valuation issues in general, have particular force when discounting of benefits is part of the picture. Even Sunstein acknowledges that the court in *Corrosion Proof Fittings* was "quite wrong" to insist that EPA produce an "apples-to-apples comparison" by discounting nonmonetary benefits. *See* THE COST-BENEFIT STATE, at 85-86.

The argument in *Corrosion Proof Fittings* that discounting should run from the date when the latent injury manifests itself makes sense to the extent that the delay in the injury results in less of a loss for the individual than an immediate disability or death would. That is the logic of the Revesz quote in this note. However, the court's argument is questionable insofar as it essentially ascribes a zero value to the benefits that people can derive from the here-and-now freedom from having to worry about a future manifestation of the disease. As Heinzerling writes in the congressional testimony cited above, "In everyday life . . . we regard the removal of a risk as a benefit as soon as it happens; we don't ordinarily react to the removal of a carcinogen in our environment, for example, by announcing that we will hold off feeling relieved until the date when we might have developed cancer had the carcinogen not been taken away."

7. *Legal constraints.* The default rule stated in *Michigan v. EPA*—allowing an agency to consider costs unless Congress has clearly indicated otherwise—probably makes sense. However, that presumption gets one only so far. In the first place, the panel in *Michigan* itself was split. One judge read the statute as rendering cost considerations irrelevant. *Id.* at 695-97 (Sentelle, J., dissenting). Moreover, both *American Trucking* and *Michigan* arose under the Clean Air Act. In *American Trucking*, Justice Scalia acknowledged that the specific provision involved in *Michigan* did allow consideration of costs, although the provision at issue in the Supreme Court case did not. 531 U.S. at 469 n.1.

Even in the absence of a formally articulated presumption, however, the winds seem to be blowing in the direction of at least *allowing* agencies to take account of costs in environmental contexts. In an opinion filed after the text went to press, the Supreme Court in a 5-4 decision took a new turn in deciding whether a vague environmental statute permitted an agency to balance costs and benefits. *Entergy Corp. v. Riverkeeper, Inc.*, 129 S.Ct. 1498 (2009). The case involved standards for cooling towers for powerplants that injure aquatic organisms. The Clean Water Act provided that the standard "shall require that the location, design, construction, and capacity of cooling water intake structures reflect the best technology available for minimizing adverse environmental impacts." EPA determined that it could utilize CBA in setting these standards. The Second Circuit (in an opinion by Judge Sonia Sotomayor) disagreed, but the Supreme Court held that EPA's view was a reasonable interpretation of the statute and upheld it under *Chevron*. Justice Breyer, who regularly supports CBA, agreed that the statute permitted but did not require CBA, but he dissented on a secondary issue. Justices Stevens, Souter, and Ginsburg dissented from the majority's view that the statute permitted CBA.

For the five-Justice majority, Justice Scalia wrote that the term "best technology available" could reasonably be read to mean either "greatest reduction in environmental impact at a cost that can reasonably be borne by the industry" (the lower court's reading) or "the technology . . . produces a good at the lowest per-unit cost, even if it produces a lesser quantity of that good than other available technologies" (the EPA's reading). The Court distinguished *Cotton Dust* and *American Trucking* (which held that the relevant statutes precluded CBA), in part because of different language in those statutes, and in part because *Chevron* mandates deference to reasonable agency construction of an ambiguous statute. Thus, *Entergy* suggests that the Court is moving toward using *Chevron* as the functional equivalent of the *Michigan v. EPA* statutory presumption.

8. *Triggering regulatory analysis.* All of the triggering requirements rest on the premise—with which we agree—that the duty to conduct a regulatory analysis should not be extended too freely. Apart from the doubts that we have already mentioned about their probative value in regulatory decisionmaking, CBAs are themselves costly to prepare. These reservations have particular force at the state level, as the Whisnant & Cherry article explains. Presumably, a state agency rule will almost always have a smaller economic impact than a similar federal rule that is applicable nationwide; thus, the burdens on the private sector that a persuasive CBA could potentially avoid are likely to be less. At the same time, the costs of preparing a formal regulatory analysis are likely to be proportionately higher in relation to the budgets of state agencies than they are in relation to the budgets of most federal agencies.

The "significant regulatory action" criteria of the executive order have a fairly close logical relationship with the justifications for conducting regulatory analysis: the possibility of a discrepancy between costs and benefits is most troubling when the rule itself is likely to prove expensive. However, the criteria in the executive order have been developed in a context of a regime in which the agency and OIRA are the only entities that have power to order an analysis. Those criteria may not work well in an APA setting in which an alleged error in failing to conduct a regulatory analysis can be litigated, as appears to be possible under at least some of the state APA regulatory analysis provisions. A court is not well equipped to resolve the elusive question of whether a proposed rule would result in costs that meet a given numerical threshold, especially in the absence of the very factual data that the analysis itself is intended to uncover.

One of the bills that emerged in late stages of the regulatory reform debate of the 1990s tried to meet these concerns. *See* Regulatory Improvement Act of 1998, S. 981, 105th Cong. § 627, S.Rep.No. 105-188, at 44, 96 (1998). It would have allowed APA challenges to an agency's refusal to find that the $100 million "major rule" criterion has been satisfied—but it also would have circumscribed this remedy by providing that the agency's negative finding would be judged by an arbitrary-capricious standard of review and could not be contested until the end of the rulemaking proceeding. For discussion, see Fred Anderson et al., "Regulatory

Improvement Legislation: Risk Assessement, Cost-Benefit Analysis, and Judicial Review," 11 Duke Envtl.L. & Pol'y F. 89, 106-08, 118-22 (2000).

The "on request" approach of the 1981 MSAPA avoids the problem of uncertainty about whether the agency's obligation to conduct regulatory analysis has been triggered. However, militating against any broadly available triggering mechanism is the risk that the power to force an analysis will be used by opponents of the agency to delay unwelcome rules or to harass the agency. The Comment accompanying MSAPA § 3-105 expresses strong concern on this score. It suggests that the governor and the administrative rules committee are the most logical holders of such power, because they are "directly elected officials with general responsibility for state government." The Comment expresses doubt about the wisdom of allowing members of the public, or local officials, to force an analysis, given the "danger that such a power . . . might be abused." One can readily imagine an external party using the threat of a demand for regulatory analysis as a bargaining chip with which to extract unrelated concessions from the agency.

A weak spot in the MSAPA system seems to be the absence of any substantive criteria on which a request for regulatory analysis must be predicated. Logically, regulatory analysis (which after all is a supplement to the regular notice-and-comment process) seems best suited for complex rulemaking proceedings in which quantitative methods of policy analysis are likely to shed some light. But nothing in § 3-105(a) requires the requesting party to base its request on the presence of that, or any other, state of affairs. This gap may leave external parties with too much room to make unwarranted requests. Even if government officials are the only eligible requesters, their political accountability may not prevent unreasonable requests if no one can point to anything in the statute that would make a particular request inappropriate.

9. *Judicial review of analysis requirements.* The debate over the 1995 regulatory reform bill had intense ideological aspects: the measure was strongly favored by business interests and opposed by beneficiary groups, especially environmentalists. But there were also principled arguments behind the opposition to judicial review of agencies' compliance with the regulatory analysis requirements that the Dole bill would have established. Those requirements (which involved not only cost-benefit analysis but also risk assessment) were lengthy, detailed, and technical—quite different from the simple terms of § 553. Courts might have had to adjudicate whether agencies had complied with provisions in the bill such as "An agency shall not inappropriately combine or compound multiple policy judgments" and "[An agency] shall describe the nature and extent of the nonquantifiable benefits and costs of a final rule . . . in as precise and succinct a manner as possible." There were doubts about the competence of

the courts to evaluate agencies' compliance with such specifications, and also about the amount of lawyers' and judges' time that would be consumed in arguments about these issues. For elaboration on these points, see Ronald M. Levin, "Judicial Review of Procedural Compliance," 48 Admin.L.Rev. 359 (1996).

10. *State-level judicial review.* As the previous note suggests, there are strong arguments against subjecting regulatory analysis requirements to any judicial review. Although MSAPA § 3-105 is less detailed and prescriptive than the Dole bill, the analyses it requires will often have to be based on unprovable assumptions, rough factual estimates, and unusually difficult predictions. Consequently, even where agencies have made a sincere and diligent effort to provide an expert regulatory analysis, their contents would be easy to challenge.

In this light, there are grounds for concern that the "good faith" test of § 3-105(f) does not go far enough to insulate agencies from litigation over whether they complied with the regulatory analysis requirements of that act. "Good faith" may well be in the eyes of the beholder. Indeed, there is no assurance that reviewing courts would necessarily limit themselves to a determination of whether the agency "actually addresse[d] in some manner all of the points specified in subsections (b)-(c)," as the Comment accompanying that section urges. The official Comments are supposed to be given deference, but the text of the Act is controlling, and in this instance the Comment's narrow reading of the "good faith" test seems somewhat strained. One could easily envision a reviewing court holding that, although an agency did mention the matters identified in subsections (b) and (c), it discussed them too superficially and thus did not act in "good faith."

From one point of view, the decision in *Methodist Hospitals* seems absurd. The Board's benefit-cost note was sheer boilerplate, couched in generalities that could just as easily have been written about any other exercise of this ratesetting power. The court's approval of this statement was tantamount to deciding that judicial review of the agency's cost-benefit note should be meaningless. Yet, as we have seen, there are good arguments for barring judicial review of CBA and leaving enforcement of this function to political oversight. If one believes that courts, particularly state courts, have little competence to evaluate cost-benefit analyses, and that the risks of delay or ossification are great, perhaps an ultra-deferential approach to review is an attractive policy. Thus, a sympathetic interpretation of the *Methodist Hospitals* case would be that the court discerned some of these risks and thought that other judicial checks were adequate. (In fact, the court went on to decide that the Board's statement of basis and purpose had been insufficient.)

11. *Specialized regulatory analyses.* Although judicial review as such

has been thoroughly covered above, this question can be used to open up issues about the overall merits of the RFA. The Act can be seen as a classic example of special-interest legislation. Agencies must in any event give careful attention to the merits of proposed rules in order to comply with § 553; why should they have a special obligation to look at the rule's impact on small business? Why has Congress not established a similar requirement to examine the impact of a proposed rule on city dwellers, or the poor, or consumers, or other groups that lack the political clout of organizations like the National Federation of Independent Business? Won't the availability of judicial review lead to more ossification without a redeeming benefit to the public interest at large?

But then, if students are buying into the notion of the RFA as special-interest legislation, ask them whether the NEPA environmental impact statement requirement is any more justifiable. Aren't environmental groups quite well organized today and capable of making their case through the ordinary notice-and-comment process? Students' likely response will be that environmental impact statements are necessary because agencies tend to focus narrowly on their respective missions and to overlook the environmental implications of their rules unless forced to study them. But that's exactly what small businesses say about *their* interests. Of course, it is entirely possible to believe that environmental values need special protection and small businesses don't, but this line of discussion may help bring home to students that such perceptions are often in the eye of the beholder and difficult to separate from one's particular political ideology.

12. *Regulatory flexibility in the states.* It seems pretty clear that the Texas consumer credit commissioner in *United Loans* gave short shrift to his responsibilities under the regulatory flexibility law. On their face his regulations looked likely to impose burdens on small business, so the statute required a substantive analysis. To this extent, the case presents judicial review in a fairly positive light—upholding compliance with a statute. On the other hand, the case illustrates concretely how the regulatory flexibility legislation adds to a rulemaking agency's burdens. In addition to the analysis already required by the standard APA, the agency must examine an issue that its enabling legislation probably does not specifically address. Moreover, the agency must do so *before* it publishes its notice of proposed rulemaking.

The court's final interpretation neatly raises the question of why regulatory flexibility laws should exist at all. From a good-government perspective, the most credible argument is that regulators will tend to overlook the special problems their rules will inflict on small businesses unless they are forced to pay attention to them. *See* Verkuil's article, cited in the note. (This is one of the few scholarly articles that have ever had anything good to say about the RFA.) On that premise, the Texas commissioner was persuasive in arguing that the statute's requirements should not come into play unless a proposed rule would have a *disproportionate* impact on small businesses. But the Texas statute is not drafted that way; to that extent, it probably has to be regarded as special-interest legislation. For a debunking of the premises of these laws, see generally Richard J. Pierce, Jr., "Small Is Not Beautiful: The Case Against Special Regulatory Treatment of Small Firms," 50 Admin.L.Rev. 537 (1998).

13. *Specialized analyses by executive order.* Here is further confirmation that analysis requirements tend to be meaningful only to the extent they are enforced. The cost-benefit analysis obligations of E.O. 12,866 are potent because OIRA cares about them and insists on compliance. But neither OIRA nor the courts press agencies to comply with the orders described in this note, so noncompliance is rife. Presumably, in issuing these directives, the White House was more interested in the appearance of getting something done than in the reality of it.

14. *Administrative guidelines.* The IQA and its progeny have been heavily criticized for threatening to contribute to the ossification of rulemaking functions. Rigorous analysis of information, such as scientific data, is desirable in the abstract, but the pursuit of it consumes scarce resources. Yet, because of the irregular process by which the Act was adopted (being drafted by a lobbyist and unobtrusively slipped into an appropriations bill by a friendly legislator), proponents of the measure never had to make a public case that such a potentially burdensome law was needed, nor did they have to temper the mandate with offsetting factors for OMB to consider. A more open legislative process might well have led to a more balanced mandate.

15. *Problem.* State regulation of cellphone use by drivers is a highly topical matter. As of summer 2009, five states and the District of Columbia require all drivers to use a headset in order to make a cell phone call while driving. A larger number of states prohibit teenaged drivers and school bus drivers from making any mobile phone call while behind the wheel, regardless of what equipment is available. Similar proposals are pending in other states. No state, however, bans all mobile phone calls by all drivers. (Fifteen states also ban text messaging by all drivers. We didn't ask about texting in our problem, but you might wish to do so.) The situation is bound to evolve, but instructors should be able to find up-to-date information at the website of the Governors Highway Safety Association, *www.ghsa.org*.

Although all of these bans have been imposed legislatively, administrative solutions have also been considered. In the *Federal Register* document cited in the problem, the National Highway Traffic Safety Administration denied a petition for regulatory action filed by the Center for Auto Safety. CAS asked NHTSA to take action in this area by using the same statutory authority that had enabled NHTSA to prescribe passive restraints in *State Farm*, § 9.4. The agency denied the petition, citing, inter alia, its "need to consider costs as well as benefits," the "lack of specific data and analysis" in the petition, and "the resources needed to conduct rulemaking."

These measures and proposals have generated a substantial literature in which authors have deployed the techniques of cost-benefit analysis and have concluded, at least in some instances, that the now-popular restrictions may not be cost-justified. Hahn is normally very supportive of cost-benefit analysis and skeptical about regulation, and the coauthored article cited in the Problem is no exception. However, he and Dudley have assembled and synthesized a good deal of material on both sides of the issue. The various factual assertions in the problem are all based on propositions that Hahn and Dudley say are supported by studies (although we do not vouch for their accuracy in any ultimate sense). On the other hand, critics of cost-benefit analysis are "amaz[ed]" by these studies and see them as a clear example of technocratic logic run amok. *See* Frank Ackerman & Lisa Heinzerling, PRICELESS: ON KNOWING THE PRICE OF EVERYTHING AND THE VALUE OF NOTHING 1-2 (2004). Of course, students themselves will have plenty of firsthand experience to bring to bear on discussions of the issue.

In the Problem, the first issue is: what are the agency's obligations if no new legislation is passed? The enabling act tells the agency to adopt "such reasonable measures as are adequate to meet the need" for vehicle safety." This language would probably be construed to require the agency to *consider* costs along with benefits. The Supreme Court reached essentially that conclusion in *State Farm*, as students will see in § 9.4. At the very least, the statute would be construed to *permit* the consideration of costs. Because the statute requires only "reasonable" measures, the court wouldn't even need to rely on the presumption articulated in *Michigan v. EPA*, nor on aggressive use of *Chevron* as in *Entergy*. So the cases like *Cotton Dust* that exclude cost-justification as irrelevant (N.7) are inapplicable here. On the other hand, the court is unlikely to conclude that a formal cost-benefit study is required by statute. *Corrosion Proof Fittings*, which did find such a requirement in TSCA, is an outlier that is unlikely to be followed. If the agency doesn't do the study, however, it might have trouble convincing a court that it was justified in rejecting the conclusions of the anti-regulation studies that the industry did submit.

Larry's legislative proposal raises the core policy questions about the merits of CBA in a straightforward fashion, and the cell phone controversy provides a concrete context for discussion. A good case can be made for the proposition that the MTD should do a cost-benefit study. The extra effort would arguably allow the agency to bring objectivity and rigor to a controversy that otherwise might be dominated by impressionistic guesswork and anecdotal accounts of horrible accidents. It is probably no coincidence that the most common path taken by states that regulate cell calls is to *allow* most drivers to make mobile calls using "hands-free" equipment, even though the same leading study that disclosed a fourfold increase in accidents stemming from cell phone use also cast doubt on the difference between the risks of handheld and hands-free phones. Hahn & Dudley, 55 Admin.L.Rev. at 140, 155. Evidently, the real source of risk is the mental distraction of the conversation, not the physical acts of dialing a number and holding the receiver, and the hands-free option does not significantly ameliorate this risk. Arguably the hands-free compromise position is a largely symbolic band-aid adopted by politicians who want to look as though they are responding to a burgeoning public safety risk, but who do not want to take the more unpopular step of prohibiting drivers from making any mobile phone calls from the road.

A host of other arguments have been made during the national controversy over bans on the use of cell phones by drivers. Would the ban force drivers to pull over to the side of the road (a sometimes risky maneuver) to take an incoming call? A cost-benefit study might at least inquire into such questions.

Conversely, the fact situation would also allow you to bring out some of the arguments against conducting the CBA study. For one thing, cost-benefit analysis itself consumes time and resources. The payoff in terms of better decisionmaking may not justify that investment. After all, the choice is not between CBA and no analysis at all. The choice is whether to superimpose CBA on top of the usual obligations of notice-and-comment rulemaking, which previous sections of the chapter have shown to be far from inconsequential. You can also touch on the methodological quandaries described in earlier notes, such as those associated with putting a dollar value on lives and measuring intangibles (like the convenience value of cell phones) by some semi-objective reference value such as willingness to pay. (In fact, the Transportation Department has published a guidance expressing its approach to determining the value of a statistical life. *http://ostpxweb.dot.gov/policy/reports/080205.htm*. According to this 2005 document, "we have determined that the best present estimate of the economic value of preventing a human fatality is $5.8 million." This was an increase from the $3.0 million figure adopted in 2003. The document contains much qualifying language to the effect that uncertainties cannot be eliminated entirely and that the guidance should be implemented flexibly.

Difficulties associated with discounting of future benefits are relatively small in this problem, although not entirely absent. In environmental law or toxic substances control, for example, agencies need to figure out how to put a present value on the curtailment of harms that build to fruition over time, such as exposure to chemicals that may eventually give you cancer, or environmental degradation that slowly but inexorably impairs the quality of life. In contrast, most of the harms associated with automobile accidents do not exist at all until a collision occurs. Or do they? Perhaps drivers, passengers, and pedestrians would feel more secure immediately if they knew that, thanks to the MTD regulation, they were less likely to be involved in a collision involving a driver who is using a cell phone. But the value of this feeling may be hard to quantify, and decision-makers might not regard this argument as a substantial factor in the overall equation anyway.

The built-in uncertainties of CBA militate a fortiori against the idea that the department should have to justify its ultimate decision on the basis of a *quantified* showing that the benefits of the ban are commensurate with the costs. Ultimately, the choice between instituting the cell phone ban and taking no action is a matter of political choice.

The judicial review provision in Larry's legislative proposal could be contested from either of two directions. On the one hand, it means that a mistaken application of the required criteria for conducting the CBA will not be fatal to the ensuing rule if the department has made its mistake in "good faith." The concept that a conceded statutory violation (which would not necessarily be "harmless") should simply be overlooked seems odd to many lawyers. On the other hand, a critic of CBA could argue that the vague "good faith" test opens up too many opportunities for vested interests such as KIT to accuse the department of corner-cutting. Indeed, given the resource constraints impinging on agencies, especially at the state level, as well as the inherent complexities of regulatory analysis, accusations of corner-cutting wouldn't necessarily be hard to make.

If you wish, you can also change the facts and ask the class to suppose that the bill specifies a dollar value as the threshold test for whether a proposed rule must undergo CBA. Suppose further that the department claims that the impact of the rule on the state's economy would not trigger that test. This scenario would implicate other reviewability questions. On the plus side, providing a judicial remedy if the agency simply refuses to perform its duty to conduct the analysis could be considered a modest step, the minimum necessary to ensure the effectiveness of the analysis requirement. *Cf. United Loans.* However, opponents of judicial review could argue in response that the court is in a poor position to be able to calculate whether a given rule will meet the dollar threshold that triggers the CBA obligation. The industry has a strong incentive to go to court and argue that the threshold will be met. Such litigation could delay the proceeding, and even the threat of commencing such a suit may give the industry leverage with which to extract a concession concerning the substance of the rule. Thus, the legislature might want to consider safeguards such as those of S. 981, described in our comments on N.8 above.

§ 5.9 NEGOTIATED RULEMAKING

Notes and Questions

1. *Legal context.* Regulatory negotiation as commonly understood involves the use of alternative dispute resolution techniques at the rule-drafting stage. A related issue involves informal settlement of lawsuits that have been brought to challenge rules in court. For discussion of the latter, see Jim Rossi, "Bargaining in the Shadow of Administrative Procedure: The Public Interest in Rulemaking Settlement," 51 Duke L.J. 1015 (2001).

2. *Reg-neg in the states.* The regulatory negotiation process appears to be as suitable for state agencies as for federal agencies, and may even have more promise in the former situation because of the smaller number and greater homogeneity of the interests affected by state agency rules, their geographically compact location, and the lower visibility and greater informality of state rulemaking processes as compared to the federal process.

3. *Candidates for reg-neg.* Negotiated rulemaking can be successful in practice only if all of the significant interests involved in a potential rulemaking can be effectively identified in advance; if the process involves adequate representatives of those interests; and the parties to the process actually believe that a negotiated agreement may provide a better solution than a rule developed wholly through the usual rulemaking process. Negotiated rulemaking is not likely to work in contexts where the only possible outcome is likely to be a zero sum game where one interest totally prevails at the expense of all other significant opposing interests. It is also not likely to work if the political value to the parties of taking, to the very end of the rulemaking process, intransigent positions outweighs any benefits that may be obtained from such negotiation, or if the past relationships of the parties with each other prevents them from engaging in meaningful negotiations.

In several ways, the DOT's disability accommodation proceeding seems to have been a good candidate for regulatory negotiation. Representatives of the affected interests (people with various disabilities, air carriers, flight attendants, airports) were identified fairly easily, and they were in a good position to contribute practical insights that might not be apparent to the DOT. In fact, the negotiation resulted in consensus on the first two issues mentioned in the note. "Air Carriers and the Disabled Struggle to Write New Rules," New York Times, Sept. 8, 1987, at B7. However, negotiations failed on the third issue, for reasons that, at least with hindsight, seem easy to understand: A department lawyer "described this issue as one viewed by 'the National Federation for the Blind as a pure and simple matter of discrimination' and by 'the carriers as a clean cut safety issue.'" 2 ADR Rept. at 119. Each side saw this issue as fundamental, and neither would yield. (Eventually, the FAA adopted a rule substantially taking the carriers' side. 55 Fed.Reg. 8054 (1990). The NFB criticized it heatedly but did not appeal.)

4. *Criticisms.* We have excerpted Funk's article at length because it so effectively highlights not only the potential disadvantages of negotiated rulemaking, but also some intriguing issues about the legitimacy and theoretical basis of all rulemaking. However, one can raise a number of doubts about his argument. To the extent that Funk contends that negotiated rulemaking deters an agency from seeking the "public interest," one might respond that the contrast with conventional rulemaking is overdrawn. The usual process of informal rulemaking is by no means a purely technocratic exercise. Political judgments are pervasive. You may wish to refer back to the "interest representation" model of agency action noted in § 1.7, which captures an element of the rulemaking process that Funk's account downplays. Certainly cases like *Sierra Club* and *ANA v. FTC*, which students saw a couple of lessons ago, assume that rulemaking agencies regularly consult with and are influenced by interest groups; political responsiveness is seen as important to the legitimacy of rulemaking.

In this connection, you might also focus on Funk's discussion of the possibility that poorly organized, diffuse segments of society will get short shrift in the reg-neg process. He certainly has a point, but you might ask whether the same is not also true to some extent in ordinary rulemaking. Non-yuppie woodstove users may not have been represented at the bargaining table, but it's unclear whether their voices would have been heard very loudly in a regular § 553 proceeding either.

Still, one must agree with Funk that decisionmaking through the conventional notice and comment process induces a degree of detached inquiry that reg-neg does not. One may, however, go on to ask whether the idea of a "public interest" has any intelligible meaning, apart from the fallible perceptions and policy biases of agency decisionmakers. Proponents of reg-neg can also argue on several grounds that the negotiating process does promote the public interest, properly understood. As the Lubbers reading indicates, the advantages include (i) an atmosphere in which participants do less posturing and more communicating about their strongest priorities, so that the ultimate decision can embody a more well-tuned tradeoff among the competing values; (ii) the acceptability of the rule to the affected interests, because they helped shape it instead of its being foisted on them; and (iii) a likelihood that the rule will actually be better because of the intensive involvement of people who are personally involved in the industry being regulated, as agency personnel often have not been. (We once heard a practitioner endorse reg-neg as a superior alternative to having rules drafted by "some agency lawyer two years out of law school." See how your students react to that!)

A narrower, but perhaps more telling, aspect of Funk's critique is the claim that the negotiating process induces agencies to give short shrift to legal restrictions and scientific investigation. Of course, as Lubbers explains, this is not supposed to happen; the agency is supposed to remain mindful of its legal constraints and refuse to accept any deal that would undermine them. But the woodstove episode, from Funk's account, suggests that reality worked out differently. Whatever the validity of his analysis of the Clean Air Act, it must at least be evident that the reg-neg process creates a temptation to cut corners in this regard, in order to serve the goal of reaching consensus and making the participants satisfied—particularly if the agency expects that it will never have to defend the rule in court.

Consider throwing out the suggestion that reg-neg can be legitimate even if it *does* foster a tendency to evade legal restrictions. After all, if a balanced committee unanimously concludes that Congress chose a shortsighted and counterproductive means of reaching an end, is there anything wrong with their agreeing to adopt an alternative approach that achieves the legislature's desired end more effectively? Proponents of reg-neg seldom if ever carry their logic to such an extreme; at some point, all will agree that one has to be willing to live within the constraints of the rule of law, even if everyone who knows the problems of the industry firsthand agrees that Congress did something stupid. Still, regulatory negotiation rests heavily on the idea that a process that emphasizes pragmatic problem-solving can serve as a legitimate surrogate for some of the formal norms of administrative law; a big unresolved question is the extent to which this is true.

5. *Judicial review.* Section 570 is a puzzling provision, and we suspect that Congress did not fully think through its implications. Judge Wald's article cited in the note contains a characteristically thoughtful exploration of these conundrums. At a minimum, § 570 probably means that the court must not permit an agency that uses reg-neg to claim wider legal authority than if it had not employed that technique. Thus, the legislature has instructed courts to disavow the concept advanced in the last paragraph of the preceding note. In the woodstove example, therefore, if a court agreed with Funk's analysis of the Clean Air Act—and found that the agency's error was so manifest as to exceed the deference normally accorded under *Chevron*—it would set aside the rule. (That is, it would do so if someone actually sought judicial review, which is rare in reg-neg.)

However, it is harder to sort out the implications of § 570 for judicial review of the factual and policy premises of a reg-negged rule. The whole point of the negotiation is that certain provisions will get into the rule because the participants have agreed on them, irrespective of whether the agency would have reached the same conclusions had it been acting alone. Is the agency, in drafting its statement of basis and purpose, supposed to pretend that the negotiation never occurred? (Funk claims that some aspects of EPA's explanation in the woodstove case were indeed disingenuous, concealing the fact that a provision was reached through negotiation.) The tactic might work, because of the *Morgan* presumption of validity, but the idea that reg-neg can survive only if agencies do not admit being influenced by it is not very conducive to broad use of this device.

On the other hand, if an agency openly acknowledges that it selected an option as a result of negotiation, a court will have to decide whether that aspect of the agency's decision was "reasonable." A court that is suspicious of regulatory negotiation might take the agency's acknowledgement as evidence that the agency has abdicated its responsibilities, and might remand the case for more "rational" decisionmaking. But a court that is more sympathetic to regulatory negotiation might reason that an agency *should* be favorably disposed towards adopting a proposal that a broadly representative group of industry and public interest advocates considers workable and will probably accept in a more or less cooperative spirit. The court might say that its own acceptance of this reasoning is not "greater deference" but simply an application of the ordinary "reasonableness" test to the actual situation that negotiation over the terms of the rule has brought into existence.

6. *"Reneging" in reg-neg.* Harter (who authored much of the scholarship that laid the intellectual foundations of reg-neg) is very critical of the *USA Group* opinion. *See* Philip J. Harter, "First Judicial Review of Reg Neg a Disappointment," Admin. & Reg.L. News, Fall 1996, at 1. He notes that the court displays a very limited understanding of negotiated rulemaking. Inherent in the very idea of reg-neg is the assumption that the agency will be presumptively inclined to adopt the negotiated agreement. One can mistrust the process on various grounds, as Funk has explained, but Congress did after all give reg-neg something of a vote of confidence in the NRA, which surely contemplates that the negotiation would constitute more than a "consultative process" in advance of notice and comment rulemaking. The suggestion that reg-neg is an "abdication" to the industry by a "captured" agency is particularly unfounded, Harter adds, because the negotiating committee, like others of its kind, drew membership not only from the loan servicing industry, but also from a broad range of interests (colleges, students, banks, etc.), as well as from the Department itself.

Nevertheless, the court's holding is clearly correct: an agency is not legally bound to adopt the committee's agreement. As Posner says, such an obligation would make a nullity of the comment period, which the NRA does preserve. Even a requirement that the agency *propose* the agreement would be unwise. If the agency already intends not to adhere to the negotiated deal, why waste everyone's time inviting comments on it? As Harter writes (*id.* at 13), the reasons for the agency to adhere are "political, not legal. If the agency repudiates agreements too often, then—as in any other situation—its word will not be worth much, and folks will not likely reach agreements with it in the future."

Then why did the Education Department "renege" in this reg-neg? Because it had not been fully committed to a negotiated agreement in the first place. Congress had *required* the agency to employ negotiated rulemaking in this proceeding. Proponents of reg-neg oppose such legislative mandates, believing that they short-circuit the important step in which an agency weighs various factors under NRA § 563(a) to determine whether the situation is really amenable to a negotiated solution. *See* ACUS, "Building Consensus in Agency Rulemaking: Implementing the Negotiated Rulemaking Act" 29, 31 (1995).

7. *Notice of variance.* Technically, the court in *City of Portland* is right: an agency has no special duty to warn participants in the negotiation that it is thinking of departing from the agreement (assuming that the final rule is a logical outgrowth of the proposed rule, which the court held was the case). However, the policy argument in the opinion is dubious. One could argue, to the contrary, that the lack of special warning impedes the ex ante attractiveness of reg-neg for stakeholders, by making it easier for agencies to depart from the agreement. Moreover, if they can't rely on the agency to at least give them a heads-up when it is thinking of abandoning the agreement, won't they always have to file rulemaking comments that are just as extensive as in any other rulemaking? That possibility will do nothing to foster the use of negotiated rulemaking, either. Finally, we would question the court's theory that if it (or Congress) were to impose this duty of notice (not necessarily telling stakeholders what the agency plans to do, just that they shouldn't refrain from commenting because of an assumption that the agency will stick with the agreement), the rules will be "easier to overturn." That would be true only if we assume that the agency won't comply with this duty.

8. *Problem.* In real life, the question of how to define economic loss was actively debated in the negotiating sessions, but the participants, and subsequently EPA, opted for the profitability test. That seems to be the more logical interpretation of "significant economic loss;" the point of this problem is to explore the extent to which the legal system should indulge the reg-neg process when consensual bargaining has led to an apparently dubious decision.

One reading of EPA's statement would conclude that the agency "abdicated its regulatory authority," in Posner's words, because it simply acquiesced in the committee's views, refusing to use its own judgment. Under a more sympathetic reading, EPA feels that the committee's interpretation is as reasonable as any, and that the purposes of the regulatory scheme will be advanced if the agency adopts a plan that has a good chance of eliciting cooperation from the principal actors in the agricultural and environmentalist sectors. Besides, the agency may have thought, the committee's endorsement suggests that the Federation is exaggerating the burdens of the proposed rule, because other industry groups with similar interests consider the plan workable and livable. How the court responds to the ambiguity in the agency's statement may depend on its overall attitude of support or doubt about regulatory negotiation, and so the broader policy debate about the virtues and vices of reg-neg can be brought into the discussion here.

A secondary issue in the case is whether the Federation is estopped to rely on its present argument because it was involved in the earlier negotiation. The response should be that no one can prevent the Federation from pressing its grievance, but other participants in the consensus can be expected to come forward to make clear that the dissenter is taking an outlier position. *See Safe Buildings Alliance v. EPA,* 846 F.2d 79, 82 (D.C.Cir.1988) (relying on consensus support for the rule as a reason to dismiss petitioner's apprehensions about it). Another twist would be to ask what would happen if the protest came from someone (say, an individual farmer) who did *not* participate in the negotiation. That scenario heightens concerns about adequate representation, but does not wholly dispel the policy argument that society benefits from consensual settlement of disputes.

You can also use the problem to raise the issues of the *USA Group* case. Posit a scenario in which the Federation persuades EPA to propose the profitability test in its notice of proposed rulemaking, contrary to the negotiating committee's recommendation. Then another participant in the negotiation, say the National Audubon Society, protests EPA's failure to adhere to the committee's draft. As we have discussed above in N.6, EPA has good reasons to try to keep the deal intact, but if on second thought it agrees with and adopts the Federation's position, the Audubon Society has no legal remedy.

CHAPTER 6

POLICYMAKING ALTERNATIVES

§ 6.1 EXEMPTIONS FROM RULEMAKING PROCEDURE

§ 6.1.1 Good Cause Exemptions

Notes and Questions

2. *Terrorism.* *Jifry* straightforwardly spells out the usual judicial reluctance to sustain claims of good cause, but it sustains one in this instance anyway. Many will probably see it as an easy case. Students will recall the sense of crisis that seized the nation following the 2001 terrorist attacks, as well as the generally shared support for putting new homeland security measures into place quickly. It is hardly surprising that the court would give the FAA and TSA wide latitude to institute protective measures on a rush basis, even though the efficacy of particular steps would be hard to predict with any certainty.

The most potentially troubling element of the story is that the FAA rule in this case was adopted well over a year after the 2001 attacks. Some might wonder whether, given the time period that had already elapsed, the TSA and FAA couldn't have waited a little more time to complete the full § 553 process. Still, the actual sequence of events described in the court's decision does not seem to us to show that the agencies were dilatory. One can understand how, with so many unprecedented security challenges presented at once, the FAA might well have taken until August 2002 to institute proceedings against Jifry and Zarie. Nor is it surprising that they would initially have used an established process of holding hearings, which had to be reexamined later when it bogged down at the prehearing conference stage. Students may need to be reminded that even a crash program can take months to institute. However, you might want to ask the class whether the court should have showed an equally indulgent attitude if the FAA had instituted a similar rule (or amended the 2003 rule) a year or two later. By that time, the overall sense of panic in the country was receding, examples of government overhyping of security threats were coming to light, and the attendant risks to civil liberties were coming into sharper focus. At some point, pleas of urgency would likely have gotten a more skeptical reception.

Regardless, the deferential opinion in *Jifry* sets the stage for a class discussion of the very different result in *Jewish Community Action*. The cases do seem distinguishable on their facts. In the Minnesota case the connections between the driver's license restrictions and the risks of terrorism seem to be real, but not nearly as direct as the anti-hijacking initiative in *Jifry*. The license restrictions will affect lots of people who have no connection with terrorism, and there is also a hint of religious intolerance in the case (the controversy about the photo ID related to women's objections to being photographed without a veil). Moreover, in contrast to the relatively simple measure instituted in *Jifry*, there must have been a variety of ways in which the Minnesota department could have framed its license requirements, and public comment could have usefully illuminated those choices.

Curiously, however, the court does not decide the case by simply finding an absence of good cause (or, to use the state statute's verbal formula, a "serious and imminent threat" to public safety). Instead, the court calls for what amounts to a detailed analysis by the agency of the reasons why notice and comment proceedings would be contrary to the public interest—a requirement that is evidently to be policed by a sort of hard look judicial review. This requirement for an in-depth exposition goes beyond what courts normally demand, and we think it is more than agencies should have to produce when they are attempting to deal with what is, by hypothesis, an emergency situation. The court might have been better advised to simply override the agency's claim of exemption (applying the familiar principle that such exemptions are "narrowly construed"), instead of imposing a procedural formula that could come back to haunt it in future cases.

3. *State law.* The language of 1961 MSAPA § 3(b) certainly sounds narrower than that of APA § 553(b)(B) and 1981 MSAPA § 3-108(a). A specific contrast is that § 3(b) appears to contain no counterpart to the "unnecessary" prong of the other two provisions. Thus, the notion that a comment period may be omitted because a rule is trivial or noncontroversial may not be viable under § 3(b). On that score, the federal and 1981 MSAPA versions seem decidedly preferable.

As for the "impracticability" and "contrary to public interest" prongs of the federal standard, it is hard to know whether the seemingly more stringent wording of § 3(b) makes a difference in practice (especially when you consider that the federal language is "narrowly construed"). All of these standards implicate the same sorts of interests, and all leave a great deal to the discretion of agencies and reviewing courts. For example, one might have thought that, in *Melton*, mere financial loss to the state would not qualify as an "imminent peril" to the public welfare. Nevertheless, the court found a sufficient emergency and upheld the commissioner's regulation. The court emphasized that the agency itself was not guilty of foot-dragging and had been given very little discretion about the contents of the regulations. The legislature had decided on the welfare cuts, and the agency was simply implementing that decision. The court's analysis seems quite similar to what a federal court would have said (if, indeed, it is not more lenient).

New Jersey's version of 1961 MSAPA § 3(b) requires consent of each house of the legislature for a rule adopted under the imminent peril exception that's in effect for more than 60 days. In *Delaware Bay Waterman's Ass'n v. Dep't of Envir. Protec.*, 697 A.2d 957 (N.J.App.Div.1997), dismissed as moot, 709 A.2d 192 (N.J.1998), the Department adopted an emergency rule banning the catching of horseshoe crabs for 60 days. Then it extended the rule for an additional 60 days with a new declaration of imminent peril. Held: the extended rule was invalid, since the Department had not sought legislative consent. The emergency justifying each of the rules was really the same--collapse of the crab population. The Department argued that the problem was not serious enough to call the Legislature into special session. The court wondered how there could be such a big emergency that the public welfare was placed in imminent peril but the emergency wasn't worthy of seeking legislative approval.

4. *Interim-final rules.* Asimow, a consultant for the ACUS recommendation discussed here, supports making post-promulgation comment mandatory, because it promotes the usual benefits of notice-and-comment and is evidently not too onerous (since most agencies already provide it). 51 Admin.L.Rev. at 733-36. One might argue that the ACUS recommendation was unnecessary, because the right to petition for the issuance, amendment or repeal of a rule in § 553(e), coupled with the § 555(e) right to receive from an agency a statement of reasons for the denial of a petition, could perform a similar function. It also could be argued that limiting post-promulgation comment on an expedited rule to the petition route would be more efficient than requiring an agency to commence a post hoc rulemaking proceeding for every such rule. However, Asimow's study strongly rejects that reasoning: "When an agency adopts an interim-final rule, it warrants that the process of public participation is continuing and that the rule is not yet set in concrete. All interested persons are invited to comment by a fixed date and the agency explicitly agrees to consider those comments as part of the process of finalizing the rule. This invitation is likely to provoke significant public participation. In contrast, the opportunity to petition the agency lacks structure and is unlikely to provoke nearly as much public participation. . . . [A]gency staff may regard petitioners as pests and the responses to petitions for rulemaking are often long delayed and perfunctory." *Id.* at 712.

Asimow sees some initial appeal in a requirement of a limited shelf-life for rules issued under the "impracticable" and "contrary to public interest" prongs of the good exemption. In the absence of such an action-forcing provision, inertia leads many agencies to neglect the task of reassessing an interim-final rule in light of comments received. When this occurs, the benefits of the commenting process are lost, and members of the public may be less likely to comment on future interim-final rules. Thus, he believes that agencies *should* proceed expeditiously to convert their interim-final rules into permanent rules, but he believes that an across-the-board sunset requirement would be likely to cause serious practical problems. For instance, it could force agencies to divert resources from more important tasks, induce hurried consideration when a deadline is at hand, and perhaps cause disruptions if an agency inadvertently lets a desirable rule lapse. *Id.* at 738-40. In any event, Asimow thinks a 120-day period is much too short: it would leave agencies with too little time for evaluation of the more complex interim rules. *Id.* at 738 n.133. (Ultimately, ACUS simply recommended that agencies *consider* imposing sunset commitments on themselves when they issue interim-final rules.)

On the question of whether a court should invalidate a properly adopted permanent rule that supplants an improperly adopted interim-final rule, Asimow's study supports the ACUS position. *Id.* at 725-26, 741. His interviews with agency officials did not uncover conclusive evidence to support the factual premises of the *New Jersey* case, i.e., that citizens submit comments at the post-promulgation stage less frequently and thoughtfully than at the pre-promulgation stage; and that agency staff take these comments less seriously at the later stage. *Id.* at 716. In any event, Asimow argues, the judicial response typified by *New Jersey* is illogical. "Whether or not the interim-final [rule] was valid, some members of the public might have been deterred from commenting on it. It would make no difference to the marginal public commentator whether a court might later find that there was no good cause. . . ." Thus, he contends, once an agency has promulgated a rule following solicitation and consideration of public comments, any grievance growing out of the agency's earlier mistaken invocation of the good cause exemption is moot, or perhaps is a harmless error. (The error would not be harmless, however, with respect to issues that pertain specifically to the time period when the incorrectly adopted interim-final rule was in effect, such as in a proceeding to impose a penalty for violating that rule. *See Paulsen v. Daniels,* 413 F.3d 999, 1008 (9th Cir. 2005).). This reasoning leads to a bright-line rule that does not depend, as the *Federal Express* approach does, on a subjective and litigation-producing inquiry into whether the agency gave the post-promulgation comments any fuller consideration than would be required in a typical § 553 case.

It is unclear why the courts have not accepted this approach, but one explanation may be a fear that evasions of normal rulemaking expectations would otherwise become too easy: "Were we to allow the EPA to prevail on this point we would make the provisions of § 553 virtually unenforceable. An agency that wished to dispense with pre-promulgation notice and comment could simply do so, invite post-promulgation comment, and republish the regulation before a reviewing court could act." *New Jersey,* 626 F.2d at 1049.

5. *"Unnecessary" rulemaking procedures.* The reason for the paucity of cases involving the "unnecessary" exemption, of course, is that rules that arguably fall within the exemption are usually too picayune to be worth litigating. Even if agencies use the exemption excessively (which, as Lavilla says, may not be the case), affected interests may not care to spend the resources to obtain judicial relief.

Jordan concedes that *Appalachian Power* and *Duquesne Power* may have been correctly decided because of the statutory deadline. Absent the time pressure, however, she would disagree with these courts. She argues that open proceedings at the state level are not a substitute for federal proceedings, because some members of the public might not have heard about the state proceedings, and others might have tailored their presentations differently if they had been addressing federal regulators.

More recently, EPA has used direct final rulemaking to adopt these state implementation plans (indeed, this was the context in which that rulemaking technique was invented). Levin, 64 Geo.Wash.L.Rev. at 4. Most plans survive the process and are adopted with a minimum of fuss, but when a plan does elicit an objection, EPA can then proceed to adopt the plan (or a revised version) through regular notice and comment procedure.

6. *Direct final rules.* Levin's article suggests that any rule that survives the direct final rulemaking gauntlet must be within the "unnecessary" branch of the good cause exemption. 64 Geo.Wash.L.Rev. at 11-15. Virtually by definition, such rules are "minor or merely technical [matters] in which the public is not particularly interested"—the legislative history's explanation of the "unnecessary" prong of good cause. An agency's unilateral declaration that a rule is noncontroversial might well be self-serving and untrustworthy; but if the agency has invited objections and received none, one can argue with some force that the declaration has been retrospectively validated. The agency has an incentive not to use direct final rulemaking excessively, because if it receives an objection and has to start over with regular notice and comment proceedings, the ultimate issuance of the rule will take longer than if the agency had never resorted to that technique.

The question of why an agency might elect to use direct final rulemaking instead of merely announcing that the rule is final by virtue of the good cause exemption can be answered on either an idealistic or hardheaded level. The idealistic answer is that "a process that smokes out unanticipated adverse reactions gives the agency precisely the benefits that notice-and-comment procedure is supposed to provide: the opportunity to avoid mistakes, to learn from others' perspectives, and to enhance the public acceptability of the ultimate product." *Id.* at 15. The more hardheaded answer is that it is a cheap means by which an agency can strengthen an argument, which it might someday have to make, that regular § 553 procedures had been "unnecessary" within the meaning of the good cause exemption. *Id.*

7. *Immediate effectiveness.* The *Gavrilovic* holding is plausible, but not unassailable. The equities supporting the defendants' interest in being allowed thirty days to cease their clandestine manufacture of a dangerous drug that had no accepted medical use would appear to be somewhat limited. And the government's sense of urgency, and its evident preference for responding to this threat through criminal rather than civil enforcement, do not seem so unreasonable, either. The debatable equities of the case highlight the extent to which the Eighth Circuit in *Gavrilovic* was determined to construe "good cause" narrowly. Interestingly, however, the court went on to endorse the position of *Rowell v. Andrus,* discussed in § 5.7 N.6, that the agency's violation did not make the rule itself void. After the thirty days were up, the rule was fully enforceable.

8. *Problem.* On the facts of this problem, Judge Gerhard Gesell (the son of the famous pediatrician Arnold Gesell) invalidated the interim-final rule in the *American Academy* case because of noncompliance with § 553, as well as for being arbitrary and capricious on the merits. The case illustrates a number of hazards in agency decisionmaking that have prompted courts to declare that the good cause exemption should be narrowly construed.

In the first place, the Secretary's assertion that lives are at risk reads too much into the "impracticable" prong of the good cause exemption. As Judge Gesell wrote, "Such an argument could as easily be used to justify immediate implementation of any sort of health or safety regulation, no matter how small the risk for the population at large or how long-standing the problem. There is no indication in this case of any dramatic change in circumstances that would constitute an emergency...." 561 F.Supp. at 401. (A similar argument would militate against a finding of "good cause" under § 553(d).)

At the same time, this case also illustrates the value of public participation in rulemaking. The court's analysis of the merits of the rule identified some issues that the Secretary, in her haste, had not considered, such as the disruptive effects of the "hotline" approach: "In a desperate situation where medical decisions must be made on short notice by physicians, hospital personnel and often distraught parents, the sudden descent of 'Baby Doe' squads on the scene, monopolizing physician and nurse time and making hospital charts and records unavailable during treatment, can hardly be presumed to produce higher quality care for the infant." *Id.* at 399.

Other problems with the regulation became evident by the time the controversy reached the Supreme Court. *Bowen v. American Hospital Ass'n,* 476 U.S. 610 (1986). By that time the government had conceded that, because hospitals normally rely on parental consent in treatment decisions, they would not be guilty of *discrimination* if they honored the parents' decision to withhold surgery from a handicapped infant. Thus, the Baby Doe incident itself had not violated federal law. A hospital's denial of food or care to a handicapped infant would be "discrimination," and thus forbidden by the Rehabilitation Act, only if it occurred over the objections of the parents. And, it turned out, the Secretary could not point to even one case in which a hospital had denied treatment under those circumstances. *Id.* at 630-36 (plurality opinion). Thus, the investigative apparatus established by the interim-final rule was addressed to a problem that did not necessarily exist at all, except as an unverified threat. (Thereafter, the government abandoned its discrimination theory in favor of a legislative solution. The Child Abuse Amendments of 1984 treats medical mistreatment of an infant's life-threatening condition as a form of child neglect and induces states to embrace this definition as a condition of receiving federal funding. 42 U.S.C. § 5106g(6).)

As for the Secretary's suggestion in her original notice that the requirement of round-the-clock access was a "minor technical change," and thus covered by the good cause exemption, the government apparently did not even argue that theory before Judge Gesell. The "unnecessary" prong of the good cause provision is reserved for basically uncontroversial decisions, which clearly was not true of this aspect of the Secretary's rule (let alone the entire rule).

Now, what about the *final* rule in the problem? One might argue that this rule too was suspect, because the Secretary could not be expected to examine the comments with an open mind after she had gone so far out on a limb politically at the interim-final rule stage. Therefore, the argument would run, the case should be remanded for a fresh look. As we have indicated in N.5 above, however, we disagree with this logic. There is little reason to believe that a third round of deliberations on the rule would have led to any different result than the Secretary had reached at the second round. The incentive for political face-saving would be about the same in either situation. The notice and comment procedure can accomplish only so much; at some point, one must remit protesting parties to other remedies, such as substantive judicial review—which in this instance proved efficacious. (This aspect of our problem is not true to life, however, because at the post-promulgation comment stage Judge Gesell had already given the hospitals the benefit, if any, of a judicial directive to the Secretary to reexamine the issues.)

§ 6.1.2 Exempted Subject Matter

1. *Proprietary matters.* As the Bonfield article cited in this note develops at length, the proprietary matters exemption is seriously overbroad. Certainly the right-privilege distinction is not a persuasive rationale for the exemption. The due process cases discussed in § 2.2.1 N.1 highlight valid reasons for the disappearance of the right-privilege distinction from the law and the public mind. Many people depend on such privileges as welfare benefits, social security, government guaranteed home loans, federal contracts, or access to public recreational facilities; they consider these benefits entitlements. Furthermore, people often have little choice but to accept such benefits, whether they are called rights or privileges.

Another justification for the §553(a)(2) exemption is that its elimination would increase work load, resulting in delay, inflexibility, and increased costs in carrying out everyday functions. Agencies also complain that without a clear-cut exemption for proprietary matters there would be uncertainty about whether rulemaking procedure must be followed, thus causing litigation or encouraging the use of those procedures where it would be unwise. The difficulty with these arguments is that they apply equally to those classes of rulemaking already subjected to the usual rulemaking procedure.

Most important, the right-privilege and proprietary-nonproprietary distinctions are not useful in evaluating whether rulemaking procedure should be employed. All government activity should be administered wisely, which suggests the utility of notice and comment rulemaking in setting policy. Responsible democratic government requires that, as a general proposition, citizens have a chance to protect their interests against administrative action that prejudices them, whether that action relates to a privilege or a proprietary matter. Nor is there any evident justification for dispensing with the delayed effectiveness requirement of § 553(d) and the right to petition in § 553(e) for all of the rules that fit within the broad proprietary matter exemption.

2. *Waiver of exemptions.* The holding in *Malek-Marzban* seems correct. If courts were to hold that an agency is "estopped" to assert a rulemaking exemption, simply because it has often waived the exemption in the past on an ad hoc basis, they would give agencies a strong incentive to shun voluntary notice and comment proceedings altogether.

3. *Proprietary matters in state law.* The proprietary exceptions in the 1981 MSAPA §§3-116(3)-(5) are narrowly drawn and are more easily justified than the overbroad federal APA proprietary exceptions. Section 3-116(3) of the 1981 MSAPA exempts rules which "only [establish] specific

prices to be charged for particular goods or services sold by an agency." The cost of conducting rulemaking proceedings every time a state operated cafeteria changes its prices for carrots and peas, or a state bookstore changes the prices of any of its books, is not worth the benefit. Similarly, § 3-116(4) exempts rules "concerning only the physical servicing, maintenance, or care" of specified "facilities or property." Without this exemption, agencies would be forced to follow rulemaking procedures for staff instructions regarding routine maintenance of agency facilities and property (i.e., how much rock salt to put on particular segments of a state highway, how often to shovel the walk in front of a particular state building, etc.). Clearly, the burden on agencies would be enormous and intolerable if ordinary rulemaking procedures had to be followed for each such rule.

One lesson that may emerge from the comparison between federal and state provisions is that the objection to the overbreadth of the former is really a matter of degree. It is in the nature of a categorical exemption to draw relatively bright lines. The result may be to exclude rulemaking procedures in some situations in which, abstractly speaking, we might want them. But the overbreadth of the federal provision is much more serious than that of the state provision, and thus criticism of the former need not carry over to condemn the latter.

4. *Agency management and personnel.* The rulemaking exemptions for matters of internal agency management are based on considerations of efficiency. The operating costs of agencies would substantially increase and their efficiency and effectiveness would substantially decrease if every time agencies gave an internal housekeeping instruction of any sort to their employees they had to follow usual rulemaking procedures. In addition, few if any benefits would accrue to the public from the use of ordinary rulemaking procedures when agencies formulate and adopt wholly internal housekeeping instructions because the public is not affected in any cognizable or significant way by most agency policies of this type. Both § 553(a)(2) of the federal APA and § 3-116(l) of the 1981 MSAPA are based upon this practical reality.

On the other hand, agencies could easily subvert usual rulemaking requirements if they could avoid those procedures for anything they called an internal directive to staff. After all, the public's rights can as easily be defined by statements formally addressed to the agency staff--"Prosecute any person who litters a public park"--as by statements formally addressed to the public--"No person may litter a public park." Application of this exemption has thus presented significant line-drawing challenges.

In *Stewart*, the dissent relied on, inter alia, the APA legislative history and the overall importance of rulemaking procedure. The majority relied on the language of § 553(a)(2), which facially seems broad enough to encompass hiring standards and had long been applied that way by the Civil Service Commission. The court also thought that the rules would not have a widespread public impact; rather, their impact would be "limited to those who seek employment."

The internal management exemptions of the federal APA (even under the *Tunik* interpretation) and 1981 MSAPA would likely exempt from usual rulemaking procedures performance criteria for agency employees engaged in law enforcement, so long as the criteria are related to the work management of the employees, rather than to a specification of the criteria defining the conduct for which members of the public may be punished. However, the government would stand on shakier ground if employee work performance criteria were to take the form of a quota of arrests or convictions, which certainly could have a direct and substantial impact on members of the public. Even the *Stewart* majority might see that case in the light suggested by its reasoning as just noted: the exemption should not apply to a rule that affects the public at large, as opposed to individuals who are directly involved in agency personnel decisions.

A rule governing agency office hours presents a similar question. Although agency office hours have an impact on the public, minor adjustments of office hours would not seem to have a "direct and substantial" impact on the rights of the public. However, such a rule might fall outside this exemption if it proposed to close an office for a substantial period of time or otherwise radically altered office hours in a way that significantly affects public access.

For a discussion of *Evans*, the lethal injection case cited in the note, see Arnold Rochvarg, "How Administrative Law Halted the Death Penalty in Maryland," 37 U.Balt.L. Forum 119 (2007).

5. *Military and foreign affairs functions.* The ACUS recommendation and the Bonfield article cited in this note urged that the military and foreign affairs exemption of federal APA § 553(a)(1) be replaced with a much narrower exemption. They proposed that matters pertaining to military or foreign affairs functions should be exempt if "specifically required by Executive Order to be kept secret in the interest of the national defense or foreign policy." This is the same standard used to exempt military and foreign affairs matters from the Freedom of Information Act. *See* 5 U.S.C. § 552(b)(1). As the text notes, the Department of Defense has more or less adopted this standard voluntarily.

6. *Problem.* Because the actual rule in *Independent Guard Ass'n* looked fairly outrageous, we have posited for discussion purposes a variation that looks somewhat reasonable (who wants armed guards to keep watch over nuclear weapons while they are stoned?). The real issue is, should such

a rule be subject to notice and comment procedure? On an ordinary language basis, the function of guarding nuclear devices can readily be termed "military" in nature. Further, the Ninth Circuit may seem to have put too much weight on the guards' civilian status and their employment by a private contractor, because under the statute it is the military *function* that counts. Still, the association can fairly argue that, because of the policy of narrowly construing § 553 exemptions, the agency should at least have to provide notice and comment before adopting a rule of this nature. Had the affected guards been soldiers, the tradition of military discipline might make rulemaking procedures look out of place, but the interaction here with workers from the private sector suggests that the government should allow public comment on the rule.

In the real case, the Ninth Circuit declined to reach the possible applicability of the personnel exemption, and it remanded for consideration of that issue. If the court follows the rationale of *Tunik* and the MSAPA, it would probably hold that the rule requires notice and comment, because of its impact—potential termination of employment—on persons outside the government. If the court follows *Stewart*, it would probably find the exemption applicable, because the drug abuse rule fits the ordinary meaning of a "personnel" matter, and the rule has no effect on the *general* public, but only on individuals who have an employment relationship with the agency (at least as closely connected with government as the disappointed job applicants in *Stewart*, if not more so).

§ 6.1.3 Procedural Rules

PUBLIC CITIZEN v. DEPARTMENT OF STATE

Notes and Questions

1. *Substance and procedure—rationale.* The FAA's practice rules, which were at issue in *ATA*, provide an apt vehicle with which you can raise the question of why the APA provides an exemption for procedural rules in the first place. Rules about discovery, the hearing process, etc., are about as procedural as you can get. The history of the *ATA* case is interesting, however. The panel held, 2-1, that the FAA rules did *not* fall within the procedural rules exemption. But in *JEM Broadcasting,* cited in the principal case, the D.C. Circuit disavowed the *ATA* reasoning, which had been heavily criticized. As the court belatedly recognized, the FAA rules at issue did implicate "value judgments," but they were not *substantive* value judgments.

The court in *Kast Metals* says that the procedural rule exemption "reflects the congressional judgment that such rules, because they do not directly guide public conduct, do not merit the administrative burdens of public input proceedings." But that virtually circular explanation does not really indicate why Congress might have made such a judgment. Likewise, the language quoted from *Batterton* begs the question. An agency should have flexibility in structuring "internal" processes, but this notion does not tell us what procedures are "internal."

Indeed, the rationale for the APA's wholesale exemption for procedural rules is somewhat mysterious: (a) Does it reflect a belief that an agency is uniquely qualified, because of its expertise, to formulate the procedures that will be used to implement and enforce the substantive law in areas within its delegated power? That argument does not persuasively distinguish procedural rules from substantive rules. With respect to both types of rules, agencies surely possess *some* expertise, but not so much that they should avoid consulting regulated parties and other members of the public, who may have information or opinions that could help agencies improve the quality of those rules.

(b) Does the exemption rest on an assumption that members of the public have no real interest in having a say in the contents of procedural rules? That doesn't wash, either. Procedural rules are often as important to regulated parties and members of the public as are many substantive rules. Trivial ones could presumably be adopted without notice and comment pursuant to the "unnecessary" branch of the good cause exception, but any assertion that procedural rules are *generally* too unimportant to deserve public proceedings seems manifestly incorrect, at least to us. After all, the Advisory Committee on Civil Rules routinely invites public comments on proposed amendments to the Federal Rules of Civil Procedure. (If you don't believe that the procedures followed by administrative agencies can be important to the citizenry, perhaps you should ask the Dean to allow you to teach some other course instead of Administrative Law.)

(c) Can the exemption for procedural rules be understood as a response to government concerns about protecting prosecutorial discretion and flexibility in enforcement planning—an inevitably adversarial process? Arguably, this is the "latitude" that *Batterton* says agencies need. But, while that point might have force in some situations, many procedural rules operate outside an enforcement context and do not raise those concerns at all.

Perhaps, therefore, the state APAs, which do not contain an exemption for procedural rules, have taken a wiser approach to this subject. In any event, an exploration of the questionable merits of the procedural rule exemption may be worth a couple of minutes of class time, because we suspect that the wide variance in the case law approaches to the exemption is related to a lack of agreement as to what purposes it serves.

2. *Competing tests.* The court in *Public Citizen* is on sound ground insofar as it criticizes the "substantial impact" test that had prevailed in early case law. As the court says, even purely procedural provisions can have significant effects on members of the public.

The "encodes" test is an improvement insofar as it turns the focus onto "substantive" as distinguished from "procedural" determinations. However, the court in *Public Citizen* seems to have misapplied its own standard. The thrust of the policy was to diminish requesters' FOIA rights. Public Citizen would of course want to receive the most up-to-date information about the Department's archiving policies. In this case the Department responded to the request three months after submittal; in other cases, the discrepancy between the submittal date and the agency's search can be much longer, due to backlogs, reluctance to comply, uncertainty about FOIA's scope, etc. That the cut-off policy applied to all FOIA requests submitted to the Department, regardless of subject matter, should have been beside the point, because FOIA itself confers a substantive right to something, namely information. *Cf. FEC v. Akins*, § 11.1.2.N.8 (informational injury in the context of standing). It is not just a procedure for implementing rights found elsewhere.

More fundamentally, the "encodes" language in the D.C. Circuit's test is frustratingly vague. It can be interpreted as exempting rules that are "basically" or "primarily" procedural, even though the agency might be motivated at least in part by a substantive agenda. In this case, for example, the cut-off policy probably was *motivated* by efficiency concerns, but the department must also have made, at least tacitly, a judgment that those concerns should trump the requesters' interest in receiving the most up-to-date records in its possession. The "encodes" metaphor is unhelpful in clarifying whether or not such a judgment takes the rule outside the exempt sphere.

3. *ACUS recommendation.* The ACUS position compares favorably with the case law tests in a couple of ways. It seems relatively easy to apply. In effect, it says that procedural rule exemption should apply only to *purely procedural* rules, as distinguished from rules that reflect judgments that partly procedural and partly substantive. Such a criterion would still pose some line-drawing challenges, but the inquiry would be relatively straightforward. (As we just discussed, the "encodes" test can also be construed this way, but the opinion in *Public Citizen* leaves room for uncertainty about whether or not that is intended.) At the same time, the ACUS test avoids the excesses of (one reading of) the "substantial impact" case law. As Lubbers and Miller explain in the article cited in text, it "has the advantage of emphasizing whether the rule has a *substantive* effect rather than a *substantial* effect." 6 Admin.L.J.Am.U. at 491.

Finally, the ACUS approach has an intelligible policy foundation. It would rest squarely on the APA values embedded in the main clauses of § 553. In this regard it would run directly parallel to the narrow-construction policy observed in the courts' application of other rulemaking exemptions, including the agency management and personnel exemption and the military and foreign affairs exemption. Any appreciable impact on substantive rights would apparently do. That policy foundation may be debatable, but at least it is discernable.

Application of this test would not necessarily change the result in *JEM Broadcasting*. In that case, the Commission's goal appeared to be purely procedural (i.e., efficiency). The FCC seemed simply indifferent to the effects of the policy on outcomes. It was going to give licenses to some applicants anyway, and there was no indication that the "hard look" policy was intended to disqualify applicants on the theory that applicants with incorrectly completed applications would be less qualified to serve as good broadcasters than other applicants would be. The policy was strict, but it was nonetheless procedural. Thus, the proper basis for challenging its stringency would have been to contest it on the merits (a mode of attack that succeeded in *Public Citizen*, although it did not succeed in *JEM Broadcasting*).

However, the ACUS test would presumably lead to a changed result in *Public Citizen*. As we discussed above, the State Department evidently concluded, without saying so, that FOIA requesters' interest in receiving the most up-to-date information was outweighed by administrative convenience. As such, the policy was partly substantive and not purely procedural.

4. *Enforcement.* Although it is true that the enforcement manual in *American Hospital* rested on a substantive value judgment that hospitals that not be able to retain excessive reimbursements, that logic proves too much. Obviously every enforcement plan presupposes that the agency wants to root out violations of the governing statute. We can see from the cases discussed above, however, that the courts are unwilling to construe the procedural rule exemption out of existence.

The extent to which a "procedural" rule can have substantive overtones without losing its APA exemption is often a matter of degree. During class discussion you might want to compare this case with the "Baby Doe" problem in § 6.1.1 N.8. In form the regulation requiring a hotline, posted warning notices, etc., was simply an enforcement scheme, but in reality its obvious purpose was to make hospitals less likely to engage in a specific form of allegedly discriminatory behavior that, at that time, was not clearly illegal (indeed, the theory of illegality ultimately was not sustained). Indeed, in the real case the government conceded that "the regulation is intended to produce 'a change in how the doctors will reach their final

329

judgments as to what to do or not to do in a given case,'" which is why Judge Gesell had no trouble holding that it was not a procedural rule. *American Academy of Pediatrics v. Heckler,* 561 F.Supp. 395, 401 & n.6 (D.D.C.1983). That rule did "encode a substantive value judgment" in a straightforward sense. In *American Hospital,* however, the court was careful to emphasize that the PRO manual did not change the standard of review for reimbursements. This distinction sets up the problem in the next note.

5. *Problem.* In the *Chamber of Commerce* case, the D.C. Circuit held that an enforcement program like the one described in the problem was outside the procedural rule exemption (as well as the policy statement exemption) and thus could not be established except through notice and comment rulemaking.

Under *Phillips Petroleum,* the rule is obviously not within the exemption, because the establishment of the CCP would surely have a "substantial impact" on the operations of companies that participated in it. However, this line of analysis would not be acceptable in the D.C. Circuit, which has disavowed the "substantial impact" analysis on the ground that even manifestly procedural rules can affect private persons. Such an analysis would fundamentally undermine the procedural rule exemption (although the reasoning in N.1 above suggests that this consequence would not necessarily be an unfortunate development).

Under the *American Hospital* test, the answer is not so clear. In the *Chamber of Commerce* case from which the problem is drawn, the linchpin of the court's analysis was the premise, apparently supported by OSHA's own past statements, that the agency was using the threat of inspection in order to pressure companies to adhere to a higher standard of conduct than the OSH Act itself did. This was a "substantive" agenda. Given its premise, the court had little difficulty dispatching the agency's further argument that the CCP did not have the force of law, because participation in the program was "voluntary." The reality was that inspections are expensive in terms of time and inconvenience, not to mention the liability risks if a violation is found, so employers have a strong incentive to avoid them. Thus the CCP would "significantly affect conduct" within the meaning of the ACUS recommendation by purposely inducing compliance with the program's high safety standards, and the program could well be said to "encode" a value judgment favoring such compliance.

However, we have made adjustments to the facts of our problem and (we think) left an ambiguity as to the critical question of whether the standards of conduct envisioned by the hypothetical CCP are indeed more stringent than what the Occupational Safety and Health Act requires. If the CCP does not promote tougher standards, but merely seeks to elicit compliance with extant standards by an unconventional route, it is more easily defended as a procedural rule. It would be much closer to the facts of *American Hospital*. (Admittedly, however, the fact that the Chamber is challenging the program through litigation suggests that it takes a more pessimistic view of the situation.)

To the extent that the court is unsure whether the CCP would effectively induce participating companies to observe more stringent safety standards than the Occupational Safety and Health Act requires, and thus whether the policy "encodes" a preference for such standards, it may want to decide the exemption question from a broader perspective. One could argue that the court should have taken a more lenient attitude in order to reward OSHA for experimenting with an innovative, "cooperative" approach to promoting workplace safety, as opposed to the traditional command-and-control model. *See generally* Sidney A. Shapiro & Randy Rabinowitz, "Voluntary Regulatory Compliance in Theory and Practice: The Case of OSHA," 52 Admin.L.Rev. 97 (2000); Jody Freeman, "Collaborative Governance in the Administrative State," 45 UCLA L.Rev. 1 (1997).

On the other hand, one can see the program as an attempt by the agency to leverage its resources by pressuring employers to adhere to a higher standard of safety than it could afford to secure through expensive rulemaking or enforcement actions. If the court disapproves of such leveraging as a circumvention of important statutory safeguards, it might want to rule against the government in this case in order to discourage similar conduct in the future. *See generally* Lars Noah, "Administrative Arm-Twisting in the Shadow of Congressional Delegations of Authority," 1997 Wis.L.Rev. 873 (a largely negative appraisal of such leveraging devices as practiced by agencies in various contexts). The *Chamber of Commerce* opinion contains language suggesting that the D.C. Circuit may have been motivated by this consideration.

The Chamber can also argue that, in any event, the goal of its suit is not to prohibit any cooperative scheme, but only to induce the agency to institute it with the safeguards of APA rulemaking procedure. A notice and comment proceeding would, for example, give the agency the benefit of outside perspectives as to alternative ways in which the CCP could be structured. This is the traditional argument behind the principle of narrow construction of rulemaking exemptions. But the modern debate over ossification has rendered the traditional strong preference for rulemaking procedure a more problematic premise than it once seemed to be.

Regardless, one lesson the problem teaches is that administration of the procedural rule exemption can be difficult and unpredictable, because the applicability of the exemption turns on agency motives or on predictions about how regulated entities will react to a rule, rather than simply on what the rule says on its face. In this respect the exemption is similar to the exemption for guidance documents, which is considered in the next section.

§ 6.1.4 Nonlegislative Rules

§ 6.1.4a Legislative and nonlegislative rules

This brief section is primarily intended to introduce students to the vocabulary and premises of the case law on nonlegislative rulemaking. Instructors should be aware that much of the older literature uses the term "interpretive rules" to denote the entire range of agency statements that we call "nonlegislative rules." *See, e.g.,* 2 Kenneth Culp Davis, ADMINISTRATIVE LAW TREATISE § 7:8 (2d ed.1979) ("An interpretative rule is any rule an agency issues without exercising delegated legislative power to make law through rules."). We have avoided that usage here. The past decade has seen increasing attention in the case law to agency policy statements, which do not fit easily into the Davis dichotomy; at the same time, the case law on interpretive rules has focused frequently (although possibly not wisely) on the question of whether an alleged statement of that kind is "derivable by interpretation." We believe that "nonlegislative rules" is a much more precise and less misleading term for the concept we have in mind.

You may find the term "guidance documents" more congenial than "nonlegislative rules." It is also in common use, such as in the OMB bulletin on "good guidance practices" discussed in § 6.1.4 N.6. Peter Strauss prefers the term "publication rules," meaning rules that can be adopted without notice and comment but must be published in the Federal Register. "The Rulemaking Continuum," 41 Duke L.J. 1463, 1467 (1992). We have avoided that term, in part because of the confusion surrounding the question of what nonlegislative rules the APA actually does require to be published. *See* § 5.7.

§ 6.1.4b Policy statements

PROFESSIONALS AND PATIENTS FOR CUSTOMIZED CARE v. SHALALA

Notes and Questions

1. *Criticisms of guidance documents.* As the text suggests, we think the dictum from *Appalachian Power* exaggerates the concept of "binding norms." A guidance document can have *some* constraining influence on agency staff without becoming binding for "all practical purposes." Nevertheless, the dictum is often repeated in the literature.

2. *Support for guidance documents.* The California APA now provides that "a penalty may not be based on a guideline, criterion, bulletin, manual, instruction, order, standard of general application or other rule unless it has been adopted as a regulation" under notice and comment procedure. Cal. Gov't Code § 11425.50(e). This section was adopted because practitioners before licensing agencies complained that many agencies had informally adopted penalty schedules that they pulled out of desk drawers and applied (or chose not to apply) in given cases. Such schedules would have been illegally adopted "underground" regulations, even under prior law, since California has no exception for non-legislative rules. But it is easier to pass laws against underground regulations than to keep agencies from issuing and relying on them in practice.

3. *Policy statements v. legislative rules.* A court that tries to apply the "binding norm" criterion can scarcely avoid a degree of speculation. Even if a document says that the agency "will" do something, does that mean "we certainly will, so don't even bring it up," or does it mean "we expect we will, unless we change our mind"? It could be either.

4. *Mandatory language.* The mental image of chemical companies paying human volunteers hundreds of dollars to gulp down pesticides is admittedly disturbing. Yet the companies insisted at the time of the *CropLife* controversy that their studies met high standards for safety, akin to those observed in clinical trials in medicine. *See* Denise Grady, "Debate Erupts Over Testing Pesticides on Humans," N.Y. Times, Jan. 9, 2003, at 18. At all events, after the D.C. Circuit decision discussed in the note, EPA did not attempt to resuscitate its moratorium, and it has continued since then to allow pesticide makers to rely on data derived from human test subjects (with exceptions for pregnant and nursing women and children). Possibly, therefore, *CropLife* can be understood as a case in which the court was relatively receptive to using a procedural rationale to attack the moratorium because it sensed that the agency had reached a dubious substantive result.

Regardless, *CropLife* is a striking example of the courts' current approach to the policy statement exemption. One would ordinarily not suppose that a press release could be a legislative rule. Yet the court's conclusion follows logically from the functional reasoning that one finds in many modern decisions. On its face the press release seems to make it perfectly clear that the agency isn't going to consider human test data, and manufacturers shouldn't even bother submitting any. That's enough for the court, even though the EPA could change its mind for various reasons (persuasion, political pressure, etc.). An important circumstance supporting the court's holding is that EPA apparently didn't even try to argue that it would be flexible about using human test studies. The case might have been very different if the agency had told the court, "Don't believe everything you read in press releases. If anybody comes forward with human study data and tries to show its procedures were safe, we'll consider the application on its merits at that time."

Of course it seems odd to apply § 553 to a mere transitional policy. But the court might respond that if the agency had wanted to defend its moratorium on the basis that it needs to put something on the books immediately, it should have invoked the good cause exemption and made the finding required by that exemption.

An incidental issue that you might wish to explore in class is whether the so-called rule in *CropLife* was exempt from § 553 due to the procedural rule exemption. In one sense, a decision about the type of evidence the agency will take into account seems to be a purely procedural matter. The moratorium doesn't rest on determinations about environmental law. On the other hand, one could argue that the adverse health consequences that were alleged to result from the testing process were indeed substantive.

The Fifth Circuit makes the *P2C2* case look easier than it is. Clearly the nine-factor formula leaves inspectors and other FDA officials plenty of room to use individual judgment and discretion in deciding whether to take enforcement action against any particular pharmacist. But the language does *not* overtly leave room for disagreement with some of its premises. It states positively that some retail pharmacies are violating the Act (i.e., that they are not exempt as a class, although a statutory foundation for such an argument might exist), and that pharmacists that engage in traditional compounding activities must be prepared to "document a history" of such activities, including the actual prescriptions. One simply cannot know whether, if a pharmacist were to dispute these propositions, the FDA would respond seriously (if reluctantly) to her argument. The mandatory language suggests not, but that is only an inference. A court that is generally suspicious of guidance documents might readily draw that inference, but a court that is more supportive might foresee a possibility that the agency would reassess those issues in light of the pharmacist's arguments, as in the *Panhandle* and *Steeltech* cases discussed in N.5.

The court seems to have gone astray in its apparent belief that if a purported policy statement leaves open the possibility of argument on *some* propositions expressed in a purported policy statement, it can treat other propositions as settled. (See the court's reliance on *Ryder Truck Lines* and the section of its opinion headed "Degree of Enforcement Discretion Accorded FDA.") This idea does not make sense. A policy statement cannot bind the public in the manner that a legislative rule would. It can, however, articulate propositions to which the agency will regularly refer when an affected person raises issues about them. It can also, to a degree not precisely defined by case law, structure its processes for contesting those positions in a manner that some members of the public will perceive to be so onerous that they cannot afford to maintain the contest. The indeterminacy that surrounds that point helps to explain the divergent results that courts reach when applying the exemption for policy statements.

5. *Binding effects in practice.* We generally agree with the materials in this note supporting the right to be heard when a policy statement is applied on an individual level. Cases such as *Flagstaff* and *McLouth* do not require a court to speculate about motives. Either the agency has responded thoughtfully to issues that the litigant has placed in controversy, or it has not; the court can decide. In fact, such review tends to merge with the "hard look" review of the agency's reasoning process that the court would provide anyway. At the same time, it differs from the way a court would review an agency's compliance with a legislative rule; in the latter situation, the agency does not need to justify its compliance with the rule, because the rule has the force of law.

Actually, however, it's a mistake to think of the "binding norm" principle in terms of judicial enforcement alone, because many controversies over the appropriate use of policy statements will never   Agencies themselves should institute policies that will prevent or deter officials from giving "binding" effect to guidance documents. The OMB "good guidance practices" bulletin discussed in N.6 contemplates such an approach.

We think the *Panhandle* and *Steeltech* cases are legitimately reconcilable with these authorities supporting the right to be heard. An agency's responsibility to consider challenges to the substance of a policy statement need not exist in isolation from the ordinary norms of the deliberative process. The agency *should* respond carefully to presentations that raise for its consideration arguments that it has not previously answered; but when a person who disagrees with a policy statement raises objections that are already answered in the statement, the agency should be able to rely directly on, or just refer to, its earlier reasoning. The insight that an agency must be prepared to defend its policy as if it had never issued the guidance document should not be pursued so singlemindedly as to make policy statements meaningless.

6. *OMB's bulletin.* The OMB bulletin is a sophisticated and generally admirable effort to define the proper role of guidance documents in agency decisionmaking. On the one hand, it recognizes that these documents can be misused. On the other hand, it acknowledges that agencies can make use of policy statements for guidance. As the court in *P2C2* asked, what would be the purpose of the statement if agencies couldn't rely on them?

A particularly interesting insight in the bulletin is its recognition that an agency *may* issue a policy statement that contains *mandatory*

335

instructions to staff, provided that these instructions "will not foreclose agency consideration of positions advanced by affected private parties." We do want frontline employees at an agency to rely on manuals from the head office. This compliance promotes regularity of administration, evenhandedness, etc. But the tradeoff is that discretion must be available at a later stage. It is legitimate for agencies to instruct employees to stick to the manual and to say to disgruntled members of the public, "I cannot change this policy. You'll have to talk to my boss." But if the manual has not been adopted through rulemaking, these employees should be told *not* to say, "This is our policy, so lump it."

Whether such a manual is "binding" may depend in part on whether the agency allows an easy appeal to supervisory personnel who do have discretion to depart from the manual. If the agency implements the instruction in such a manner that it binds everyone in the agency, the document becomes equivalent to a legislative rule and thus vulnerable to the kind of critique reflected in *McLouth*. The court in *CropLife* appeared to assume that the press release implied that the moratorium was not subject to reexamination at any level of the agency—which is why its holding is potentially reconcilable with the *Panhandle-Steeltech* line of cases. But the lines in this area are not bright. The "will not foreclose consideration" caveat in the OMB bulletin seems to invite case-by-case determination of whether various uses of guidance documents within an agency are "binding" in their respective contexts.

8. *Problem.* On facts similar to those of the problem, the court in *U.S. Telephone* held that the FCC had actually promulgated a legislative rule. However, we have changed the numbers in the problem in order to give the agency a more respectable argument. In the original case (and in the version of this problem in our second edition), the track record was that the FCC had adhered to the penalty schedule in at least 295 out of 300 cases, and only five were in the indeterminate category. Regardless, the problem illustrates the inherent fuzziness of the "definitiveness" test that courts use in implementing the policy statement exemption. "Binding effect" can be a matter of degree.

That the announcement was labeled a policy statement and contained assurances of flexibility were points in the agency's favor; but, the court said, the document certainly did not look like a mere guideline for the exercise of discretion. Its detailed, specific numerical benchmarks seemed calculated to limit discretion to a large extent. The record of actual experience under the guidelines was also equivocal. The apparent existence of some departures from the penalty schedule indicated that they were not *totally* binding, but the rarity of such departures also tended to suggest that the schedule was being used fairly mechanically and that the agency was giving the issue of penalties little if any original independent consideration at the implementation stage.

The facts are close enough to invite attention to policy considerations here. The agency can argue that it need not have announced a penalty schedule at all, and thus it should not be penalized for this effort to regularize its sanctions policies. In addition, the agency can argue that penalty schedules of this type must be frequently adjusted in light of changing law enforcement and market realities. Experience with the schedule may show that some penalties are too high or too law. Yet, because notice and comment rulemaking is costly and takes a long time, the agency would be unable to fine-tune the schedule. Indeed, the costs of rulemaking are such that the agency will probably leave an outdated penalty schedule in place for years rather than make resources available for changing it. There will always be higher priority use of resources.

The plaintiff association, however, can argue with some force that it has a substantial grievance about harsh treatment relative to broadcasters, and the FCC appears unwilling to come to grips with it in the course of either promulgating or implementing the schedule. As the court drily remarked, "It seems that the Commission has sought to accomplish the agency hat trick—avoid defense of its policy at any stage." 28 F.3d at 1235.

On the whole, this case appears similar to *McLouth*: the terms of the purported policy statement may have been open-ended enough to enable the FCC to resist reversal when the penalty schedule was first announced (had judicial review been sought at that time), but subsequent experience indicates that they are proving to be binding in practice. If the court in the problem reaches that conclusion, what should it do? The plaintiff's particular objection to the penalty structure seems generic in nature and not likely to be examined very closely in an individual adjudication (to uphold the association's position would mean rewriting the entire schedule), so it would appear that the only plausible relief is to remand the statement itself for notice and comment. In such situations, a court might permit the agency to continue to use the existing penalty schedule pending adoption of a new one, provided that the agency conducts a good faith notice and comment proceeding with reasonable dispatch.

A good question to ask the class is whether the plaintiff association could have succeeded if it had brought a judicial challenge to the penalty schedule immediately after it was promulgated. Perhaps so. The penalty schedule arguably *looks* as though it is designed to be applied with, at the very least, a strong presumption in favor of the specified values. But if the FCC says at that time that it intends to apply the schedule flexibly, perhaps a court would have to give the agency the benefit of the doubt. In such a case, deference to the agency, even if "not overwhelming" (a phrase that originated with then-Judge Scalia), might prove dispositive.

§ 6.1.4c Interpretive rules

HOCTOR v. UNITED STATES DEPARTMENT OF AGRICULTURE

As background to *Hoctor*, you might want to mention that on Christmas Day 2007 a 243-pound Siberian tiger named Tatiana escaped from its enclosure at the San Francisco Zoo and attacked three young men before being shot by police. One of the victims was killed, and the other two were seriously mauled. A suit filed by the survivors is currently resolved. Among the plaintiffs' claims is an allegation that Tatiana escaped because the wall surrounding the enclosure was only about twelve feet high, although the Association of Zoos and Aquariums recommends a minimum of sixteen feet. The zoo is arguing that the victims teased and provoked Tatiana, causing her to become enraged and to spring and claw her way over the wall.

Notes and Questions

2. *Intent to make law.* In principle, a focus on the agency's intent is appropriate, because an agency might possess legislative rulemaking authority on a certain subject, but elect not to use it. That is, it may simply want to put an interpretation on paper, for the information or guidance of the public (or at least its staff), without undergoing the hassles that the legislative rulemaking process would entail. The problem is to figure out the agency's intention in a given instance. This mode of analysis inherently lends itself to placing a degree of reliance on an agency's own label for its action. This makes a certain amount of sense, because of the presumption of regularity. It also has some appeal in practical terms, because it tends to shield agencies from reversal and thus encourages the free flow of interpretive statements that benefit the public.

However, courts realize that an agency has an obvious temptation to try to have it both ways—issuing a guidance document without rulemaking procedure, but using it as if it were a legislative rule. Thus it is not too surprising that the courts frequently reject an agency's label, if their study of the substance of the rule, or the way in which it is used, persuades them that the rule *cannot* be a valid interpretive rule.

Reference to the facts of the *Hoctor* case may help drive home the point that the intent standard is hard to apply. We don't know much about what USDA was thinking. We know that the rule was called an interpretive rule, which should be a point in the agency's favor. For a variety of reasons explored below, however, that seems to be a tenuous characterization. In those circumstances, the court quite naturally finds itself drawn towards sticking up for the principle of public participation in agency decisionmaking. Indeed, the social benefits of such participation are conspicuously mentioned in the court's opinion. Despite himself, however, Judge Posner does ultimately come around to placing some weight on the agency's intentions, as we discuss in our comments on N.6.

3. *"Interpretation" v. "arbitrary choice."* It is difficult, perhaps impossible, to make sense out of the *Hoctor* opinion. Judge Posner writes at length about the sort of "interpreting" that a court does, and juxtaposes that mode of reasoning with the more "arbitrary" or "legislative" line-drawing function that an agency commonly performs in its legislative rules. Ultimately, however, when he gets around to discussing the *American Mining* case, he virtually concedes that this sort of argument proves too much. Holdings like *Guernsey* and *American Mining* illustrate how far the "interpretive" function can extend beyond mere parsing of words. The rules in those cases were, indeed, as much interpretations of regulatory legislation as the Miranda ruling is an interpretation of the Constitution (to use an analogy that Judge Posner mentioned earlier, without exactly explaining why it was inapt). There is no conceptual stopping point at which an extrapolation from a statute *cannot* be interpretation, just as there is no sort of determination that is *so* interpretive that it cannot be the subject of a legislative rule (recall our example of the *Chevron* case in N.1). As Judge Williams says in *American Mining,* "the difficulty with the distinction [between `construing' a statute and `supplementing' it] is that every rule may seem to do both." 995 F.2d at 1110. That is the point made by Manning in his excellent article cited in this note, and we do not think Judge Posner, or other judges, have a satisfactory answer.

To be sure, Judge Posner might have said that the eight-foot standard could not reasonably be an interpretation of the structural strength regulation because it is a farfetched reading of a regulation that appears to be plainly concerned with other matters. If he had said that, this case would have been like *National Family Planning* in the next note. But he denies that this is the basis of his position. Although he does not conceal his "doubts" about the plausibility of USDA's interpretation, he does not want to rely on this ground—understandably, in light of the deferential standard of review that he would have to overcome.

It seems, therefore, that the *Hoctor* opinion is unpersuasive in its attempt to dispose of the case on the basis that the eight-foot standard "cannot be derived by interpretation." Possibly Judge Posner should have rejected the § 553 challenge, concluding that the internal memo was at least an attempt at an interpretation, and then gone on to decide whether it was a tenable interpretation, i.e., whether his "doubts" about the merits were grave enough to render the agency's decision substantively invalid.

4. *Inconsistency with the interpreted provision.* Logically, it would

seem that the court in *National Family Planning* could just as well have used a substantive rationale. The procedural holding seems superfluous at best, and perhaps dubious under the logic of *Fertilizer Institute,* which is rather persuasive in its suggestion that an erroneous interpretation is nevertheless an interpretation.

Logic is not the only factor at work here, however. Courts may prefer to rest their decisions on the lack of rulemaking procedure because that rationale sounds more politically neutral than overt disagreement with the agency's construction of the underlying text. The procedural hook has less of the odor of judicial substitution of judgment for that of executive officials (although, in fact, the same substitution of judgment occurs either way). For instance, in *National Family Planning,* one could plausibly guess that the three judges of the D.C. Circuit panel, all of whom were Democratic appointees (Wald, Mikva, and Edwards), did not want to appear to be taking sides against President Bush on the sensitive abortion issue, nor to suggest that his administration had misinterpreted its own gag rule. It was easier to say that the administration had failed to observe the APA. (Actually, one doesn't need to guess, because the author of the opinion has acknowledged that this was indeed her motivation. *See* Patricia M. Wald, "The Rhetoric of Results and the Results of Rhetoric: Judicial Writings," 62 U.Chi.L.Rev. 1371, 1415-16 (1995).)

5. *Interpretive reversals.* The cited article by Murphy, written in his characteristically whimsical style, provides a brief but incisive review of the perplexing *Alaska Hunters* doctrine. He notes the criticisms that most administrative law scholars have used to condemn the doctrine: As a matter of logic, one would think that if the initial interpretation of a provision falls within the interpretive rules exemption to § 553, so should a later one. Moreover, as a practical matter *Alaska Hunters* contributes to ossification by making it hard for agencies to change their interpretations when circumstances warrant. Finally, the courts' de facto amplification of agencies' procedural obligations, in a manner that seems so far removed from what the text of the APA says, is in serious tension with *Vermont Yankee.* Murphy also finds no plausible justification for the fact that courts apply the doctrine when agencies reinterpret regulations but not when they reinterpret statutes; the discrepancy contributes to the impression of incoherence.

The most charitable interpretation of *Alaska Hunters,* according to Murphy, is that judges believe that agencies do not sufficiently appreciate the value of stability in regulatory matters. From this standpoint, the case can be seen as rooted in a desire to make it harder for agencies to alter their interpretations. In other words, this argument would see the ossifying tendencies of the case as a feature, not a bug. Murphy admits, however, that courts have available a less drastic means of pursuing this objective.

340

They could simply, as a matter of "administrative common law," be more aggressive about enforcing the existing administrative law principle that agencies must provide strong justifications when they wish to depart from existing policy or precedent. They shouldn't be obliged to go through the full rulemaking process in order to adopt such a change.

6. *Lack of binding effect.* Practical considerations do tend to support the emerging tendency to blur the distinction between interpretive rules and policy statements. An agency's interest in advising staff members, regulated entities, and the general public about its interpretations is similar to its interest in advising them about its discretionary policies. And, conversely, the interest of members of the public in contesting agency interpretations that have been adopted outside the legislative rulemaking process but are, in practice, "treated as establishing a binding norm" is similar to their interest in contesting agency policies that have been adopted and applied in the same fashion.

The OMB bulletin does, however, highlight one valid distinction between the two types of nonlegislative rules. We saw in *P2C2* that an agency's use of mandatory language in a so-called policy statement is a strong tipoff that the document may be better characterized as a legislative rule. In the case of interpretive rules, however, this is not so. Naturally, an agency will often couch its interpretations in mandatory language for the simple reason that the agency's *position* is that the statute or regulation contains a mandatory obligation. As the cited passage from *American Mining* says, ""Interpretation is a chameleon that takes its color from its context; therefore, an interpretation will use imperative language—or at least have imperative meaning—if the interpreted term is part of a command; it will use permissive language—or at least have a permissive meaning—if the interpreted term is in a permissive provision." However, the fact that the agency takes the *position* that a statute contains a certain command does not necessarily mean that it should be entitled to enforce that position without allowing persons who disagree with that position to contest it at the administrative level. Arguably, it only means that in the interpretive rule context, as distinguished from the policy statement context, a court would have a greater need to look at the agency's actual practices when it seeks to determine it will be applied as a binding norm.

Whatever the merits of these observations as an academic matter, however, the case law is a long way from embracing the thesis that the tests for distinguishing interpretive rules and policy statements should be fundamentally the same. When an agency claims that the document in dispute is an interpretive rule, most courts will frame the issue as being whether the rule "interprets existing law" or "makes new law." Students should understand that this is at least perceived to be distinct from the "binding norm" issue in cases like *P2C2*.

7. *Rationales for the exemption.* The Posner argument from agency expertise is quite weak. Agencies know a great deal about the statutes they administer, but they are not omniscient. The whole point of § 553 is that rules will be more insightful and informed (and more legitimate) if the agency hears the public's views before it acts. Furthermore, as we have pointed out at N.1 above, interpretive rules do not necessarily differ in their *subject matter* from legislative rules. In addition, even if one grants, as at least a rough generalization, that interpretive rules tend to focus on "legal issues," Judge Posner appears to have his comparative expertise argument backwards. Agencies have *less* of an edge over courts in regard to legal issues than in regard to factual and policy issues, so why would agencies deserve *more* procedural leeway in making interpretive rules than other rules?

The argument that plenary judicial review justifies the exemption is also shaky. Saunders makes a valid point: judicial review of an agency's interpretation is not entirely plenary. To that extent, giving private citizens a right to present their arguments on the merits to a court does not seem to be a completely satisfactory substitute for the opportunity (which may be withheld pursuant to the exemption) to present those arguments to an agency before it issues its interpretive rule. To avoid complicating this discussion unduly, we have avoided mentioning in this connection a related but more esoteric doctrine: Under prevailing case law, an interpretive rule deserves *less* judicial deference than a legislative rule. *See* § 9.2.4. In scope-of-review jargon, the legislative rule is entitled to *Chevron* deference, while the interpretive rule is merely entitled to *Skidmore* deference. Should that distinction come up in class, however, you can note that it does not fundamentally change the analysis. Even assuming that these two levels of deference differ in practical operation (a premise that many lawyers would question), the more important point in this context is that *Skidmore* deference is different from no deference at all.

A separate difficulty with the Senate committee argument that plenary judicial review is a substitute for the opportunity to be heard at the administrative level is that most interpretive rules never reach the courts at all. The limited standard of review is one reason for that, of course, but there are many others, such as the expense, delay, and travail of pursuing an appeal.

The "lack of binding effect" analysis identified in this note appears to be the strongest rationale for the exemption (taken in conjunction with the utilitarian arguments mentioned at the beginning of the note). In essence, it suggests that the interpretive rule exemption is legitimate for roughly the same reasons that the policy statement exemption is. It also has the advantage of focusing on what happens on the administrative level, instead of assuming, unrealistically, that affected persons necessarily will go to court to vindicate their interests.

8. *Problem.* A premise of this problem is that the guidelines' requirement of instruction in social studies and science is a plausible reading of the Nonpublic School Act's mandate that courses in home schools must meet the "same standard" as public schools, but that the 180-day requirement is extremely dubious and probably erroneous under the substantive law. Such were the views of the Michigan Supreme Court in *Clonlara.*

A wide range of approaches to the APA interpretive rules exemption can be explored through this problem. The simplest analysis would be that the guidelines are interpretive rules, not legislative rules, because the Board describes them as such and they are worded as purported explanations of existing law. A variation on that approach would be to say that the curricular requirements are valid under that analysis, but the requirement of 180 days of class is invalid under *National Family Planning,* because it is not a reasonable inference from the school aid statute. The latter holding might be rendered under § 553(b)(A), as a conclusion that this element of the guidelines is not a valid interpretive rule; or it could be a pure holding of substantive law, as in *Fertilizer Institute.*

It's not clear where Judge Posner's approach leads in this problem. The 180-day requirement may well be erroneous, yet it falls easily within the bounds of what one would normally consider "interpretation" of statutory provisions. On the other hand, consider the Board's curriculum choices. They do not seem intrinsically unreasonable as an explication of the Act's "same standard" criterion, but are they "interpretation" in the *Hoctor* sense? One can assume that the Board was mindful of the statutory text and purpose of the Act, but obviously its curricular choices stem primarily from professional judgment and experience in the world. We think that the facts of this problem highlight the unwieldiness of the *Hoctor* effort to isolate the "interpretive" element of agency policy development for purposes of applying the § 553(b)(A) exemption.

Finally, the problem lends itself to analysis under the "binding norm" test applied by some of the cases. Here, although the Board represents that its guidelines are nonlegislative, they certainly don't sound tentative or flexible. Moreover, if the Nonpublic Schools Act is enforced through administrative proceedings, Irene may be able to show that the Board has no intention of reconsidering its position in such proceedings.

On the other hand, suppose the Board has no adjudicative role, and any enforcement proceedings under the Act would have to be brought in court by the local prosecutor. Presumably, since the guidelines do not purport to be legislative, the government would have to prove a violation of the statute, not of the guidelines as such. Under these circumstances, the state is in a relatively strong position to argue in the present litigation that the guidelines have no cognizable binding effect. (To be sure, the court in such an enforcement action would probably give weight or deference to the Board's guidelines; but if that were enough to trigger notice and comment obligations, the interpretive rules exemption would be almost a nullity, because such deference is exceedingly common.)

Many of the principal policy arguments surrounding the exemption stand out fairly clearly on the facts of the problem. One has to believe that these guidelines will have a huge impact in the real world, despite their interpretive garb. Very few home-schooling parents are likely to engage counsel to explore all their legal options; the vast majority will simply submit to what the Board says. This predictable pattern does not resolve the § 553(b)(A) issue on its own, but it dramatizes the stakes on each side. One who is generally wary of agencies' use of guidance documents can argue that the Board is effectively imposing a new obligation and that the guidelines are actually a legislative rule. The de facto coercive impact of the guidelines supports this argument. Besides, there is powerful equitable appeal to the idea that these guidelines, touching as they do upon the critical and sensitive issue of children's education, are exactly the sort of document that *should* be developed after extensive public input and consultation. Members of the public could have quite a lot to contribute to the decision

On the other hand, one who is more sympathetic to the use of guidance documents can argue that the Board ought to do *something* to promote the public policies embedded in the Nonpublic Schools Act; informal guidelines by which a politically accountable Board gives specific content to the vague contours of the Act may be much better than just letting parents do whatever they want in their home schools (which would probably mean that they would ignore the Act entirely). And, although in an ideal world one would prefer public input on guidelines such as these, state education budgets aren't always lavish, and the Board's resources may be stretched very thin. If the choice is between informal, nonbinding guidelines and no guidelines, the Board may be reasonable in opting for the former.

The majority in *Clonlara* responded to a suit like Irene's in what we would consider a very straightforward way. Michigan's APA, like the federal one, has an exemption for interpretive rules. Unlike the situation posited in the problem, however, the real board in Michigan had no authority to promulgate legislative rules. Thus, like the EEOC rules discussed in N.1 of this section, the home-schooling guidelines necessarily fell within the exemption. Thus, although the 180-day requirement was invalid under the substantive law, the guidelines were not procedurally defective, and the curricular requirements could stand.

The dissenters in *Clonlara,* however, insisted that the 180-day portion of the guidelines were also *procedurally* invalid. Because the 180-day requirement could not be found in Michigan's statutes or any legitimate interpretation thereof, the guidelines were in this regard an unlawfully promulgated "legislative" rule. We aren't exactly sure why the dissenters made such an issue of this APA argument (given the court's unanimous view that the 180-day requirement was a misreading of the statute anyway), but apparently they wanted to go on record as condemning the bureaucracy for giving a coercive, "practical binding effect" to a supposedly interpretive, nonbinding statement. The dissent relied heavily on quotations from Anthony's Duke Law Journal article (cited in N.1 of the policy statement unit). In our view, however, a better response to the dissent's concerns would be to insist that, in any administrative proceedings to enforce the guidelines, the Board must allow home-schooling parents to contest any aspect of the guideline with which they may disagree.

§ 6.2 REQUIRED RULEMAKING

NLRB v. BELL AEROSPACE CO.

1. *Bell Aerospace.* In the article cited in the introduction to this section, Bonfield presents an extensive case against the *Bell Aerospace* principle. Bonfield's position rests on the premise that rulemaking is generally a much better instrument for administrative policymaking than is adjudication. Therefore, he believes, the current freedom of agencies to elaborate their law by adjudication rather than by rulemaking is too broad. Agencies should, instead, be required to make their law and policy by rule, rather than by order, unless rulemaking is infeasible or impracticable in the circumstances.

A supporter of the current federal doctrine, while perhaps agreeing as to the advantages of rulemaking, might disagree with Bonfield's view for essentially two reasons. First, an agency's determination whether to engage in rulemaking in a given situation can be seen as an inherently judgmental issue, closely related to priority-setting, resource allocation, and other matters that arguably are beyond judicial competence. This notion is the crux of the issue considered by a host of articles, including the ones cited in this note, and we tend to think that Manning has the better of the argument. (For further analysis of this issue, see the discussion below in N.10 of this section.) We don't think Bressman can solve the problem by reframing it as a requirement that an agency must *give reasons* when it chooses to make policy through adjudication. To give the requirement any teeth, the courts would still have to decide what reasons are good ones, a task that would entail the same sort of linedrawing difficulties.

Second, required rulemaking is generally not necessary to protect the interests of individual litigants. Although individuals subjected to a case law "rule" sometimes have valid complaints about unfair treatment, courts generally can rectify those problems without having to tell the agency to launch a rulemaking proceeding. More specifically, the individual right to be heard can be protected within the context of later adjudications, and the right to be free of unfair surprise or unfairly retroactive agency policies can be protected by holding the individual order arbitrary and capricious. This second argument is developed below in NN.3-4.

2. *Purely prospective adjudication.* It can be strongly argued that, notwithstanding the plurality's insinuation that the Board had treated the *Excelsior* list requirement as a "rule," *Wyman-Gordon* did not interfere in any serious way with the Board's ability to continue making law through the adjudicative process. The plurality evidently assumes that the Board's use of what may have been an inferior decisionmaking method is not, standing alone, grounds for reversing the agency. Presumably the plurality thinks that Wyman-Gordon may not complain about that choice because the company was not prejudiced by it. In other words, although the Court may wish the Board had been better informed, the respondent was entitled to press any objections it wanted at the Board level and will not be heard to argue that others might have advanced better objections than its own. In that respect, the disposition of this case anticipated Justice Powell's remark in *Bell Aerospace* that the parties to that litigation had received a full opportunity to be heard and thus could not prevail on the basis of the Board's failure to allow others to participate. If the Board gives that opportunity to future respondents, it is apparently free to continue to make policy on a case-by-case basis.

One sees here a sharp difference between the federal and state cases. Although Friendly's opinion in *Bell Aerospace* (summarized at the beginning of the excerpted opinion) is an exception, most federal case law focuses on the immediate interests of the challenger, and the usual result is a finding that those interests can be protected without a mandate to conduct rulemaking proceedings. A number of state cases, on the other hand, effectively treat challengers to agency actions as private attorneys general who can enforce the general social interest in broad use of rulemaking proceedings. *See* N. 9.

The plurality in *Wyman-Gordon* was also bothered by the fact that the Board had not enforced the *Excelsior* list requirement against the companies involved in that very case. Arguably *Wyman-Gordon* retains vitality as a bar to purely prospective administrative adjudication. Yet it is not clear why one would want such a bar to exist. As Justice Black recognized in his concurring opinion in that case, *Excelsior* was validly commenced as an adjudication, and the issue of whether to apply the rationale retroactively did not even arise until the Board had found the facts, determined the appropriate legal and policy principles, and finally had to consider whether equity justified letting this respondent off the hook because of the newness of the controlling doctrine. It would be anomalous if an affirmative answer to the last question required the Board to start the proceeding all over again as rulemaking. Besides, the plurality's position would give the Board a perverse incentive to apply a new adjudicative doctrine retroactively, in order to prevent some court from reclassifying the proceeding as a disguised rulemaking. That would encourage the Board to engage in precisely the kind of unfair retroactivity that *Retail Union*, summarized in N.4, is intended to discourage (but cannot totally prevent because of its deferential standard of review).

In the civil litigation system, prospective-only decisions seem to be on the way out, because the Court sees them as being in tension with the principle that the law should apply equally to everyone. Judges don't like to acknowledge the reality that they are changing the law when they overrule their precedents. But administrative agencies are generally understood as wielding quasi-legislative authority, and there is no conceptual problem at all when they adopt new case law principles, or even when they overrule their own precedents. They don't have to pretend that the newly endorsed principles were really required by law all along. *See NCTA v. Brand X Internet Services*, § 9.2.4 N.7. So the Court's developing reservations about prosective-only judicial decisions should not cast a shadow over prospective-only administrative adjudication. there is less reason to question prospective-only decisionmaking in administrative adjudication than in civil adjudication. *See Laborers' Int'l Union v. Foster Wheeler Corp.*, 26 F.3d 375, 385-89 (3d Cir.1994); Ronald M. Levin, "'Vacation' at Sea: Judicial Remedies and Equitable Discretion in Administrative Law," 53 Duke L.J. 291, 358 n.304 (2003).

3. *Willingness to reconsider.* The Board did not necessarily do anything wrong in *Mercy Hospitals;* the court's basic objection is to the Board's unwillingness to rethink the *Mercy* principle when it was challenged in *St. Francis*. The court did not say that the Board may never adopt a per se principle through case-by-case adjudication. Rather, its point was that when the Board adopts such a policy through the adjudication route, it must give affected persons the chance to contest the policy in later adjudications and must respond to substantial challenges to the validity of the policy. The case is thus different from *Bell Aerospace*, in which Powell emphasizes that the parties were "accorded a full opportunity to be heard," which presumably included consideration of the points they raised.

If an agency's policy is one that the courts are not disposed to overturn, isn't the right to request an agency to reexamine its precedent pretty worthless? Possibly, you could distinguish a precedent by arguing that the facts of the two cases differ. But suppose it is squarely in point—are you out of luck? In the short run, probably so. The most you could hope for would be to persuade the agency that it had overlooked some important arguments in its earlier decision—normally a futile endeavor. Over time, however, precedents become more vulnerable. The legal landscape changes, conditions in the country change, and, most importantly, agency personnel are replaced. Under such circumstances, exhortations to reconsider precedents will not necessarily fall on deaf ears. To be sure, the agency might decide that the social interest in stability and predictability militates in favor of stare decisis, but agency officials are sometimes quite willing to scrap existing precedents in response to a reasonable request (or even without a request).

The *American Hospital* case cited in this note upheld the Board's first post-*Bell Aerospace* experiment with legislative rulemaking. It presented almost exactly the same substantive issue as *St. Francis* did. The point to notice here is that when the Board adopts a legislative rule, like the one in *American Hospital,* it eliminates private parties' right to expect any consideration of the merits of the rule at the administrative level. Such a rule is binding, and the agency couldn't decline to follow it even if it wished to do so. All the private party can do is to petition the agency to amend or rescind the rule, or perhaps to grant a waiver (*see* §§ 6.3, 6.4). Thus, to the extent that the Ninth Circuit's holding in *St. Francis* depends on its criticism of the Board for failing to allow the hospital to argue against the nurses-only bargaining unit, the Board might indeed have been on stronger ground if it had used legislative rulemaking.

4. *Reliance and retroactivity.* People who generally like the idea of an enforceable duty of required rulemaking will probably endorse the view of the lower court in *Bell Aerospace,* because retroactive application of a new precedent to persons who relied on prior case law seems one of the most oppressive forms of agency lawmaking through adjudication. However, people who generally support *Chenery II* and *Bell Aerospace* can be expected to be quite satisfied by the *Retail Union* solution. It respects the principle of agency autonomy in regard to lawmaking modality, while curing retroactivity and reliance problems in a narrowly tailored way. It also avoids giving a windfall to future litigants who *do* have timely notice of the changed policy.

5. *Abuse of discretion.* Although *Bell Aerospace* said that in some situations an agency's choice of adjudication over rulemaking might be an abuse of discretion, the important question is whether *Ford Motor Co.* identified any circumstances that would persuasively distinguish that case from *Bell Aerospace* itself. Most, if not all, commentators have thought that it did not and could not. The Ninth Circuit appears to suggest that an agency may not proceed by ad hoc order when it makes a change in existing

law that will necessarily have widespread application. But agencies use adjudication in that fashion all the time, and they certainly did it with Supreme Court approval in *Chenery* and *Bell Aerospace* (and arguably in *Wyman-Gordon*). *See also* Berg, 38 Admin.L.Rev. at 155-58, reviewing other "special circumstances" of *Ford Motor Co.* that might arguably set it apart from the Supreme Court cases and concluding that they "really do not seem to add up to much."

6. *Benefit programs.* Without doubt, *Ruiz* has been less than influential, but it may be interesting to ask the class how far its result can be defended without totally disavowing the main line of cases leading up to *Bell Aerospace.* Perhaps the most plausible distinction is that *Ruiz,* unlike all the other cases discussed in this section, involved a spending program rather than a regulatory program. A budgetary allocation is a finite resource. Thus, if the BIA passes out funds on a haphazard basis, it may run out of money before Ruiz comes around, even though his might be among the most deserving of cases. This possibility suggests the need for some central planning to ensure that the spending follows rational priorities. In this respect *Ruiz* bears a resemblance to some of the due process cases discussed in N.8, and it is distinguishable from the regulatory cases, in which the agency could potentially give a hearing to any number of respondents. Moreover, although in theory the BIA could develop such standards in the course of deciding individual applications for money, one strongly suspects that Snyder Act adjudications are too informal to make that possibility very realistic.

Having said that much, however, we see little justification for the suggestion in *Ruiz* that standards must be developed through a *legislative* rule. What if the government is amenable to promulgating some general guidelines, but believes that local offices should have discretion to use their judgment on a case-by-case basis, as with the policy statement in *P2C2*? To the extent that the *Ruiz* opinion forecloses that option, it seems indefensible. Perhaps, as some have suggested, *Ruiz* is driven primarily by sympathy for impoverished Indians, towards whom the federal government has important fiduciary obligations. But the courts could have real difficulty if they were to try to resolve required rulemaking cases on the basis of such overt substantive value choices. After all, Mr. Chenery lost 4.5 million dollars as a result of the SEC's lawmaking-by-adjudication in his case; how could the Court brush that interest aside as trivial? Maybe the general tendency to ignore *Ruiz* is just as well.

7. *Judicial presumption.* On its own terms, *Megdal's* interpretation of legislative intent is not very difficult to justify. Justice Linde's strongest argument is that Oregon has thirty-odd occupational licensing statutes that seemingly are indistinguishable from the dentists' statute, and many of them contain an explicit rulemaking requirement. Courts do not always

indulge the inference that the legislature would have treated like situations similarly if it had stopped to think about the matter. *See West Virginia University Hospitals, Inc. v. Casey,* 499 U.S. 83, 100-01 (1991). But in *Megdal* the court faces that issue directly and makes a plausible case that the difference could not have been deliberate: "The difference of the potential impact, when one occupation is given fair notice of obligatory standards for propriety by prior rulemaking and another occupation is given no such prior notice, is too pronounced to be attributed to the legislature without some showing that it was intended." More generally, the court emphasizes the need to assure fair notice to licensees of the specific conduct that might cause loss of their licenses. Rulemaking might not be the only way to give notice, but it is certainly the most effective way.

If one reads *Megdal* as standing for a broad presumption favoring rulemaking, as espoused by Bonfield, however, the arguments just mentioned will not suffice. In most situations in which an agency has been authorized, but not specifically directed, to implement a vague statutory mandate through rulemaking, one will not be able to point to a series of parallel statutes that do explicitly command the use of rules. And in some contexts the fair notice rationale carries much less weight than it did in *Megdal;* that was Justice Powell's point in *Bell Aerospace,* where the potential obligation to comply prospectively with a bargaining order did not trigger such intense concerns about prior notice. And, most fundamentally, it is hard to get past the fact that legislatures frequently do instruct agencies that a given decision must be made through rulemaking; if a statute on its face allows an agency to evolve its policies through either rulemaking or adjudication, one might well infer that the legislature meant for the agency to have a choice. Against this background, the limited scope given to *Megdal* in subsequent cases is not surprising. Apparently, even courts that have been receptive to ad hoc experimentation with required rulemaking, as discussed in N.9, do not want to commit themselves to an across-the-board shift in the direction of rulemaking.

8. *Due process.* The extent to which due process may require administrative rulemaking is discussed at some length in Bonfield, 42 Admin.L.Rev. at 165-72. That discussion concludes that only in rare instances, at most, will due process require agencies to elaborate their law by rule, rather than by order, where the agency process is of a nonpenal character. The inertia of existing law on this subject, and the presumption favoring the constitutionality of agency action, militate against expansive use of due process in this context. In any event, proponents of required rulemaking are not likely to find due process a very dependable lever for reform, because the prevailing methodology of due process adjudication, the *Mathews v. Eldridge* balancing test, is highly unpredictable in its application. So, Bonfield concludes, while due process may be of some marginal utility in efforts to increase agency lawmaking by rule, it is not

likely to be an effective tool with which to establish a clear mandatory general preference for administrative rulemaking.

There are also more substantive reasons to be wary of the due process approach to this issue. When courts rely on the Constitution to hold that agencies must use rulemaking in particular contexts, the legislature can't override their decisions if the consequences prove unsatisfactory. Moreover, broader use of the due process clause in forcing agencies to develop law through rules would likely result in an expanded role for the *federal* courts in supervising *state* administrative action. Although that prospect may be pleasing to people who have little or no faith in state government, modern federal constitutional jurisprudence is not at all antagonistic to federalism values—the trend is much more in the opposite direction. We think that both federal and state courts would be reluctant to endorse a doctrinal shift that might trigger a cascade of suits under 42 U.S.C. § 1983 against state agencies that have chosen, for one reason or another, to adopt in adjudication principles of law that arguably should have been developed through rulemaking. Indeed, the lack of significant decisions in that direction since the 1970's speaks for itself.

9. *Other state cases.* Even proponents of required rulemaking may well wonder about the soundness of the *Bessemer* case. In one breath the court suggests it may be impossible to write rules on this subject; in the next, the court faults the agency for failing to do it! The qualifying language "as soon as feasible and to the extent practicable" in 1981 MSAPA § 2-104(3) was included in order to induce courts to focus on the question of whether, at a given point in the development of a program, the subject matter really is susceptible of as much refinement as they might ideally desire. The Wyoming court seems not to have considered that question. This might well be the sort of case in which the EQC decision deserved to be sent back for further consideration (if it failed to disclose the criteria that led the agency to treat the mountain as "rare or uncommon"), but in which it was too early to expect the agency to have settled on criteria that would be durable enough to warrant promulgating in a regulation. The *Chenery II* "muddling through" approach might have been as much as the agency could manage at that time; at least, the court's opinion offers little basis for believing otherwise.

10. *1981 MSAPA.* The essence of the case for § 2-104(3) is the claim that rulemaking is far superior to adjudication as a device for making agency law and policy. The official Comment to the section emphasizes, for example, that when law or policy are expressed in rules rather than orders, it tends to be more accessible to the public, easier to understand, and more amenable to public participation and political oversight. Students can be referred back to § 5.1 of the casebook for a fuller exposition of the advantages of rulemaking. At the same time, § 2-104(3) has been

deliberately framed in terms that avoid expecting the impossible from agencies. The mandate is only to issue rules "as soon as feasible and to the extent practicable." (The dictionary meanings of "feasible" and "practicable" are equivalent, but the MSAPA uses the former to refer to the timing of rulemaking and the latter to refer to the extent of detail required. We employ the same usage here.)

Weighing against the advantages of § 2-104(3) are the points made in *Chenery II*. Some issues do not readily lend themselves to rulemaking, because their implications have not yet become clear or are simply too unforeseeable or elusive. Thus, even if one believes that agencies should resolve legal and policy issues through rulemaking to a greater extent than they do today, one might think that a mandate to do so "to the extent practicable" could result in more than the optimal amount of rulemaking. Of course, a defender of § 2-104(3) would respond that the qualifying language "as soon as feasible and to the extent practicable" was included precisely in order to take account of reservations such as those of *Chenery II*. But there is a limit to how broadly those qualifiers can plausibly be read. A completely open-ended interpretation would undermine the reform thrust of the legislation; surely § 2-104(3) means more than that the agency must resort to rulemaking when and to the extent it thinks that such procedure would be a good idea. In short, there is a built-in tension between the basic mandate of the provision and its qualifying language, and no one knows for sure how their competing thrusts will work out in practice.

What about Auerbach's suggestion that the courts may not be qualified to administer § 2-104(3), and Bonfield's rebuttal, which relies on an analogy to the arbitrary-capricious standard of review? Bonfield's argument is similar to the point made by Magill in the article cited in N.1. Although scholars obviously have no consensus on this issue, a substantial argument for Auerbach's side is that the judgments that courts would have to make under § 2-104(3) involve the sort of inherently judgmental, polycentric considerations that they may have the least capacity to evaluate. They implicate determinations about relative priorities, resources, and the ripeness of an issue, which may be less suited to judicial determination than questions such as what a statute means or whether the facts in a record support a finding. (Compare the presumptive unreviewability of enforcement discretion, as prescribed in *Heckler v. Chaney*, § 10.5, and the lenient standard of review prescribed for agencies' denials of rulemaking petitions, § 6.3.) Sometimes an agency and the various constituencies to which it is accountable (including political leaders as well as regulated interests and beneficiary groups) simply have no consensus about how a given problem should be resolved, and judges may be in a poor position to decide whether the question has percolated long enough. Courts have enough trouble deciding whether an issue is ripe enough for *themselves* to resolve. (*See* § 11.2.4.) Deciding whether it is ripe enough for *some other* body to resolve would seem to be even trickier.

But the ultimate answer by proponents of § 2-104(3) will be that the goal of effecting a shift toward regular use of rules rather than orders for policymaking is important enough that the risk of some judicial misjudgments along the way is a price worth paying.

11. *The Florida rulemaking counter-revolution.* Florida's experience with "presumptive rulemaking" is difficult to evaluate from afar. No doubt the record is a mixed one. For example, the decision in *Matthews v. Weinberg* will strike many, probably most, students as a positive development.

However, the 1996 APA amendments in Florida could support a more pessimistic appraisal. They suggest that the grievances and complaints that led to the Florida rulemaking counter-revolution may have been, in fact, well founded. Does the presumptive rulemaking law induce agencies to promulgate hasty, ill-considered rules? In theory it should not do so, because it calls for rulemaking only where "feasible and practicable," but perhaps real-world pressures have caused it to work out differently. Perhaps risk-averse agencies have been so eager to avoid being sued for noncompliance with the new law that many of them have responded with rules that are at best marginally satisfactory on the merits. (Compare the reasoning of *Vermont Yankee*, § 5.4.3, suggesting that the unpredictability of judicial reversal under the hybrid rulemaking case law would ultimately have led to the overproceduralization of informal rulemaking.)

In any event, Florida seems at first glance to have acted paradoxically in 1996: First it imposes a duty to engage in rulemaking, then it dumps a barrage of constraints on the rulemaking function, such as a broad private right to waiver of rules. Rossi argues that the common theme in these seemingly contradictory measures is the erosion of agency discretion. He predicts that this situation is inherently unstable: "Eventually, pressures toward delegation will likely lead regulatory reform to shift its focus toward restoring some discretion to agencies." 49 Admin.L.Rev. at 375. That argument sounds logical, but the subsequent amendments to the Florida APA in 1999 and 2008 suggest that the political impulse to constrain the rulemaking process has by no means abated, and that the state's experiment with presumptive rulemaking is not going away any time soon.

12. *Problem.*

(a)(i). *Mark's case under federal law.* If MU is a federal agency, it is free, under *Bell Aerospace*, to elaborate its law by rule or by order, so long as it does not abuse its discretion. Consequently, MU could choose to proceed by ad hoc order to determine that an excessive number of parking tickets is "conduct inappropriate for a student." The question, however, is whether or not making that law ad hoc in Mark's case is an abuse of MU's discretion in light of its retrospective application to Mark, who may not have had fair notice that an excessive number of parking tickets would be sanctionable as "conduct inappropriate for a student."

There is no evidence that this is a case where Mark had relied in good faith on past decisions of the agency; and this is not a situation in which fines or damages are involved. So it does not fit squarely within the *Bell Aerospace* examples of impermissible or misused ad hoc agency lawmaking. The factors listed in the *Retail Union* case also seem to suggest that MU could announce this new law in Mark's case: 1) Mark's case is one of first impression—it does not overrule a prior case holding to the contrary; 2) since the facts do not indicate that MU has in the past faced such an extreme case of parking violations (185 tickets), the new policy that parking tickets can lead to suspension is not an abrupt departure from past practice but, instead, only fills a void in an unsettled area of the law; 3) there is no evidence Mark relied on any prior law to the contrary; 4) the interest of the school in applying this new law to Mark's case seems considerable, in light of the huge number of tickets he received, his flagrant disregard of the school's parking rules, and the likely effect on other students of his continuation in school under the present circumstances.

On the other hand, it could be argued that ad hoc lawmaking was unfair here because the burden on Mark from retroactive application of this new law to his case is considerable—a six month suspension from school. Also, if one thinks of the SDB and the university parking authority as part of a single entity, namely MU, Mark may be able to show that the university has long turned a blind eye towards behavior like his, and thus his suspension *is* an "abrupt departure from well established practice." In any event, if Mark does obtain relief from his suspension, that outcome will not necessarily mean that the legal principle established by SDB in his case will no longer be regarded as a precedent.

Another argument for setting aside the result in Mark's case is based on *Soglin v. Kauffman*, 418 F.2d 163 (7th Cir. 1969), discussed in N.8 of this section. *Soglin* held that a public university could not expel university students for "misconduct" wholly on the basis of an ad hoc elaboration of that standard in the case at hand; instead, the university had to issue rules giving content to that standard in advance of sanctioning students thereunder, so that they would have fair notice of the prohibited "misconduct." It could be argued on the basis of *Soglin* that the MU disciplinary action in Mark's case was penal in nature and, therefore, triggers due process safeguards. But let's face it: *Soglin* and the other due process cases discussed in this section are all more than thirty years old and have gone nowhere since, so it's not clear that they would be followed today in any event.

(ii). *State law.* You might start by assuming, contrary to the implication of the Problem, that MU is a state institution but is not bound by a statute based on 1981 MSAPA. That might occur because MU is a local institution or because Madison's APA is inapplicable to state universities-- which is not uncommon, by the way. In that situation, Mark would have to fall back on cases like *Megdal*, arguing that the statute authorizing MU to adopt discipline rules should be construed to require that vague provisions like "conduct inappropriate for a student" be fleshed out by more specific rules.

But whatever the merits of the *Megdal* principle generally (and even Oregon has backed away from its full implications), it probably won't work here because the vague term is found in existing agency rules, not in a statute. We have no information about the underlying statute (which probably just authorized MU to adopt appropriate rules) nor about other state statutes that could arguably send a message that more precise rulemaking is needed (like the other licensing statutes in *Megdal*). It's not very plausible to argue that the drafters of the MU rules were sending a message to future disciplinary boards that they ought to adopt additional rules fleshing out the "conduct inappropriate for a student" standard. If they felt that way, they should have done it themselves when they first adopted the rules.

If MU is governed by 1981 MSAPA § 2-104(3), Mark's legal position is much improved. He would assert that MU failed, "as soon as feasible, and to the extent practicable," to elaborate the meaning of "conduct inappropriate for a student." It would have been very easy to codify the principle that 150 tickets is grounds for suspension, if that is what the Board believes. At the very least, he could say, MU could have previously indicated by rule the kinds of factors that would be considered in individual cases when the SDB made its decisions under that vague standard. For example, MU could have indicated by rule that a pattern of wholesale, flagrant disregard of any university rule or certain types of university rules would be regarded as "conduct inappropriate for a student." Or it could have specified that parking or traffic violations would be treated as such conduct in certain types of circumstances, or that it would consider specified factors in making that determination.

MU would respond that rulemaking had been neither "feasible" nor "practicable" when the SDB acted on Mark's case. The university would say that it is unreasonable to expect the SDB to have promulgated rules concerning the parking issue, when such a case had never even arisen before, even once. Don't the members of a part-time board composed of faculty and students have better things to do (like, for example, preparing for class?) than to sit around writing rules to cover hypothetical situations? True, they could have written rules like the ones suggested in the preceding paragraph, addressing "inappropriate conduct" on a general level, as opposed to parking offenses in particular. But such rules might have been so abstract and open-ended as to be meaningless, and at any rate wouldn't give students meaningful guidance about what they can and can't do. Why spend a lot of time substituting one set of platitudes for another? MU would argue that the SDB acted sensibly, or at least lawfully, in leaving these questions for case-by-case determination.

(b) *Belinda's case.* If MU is a federal institution, the SDB could argue that the sanction imposed on Belinda is sustainable regardless of whether the principle adopted in Mark's case was procedurally valid or not. Under *Wyman-Gordon,* it would say, Belinda received a proper adjudication, and that fact cures any arguable error in not using rulemaking procedure earlier. However, Belinda could rely on *St. Francis Hospital* to argue that the SDB improperly treated Mark's case as binding. The Board may be correct in saying that it can't distinguish between 185 tickets and 175 tickets (or if your class disagrees, change the facts so that she has 190). But under *St. Francis* the SDB should also have been willing to entertain the argument that the earlier Board decision was too strict and should not be followed. The second SDB opinion can be read as saying that the Board wouldn't even consider that possibility.

If MU is a state university governed by the MSAPA, Belinda has an almost unbeatable argument that the Board violated § 2-104(4). Once the Board had decided in Mark's case that accumulating 150 tickets is grounds for suspension, codification of that conclusion would almost certainly have been "feasible" and "practicable." The Board wouldn't even have needed to allow notice and comment first, because rules pertaining to students in educational institutions are exempt from rulemaking procedural obligations. § 3-116(6). The only way the Board might prevail here would be to argue that, on second thought, it does not really subscribe to the bright-line rule suggested by casual dicta in Mark's case. (Or, the new Board does not agree with the bright-line principle favored by the old Board.) Instead, it thinks that the question of suspension vel non should depend on a variety of factors in addition to the number of tickets—such as whether the accused student received actual warnings about what might happen to her, whether she shows remorse, whether she has been in any other trouble, etc. On this premise, the Board could tenably argue that the issue is too complicated to admit of codification, at least as of now. But the language of its opinion in Belinda's case makes the credibility of this defense highly suspect.

Alternatively, Belinda could attack the suspension directly as unjust or extravagant. On the facts as given, the link between the Board's violation and any prejudice to Belinda is unclear. If she cannot show substantial prejudice resulting from the violation, she may lose on that basis alone. § 5-116(c) (introductory clause). Perhaps, however, she can show that she might have avoided running up so many parking offenses if she had been given better notice of the Board's position. If so, she can argue that the sanction is unwarranted, or at least excessive, in that the unfair surprise to her outweighs the public interest in the sanction itself. The *Retail Union* case in N.5 provides support by analogy for such an argument, although the analogy is imperfect because her complaint is not that the case law was actually unclear but that she was not given adequate notice of it. A case that would support this argument even more directly is *General Electric v. EPA,* § 4.4.3 N.5.

§ 6.3 RULEMAKING PETITIONS AND AGENCY AGENDA-SETTING

MASSACHUSETTS v. ENVIRONMENTAL PROTECTION AGENCY

Notes and Questions

1. *"Extremely narrow" judicial review.* The notion that the standard of review for petition denials should be unusually limited has valid justifications, at least under some circumstances. One is that such denials often rest on determinations that courts cannot effectively supervise, such as resource allocation and priority-setting. This line of argument is developed in the quote from *NRDC v. SEC* in this note. Moreover, the record before the agency will normally be quite skimpy; thus, the court must be amenable to upholding the agency without insisting on the sort of detailed analysis that "hard look" review would normally require. The "right whale" apparently exemplifies the judicial restraint envisioned by these pronouncements. It is hard to see how the agency's explanation could have stood up against the usual hard look scrutiny.

When Luneburg raises doubts about the narrow standard of review, he has in mind a situation in which a challenger claims that an agency declined to engage in rulemaking because it misinterpreted its legal authority. As to that sort of case, he appears to be right. The *NAACP* case discussed in N.3 is an example of a petition denial case in which it is not meaningful to talk about a "narrow" standard of review. To say that "the scope of review is narrow" in that kind of case is usually just another way of saying "the agency's statutory authority is broad." At the same time, however, Luneburg acknowledges that resource allocation decisions are normally beyond a court's ability to second-guess. Moreover, he says, although an agency *might* be courting reversal if it tries to use this excuse to avoid administering a program at all, resource allocation *might* be a sufficient justification even in that situation. The agency might say that it is giving short shrift to one program because it believes that its limited time, funds, and personnel are better devoted to other programs that it also has been charged with administering.

2. *Massachusetts v. EPA*. The global warming case is an interesting attempt to have it both ways—the Court claims to be implementing a standard of review that is "narrow" but nevertheless searching enough to allow for reversal in this case. Justice Stevens maintains that the EPA relied on considerations that were not authorized by statute. More specifically, the Court reads the Clean Air Act to mean that EPA's decision has to rest on science and not on extraneous political considerations. Thus, the Court would defer to a science-based determination, but not to the one that EPA actually made.

Justice Scalia may be right that major regulatory statutes are typically read flexibly enough to allow an agency to take at least some account of the President's broad regulatory strategies and the United States's relations with other countries. *This* statute, however, is designed to be action-forcing. If carbon dioxide is an "air pollutant" and EPA makes an endangerment finding, regulatory action is expected, or at least strongly presumed. Scalia's argument that the Act gives the agency discretion to decide *whether* to make a finding comes across as a strained effort to avoid this legislative mandate.

That said, however, it would be difficult to argue that this 5-4 case could have come out only one way. The "common sense" premises of the decision are all too evident. The majority evidently believes that climate change represents an urgent challenge, according to respectable scientific opinion, yet the administration refuses to acknowledge this "inconvenient truth." Therefore, the Court's usual deference to administrative expertise cannot carry the day in this case. The dissenters, on the other hand, seem more comfortable relying on the specialized agency.

The *Massachusetts* decision did not, of course, elicit immediate action by EPA to regulate vehicular emissions of greenhouse gases under the Clean Air Act. The Bush administration's methods of avoidance were by no means subtle. For example, when EPA submitted its finding that greenhouse gases are an "air pollutant" under the Act, together with its recommendations for action, the White House initially refused to open the e-mail message containing the finding. It induced the agency to dilute its proposals, and then it solicited opinions on the EPA analysis from several other agencies, resulting in further delay. That the administration managed to "run out the clock" until it left office could be taken as a sign that the judiciary ultimately cannot force a recalcitrant agency to engage in rulemaking that it does not want to pursue.

But one could equally well argue that, in fact, the *Massachusetts* case did make a real difference. It stimulated congressional pressure, helped firm up public opinion in support of regulation, and possibly contributed to the political reaction that swept into office an administration that was likely to take a much more proactive approach to the climate change issue. (In fact, the Obama administration did quickly make an endangerment finding as contemplated by this case. 74 Fed.Reg. 18,886 (April 24, 2009). In short, accountability for arbitrary decisionmaking can be real even when it stems from a complex interaction of multiple political forces.

3. *Jurisdictional issues.* The *NAACP* case obviously has a kinship with *Massachusetts*. Both decisions rested on the idea that, although a court cannot monitor an agency's resource allocation decisions, it can at least intervene when an agency's rejection of a rulemaking petition rests substantially on a misinterpretation of its statutory authority. However, *NAACP* was in a way a simpler situation, because it involved a bilateral choice. The FPC thought it lacked jurisdiction, and the court decided otherwise. In *Massachusetts*, however, the Court had to do more interpretive work in order to define the relative spheres of administrative and judicial responsibility.

4. *State case.* The surprising *Rios* case arose from a regulatory regime modeled on that of OSHA. The department had already studied the issue of blood testing for agricultural workers who handle pesticides. In 1993 it had adopted a voluntary blood testing program, rather than a mandatory one. In a separate section of the *Rios* opinion, the court held that the 1993 rule was reasonable in light of the record that had existed as of that time. Post-1993, however, the department's technical advisory group concluded that a mandatory program was feasible after all, but the department declined to take further action, pleading resource limitations. The court reversed. Essentially, the court reasoned that, because the department had put so much work into this particular monitoring program already, the usual judicial deference to agencies in their resource allocation decisions need not apply.

To say the least, the court was treading into dangerous territory here. The additional steps the department would have to take in order to complete the rulemaking ordered by the court do not seem minimal. The assistant director who had declined to go forward had "focused primarily on the Department's limited resources, noting in particular the budget and staff constraints in the rulemaking section of his division, and he stressed the importance of setting priorities for the allocation of scarce resources. In his view, 'any substantial new rulemaking project would require new budget or the displacement of other agency activities." Because the subject area was contentious, the department would need to "develop and evaluate a voluminous record, and to prepare for likely litigation." Moreover, as the dissent in the Washington Supreme Court observed, the department had no experience in designing medical monitoring requirements, because in the past it had simply copied from models already adopted by OSHA. As the director noted, "it is not unusual for an OSHA rule of this complexity to require 10 to 15 years from start to finish, and thus the Department does not undertake lightly to engage in rulemaking for which there is no OSHA standard." 39 P.2d at 981 (Madsen, J., dissenting). Consider, also, the potentially perverse incentive effects of the majority's holding. If investment of resources to study a problem can lead to a judicial mandate to take action on the study, the department may be a lot less amenable to conducting preliminary studies of other workplace risks in the future. *See id.* at 980. Even if we assume that some of these dire warnings were exaggerated, we believe that they accurately reflect the *types* of hazards that a judicial holding of this kind may bring about.

5. *Deadline for response.* The idea of requiring an agency to respond to a petition for rulemaking within a specified period is reasonable. The agency may not have to give a very lengthy response, especially if the petition itself is on the perfunctory side; but, arguably, the agency should at least give a yes-or-no answer within some determinate period. (Section 555(e) does require "prompt notice ... of the denial" of such a petition, but, aside from the vagueness of the term "prompt," this language does not necessarily mean that the agency must *make a decision* promptly. In practice, the agency may not make one at all.)

However, some federal regulatory legislation already contains such deadlines, and Luneburg finds them problematic:

[E]ven where these statutory deadlines exist, they are often not met by the agency because, to the extent Congress contemplated that a grant or denial should be preceded by more than cursory examination, they may be unrealistic in view of the difficult issues raised by some petitions. To the extent the agency tries meeting the deadline in most cases, its ability to pursue its own regulatory agenda may be substantially undermined. If the deadlines are met, it may only be because the agency considers that a grant involves no more than a polite "thank you" for an idea that may be worthy of further consideration, without any legal obligation for the agency to formally commence a rulemaking by the issuance of [a § 553(b) notice]. The grant may seem to be the least risky course to follow since a denial may prompt the disappointed petitioner to seek judicial review. However, the agency may opt for a summary dismissal where judicial review seems unlikely and the agency considers meeting the statutory deadline to be more important than evaluating the merits of the petition to the degree which it may deserve. In neither case does the statutory deadline necessarily accomplish much in forcing an agency to consider seriously an outside proposal.

1988 Wis.L.Rev. at 16. Luneburg suggests that a more effective solution would be for agencies to impose targets on themselves. *Id.* at 17. The ACUS recommendation cited in N.6 endorsed that idea. Later, ACUS reaffirmed that position—but then it added that, "if necessary, the President by executive order or Congress should mandate that petitions be acted upon within a specified time." ACUS Recommendation 95-3, 60 Fed.Reg. 43109 (1995). The preamble suggested 12-18 months as a suitable time limit. This later ACUS recommendation seems to have been intended to head off the even stricter provisions of then-pending regulatory reform bills. *See, e.g.,* S. 343, 104th Cong. § 553(e)(4), S.Rep.No. 104-90, at 4 (1995) (180-day limit).

6. *Agency procedures for dealing with petitions.* Luneburg thinks the issue of regular comment periods for rulemaking petitions poses a "close question." 1988 Wis.L.Rev. at 30-31. Public input could help overcome bureaucratic inertia; it may also promote rigorous analysis, because the courts would expect a reasoned response to any thoughtful comments. But comment periods also may elicit minimal or unhelpful responses, the value of which may be outweighed by the delays and costs they would add to the process. Moreover, he notes, petitioners themselves typically have means of stimulating public debate and submissions to the agency, and it may be fair to place the burden of generating supportive comment on them rather than on the agency.

7. *Reexamination of existing rules.* The idea of a systematic, action-forcing mechanism to stimulate rule review is attractive, because of the inherent tendency of agencies to undervalue this function. However, while systematic approaches permit agencies to plan their activities, they could lead to overbreadth problems. Because they consume scarce resources (not only dollars, but time and attention of key personnel), it is important to define their scope carefully. In that context, a requirement that agencies must review all of their regulations within some relatively short defined period seems extravagant. It works at some agencies, according to Eisner and Kaleta, 48 Admin.L.Rev. at 143, but at others it would be a waste. Some regulations will be functioning satisfactorily to everyone concerned and require no serious attention. The GAO's finding that voluntary reviews are more likely to lead to actual regulatory changes than are mandated reviews should surprise no one. Thus, a better system for reexamination of existing rules may be one that requires a serious review commitment but allows agencies to make their own selections of the rules that most need review, or to accept nominations from the regulated public.

In *Cellco* the D.C. Circuit upheld the FCC's interpretation of the biennial regulatory review provision of the Telecommunications Act. The court said that the similarity in wording between that provision and the Commission's basic rulemaking authority suggested that the word "necessary" in the two provisions should be given a similar meaning. Or at least the language was ambiguous enough to allow the Commission to reach that result under *Chevron.* As for the deregulatory purposes of the 1996 law, the court said that the language of the biennial review provision embody that purpose as fully as the petitioner in *Cellco* claimed. Rather, the duty (or presumptive duty) to repeal a regulation would arise only *after* the rule had been deemed not to be "necessary in the public interest." The goal of deregulation did not have to dominate the Commission's consideration of the "necessity" issue itself.

8. *Delay in completing rulemaking proceedings.* When a scholar like Richard Pierce, who is usually a harsh critic of tight judicial control over the rulemaking process, calls for the courts to get tougher, one certainly should pay attention. His stance apparently stems from the high value that he places on political accountability in a democracy. Elected legislators are accountable, so let them either take the heat or fix the problem. However, we think that this line of argument is strongest when a *specific* issue is squarely before the legislature. It is less persuasive when the critique pertains to an endemic tendency arising out of the collective action of numerous committees. Each committee may think well of the mandates that it originated, despite the harmful effects of the overall pattern. Furthermore, the proliferation of statutory deadlines bears many earmarks of the familiar legislative propensity to claim credit for taking a strong stand while blaming agencies for failing to do what Congress instructed—hardly the political system working at its democratic best.

In this context, we see force in Judge Wald's doubts about the feasibility and desirability of strictly enforcing all statutory deadlines: "The problem with this `high road' approach is that the too hastily conceived or executed rule will probably stand a greater risk of being thrown out eventually for lack of reasoned decisionmaking and, thereby, add to that resource-skewing pool of remands about which Pierce is worried." 49 Admin.L.Rev. at 664. She makes clear that courts cannot simply accept agencies' blanket assertions that they have delayed a rule because they are overworked (she was a member of the panel in the *Chemical Workers* case cited in this note). She suggests, however, that if an agency came forward with a rational plan that rank-ordered statutory deadlines according to a comparative assessment of the public benefits expected from various pending rules, a court might do well to acquiesce in it.

9. *Lapse of rulemaking proceedings.* In his treatise, Bonfield supports the time limit for the reasons stated in the official 1981 MSAPA Comment. In his view, it bolsters the political function of rulemaking proceedings, i.e., ensuring that rules will be acceptable to the community at

large. He adds that the six-month period "would appear to be long enough for a state agency to adopt even the most complex rule that is likely to be before it." Arthur Earl Bonfield, STATE ADMINISTRATIVE RULE MAKING 230-32 (1986).

We, however, are more inclined to think that an agency might be legitimately unable to finish a particular rulemaking within a limited period, due to staff shortages or staff turnover or a flood of public comments. Or the agency might be pursuing extended consultations with political and community leaders, in order to craft a compromise that might *improve* the public acceptability of the final product. In such cases, it would be wasteful or counterproductive to compel the agency to start all over again. Moreover, an agency that suddenly adopts a long-forgotten rule could be expected to pay a political price for that tactic. Since, by hypothesis, the agency is assumed to be sensitive to public opinion, it would have an incentive not to repeat the maneuver very often.

Note that the 180-day figure in the MSAPA is bracketed, so in principle a state could adjust the length of the period to suit its particular needs. The argument about the time limit really comes down to deciding which kind of risks one is more willing to take. On the whole, the time limit approach will probably work best in states with agencies that have an undemanding workload. As the complexity of agencies' assignments increases, the rulemaking process becomes more ossified, and budgets shrink, the costs of the time limit are likely to look increasingly troublesome.

10. *Problem.* In *AHPA* the court reaffirmed the usual case-law admonition that reversal of a rulemaking petition denial is reserved for the "rarest and most compelling of circumstances," but went on to find that this was such a case. The availability of new information may not be enough to warrant disturbing the Secretary's decision. He could possibly believe that the university researchers' findings were not conclusive enough to justify launching a new proceeding. (We have not included in the problem some of the aggravating circumstances of the real *AHPA* case, which involved the department first embracing, then backing off from, the implications of the university study.)

More troubling is the Secretary's suggestion that "retaining the desired gait" is one of the objectives he is supposed to pursue. As the court said, the Horse Protection Act appears designed to end soring, with no suggestion of solicitude for owners who favor that practice. Thus, the Secretary's decision suggests that he has proceeded on an incorrect legal premise, thus committing an error resembling that of the FPC in the *NAACP* case discussed in N.3. Put that problem together with the basically conclusory nature of the Secretary's decision, which does not seem adequate to enable the court to perform its reviewing role, and one sees a fairly strong case for reversal. After all, the Secretary did not argue that his resources were too limited to allow him to conduct further rulemaking to curb soring.

Luneburg concludes from *AHPA* that the court's analysis and result belied its claim to be applying a "narrow" standard of review. 1988 Wis.L.Rev. at 53-54. One could say in the court's behalf that *AHPA* was simply an unusual *kind* of case, presenting circumstances different from the more common situation in which an agency pleads competing obligations. Either way, students should see from this exercise that general pronouncements about a "narrow" review standard don't resolve concrete cases.

On the relief issue, the D.C. Circuit opted for a remand for a better explanation, not a mandate to commence rulemaking forthwith. That choice seems appropriate. Lack of satisfactory explanation is a big part of the problem with the Secretary's decision; therefore, he should be asked to provide a better one. Perhaps he can make a case that the facts are more ambiguous than HDA maintains, or that competing priorities require greater attention. HDA might argue here that the Secretary's previous misreading of the statute shows bad faith and justifies a firm judicial line. But, as one sees in the "delay" cases, courts are usually pretty tolerant of inaction; the Secretary now has one strike against him but most courts wouldn't say he has struck out.

After the remand, however, the Secretary again rejected AHPA's petition, and AHPA appealed again. This time, the district court directed the department to commence rulemaking immediately. *AHPA v. Lyng,* 618 F.Supp. 949 (D.D.C.1988). The judge was clearly disturbed by what he saw as the department's "lame attempt" (sic) to discredit with nitpicking criticisms a study that the agency itself had commissioned.

§ 6.4 WAIVERS OF RULES

WAIT RADIO v. FCC

Notes and Questions

2. *Must waivers be available?* There is language in *WAIT Radio* that can support the position of cases like *BellSouth* and *Turro* (e.g., "the agency's discretion to proceed *in difficult areas* through general rules is intimately linked to the existence of a safety valve procedure" (emphasis added)). But the impression conveyed by the earlier opinion as a whole is that the court strongly expected an agency to entertain waiver petitions seriously in a wide range of cases. Much has changed since then. *WAIT Radio* is a classic Leventhal essay that projects confidence that courts can

help agencies strike a judicious balance between generality and particularity of treatment. Today's judicial sensibility is much more cautious.

Realistically speaking, rules without exceptions are part of everyday life. It is not surprising, therefore, that the FAA was able for so long to maintain its bright-line rule in the highly sensitive area of air safety. The strict age-60 rule had remarkable staying power. A critical factor that led to its demise was the decision by the International Civil Aviation Organization, a United Nations group, to allow pilots to fly until age 65. When that standard took effect in November 2006, older pilots employed by foreign airlines were able to fly into and out of American airports. This made the enforcement of an age 60 retirement age for American pilots hard to justify as a safety measure. The FAA commenced a rulemaking proceeding to raise the retirement age the following January. That proceeding was expected to take at least a year and a half to conclude, but Congress cut it short by passing the so-called Fair Treatment for Experienced Pilots Act in December 2007.

3. *Abuse of discretion review.* *Alizoti* is a curious case, because the petitioner loses even though the panel majority all but acknowledges that she deserved her waiver. The issue quickly comes down to a debate about the limits of the judicial role. The majority thinks it is being asked to provide "*de novo* review." While it may be correct that complete substitution of judicial for administrative judgment could bring "chaos to the review process," relief in this case would not have required the court to go so far. The panel decision (written by a district judge from the Western District of Kentucky, sitting by designation) seems to discern no middle ground between de novo review and a completely hands-off attitude. We think the dissent had the better of this argument. Oddball cases like this one, involving an apparently innocent petitioner whose case was simply mishandled by various bureaucrats, probably don't come along very often. When they do, a judicial willingness to conduct serious abuse of discretion review is part of our system.

6. *Florida provision.* Rossi supports programs through which agencies are *permitted* to grant waivers, as his article on FERC (quoted in N.1) indicates. However, he has doubts about the Florida statute's unique directive that agencies *shall* allow waivers or variances under the statutorily specified conditions:

> Florida's new waiver provision potentially goes from one extreme—no waiver—to another—mandatory waiver. The result may be to open agency floodgates to requests for special treatment from regulated persons. Moreover, regulated interests will face increased incentives to appeal to the [state's central hearing panel] or to courts, inviting these non-political institutions to second-guess agency judgment as

to a regulatory program's goals.

> To the extent that regulated parties begin to perceive an entitlement to waiver, the new Florida provision may undermine its flexibility objective. The provision will have reduced, not increased, agency discretion.

49 Admin.L.Rev. at 357. Rossi adds that the magnitude of these costs may depend on how deferentially the statute is applied. *Id.* at 358. As written, however, the provision seems to be less concerned with "flexibility" than with pushing Florida in the direction of deregulation. Or, to put it another way, it can be expected to promote flexibility for the *regulated*, but not necessarily for the *regulators*.

7. *Problem.* (a) *HSL case.* The court decision in the HSL case is more or less identical to the *Advocates* case. It provides an opportunity to explore the point that, while waiver programs serve admirable purposes, they can also conflict with important regulatory objectives. The fact situation is a good illustration of this tension. Most people want reasonable accommodation of the disabled, but they also want the drivers of eighteen-wheelers passing them on the freeway to be fully qualified. The material in N.5 can be discussed in this connection. In the problem a public interest group was ready, willing, and able to jump into the fray on the pro-regulation side, but students should be able to see that this won't always be the case, and waivers may serve to undercut legitimate requirements that protect the public.

(b) *Bert's case.* One could see the FHWA's response to Bert as similar to the agency explanation that led to reversal in *WAIT Radio*—i.e., as saying little more than that the agency is hostile to waivers and doesn't intend to take seriously any request for one. As the Eighth Circuit put it in *Rauenhorst,* the agency's reasoning "completely defeats any statutory provision for waivers for cause," 95 F.2d at 722. This premise could lead a reviewing court to follow *WAIT Radio* by declaring that requests for waivers are fundamental elements of a regulatory system and deserve a substantive response. The Eighth Circuit certainly thought Mr. Rauenhorst had a credible case. It held that the FHWA had been arbitrary and capricious in refusing the petitioner a waiver. The opinion leaves little doubt that, in the court's view, the FHWA had been dragging its feet in failing to come to terms with overwhelming evidence that people like Rauenhorst deserved to be accommodated.

However, it is also possible to see the FHWA's response in a more sympathetic light. After all, the agency's fear that "if we do it for you, we'll have to do it for everybody" was not fanciful. *See* § 4.4.2 of the casebook. (In fact, it was somewhat corroborated by the Eighth Circuit's decision itself.

Another monocular driver, Breth, had previously been turned down for a waiver and had brought suit. In a settlement agreement the FHWA had admitted him into the experimental program. So the Eighth Circuit said: if that was okay for Breth, why not for Rauenhorst?) The point that the agency tried to make, to no avail, was that the right way to revise its safety regulation was through the § 553 rulemaking process, and that the orderly unfolding of that process, including the ongoing controlled experiment, would be undercut if the agency had to resolve the same issues through the waiver process. (As for the Eighth Circuit's suggestion that the agency was simply being dilatory in the face of the obvious obsolescence of its rules, remember the D.C. Circuit's conclusion only two years earlier that the agency appeared to be putting *too little* emphasis on safety. You can imagine how the agency must have felt about receiving these judicial mixed signals.)

In any event, the most that Bert is likely to get from a federal court is an order directing the FHWA to consider his waiver application on some individualized basis. The court is less likely to second-guess the agency on the ultimate question of whether Bert in particular deserves the waiver. (Remind students that in *WAIT Radio* itself, the FCC wrote a more substantive decision on remand, again denying the station's application for waiver, and the court affirmed.) However, disability law principles might spur the court to take a more assertive position. *Cf. Parker v. USDOT*, 207 F.3d 359 (6th Cir.2000), holding that FHWA's rejection of the plaintiff's (timely) application to participate in the waiver program was arbitrary and capricious. He not only was monocular but also had lost part of his left arm—but he did have a good driving record. The court's point was that he was entitled under the Rehabilitation Act to an individualized determination and could not be excluded on the basis of a per se rule against giving waivers to persons with multiple disabilities. So, again, the court did not overtly second-guess the agency's judgment on the individual level (though it came close).

This discussion sets up the question of how well Bert could do under a state law like Florida's. His prospects look pretty good. Clearly he can meet the "substantial hardship" test of the Florida statute. He also can argue that he intends to satisfy the "purpose" of the regulation by driving carefully, in a manner that compensates for his disability—as monocular drivers have apparently been doing with much success for some time. That logic calls for a slightly strained interpretation of the "purpose" clause of the Florida statute, but it seems well within the spirit of that clause. Thus, a court would probably conclude that his waiver application falls within the facial scope of the statute.

The critical question is whether Bert will be able to show that he can *in fact* drive safely enough to meet the purposes of the regulatory scheme.

The agency is not currently disposed to believe this. But since the statute seems to be worded in such a manner as to create an entitlement, judicial review might prove quite intrusive. The policy issues surrounding the Florida statute—whether we should be more concerned about inflexible bureaucrats than about inexpert courts and a flood of applicants—are certainly implicated here.

For example, suppose Bert shows that he can drive *almost as safely* as commercial drivers who are not covered by the rule. The outcome would probably turn on how deferentially the court reviews the agency's determinations under the waiver statute. He might win, if a court were to consider his almost-as-good driving *safe enough* to meet the statutory purpose.

Postscript. Teachers with knowledge of disability law may notice that the regulatory program in this case was also the subject of a Supreme Court case on the Americans With Disabilities Act. In *Albertson's, Inc. v. Kirkingsburg*, 527 U.S. 555 (2000), an interstate carrier fired a monocular driver for failing to meet federal vision requirements, and it refused to rehire him even after he had obtained a FHWA waiver. The Court said that the employer was entitled to rely on the FHWA regulation as stating a valid safety qualification, even though the agency was taking tentative steps toward modifying it through the experimental waiver program. Thus, the employer had not violated the ADA.

Subsequent to the events in the problem, the relevant duties of the FHWA have been transferred to the Federal Motor Carrier Safety Administration (also part of DOT). The FMCSA has been given new statutory authority to grant waivers on an individualized basis "if the Secretary determines that it is in the public interest to grant the waiver and that the waiver is likely to achieve a level of safety that is equivalent to, or greater than, the level of safety that would be obtained in the absence of the waiver." 49 U.S.C. § 31315(a). It now exercises that authority on a regularized basis, having decided that the experimental waiver program was a success. *See, e.g.,* 71 Fed.Reg. 30,227 (2006) (granting waivers).

CHAPTER 7: CONTROL OF AGENCIES BY THE POLITICAL BRANCHES OF GOVERNMENT

§ 7.2 DELEGATION OF LEGISLATIVE POWER TO AGENCIES

§ 7.2.1 The Nondelegation Doctrine and Federal Agencies

§ 7.2.1a From *Field* to the New Deal

Field is an early example of the Supreme Court talking out of both sides of its mouth. It asserts that Congress cannot delegate the power to make law—and then upholds a delegation to the executive branch of a difficult and highly political legislative decision.

Field presents a typical example of the need for delegated legislation—Congress was moved to action by an international trade problem caused by perceived unfair foreign trade practices. However, it could not solve the problem itself by either imposing trade sanctions or establishing a clear formula identifying the events that would trigger sanctions. Matters had to be left to an executive branch actor, here the President, who (operating under a vague standard) could stay on top of changing developments, engage in quiet and complex negotiations with foreign powers, make the necessary economic studies, and take appropriate action at the appropriate time reflecting highly complex domestic and international political calculations. It would also be typical of the legislative process that the measure represented a compromise between those members who wanted immediate sanctions against foreign nations and those who wanted none at all.

Because the nondelegation doctrine in the bald form stated by the *Field* Court plainly could not be accommodated to modern government, the Supreme Court declined to enforce it literally in *Field* and subsequent cases. While asserting that the principle was "vital" to the "integrity" of constitutional government (without citing any authority for that proposition), the Court was obviously unable to follow it.

The rationale for a standards or intelligible principle requirement is that it allows the court to pretend that no "delegation" really occurred. By providing standards, the legislature purported to limit administrative discretion. Standards also permit a reviewing court to assess whether the agent carried out legislative intent. Thus, the principle of checks and balances is satisfied. However, the effect of such "standards" can be purely cosmetic. Many modern regulatory statutes involve such empty standards that this rationale is a sham. An agency would hardly claim to have power to adopt rules that are not in the "public interest" or to prevent practices that are "fair" or adopt rules that are not "feasible." Instead, these statutes are delegations of power to agencies to do good and prevent bad—and give no more guidance than that. In *Industrial Union,* Rehnquist makes this point very well.

The decision in *Panama* seems downright silly. The President's power was narrowly circumscribed, and in context, there was abundant evidence of what Congress wanted. The delegation was even narrower than in *Field*, where the President had to make elaborate economic studies and political calculations before taking a specifically defined act. *Panama* could be consistent only with an idealized vision of government in which no legislative power could be delegated at all. *Schechter*, on the other hand, is not so absurd. The breadth of the delegation was breathtaking—a delegation of authority to do just about anything in the economic sphere, in the hope that it might work to turn the economy around. The difference in the breadth or scope of the delegations in *Panama* and *Schechter* explains the difference in Cardozo's position. If one believes in a judicially enforceable nondelegation doctrine, *Schechter* was the ideal case to assert it.

Later cases sought to explain *Panama* and *Schechter* by pointing to the severe procedural defects of NIRA—a point made obliquely by Cardozo at the end of the quoted material. This supports the argument, to be developed later in the text, that safeguards, such as fair administrative procedures, can be more important than legislative standards. In the case of NIRA, there was no defined agency to adopt and to administer the codes. There was no formal publication of the codes of fair competition and no formal process for obtaining public comment on the codes. Indeed, the administration of NIRA was characterized by a huge output of material (codes and interpretive material on the codes) and vast confusion. For example, it appeared that the enforcement provisions of the "petroleum code" involved in the *Panama* case had been accidentally amended out of existence. The lack of a centralized system for publishing important federal documents, which was highlighted in the NIRA cases, led to the adoption of the Federal Register Act. *See* § 5.7.

Another important point about *Schechter* is that, in practical operation, private companies were regulating their competitors. Trade associations, often controlled by a few dominant enterprises, proposed and wrote the codes without any process for public input or any hearings. Nor, as a practical matter, was there much intervention by federal officials (who were under intense time pressure to produce codes governing the entire economy). The "poultry code," for example, was used by chicken wholesalers to force an unwelcome practice on retailers—they had to take whatever "sick chickens" were offered to them. The anti-competitive elements of such a scheme of regulation are obvious and objectionable. We discuss delegation to private parties further in § 7.2.2.

§ 7.2.1b From the New Deal to the Present

The notions that the courts had an obligation to protect the free market from legislative regulation and to protect state economic regulation from federal interference were already history by the time *Yakus* came to the Supreme Court in 1944. The Court remembered well the hard lessons it had learned (such as Roosevelt's Court-packing plan) when it had tried to thwart the New Deal. Thus, only Justice Roberts dissented on delegation grounds. It is important to emphasize Stone's argument that the Constitution does not demand the impossible or impracticable; we have to be practical and flexible—and that requires a flexible nondelegation doctrine.

In *Yakus*, the Court failed even to mention *Panama* and distinguished *Schechter* on the spurious ground that NIRA provided no standards. In fact, the 1942 price control act gave no meaningful guidance for solving the infinite number of tough decisions invariably attending the process of price control—how much do you accommodate individual differences between producers, how much profit should you allow, how much advertising should be permitted, how do you balance the need for stable prices with the need for production incentives or for suppressing demand, etc. Congress wanted to stop wartime inflation, it suggested October, 1941 prices as a consideration, and it turned over the whole job to the Administrator.

As a practical matter, there was little difference in the guidance furnished by Congress in *Schechter* and in *Yakus*. The *Yakus* delegation was quite as sweeping (it covered prices and rents in the entire economy). As in *Schechter*, there was an economic emergency. Congress had to act, but could not even begin to deal with the problem itself. Only a delegation of great breadth could possibly address such a problem. This time the Court was prepared to let Congress do what it had to do. True, Congress acted under the war power rather than the commerce power, and that may provide a ground for distinguishing the cases.

The *Yakus* opinion observed that the statute required a statement of considerations for adopting price regulations, which distinguished the case from *Schechter*. However, there was no requirement of any prior hearings, or even any public notice and comment, before the agency adopted regulations (although the statute provided for a protest procedure after they were adopted). Judicial review was available—but only if one protested the regulation, and only within sixty days after the protest was rejected. No judicial review of a price standard was available upon criminal prosecution for violating the standard. Thus the procedural protections for persons harmed by the standards were not at all adequate, at least by present standards.

Yakus also observed that the purpose of requiring standards was to facilitate judicial review of the agency's action. However, as just noted, judicial review was very much restricted under the Emergency Price Control Act. *Yakus* held that it was constitutional to preclude judicial review of a regulation upon the criminal prosecution of a violator. In any event, there was an absence of legislative discretion-restricting standards in the Price Control Act, and the statute, therefore, contributed very little to facilitating judicial control.

§ 7.2.1c Revival of the Nondelegation Doctrine

INDUSTRIAL UNION DEPARTMENT, AFL-CIO v. AMERICAN PETROLEUM INSTITUTE

WHITMAN v. AMERICAN TRUCKING ASS'NS

For a doctrine often described as moribund, the nondelegation doctrine shows flickering signs of life. It's almost as though the Supreme Court is trying to keep the *Schechter* and *Panama* decisions around, just in case they might need them some day to invalidate some particularly obnoxious piece of legislation (see the problems below for possible candidates for such treatment). Supreme Court dissenters argue that the nondelegation doctrine should be applied to the case at hand, including both Rehnquist and Burger in *American Textile Mfrs. Inst. v. Donovan*, 452 U.S. 490 (1981). Thomas suggests in his *American Trucking* dissent that he'd like to broaden the doctrine by invaliding statutes that contain intelligible principles but are otherwise too vague and sweeping (as many of them are, of course). *Industrial Union* twisted the statute, supposedly to avoid holding that it violated the nondelegation doctrine. Scalia's opinion in *American Trucking* specifically endorsed both *Panama* and *Schechter* and went on to say:

> It is true enough that the degree of agency discretion that is acceptable varies according to the scope of the power congressionally conferred. While Congress need not provide any direction to the EPA regarding the manner in which it is to define "country elevators," which are to be exempt from new-stationary-source regulations governing grain elevators, it must provide substantial guidance on setting air standards that affect the entire national economy.

This "substantial guidance" standard could be wielded as a weapon against legislation that delegates so much unaccountable power to the Executive that the Court decides it should be struck down. For another sign of the nondelegation doctrine's life, see the dissenting opinion of Judge Janice Rogers Brown in *Michigan Gambling Opposition v. Kempthorne*, 525 F.3d 23 (D.C.Cir.2008), which argued that the provision allowing the

Secretary of the Interior to take lands "for Indians" violates the nondelegation doctrine, since it states no standards at all. (The Secretary of the Interior placed 147 acres of rural land into trust to enable a tribe to build a casino.)

Another possible explanation for the Supreme Court's failure to launch a full-scale assault on the venerable nondelegation doctrine is that they simply see no need to do so. In any given case, they can just as easily hold that a challenged statute satisfies the doctrine's not-very-confining requirements.

Notes and Questions

1. *Purposes of the standards requirement.* Rehnquist makes several arguments in favor of the nondelegation doctrine and its standards requirement. First, the nondelegation doctrine ensures that "to the extent consistent with orderly governmental administration . . . important choices of social policy are made by Congress, the branch of our government most responsive to the popular will." This argument asserts that elected legislators (rather than unelected administrators) should make the tough calls. It is a variation on the idea that ours is a government of laws, not of men; by giving excessive discretion to the "men" who run agencies, we are not being governed by "laws." This argument is often phrased in terms of accountability—the people should be able to use their votes to give credit for political decisions they like or to assess blame for decisions they dislike. When Congress makes the tough calls, this is possible; when Congress ducks them by passing them on to unelected agents, it is more difficult for the people to hold anyone accountable.

Of course, nothing prevents the people from blaming or giving credit to Congress for delegating particular decisions to agencies and for the particular agency decisions executed under such delegations. One might also argue that the people want Congress to take action against perceived problems. If Congress discovers that it needs to delegate broad authority to agencies in order to solve those problems, or because it believes an expert agency is in a better position to solve those problems, a majority of the voters might well approve such a course of action.

Second, Rehnquist says, the nondelegation doctrine ensures that there is a legislative standard, an "intelligible principle," to guide the agency in its exercise of the delegated discretion. Third, the doctrine ensures that reviewing courts can test exercises of delegated discretion against ascertainable legislative standards. As noted earlier, the "standards" or "intelligible principles" that have actually been upheld by the courts are often totally indeterminate. Many leave so much discretion to agencies that any rational exercise of the delegated power is at least arguably consistent with the standards. The question then becomes whether the nondelegation doctrine should be "revived," so that Rehnquist's objectives might be more fully realized.

Standards to constrain the administrator may be found in the legislative history of the enabling act, in the purpose of that statute, in other statutes that may be read in pari materia with the enabling act, in the nature of the subject matter, in the past pattern of agency action under the enabling act, and in the constitutional and common law concepts of reasonableness. *See, e.g., Michigan Gambling Opposition, supra*, holding that the phrase "for Indians" (in a statute allowing the federal government to take land) provides an intelligible principle, because the history and structure of the statute and its legislative history show that its purpose is to further Indian economic development and self governance. The court also quoted the language from *American Trucking* that "the degree of agency discretion that is acceptable varies according to the scope of the power congressionally conferred," noting that this case involved taking specific parcels of land for a casino, a power that is not so broad as to require limiting principles more specific than pursuing Indian economic development. The court also relied on the President's traditional authority in conducting relations with Indians. Judge Brown's dissent argued that the implications of taking land are vast (because it removes the land from state jurisdiction and taxation) and that the majority had conjured standards out of thin air. "To say the purpose is to provide land for Indians in a broad effort to promote economic development . . . is tautology on steroids." 525 F.3d at 37.

Courts have often required more precise standards in a legislative delegation when the statute threatens a fundamental right such as freedom of speech. *See Shuttlesworth v. Birmingham,* 394 U.S. 147 (1969), which invalidated a delegation to issue a parade permit "unless in [the City Commission's] judgment the public welfare, peace, safety, health, decency, good order, morals or convenience required that it be refused." Distinguishing cases in which such vague standards as these have been upheld in cases involving economic interests, *Shuttlesworth* insisted that "narrow, objective, and definite standards [are necessary] to guide the licensing authority" in the First Amendment area.

Shuttlesworth calls for especially precise standards when a legislative delegation affects a fundamental constitutional right such as freedom of speech. In a way, this requirement is attractive, because of the societal consensus that rights of that kind deserve special protection. The danger to such a right from a standardless delegation is quite severe. The idea that delegations implicating First Amendment concerns (such as exclusions from public fora) must be limited by objective and definite standards was reprised in *Arkansas Educ. TV Comm'n v. Forbes,* 523 U.S. 666 (1998), which upheld a public television station's exclusion of a minor party candidate from a campaign debate. The majority paid little attention to the nondelegation doctrine, but it is discussed extensively in Justice Stevens's dissent. Stevens objected that the station was unconstrained by any standards in deciding which candidates to include or exclude. This made it possible for the exclusion decision to be based on improper grounds such as viewpoint discrimination. The majority's unwillingness to apply *Shuttlesworth* here may be related to the exceptional status of public broadcasting stations. Although they are engaged in "state action" for First Amendment purposes, they are deliberately given more autonomy than the average state agency enjoys, so that they can exercise what the Court called "editorial discretion."

2. *Safeguards and nondelegation.* The nondelegation doctrine and its legislative standards requirement is calculated to make agencies political and judicially accountable and prevent abuse of discretion. Safeguards in the form of protective procedures, judicial review, and agency-created standards may perform those same functions. Rulemaking procedures (such as notice and comment, a reasons requirement, and a publication requirement) help to insure that agency action is politically acceptable and not arbitrary. Similarly, the requirements of notice, hearing, and findings in adjudication may minimize the likelihood of arbitrariness. Judicial review is a critically important safeguard against arbitrary actions. Thus procedural safeguards plus judicial review may provide for a checking function that substitutes for the presence of statutory standards. However, the safeguards approach involves the same problems as the standards approach—how many safeguards are enough? If, for example, the notice and comment requirements don't apply because of an APA exception (such as the good cause requirement), and the statute precludes judicial review, would that render the statute unconstitutional? (See the "bird flu" and "blanket waivers" problems below).

Davis points out that if legislative standards fail to constrain agency discretion, agency-created standards may accomplish the same result. Agencies are in a position to progressively refine the broad statutory standards under which they operate as they gain experience in implementing the statute. Such agency-generated discretion-limiting standards may serve a checking function that substitutes for the presence of statutory standards. And these agency-generated standards could be applied when the rules are subjected to judicial review. However, the Supreme Court in *American Trucking* rejected the lower court's decision that agency-created standards could substitute for a lack of statutory standards. Scalia explains that if the statute violates the nondelegation doctrine, the defect cannot be repaired by the agency (however, the statute itself passed muster, so the discussion of this issue was not necessary to the result). Sunstein criticizes this aspect of *American Trucking*. Cass R. Sunstein, "Is OSHA Unconstitutional?" 94 Va. L. Rev. 1407 (2008).

The Supreme Court's hesitation on this point is understandable. If agency-created standards can substitute for statutory standards, courts will be encouraged to apply the nondelegation doctrine to vague legislation and to remand cases to agencies to supply discretion-limiting standards (as the lower court did in *American Trucking*). However, generations of experience have taught the Supreme Court (and even Justice Scalia!) to shun the nondelegation doctrine. As Richard Stewart points out, the doctrine simply doesn't work, because you can't say how much delegation is too much, and the resulting uncertainty invites endless litigation and highly politicized decisions. The same problem would apply to a requirement of agency-created standards, and the result would be a swamp of conflicting and politicized decisions. This approach would invite regulated parties to challenge every broad delegation-authorizing statute, and that, in turn, would gravely imperil the operation of regulatory and health and safety statutes. Moreover, the Davis approach leads to the odd conclusion that a statute might be valid when passed but later (perhaps years later) become invalid because the agency has failed during that period to adopt discretion-confining standards.

Davis seems to contemplate aggressive use of the thesis that procedural safeguards and agency-created standards can legitimize agency action in the same manner as legislatively created standards. But it is not clear that Davis' proposal has much to do with unlawful delegation of legislative power. He argues that agency action under a delegation should be invalidated if not accompanied by adequate procedural and substantive safeguards, and that if the legislature does not provide those safeguards, the agency may subsequently do so, thereby legitimating its action under that delegation. If so, Davis is really offering a solution for potentially abusive agency action under a delegation, rather than for improper legislative action in transferring authority to the agency in the first place.

3. *Arguments for reviving nondelegation doctrine.* The general reasons for revival of the nondelegation doctrine suggested by Rehnquist in *Industrial Union*, and by Schoenbrod and Scalia, have some merit, but it would be difficult to achieve these benefits in practice, as Stewart argues in N.4.

The idea that courts should overturn delegations because the legislature is institutionally incapable of making the tough decisions itself is both attractive and dangerous. It is attractive because a serious revival of the nondelegation doctrine could force Congress to shoulder its proper decisionmaking responsibilities. On the other hand, revival of the legislative standards doctrine might leave our political community unable to deal with the sort of extremely complex and highly politicized problems that the legislature could only solve through very broad delegations.

Scalia argues that the current law legitimates delegation of legislative authority to the courts who must "ultimately determine the content of standardless legislation," rather than to the agencies, and that revival of the nondelegation doctrine would diminish judicial rather than administrative authority. There is an element of truth in this. The Stevens opinion in *Industrial Union* is illustrative. The plurality's "significant risk" test is not an obvious construction of the words of the statute and appears to rest on the Court's belief that the statute sweeps too broadly and needs to be curtailed somehow. However, a revived nondelegation doctrine would transfer far more power to courts than they have now, since they would have to examine every single delegation in every federal statute to see whether Congress should have done more than it did.

An article that makes public-choice oriented arguments similar to Schoenbrod's is Peter Aronson, Ernest Gellhorn, & Glen Robinson, "A Theory of Legislative Delegation," 68 Cornell L. Rev. 1 (1982). These authors argue that the nondelegation doctrine should be revived in order to block the enactment of laws dictated by special interests. Granted, a stern non-delegation doctrine would impede passage of a great deal of legislation; but these authors accept that result because they believe that most legislation should not be passed. They believe that most legislation involves private special interests redistributing wealth to themselves. Other legislation is passed at the urging of "high demanders" who seek costly and inefficient legislative solutions to real problems. We think Mashaw effectively demolishes the attempt to correlate broad delegations with rent-seeking legislation.

It would surely be preferable for Congress to make the tough calls. This would serve the cause of accountable government. It would probably be better to conduct the struggles over public policy at the more visible and politically responsive level of the legislature—rather than at the less visible and less politically responsive level of the agency. Nevertheless, broad, vague delegations seem inevitable in modern government. A serious non-delegation doctrine based on a legislative standards requirement would block enactment of a great deal of legislation deemed necessary by the political community, and would drastically cripple the effectiveness of much legislation that does pass. Consequently, many of the attempts to revive the doctrine may really be attempts to prevent legislative efforts to deal with serious social or environmental problems.

4. *Arguments against reviving nondelegation doctrine.* Stewart's critique is convincing. Legislatures cannot anticipate and answer all of the policy questions that may arise in relation to authority they have delegated to agencies, and legislatures have every reason to fuzz many of these policy questions in order to get legislation passed. Indeed, excessive specificity by the legislature can sometimes make a program totally ineffective, because

it inhibits adjustment to unforeseen circumstances.

Courts that take the nondelegation doctrine seriously will be engulfed with delegation cases since so many federal statutes contain so many different delegations. Judges who must decide whether a particular delegation is constrained by an intelligible principle or primary standard will seem partisan, because there is no intellectually respectable way by which a court can distinguish a necessary from an unnecessary delegation and an adequate from an inadequate legislative standard. It really is not possible to give a principled answer to the question of whether Congress went as far as it reasonably could in furnishing specific guidance to the agency. Thus it seems likely that Rehnquist's opinion in *Industrial Union* and Thomas's opinion in *American Trucking* flowed, in part, from doubts as to the wisdom of the underlying regulatory legislation (or the regulations themselves)— just as the Supreme Court's opinions in *Panama* and *Schechter* also flowed, undoubtedly, from judicial hostility to legislation that tampered with free markets.

Mashaw's pro-delegation argument seems to us to have much merit. The President is politically accountable for what agencies do in a much sharper way than Congress is accountable for passing broad or narrow legislation. And it makes sense to allow the President some elbow room, through broad delegations, to change agency policy inherited from a prior administration. That's what the President was elected to do.

Posner and Vermeule's article attacking the historical legitimacy of the nondelegation doctrine is also persuasive, in our opinion. The Supreme Court never properly considered whether the nondelegation doctrine, which is derived from the law of principal and agent, made any sense in the realm of separation of powers. The Court just adopted it in dictum in *Field v. Clark*—yet never actually applied it (except for the two 1935 cases). Nothing in the Constitution's history, the arguments of the founders, or the Federalist Papers lends the least support to the doctrine. In fact, early Congresses adopted numerous statutes containing extremely broad and standardless delegations which were unquestioned in court, indicating that both the founding generation and the early courts saw no problem with delegations to the executive. *See also* Ronald Levin, "One Last Haul, Via American Trucking," Admin. & Reg.L. News, Summer 2001, at 2 (nondelegation doctrine is unworkable and should be discarded, because the existing case law encourages lower courts to keep applying it).

5. *Narrow construction of statutes.* You may wish to discuss the implication of *Chevron* to the debate about whether courts should enforce a nondelegation canon. *Chevron* is a pro-delegation canon—it requires that courts uphold an agency's reasonable interpretation of an ambiguous statute. It is difficult to reconcile *Chevron* with the existence of a non-

delegation canon.

Driesen contends that the doctrine that broad delegations of authority should be construed narrowly to avoid the nondelegation doctrine suffers from all the same defects as the nondelegation doctrine itself. True, courts have often construed statutes to avoid "grave doubt" about a statute's constitutionality, but this involves constitutional values other than nondelegation, such as First Amendment or perhaps preemption or retroactivity. The moribund nature of the nondelegation doctrine suggests that there really is little doubt about the constitutionality of statutes that delegate broad powers with meaningless standards. Moreover, as *Rust* and *American Trucking* illustrate, courts can give only "reasonably available" constructions to statutes that might raise constitutional issues. Narrowly construing statutes in ways that are not "reasonably available" encourages politicized decisions by judges who disagree with the particular statutes or regulatory schemes they are called upon to interpret.

In particular, Driesen points to the holding of *American Trucking* that the nondelegation problem (if there is one) can't be solved by remanding the case to the agency to build an intelligible standard into a statute that lacks one. The Court said: "The very choice of which portion of the power to exercise—that is to say, the prescription of the standard that Congress had omitted—would itself be an exercise of the forbidden legislative authority." In other words, the fundamental policy decision must be made by Congress, not by the delegatee of the power. Asking the agency to save the statute by construing it narrowly would undermine the purpose of the nondelegation doctrine which is to force Congress to make the hard calls. But, Driesen points out, 64 U.Pitt.L.Rev. at 48-58, the same problem arises when a court narrowly construes a statute to avoid the nondelegation problem. How can the court save a statute by making the fundamental policy decisions that Congress failed to make and that the nondelegation doctrine requires Congress to make? Doing so is judicial legislation.

It's worth discussing whether the plurality opinion in *Industrial Union* makes sense. The plurality opinion reads a "significant risk" standard into the OSHA statute to save it from a nondelegation challenge. The plurality plus Rehnquist seem to be saying that OSHA had too much power, the statute should have permitted consideration of costs, and the benzene rule just went too far. In other words, *Industrial Union* was as politicized a decision as one invalidating the statute on nondelegation grounds. Others might argue that the sequence of events leading up to the rather heavy-handed judicial innovation in *Industrial Union* was an acceptable resolution of the problem of vagueness in the Act. OSHA was able to begin operating, and to generate some experience, before the question of the statute's scope had to be resolved. In a practical (if not legal) sense, that question may not been ripe for resolution any sooner. And, after all, if Congress didn't like the significant risk test, it was free to overturn that construction by amending the statute.

So one can argue that this sort of dynamic interplay among the branches of government compares favorably with a constitutional doctrine invalidating OSHA unless and until Congress resolves all the important legal issues the agency would ultimately face (or, more accurately, all issues that some judge might later decide were so important that Congress should have decided them). In short, even if, in the abstract, it would have been better for Congress to have resolved the coverage question initially, we prefer Stevens' approach to the legislature's default over Rehnquist's.

For an article supporting the D.C Circuit's approach in *American Trucking,* see Ernest Gellhorn, "The Proper Role of the Nondelegation Doctrine," 31 Env.L.Rptr. 10231 (Feb. 2001). Gellhorn contends that the D.C. Circuit was right in allowing the EPA to provide a narrowing construction of the statute. This was an application of the *Chevron* approach that requires courts to uphold reasonable agency interpretations of ambiguous statutes. (*See* § 9.2). In a thoughtful article, Sunstein discusses the interplay between *American Trucking* and *Industrial Union.* He criticizes the *American Trucking* holding that delegation problems can't be solved by narrowing standards adopted by the agency. With that option off the table, he suggests that OSHA should be interpreted to include a requirement that costs and benefits of health and safety standards must be at least proportional. Cass R. Sunstein, "Is OSHA Unconstitutional?" 94 Va. L.Rev. 1407 (2008).

6. *Problem—bird flu.* We assume that instructors would choose one of the problems in this section; few would find the time to tackle both problems. Obviously, quarantine laws raise many legal and policy issues. For a comprehensive bibliography, see http://biotech.law.lsu.edu/cases/pp/ quarantine.htm. As this manual goes to press, the crisis du jour is swine flu, not bird flu, but the problem will work as well in either case.

Presumably, Mary can raise the various arguments about invalidity of the regulations in defense of her criminal prosecution (absent some provision precluding review, as in *Yakus,* or requiring that challenges to a regulation be filed within a short period such as sixty days). This was the method used to challenge a person's draft classification under the Selective Service laws. One had to exhaust all administrative remedies before the draft board, then refuse induction and raise defenses at the time of criminal prosecution.

Are the rules valid without APA compliance? The first rule does not seem to qualify for the good cause exemption of APA § 553(b)(B), since, so far as the problem indicates, there was no emergency at the time the rule allowing the imposition of quarantines was adopted. Of course, you could add facts here suggesting that bird flu was seen as an impending crisis because cases had been reported all over the world and it could strike here at any time. Consequently, there would have been insufficient time to conduct notice and comment and then to put the quarantine procedure into place. However, it seems clear that the second rule—imposing the Oak City quarantine—is a valid emergency rule. That same emergency would also permit the agency to dispense with the 30-day pre-publication rule under the good cause exception, § 553(d)(3). Note that the APA requires that PHS must separately explain the basis for claiming the good cause exemption both for dispensing with notice and comment and disregarding the 30-day rule.

Statutes that authorize regulations and make violation of the regulations criminal are quite common. In themselves, they don't violate the nondelegation principle. *See, e.g., Grimaud v. United States*, 220 U.S. 506 (1911).

It seems unlikely that the court would invalidate the statute because of the nondelegation doctrine. There is just too much history here in which courts have refused to apply the doctrine. The statute doesn't state a standard (intelligible or otherwise), but the history of public health regulation supplies the standard. The regulations must do whatever is "appropriate and necessary" to protect the public health in the case of some type of emergency. That is more than sufficient. (There may also be helpful legislative history that indicates the nature of the powers conferred on the PHS).

However, it seems appropriate to question the particular terms of the Oak City quarantine. Here one can utilize the approach taken in *Industrial Union* or *Kent v. Dulles* and referred to as "nondelegation canons" by Sunstein. The statute is valid but should be construed in a way that avoids constitutional problems. We've already decided to construe the statute to contain the limiting words "appropriate and necessary" so that it contains an intelligible standard. But this regulation appears inappropriate and unnecessary. It verges on something that is a violation of substantive due process, because it is so arbitrary and extreme, and it perhaps interferes with the right to travel. The fact that a criminal violation and jail time are involved only magnifies the seriousness of the problem. To underline the point, what if the regulations had authorized the police to shoot on sight anybody violating the quarantine? At that point, you'd have to have some serious reservations about the validity of the regulation. (You might wish to discuss substantive due process or arbitrariness of the regulation as a separate subject from delegation.)

Surely there must be an exception for someone who must leave her home to get food for her family or to deal with some other personal emergency like going to the hospital to have a baby. Perhaps the regulation should have required that persons wear a mask when they leave their home to deal with an emergency, that they minimize contact with other people while doing so, and that they return home as soon as possible. Despite the extreme seriousness of a bird flu epidemic, this quarantine is just too rigid and a court should invalidate the regulation as applied in this case, even if it would not be prepared to invalidate the regulation on its face. It could do so using normal arbitrary-capricious review under the APA (since the strictness of the quarantine provision is not supported by the rulemaking record) or under the narrow construction approach advocated by Sunstein.

A case that illustrates narrow construction reasoning is *Boreali v. Axelrod*, 517 N.E.2d 1350 (N.Y. 1987). The case involved a similar standard-less delegation to a state public health agency (authorizing it to "deal with any matters affecting the . . . public health"). The court declined to consider whether the grant of authority violated the state's nondelegation doctrine. However, it invalidated rules adopted under authority of that statute which imposed smoking bans in public places. The court's reasoning in *Boreali* seems dubious, but the opinion makes one good point: the legislature has consistently failed to enact anti-smoking bans (forty separate bills had failed), so it seems strange that an agency could adopt them under authority of such a vague statute.

7. *Problem–blanket waivers.* Most nondelegation cases (like *Industrial Union* and *American Trucking*) grow out of an attempt by business to resist health and safety legislation. However, this isn't always the case. The blanket waiver provision of the Real ID Act is being attacked by environmentalists because it confers too much power on the government. Here it's the liberals, not the conservatives, who are entertaining the idea that a statute might violate the nondelegation rule.

In the *Defenders* case, the district court held that § 1103(c)(1) did not violate the nondelegation doctrine. The waivers had to be "necessary to ensure expeditious construction," a standard similar to that upheld in *American Trucking*. The fact that the Secretary was authorized to waive an unlimited number of laws didn't matter, because an otherwise permissible delegation of authority does not become invalid because of its broad scope. The court bolstered its analysis by pointing out that the nondelegation doctrine does not apply to areas in which the executive branch traditionally exercises constitutional authority, in this case immigration control and foreign affairs. Note that the effect of §1103(c)(1) is to allow the Secretary to choose between border security and environmental protection, and it prohibits the courts from questioning the determination that waivers are "necessary to ensure expeditious construction" as arbitrary and capricious.

Defenders of Wildlife also upheld §1103(c)(1) under the rule in *Clinton v. New York*, 524 U.S. 417 (1998), which is discussed in § 7.4.1 N.10. *Clinton* held that Congress could not delegate authority to the President to repeal appropriation measures (the so-called line-item veto). But the court held that suspensions of existing statutes in particular cases are not equivalent to repeals, citing the vast number of statutes that authorize agencies to waive the application of federal laws.

If one believes in the Davis approach to nondelegation, the *Defenders* situation provides a good target. The Secretary's discretion is total and unconstrained. There are no procedural safeguards whatsoever. The government is encouraged to just dispense with all inconvenient laws to build the fence quickly, regardless of the costs to other interests, and the the public has no way to influence the decision through notice and comment or otherwise. Damage to resources (such as the environment, endangered species, or Indian historic sites) will be permanent, not just temporary. There is not even a requirement that the Secretary explain why it is necessary to waive a particular law, so no ability for the agency to develop a consistent practice. So much simpler to just waive all of them.

In addition, there is a complete preclusion of judicial review of the merits of the decision; litigants can only question its constitutionality, but it is difficult to see what constitutional objection there can be (aside from the nondelegation issue) to waiving the statutes like NEPA or the Endangered Species Act to build a border fence. As a result, there is little accountability, which gives rise to concern under a checks and balances approach. We take judicial review almost for granted as a vital checking mechanism, and a preclusion of review of the merits of these important decisions is disturbing. (See discussion of preclusion of judicial review in chapter 10). Congress could, of course, oversee the decision to waive the various statutes, but any such interference would likely come too late to save the resource from destruction. Presidential control is also a possibility, but it doesn't seem likely that the President is going to interfere with a waiver decision. Under George W. Bush, the presidential policy was to build the fence as rapidly as possible.

So if there was ever a statute that would be invalid under the Davis approach, this is it. However, it also seems very unlikely that the court would follow the Davis approach. This is especially true after *American Trucking*, which rejected Davis's idea that an agency could save a statute that was invalid under the nondelegation doctrine by adding its own narrowing construction.

Prospects for a nondelegation attack on the statute appear slim, even putting aside the fact that broad delegations are even more acceptable in the areas of immigration or foreign relations than in terms of strictly domestic legislation. The standard that waiver of the laws is "necessary to ensure expeditious construction" gives at least as much guidance as "requisite to protect the public health" in *American Trucking* and countless other decisions. Thus to uphold the nondelegation argument here would break sharply with all of the cases decided since *Yakus* back in 1944. It's just not going to happen.

It's also worth noting that the statute doesn't coerce anyone to do anything, or impose any penalties on individuals, unlike the economic, environmental or safety statutes involved in *Schechter, Yakus, Industrial Union* or *American Trucking*. That factor lessens the need to apply the nondelegation doctrine. (The lack of coercion was a factor in deciding that a decision not to enforce the law was judicially unreviewable—see *Heckler v. Chaney*, § 10.5.)

Another possibility to consider is that the court could give a narrowing construction to the Act, as in *Industrial Union*. Presumably the court would find that the waiver authority in the REAL ID Act has *some* boundaries. (You can dream up your own hypos: could the Secretary use his waiver authority to empower departmental personnel to dishonor contracts? Ignore traffic laws? Discriminate in employment? Shoot trespassers on sight?) The court might say, for example, that the waiver authority applies only to federal laws, not state laws, because Congress would not use the term "waiver" to refer to laws that it did not itself enact. (The actual order in *Defenders* was ambiguous on this point. The Secretary waived "all federal, state, or other laws, regulations and legal requirements of, deriving from, or related to the subject of, the [listed federal statutes].) Or perhaps the court could say that the Secretary may waive only laws pertaining to official decisions by the project, not the random actions of individual employees.

It seems unlikely that the court could use its interpretive power to eliminate all worries about delegation from the litigation. True, in *Industrial Union* the Supreme Court chose to narrow OSHA's broad powers despite the lack of statutory language that could easily be invoked to serve that purpose. But this case looks more like *American Trucking*, in which the Court did provide guidance about the scope of CAA § 109(b) but reached the constitutional challenge anyway, because a court may choose only among "reasonably available interpretations of a text."

Still, the possibility of a narrowing construction means that, even if Defenders is fated to lose its constitutional challenge, it might win a "consolation prize" in the form of a judicial declaration of limits to the Secretary's power. (In this particular instance, the court's ruling would have less force than usual, due to the Act's blanket preclusion of judicial review of the merits of suspension decisions, but Defenders could nevertheless invoke it in other fora, including congressional oversight committees and the court of public opinion.) Indeed, the opportunity to win such a consolation prize is probably one reason why litigants continue to lodge nondelegation challenges despite the miserable track record of the constitutional doctrine. The "significant risk" holding of *Industrial Union* has, after all, been a tremendous boon to business in subsequent OSHA proceedings.

§ 7.2.2 The Nondelegation Doctrine and State Agencies

Many states still apply (or at least purport to apply) the nondelegation doctrine, even though the doctrine is moribund at the federal level. As a result, state delegation cases provide a useful point of comparison. Why is the nondelegation approach routinely applied in many states even though most judges and scholars consider it unworkable at the federal level?

Some possible hypotheses: Perhaps state court judges, especially in small or rural states, are less sophisticated about administrative law than their federal counterparts and therefore take the rhetoric about the need for standards or intelligible principles seriously. Perhaps some of their pronouncements are just that—rhetoric—and the judges would not actually invalidate any but the most extreme standardless laws. (Obviously *Thygesen* in the text would be an exception to that generalization.) Perhaps the state nondelegation doctrine cases reflect the substantive views of conservative judges who disagree with particular regulatory measures (which they can't find some other constitutional basis for overturning). *Thygesen* could be an example of that. Finally, as mentioned in the text, another factor may be language in state constitutions that appears to require strict separation of functions. However, Rossi's article cited in N.1 of the text found little correlation between whether the states enforced a strong, weak, or moderate version of nondelegation and the presence of strict separation of powers language in the state constitution. 52 Vand. L. Rev. at 1190, 1201.

Rossi believes that state courts might be justified in applying the nondelegation doctrine, because the problem of agency accountability is more severe at the state than the federal level. For example, the quality of state legislation and the quality of legislative oversight of agency action is lower than that of federal legislation, because legislative sessions are much shorter, fewer legislators have adequate staff, and special interests can mobilize more effectively and cheaply than at the federal level. Moreover, states usually lack the unitary executive characteristic of the federal executive (many state executive officers are separately elected), so it is less possible to hold the governor accountable for agency action. Moreover, many states lack arbitrary/capricious review of agency rules, so that judicial oversight is less extensive than at the federal level. All of these factors

385

exacerbate the problem of the lack of accountability of state agencies and justify a serious nondelegation doctrine. *Id.* at 1223-29. Similarly, in many states, agencies are more likely to be captured by private interests (or even run by parties representing specific private interests) than are federal agencies, thus justifying more stringent delegation analysis. *Id.* at 1234.

Perhaps state court judges believe that it is feasible to compel state legislatures to make the difficult political choices when they pass legislation, even though it has long since become clear to most observers that it is infeasible to expect Congress to do so. Some cases seem to reflect the view that the legislature was downright lazy. Some cases merge consideration of delegation and void for vagueness claims. *Kwik Shop, Inc. v. City of Lincoln,* 498 N.W.2d 102 (Neb. 1993) (invalidity of vague multi-factor test for issuing liquor licenses).

We, at least, do not believe that a state nondelegation doctrine is any more useful or workable in improving agency accountability than the federal doctrine. The criticisms of a federal nondelegation doctrine, such as the likelihood that it would obstruct passage of necessary legislation and the inability of courts to administer it without seeming politicized, seem to us equally applicable in the states.

Numerous state court decisions adopt narrowing constructions of broad delegations, a tactic similar to that discussed in § 7.2.1 N.5. *See, e.g., Boreali v. Axelrod,* 517 N.E.2d 1350 (N.Y. 1987) (state agency operating under broad delegation of power to "deal with any matters affecting the . . . public health" lacked power to ban smoking in public places, which legislature had often tried and failed to do so); *D.A.B.E. Inc. v. Toledo-Lucas County Bd. of Health,* 773 N.E.2d 536 (Ohio 2002) (regulations issued by local board of health prohibiting smoking in public places unauthorized by state statute). This approach may be more useful in dealing with objectionable regulations than invalidating statutes under the nondelegation doctrine.

THYGESEN v. CALLAHAN

Notes and Questions

1. *Delegation in the states. Askew* criticizes federal courts for failing to apply the nondelegation doctrine. The decision says that it is required to take the doctrine seriously in light of the separation of powers language in the Florida constitution (mentioned in text preceding *Thygesen*). *Askew* was followed in *Bush v. Schiavo,* 885 So.2d 321 (Fla.2004), which arose out of the famous Terry Schiavo case. The case invalidated under the nondelegation doctrine a statute giving the governor power to impose a stay upon a court decision that upheld a hospital's decision to deny nutrition or hydration to

386

an incompetent patient (or to remove such a stay). The court said that the statute was completely lacking in intelligible standards. This seems a good example of how the nondelegation doctrine can operate as a handy tool for the court to invalidate action by the legislature or the executive that it wishes to overturn for other reasons.

Thygesen indicates that Illinois is a strong nondelegation state. However, *Thygesen* seems a remarkably insensitive application of the doctrine. The harm that the legislature had in mind was completely obvious. Check cashing services prey on the poor, who have no other way to cash checks. Such services often have de facto monopoly power, since poor customers are likely to lack mobility. As a result, the services can charge pretty much what they want. Requiring this to be stated by the legislature is pure formalism.

Similarly, the court's concern that the "means" have not been stated is peculiar. Ratemaking statutes from time immemorial have included a standard no more precise than that the rates be "just and reasonable." It seems very dubious at this late date to invalidate a ratemaking statute on this basis. One is left with the suspicion that the court simply disagreed with the statute on the merits. A subsequent lower court case seems to conflict with *Thygesen* which it purports to "distinguish." In *South 51 Development Corp. v. Vega*, 781 N.E.2d 528 (Ill.App.2002), the court upheld a delegation to a state agency to adopt rules regulating payday loans. The rules had to be "necessary and appropriate for the protection of consumers." The court held that "harm" and the "means" were all clear from the legislative history (a detailed study of the payday loan industry). It was obvious that the rules were intended to protect borrowers from the endless cycle of debt they couldn't pay off. *South 51* was affirmed by an equally divided Illinois Supreme Court. 809 N.E.2d 122 (Ill.2004).

In Rossi's weak states, procedural safeguards are more important than standards. In his moderate states, courts take account of procedural safeguards such as APA rulemaking procedures along with standards or legislative declaration of policy. Rulemaking procedures make unsound agency action less likely; they facilitate judicial review on procedural grounds as well as on substantive grounds; and their applicability facilitates a political process that is a good substitute for the legislative process.

The authors of this casebook believe that the nondelegation doctrine does more harm than good at both the federal and state levels. It is not possible to articulate how much legislative standard-setting is "enough." In many cases legislatures simply cannot articulate meaningful standards (either because they lack the time, information, or political will do to so) and must confer vast discretion on agencies through the equivalent of blank checks. Judicial attempts to apply the doctrine expose judges to the charge that their decisions are unprincipled and politicized (especially because judges in most states are elected or subject to other political checks). We agree that legislatures should make the tough policy calls, but we would not enforce that normative view through the judicial nondelegation doctrine. Similarly, we believe that agencies should be constrained by procedural safeguards and by judicial review, but we would not strike down delegations lacking such safeguards under the nondelegation doctrine, because it is not possible to say how much procedural protection is enough.

At the same time, we believe that in the real world such blank checks seldom exist. The general purposes of the regulatory legislation, its structure and background, and the larger legal context usually supply guidance to administrators and a foundation for judicial review. And if they don't, it is legitimate for the agency and ultimately the courts to imply (i.e., invent) such guidance through narrowing constructions of the statute. As indicated above, the court in *Thygesen* could surely have found meaningful limits on the agency had it been so minded. See § 7.2.1 N.5 for discussion of the nondelegation canon and judicial narrowing of overbroad statutes.

2. *Delegation of rulemaking and adjudicatory authority to private persons.* The federal securities cases at least suggest that delegations of governmental rulemaking authority to private persons or entities may be proper, if they occur in contexts adequate to ensure that the rules adopted actually serve the public interest rather than only the interest of the private persons or entities formulating them, and if there are adequate safeguards to ensure that the private action will not be carried out in an arbitrary and capricious way. *Todd* indicated that the SEC's power to approve or disapprove the rules was critical.

Discussing federal law, Harold Krent has argued that even if delegations to private individuals survive scrutiny under the nondelegation doctrine, as they probably will, they raise troubling questions under the separation of powers doctrine, because of their intrusions on executive branch prerogatives. *See* Harold J. Krent, "Fragmenting the Unitary Executive: Congressional Delegations of Administrative Authority Outside the Federal Government," 85 Nw.U.L.Rev. 62 (1990).

The *Boll Weevil* case was distinguished in *Texas Workers Comp. Comm'n (TWCC) v. Patient Advocates*, 136 S.W.3d 643 (Tex.2004), which involved a process by which workers' comp insurance carriers audited claims and set reimbursement rates for medical procedures that weren't already fixed. The Court determined that there was no delegation, as TWCC maintained the power to audit claims and set rates; it had merely sought the assistance of the carriers in carrying out its statutory chores.

The *Boll Weevil* case is critically discussed in Brian M. Jorgensen,

Note, "Delegations in Danger," 29 Tex.Tech.L.Rev. 213 (1998), contending that it jeopardizes numerous other delegations to private bodies. The court in *Boll Weevil* was reluctant to overturn the program and was sharply split. The legislature obviously wanted a program run by and for farmers with little involvement by state officials. Probably it felt that the program could be run efficiently, like a private business, without a lot of legal constraints and bureaucracy. Indeed, in these days of distrust of government, perhaps this was necessary to get the program through the legislature at all.

The legislature might try to restructure the program, and preserve its private character, if i) the Foundation's rules were subject to approval or disapproval by a state agency, ii) the criminal enforcement elements were removed, iii) some procedural due process was provided before enforcement action was taken, iv) judicial review of both rules and adjudications was provided, v) the board members were required to have experience or educational qualifications, vi) the board members would not themselves be cotton farmers, vii) the program would be in effect for only limited duration—perhaps two years, viii) the amount of assessments was limited by statute, ix) the legislature wrote clear standards into the act. In fact, according to the Texas Tech note, the legislature did restructure the program by placing it under the supervision of the Commissioner of Agriculture and providing for administrative review of adjudicative decisions.

3. *Privatization of government functions.* The Robbins article contends that private delegations to manage a program are more likely to pass judicial muster than private delegations of rulemaking or adjudicatory authority. The danger to individual interests and the public interest is significantly less in the former situation than the latter.

Robbins suggests that a delegation to a private entity to run a federal prison may be valid if the federal corrections agency formulates the prison disciplinary procedures and controls the disciplinary proceedings. If the private body were also authorized to make disciplinary rules or to impose disciplinary penalties, Robbins says the courts might follow *Todd* and ask: 1) whether the correctional agency retained the power to approve or disapprove those rules; 2) whether the agency could make de novo findings of fact aided by additional evidence, if necessary; and 3) whether the agency could make an independent decision on the violation and the penalty. One important factor would be whether the private prison manager seemed to have a conflict of interest in deciding disciplinary cases (it might have a financial interest in hanging on to a prisoner as long as possible). Another important factor would be the presence of judicial review, especially of adjudicatory decisions.

On the other hand, the *Todd* test might be inapplicable to a delegation that affects fundamental liberty interests as opposed to property interests. Indeed, the incarceration of prisoners is such a core governmental function that it may be considered to be entirely non-delegable.

State law typically contains provisions relating to which functions can legally be privatized. These statutes, often passed at the instance of organized labor, might well prohibit privatization of prison management. Moreover, state nondelegation rules tend to be stricter than those at the federal level.

Any federal or state privatization plan for prisons must specially ensure that the delegatee's private interests will not be preferred to the interests of affected prisoners or the public. Where the potential for such conflicts exist, courts might invalidate the delegation whether or not there was judicial review. In the end, Robbins concludes that there are no clear precedents on the lawfulness of delegating the incarceration function to private bodies and, therefore, that the issue remains unclear.

4. *Incorporation by reference of future federal law.* When a state statute or rule incorporates future changes in federal law, the effect is that the state lawmaking power has been delegated to the federal government, an entity wholly outside the control of the state political process. However, following Rochvarg's analysis, where federal interests parallel state interests (as in the case of a jointly administered welfare program), this delegation seems acceptable, since it is likely to yield the same results as would have been achieved by a state agency rulemaker. *But* see *Clemens v. Harvey*, 525 N.W.2d 185 (Neb.1994) (state welfare law could not incorporate future changes in federal law—dictum).

A recent example of a delegation to the federal government that was upheld by a state court is *State v. Klink*, 541 N.E.2d 590 (Ohio 1989), involving a criminal statute that listed illegal drugs. The statute incorporated any future revisions made by the Attorney General to the federal controlled substance law. In a split decision, the court upheld the conviction of a person who used a substance that had been added by the Attorney General to the list. This case might be justified under Rochvarg's approach, since analysis of newly developed chemicals is technical and requires constant revision.

Oklahoma City was criticized by Bernard Schwartz, "Administrative Law Cases During 1995," 48 Admin.L Rev. 399, 402 (1996). Schwartz noted that the federal Davis-Bacon Act contains adequate standards that guide the Labor Department; these should be good enough for Oklahoma's purpose. He questions what is wrong with the state enlisting for its own convenience an arm of the federal government to make prevailing wage determinations; undoubtedly the Labor Department has superior resources, experience, and methodology for making such determinations as compared to a small state agency. Certainly the delegation can be justified under Rochvarg's analysis, because of the superior efficiency and resources of the federal agency and the need for constant revision in the determinations.

In tax cases, state courts are suspicious of state statutes that incorporate future changes in federal tax law, since such future federal changes often are based on political or social calculations. Thus *Wallace v. Commissioner of Taxation*, 184 N.W.2d 588 (Minn.1971), overturned such a provision in the state income tax. The tax commissioner sought to apply a provision in federal law (enacted after the state law) which required a 30-day waiting period before sick pay became excludible from income. Previous federal law excluded sick pay immediately. This is the sort of political judgment, the *Wallace* court believed, that should be made by the state legislature, not by Congress. *McFaddin*, cited in the text, is to the contrary, and cites a number of cases going both ways on the issue.

McFaddin seems right. An important state interest is served by having identical state and federal tax laws—convenience of the taxpayer in not being required to master two conflicting sets of tax laws and to file different forms. State courts should defer to the judgment of the state legislature that ease of administration is more important than having every tax law call made by the state legislature. However, Rochvarg's analysis might suggest agreement with *Wallace* rather than *McFaddin*.

The cases upholding delegation to the federal government all are based on a valid and defensible state purpose: ease of tax administration, regulatory conformity in administering a welfare program, or having identical criminal drug laws or citrus grading standards with the federal government. Such delegations seem much more justifiable than a delegation to private entities, as discussed in the previous note, yet delegations to private entities are frequently upheld. If the list of factors in *Boll Weevil* were applied to cases like *Oklahoma City* or *Wallace*, the delegations to the federal government would probably be upheld.

5. *Problem*. *Chiles* overturned a similar statute as an unlawful delegation of legislative power. Recall that Florida is one of the states that still takes the nondelegation doctrine quite seriously and does not allow safeguards to substitute for standards. *Askew v. Cross Creek Waterways*, cited in text, N.2. *Chiles* ruled that the law was a standardless delegation of power to set fiscal priorities and therefore violated the non-delegation doctrine. The statute failed completely to indicate what sort of budgeting priorities the Commission should follow.

The Florida decision bears an obvious resemblance to *Clinton v. City of New York*, 524 U.S. 417 (1998), which struck down the federal Line Item

Veto Act. *See* § 7.4.1 N.10. Indeed, *Chiles* contains a good deal of separation of powers language. The court argued that the Commission's power was equivalent to a power to appropriate funds—yet only the legislature can exercise that power, and only through the legislative process. Bills are supposed to be passed by both houses, then either signed or vetoed by the governor. This statute, on the other hand, permitted the Commission to alter appropriations without any of those required procedures.

On the other hand, there are also important differences between the two cases. *New York* rested primarily on the notion that the chief executive (the President) was exceeding his proper role in the constitutional system. *Chiles* was written differently, perhaps because the budget cuts in that case were technically made by a commission, not just by the governor. Admittedly that distinction may be somewhat artificial, because the Florida commission consisted of the governor and his cabinet. But *Chiles* did refer to the challenged statute as an improper delegation of legislative power, and it relied directly on nondelegation doctrine precedents such as *Askew*. In our fictional problem, the budget commission is identified simply as an executive agency. Thus, we think the nondelegation doctrine provides a logical point of reference for analysis of its constitutionality.

If there is to be a viable nondelegation doctrine at all, this seems to be a good case in which to apply it. Where to cut the budget is an intensely political decision. Obviously the political priorities of Commission members will determine whether to cut housing for the homeless, as opposed to something else such as spending on the state tourism bureau. The case seems to present a serious lack of accountability—this way of dealing with the problem allows both the legislature and the governor to duck responsibility. (You might ask students, however, whether the statute would be invalid if the commission were constituted like the Florida one. The governor can be held politically accountable for actions taken by a decisionmaking body consisting of himself and his cabinet. Compare Mashaw's defense of delegation as a device that vests authority in a politically accountable President.)

Neither *Chiles* nor the problem says what procedures, if any, the Commission is to follow. In Florida, this would be immaterial (since *Askew* rejects the relevance of safeguards). It's worth discussing here, however, since we don't know what Madison law is. Chances are, there would be no safeguards for Commission action. The Commission probably would not be required to observe rulemaking procedures, since those would be too time-consuming to deal with an emergency situation (the longer you wait to cut to cut the budget, the deeper the cuts would have to be). Nor is it clear that the commission's cuts would be subject to any meaningful sort of judicial review on the basis of ultra vires, since this case might well be held to involve action committed to agency discretion. Nor is it likely that the

Commission will develop internal standards to guide their action; each year's budget crisis will probably be dealt with ad hoc.

When you combine the lack of safeguards with the lack of accountability and the legislature's sloth, you have a statute that's pretty vulnerable to attack. It doesn't hurt that the plaintiffs are homeless kids either.

How might the statute's constitutionality be defended? The statute contains several standards, although these seem too general to furnish useful guidance to anyone. The standards are similar to those employed in the statute underlying *New York*. Breyer's dissent in *New York* uses the history, purposes, and legal context of the federal law to flesh out its rather meaningless substantive criteria. Basically, the government would say, everyone knows that the purpose of the Madison statute is to cut the least essential items from the budget and thereby eliminate the deficit. The public could judge whether the Commission's decisions furthered this obvious purpose.

The lack of express procedural safeguards in the Madison statute may also be a problem. Breyer said the lack of rulemaking obligations and judicial review in the federal act was acceptable, because at least the President is politically accountable. Without more facts about the Madison commission's membership, we can't say the same about it. The statute does not contain language excepting the Commission from notice and comment rulemaking nor does it preclude judicial review. *Cf. Touby v. United States*, 500 U.S. 160 (1991) (rejecting nondelegation doctrine challenge to drug control statute, but only after adopting narrow construction of preclusion-of-review statute). As explained above, however, procedural constraints may not be very practical in the context of the way this statute would have to operate.

There may, however, be accountability through the political process. The governor and the legislature will be keeping a close eye on the commission, making sure that it doesn't make any cuts that would lead to unacceptable political consequences for the state's elected leadership. There aren't enough facts to discuss this concretely, but you can use this possibility to preview themes that will dominate later sections of this chapter. The effectiveness of oversight as a constraint on the Commission will depend on matters such as who appoints the commissioners, who can fire them, and whether and how the governor and legislature can overrule their decisions.

Finally, you can discuss the "floodgates" objections to application of the non-delegation doctrine. Use of the doctrine may look attractive on these facts, but will the court be able to avoid triggering a flood of new cases challenging delegations of other issues that some litigant thinks the legislature should have decided?

§ 7.3 DELEGATION OF ADJUDICATORY POWER TO AGENCIES

You might ask the class why a legislator might wish to transfer decisionmaking in particular classes of cases from courts to agencies. Agency adjudications may be preferred because they:

a. Are speedier
b. More informal
c. Less expensive
d. Permit use of expert decisionmakers
e. Permit use of specialized decisionmakers
f. Facilitate policy development by vesting adjudication in the same body that makes the rules and enforces them
g. Avoid judicial bias against a regulatory program
h. Avoid juries or costly criminal procedure protections
i. Avoid need to expand the life-tenured federal judiciary by instead creating a group of non-tenured judges who could be assigned to other business or terminated if they were no longer needed.

COMMODITY FUTURES TRADING COMMISSION v. SCHOR

Notes and Questions

1. *Public and private rights.* The exact nature of the distinction between "private rights" and "public rights" is often unclear. Most frequently the courts appear to describe public rights as disputes involving government versus private persons, whereas private rights concern disputes between private persons. Public rights in that sense vindicate the interests of the community as a whole, while private rights vindicate only personal interests. Public rights are typically created by statute, while private rights are typically created by common law.

However, the distinction between public rights and private rights presents difficulties and may be illusory. All rights created by the law—whether created by statute or common law, and whether calculated to vindicate the rights of the public at large or the rights of private persons, are intended to advance the public interest. Even common law principles of contract or tort are calculated to maximize the interests of the community at large.

Furthermore, even if the public rights/private rights dichotomy is viable, that distinction appears to point the wrong way. If the purpose of Article III is to ensure unbiased consideration of cases and an adequate system of checks and balances between the three branches of government, judicial independence should be a *greater* concern in cases involving public rights than in cases involving private rights, where the government is not involved as a litigant. Cases involving ordinary contract disputes like that presented in *Northern Pipeline* or the counterclaim in *Schor* seem the least likely subjects for improper interference by the nonjudicial branches of government.

Moreover, private rights disputes are the cases least connected to the judicial power defined in Article III. Most private rights cases arise in the diversity jurisdiction or the bankruptcy jurisdiction of the federal courts—only tangentially arising out of a federal statute. On the other hand, questions involving public rights usually arise directly from the provisions of federal statutes. Finally, since it has been deemed proper to dispose of a vast array of public rights cases (like welfare) with administrative hearings plus judicial review, why should private rights cases require any greater judicial involvement?

The majority and dissenting opinions in *Northern Pipeline* and *Schor* reflect the two different judicial styles of handling separation of powers issues: the formalist approach and the pragmatic (or functionalist) approach. These are described in § 7.1, and we will see examples of the two styles throughout the balance of this chapter. Pragmatism won the day in *Schor,* as the majority opted for an adjudicatory structure that seemed to make solid practical sense and didn't create a serious problem of incursion into the turf of Article III courts. Whereas the *Northern Pipeline* majority (and *Schor* dissent) take a formalist approach: private rights disputes can't be delegated.

White's dissent in *Northern Pipeline* is an example of pragmatism. He suggested that Article III disputes should be resolved by a balancing test rather than by a public rights/private rights dichotomy, which he argued was unprincipled and historically unsound. Balanced against Article III concerns would be Congress's reasons for assigning the function to non-Article III judges, and the dangers of possible abuse. In bankruptcy cases, there were strong practical reasons for centralizing all bankruptcy adjudication in bankruptcy judges, and for not giving them Article III status. Because judicial review of their decisions was preserved, and because improper interference by the nonjudicial branches of government was unlikely, White saw no reason to upset the carefully wrought congressional scheme. Indeed, it is puzzling why six Justices in *Northern Pipeline* felt impelled to invalidate the delegation to bankruptcy judges, thus causing chaos in the bankruptcy system and provoking a real crisis. The reason must lie in a concern by the Justices that they have to draw some kind of line, lest Congress strip them of their entire jurisdiction, in which case Article III would become an empty shell.

Fallon argues in the article cited in text that Article III values can be protected if an Article III court provides appellate review of cases decided by non-Article III tribunals created by Congress. Fallon identifies Article III values as the protection of the virtues implicit in the separation of powers concept, an assurance of fairness to litigants, and protection of the integrity of the adjudication process. Fallon criticizes the amorphous balancing test used by the Supreme Court in *Schor* to determine the validity of delegations of adjudicatory powers to non-Article III bodies. He prefers his more predictable and neutral appellate review theory to the uncertain and potentially non-neutral balancing theory of *Schor*.

Fallon contends that when Congress delegates civil matters to non-Article III tribunals, it must provide judicial review of those tribunals by an Article III court. The appellate review required for this purpose includes de novo review of all constitutional issues and review on an independent judgment basis of all questions of law. (Query whether *Chevron* step two review qualifies under this approach.) Fallon says there is a general presumption against the need to have an Article III court review questions of fact. Nevertheless, he contends, an Article III court must be able to review factual determinations by administrative bodies when the statutory scheme does not provide adequate protection for Article III fairness values. While such review may be limited with respect to ordinary facts, it must be permitted on a de novo basis with respect to constitutional facts.

After *Schor* it appears that few delegations of adjudicatory power to federal agencies are likely to violate the mandate of Article III that judicial power be vested in Article III courts. *Schor* stresses that the constitutionality of such delegations will be determined in light of Article III's purposes: the protection of the role of an independent judiciary and the protection of the right of litigants to have their claims decided by judges free from the domination of the other branches of government. The majority opinion in *Schor* states that the court will consider the following factors in determining the validity of a delegation of adjudicatory authority to a non-Article III body:

    i. the extent to which the essential attributes of judicial power are reserved to Article III courts;
    ii. the extent to which the non-Article III forum exercises the range of jurisdiction and powers normally vested only in Article III courts;
    iii. the origin and importance of the right to be adjudicated; and
    iv. the concerns that drove Congress to depart from the requirements of Article III.

Application of these factors will involve an ad hoc balancing process. Thus it is hard to predict results with any certainty. Adjudication of criminal charges cannot be delegated to non-Article III tribunals, because of both Article III concerns and Bill of Rights limitations. Beyond that, application of the four *Schor* factors will probably be difficult.

Following the Fallon article, a delegation of adjudicatory powers to an agency is most likely to be held invalid where it also seeks to exclude judicial review by an Article III court and where the parties to such an adjudicatory proceeding did not consent to its resolution by that non-Article III tribunal. In this connection Fallon notes:

> *Schor* rightly upheld the CFTC's jurisdiction over state law counterclaims, because the statute provided for de novo review of questions of law by an article III court. The Supreme Court in *Schor* also relied heavily on a waiver analysis, because the parties had consented to the jurisdiction of the CFTC. The case thus suggests a question—which would have been presented directly had full appellate review not been provided—about the legitimacy and effectiveness of waivers of article III rights in the absence of appellate review. As long as the waiver is not procured by any form of illegitimate pressure, waiver ought to be held permissible within an appellate review theory. Waiver substantially alleviates any concern of unfairness to the parties. Moreover, when both parties are satisfied that the adjudicatory scheme treats them fairly, there is substantial assurance that the agency is not generally behaving arbitrarily or otherwise offending separation-of-powers values. Judicial integrity is not at risk. The implications of *Schor*, as much as its holding, thus seem wholly defensible.

101 Harv.L.Rev. at 991-92.

3. *State cases and adjudication of private rights. Wright* and *Opinion of the Justices* seem questionable. Why shouldn't medical malpractice or automobile accident disputes be initially delegated to agencies, subject to appropriate safeguards and with adequate judicial review? Perhaps an expert agency could do a better job with med mal cases than the courts do. The fact that workers' compensation schemes administered by agencies have been upheld in all states suggests a general agreement that a common law tort action can be reshaped into a statutory cause of action and, subject to adequate safeguards including protective agency procedures and judicial review of agency action, be administered initially by a body other than a court.

However, there is a distinction between workers' compensation (which is a new strict liability created by statute) and the traditional common law theories of medical malpractice or auto accidents. If these common law cases can be transferred to agencies, then all civil cases can be transferred—leaving the courts with nothing to do except criminal cases (and many of these could possibly be decriminalized and transferred to agencies, as discussed below).

Schor can be distinguished from the situations discussed in these state cases on the ground that the parties in Schor consented to the jurisdiction of the CFTC. Moreover, the adjudication of contractual counterclaims was a necessary incident to a general scheme of administrative adjudication of reparation claims. But in Crowell v. Benson there was no voluntary waiver by the parties and no independent regulatory scheme; yet the Court upheld the act vesting adjudicatory authority in the agency.

As a sidelight, the Australian High Court rejected Crowell. It ruled that under the separation of powers provisions in the Australian constitution, the legislature could not transfer adjudication of private disputes to an agency—not even rights created by statute. As a result, only a court, not the Human Rights and Equal Opportunity Commission, can adjudicate claims of race or sex discrimination. Brandy v. Human Rights and Equal Opportunity Commission, 183 C.L.R. 245 (1995). The result is that the entire federal system for enforcing the anti-discrimination law collapsed.

5. *Remedies and penalties.* Making it a crime to violate a lawful agency order may be a good idea, particularly in areas of public concern. For example, one might favor a statute criminalizing the dumping of toxic wastes into drinking water in violation of an agency order. A criminal proceeding in court would furnish all necessary procedural protections. It would be essential to allow review of the underlying agency order in the criminal proceeding (unless it had already been reviewed).

As background to *McHugh*, the Santa Monica rent control ordinance was and remains controversial. It was adopted by an initiative and its terms were tough on landlords (and generous to tenants). For years, a building at the city's border had a large sign emblazoned "welcome to the people's republic of Santa Monica." The ordinance lacked vacancy decontrol provisions, made it difficult to raise rents even where the landlord had improved the property, and prohibited landlords from converting apartments to condominiums. Most important, the rent control board was elected, and there are a lot more tenants than landlords in Santa Monica. Consequently, members of the board ran on a tenants'-rights platform and had to deliver once in office. All this was well known to the California Supreme Court. (Some of the provisions of the ordinance, such as the lack of vacancy decontrol, were changed by a state statute that preempted various provisions in local rent control ordinances).

Assuming that an agency can assess civil money penalties, payable to the government, and assuming that agencies can award restitutionary or compensatory damages to private individuals, it's hard to see why agencies can't award penalties (such as treble damages or punitive damages) to private individuals. True, those remedies involve punishment, and we may be uncomfortable about nonjudicial imposition of punishment. But realistically, civil money penalties are punishment also, and agencies can impose them. And many agency remedies, although remedial in nature, are extremely drastic in effect (such as license revocation). So what's the constitutional problem with allowing agencies to impose punitive damages payable to victims (so long as the punishment lacks the stigma associated with criminal penalties)?

Punitive awards may be necessary to make a regulatory scheme work. One can imagine landlords under rent control who persistently abuse tenants, on the ground that their maximum exposure is to refund the rent; or employers who persistently commit civil rights violations on the theory that their maximum exposure is backpay. True, these agencies could be empowered to assess civil money penalties, but these would be retained by the agency and thus there would be little incentive for victims to come forward and complain.

The *McHugh* holding that prohibits the agency from using rent withholding as a remedy is also suspect. Rent withholding is an effective remedy for tenants to collect the amount of rent that they've been overcharged without having to go to court. The amounts owed might be too small to justify litigation; moreover, there might be long delays before anybody could get into court. Thus landlords would be encouraged to refuse to pay restitutionary amounts awarded by the Board until forced to do so by a court. Thus rent withholding was a remedy that would promote the purposes of the rent control law. The court's rationale was that the withholding remedy is self-executing, because it has immediate practical and legal effect. If the withholding remedy were permitted, the landlord would have to go to court and sue the tenant to get the money back (but the tenant would often would be judgment-proof).

You may want to discuss the general rule prohibiting agencies from holding parties in contempt or otherwise enforcing their own orders without the need to get a court order. The traditional rule is based on concern that agencies may have a built-in institutional interest in the outcome of their adjudications, because agencies are responsible for implementing particular regulatory programs.

However, an argument can be made in favor of giving agencies the contempt power (so long as the order is subject to judicial review). The agency may encounter problems in controlling its proceedings (for example, there might be disruption of a hearing or a litigant may refuse to obey an ALJ's rulings). These are the same problems that courts sometimes encounter. Furthermore, as discussed in § 4.1.2, there is a good argument for giving agencies the contempt power in the case of refusals to cooperate with lawful agency investigations. Otherwise, the agency must go to court to get a compliance order, which gives obstructive litigants a free bite. So long as the contempt order is judicially reviewable for abuse of discretion, it is difficult to see why agencies should be denied the contempt power when they are permitted to exercise so many other discretionary powers with a great impact on members of the public.

6. *Problem. Rosenthal* upheld a state statute delegating adjudication of traffic and parking offenses to an agency. Some important factors in the decision were that the offenses were decriminalized and the only penalty was the imposition of a civil fine. In addition, the standard of proof to establish a violation was clear and convincing evidence; the delegation was surrounded by adequate procedural and substantive standards; judicial review was available; and the volume of traffic infractions handled by the courts as criminal proceedings was so large that the prompt and judicious handling of these cases in the courts was no longer possible.

Van Harken was a due process attack on a Chicago ordinance decriminalizing parking violations with a maximum $100 penalty. *Van Harken* might be distinguishable in light of the higher penalties in the problem and the more serious implications (such as insurance cost) of being convicted of a moving violation.

The *Van Harken* court did not discuss whether the statute violated separation of powers under the Illinois constitution. As far as due process is concerned, the court saw no reason why a formerly criminal process could not be converted to an administrative one imposing civil penalties. "The traditional system, mindlessly assimilating a parking ticket to an indictment for murder, was archaic and ineffective." The court then applied a straightforward cost/benefit equation under *Mathews v. Eldridge* and upheld the scheme. It did so even though i) the police officer who wrote the ticket does not appear in court (because the cost to the city of having cops appear at all hearings outweighs the benefit to drivers), ii) the hearing officers are private lawyers who can be fired at will (they are paid $35 per hour without benefits), iii) the hearing examiners are instructed to cross-examine the drivers, iv) judicial review is available but the filing fee exceeds the maximum fine.

It does not seem significant that in the problem the burden of proof in a proceeding to establish a violation is preponderance of the evidence, while in *Rosenthal* it was "clear and convincing evidence." The trial of Ralph's case by the agency will probably be deemed lawful so long as judicial review is available, there are adequate procedural safeguards in the adjudicative proceeding before the agency (whether in the state APA or in other applicable law), and some express or implied standards may be discerned to guide agency action in his case. Remember, also, that traffic and parking violations are meant to vindicate public rights as opposed to private rights. If your jurisdiction emphasizes that distinction as a basis for permissible delegation of adjudicatory authority to agencies, this scheme should pass muster. Consequently, Ralph cannot successfully object to the trial of his case before the Traffic Agency.

The result should be the same if the Traffic Agency were a federal agency, and for the same reasons. The *Schor* balancing test applied here would appear to be satisfied in light of the decriminalization of these offenses, the availability of judicial review, the adequacy of the surrounding safeguards, the great need for administrative adjudication of these offenses, and the fact that this scheme was calculated to vindicate public rights. Even though the scheme involves matters that were traditionally handled by criminal adjudication in court, the offenses have been decriminalized. Thus the case seems more like *Crowell v. Benson* (involving the transformation of a traditional tort action for workplace injuries into a strict liability scheme) than like *Northern Pipeline* (which involved traditional contract claims).

§ 7.4 LEGISLATIVE CONTROLS

§ 7.4.1 The Legislative Veto and Control of Federal Agencies

IMMIGRATION AND NATURALIZATION SERVICE v. CHADHA

1. *"Legislative" acts.* The main line of reasoning in Burger's opinion is quite weak and easy to debunk. The Court calls the veto "legislative" because it "had the purpose and effect of altering the legal rights, duties and relations of persons . . . outside the legislative branch." Of course, the assumption that Chadha's rights were "altered" begs the question: one could just as easily say that there was no legal right to suspension of deportation until Congress failed to veto it. Moreover, even if one agrees that the veto did bring about an alteration of legal rights, that effect is hardly unique to "legislation." Every administrative adjudication or rule would meet that standard as well. As for the Court's "presumption" that a given branch of government is acting within its assigned sphere, such a presumption may make sense when it is used to *support* the constitutionality of that branch's actions; but it seems perverse when, as here, it is used as a starting point for an argument that the branch is acting *unconstitutionally*.

On a more fundamental level one might question the Court's assumption that the § 244(c)(2) power has to fit into one of the three traditional categories of separation of powers doctrine—either legislative, executive, or judicial. The Court does not confront the possibility of thinking about it as none of these, but simply as a device that Congress has created, using its necessary and proper clause power, as a check on the bureaucracy. Instead, the Court insists on categorizing the legislative veto using the traditional terms, and then accomplishes that categorization through patently circular reasoning: The House had to comply with Article I, § 7 because it was legislating, but the reason the decision was legislative was that a house of Congress made it.

Capping off the flaws in the Court's use of the "legislative" label is the fact that the House's action in *Chadha* really did not seem very much like legislation--it applied only to named persons on the basis of fixed facts and contained no general principles for future application. It seems more like adjudication. Even if one does not agree with Justice Powell that such individualized action is inherently off limits for Congress (*see* N.3 below), the factual setting of *Chadha* presented a particularly weak context for Burger's assertion that a one-house veto is essentially legislative in nature.

2. *Legislative veto versus delegation.* At first blush, White's comparison between the one-house veto and a routine delegation to an administrative agency seems very strong. However, the majority provides a somewhat credible answer in footnote 16. There the Court explains that executive actions are bounded by the original statutory mandate, by judicial review, and by Congress's ability to modify or revoke the power it has conferred. The congressional power leveled against Chadha, however, was bounded by none of these checks. It was totally standardless, unconstrained, and unreviewable. When Congress exerts that kind of power (acting, as the Court said later in the opinion, with "the unreviewable force of law"), the Court's insistence that it must at least comply with the bicameralism and presentment safeguards makes a certain amount of sense. This is a separation of powers rationale, derived not so much from constitutional text as from a judgment about the need to put some sort of brake on the exercise of Congress's virtually plenary substantive authority. In other words, the strict limitations of *Chadha* are an offset to the congressional primacy recognized in *Youngstown* (discussed in § 7.6 N.1).

The Court's sweeping ban on the legislative veto seems at least somewhat defensible if one combines the reasoning in the preceding paragraph with a couple of other considerations: (a) The historical material cited by the Court does attest to the founders' deep concern about potential excesses of legislative authority. Even if one agrees that modern conditions could justify discounting the original intent, the historical material lends weight to the Court's argument. (b) The usual judicial deference to Congress' exercise of judgment under the necessary and proper clause seems out of place here, because the legislative veto serves the institutional interests of Congress itself in its ceaseless rivalry with the other branches. As other material in this chapter illustrates, the Court has usually (but not always) been more deferential to Congress in other separation of powers disputes in which the legislative branch's self-interest is less deeply implicated. *See* § 7.5.2b N.3. Congressional "aggrandizement," as it is known in the separation of powers literature, deserves minimum deference. (Note that the Court pays lip service to the presumption of constitutionality but doesn't really display much deference.) (c) Finally, the policy critique of legislative vetoes, discussed in N.5 below, may have bolstered the Court's confidence in its broad holding.

However, since the above objections to the legislative veto are based on a prudential weighing of the risks and benefits of the device, one could very well reach a different judgment concerning other control devices that are arguably distinguishable from the legislative veto. Thus, for example, later in this section we discuss variations on the legislative veto that seem to us at least somewhat more defensible than the devices that fall squarely within the *Chadha* ruling.

If one tentatively accepts this rationale as support for the *Chadha* principle, the fact that the legislative veto was established through a procedurally valid statute doesn't carry much weight. In the first place, one can't argue that the President signed off on the legislative veto in § 244(c)(2), because the 1952 Act was passed over Truman's veto. *See* 462 U.S. at 993 (White, J.). Second, even with respect to other legislative vetoes in bills that Presidents *have* signed, the separation of powers objection to those provisions exists for the benefit of the public, not the chief executive as such. The objection rests on what courts perceive to be a *continuing* unhealthy concentration of power. Finally, consider the obvious fact that presidential administrations change. One could question whether all future administrations should be bound by the decision of one President, in the middle of a single political struggle, to agree to a legislative veto as one element of a package that he otherwise desires (or fears resisting).

3. *Legislative vetoes of agency adjudications.* The use of a veto provision in the deportation suspension statute seems explainable largely by historical factors. In the past, Congress had granted relief to aliens through private bills. This became cumbersome, so the suspension power was delegated; nevertheless, Congress wished to retain a vestige of its historic role in making such decisions. As Powell argued, there was much to criticize about the § 244(c)(2) procedure. The INS proceedings are on the record and are judicially reviewable; Congress' decision was neither. Indeed, the House's poorly explained, last-minute veto was extremely harsh in its effect on Mr. Chadha and seems unfair. Usual notions of appropriate judicial procedure and separation of functions are offended by this sort of action. It is close to being a bill of attainder (a legislative act visiting

penalties on a named individual without a judicial trial). Thus Congress' action does not seem like legislation at all.

Nevertheless, the adjudicative nature of the House's action was not clearly unconstitutional. Congress's use of private bills, which § 244(c)(2) replaced, had been longstanding, and the bill of attainder clause was probably not applicable, because it is violated only where a legislature engages in "punishment" of individuals, a term that might not apply to a congressional determination that Chadha could be deported without "extreme hardship."

More to the point, the Court's failure to rest its decision on this basis can be explained by the fact that this rationale would have given the Court very little leeway, if any, to speak to the general problem of legislative vetoes as such. Nothing in Justice Powell's opinion suggests that he would have viewed the case any differently if bicameralism and presentment procedures had been added to § 244(c)(2). To be sure, those procedures would have furnished some protection against hasty action; but Powell does not even mention them, presumably because they would not have furnished the judicial-type safeguards that he appears to believe were necessary. The Court would have been hard pressed to argue that the full legislative process would have satisfied his concerns. Thus, endorsement of the Powell position would effectively have meant postponing a decision about the validity of the legislative veto until another day. Presumably, the majority decided that, since it was planning (for better or worse) to declare that all legislative vetoes were unconstitutional, it might as well use Chadha's case as the vehicle for its announcement, because the congressional abuse of power was so palpable in his case.

5. *Policy issues.* Among the objections listed (which by no means exhaust Bruff and Gellhorn's charges against the legislative veto), the one that comes closest to being an implicit attack on legislative oversight itself is the claim that members of Congress do not have as much familiarity with the issues as agencies have. It's undoubtedly true, but if there is to be legislative review at all, Congress's comparative lack of information is something we have to accept.

The risk of stalemate is to some extent a product of the legislative veto mechanism itself, in that the purely negative nature of a veto allows members of the legislature to avoid coming to grips with the question of what the agency *should* do. Notice, however, that the Congressional Review Act suffers from the same vice, even though it conforms to the strictures of Article I, § 7.

Finally, Bruff and Gellhorn's concerns about the disproportionate influence wielded by small groups of legislators (or their staffs) and by powerful interest groups seem to be directly related to the constitutional weaknesses of the legislative veto, because these are exactly the sort of influences that the bicameralism and presentment clauses are designed to counteract. Bruff and Gellhorn are not the only authors to find special risks of interest-group influence under the legislative veto. A study of the practical effects of the veto in several states, in both Democratic- and Republican-controlled legislatures, found that although legislative review committees were highly sensitive to political forces, "the balance of support and opposition in the oversight process most often favors regulated and client groups," and thus "may simply create a new access point for interests already successful in obtaining influence." Marcus E. Ethridge, "Consequences of Legislative Review of Agency Regulations in Three U.S. States," 9 Legis.Stud.Q. 161, 174 (1984). A more recent study asserts that the presence of a legislative review mechanism in a state "reduces regulatory compliance costs," which sounds like the same finding with a more positive spin. Dorothy M. Daley et al., "Checks, Balances, and the Cost of Regulation: Evidence from the American States," 60 Pol.Res.Q. 696 (2007).

6. *Reality check.* Although Presidents often acquiesce in legislative veto provisions in appropriations measures, they do not always do so. Sometimes, they declare in a signing statement that they will construe the congressional directive as merely requiring notification to the relevant committee, rather than congressional permission. *See, e.g.*, GAO B-308603, "Presidential Signing Statements Accompanying the Fiscal Year 2006 Appropriations Acts" 9-10 (June 18, 2007) (identifying two such incidents during the past year).

7. *Congressional Review Act.* The short answer to the constitutional question is that the Act meets *Chadha* standards, because a joint resolution of disapproval cannot pass without bicameral action and presentment to the President. (Note that a *joint* resolution differs from a *concurrent* resolution, which is not presented to the President and thus could not support a legislative veto. *See U.S. Senate v. FTC,* noted above in N.4.) Even with respect to major rules, which are delayed at least sixty days under the Act, the CRA is basically a "report and wait" statute, following a model that has long been used to give Congress an opportunity to study proposed revisions to the Federal Rules of Civil Procedure. *Chadha* expressly recognized the validity of this arrangement. 462 U.S. at 935 n.9.

The breadth of the Act seems decidedly unwise. The amount of paper flowing into the Capitol is grossly out of proportion to the number of rules that Congress has the time or desire to review. The overbroad reporting obligation also imposes large unnecessary burdens on agency resources. Congress would have done better to limit the scope of the automatic review process to a more manageable universe, while relying on "fire alarm" devices to bring other questionable rules to Congress's attention. ("Fire alarm" oversight means reacting to interest groups or other constituents who bring problems to the legislature's attention, as distinguished from "police patrol" oversight, in which the legislature goes out to uncover problems on its own. *See* § 1.6.)

As for the broader question about the overall wisdom of the congressional review power, any generalization may be hazardous, given the infrequency with which the power is actually used. This is not to say that the CRA has had no effects on rulemaking proceedings in which Congress took no formal action. On the contrary, there are a few reports of situations in which the Act gave members of Congress leverage with which to extract concessions from agencies informally. Nevertheless, reliable information about these effects is not easy to acquire.

If one cares to speculate, however, the Bruff and Gellhorn study discussed in N.5 could support some pessimistic predictions. The restoration of bicameralism and presentment checks, which were absent from the traditional legislative veto, provides some protection from extravagant legislative intrusions. But the CRA still embodies one of the structural vices of the older veto schemes: members can vote *against* a rule without having to take responsibility for figuring out what solution they would *favor* (or indeed whether anyone could improve on the agency's solution). Thus, the CRA still poses risks of contributing to stalemate and non-constructive intervention. Cohen and Strauss also argue that the Act virtually goes out of its way to *avoid* political accountability for any review that legislators may conduct, because of its provision that a court may not infer anything from Congress' failure to override a rule. 49 Admin.L.Rev. at 105-06. (One could argue, however, that in the court of public opinion Congress will be more accountable nevertheless.)

8. *Effects of CRA disapproval.* The assumption behind the "void ab initio" provision of the CRA, § 801(f), seems to be that Congress will disapprove only "really bad" rules, and no one should get into trouble for having violated such a rule, even if the violation occurred before Congress got around to acting. This idea has some appeal in the abstract, but Congress didn't think through the practical implications, as illustrated by the absurd consequences of the situation in Cohen and Strauss's hypothetical about fishermen's nets.

We would hope and expect that, even without § 801(f), an agency would simply decline to bring an enforcement action against the fishermen and other regulated persons who are in a similar situation. However, it can be strongly argued that such people deserve assurance in advance that they will be protected. The ABA resolution cited in N.7 offers an attractive solution: it proposes that § 801(f) be amended to provide "that no person may be subjected to legal liability for activity taken in reasonable reliance on the rule during any period in which it has, in fact, been in effect."

The CRA provision forbidding an agency to promulgate a rule that is similar to the disapproved rule, § 801(b)(2), will at a minimum lead to confusion over how different the second rule has to be. In effect, the joint resolution would effect a pro tanto amendment of the agency's governing statute, and unelected judges would have to decide the scope of that amendment without any real congressional guidance. (The disapproval resolution would not be helpful. The Act provides that every such resolution must follow a set format, which would contain only uninformative boilerplate.) Also troubling is the possibility that Congress might have disapproved the first rule because of unresolved factual questions, or the agency's failure to consult sufficiently with affected interest groups. *See Mead v. Arnell,* 791 P.2d 410 (Idaho 1990), discussed in § 7.4.2 N.4. In these scenarios, the § 801(b)(2) prohibition might have the perverse result of preventing the agency from issuing a rule that Congress could easily support in the second round, after the original problem has been cured.

The ABA resolution strikes us as an excellent cure for these problems. It would remove all *legal* constraints on the kind of rule that could be issued in the second round. The fear that this would give agencies too much room for manipulation seems unfounded, because the second rule would *also* be subject to congressional review. When an agency submits to Congress a rule that has already been disapproved by joint resolution, one can be confident that the legislature will scrutinize it closely (and its scrutiny would be aided by the explanatory statement prescribed by the ABA proposal). If the substitute rule survives such scrutiny, the courts would have no good reason to throw it out on the basis of the prior disapproval. In short, the ABA approach puts the responsibility for monitoring the situation squarely on Congress—which is appropriate in light of the fundamentally political nature of legislative review.

9. *Separation of powers.* Logically speaking, the *Bowsher* and *MWAA* decisions appear to rest on a more secure footing than *Chadha* does, because the separation of powers doctrine provides a more persuasive basis for curbing congressional control over administration of the laws than the bicameralism and presentment clauses do. This does not mean, however, that these particular applications of separation of powers principles have necessarily been wise. Although the *MWAA* case can be seen as having intercepted a fairly transparent attempt to circumvent *Chadha, Bowsher* rested on a rigid and at best controversial assessment of the risks of congressional involvement in the *potential* (but never actually exercised) removal of the Comptroller General. *See* § 7.5.2b N.3.

Still, *Bowsher* and *MWAA* remain as firmly rooted within the formalist mode of reasoning as *Chadha* was. The case for this inflexible approach to separation of powers may be at its strongest when directed at statutes that attempt to strengthen the legislative branch at the expense of other branches. Since legislatures are constantly tempted to adopt statutes that serve their own institutional self-interest, the Court has some reason to try to maintain the checks and balances system through holdings that are relatively easy to apply. It is arguable, though scarcely beyond debate, that a certain amount of overbreadth is an acceptable price to pay for such clarity.

10. *Presidential revision.* The rationale for formalism just mentioned does not, however, work very well in relation to *Clinton v. New York.* The Court emphasized in that case that it was not relying on policy considerations, but only enforcing the strict rules of the constitutional system. Yet this doggedly formalist holding occurred in a context in which Congress had not sought to aggrandize its own power, but rather had voluntarily surrendered power to the executive branch.

Conspicuously absent from the Court's opinion was any attempt to demonstrate that the President's authority under the Act threatened to lead to abuses of power by the White House, or to a dangerous shift in the balance of power between the branches. Perhaps, since both the President and Congress were supporting the Act, the justices felt that a purely formalist argument was the only rationale they could plausibly advance.

Justice Kennedy's concurrence clarifies the possible separation of powers problem. To put the point more bluntly than he did, a President could have used the line item veto selectively to kill spending in districts represented by representatives from the opposing party, or to say to a senator, "vote for my foreign aid package or you'll lose your highway money." This focus on the largely unchecked power of the President under the Act recalls our suggestion, in N.2 above, that *Chadha* can be seen as resting on a barely articulated separation of powers basis, i.e., as reacting against the largely unchecked power that the legislative veto would have vested in Congress. We would have found the Kennedy rationale a somewhat more persuasive basis for the *New York* holding. But the extent to which the majority tacitly agreed with it is unknowable.

11. *Rulemaking as proposing.* The main purpose of this note is to lay a foundation for the Problem in the next note. We would add, however, that Verkuil's proposal arguably raises less troubling constitutional concerns than a generic legislative veto statute would. One of the main problems with the latter is that agencies produce so many rules that the legislature can't meaningfully address them. Thus, inordinate power devolves upon committees that may be unrepresentative of the legislative body as a whole. But it is less farfetched to think that Congress could meaningfully review

the 75-100 major rules that are promulgated each year. Even so, a court might find that the system would pose a constitutional problem if it were convinced that this review process would be so superficial and contaminated with interest group pressure as to result in an unacceptable intrusion on executive authority.

12. *Problem.* The idea behind this problem is that the imaginary legislative review scheme replicates the substance of the legislative veto provision in *Chadha*, but does so in a manner that arguably satisfies the formal requirements of Article I, § 7. The question then is whether the policy problems associated with the legislative veto are severe enough to justify a conclusion that the scheme violates separation of powers principles. The scheme is based on a serious proposal by Rosenberg (and to a lesser extent by Breyer in the article cited in the preceding note), but we have doctored the details in order to make the potential objections to the FDA legislation more glaring.

The inspiration (or conceit) behind the plan is that, since the FDA has no rulemaking power but only the power to propose a rule, a rule cannot become law unless it is "passed" by both Houses of Congress and signed by the President—just as Art. I, § 7 envisions. The procedure by which a bill is automatically introduced in Congress and deemed passed unless a House votes it down is admittedly unusual, but the Rules of Proceedings Clause of the Constitution seems broadly worded enough to permit it, at least prima facie. Indeed, Rosenberg notes that the House rules already provide for a similar device to initiate an automatic joint resolution to adjust the national debt limit. Rosenberg, 51 Admin.L.Rev. at 1084 n.162; *see* House Rule XXVIII ("Upon adoption by Congress of a concurrent resolution on the budget . . ., the Clerk shall [when necessary] prepare an engrossment of a joint resolution increasing or decreasing, as the case may be, the statutory limit on the public debt . . ., and the joint resolution shall be considered as passed by the House"). There is also a possible argument that the system does violate *Chedha* principles, because it allows twenty percent of the membership of the House or Senate to delay the approval of a rule-adopting bill. However, that argument does not seem to be a winner, because parliamentary rules often have similar effects (think of filibusters, holds, quorum calls, etc.)

In reality, however, the FDA review scheme would mean that the FDA would adopt a rule in the usual fashion, but either House could unilaterally kill the rule. To the extent that a one-House veto leads to interest group capture, legislative thoughtlessness, etc., those problems would be revived. On these facts, the pharmaceutical lobby clearly acquires an enhanced opportunity to exert influence on FDA rules by working in the legislature. The issue for students to discuss would be whether these concerns are outweighed by the benefits of stronger legislative participation in the rulemaking process.

For Rosenberg (as well as Breyer and Verkuil), the idea of recasting agency rules as mere "proposals" is linked to an expectation that Congress would have to take an up-or-down vote on all of the "proposals." In our problem, however, this is not so. Each House can consider killing a rule, but it need not take responsibility for its contents. Moreover, as in the CRA, courts are prohibited from ascribing significance to the failure of an override vote to pass.

We can picture a court saying that if Congress thinks that FDA rulemaking in the area of drug labeling is especially troubled, it should have latitude to subject those proceedings to special oversight. But we can also picture the Court taking a stand against the plan. If the Act were to be upheld, the next step might be for Congress to extend it government-wide. The Court might well conclude that the notion that Congress can treat all agency rules as "proposals" would be too obvious a fiction to take seriously. One lesson that can be drawn from *MWAA* and *Clinton v. New York* is that the Court doesn't like clever legislative innovations that threaten to change the balance of powers among the branches in fundamental ways. Thus, perhaps the Court would choose to ban the rulemaking-as-proposing device before it has a chance to spread.

The *Meadows* case cited in this note may foreshadow the Court's response to the rulemaking-as-proposing approach. The West Virginia court held that a "proposal" system for all agency rules violated the state constitution. The court did not rely directly on *Chadha*. Instead, it relied on a separation of powers rationale, charging that the West Virginia APA provision encroached on the authority of the executive branch. Although the court acknowledged the theory, that a legislature could elect not to empower an agency to act through rules at all, the court looked through form to substance and noted that the state's APA contained all the standard elements of rulemaking (as in our problem). Thus, the reality was that the legislature was trying to keep a tight grip on the law-implementing function, in addition to its unchallenged supremacy in law-writing. To the court, that combination of powers offended checks and balances principles. The court was probably influenced by the facts of the case, in which a few powerful legislators had prevented the state's health care agency from finalizing regulations that were needed if the state was to remain in compliance with federal law.

§ 7.4.2 The Legislative Veto in the States

1. *State legislative vetoes.* Devlin makes a thoughtful argument (perhaps not fully done justice in our excerpt), but we are inclined to believe

that the similarities between state and federal legislatures outweigh the differences, at least in relation to the most typical forms of legislative veto. At both levels, the salient problem is the essentially unrestrained power of a legislative body, often exercised by a rather small committee. The situation opens up significant opportunities for caprice and interest-group influence, normally without much exposure to external check (although in *Mead v. Arnall* the Idaho court did review a specific exercise of a legislative veto "on the merits," as discussed in N.4).

As to the specifics of Devlin's argument, his most vulnerable assertion appears to be the claim that states have to live under the shadow of federal law as enforced by federal courts. Virtually all of the same constraints also apply to federal agencies, so his distinction between the two levels of government seems thin. The observation that legislatures have short sessions and small staffs may carry more weight, particularly in relation to the *temporary* suspension devices discussed in N.3. Yet we believe that state legislatures do not really need a legislative veto in order to maintain a pretty strong influence over administrative rulemaking. The contrary perceptions of many state legislatures can be seen as self-serving and should be viewed with skepticism.

2. *Legislative vetoes in limited contexts.* In his "Baby in the Bathwater" article, Strauss praises the New Jersey cases and argues that the Court should have drawn a distinction between statutes that use legislative vetoes to constrain the chief executive directly (like War Powers, executive branch reorganization, impoundment control, or control over spending under year-by-year appropriations) and statutes that use legislative vetoes in regulatory contexts. He argues that the Court should have reserved decision on the former type of legislative vetoes and, when the issue presented itself, perhaps upheld them. He views such legitimate vetoes as arising in areas in which legislative and executive functions are shared, the interests of private individuals are not directly threatened, and judicial checks are usually unavailable. In such situations, he suggests, the government gains in flexibility, and the veto is a necessary part of a compromise which enhances (rather than threatens) unitary Presidential control over the executive branch.

3. *Suspensive veto.* Under *Chadha* it would be hard to draw a constitutional distinction between legislative vetoes that suspend agency action for a defined period and those that invalidate it permanently. In either case the effect of the veto is to alter the present legal rights of individuals outside of the legislative branch. In that sense a suspension is simply an invalidation of agency action for a fixed period. Here, the suspension would have been beneficial to migrant workers (who moved from job to job and were thus particularly disadvantaged by the sub-minimum wage), but detrimental to their employers. Frickey's article, relying on

Chadha and public choice reasoning, makes a strong and straightforward argument for the unconstitutionality of the suspensive veto. Indeed, some of the court's arguments are weak—particularly the suggestion that anything should turn on whether a state has an *express* separation of powers provision. All state constitutions presuppose the same basic model of separation of powers, and a given state's decision to make it explicit says little if anything about how the model should be applied. *See* Devlin, 66 Temp.L.Rev. at 1236-41.

But *Chadha* is not binding on state courts, and from a functionalist perspective one could make a reasonable case that the suspensive veto is more tolerable than the classic legislative veto and ought to be upheld. The strongest argument in its favor derives from Devlin's observation that many state legislatures have short, intermittent sessions. The suspension can be rationalized as merely giving the legislature an adequate opportunity to react to a rule before it goes into effect and becomes too hard to dislodge. *Cf. Ameron, Inc. v. United States Army Corps of Engineers*, 809 F.2d 979, 995-98 (3d Cir.1986) (upholding Comptroller General's power to stay performance of government contracts temporarily, as a reasonable accommodation to Congress' power of oversight), *cert. dismissed*, 488 U.S. 918 (1988).

At the same time, the suspensive veto gives only limited bargaining power to a legislative committee. Both legislators and administrators will know that if the committee can't put together enough support to surmount the bicameralism and presentment hurdles, the rule will go into effect eventually. Thus the suspension gives the committee some room to extract concessions, but perhaps not so much as to disrupt the balance of power between branches to an extent that functionalist analysis would regard as unacceptable. The temporal limits on the suspension prevent it from placing *unchecked* power in the hands of a small group of legislators. (In *Martinez* the court claimed that the list of criteria in the statute also provided a check on the committee, but for reasons discussed in the next note we find that claim much less persuasive.)

We do not mean to say that the case for a suspensive veto is airtight. This variation on the legislative veto still poses risks of interest group capture, of a committee's being unrepresentative of the entire legislature, and of simple perverseness on the part of a small group of legislators. Moreover, the alleged need to take action between legislative sessions could be exaggerated. Ordinarily, one suspects, the committee will know all about the rule well in advance of its adoption, whether through the notice opportunities provided by the rulemaking process or through the informal contacts between agencies and legislative oversight committees that go on all the time. In the real world, most legislative influence on rulemaking occurs through informal negotiations in advance of the actual agency action; this sort of interchange may be feasible even when the legislature isn't formally in session. Finally, Frickey reports that the now-repealed Minnesota suspensive veto, unlike Wisconsin's, could be invoked *repeatedly*. 70 Minn.L.Rev. at 1241 n.22. In a jurisdiction where that is true, the argument that the suspensive veto is just a means of giving the legislature adequate time to respond to a new rule certainly won't fly.

4. *Grounds for objection.* A provision stating that a legislative committee may invoke a veto-like device only against *unlawful* rules can be understood as part of a compromise that aims to prevent the device from sweeping too broadly. But such limits do not easily fit together with an assessment of legislators' strengths and weaknesses:

> It is fundamental that courts, not Congress, have the ultimate responsibility to interpret the law. To the extent that congressional review of rules duplicates the function of the courts, it does not seem a wise use of congressional time. Moreover, Congress is ill-equipped, both by inclination and competence, to determine its own former intent with the care and restraint customary in judicial review. The members of Congress have less time and no better resources (briefs, memoranda of law) than the federal courts. . . . The more appropriate role for congressional review is policy review, because it is a natural part of the legislative process that is not engaged in by the courts.

Bruff & Gellhorn, 90 Harv.L.Rev. at 1429-30. Weighing the other way might be the argument that legislators at least have firsthand knowledge of what they meant when they wrote the statute being implemented. But *Barker* is right: their recollections of what they meant will surely be deeply colored by current political imperatives. Moreover, many regulations implement statutes that have been on the books for decades; in that situation, obviously, the committee will not have personal knowledge of what the statute was intended to mean.

One of the main reasons to encourage political oversight is to promote democratic values and political legitimacy, by bringing the actions of unelected administrators into line with the goals and values of the public. Whatever their limitations, politicians at least can claim to have a feel for what the public will accept; this is one of the main strengths that a legislator brings to the oversight role. Arguably, therefore, if an oversight mechanism in the nature of a legislative veto is to exist at all, a state should not try to restrict the bases on which the reviewers may intervene (let alone try to impose a sort of "hard look" review on a fundamentally political decision, as the court in *Mead v. Arnell* did). Rather, it should rely on other constraints on the process to safeguard separation of powers values, such as the time limits built into most suspensive veto schemes, or the bicameralism and presentment safeguards preserved in the Congressional Review Act.

5. *Burden-shifting.* Our analysis of the constitutionality of § 3-204(d) is similar to that regarding the suspensive veto. Under a straightforward application of *Chadha,* the provision would be vulnerable, because if the burden shift has any significance at all, it must necessarily result in an alteration of legal rights without bicameralism and presentment. The fact that legislatures have traditionally regulated burdens of proof would not, standing alone, justify a different result, because the ARRC is not the legislature; indeed, the whole point of *Chadha* is that a part of the legislature cannot be equated with the whole of it (and still less can it be equated with the combination of legislature plus gubernatorial signature). Again, however, if one applies a more functionally oriented approach to separation of powers, it could be argued that the burden shift is quite limited in effect and thus does not really disrupt the relationships among the political branches to the point of unconstitutionality. Indeed, one might say that the MSAPA provision is even less disruptive than a suspensive veto, because a committee objection does not prevent a rule from going into effect, even temporarily.

The text spells out the principal policy arguments that favor the MSAPA provision. One potential criticism of § 3-204(d) is that the committee is permitted to object only to the lawfulness of the rule (as to which it has fewer qualifications to make a judgment than the court itself has), not to its political soundness (as to which it *would* have an institutional advantage). The basis for this criticism is spelled out in N.4 above. Secondly, one could argue that the actual effect of the burden shift in a given situation would be quite difficult to predict in advance. Thus, in the informal negotiations in which disagreements between the agency and the ARRC would usually be hammered out, both sides might sense that a committee objection would put the rule in greater jeopardy of being overturned in court, but neither side would know whether, or how far, the objection would make a difference. How this sort of mutual speculation would play out in practice is anyone's guess.

6. *Problem.* For instructors who regularly teach using the problem method, this brief fact situation provides a gateway into the issues of whether a suspensive veto is valid and whether the grounds on which legislative reviewers may rely should be restricted. Those are the most important questions about legislative review devices at the state level. We refer you to our comments on NN. 3 and 4 for discussion of those questions.

§ 7.5 EXECUTIVE CONTROL: PERSONNEL DECISIONS

§ 7.5.1 Appointment of Officers

BUCKLEY v. VALEO

Notes and Questions

1. *Buckley.* The unanimity of the Court in *Buckley* on the Appointments Clause issue can probably be explained by the fact that the text of the Constitution appears to dictate the result in unequivocal terms. In practice, however, common sense has prevailed. Presidents have recognized that the credibility of the FEC would be totally undermined if they were to stack the Commission with their own loyalists (and turncoat members of the opposition party). So they have continued to appoint commissioners selected by the congressional party leaders, even though they are not legally obligated to do so.

2. *Principal versus inferior officers.* The majority could not decide whether "inferior" meant "minor" or "subordinate" or both. As a factual matter, the former approach was shaky in the context of *Morrison* itself, and hindsight makes that flaw even clearer, for experience demonstrates that the position of independent counsel can be exceedingly powerful and long-lasting (as the examples of Lawrence Walsh and Kenneth Starr must confirm). Besides, there was force to the dissent's argument that Congress should not be able to undermine the President's appointment power by merely splitting up into small pieces positions that he would otherwise be entitled to fill. The subsequent *Edmond* case appears to reflect an abandonment of this approach to defining "inferiority."

This is not to say, however, that the dissent was necessarily right in arguing that the independent counsel could not be "inferior" because of the restrictions on her potential removal. It doesn't seem farfetched to describe Morrison as ranking below the Attorney General, in an organization-chart sense, even though he would have had trouble discharging or controlling her. Her situation doesn't seem very different from that of administrative law judges, who are appointed by department heads but enjoy considerable independence after their appointments. Scalia's reasoning might mean that the Attorney General could not even have appointed a special prosecutor to investigate presidential misconduct if the removal protection were contained in Justice Department regulations rather than a statute. Did the Constitution require that Nixon himself appoint Archibald Cox and Leon Jaworski, or that Clinton appoint Robert Fiske (Starr's predecessor, before the Ethics in Government Act was renewed)? We tend to think that the *independence* of the independent counsel is not necessarily incompatible with the *subordinateness* that Scalia himself thinks identifies an "inferior" officer.

The Court's further conclusion that the judiciary may appoint executive officers was understandable in light of the history cited by the Court, as well as the unconfined language of the Appointments Clause itself. Probably, however, the notion of "incongruity" will be used to keep the universe of such appointments small. And such appointments *should* remain infrequent, because they have such a potential for embroiling the courts in executive affairs. It was foreseeable even at the time of *Morrison* that judicial appointment of executive branch officials such as special prosecutors could potentially draw the judiciary into political controversies that could impair the public's perceptions of them as nonpartisan and impartial. Subsequent experience has, of course, borne out those dangers.

3. *More inferiority complexities.* In the *Libby* case Judge Walton assumed that *Morrison* and *Edmond* are both good law and should be harmonized. That assumption supported the constitutionality of the special counsel appointment in this case, because Fitzgerald, like Morrison, had a temporary appointment of limited scope. The issue gets more interesting, however, to the extent we assume, at least for the sake of argument, that *Edmond* provides the main point of reference.

Even with that assumption, however, Libby's argument was tenuous. One possible basis for rejecting it was that Fitzgerald had already been appointed by the President and confirmed by the Senate in his capacity as a U.S. Attorney in Chicago, and the CIA leak investigation was simply a new assignment within the scope of the original appointment. *Cf. Weiss v. United States*, 510 U.S. 163 (1994) (judges on Court of Military Appeals did not have to be appointed pursuant to Appointments Clause, because they had earlier been properly appointed as commissioned military officers).

Judge Walton did not rely on this argument. Instead, he argued that, even though Fitzgerald was not subject to day-to-day supervision by top Justice Department officials, he did have to comply with standard Justice Department prosecution policies (or rather, the court construed his letter of appointment as requiring him to comply). Moreover, Fitzgerald was removable at will. If the Attorney General had wanted to fire him, he could simply have revoked the Comey letter. The real source of Fitzgerald's job security was the political price that the administration would have paid if it had ousted him. One can rationally contend that this set of constraints was still not enough to satisfy the "supervision" element of *Edmond*. But that contention was never likely to fare well. By the time the court ruled on the Appointments Clause issue in *Libby*, court testimony had already made clear that White House officials had been deeply involved in some of the leaks that had triggered the investigation. Conflict of interest concerns obviously militated against a constitutional holding that only the President could appoint a prosecutor to investigate the leak.

In any event, Libby later moved to be released on bail on the basis that he could at least raise a substantial question of law or fact on appeal. The D.C. Circuit denied the motion and stated that he had not met that test. *United States v. Libby*, 2007 U.S.App. Lexis 16090 (D.C.Cir.2007). This decision led directly to President Bush's commutation of Libby's prison sentence.

4. *Courts of law and department heads.* We think the concurrence in *Freytag* is far more persuasive than the majority opinion. Footnote 4 in Justice Blackmun's opinion is the giveaway that his analysis is shaky: The idea that the Appointments Clause limits "Heads of Departments" to Cabinet agencies is simply not credible if it means that the top officials in the independent agencies (who would be "principal" officers) cannot appoint their own subordinates. The Constitution should allow the chair (or the members) of the FCC, for example, to appoint bureau chiefs and a general counsel for the Commission—just as Cabinet officials can do within their respective agencies. That Justice Blackmun is uncertain as to whether the SEC, or the Federal Reserve Bank of St. Louis, is a "department" casts a great deal of doubt on his notion that the Clause is intended to keep the appointment power confined to a small number of entities. That notion seems obsolete in light of the realities of our modern, far-flung federal establishment.

The idea that the Tax Court is one of the "Courts of Law" mentioned in the Appointments Clause seems to be a strained attempt to adhere to the theory just mentioned while carving out a narrow basis for upholding the obviously sensible arrangement under which the Chief Judge of the Tax Court appoints special trial judges for that court. As Scalia says, the constitutional phrase "the Courts of Law" is most naturally read as referring to Article III courts. Justice Blackmun's argument that the Tax Court fits that phrase because it adjudicates cases would appear to imply that all other executive agencies that engage in administrative adjudication are also "Courts of Law"—which seems absurd. (The majority distinguished those bodies by noting that the Tax Court *only* adjudicates cases and "is neither advocate nor rulemaker." 501 U.S. at 891. But the alleged basis for the Tax Court's appointment authority is that it exercises "judicial power;" it is not clear why an agency that exercises that power *as well as others* stands in a different position for Appointments Clause purposes.)

5. *Employees.* Notice how the majority opinion in *Freytag* has led directly to the difficulty underlying *Landry*. If the FDIC could readily be characterized as a "department," the ALJs could be treated as "inferior officers" appointed by the head of a department. But *Freytag* suggests that the FDIC cannot be a department, and the agency itself ultimately

abandoned any effort to claim such a status. 204 F.3d at 1133 n.2. In this instance the court was able to steer around that difficulty by finding that the ALJs were not even inferior officers, but mere employees. The fact that their decisions were only recommendatory made that strained argument possible. But most ALJs do have the authority to make "initial" decisions (which become final if not appealed), and that escape route from *Freytag* would not be available. It may not be long before we see another case in which the Court will be forced to revisit its limiting interpretation of what a "department" is.

As for legislative appointment of "employees," we know from *Morrison* that the Court is unwilling to erect a strict rule that all executive appointments must be made within the executive branch. With respect to appointments by legislators, however, *Bowsher* and *MWAA*, discussed at § 7.4.1 N.9, strongly suggest that the modern Court would reach the same result as in *Springer*, at least in most circumstances. The Scalia concurrence in *Freytag* contains colorful historical material regarding the Founders' support for this position, and nothing in the *Freytag* majority opinion directly cuts the other way.

6. *State appointments.* As this note explains, constitutional constraints on the appointments power in some states (though not all) are much looser than in the federal system. The *Marine Forests* decision is a good illustration of this divergence. In addition to the points made in the court's opinion, as summarized in the note, one practical factor that supported the practice of legislative appointments to the coastal commission was the inherently political nature of the commission's decisions. Land use planning involves numerous tradeoffs among incommensurable values, such as environmental protection versus commercial development. In such a system, participation by locally based political figures in the commission's staffing has some pragmatic appeal. But the fundamental issue is whether to allow functional considerations of this kind to affect the constitutional debate in the first place.

7. *Regulating politics.* *Parcell* presents a functionalist approach to appointments issues in a relatively appealing context. Providing a counterpoint to *Buckley,* it rests on a plausible public policy interest in not giving the governor total control over appointments to a body that regulates the political campaigning process. According to Devlin, the *Parcell* decision illustrates both the attractive and troubling features of a functionalist analysis of appointments issues:

> Classification of governmental functions is always difficult, and the answer to other questions posed—questions such as whether a particular level of influence by one branch over another rises to the level of "coercion," or whether the legislators' intentions are benignly

cooperative or hegemonic—appear to reside primarily in the eye of the beholder. Nor is it obvious why *these* four factors were chosen. . . . [T]he factors identified by the court appear only indirectly relevant to the concerns of efficiency, accountability, or abdication that ought to lie at the heart of distribution of powers analysis at the state level. Nevertheless, the . . . analysis seems far better able [than a formalist approach] to accommodate the evolving needs of state governance, while at the same time preserving the necessary core of autonomy that each branch must retain.

66 Temp.L.Rev. at 1250.

Green is a much more suspect decision, because it looks much more like a legislature trying to supersede the executive branch. Although the board may not have remained under the direct control of the legislature, its membership—consisting almost entirely of legislative appointees—hardly seems conducive to maintaining a strong checks and balances system. Instead of safeguarding against conflicts of interest, here the act seems to create one: it looks as though the legislature wanted to make sure that it would not be threatened by vigorous enforcement action by appointees of a different branch of government. (Or could the legislature have thought that Louisiana has such a tradition of clean politics that it didn't *need* a strong election enforcement board?)

Spradlin's reasoning is the polar opposite of *Parcell*'s: It has the virtue of predictability and the vice of potentially excessive rigidity. But the case probably reached the right result. The appointment of an ethics commission member by the chief justice has the disadvantage of entangling the judiciary in political controversies outside of the context of litigated cases. And what is the advantage of the arrangement? If its rationale was that the commission should include a member who won't be identified with any political faction or cause, experience under the federal independent counsel statute should remind us that an appointee selected by a judge will not necessarily be an apolitical figure.

8. *Legislators as appointees.* Devlin, 66 Temp.L.Rev. at 1256, is appropriately critical of *Allain*: "The grounds for this holding appear to be wholly conceptual—issues of whether such an arrangement posed any real danger to the state, whether it obscured political accountability for budgeting decisions, or whether it allowed any branch to avoid its responsibilities were all left undiscussed." Budgetary decisions routinely involve direct negotiations between the governor's office and the legislature, just as the White House and Congress regularly negotiate the outlines of a budget each fiscal year. It is hard to see how a state's formalization of such arrangements through a commission would have offended any legitimate concerns about separation of powers.

9. *Qualifications.* Legislatively prescribed qualifications for office are commonplace and usually accepted without controversy. We would suppose that Congress has broad authority under the Necessary and Proper Clause to adopt reasonable qualifications for executive offices, at least where it is not aggrandizing its own powers (such as where the qualifications are so confining that they are equivalent in substance to legislative selection of particular individuals to serve in the position). There is surprisingly little judicial precedent delimiting the scope of this authority. To that extent, President Bush's signing statement questioning the qualifications that Congress had prescribed for the FEMA Administrator may have been legally tenable, but it was certainly injudicious. The question has to be seen against the backdrop of FEMA's notorious failure to prepare adequately for Hurricane Katrina in New Orleans in 2005 and the questions raised at that time about the competence of its leadership. In that context, Congress's declaration that the next Administrator must be a person with experience and ability in the area was understandable, and the President's gesture of defiance made little sense.

10. *Problem—inferior officers.* We have provided two teaching problems in this section because federal and state law are largely divergent. This problem focuses on federal law. The FAB in the problem is based directly on the Public Company Accounting Oversight Board or PCAOB (commonly pronounced "peekaboo"). In *Free Enterprise Fund*, the D.C. Circuit upheld its constitutionality over a strong dissent by Judge Kavanaugh. After the casebook went to press, the Supreme Court granted cert. to review the decision. 129 S.Ct. 2378 (May 18, 2009).

Congress stumbled into deep constitutional waters in setting up the PCAOB because it thought it didn't need to adhere to the Appointments Clause. It structured the Board as a private corporation, somewhat like the New York Stock Exchange. Unfortunately, that was a miscalculation. At some point, everyone apparently figured out that a quasi-public corporation that wields governmental power does have to comply with the obligations of governmental entities. *See Lebron v. National Railroad Passenger Corp.*, 513 U.S. 374 (1995) (treating Amtrak as part of the government); Donna M. Nagy, "Playing Peekaboo with Constitutional Law: The PCAOB and its Public/Private Status," 80 Notre Dame L.Rev. 975 (2005). In *Free Enterprise Fund* the Board conceded in district court that the private entity rationale wouldn't fly, and the court of appeals didn't even mention that issue. The stage was thus set for a classic Appointments Clause dispute.

The first problem for Debitz will be to establish that the FAB members are not "employees" but "Officers of the United States" who must be appointed in conformity with the Appointments Clause. To some degree their situation is like that of the ALJs in *Landry*, whose decisions were mere recommendations to the FDIC. Here, too, the SEC can freely second-guess the FAB's adjudicative decisions and also its rules. However, Debitz has a strong argument that the Board does exercise "significant authority pursuant to the laws of the United States," making its members at the very least "inferior officers." The investigation in which the company is now embroiled was launched by the Board without any evident SEC participation or control. From Debitz's point of view, according to the facts of the problem, that decision was truly "significant."

Assume, then, that the Board members' appointments do have to comply with the Appointments Clause. Clearly, they do not comply unless the SEC is a "department"—an issue that *Freytag* expressly left open. Judge Rogers, for the majority in *Free Enterprise Fund*, said that the SEC is "Cabinet-like" in the range of powers it exercises. Her strongest argument was that a contrary holding would be impractical—the Commission, and by extension other independent agencies, surely ought to be able to appoint its own subordinate officials. That proposition seems persuasive (at least the SEC is more "like" a Cabinet department than the Tax Court is), but *Freytag* does not provide any sure guidance on this issue. A secondary issue is whether, assuming it is a department, its head is the full Commission or only its Chair. Judge Rogers saw no difficulty with the concept that a "Department" could have multi-member heads, and longstanding practice supports that assumption.

Judge Kavanaugh agreed with the majority on the points noted in the preceding paragraph (537 F.3d at 712 n.24), but he dissented on the ground that the members of the PCAOB are actually *principal* officers, who must be appointed by the President and confirmed by the Senate. In the problem, Debitz can argue that *Morrison* is easily distinguishable. The FAB members have regular jobs with the government—not a special, one-shot assignment, as an independent counsel had. Moreover, the special equities that underlay *Morrison* are not implicated here. The goal of improving corporate audits does not implicate the conflict of interest difficulties that demanded that the President be barred from appointing an independent counsel. Debitz also has valid grounds for distinguishing *Edmond*. The FAB is subject to less supervision than the Coast Guard court in *Edmond* was. The latter entity was supervised in both its decisions and its day-to-day operations, but the FAB is supervised only in its decisions (both adjudicative and rulemaking). Since members of the FAB can be removed only for good cause, the SEC could have had little say in, for example, the Board's decision to conduct an intrusive investigation into Debitz's affairs.

The Board also has good arguments, however. In the first place, the SEC's appointment power surely creates no "incongruity" of the kind contemplated in *Morrison*. If any administrative body is to appoint the members of the FAB, the Commission is the most logical candidate. Furthermore, *Edmond* is entirely unclear as to the amount of "supervision" that is required in order to make an officer "inferior." The powers that the SEC does have give it quite a bit of leverage over the Board. If it discerns a pattern of overly zealous investigations, it can modify the Board's rules to circumscribe them. Perhaps, therefore, the court should defer to Congress's judgment and uphold the Act.

It should be obvious that this fact situation also raises serious constitutional issues about the removal power. The President does have some control over the FAB, but it is two steps removed from direct supervision. He has only limited control over the SEC, and the SEC has only limited control over the Board. Instructors may wish to return to this fact situation when they teach the next unit. The D.C. Circuit majority and dissenting opinions discuss that issue comprehensively as well. It is possible, therefore, that the Court won't reach the Appointments Clause issues at all in its upcoming decision in this case.. If it does resolve them, we'll replace the problem in an upcoming supplement or new edition.

11. *Problem—judicial appointment.* In *Melott* the Supreme Court of North Carolina held that a statute like the one in the problem was constitutional. The court made the quite dubious argument that the appointment power is not an executive function; therefore, even if the position of OAH Director was executive in nature, the legislature could entrust it to someone other than the governor. (We have been told informally that the real motive for the statute was that the governor was a Republican, and the Democratic-controlled legislature didn't want to give him the appointment.)

Since states don't adhere to the intricacies of the federal Supreme Court's Appointments Clause case law, you can use class discussion of this problem to explore broad separation of powers themes. Proponents of a strict approach can argue that governors cannot effectively execute the laws unless they can put people into top positions who agree with their policies and whom they trust; and that such an arrangement improves accountability. Opponents of such an approach can say that, while the foregoing points may be valid as a general matter, the range of possible offices needing appointments is so broad that the court should read the constitution flexibly, reserving the separation of powers doctrine for specific occasions on which the legislature clearly overreaches. Consider, also, Devlin's policy arguments for giving state legislatures more leeway than Congress has (*see* N.7).

Probably, however, Madison has *some* category of "inferior officers" who don't have to be appointed by the governor personally. If Gunther is deemed to fall into that category, the remaining question would be whether his appointment by the Chief Justice could be considered "incongruous" (to use the terminology of *Morrison*). Superficially it is not, because an ALJ acts "judicially" and a supreme court justice can feasibly understand the job and pick a competent person to fill it. Nevertheless, there is little precedent in this country for courts choosing ALJs of agencies, and the general policy of keeping the courts separate from the political fray would suggest reasons to question the propriety of the statute.

The ultimate legal question is whether, in these particular circumstances, the Chief Justice's appointment of the state's head ALJ violates separation of powers notions. In *Melott* a concurrence and a dissent debated this question in terms of whether the Director's position was "executive" or "judicial." The concurrence said that the job was predominantly "judicial" or "quasi-judicial," and thus could be filled by the Chief Justice. The Director's administrative duties were incidental, and case-deciding was the heart of the job. Possibly one could add that, if one cares enough about the independence of the ALJ corps, selection by a relatively non-political figure makes sense.

The dissent said that this use of the "judicial" label was extravagant, because numerous agency officials in the executive branch also frequently sit in contested cases; you can't plausibly say that all of them could be removed from the governor's control (let alone entrusted to the state's chief justice). Moreover, the executive functions of the Director shouldn't be brushed aside. They call for policy decisions that shouldn't be the concern of the state's head jurist (*cf. Spradlin*); and there should be political accountability, such as through the governor, if OAH isn't functioning properly. The problem doesn't say whether the Chief Justice faces periodic retention elections. If she does, it might be suggested that S.B. 234 does leave room for some political accountability. But that's unconvincing, because even elected jurists don't have the continuous contact with interest groups and the systematic marshaling and consolidation of political support that is customary in the "political" branches.

If one wants to apply the *Parcell* four-factor formula here, the labeling game played above speaks inconclusively to the first factor. We would suppose that S.B. 234 is unconstitutional under *Parcell*, because, although the legislature itself isn't usurping the governor's power, the goal of the statute is to entirely displace the governor from this corner of running the government, instead of simply working with the governor in a "cooperative" arrangement (factor two). Moreover, the policy justifications for superseding the chief executive's normal role (factor three) are not overwhelming here. We haven't enough facts to know how the system works in practice (factor four).

§ 7.5.2 Removal of Officers

§ 7.5.2a The Rise of the Independent Agency

HUMPHREY'S EXECUTOR v. UNITED STATES

2. *Supreme Court analysis.* Even though the Court in *Morrison* was very critical of the analysis of *Humphrey's Executor,* the earlier decision is worth some class time, because it is still an influential case, and indeed the institution of independent agencies has grown up on the basis of it. Its analytical structure is weak, however, and it's no wonder that by the time of *Morrison* no Justice had a kind word to say for it.

You might start the discussion by exploring why, as *Myers* argued, there must be *some* limits to Congress' power to shield administrative officials from presidential removal. In the case of a sensitive position like Secretary of State, it seems obvious that a President should not have to put up with the previous administration's appointee, no matter what Congress may have provided. An administration can hardly function well unless its key officeholders are people who are committed to the President's policies and enjoy the President's trust.

Although the sweeping language of *Myers* may have needed some curtailment, the conceptual distinction in *Humphrey's Executor* between "executive" functions, on the one hand, and "quasi-legislative" and "quasi-adjudicative" functions, on the other, was quite troublesome. *See* Strauss, 84 Colum.L.Rev. at 611-16. The New Deal assumption that an agency like the FTC could simply apply expertise and experience, enforcing "no policy but the policy of the law," seems hopelessly outmoded. Obviously the agency does make policy judgments, and those judgments are not very different from the kind of determinations that normally accompany the *execution* of the law. Indeed, executing any important statute will normally entail extensive rulemaking and adjudication, which are "quasi-legislative" and "quasi-adjudicative" respectively.

Looking at the issue on a more pragmatic level, one could see a justification for independence in the case of an agency with a narrowly confined adjudicative role (*see* N.3). In those early days the FTC was considered to have a very narrow role. But *Humphrey's Executor* has come to be understood as supporting the independence of agencies like the FCC, SEC, and modern FTC, which obviously do make important policy judgments through both rulemaking and adjudication. Rulemaking in particular, a "quasi-legislative" function, is manifestly a political enterprise, and the *Myers* reasoning had far more relevance to it than the Court in *Humphrey's Executor* was willing to acknowledge.

This is not to say that the independent agency concept has nothing to it. In the article cited in this note, Shane reviews the arguments for the strict unitary executive theory but finds them insufficient. Presidential control over the agencies has benefits in terms of political responsiveness and policy coordination, but the independent agency model contributes to the primacy of Congress in domestic matters and also serves to promote what may be a healthy diffusion of power within the executive establishment. 57 Geo.Wash.L.Rev. at 621-23. Shane also rejects the textualist argument that the Constitution's vesting of "the executive power" in the President means that the President must have total control over executive functions; in his view, the Necessary and Proper Clause clearly indicates that Congress has broad latitude to regulate or limit the President's exercises of that power. *Id.* at 599-602.

But even if the idea of independence has some merit, there seems to be little logic to the present distribution of functions between independent and executive agencies. Indeed, it is hard to see a difference of constitutional dimension between the functions of, for example, the FCC and SEC ("independent"), on the one hand, and the EPA and Transportation Department ("executive"), on the other. In practice, the decision about which entities will be independent has been resolved in the political arena by Congress and the President on the more or less random basis of their relative political strength or bargaining power at a given time.

In a thoughtful article, Paul Verkuil has suggested a realignment of functions as between independent and executive agencies that might make sense of the jumble. Essentially, he would concentrate adjudicative functions in multi-member independent agencies (including some functions now performed by executive agencies), and he would transfer many of the policy duties of independent commissions to agencies that would be headed by a single administrator, in some cases protected by tenure. Paul R. Verkuil, "The Purposes and Limits of Independent Agencies," 1988 Duke L.J. 257, 275-79. But political actors seem satisfied with the chaotic status quo.

3. *Removal of adjudicators.* *Wiener* has been a relatively uncontroversial precedent, because presidential control over purely adjudicative bodies would raise due process problems, as even *Myers* seemed to acknowledge; and control over these functions has not been a priority for Presidents anyway. *Wiener* would prove too much, however, if it were read to stand for the proposition that Congress is presumed to give—or constitutionally *could* give—tenure to the members of any agency that engages in adjudication. Even the Attorney General has some adjudicative responsibilities (such as in the immigration area). When an adjudicative role is combined with policymaking responsibility, as in the more typical independent agency, the presidential interest in having a say in the agency's

decisionmaking becomes much stronger than was the case in *Wiener*. In short, *Wiener* was an easy case that did not force the Court to confront the highly problematic aspects of the independent agency concept. (Since the War Claims Commission was only given a three-year life span, the Court in *Wiener* also didn't have to face the question, raised in later cases, of whether a fixed term of office implies a legislative desire to protect agency heads from arbitrary removal.)

§ 7.5.2b Removal Issues in the Modern Era

MORRISON v. OLSON

1. *Morrison.* The *Morrison* opinion goes to some lengths to compare the independent counsel with the independent agencies and thus to reaffirm the constitutionality of the latter. Yet, even as the Court acknowledges that the *Humphrey's Executor* reasoning is a shaky basis for removal restrictions, it offers a substitute rationale that is also quite vulnerable to attack, or at least quite perplexing. The heart of this rationale is that the "good cause" removal restrictions are not *really* much of an impediment to the President's ability to fulfill his constitutional duties. It is an odd assertion, because the very point of the removal restrictions is to tie the President's hands. As Justice Scalia quips, this "is somewhat like referring to shackles as an effective means of locomotion."

More fundamentally, this basis for the Court's willingness to accept an agency's freedom from presidential control has no obvious stopping point. The implication might be that the President's constitutional duties are really quite modest, so that Congress has broad power to carve agencies out of the presidential domain. On the other hand, the Court does reaffirm *Myers,* so there must be some limits to Congress's ability to create "independence." We just can't tell where they are.

What is truly surprising about the *Morrison* opinion is that it puts so little emphasis on what most people would have thought was the most powerful argument supporting the independent counsel statute: the idea that the executive branch cannot be trusted to investigate its own wrongdoing. In fact, the Court barely mentions this point. The only allusion to it appears at the end of the Court's discussion of the removal restriction as such, just before the Court turns to appraising the Act "taken as a whole." The opinion notes that "[h]ere, as with the provision of the Act conferring the appointment authority of the independent counsel on the special court, the congressional determination to limit the removal power of the Attorney General was essential, in the view of Congress, to establish the necessary independence of the office." 487 U.S. at 692-93. Even then, you have to turn back to the section of the opinion on appointments to uncover the observation that "Congress of course was concerned . . . with the conflicts of interest that could arise in situations when the Executive Branch is called upon to investigate its own high-ranking officials." *Id.* at 677 (quoted in § 7.5.1 N.2 of the casebook).

One could have imagined an opinion focusing on this specific concern. The Court could have used the *Nixon v. Administrator of General Services* test, arguing that, in the language of that opinion, the Act's "potential for disruption [of executive branch functions] is justified by an overriding need to promote objectives within the constitutional authority of Congress." Such a rationale would have been reasonably persuasive on its own terms— although it would still have been vulnerable to Justice Scalia's charges that it is too subjective and that it gravely weakens the presidency.

Instead of deciding the case on that narrow basis, however, the Court seemingly went out of its way to discuss the status of the special prosecutor in terms that could easily be extended to other independent agencies. *See* Glen O. Robinson, "Independent Agencies: Form and Substance in Executive Prerogative," 1988 Duke L.J. 238, 240-41. Possibly this is one of those occasions when one can assume that a rationale not stated in the Court 's opinions *must* have had something to do with the outcome. But the opinion as written constitutes a strong affirmation of the independent agency concept. Unfortunately, it doesn't do much to delimit the permissible boundaries of "independence;" the Court seems willing for now to leave that question open for resolution within the political process. (However, the suggestion in footnote 30 that independence may be justified where "necessary to the proper functioning of the agency or official" seems reasonably intelligible. In context, it appears to mean that Congress may confer tenure on "quasi-judicial" officers like those in *Wiener*. How much further this argument could extend remains uncertain.)

As a practical matter, *Morrison* seems to have quelled the broad-gauge assault on independent agencies in the courts. As the note indicates, however, the unitary executive theory has retained its strong supporters outside of judicial circles down to the present day. *See* Stephen G. Calabresi & Christopher S. Yoo, THE UNITARY EXECUTIVE: PRESIDENTIAL POWER FROM WASHINGTON TO BUSH (2008).

Incidentally, students may be confused by the Court's remark that "*Myers* was undoubtedly correct in its holding." The Court surely did not mean to imply that a President's inability to remove a postmaster in Oregon is more of an obstacle to a successful presidency than his inability to discharge a special prosecutor who is investigating a high-ranking member of the administration. Common sense belies that notion. Nor could the Court have meant to rely on the fact that a postmaster does not legislate or adjudicate; *Humphrey's Executor* had relied on that distinction, but *Morrison* obviously means to disavow it. Rather, the Court's point must be that the actual holding of *Myers* was that the Senate could not reserve *for itself* the right to veto the dismissal of the postmaster. Rehnquist had no difficulty suggesting that the legislature may not participate in the decision about whether to remove a specific individual from office, because *Bowsher* had reaffirmed that aspect of *Myers* only two years earlier. This analysis might provide you with a jumping off point for a discussion of the *Bowsher* decision.

2. *Demise of the independent counsel statute.* The constitutional question in this note provides a good opportunity to challenge students to think carefully about the reasoning of *Morrison*. The question is more difficult than it may seem. Scalia's apprehensions about the practical consequences of the independent counsel statute have come to be seen as prophetic, but the claim that he was right about the constitutionality of the statute may carry more far-reaching implications than many people realize.

The world now knows, if it did not know before, that the independent counsel statute certainly can "impede the President's ability to perform his constitutional duty," in the sense that it can result in a major intrusion on the time and attention (and pocketbooks) of key members of the administration, including the President personally. But these costs would appear not to be the sort of "impediments" that *Morrison* was talking about. Rather, *Morrison* was referring to the "impediment" that results when a President cannot remove, and therefore cannot control the discretionary decisions of, a subordinate officer. And, while the discretionary decisions of an independent counsel were surely important ones, they were not clearly more important than the policy decisions of the heads of the FTC, FCC, SEC, and so forth. The Court clearly did not want to abandon the independent agency concept wholesale. It may have been for the best, therefore, that the design flaws of the Ethics Act were ultimately rectified through legislative change rather than through judicial reconsideration of the constitutional issue.

3. *Legislative removal.* On a relatively concrete level, the *Bowsher* holding does not seem unreasonable. The principle that Congress may not remove agency officials dates back to *Myers*. And, while the extension of this principle to a potential but never-exercised element of congressional "control" might seem overly dogmatic, there were significant reasons to conclude that the Gramm-Rudman Act presented separation of powers problems. Basically, as the concurrence in *Bowsher* argued, the Comptroller General is a congressional functionary. (*See* § 7.4.3 N.b for a discussion of the GAO's usual duties.) Congress gave him the job of estimating the anticipated deficit because it didn't trust the Reagan administration to produce honest numbers. That mistrust may have been justified, but the job of implementing Gramm-Rudman was not fundamentally different from the job of implementing other legislation. If Congress could withhold that task

from the executive branch, on what basis could the Court thereafter limit the legislature's ability to keep any of its other initiatives out of Reagan's hands? Such line-drawing would have been difficult. In that light, the Court's preference for a flat constitutional rule may have been understandable. (The premise that Stevens was right about the role of the Comptroller General also explains why, in our view, Blackmun was wrong. The Comptroller General's ties to Congress were so numerous that merely severing the removal provision wouldn't really have cured the separation of powers difficulties with Gramm-Rudman.)

An interesting sidelight on this case is that Chief Justice Burger, in the first draft of his majority opinion, tried to rest the decision on a unitary executive theory. The draft argued that the fatal flaw in the Act was that the *President* would have no power to remove an official with "executive" responsibilities. A chorus of Justices immediately objected that this argument was unacceptable because it would cast doubt on the constitutionality of the independent agencies. Burger was forced to back down and adopt a different rationale. *See* Bernard Schwartz, "An Administrative Law `Might Have Been'—Chief Justice Burger's *Bowsher v. Synar* Draft," 42 Admin. L.Rev. 221 (1990).

4. *Functionalism. Morrison* distinguished *Bowsher* on the ground that the earlier case had involved an attempt by Congress to aggrandize its own power. Crude as it may seem, this simple distinction does a pretty good job of explaining most of the Court's recent separation of powers holdings: the Court has used formalism in cases of congressional aggrandizement (*Buckley, Chadha, Bowsher, MWAA*) and functionalism in cases in which Congress has regulated the other branches (*Schor, Morrison, Mistretta*). The distinction also has a certain logic to it. Where Congress is seeking to advance its own institutional interests, a strict approach to separation of powers promotes the principle of checks and balances; elsewhere, Congress's authority under the necessary and proper clause invites greater judicial deference. Nevertheless, *Clinton v. City of New York,* the line item veto case, shows that the absence of congressional aggrandizement doesn't guarantee that an innovation will survive.

Another arguable justification for *Bowsher* is that the main point of the principle of separated powers is that law-writing should be kept separate from law-implementing. Since Congress has such wide control over the former, a principle that denies Congress any power over the latter may be defensible. At least, the Court appears to have proceeded on this assumption in its modern cases, and the *MWAA* case (which was post-*Morrison*) indicates that the Court has not changed its mind on this score. This line of argument does jibe pretty well with *New York,* which can be seen as making the converse point (sub silentio): since the President has broad control over law-execution, his law-writing role should be strictly confined to what Article I, § 7 gives him. (That rationale for *New York* doesn't fully answer the dissenters' point in that case that the line item veto was similar to a delegation, but at least the majority faced that issue and did its best to distinguish the two situations. *See* § 7.4.1 N.10.)

5. *State constitutions.* As the federal experience attests, removal controversies arise in a wide variety of contexts, ranging from situations in which plenary removal authority for the chief executive makes a lot of sense to situations in which it makes very little sense. Not surprisingly, state constitutional provisions that prescribe (or are construed to prescribe) a single principle to govern all situations are bound to generate some anomalies.

Thus, *Wilcox* took liberties with explicit constitutional language in light of powerful policy arguments that a governor ought to be able to remove key members of his administration who are not effectively promoting his policies. *See Lunding,* 359 N.E.2d at 97. "'[I]f one of the governor's cabinet members, a director of a major department, developed either a major policy difference with the governor or even simply a major personality difference with the governor, . . . the governor ought to be permitted to remove him. . . .'" *Id.* at 100 (quoting state Sen. [and Prof.] Dawn Clark Netsch). In *Lunding,* however, the court saw that *Wilcox,* too, might be too extreme. An election board is a paradigmatic example of an agency that should not be too heavily influenced by an incumbent governor. Both of the court's holdings make sense to us as reasonable efforts to cope with overly rigid constitutional language.

A related issue in most of these cases has been whether the appointee has a due process right to be heard before being removed. You could raise this issue for review purposes here—or you might find that it makes a good exam question. Three capable opinions in *Adams* develop both sides of the due process question. Analytically, *Roth* seems to imply that the criteria stated in the constitutional provision (incompetence, neglect of duty, malfeasance) create a "legitimate claim of entitlement," even if judicial review of the merits was unavailable. *See* § 2.2.1. But the majority in *Adams* argued that *as construed by the state,* these criteria were meaningless. (Note the parallel between the reasoning of Judge Stevens, concurring in *Adams,* and that of Justice Stevens in *Bishop v. Wood,* § 2.2.2 N.3.) The majority simply could not believe that the occupant of a sensitive policymaking position in the government could have "property rights" in his job. The opinions in *Adams* also contain good analyses of the "stigma" issue. To the majority, removal for "neglect of duty" was widely understood as boilerplate—it was recited in order to satisfy the constitutional provision, but actually meant nothing more than "I can find a better commissioner." 492 F.2d at 1008. The dissent forcefully argued that this subtlety might be lost on bar disciplinary authorities and the general newspaper-reading public, so the stigma was real. *Id.* at 1014-17 (Pell, J., dissenting).

6. *Good cause.* In the cited article, Lessig and Sunstein read the language of *Morrison* and *Bowsher* at face value. They suggest that a statute that allows dismissal only for "good cause" can legitimately be interpreted as leaving the President "a large degree of removal and supervisory power." Their argument is presented ingeniously and with full acknowledgment that it is contrary to conventional wisdom, but we are skeptical about it. The government operates from day to day on the generally shared assumption that a "cause" criterion confers a high degree of job security. We doubt that some incautious language in a few Supreme Court opinions should be interpreted to dislodge that customary assumption (although of course it *can* be so interpreted).

The opinion of the Massachusetts court in *Levy* is insightful insofar as it recognizes that some gubernatorial findings of "cause" require closer judicial scrutiny than others. Essentially the court is drawing the same distinction as the one drawn in the Illinois cases discussed in N.5. Independence is more important for some state agencies than for others. The actual outcome of the case may be debatable, as the 4-3 vote reflects. Even with respect to independent agencies, a "cause" standard must mean something, and an allegation of fiscal irresponsibility might qualify as such, as the dissenters maintained. On the other hand, the majority made a credible case that the rhetoric about irresponsibility was somewhat overheated. Regardless, even the dissenters did recognize that a dismissal of an MTA member for "cause" would have to rest on a more compelling basis than a mere policy disagreement with the governor. Thus, the Lessig-Sunstein view did not find support on this court.

Incidentally, the MTA in this case is not the subway operator featured in the well-known Kingston Trio song that exhorted the citizens of Boston to "fight the fare increase . . . and get Charlie off the MTA." That was the Metropolitan Transit Authority (now Massachusetts Bay Transit Authority).

In the abstract, the remarkable *Bouton* case about the dress code may seem to be evidence of a robust executive power to find "cause." (After all, doesn't it get pretty warm in the Virgin Islands?) More likely, however, the case should not be taken very seriously. Its finding of "cause" is announced fleetingly in a nonprecedential opinion, with no supporting reasoning. Perhaps the court simply assumed, without thinking about it, that it could give the "cause" standard an employment law meaning, ignoring the somewhat higher standard customarily associated with that term in a statute that is designed to protect the independence of administrative officials.

7. *Inferring tenure.* A statutory provision under which an appointee "shall serve a term of X years" can easily be read to imply that an appointing authority may not remove the appointee without cause before the X years have expired. But the inference is not inescapable. The provision could simply mean that the legislature wants regular turnover (or at least the possibility of regular turnover) in the agency's leadership. Fixed terms allow a chief executive to accomplish this objective gracefully, without the trauma of a "dismissal," but are not necessarily incompatible with a policy of allowing the chief executive to replace the agency head immediately if she wishes. *See Adams,* 492 F.2d at 1007. This seems to be the basis for the *Parsons* decision. For a discussion of *Shurtleff* and *Parsons* as illustrating how background principles of administrative law can trump plain meaning in statutory construction, see Jonathan R. Siegel, "Textualism and Contextualism in Administrative Law," 78 B.U.L.Rev. 1023, 1035-37 (1998).

The U.S. Attorneys scandal does not necessarily suggest that *Parsons* should be reconsidered. The episode illustrates a point of which students should be aware: political remedies can often lead to accountability when judicially enforceable rights cannot. In this instance, the firings led to the inspector general's report cited in the note, as well as highly visible congressional hearings, proceedings in the legislative ethics committees, grand jury probes, etc. The upshot was multiple resignations and considerable political damage for the administration. Whether these repercussions were "enough" can be debated, but certainly this was one episode in which political accountability did not depend on whether the dismissed U.S. Attorneys could litigate to get their jobs back.

8. *Inferring tenure in the states.* The *Schluraff* plurality's distinction between fixed staggered terms and fixed concurrent terms seems labored. True, the distinction finds some support in the language of *Watson,* which argues that a plenary removal power would undercut the legislative objective (implied by staggered terms) of always having some experienced members on the board. 125 A.2d at 357. Nevertheless, the separate opinions in *Schluraff* are persuasive in suggesting that if staggered terms imply tenure, so does any fixed term.

The Pennsylvania cases could be considered another example of overly mechanical jurisprudence. Had the court taken a more functional analysis, it could have argued that a real estate assessment board is an almost purely judicial body that should operate free of political influence. In other words, the logic of *Wiener* would have invited a different result here. On the other hand, the Pennsylvania approach is easier to apply than the intricacies of federal law. It does, therefore, at least have the virtue of letting appointees and governors know what their legal rights will be in the event of a falling out.

9. *Problem*. Although federal and state law cannot be sharply distinguished in the removal area, we have divided our problem into federal and state components so that classroom discussion does not have to be confined to an analysis of the current federal case law (assuming anybody can figure out what it means!). The teacher can also ask what principles the state of Madison *should* adopt.

In the real *Pievsky* case, the background circumstances suggest that Governor Tom Ridge's forceful actions may well have been a good-government move. His dismissals followed a series of newspaper exposés disclosing a pattern of patronage, one-bid contracts, and mismanagement (i.e., squandering most of the reserves) attributable to a Democratic faction that dominated the port authority. To clean house, Ridge sought to get rid of the old guard. *See* Nancy Phillips, "Ruling Lets Ridge Pick DRPA Team," Philadelphia Inquirer, April 13, 1996. The judges probably knew about these allegations, but they do not appear in the opinion. Thus, the case proceeded on the assumption that the governor had to show that he could replace the commissioners without showing "cause," and our problem rests on the same assumption.

Analytically, there are two issues here. First, should the five-year term provision be read to imply that the commissioners may be removed only for cause? Second, if it is read that way, is it constitutionally suspect? In practice, however, these issues would blend together, because the court's view of constitutional policy could of course influence its interpretation of this ambiguous statute.

In *Pievsky*, the Third Circuit supported the governor on every issue. Citing *Parsons*, the court said: "It is a long-standing rule in the federal courts that a fixed term merely provides a time for the term to end. The fixed term is merely a `cap' with the appointee removable at will." 98 F.3d at 734. Also, the case involved Pennsylvania officials, and the court relied on *Schluraff* as an expression of Pennsylvania law (which the court said was not controlling but deserved "deference"). *Id.* at 738-39. Although the court appears to have overstated the federal "rule," its construction is at least reasonable. See our discussion above in N.7. The relative merits of a fixed rule of thumb versus a more functional analysis can be explored here.

Turning to the constitutional issue, let's first assume that under federal law—or at least Madison law—the court may look to the principles of *Myers* and *Humphrey's Executor*. In *Pievsky* the Third Circuit made a fairly strong argument that the port authority fell on the *Myers* side of the line rather than on the *Humphrey's Executor* and *Wiener* side. The court argued correctly that this analysis turns on the character of the agency's functions. Although the actions of the agency may technically be "adjudication" in the sense that they are not rulemaking, they involve

433

basically discretionary and policy judgments, as opposed to applying some supposedly neutral rule of law to factual disputes. In *Pievsky* the court described the DRPA (Delaware River Port Authority) as "a politically sensitive body that must be responsive to the programs and policies of the administration presently in office." The court quoted from one of its earlier decisions in which it had said:

> The policy and political issues, including economic considerations, arising in an entity such as the DRPA are many. If tolls are raised, bridges fall into disrepair, or traffic is congested, there are surely political consequences. Whether decent roads and transit systems will be made available to all segments of the communities, or will be provided in a manner perceived as favoring some or excluding others, raises important and sensitive social, economic and political questions.

Id. at 735. Thus, the "ability of the Governor to remove DRPA Commissioners ensures that the commissioners are politically accountable to each state's administration." *Id.* at 736. In the court's eyes, this reasoning distinguished the DRPA from the FTC in *Humphrey's Executor,* which the Supreme Court had envisioned as a nonpartisan body, and from *Wiener,* in which the agency's tasks were better described as adjudicatory in the narrow sense. We find this analysis fairly convincing. It rests, however, on the premise that the governor has political responsibility for the port authority. That premise is evidently not shared in all jurisdictions. The *Levy* case in N.6 proceeds on a contrary premise, and so does *Alcorn*, the Virginia-based case cited in the problem, which reached a result contrary to *Pievsky*'s on very similar facts.

But would the answer change under *Morrison*? In *Pievsky* the court said no, because "the Governor's inability to remove DRPA Commissioners prior to the expiration of their terms would impede his ability to carry out his functions as Chief Executive." *Id.* at 737. Maybe so, but why is that impairment any more grave than the impairment of the President's functions in *Morrison*? The difficulty, or perhaps impossibility, of answering that question shows why *Morrison* is such a frustrating opinion. Surely the "control" that the Court said the President could exercise over the independent counsel does not distinguish the cases, because presumably the PRPA commissioner in our problem could at least be removed if "cause" were shown. And, as we have emphasized above, the conflict of interest aspect of *Morrison,* which might have furnished an easy way to distinguish the cases, got barely a whisper of attention from the Supreme Court.

§ 7.6 EXECUTIVE OVERSIGHT

In the previous edition of this casebook, we split our coverage of E.O. 12,866 between § 5.8 and this section. In the current edition, most of the coverage is consolidated here. In addition, because of the importance to the present unit of the executive oversight discussion in *Sierra Club v. Costle*, § 5.5.2, along with N.5 following that case, you should consider noting on your assignment sheet that students should review that material.

EXECUTIVE ORDER 12,866

For the principal reading for this section, we have excerpted E.O. 12,866 in the form in which President Clinton originally promulgated it. That version was in effect when the casebook went to press. Thus, the reprinted version does not include the amendments that President Bush made in 2001 and 2007, because President Obama rescinded them shortly after taking office. Some of those amendments are, however, discussed in NN. 2 and 9. Presumably the Obama administration will revise or replace the executive order soon.

Notes and Questions

1. *Case law background.* Justice Jackson's concurring opinion in *Youngstown* is the iconic pronouncement in this area. It doesn't settle any specific issues, but it does provide a very useful framework for analysis. We give it only minimal attention here, because we assume that the general topic of separation of powers between the President and Congress—as distinguished from its specific application in the context of administrative agencies— is covered in the constitutional law course.

2. *Evolution of OIRA oversight.* It is interesting to notice that the Clinton executive order was acceptable enough to the subsequent Bush administration that the latter was willing to live within its basic structure, subject to a few amendments. One reason for the durability of E.O. 12,866, we think, is that it was a sophisticated synthesis of competing perspectives. It maintained the Republicans' commitment to the principle of executive oversight, but eliminated many of the procedural deficiencies that had antagonized Democrats. Both administrations have recognized that they could improve the acceptability of their operations by taking steps in the direction of greater transparency.

3. *Merits of executive oversight.* As the literature surveyed in this note suggests, the merits of OIRA review are much debated. Our own reaction, however, is largely favorable to the process. At the margins, presidential review can infuse a democratic element into a rulemaking

proceeding, because of the administration's contacts with the political process on an ongoing basis. Even lame-duck Presidents are usually highly attentive to public opinion, because of their desires to preserve their personal popularity and that of their party; and of course this tendency is even more marked among Presidents who can run for re-election. Thus, one should expect the White House to use the oversight process to influence agencies to modify particular proposed regulations at the margins, so as to bring these rules into closer harmony with the President's overall political program (although that program is itself likely to be an amalgam of conflicting elements and uneasy compromise positions, and to be variable over time).

4. *Legality of executive oversight.* The prevailing reading of *Kendall* and *Myers* is that when an administrative decision is delegated to an agency official, the official has the final legal responsibility to make the decision and the President cannot lawfully order her to make one of his own choosing. This is clearly the assumption underlying *Sierra Club*: the court's affirmation that the President may exert "influence" makes sense only in the context of an assumption that the President cannot make the decision unilaterally. Even *Myers,* a notably pro-presidential decision, acknowledges this limitation on the chief executive's power (see the last paragraph of the quote from *Myers* in § 7.5.2a). On the other hand, at least in the case of *executive* agencies, the President certainly may fire an agency head if he disagrees with her decision. The President doesn't need to have a "good" reason, because the whole point of *Myers* was that the agency head may be fired for *any* reason. (Regarding independent agencies, see N.7 below.)

An attractive aspect of the notion that the President may influence but may not command an agency head to act in a certain way is that it preserves roles for both political responsiveness and bureaucratic rationality in the rulemaking process. The White House presses its political concerns, the agency takes a stand on the basis of its expertise and technocratic values, and then the two sides negotiate to resolve their differences. Each side may win some battles and lose others. The outcome in a particular context will depend in part (one hopes) on the relative strength of these competing considerations in that context.

5. *Where the buck stops.* On its face, E.O. 12,866 is ambiguous about whether the President (or Vice President acting for the President) can overrule an agency. The first paragraph of § 7 says that one of these elected officials will resolve conflicts "with the relevant agency head," suggesting a collaborative approach. The last paragraph sounds much more hierarchical: the President or Vice President "shall *notify* the affected agency and the Administrator of OIRA of the President's decision with respect to the matter." Yet this provision co-exists with others that affirm the agency's decisionmaking authority (§§ 2(a), 9), not to mention the frequent

reminders, including one in § 7, that the order only applies "to the extent permitted by law."

As we suggested in the preceding note, to the extent the order is ambiguous, the preferable answer in principle is that the agency head has the legal power to decide, and the White House is at most free to exert influence. This aspect of the order is well discussed in Pildes & Sunstein, 62 U.Chi.L.Rev. at 24-28. They note that, in practice, the agency head is likely to want to be a team player. Her acceding to the White House's desires is not necessarily bad, if the underlying statute permits such a choice. Again, when each side decides how hard to press for its preferred outcome in a particular instance, it makes that judgment in the context of an ongoing working relationship between the President and agency, in which each is in a position to help or hurt the other.

6. *Presidential administration.* As the preceding notes imply, we are skeptical about Kagan's suggestion that a court should review a presidentially-directed action, at least in the sense of acting as though the President has stepped into the agency head's shoes. *See* 114 Harv.L.Rev. at 2351. (Kagan is now serving as U.S. Solicitor General.) Even taking the general thrust of her reasoning as a given, she could have taken a more moderate approach to it. She might instead have suggested that the courts should continue to treat the agency head as the relevant actor, but that the agency head's statement that "the President told me to do it" should be accepted as a legitimate factor for the agency head to have considered, where the statute otherwise permits such a reading. Kagan's proposed default principle of statutory construction would be a bit less of a stretch this way.

In fact, this type of reasoning is not very different, if different at all, from today's operative principles. *See, e.g., Whitman v. American Trucking Ass'ns,* 531 U.S. 457 (2001). After the Court upheld the Clean Air Act against nondelegation attack, as discussed in § 7.2.1c, it reviewed EPA's selection of a strategy for implementing the ozone standard. Although the Court openly recognized that the strategy had come about at the "request" of the White House, it treated the action before it as the action of EPA. 531 U.S. at 477-79.

Continued adherence to the premise that the agency head remains the decisionmaker, at least formally, would also harmonize better with the fundamental APA principle that the agency must be accountable for giving "consideration" to (§ 553(c)) and responding to public comments. That accountability is important, both in a judicial review context and in a more general good-government context. We can appreciate the force of Kagan's point (114 Harv.L.Rev. at 2360) that the big-picture decisions will often be made at a level of government where public comments will for practical purposes be "show." Even so, outside groups should be able to expect that their comments might influence the details of the rule at the margins, and under current law that assumption will frequently be realistic.

7. *Independent agencies.* Certainly, Congress's designation of an agency as "independent" implies a desire to remove it, at least in part, from presidential influence. Extension of OIRA oversight to such agencies would be somewhat at odds with that desire. However, the ABA and ACUS recommendations supporting such an extension appear to rest on a perception that the distinction between executive and independent agencies is incoherent anyway, and thus should not be given a great deal of deference. The strongest arguments for independent status usually focus on a desire to remove *adjudicative* functions from politics. *See* § 7.5.2. But OIRA review deals with the writing of *rules*—and economically "significant" rules, at that. This is an inherently political activity. Congress itself would never agree to keep its fingers out of most such proceedings, so the suggestion that the President should have no say in them seems rather hypocritical.

In that context, there is force to Strauss and Sunstein's argument that independent agencies' rulemaking should be subject to OIRA oversight for the same reasons that executive agencies' rulemaking is. The benefits to the government of coordinated policymaking and of OIRA's policy analysis capabilities are directly implicated here. As we said above, such oversight should proceed on the basis that the ultimate decisional authority belongs to the agency and the President is only allowed to exert "influence" over it. In the case of independent agencies, that influence may be reduced by virtue of the legal limitations on the President's ability to fire the agency head(s). Nevertheless, although he cannot threaten to discharge independent commissioners, he has other tools at his disposal, such as his control over budget decisions affecting them, with which he can attempt to elicit their cooperation. *See* § 7.5.2a N.4.

In staking out this position, we do not ignore the criticisms of the OIRA process voiced by Bagley and Revesz among others. Those criticisms would, however, be just as applicable to review of executive agencies as opposed to independents, and the debate over any needed reforms of the oversight process is not directly relevant to the domain question. (At least not in principle. On a more pragmatic level we could easily envision someone saying, "don't extend OIRA review to new agencies until you've fixed what's broken.")

Bruff agrees that the White House has a substantial interest in bringing independent agencies within the OIRA fold, but he also points out that there are some "kinds of rulemaking programs for which presidential supervision is not appropriate." As examples, he mentions Federal Election

Commission rulemaking that affects political campaigns and the Federal Reserve Board's control over the money supply. 57 Geo.Wash.L.Rev. at 591-92. He has a fair point there. Thus, if the overall exemption for independent agencies were rescinded, the White House would have to give serious consideration to writing narrower exemptions for functions such as these.

8. *Beyond OIRA.* In his "Presidential Rulemaking" article, Peter Strauss makes a case against the idea that adoption of a rule should be viewed as an act attributable to the President personally. This view subverts the checks and balances system, he suggests, in part because an agency is subject to congressional and judicial checks that are much less effectively deployed against the chief executive. We would add that the drift of responsibility for executive oversight from OIRA to the President and his policy staff may be significant in and of itself. Arguably OIRA has a comparatively orderly process and a technocratic culture that does not characterize what is loosely called the West Wing. But the force of that distinction is hard to gauge without better information than is readily available.

In any event, the dialogue cited here between Kagan and Strauss related to the Clinton years. By all reports, the same trend prevailed during the subsequent Bush years, with the White House dictating numerous policy decisions to the mainline agencies. And, although we expect the Obama presidency to differ from the Bush presidency in many ways, we do not think the trend toward concentration of responsibilities at the presidential level will necessarily be reversed. Indeed, the incoming President has appointed a number of "czars" to coordinate policy development in various areas, including, no doubt, issues that could potentially have been left largely to the agencies. *See, e.g.,* Tom Hamburger & Christi Parsons, "White House czar inflation stirs concern; as the 'super aides' multiply, Congress and others worry about the accumulation of power in the presidency," L.A. Times, March 5, 2009, at A1.

9. *The vision of a unilateral executive.* The Regulatory Policy Officer provisions of E.O. 13,422 (which is cited in N.2) spurred a variety of objections. Commonly heard complaints were that (a) the RPO's responsibility for planning choices would necessarily detract from the agency head's authority and discretion; (b) the order did not say that the RPO would necessarily report to the agency head—rather, the RPO would report to the President, who would thereby acquire the greatest control over the RPO's discretionary decisions; (c) the order did not require that an RPO must be an official who had been confirmed by the Senate, and so it would weaken the relationship between policy planners and the legislative branch; and (d) the order could be read as requiring the independent agencies to designate a presidentially-appointed RPO, which would amount to a

substantial extension of presidential oversight of those agencies.

These objections would seem to have been well taken in principle; and, in light of the overall track record of the Bush "unilateral" presidency, the alarmed reaction of the administrative law community is easy to understand. As the dust settled, however, some of the objections just mentioned seemed to fall by the wayside. OMB published an "implementation memorandum" that stated that the administration did not regard the amended order as requiring independent agencies to name a presidentially appointed RPO. The memo also stated that the RPO would indeed report to the agency head. OMB Memorandum M-07-13, at ¶¶ 28-29 (April 25, 2007), *reprinted in* William F. Funk et al., FEDERAL ADMINISTRATIVE PROCEDURE SOURCEBOOK 360, 375 (ABA 4th ed. 2008). Moreover, it turned out that nearly all executive agencies already had RPOs who had been appointed by the President with Senate confirmation, so the amended order did not significantly alter that state of affairs.

The biggest remaining problem among those listed above, therefore, would seem to have been item (a). By purporting to entrust responsibility for approving the agency's regulatory priorities to someone other than the agency head, the plain thrust of the order was to fragment authority within the agency and make it less able to resist pressures from the White House. Moreover, that transfer of responsibility seems incompatible with the (usual) congressional decision to vest responsibility for policy in the agency head. The agency head could, to be sure, override the RPO's choices, but only by expending extra political capital in order to do so. We do not see a valid justification for the order's attempt to impose those additional costs. *See* Strauss, "Overseer, or 'The Decider'?," 75 Geo.Wash.L.Rev. at 735. In this respect, at least, the new administration's rescission of E.O. 13,422 is welcome.

A variety of circumstances may induce a President to sign a bill but simultaneously suggest that he might not enforce all of it according to its terms. In some of those situations, the constitutional theory underlying the President's declaration is itself wrong, and the statement deserves criticism. (An example is President Bush's signing statement that dubiously questioned Congress's right to prescribe qualifications for the position of FEMA Director. *See* § 7.5.1 N.9.) In other situations, the statute really does have a constitutional problem, and a President has good grounds for voicing doubts about it. A recurring example is a congressional requirement that the President must not take a particular action without getting clearance from a particular committee chair. These provisions are obviously questionable under *Chadha*, and Presidents will sometimes respond by stating that they will construe the provision as merely requiring notification. *See* § 7.4.1 N.6 and accompanying manual discussion. Such a response is not exactly compatible with the congressional directive, but it is understandable in terms of the executive branch's legitimate defense of its prerogatives. Another example, not so common but certainly possible, would be a congressional provision that purported to limit unduly a President's removal authority. We know from *Myers*, § 7.5.2a, that some such provisions would be unconstitutional.

In this light, we agree with the position expressed by Bradley and Posner as quoted in this note. Many of President Bush's signing statements rested on extravagant theories of presidential powers, and they were open to criticism on that basis. We do not, however, agree with the view that a President who signs a law, instead of vetoing it, should always be expected to carry it out according to its terms. That view is too inflexible for the modern era, in which Presidents are often presented with omnibus bills that contain a huge number of provisions, some small fraction of which may raise a constitutional problem. A signing statement that gives notice to the world (including agency officials who will implement the law) of the President's objections is a reasonable alternative. This position was shared by the Clinton administration, *see* Walter Dellinger, "A Slip of the Pen," N.Y. Times, July 31, 2006 (an op-ed by the former head of the Office of Legal Counsel under Clinton), and it has now been endorsed in essence, by President Obama. *See* 74 Fed.Reg. 10,669 (2009).

10. *State executive review.* The New York system condemned in the *Rudder* dissent is distinguishable from the federal model. OIRA has the power to delay issuance of a rule pending further analysis, and this is by no means a small power, but it does not have authority to disapprove a rule outright. The executive order leaves that role to the President or Vice President. New York, however, entrusts a veto power to the governor's delegates—officials who are not elected and who also are not the designated decisionmaker under the applicable substantive statute.

To be precise, the disapproval authority in New York is vested not in GORR itself but in a committee composed of the governor's secretary, counsel, budget director, and director of state operations. This is the "Governor's committee" referred to by Mercure, J. Of course these top officials are highly unlikely to do anything the governor doesn't want them to do, but the governor doesn't have to take personal, public responsibility for their actions.

It would be reasonable to argue that the distinction just stated is too hair-splitting, and that the GORR system is not different in its essential nature from other oversight systems including the federal one. Fair enough. After all, writers often refer to "OIRA review" and "White House review" more or less synonymously. If one takes that view, the *Rudder* dissent starts to look more like an outright rejection of typical executive oversight.

11. *Executive review in California.* For reasons similar to those suggested by Pierce in N.3, we think OAL plays a valuable role despite the availability of judicial review. It largely replicates what a court would do, but it does so immediately and without the need for private and government actors to expend huge sums in litigation. And it tries to negotiate out the problems when it finds them—which is far better than waiting for a court to reject the rule years later. OAL's efforts to clarify the writing of rules are also worthwhile.

Nevertheless, we would not urge the federal government to emulate the California model. We think OIRA's focus on methodology and on political control and coordination is healthy and necessary. To turn OIRA into a mini-court or an English teacher like OAL would detract from that function. If applied aggressively, as OAL did in California in the late 1980's, it would give staffers in OIRA too much power and could be used to thwart any rulemaking effort with which the staffers disagreed. If applied benignly, as OAL does in California now, it would serve relatively little purpose in an environment in which many rules are subject to judicial review. Given the problem of ossification of the rulemaking environment, it would be unwise to pile a checking function like that of OAL onto the political oversight function of OIRA. And of the two different functions, we believe OIRA's is far more important.

12. *Gubernatorial vetoes.* The power exercised by several governors to cancel or disapprove a rule outright presents a striking contrast with federal jurisprudence, under which a President may attempt to persuade but the agency head has the final authority to decide. *See* our comments to N.4. Presumably judicial and legislative checks will be somewhat less potent as against a governor than against a typical rulemaking agency. One can fairly ask whether the governor's distinctive political accountability is a satisfactory substitute for the reduced efficacy of those checks and for the specialized expertise of the agency. But one might also argue that the context is significantly different at the state level—for example, because judicial checks on agency rulemaking tend to be weaker than at the federal level, or because governors tend, in fact, to be "closer to the people" than Presidents by virtue of the smaller size of the electorate.

13. *The plural executive.* As Marshall discusses in the cited article, the divided executive structure that characterizes most states gives rise to fascinating questions as to who can speak for the state. Most cases take the attorney general's side in these disputes. This is not surprising in light of the typical state constitutional provision that puts the attorney general in charge of litigation on behalf of the state, but the client agencies often resist their counsel's control and seek independent representation. *See, e.g., Ex parte Weaver*, 570 So.2d 675 (Ala.1990) (with discussion of case law from various jurisdictions, and also a heated dissent). *But see Wilder v. Attorney*

General, 439 S.E.2d 398 (Va.1994) (allowing the governor to hire special counsel). Marshall notes that the divided executive provides a check against overreaching in the executive branch, but it also "potentially undermines the virtues of energy and efficiency, political accountability, and separation of powers that the Framers of the Federal Constitution associated with the unitary executive model." 115 Yale L.J. at 2448. He goes on to raise the provocative question of whether an independent attorney general model could work at the federal level. He suggests that the idea should be seriously considered.

14. *Problem.* This problem is based only loosely on *New York v. Reilly,* a case in which the D.C. Circuit found that OIRA had exerted some influence on the recyclables decision, but not enough to have displaced EPA's discretion, as far as the record showed. The court upheld that decision. EPA's failure to proceed with the batteries proposal did not raise an issue of OIRA interference, but the court held that the agency's decision was arbitrary and capricious on the merits.

In the casebook problem the outcome of the batteries deliberation is a relatively benign example of executive oversight in action (like the recyclables decision in the real case, as just described). Bonita's recommendation has a technocratic flavor, reflecting the expertise in policy analysis that MOIRA supposedly brings to the table. Moreover, Chad's desire to "be seen as a team player" is the kind of tractability that a gubernatorial administration would naturally seek to enlist in the interest of promoting the governor's policies. Under current practice, all this is allowed.

In fact, the situation would be similar to the one envisioned in *Sierra Club v. Costle,* § 5.5.2: "Of course, it is always possible that undisclosed Presidential prodding may direct an outcome that *is* factually based on the record, but different from the outcome that would have obtained in the absence of Presidential involvement. In such a case, it would be true that the political process did affect the outcome in a way the courts could not police. But we do not believe that Congress intended that the courts convert informal rulemaking into a rarified technocratic process, unaffected by political considerations or the presence of Presidential power." The difference is that the "prodding" was by the oversight agency rather than the chief executive personally, but that difference is not considered determinative in the administrative state as currently practiced in the federal government and a number of states.

On the other hand, it is possible to argue that even this much "interference" by MOIRA is too much, because it results in an outcome that the agency head does not really want. This is tantamount to doubting that such oversight should exist at all, a proposition that you may want to

443

explore with the class. After all, the intervention did result in less environmental protection, arguably a tendency built into the oversight agency's DNA (or so say Bagley and Revesz regarding the federal OIRA).

Regardless, the batteries incident in the problem can be usefully juxtaposed with the agency's decision regarding recycling of newsprint. If the journalistic account is true, the officials would seem to have erred by treating the latter decision as one on which the governor had the last word. *See* NN.4-5. Or is that an error? Here you can discuss Kagan's default rule under which the President *would* have the last word unless Congress was explicit to the contrary. *See* N.6. In some of the states, moreover, the governor can indeed have the last word, and in New York the governor's oversight entity itself can. *See* N.10. (The recyclables incident did not directly implicate the governor's veto authority, but the existence of that authority in these states suggests that they would not follow the prevailing federal perspective on the limits of presidential administration.)

CHAPTER 8: FREEDOM OF INFORMATION AND OTHER OPEN GOVERNMENT LAWS

§ 8.1 FREEDOM OF INFORMATION ACT

On the often ignored requirement that agencies index their informal adjudicatory decisions, see Margaret Gilhooley, "Availability of Decisions and Precedents in Agency Adjudications: Impact of the FOIA Publication Requirements," 3 Admin.L.J. 53 (1989).

Like Connecticut, Minnesota and Utah, Australia entrusts enforcement of its FOIA to an agency—the Administrative Appeals Tribunal, an independent tribunal that provides hearings for hundreds of different administrative schemes. Judicial review of AAT decisions is available in the Federal Court. Transferring enforcement of FOIA to an administrative tribunal independent of the agency that has refused disclosure enables courts to shed a time-consuming and often tedious task (considering such cases on the record at the judicial review phase is far less time consuming). But assuming difficult cases will be judicially reviewed, the addition of an administrative decisionmaker extends the time that will be consumed before the requestor finally gets the documents.

Early in his first term, President Clinton issued a memorandum calling upon agencies to "renew their commitment" to FOIA. Under the Clinton approach, the Department would apply a presumption of disclosure. Only where disclosure would be harmful to an interest protected by an exemption would government assert that the exemption applies. The Bush administration reversed the Clinton policy. It announced that there is no presumption of disclosure and informed agencies that it would defend any non-disclosure decision that had a substantial legal basis. On his first day in office, however, President Obama issued a memorandum that reversed the Bush FOIA policy and called for all agencies and departments to "adopt a presumption in favor" of Freedom of Information Act requests. 74 Fed.Reg. 4683 (2009).

On the subject of the costs and benefits of FOIA, see Edward A. Tomlinson, "Use of the Freedom of Information Act for Discovery Purposes," 43 Md.L.Rev. 119, 124 (1984), pointing out that the FBI is compelled to assign hundreds of professional agents to review closed investigatory files on a line-by-line basis, at the behest of federal prisoners, to determine which portions it may safely release. It is certainly questionable whether this is the best use of such a scarce resource. For a contrasting perspective, see Seth F. Kreimer, "The Freedom of Information Act and the Ecology of Transparency," 10 U.Pa.J.Const.L. 1011 (2008). Kreimer argues that FOIA, along with many other checking institutions in government, was quite significant in uncovering abuses in the War on Terror.

The question of whether we should try to limit the costs of FOIA, and if so, how to do it, is a large and important one. Besides broadening the exemptions, one might refocus the entire act by requiring that the requester demonstrate why the information is needed and simply rule out some purposes such as business advantage or curiosity. Or you could limit FOIA to its "central purpose" to "ensure that the Government's activities be opened to the sharp eye of public scrutiny, not that information about private citizens that happens to be in the warehouse of Government be so disclosed." *US Dep't. of Justice v. Reporters Committee for Freedom of the Press,* 489 U.S. 749, 774 (1989).

§ 8.1.1 Protecting Deliberation: § 552(b)(5)

NLRB v. SEARS, ROEBUCK & CO.

Sears offers an opportunity to discuss the prosecutorial independence of the general counsel, which is characteristic of the NLRB and some other labor law agencies. In most agencies, the agency heads decide to issue a complaint, then later make the final decision. The NLRB's arrangement promotes separation of functions but has historically caused problems when the general counsel disagreed with the Board majority. If the general counsel refuses to issue a complaint, the Board cannot overturn that decision. This makes the general counsel's decisions important to labor law practitioners—hence the *Sears* case. Memos between agency prosecutors in other agencies would be of far less importance. That may explain the unusual holding that the NLRB GC's decision not to prosecute is a "final opinion."

Notes and Questions

1. *FOIA Exemption (5)—deliberative documents.* As explained in *Sears,* the rationale for the deliberative process exemption is to encourage candor in government decisionmaking. People engaging in that process should be encouraged to express even unpopular views without inhibition. If you knew your memo would likely appear in the New York Times, you might express your views orally rather than write them down, or you might pull your punches. People are already cautious enough in government about expressing controversial views; if all written memoranda about policy formation were public, there would be a severe chilling effect.

It could be argued that the state versions of the exemption, which balance the interests in confidentiality against the interests in disclosure are inadequate; a person writing a memo cannot know how a court will later strike this balance. Therefore he or she would often decide to express views in a guarded manner and convey the actual message orally. *Sears* also mentions additional reasons for the FOIA exemption, such as avoiding

446

confusion when the memo states arguments that the agency chooses not to rely on when it makes a final decision. For discussions of deliberative process privilege in evidence law and under FOIA, see the Kennedy article cited in N.4 of the text; Russell L. Weaver & James T. R. Jones, "The Deliberative Process Privilege," 54 Md.L.Rev. 279 (1989).

You might tie this discussion to subjects previously raised, such as separation of functions (§ 3.3.4). Under the general rule, there is no prohibition (or required disclosure) of communications to agency heads from staff advisors, provided the advisors haven't been adversaries in the particular case. This is to assure that agency heads can get candid advice from the staff. Similarly, *Morgan IV,* § 3.3.1, protects agency decisionmakers from judicial scrutiny of their thought processes or of the substance of the advice they listened to or disregarded. This guards the autonomy of agency decisionmakers and again helps to insure uninhibited advice.

In our opinion, there is a compelling reason for maintaining this FOIA exemption, even though it dramatically lessens the value of FOIA as a political check on agencies. For example, a journalist or scholar wishing to criticize agency policy would benefit enormously from access to the thinking of staff members that lies behind a crucial decision, especially if it disclosed dissenting views. But there's a paradox here: a democratic government requires that the populace be well informed; yet to have a government that works, we need to dispense with transparency when we talk about agency decisionmaking.

The deliberative process exemption does not generally cover factual materials, but one could argue that it should, because document producers might not be candid about embarrassing or politically sensitive facts if they know that the document may be disclosed. You might be tempted to fudge the facts in that situation, relying on oral communications to convey the true picture. Consequently, the courts have said that the disclosure of factual material is exempt if its disclosure may so expose the deliberative process within an agency that the material should be privileged.

Note the dissonance between the deliberative process exemption and the Sunshine laws discussed in § 8.2.1. Of course, the effect of open meeting laws is exactly what the FOIA deliberative process exemption is intended to prevent. Sunshine acts tend to prevent candid discussion of issues that agency decisionmakers are supposed to be deliberating about.

2. *Final opinions and exemption (5).* In applying exemption (5), cases like *Sears* distinguish pre-decisional and post-decisional memos. The idea is that the writer of a document prepared after a decision has been made and that explains that decision, would not be inhibited by disclosure

447

of the document. Even if the writer would be inhibited, the quality of the decisionmaking would not be affected, since the decision has already been made. However, the distinction might be questioned. A memo explaining a controversial decision already taken (i.e. ordering a regional director not to issue a complaint) might be far more candid about the real reasons for the decision if it can be kept within the agency's walls. And, of course, a post-decisional memo in one case is really a pre-decisional memo in the next case that presents a similar issue.

The public is thought to have a greater interest in documents that explain decisions already made (otherwise such decisions would be "secret law") than in documents that are part of the process of making that decision (which might rely on arguments that do not appear in the decision itself). This argument might also be challenged: the public might have a great interest in learning about the intra-agency struggles that led up to a decision but which are papered over in the final decision.

Secret law is odious because it tends to be known only to agency staff and to a relatively few highly knowledgeable outsiders, who thus have an advantage over everyone else. It can be too easily manipulated by the staff, who will use it or ignore it as they see fit. Moreover, secret law cannot be discussed and criticized by scholars. Thus, there are strong arguments in favor of the publication and publicity provisions of § 552(a)(1) and (2) that do not necessarily apply to most document requests under § 552(a)(3). Moreover, § 552(a)(1) and (2) are more easily and routinely complied with than (3), because (3) requests are personalized.

Note that the work-product privilege also served as a reason for non-disclosure in *Sears*. The General Counsel's memo ordering a complaint to be filed is part of a lawyer's work in a case. General Counsel must prosecute the case and should not have to disclose to adversaries the research and theory behind the case. As the next note points out, a large amount of FOIA requests are really part of the discovery process for litigation, and must be assessed in that context. Perhaps the work product material is "reasonably segregable" from the parts that set forth the law the general counsel applied (FOIA § 552(b), last paragraph), so that the latter could have been disclosed. But if the meaning of the underlying Board case law was debatable, the memo writer's exploration of what "legal theories" the writer might be able to advance successfully in the case would fall squarely within the scope of work product privilege. Fed.R.Civ.P. 26(b)(3).

3. *FOIA as discovery.* In the NLRB context, Sears might be greatly interested in the reasons why the general counsel ordered a complaint to be filed—because these reasons might be entirely different from those stated by the Board in its final decision. They might contain material about whether the Board should assert jurisdiction when it has discretion not

to—an issue that might not be described in the Board's final decision. Sears wants to understand the general counsel's discretionary decision-making and it needs to know his reasons both for filing complaints and refusing to file them. And the Court concedes that a general counsel's decision to file a complaint really is a final disposition with real operational effect. For these very reasons, the NLRB might wish to keep the memos confidential, so that people will be kept guessing about exactly how the general counsel makes its decisions to prosecute or to let other potential violations go unprosecuted.

Tomlinson argues that it is neither desirable nor workable to deny litigants the same access to information that is available to anyone else. He explains that litigants often use FOIA to obtain access quickly to a large volume of agency material. They can get it before litigation begins (and thus use it to help decide whether litigation would be fruitful or frivolous). The requester is entitled to everything she asks for, regardless of relevance or burden, unless it falls under an exemption. And who knows—perhaps a low-level FOIA clerk will disclose material that, in fact, would have qualified for an exemption.

If the agency refuses to disclose because it claims an exemption is applicable, it ordinarily must prepare a *Vaughn* index—a detailed breakdown of each document and an explanation of precisely why an exemption is claimed. In complex cases the government has a considerable burden of persuasion to establish its right to an exemption, and courts are reluctant to conduct burdensome in camera reviews (although they frequently conduct them in connection with discovery disputes). The indexing procedure is named for the case that initiated it. *Vaughn v. Rosen*, 484 F.2d 820 (D.C.Cir.1973). Indexing shifts much of the analytical work to the agency and thus makes the judicial task more manageable.

§ 8.1.2 Confidential Private Information: § 552(b)(4)

CHRYSLER CORP. v. BROWN

Notes and Questions

3. *Disclosure of confidential material.* There is a strong argument for amending FOIA to restrict the ability of business to extract information about its competitors. Perhaps there should simply be blanket protection for information submitted to the government under a confidentiality agreement. The use of FOIA to secure competitive advantage serves only marginal public interests, imposes large burdens on agency staff, and probably contributes significantly to the difficulties government has in gathering information. At the least, perhaps the fees charged for this type of requestor should be much higher than for other FOIA requests, so that taxpayers do

not subsidize competitive activity. As O'Reilly points out:

> Suzuki Motor Company has been an effective collector of Toyota's submissions to the U.S. government in 1981, though neither firm would enjoy access to the other's data in Japan. A food processor which saves tens of thousands of dollars of its filtration costs because of its innovations may never enjoy the . . . advantages, because its blueprints were photocopied last week at a regional office of the EPA and mailed to its larger competitor for ten cents per copy. And the small inventor with the archetypal better mousetrap finds that contracting or proposing to contract with the government opens detailed design data to larger competitors, who can enter the market more quickly and dispose of both mice and the innovator.

> The FOIA was meant by all its sponsors to keep agencies accountable for their workings and official conduct. By 1982, the quarter of a billion dollar cost of the Act was subsidizing Swedish ball bearing makers in their searches at [the] FTC, French aviation firms at [the] DOT, and competitive searches throughout the government.

James O'Reilly, "Regaining a Confidence: Protection of Business Confidential Data through Reform of the Freedom of Information Act," 34 Admin.L.Rev. 263, 263-64 (1982).

4. *Reverse FOIA and the Trade Secrets Act.* Chrysler deals with some rulemaking fundamentals that might be a handy review: OFCCP's regulation was not "law," and could not justify disclosure of material covered by the trade secrets law, because it was not a valid legislative rule. Thus the case reaffirms that legislative rules are "law" as much as statutes, whereas non-legislative rules are not "law." The regulation in question could have been an enforceable legislative rule (and thus "law") because it "affected individual rights and obligations." Why wasn't it?

i) The Court held that OFCCP lacked delegated legislative power to adopt information disclosure regulations. Note that it didn't reach the issue of the validity of the Executive Orders and their information disclosure requirements, issues that would probably have divided the Court.

ii) OFCCP had not used notice and comment procedure. But why did it have to? See APA § 553(a)(2)—APA rulemaking provisions are inapplicable to matter relating to agency "contracts."

iii) At the time the rule was adopted, OFCCP claimed it was interpretive, a policy statement, or procedural. Thus it never intended to adopt a legislative rule. The rule in question seems like a policy statement, since it describes how the agency will probably exercise its discretion when it receives a request for information. An agency cannot get legislative effect for its rule if it did not intend to adopt a legislative rule. *See* § 6.1.4.

One reason why submitters of information are less happy with *Chrysler* than with the reverse-FOIA theory the Court rejected is a difference in scope of review. Under FOIA, courts decide the applicability of exemptions de novo. But *Chrysler* holds that submitters can seek review of a § 1905 violation through an action under the APA; however, the scope of review of the agency's decision that § 1905 is inapplicable would be the arbitrary and capricious standard. Thus, as *CNA* (see text N.3) showed, the agency enjoys greater judicial deference in an action based on a § 1905 violation than in a reverse-FOIA action. In addition, of course, the agency can adopt a regulation allowing disclosure under the Trade Secrets Act.

5. *Privacy exemption—judicial weighing.* If the sort of weighing of interests employed under the *Dep't of Defense* case (and other exemption (6) cases) were employed for purposes of exemptions (4) or (5), less information would be disclosed. The courts would actually have to determine whether there was any significant public interest in having the information disclosed (i.e. in the public's learning what government is up to). Recall the state cases discussed in the text at § 8.1.1 N.1 that employ this form of balancing. In general, agencies would raise the balancing defense in a great many cases and would disclose much less information voluntarily. Particularly under (4), many requests are by competitors of the firms submitting the information; there is little public interest in disclosure and substantial privacy interests in non-disclosure.

Since FOIA cases already call for close judicial scrutiny, this sort of balance might not greatly enhance the burdens on the courts in enforcing FOIA. Indeed, it might save the courts time, because the balancing test could be used to turn aside extremely burdensome and costly requests for information; the courts might be able to avoid in camera review in those cases. However, this would be a huge change in underlying philosophy; since its enactment, the basic idea of FOIA has been that all the information in the government's possession is public property unless one of a few narrow exemptions apply to it. The public interest in disclosure is presumed; if the requestor wants the information, it's assumed that there is a public interest in disclosing it.

6. *Problem.* a) NIMH would rely on FOIA exemptions (4) (with respect to the application) and (5) (with respect to the committee report and John's report).

Washington Research Project held that the information is neither a "trade secret" nor "commercial or financial" and thus is disclosable despite (4). It observed that FOIA exemptions must be construed narrowly. The Restatement of Torts defines "trade secret" as information used in business which gives an advantage over competitors. And Gloria is not "in business." Later, the court interpreted "trade secrets" even more narrowly, as information actually used in the production process. *Public Citizen Health Res. Group v. FDA*, 704 F.2d 1280 (D.C.Cir.1983).

Since Gloria is not in business, the court said that the information is neither commercial nor financial, even if, as the court said, researchers "are really a mean-spirited lot who pursue self-interest as ruthlessly as the Barbary pirates did in their chosen field." 504 F.2d at 244. Later cases seem somewhat more generous in defining "commercial." The term is not limited to records that reveal basic commercial operations or reveal the income-producing aspects of a business. It applies when the provider of the information has a commercial interest in the information submitted to the agency. *Baker & Hostetler LLP v. U.S. Dep't of Commerce*, 473 F.3d 312, 319 (D.C.Cir. 2006) (treating letters sent to Department by U.S. lumber companies that concern lumber market conditions as commercial). Still, the test seems to require that the submitter be in business.

Of course, these conclusions are debatable. Gloria could be said to be in the business of being a professor. For a professor, doing research is part of your business. Good research can earn you promotions and job offers from better schools. Bad research can do just the opposite. Good research might translate into a book proposal, and book royalties are certainly business income. Thus it doesn't seem unreasonable to say that research plans are trade secrets or that the information in grant applications is commercial.

Moreover, Bob is acting a bit like a Barbary pirate in trying to secure Gloria's research design before her conclusions are published. He deserves little sympathy, but under FOIA, a particular requester's motives are irrelevant. All this suggests that perhaps exemption (4) should be amended so that it covers all information submitted by private parties to the government in confidence (whether voluntarily or under compulsion). NIMH's promise of confidentiality should be respected. Such an amendment would eliminate the problem of defining "trade secrets" as well as "commercial" or "financial" as well as avoid the difficulties in applying the *Critical Mass* tests.

Assuming the information was commercial or a trade secret, was it provided to NIMH voluntarily or under compulsion? Under *Critical Mass*, a different test applies in these two situations. You can argue either way—Gloria wasn't compelled to submit the material but she certainly would not get a grant without having done so. As a result, disclosure of the information probably would not impair the agency's ability to get such information in the future. Grant applicants really have no choice but to submit it. Therefore, probably the test should be the one relating to information submitted under compulsion: would disclosure cause substantial harm to her competitive position? It could be contended that Bob might beat her to the punch if he finds out what she is doing before she publishes, which would cause substantial harm to her competitive position.

If the information was provided voluntarily, however, the test is far more lenient: it is information that would not customarily be released to the public. Clearly Gloria doesn't go around releasing to the public her plans for future research.

Exemption (5) should be applicable to the committee's recommendation to John. As explained in *Sears*: disclosure would discourage the peer reviewers from making candid appraisals of their colleagues' applications (and of the applicants' prior work, and anything else that might be relevant). It would be difficult for Gloria's colleagues to face her at a convention if she knew that they had panned her work.

Sears explained that a second rationale for the exemption is that the public has little need for memos that recommend action that might be taken for a different reason by the ultimate decision-maker. However, that seems questionable both in *Sears* and here: the important "law" of how grant applications are screened and prioritized might be in the committee's evaluations, not in John's report.

Note that exemption (5) ordinarily does not apply to factual materials, just to "deliberative" materials such as evaluations, policy recommendations and ideas. There might be a good deal of purely factual material contained in the committee's report. The *Washington Research* case held that factual materials (such as summaries of the original grant application) in the committee report were so intertwined with evaluative materials that none of the factual material should be released. Similarly, see the *Trentadue* case in text and *Dudman Communications Corp. v. Dept. of Air Force*, 815 F.2d 1565 (D.C.Cir.1987).

You may also want to discuss whether the meeting of the peer review committee (if federal) would be covered by the Federal Advisory Committee Act, which would require that its meetings be held in public. This would also make the entire peer review system unworkable. *See Animal Legal Defense Fund v. Shalala*, discussed in the manual at § 8.2.2, which held that meetings of a peer review committee were subject to FACA. NAS got the decision reversed by statute but other grant making agencies might still have this problem.

Finally, John's report should be released. Indeed, this should be done automatically and the reports should be indexed. As defined in *Sears*, John's report is a "final opinion" and it is post-decisional, so it does not come under exemption (5). Disclosure of memos that explain decisions already made will not, according to *Sears*, inhibit candor in decisionmaking. Query, however—if John knows the report will be public, he might pull his punches in criticizing individual applications.

b) *Chrysler* held that FOIA does not prevent disclosure, but § 1905 may. Gloria may raise the issue by bringing a district court action under the APA challenging the disclosure. Sec. 1905 has no bearing on the deliberative materials; if NIMH wants to release them, Gloria has no remedy. As to her application, if it is not protected under exemption (4), as *Washington Research Group* held, then § 1905 does not apply to it, because courts have held that § 1905 covers the same ground as exemption (4).

But suppose that *Washington Research Project* is wrong and that Gloria's original application is protected from disclosure under (4). If the documents satisfied the competitive injury test of *Critical Mass, CNA* and *Chrysler* indicate that they could not be disclosed unless NIMH adopted a valid legislative regulation allowing disclosure. One might speculate on whether NIMH could do so (i.e. what kind of legislative authorization would be required to enact such a rule and whether the rule would be found substantively valid).

§ 8.2 THE SUNSHINE AND ADVISORY COMMITTEE ACTS

§ 8.2.1 Sunshine Acts

a. *Costs and benefits of sunshine laws.* James Madison, among numerous others, believed in the arguments summarized in the *Common Cause* case. Madison wrote: "A popular government, without popular information, or the means of acquiring it, is but a prologue to a farce or a tragedy; or perhaps both." Brandeis said: "Publicity is justly commended as a remedy for social and industrial diseases. Sunlight is said to be the best of disinfectants; electric light the most efficient policeman." James H. Cawley, "Sunshine Law Overexposure and the Demise of Independent Agency Collegiality," 1 Widener J.Pub.L. 43, 45 (1992).

As a practical matter, it is unlikely that open meeting laws function as a significant political check on agency action. There are too many ways to get around such laws, and to keep controversial discussions out of the public eye, as the text explains. The costs of such statutes, in inhibiting frank discussion among agency members, are very real. For a blistering attack on sunshine laws, which includes statements of numerous well-informed agency heads, see Cawley, *supra*, urging that sunshine acts be amended to permit off-the-record policy discussions. Similarly, see Jim Rossi, "Participation Run Amok: The Costs of Mass Participation for Deliberative Agency Decisionmaking," 92 Nw.U.L.Rev. 173 (1997), concerning the manner in which sunshine laws impair collegiality in multi-member agencies, thereby degrading the decisionmaking function.

One of the authors was told by a state public utility commissioner that the members of the commission were afraid to have lunch together, lest someone see them and think they were violating the open meeting law. The commission in question was so hobbled by the requirement that all deliberations occur in public that it could not establish an agenda, set priorities, control ongoing cases, or make policy. The commissioner affirmed that his agency's public meetings consisted only of the most perfunctory discussion. Yet the chances of securing relief through a statutory amendment were considered nil, because of the political popularity of the sunshine concept.

b. *Definition of meeting.* By statute, California takes the same approach as Minnesota—information-gathering or informal discussion meetings are subject to the open meeting law. The Minnesota/California approach makes sense if the objective is to use open meeting statutes as a political check on agencies. But the *ITT* rule, which sharply limits the scope of the Act, makes good practical sense in light of the experience of most agencies that candid exchanges do not take place at public meetings. As a result, the authors believe that all agencies should be permitted to adopt the *ITT* approach and close to the public meetings at which discussions, as opposed to deliberations, will take place. Only if the meeting will or may take official action, for example by adopting rules, should the sunshine act apply and the meeting be open to the public as a matter of right. Of course some discussions will be of such a nature that public attendance would be welcome or at least innocuous, but the agency should have a choice about whether to open it up.

Booth Newspapers, Inc. v. Univ. of Michigan, 481 N.W.2d 778 (Mich.App.1992), is an example of the sort of practice that the *Moberg* decision suggested could be a violation of the open meeting law. In picking a new president of the University, the Regents deliberately broke themselves into committees, each consisting of less than a quorum of the whole board, to consider applications. One regent coordinated the whole process. The use by defendant of overlapping, intercommunicating, subquorum groups in its presidential selection process violated the Act. The entire process (including candidate interviews) must be in public (except, under a narrow exception, for consideration of applicants' qualifications after the applicant has requested confidentiality). However, the court did not set aside the presidential selection but merely enjoined the board from acting that way in the future (it also awarded attorneys' fees to the plaintiff newspaper). It's interesting to speculate about how different these interviews would have been if conducted in public (for example, in people's willingness to raise and to answer questions about controversial issues like affirmative action).

Similarly, by statute, California prohibits the use of seriatim meetings conducted by member-to-member contacts, or the use of intermediaries or telephone conference calls, to circumvent open meeting laws. Cal. Gov't Code § 54952.2.

d. *Exemptions.* For treatment of exemptions to state open meeting laws, see John Peterson, Note, "When Open-Meeting Laws Confront State Legislatures: How Privacy Survives in the Capitol," 10 Nova L.J. 106, 110-14 (1985). In some states, there is a much broader blanket exemption. In Nebraska, for example, a meeting can be closed if "clearly necessary for the protection of the public interest or for the prevention of needless injury to the reputation of an individual." For a strict construction, see *Grein v. Board of Educ.*, 343 N.W.2d 718 (Neb.1984).

§ 8.2.2 Federal Advisory Committee Act (FACA)

The Croley & Funk article contains an excellent rundown of the interpretive problems that have arisen in applying FACA, as well as a set of recommendations that were to have been presented to ACUS but were aborted by ACUS's defunding.

For an argument that FACA violates the separation of powers by interfering with the President's ability to get advice, see Jay S. Bybee, "Advising the President: Separation of Powers and the Federal Advisory Committee Act," 104 Yale L.J. 51 (1994). A brief account of the history of FACA appears in Michelle Nuszkiewicz, Note, "Twenty Years of the Federal Advisory Committee Act," 65 So.Cal.L.Rev. 957 (1992). The author points to the unresolved problem of the application of federal criminal conflict of interest laws to members of advisory committees. FACA requires that committees have "balanced membership," meaning members representative of all sides of a controversy. Some of them are likely to have actual or at least apparent conflicts of interest, but they may never be informed of the risk of violating the criminal statute.

In *Center for Policy Analysis on Trade & Health v. Office of U. S. Trade Rep.*, 540 F.3d 940 (9th Cir.2008), the Center complained that an advisory committee appointed by the Trade Representative failed to satisfy the "fairly balanced" requirement of FACA (and corresponding provisions of the Trade Act), because the committee had no representative of the public health community. *See* § 8.2.2. The court held that there were no standards by which it could decide whether the committee was fairly balanced or whether or not it should include a public health representative. Consequently, the action in question was committed to agency discretion and hence unreviewable. *See* § 10.5.

The *Public Citizen* case adopts a dubious construction of the statute. FACA applies when the President or an agency "established or utilized" a committee. The Court basically reads the words "or utilized" out of the statute. This construction sharply narrows the reach of FACA. Nevertheless, the decision is defensible from a policy standpoint. Aside from the constitutional problems that a contrary construction would raise, there are real practical problems of applying FACA to the deliberations of the ABA's Standing Committee on the Judiciary. The Committee simply cannot meet in the open to discuss nominees whose names haven't been disclosed, or open its records to disclose the candid discussions of the nominees' qualifications. It solicits views of lawyers, judges and others on a confidential basis. If FACA applied to the Committee, it could not continue to render advisory services to the President. Similar concerns apply to a vast number of contacts between the Government and individual groups that exist independent of the Government but that can render valuable advice to government agencies. Either the bureaucratic FACA rules would be too costly for such groups to comply with, or the openness required by FACA would prevent their giving confidential advice.

As an example of the sort of "utilization" of an advisory committee that would be covered by FACA, the Court in *Public Citizen* referred to groups "formed indirectly by quasi-public organizations such as the National Academy of Sciences 'for' public agencies as well as 'by' such agencies themselves." In a subsequent case, the Court of Appeals applied this dictum to a committee (the "Guide Committee") composed of eminent scientists and ethicists. The Guide Committee had been formed by the National Academy of Sciences (NAS) to update the "Guide for the Care and Use of Laboratory Animals," a highly regarded and heavily used reference work. The Committee believed that it was not covered by FACA, because no government agency controlled its deliberations. Accordingly, it adopted a confidentiality agreement and refused public access to its meetings.

However, the court disagreed, holding that the absence of governmental control of the Guide Committee was irrelevant in light of the Supreme Court's dictum in *Public Citizen*. *Animal Legal Def. Fund, Inc. v. Shalala*, 104 F.3d 424 (D.C.Cir.1997). NAS pinned its hopes on Supreme Court reversal of this decision, but cert. was denied. NAS claimed that its entire advisory committee structure would collapse as the result of the decision (since there is no way to perform functions such as peer review of grant applications in an open meeting). NAS successfully lobbied Congress to overturn this decision and exempt itself from FACA. Pub.L. 105-153 (1997).

For an interesting treatment of the statutory requirement that a committee be "fairly balanced," see *Public Citizen v. National Advisory Committee on Microbiological Criteria*, 886 F.2d 419 (D.C.Cir.1989). The plaintiff complained that the Committee lacked consumer representation. Judge Edwards agreed with the plaintiff; Judge Friedman disagreed. Judge Silberman thought the plaintiff lacked standing and that the "balance" requirement was nonjusticiable because committed to agency discretion. Since the class hasn't reached the issues of standing or commitment to agency discretion yet, it's probably premature to take up this case here. However, it might make a good exam question. *See* Croley & Funk at 493-502.

As *Cheney* in the text shows, FACA does not apply to "any committee which is composed wholly of full-time officers or employees of the Federal Government." An earlier case, made obsolete by the Supreme Court and D.C. Circuit decisions in *Cheney,* is nevertheless quite interesting. President Clinton's Task Force on National Health Care Reform consisted of high level federal employees and was chaired by Hillary Rodham Clinton. Was Mrs. Clinton, then the First Lady, a full-time officer or employee of the Government? In *Association of American Physicians and Surgeons v. Clinton,* 997 F.2d 898 (D.C.Cir.1993), the Court held that she was. As a result, the Task Force was not required to comply with FACA and open its meetings to the public.

The court had to stretch to classify Mrs. Clinton as a federal officer or employee, since she did not get paid and was never formally appointed to any position. The court's theory was that in a different statute Congress had recognized that the First Lady acts is the functional equivalent of assistant to the President. Once more, the subtext of the decision was that serious constitutional problems would be raised if the Task Force were made subject to FACA, in light of its close proximity to the President and the President's need for confidential advice. A dissenter disagreed with the statutory interpretation that treated Mrs. Clinton as a federal officer or employee; he would have reached the same ultimate result by ruling that FACA cannot constitutionally be applied to the Task Force.

The court in the *Clinton* case also wrestled with whether FACA applied to the Working Group that advised the Task Force. The Working Group consisted of about 300 federal employees from the executive branch and a number of private consultants who attended working group meetings. The court remanded the case to the lower court to determine whether the private consultants or part-time federal employees required the Working Group to be classified as an advisory committee that would be regulated by FACA. The court described a continuum. At one end, a formal group consisting of a limited number of private citizens (whether or not described as consultants) are brought together to advise the government. FACA would apply to this group. At the other end of the continuum is an unstructured arrangement in which the government seeks advice from a collection of individuals who do not interact with each other. Such an arrangement would not trigger FACA. The D.C. Circuit decision in *Cheney* is inconsistent with this de facto membership approach. Since none of the outsiders could vote on Task Force determinations, they should not be considered members; consequently, the Task Force was not subject to FACA by reason of their participation.

CHAPTER 9

SCOPE OF JUDICIAL REVIEW

§ 9.1 SCOPE OF REVIEW OF AGENCY FINDINGS OF BASIC FACT

§ 9.1.1 The Substantial Evidence and Clearly Erroneous Tests

It can be argued that the various gradations--all the way from independent judgment down to some evidence--make little practical difference. If counsel persuades the court that an injustice has been done, the court will find a way to reverse--if not on the facts, then by finding a procedural error (such as inadequate findings). Nevertheless, we believe that the different standards do matter and that conscientious judges do exercise different levels of scrutiny depending on the test. We are convinced, for example, that a court exercising independent judgment under the California standard is much more likely to reverse on the facts than the same judge applying substantial evidence. Whether there is a comparable practical difference in outcomes between cases reviewed under clearly erroneous as opposed to substantial evidence, however, is less clear. See further discussion in N.6.

For a pungent comparison among the various review standards, some may like Judge Jerome Frank's puckish comment in *Orvis v. Higgins*, 180 F.2d 537, 540 n.7 (2d Cir.1950):

> A wag might say that a verdict is entitled to high respect because the jurors are inexperienced in finding facts, an administrative finding is given high respect because the administrative officers are specialists (guided by experts) in finding a particular class of facts, but, paradoxically, a trial judge's finding has far less respect because he is blessed neither with jurors' inexperience nor administrative officers' expertness.

The "some evidence" test used by the Ohio Supreme Court in reviewing workers' comp. cases is explained by the fact that the court is deluged by these cases. They are heard by writ of mandamus directly in the Supreme Court, and jurisdiction is mandatory. *See* Ronald T. Bella, "Judicial Review of Decisions of the Industrial Commission of Ohio: Is Some Evidence a Non-Existent Standard?" 12 U. Dayton L.Rev. 535 (1987). Thus the "some evidence" approach discourages at least some litigants from seeking writs and allows the court to summarily affirm most of the cases.

Notes and Questions

1. *Rationales for the substantial evidence test.* Louis Jaffe suggests that a reviewing court's power should be broader over agency fact finding than over a jury verdict, since a jury is intended to reflect community views of justice, whereas an agency is not supposed to reflect community prejudice but to apply expertise. Consequently, it must justify its findings by reasoning from the evidence, using the logic of experience, as opposed to merely expressing a socially approvable conclusion. JUDICIAL CONTROL OF ADMINISTRATIVE ACTION 596-98, 616-18 (1965) (quoting statements made by Justices Frankfurter and Black in oral argument of *Universal Camera* to the effect that the "whole record" test does not apply to jury verdicts). In this observation lie the seeds of hard look review.

The class might be asked to evaluate the several rationales for the substantial evidence test that are suggested in the text:

I. *Expertise*: This rationale is more persuasive with respect to findings on scientific or technical matters than on questions of basic fact on which judges are as qualified as agency fact-finders. However, an agency that hears labor cases every day, and is accustomed to dealing with testimonial conflicts in such cases, may be better qualified than a trial judge to sort out who is lying (whereas an appellate court is no better qualified to find facts than a trial judge). This tends to explain why reviewing courts must give more respect to an agency's findings than to those of a trial judge. *See* Robert L. Stern, "Review of Findings of Administrators, Judges and Juries: A Comparative Analysis," 58 Harv.L.Rev. 70, 82-83 (1944).

Frankfurter describes the NLRB as "one of those agencies presumably equipped or informed by experience to deal with a specialized field of knowledge, whose findings within that field carry the authority of an expertness which courts do not possess and therefore must respect." 340 U.S. at 488. But Jaffe cautions: "The usual court . . . demands, and properly so, that the agency convince the court that its 'putative' expertness is in fact relevant to the finding in question; and even then takes this expertness as but one factor in the agency decision which must run the gauntlet of its common sense." Jaffe, *supra*, at 614-15.

ii. *Delegation*: This rationale begs the question. Why is it so clear that the legislature wished to delegate such broad power over fact finding? Perhaps an agency should not be implementing a policy when it finds facts, but should function like a court that is indifferent to the result.

Yet the delegation rationale seems the soundest explanation for the substantial evidence test. There are good reasons to attribute to the legislature a desire to delegate broad power over factfinding to agencies. These reasons include agency expertness as well as reduced cost and the need to coordinate factfinding with policymaking.

An adjudicating agency is not part of the judicial branch. Respect for other branches indicates that a reviewing court should have lesser powers over agency decisions (even over their factual determinations) than it has with respect to trial courts. Note that the concept of delegation links together all the parts of this chapter--scope of review of facts, law, application, and discretion. In each case, delegation helps to explain why the reviewing power of the courts is circumscribed; however, as in the case of *Chevron*'s delegation rationale, there is sometimes an uneasy feeling that the court has created a delegation from thin air.

iii. *Discouraging appeals*: Though this rationale has intuitive appeal, it is at best an incomplete explanation for the substantial evidence test, because it does not supply a reason to distinguish between appeals from trial judges (clearly erroneous standard) and appeals from agencies (substantial evidence standard). A related explanation is that the substantial evidence test "frees the reviewing courts of the time-consuming and difficult task of weighing the evidence . . . and it helps promote the uniform application of the statute." *Consolo v. FMC*, 383 U.S. 607, 620 (1966) (a footnote says that the same policies are behind the primary jurisdiction doctrine). But it can be argued that this argument is overbroad: it suggests that a reviewing court should also be "freed" when it reviews the findings of trial courts without juries.

iv. *Differing politics*: Judges may have sharply divergent political views from administrators. One need not be unduly cynical to conclude that political views and institutional bias may color fact-finding. If a court suspects that an agency is fired with zeal for a particular program, it may be suspicious of the agency's fact findings.

In *Elliott* the majority strongly rejected Judge Easterbrook's suggestion in dissent that the court could discount the CFTC's findings because the only commissioner who had actual experience in the industry had dissented from them. Judge Cudahy wrote for the majority:

> The expertise or specialized knowledge of the agency is institutional, not personal. The dissent is off-base in exploring the occupational backgrounds of members of the Commission. As the dissent illustrates, it is a tempting but ultimately unrewarding exercise to make this a contest between the expertise of the commissioners and the expertise of the judges. The agency employs experts in the various subjects with which it must grapple and some of its staff

advise the commissioners. Courts, on the other hand, employ no experts to advise the judges. . . .

Of course, the statutory requirement of substantial evidence review applies even if the court thinks that the agency decisionmakers are underqualified political appointees, and the Seventh Circuit could hardly have been expected to say otherwise. But one should not rule out the possibility that judges sometimes follow Easterbrook's reasoning without acknowledging it.

2. *The whole record.* If substantial evidence is applied without the "whole record" gloss, review becomes pretty much of a rubber-stamp, equivalent to the "some evidence" standard mentioned in the note at the beginning of this subchapter. Notice that the court in *Yao* could not refrain from engaging in whole record review even as it insisted (on slender evidence of legislative intent) that it had no obligation to consider the evidence on both sides.

Although it may seem patently obvious that a court should look at the evidence presented by both sides in deciding whether there is substantial evidence to support the decision, this is not obvious to everyone. In fact, a 1993 report by the ABA Section of Torts and Insurance Practice asserted that at least fifteen states have failed to adopt the "whole record" approach. And progress comes hard: when New Mexico switched to using the "whole record" approach, litigants had a lot of trouble figuring out how whole record review was different from judicial reweighing of the evidence. *See Tallman v. ABF*, 767 P.2d 363 (N.M.App.1988).

3. *Disagreement between agency and ALJ.* An ALJ's conclusions should be entitled to less weight than a master's, because of the responsibility placed by statute on the agency to decide the case and, if necessary, to use it for the purposes of policymaking. Note, for example, that the agency heads have broader powers to consult uninvolved members of the agency staff than do ALJs. *See* APA § 554(d).

But an ALJ's conclusions (particularly on credibility) should not be ignored by reviewing courts. The APA upgraded the status of ALJs by protecting their independence (5 U.S.C. §§ 3105, 7521, 5372) and enhancing their status. *See* § 3.4. If agencies could ignore their fact findings, ALJs would be converted into mere takers of evidence, contrary to the objectives of the APA.

The Court found a middle ground between ignoring an ALJ's findings and making them as unassailable as a master's. A reviewing court must treat an agency reversal of ALJ findings as a factor detracting from the substantiality of evidence that supports the agency's findings (a "minus factor" is what we call it in the text). Obviously, to the extent that an ALJ's findings concern credibility, particularly credibility as judged by a witness's demeanor, the findings are entitled to more deference than if they concern the inherent plausibility of testimony, or the qualifications of an expert witness, or inferences arising from that testimony, or issues of discretion or policy.

However, an ALJ's findings can be important on judicial review even where credibility is not at issue. (*Universal Camera* says that the significance of the ALJ's report "depends *largely* on the importance of credibility in the particular case" [emphasis added], not that the report's significance depends "exclusively" on this factor.) In the FTC antitrust hypothetical mentioned in the text, suppose the ALJ writes a painstaking, detailed 100-page opinion analyzing economic data pertaining to two companies that want to merge, and the Commission reverses in a cursory 10-page decision. One can be pretty sure that the court of appeals will give a lot of weight to the more careful piece of work.

And even if the ALJ's initial decision and the commissioners' decision look equally conscientious, a disagreement between the two can impair the agency's moral authority, and thereby lessen the agency's chances of prevailing on appeal. You could compare the significance of the initial decision with that of a dissenting opinion at the commission level. The dissenters' opinion carries no *legal* weight at all, but any private party would rather appeal from a 3-2 commission decision than from a unanimous one. In a similar sense, the "probative force" that the initial decision "intrinsically commands" (to use Frankfurter's language) can derive from its very existence.

Reviewing courts seem to have little problem applying *Universal Camera*. In addition to the "heightened scrutiny" formula of *Aylett*, another formula calls for the court to "examine the evidence more critically in determining whether there is substantial evidence" when ALJs and agency heads disagree about credibility. *Bechtel Constr. Co. v. Secretary of Labor*, 50 F.3d 926, 933 (11th Cir.1995) (affirming Secretary's decision about reason a person was fired, despite conflict with ALJ).

One interesting body of research tends to debunk *Universal Camera*. It suggests that the clues we extract from actually seeing a witness are more likely to mislead than to give correct results. As a result, readers of a cold record may do *better* in detecting truthtelling than the person who hears and sees the witnesses. *See* Olin Guy Wellborn III, "Demeanor," 76 Cornell L. Rev. 1075 (1991).

You can have quite a bit of fun with this material in class; some of the studies cited by Wellborn are quite amusing. On the other hand, it is not clear that those studies really apply to professional fact finders like

ALJs. Moreover, an ALJ stays with a case for days or weeks; this makes the ALJ more capable of resolving credibility questions than someone who hits the dispute cold, like the subjects of the studies discussed by Wellborn. Also, a subsequent article claims Wellborn overreached his data; the clues we get by listening to people (tone of voice, etc.) actually are helpful in deciding whether they're telling the truth, even though visual clues (like fidgeting) are not. Jeremy A. Blumenthal, "A Wipe of the Hands, A Lick of the Lips: The Validity of Demeanor Evidence in Assessing Witness Credibility," 72 Neb.L.Rev. 1157 (1993).

4. *Agency-ALJ disagreements in the states.* The Wisconsin approach in *Rucker* makes sense; it forces the heads to face up to the fact that they're disagreeing with a credibility assessment and explain why their view (based on a cold record) is better than the ALJ's. Many times they can do so, especially if the case involves expert witness testimony.

The Florida approach greatly upgrades the status of the ALJ vis-à-vis the agency heads. It creates distinctions that have proved difficult in practice. The *Johnston* case, in our opinion, gives too much weight to an ALJ's views about what is acceptable medical practice; even if "ordinary methods of proof" are used, the ALJ's views on this issue aren't entitled to much weight as compared to the physicians who are serving as agency heads. However, the full opinion in *Johnston* suggests that the court thought the agency was picking on the doctor without any justification, which helps to explain the holding.

See also McDonald v. Dept. of Banking & Fin., 346 So.2d 569 (Fla.App.1977), which takes a different approach to the Florida statute. "At the other end of the scale [from findings based on credibility], where the ultimate facts are increasingly matters of opinion and opinions are increasingly infused by policy considerations for which the agency has special responsibility, a reviewing court will give correspondingly less weight to the hearing officer's findings in determining the substantiality of evidence supporting the agency's substituted findings."

In addition, the Florida courts have had trouble figuring out which ALJ conclusions are factual (to which the statute applies) and which ones are legal (to which the statute would not apply). It seems that questions of application of law to fact are treated as fact for this purpose. *See Berger v. Dep't of Prof. Reg.*, summarized in the Manual's discussion of the problem below; *Goin v. Commission on Ethics*, 658 So.2d 1131 (Fla.App.1995). In *Goin*, the FSU athletic director got a bargain-price roofing job from a roofer who was bidding on a big job for the FSU athletic facilities. The statute prescribed sanctions if an employee "knows, or with the exercise of reasonable care, should know" that he is receiving a thing of value given to influence his official action. The ALJ found that Goin knew enough to conclude he might be getting a good deal on the roofing job, but that this was not sufficient to meet the statute--he should have seen a yellow light. but there was not evidence he should have seen a red light. The agency heads reversed, holding that these facts established that with the exercise of reasonable care he should have known that the deal was given to influence his action. The court held that this was fact, not law, and reversed.

Administering the tests stated in *Johnston* and *McDonald* has caused a lot of problems for Florida appellate courts. *See* Michael Asimow, "Toward a New California Administrative Procedure Act: Adjudication Fundamentals," 39 UCLA L.Rev. 1067, 1122-24 (1992). The *Universal Camera* approach is better; it does not require drawing any bright lines or tight classification of issues; on a case-by-case basis, it allows the appellate court to detract from substantiality of evidence to an appropriate degree where an ALJ and agency heads disagree, especially on credibility findings.

The California statute is part of a revision of the APA relating to adjudication; it is the only provision in the statute that relates to judicial review. However, based on experience under the Florida statute, the drafters found it easier to codify the *Universal Camera* standard as a judicial review test than as a test directed at the agency heads. The change was bitterly resisted by a number of agencies (especially labor agencies like the Public Employee Relations Board) and by the Attorney General. It was strongly supported by private sector professionals who have often resented the process whereby agency heads manipulate credibility findings in order to reverse ALJ decision with which they disagree on policy grounds.

The California statute was intended to codify *Universal Camera,* but it can be read to go further and to basically adopt Hand's position in *Allentown* (which the Supreme Court rejected). Note also that the California statute applies *whether or not* the ALJ and the agency heads disagree about credibility. This becomes very important when the new statute is applied to California independent judgment judicial review. *See* § 9.1.2.

It would seem that the *Universal Camera* analysis is, if anything, even more applicable to clearly erroneous than to substantial evidence. *See Clowes v. Terminix Int'l*, Inc., 538 A.2d 794, 800-01 (N.J.1988), in which the court applies a clearly erroneous test (although the statute apparently does not prescribe any particular scope of review). It strongly discounts a civil rights agency's finding of handicap discrimination because the agency heads overturned the ALJ's credibility findings.

5. *Supreme Court review of court of appeals.* Originally, the language in *Universal Camera* regarding Supreme Court oversight of the courts of appeals was probably intended to be only a statement about the Court's certiorari policy, not a pledge to defer to the courts of appeals.

Conceptually, one might prefer that approach, because the deference model seems rather confusing ("Could the court of appeals have reasonably believed that the agency could not have reasonably believed that. . . .?"). Also, if the Supreme Court applies the same substantial evidence test that the lower courts do, it can write opinions showing by example how that test should or should not work, as in *Allentown Mack*.

However, conceptual purity is not the only value at stake here. Pragmatic considerations are also relevant. The Supreme Court can simply deny certiorari in an unimportant case, but many other appellate tribunals have mandatory jurisdiction. In these courts there is much to be said for the deferential, *Standard Oil* approach to substantial evidence review. Intense review of the records in individual adjudications by state supreme courts seems like a waste of time and resources of both the courts and public litigants. In fact, the same thing is true if the initial judicial review takes place in a trial court; there is little need for a state intermediate court of appeals to conduct the same review over again.

Re-review of the facts by appellate courts encourages disgruntled litigants to keep appealing. Generally the substantial evidence test is very case-specific; individual cases aren't precedents for future cases. Careful scrutiny of the record by one court is probably sufficient.

The New Jersey model (giving greater scrutiny when the lower court has overturned an agency decision than when the lower court upheld the agency) seems asymmetrical and unfair. The New Jersey rule is not calculated to increase public confidence in the judiciary.

6. *"Clearly erroneous" review.* In principle, the distinction between clearly erroneous and substantial evidence review ought to make sense. "Clearly erroneous" implies that the appellate reviewer is free to make the same *kinds* of judgments that the decisionmaker below makes, although the appellate judge should display restraint before substituting judgment. "Substantial evidence" implies that the appellate judge's perspective is deemed to be somehow qualitatively different from that of the decisionmaker below; therefore, substitution of judgment at the appellate level would subvert the legal system's intention to infuse that "something different" into the decision.

In practice, however, clearly erroneous and substantial evidence tend to merge. As Judge Posner suggests, "cognitive limitations" are one reason for this convergence—the judicial mind can't necessarily split this legal hair successfully under the fact pressure of a given case. Another reason is probably a degree of skepticism about the underlying premise mentioned in the preceding paragraph. To the extent that one harbors mistrust of juries, on the one hand, and agencies, on the other, there will be strong temptations to apply substantial evidence review in a manner that approaches a stricter test.

The issue floated in the last paragraph of the casebook note is important, however. Practitioners and judges (and, let's face it, academics) frequently *act* as though the choice among standards of review is vitally important. The disputation occurs not only in legislative drafting situations, but also in individual cases in which the appropriate standard of judicial review is in doubt. The issue isn't confined to fact review. Think about the unending "Step Zero" debate in the *Chevron* context, a game that may or may not be worth the candle, *see* § 9.2.4 N.2, as well as the debate over whether substantial evidence review is stricter than arbitrary-capricious review, *see* § 9.4 N.5.

In all of these situations, the dispute is in part over atmospherics. Government litigants normally want to clothe their arguments in the garb of a "highly deferential" standard of review. Private litigants have an incentive to say that the standard of review in their case is particularly demanding. After all, these competing advocates can *hope* that the choice of a particular standard will have some influence on the judges who will decide the appeal. And who knows? It *might.* Moreover, even if one agrees with Judge Posner and Justice Breyer that the statement of a nominal standard of review won't really make much difference, the debate may not be totally futile. Judges may think that they can at least get some rhetorical mileage out of being able to write some pro-deference language into an opinion that upholds an agency, or that they can make an opinion reversing an agency look more credible if they can characterize the standard of review as relatively strict. So litigants have an incentive to brief the issues in a manner that will give judges the latitude to play the deference or non-deference card.

7. *Problem.* In *Blanding*, there was no hearing officer decision; the CRC found for the member, and the court affirmed under the substantial evidence test. The Health Club tried to defend on the basis of the first amendment's free exercise clause (of religion--not of muscles!), since its owners were born-again Christians who objected to homosexuality. The court held that the respondent was a corporation, so that the religious beliefs of its stockholders were irrelevant, and that the burdens of the anti-discrimination law did not violate free exercise.

You might want to make these points:

I) On the Club's appeal, the issue is whether there is substantial evidence for the conclusion that (i.e. could a reasonable person find that) Ted proved by a preponderance of the evidence that he was terminated because of affectional preference rather than conduct.

ii) Gloria's conclusions in part rest on credibility determinations. She believed Mark's testimony that he terminated Ted because of his conduct and for refusing to discuss it, not because of his affectional preference. Under *Universal Camera*, this detracts from the substantiality of evidence in support of the CRC's decision. Presumably, under the clearly erroneous test, the disagreement between Gloria and the CRC would weaken the CRC's conclusions even more.

iii) CRC's decision may rest on more than a credibility determination. The agency may have concluded that the conduct involved (making a date) could not be the basis for terminating a health club member--even if Mark found it offensive and inappropriate.

In other words, employing its expertise in anti-discrimination law (and perhaps adopting a presumption to assist in future cases), the CRC may have decided that termination purportedly based on trivial and objectively inoffensive conduct and upon a refusal to discuss that conduct was probably a cover for affectional preference discrimination. It seems unlikely that a man would be kicked out of the Club for making a date with a woman member.

To impress a reviewing court, this conclusion should be clearly spelled out and justified in the CRC's decision. Assuming it is, the conclusion does not seem arbitrary, and a court should not overturn it for want of substantial evidence. However, a court could overturn it as a matter of law, if it holds that the statute does not permit an agency to adopt a presumption that unlawful discrimination has occurred.

See, however, *Berger v. Dep't of Prof. Reg.*, 653 So.2d 479 (Fla.App.1995). Berger had a business as a dental-legal consultant. As Berger explained in his hearing, "I speak law and I speak tooth. I can explain the law to dentists in words they understand. I can explain dentistry to lawyers in words they understand." But the Department believed Berger was engaged in the unauthorized practice of dentistry because his letterhead identified him both as a J.D. and "D.D.S." (an academic degree which in fact he had earned). The ALJ found that the use of the initials D.D.S. did not represent to the public that Berger was licensed to practice dentistry. The agency heads reversed this as an incorrect finding of law. The court reversed, stating that an agency could not circumvent the requirements of the Florida statute (discussed in N.4) by characterizing findings of fact as legal conclusions.

iv) To the extent that the decision relies on the CRC's findings (in conflict with Gloria's about credibility), there may nevertheless be substantial evidence to support CRC's conclusion—although less substantial than if Gloria had found that Mark was lying. The decision may rest on more than just disbelieving Mark. The difficulties the Club was having with its heterosexual members suggest that the Club was seeking ways to get rid of its homosexual members and might seize on any trivial piece of conduct to do so.

v) Awarding punitive damages could be an abuse of discretion. There are probably other health clubs in town that do the same thing, the Club seems to be a first offender, and the case is pretty close. Note discussion of whether an agency can be empowered to award punitive damages in § 7.3 N.5.

vi) Under a clearly erroneous standard, a court would have greater power and could easily conclude that Ted had not satisfied his burden of proof on the factual questions. However, to the extent the decision relies on an alternative ground--a "rule" adopted in the course of adjudication that a discharge resulting from this sort of conduct is prohibited discrimination-- the court should either affirm the decision or overturn the "rule" as arbitrary or contrary to law.

vii) It is useful to flip the question and ask what happens if CRC ruled for Club rather than for Mark--in other words, found that the Club terminated Mark for his conduct rather than for his affectional preference. Clearly there is substantial evidence for this conclusion, even taking account of the contrary evidence in the "whole record." But a court disposed towards strong enforcement of the anti-discrimination law probably could hold such a decision clearly erroneous anyway.

§ 9.1.2 Independent Judgment and De Novo Review

1. *Constitutional and jurisdictional fact. Ben Avon* is still followed in a minority of states and has elicited this harsh appraisal:

> The patently undesirable effect of this rule is to undermine the finality and authority of administrative rate-making by permitting utilities to entirely ignore such rates by crying `confiscation' and seeking judicial review. The courts are then faced with the onerous task of sifting through volumes of economic data and generally contradictory expert testimony without the refined expertise of the specialists who sit on public service commissions and attempting to arrive at a more enlightened judgment than the administrative body that has already undertaken the task. . . . If the inherent unsoundness of the rule were not bad enough by itself, the problem has become even more complex due to the uncertainty that surrounds its very existence. . . when there is widespread

doubt as to whether a rule exists at all, the result is often disastrous.

Leslie A. Glick, Independent Judicial Review of Administrative "Rate-Making: The Rise and Demise of the *Ben Avon* Doctrine," 40 Ford.L.Rev. 305, 306 (1971).

Jaffe traces the roots of the jurisdictional fact notion to English and American certiorari cases, which distinguish the issue of whether a tribunal was within its jurisdiction from other disputes and permit trial by affidavit of jurisdictional facts. JUDICIAL CONTROL OF ADMINISTRATIVE ACTION 624-35 (1965).

Crowell illogically singled out two particular factual questions (employment relation, navigable waters) for independent review. It is difficult to see why the employment issue has any constitutional significance. Surely, Congress could have determined that there should be no-fault liability toward maritime independent contractors as well as employees. Still, some issues with great constitutional significance could justifiably be singled out for special review--e.g. citizenship in the *Ng Fung Ho* case. Jaffe defends *Ng Fung Ho* by agreeing with Brandeis (in his *Crowell* dissent) that questions of personal liberty may be on a different plane than property rights. Moreover, Jaffe suggests that citizenship (a clear-cut yes-no question entailing great personal harm to a person and requiring no special expertise) is different from the *Ben Avon* issue. In a ratemaking case, the initial decision must be made by a specialized, expert tribunal, and there is a large zone in which different conclusions can be reasonably justified. The danger of political bias in immigration cases is also a factor arguing for enhanced review. *Id.* at 641-47.

On independent review of sensitive constitutional issues, Monaghan's cited article tentatively supports independent review of the application of constitutional standards to the facts when administrative agencies have made the initial determination, but not where trial courts have done so. He draws that distinction because agencies, unlike courts, suffer from a "legitimacy gap"-- they aren't mentioned in the Constitution. This is a distinction that may appeal more to constitutional scholars than to administrative law scholars. For a more recent discussion, see Adam Hoffman, Note, "Corralling Constitutional Fact: De Novo Fact Review in the Federal Appellate Courts," 50 Duke L.J. 1427 (2001).

2. *De novo review in federal courts today.* The food stamp and IDEA judicial review statutes are anomalous and create a lot of unnecessary work for hard-pressed courts. They occur because of legislative compromises in which some special interest group manages to win special procedural protections for itself. In the case of food stamps, perhaps it was the retailing

industry that wanted to make it hard for USDA to reject applications or to revoke certification for accepting food stamps.

In the case of IDEA, proponents of the legislation obviously feared that school boards would refuse to accept costly placements for disabled kids, and they wanted strong judicial review to offset this strategic disadvantage. Generally, it would be pretty easy for a school board to come up with substantial evidence and good reasons for any particular placement that it wanted to make. Thus it would be difficult for a parent to fight this decision without an elevated judicial review standard. But it really isn't good policy for federal district courts rather than school boards to make the placement decisions for disabled kids.

In *Ojai*, cited in text, the court said:

> Thus, judicial review in IDEA cases differs substantially from judicial review of other agency actions in which courts generally are confined to the administrative record and are held to a highly deferential standard of review. . . . "Congress intended courts to make bounded, independent decisions-- bounded by the administrative record and additional evidence, and independent by virtue of being based on a preponderance of the evidence before the court. . . ." Nevertheless, when reviewing state administrative decisions, "courts must give `due weight' to judgments of education policy. . . . Therefore, the IDEA does not empower courts to `substitute their own notions of sound educational policy for those of the school authorities which they review. . . . " How *much* deference to give state educational agencies, however, is a matter for the discretion of the courts.

> Here conducting its review of the administrative proceedings with this unusual mixture of discretion and deference, the district court decided to grant the school official's motion for summary judgment. . . .

4 F.3d at 1471-72 (citations omitted).

De novo review under FOIA is obviously predicated on the belief that agencies cannot be trusted to disclose what may be embarrassing information even when the Act requires it. The debate over whether the benefits of firm FOIA enforcement outweigh the costs are reviewed in the introductory discussion in § 8.1. But recall Verkuil's finding that, despite the supposedly de novo standard of review, the government wins ninety percent of its cases in FOIA actions. This is a good object lesson regarding Congress's limited capacity to adjust outcomes by legislating an exceptional standard of review.

3. *State law.* The Texas substantial evidence de novo procedure does seem pretty "crazy." It is hard to see any logic in a system in which the jury decides the reasonableness of a decision by using its own judgment without necessarily taking account of the reasoning of the administrative agency. (Schenkkan doesn't address whether an appellate court would then decide whether the jury was reasonable in deciding whether the agency was reasonable, but the question itself seems "crazy.") It does seem that the Texas approach is a product of history much more than logic. In addition to the points he makes in the quote, Schenkkan points out that the Railroad Commission cases in which the system developed were all assigned "to the trial courts of Travis County. In a town as small as Austin was then, 88,000 in 1940, with little economic base beyond state government and the University of Texas, every one of the handful of judges and potential jurors, drawn from the white male population, was likely to know or think he knew what had 'really' happened in a high-profile Railroad Commission case." 7 Texas Tech.Admin.L.J. at 302.

Anyway, the narrative recounted in this note does highlight, in stark terms, a fairly legitimate point: a credible decisional process at the administrative level is often considered a sine qua non for deferential judicial review. The teachings of *Christensen* and *Mead*, § 9.2.4, can be interpreted as illustrating the same relationship.

4. *California independent judgment rule.* The California "independent judgment" test is discussed in detail in Michael Asimow, "The Scope of Judicial Review of Decisions of California Administrative Agencies," 42 UCLA L.Rev. 1157 (1995). The effect of independent judgment is that the decisions of the ALJ (often from a central panel in California) and the agency heads count for nothing; the only function of the agency proceedings was to make a record. The court makes all the calls, including close questions of credibility.

Asimow argues that the *Bixby* rhetoric is not persuasive. *Id.* at 1177-80. True, licensing agencies may be controlled by the industries they regulate, and they sometimes treat harshly licensees who rock the boat. Also such agencies sometimes go on prosecutorial rampages, picking on licensees for relatively minor conduct. But such cases are rare; most licensing boards are pathetically understaffed and prosecute only the most egregious violations, if they prosecute anybody at all. When there is a prosecutorial abuse by a licensing agency, it is questionable whether independent judicial judgment is really needed to correct the problem. Substantial evidence review does the trick in other states and in federal law.

Against the benefits of independent judgment review must be

weighed the costs: I) substituting judgment of unqualified trial judges for qualified and specialized boards on questions of basic fact; ii) enormous commitment of resources by trial courts that have to read, analyze and weigh every word of the transcript (as opposed to substantial evidence, which imposes much lower judicial burdens); iii) substitution of the court's political point of view for that of the agency--frequently home town trial court judges override decisions of licensing agencies; iv) the encouragement it offers to losing litigants to seek judicial review in every case at considerable cost to courts, agencies, and litigants; v) the confusion about when independent judgment will be provided..

Even if one accepts *Bixby*, one must question *Frink*. It is possible, of course, that welfare bureaucracies are subject to political pressure to keep people off the rolls, but it seems poor policy for courts to substitute judgment on questions of whether someone is faking disability. Moreover, a serious defect of California law is the constant confusion about whether independent judgment or substantial evidence should apply. There are countless cases on the point and the borderline seems to be shifting. *Id.* at 1171-76.

The most recent evidence of the doctrinal disarray comes from *Termo Co. v. Luther*, 86 Cal.Rptr. 687 (Ct.App.2008), extending independent judgment to an order requiring the corporate operators of oil wells to plug the wells because they had been abandoned for seven years and were likely to be unproductive if reopened. The right to pump oil was "vested" because the wells had previously been operated and was "fundamental" because of the order's economic impact and "effect in human terms." Surely this use of independent judgment to protect corporate profits is a far cry from the rationale of *Bixby*, such as it was.

On the other hand, the California statute requiring courts to give great weight to properly labeled credibility findings, *see* § 9.1.1 N.4, applies in both substantial evidence and independent judgment cases. In independent judgment cases, the statute greatly limits the ability of the reviewing court to substitute its judgment on credibility findings for those of an ALJ. Note that this statute applies whether or not the agency heads disagree with the ALJ's credibility findings; thus it goes far beyond *Universal Camera*. In the vast majority of cases, the agency heads adopt the ALJ's credibility findings; courts reviewing the decision no longer can ignore what the agency has done, but instead are pretty much stuck with the ALJ's findings on credibility.

5. *Problem.* As to Ted, although the discrimination was no doubt humiliating and might be financially damaging (if other clubs are more expensive or otherwise unsuitable), it is hard to see the loss of health club membership as sufficiently "fundamental" as *Frink* uses that term--even if it was "vested." However, *Kerrigan v. FEPC*, 154 Cal.Rptr. 29 (App.1979),

held that an agency's denial of a claim of age discrimination in employment triggered independent judgment review for the employee. The case turns on the importance of a job in the individual's life situation. Perhaps the court would say that the evil of prohibited discrimination, even as to club membership, is so great that independent judgment is required. Who knows--it's that sort of doctrine.

A decision in Ted's favor, ordering him reinstated to the Club, does not infringe a fundamental right of the Club. *L. A. Dep't of Parks v. CSC*, 10 Cal.Rptr.2d 150 (App.1992) (reinstatement to job because of racial discrimination--substantial evidence, not independent judgment). Thus the test is asymmetrical--an employee claiming discrimination gets independent judgment; an employer denying discrimination does not. However, an administrative decision imposing a pecuniary penalty on a business does infringe a fundamental right; therefore the financial penalties imposed by the CRC would trigger independent judgment. *Interstate Brands v. Unempl. Ins. App. Bd.*, 608 P.2d 707 (Cal.1980).

If the Club had a license, and it was revoked because of prohibited discrimination, it is likely that it would receive independent judgment. Generally, revocation of professional licenses has been the most important trigger of the fundamental rights doctrine, and a Club's business license should be in the same category. Revocation puts it out of business, and that should be sufficient to trigger independent judgment. *See Goat Hill Tavern v. City of Costa Mesa*, 8 Cal.Rptr.2d 385 (App.1992) (independent judgment to review city's refusal to renew saloon's conditional use permit).

Note that the ALJ's decision in the Club's favor was based on a credibility determination of why the Club terminated Ted's membership. Under the California APA provision discussed in § 9.1.1 N.4, the reviewing court would have to give great weight to this determination, assuming that the ALJ properly labeled it as a credibility determination based on demeanor and identified the elements of the demeanor, manner, or attitude of the witness that supported her determination. This very much cuts into the independent judgment test.

§ 9.2 SCOPE OF REVIEW OF ISSUES OF LEGAL INTERPRETATION

Special note: The case law and academic literature on judicial deference to agencies' legal interpretations is voluminous and deeply controversial, but some teachers will want to spend more time on it than others. We have, therefore, organized this section in a manner that will accommodate various preferences. The core material, centering on the *Chevron* case, is in § 9.2.2, and presumably all will want to teach it. Most will probably also want to cover the *Skidmore, Christensen,* and *Mead* cases in § 9.2.4. However, § 9.2.3 is an optional section. It offers extra coverage for the true *Chevron* aficionados, but instructors who have less interest can skip it, because § 9.2.2 makes all the essential points. In addition, instructors who favor this casebook's special emphasis on state law will find ample coverage in § 9.2.1, but those whose interests are more focused on federal law can assign only selectively from that section or omit it entirely.

* * * * * * * *

The ambiguity of the word "deference" often makes it difficult to know whether a court is taking a reasonableness or a substitution of judgment approach. Still, the difference between the approaches is important, at least in theory. Under a substitution of judgment or weak deference approach, deference serves as a thumb on the scale. It is contextual—the weight of the thumb varies with the circumstances. But the key point is that the court maintains a relatively intrusive checking power and does not treat the agency as exercising a delegated power to interpret.

In contrast, a reasonableness or strong deference approach does concede to the agency delegated power to interpret an ambiguous text. Thus the court is bound by the agency's reasonable interpretation, even if it thinks another interpretation would be better. The court's checking power is thereby diminished. You can, therefore, relate the choice of interpretive approaches to the role of courts in the checks and balances system; this links Chapter 9 with Chapter 7 on checking of agencies by the other branches of government.

As with any other scope of review topic, there is always room for skepticism as to how far courts actually are influenced by deference principles--let alone by subtle distinctions between competing principles. We've mentioned this issue of skepticism in the preceding section and will return to it periodically in this one. The models that we call "strong" and "weak" deference may not work out very differently from each other in practice. Where the stakes are high and the social conflicts most sharply drawn, you especially have to take judicial pronouncements about the standard of review with a grain of salt. But we believe that the doctrine has some influence, especially in the less passion-inspiring cases.

In any event, the material in this section has obvious professional importance for your students. In practically every administrative law case they may ever litigate, their briefs will have to address the applicable standard of review. Administrative lawyers have to become familiar with the rhetoric of scope of review, whether they believe in the potency of these formulas or not.

476

CONNECTICUT STATE MEDICAL SOCIETY v. CONNECTICUT BOARD OF EXAMINERS IN PODIATRY

Notes and Questions

1. *Independent judgment.* The *Connecticut Medical* opinion begins with a catalogue of the review standards codified in the Connecticut APA. You might use this passage as a good excuse to walk your students through 5 U.S.C. § 706, or your own state's APA provision on scope of review, or both. Most such statutory standards are unilluminating analytically, but they have to be invoked in a litigation context, and students ought to know about them. At least the statutory formulas reinforce the insight that a given case typically presents a variety of issues that have to be evaluated in different ways. Here the court is dealing with a pure question of law.

The court goes on to say that, on such an issue, it exercises "independent judgment," and the note asks some basic questions about the justification for that test. At least some of the reasons for deference that were explored in the preceding section seem applicable here. In some sense the members of the podiatry board may be more experienced and "expert" in the intricacies of the regulatory framework than a generalist court would be. They work with § 20-50 on a regular basis, and a court almost never does.

But that line of argument is unsatisfying. The court's authority to substitute judgment on issues of law is an important element of the checks and balances system. Independent scrutiny of a separate branch of government serves to uphold the rule of law. It is also a safeguard against industry capture, political agendas, and mere caprice. And, in any event, the imbalance in "expertness" between the court and the agency is at least *less* than in regard to factual and policy issues.

An obvious problem with deferring to the podiatry board's reading of § 20-50 is that the board, like many other state licensing authorities, may be overly solicitous of the industry it is charged with regulating. We drew attention to this problem in another context above. *See* § 3.3.5 N.2 of this manual. *See generally* Walter Gellhorn, "The Abuse of Occupational Licensing," 44 U.Chi.L.Rev. 6 (1976). Naturally, podiatrists themselves will be receptive to the proposition that they can treat sprained ankles. It is certainly possible that the legislature wanted them to take on that additional business, but that proposition should be subject to scrutiny from an independent branch of government.

At the time of this case, the podiatry board's enabling statute provided that the board should be composed of three practicing podiatrists and two public members. Domination by the regulated industry was built into its structure. Moreover, at the time of the declaratory ruling that was contested in this case, the two public members' seats were *vacant*. *See Fleishman v. Connecticut Bd. of Ex'rs in Podiatry*, 576 A.3d 1302, 1305 (Conn.App.1990). Thus, a safeguard for the public interest that the legislature itself had prescribed was going unheeded. This fact isn't mentioned in the principal case, and the court may not have known about it, but at the very least it highlights one of the pathologies that independent judicial review of an agency's legal interpretations can counteract.

2. *Interpretive weight.* Justice Brown's pointed and precisely phrased formulation of a standard of judicial review for agency legal interpretations relies directly on Asimow's report to the California Law Revision Commission. Naturally, we find her approach attractive. There are good reasons for giving deference to agency interpretations when appropriate, as opposed to deciding the interpretive question as if the agency's interpretation did not exist. *See* Asimow, 42 UCLA L.Rev. at 1203-06 (justifying weak deference in terms of accuracy and efficiency criteria, especially the need for uniform constructions and praising the incentives provided by the weak deference rules for agencies to provide reasoned interpretations). Your authors are in accord on this general proposition. *See* David R. Woodward & Ronald M. Levin, "In Defense of Deference: Judicial Review of Agency Action," 31 Admin.L.Rev. 329 (1979) (criticizing the proposed "Bumpers Amendment" to the federal APA, which would have purported to abolish such deference).

Justice Brown also makes clear that this "weak deference" is supposed to be different from the reasonableness review that might be associated with *Universal Camera.* How much difference that distinction makes in practice is a troublesome question. We take up this issue in § 9.2.4.

In *Connecticut Medical*, how do the weak deference factors point? As to the factor of comparative institutional competence, the issue seems pretty non-technical. It isn't clear that the agency has greater competence than the court to decide what the legislature meant by the word "foot." And the court is construing a statute, not a rule (agencies are thought to have particular competence in interpreting their own rules).

As to the reliability of the particular board interpretation in this case, a couple of factors support the agency: The issue was decided in an adversarial adjudicative procedure and apparently was thoroughly considered by the agency. The agency's view is not inconsistent with a prior interpretation. On the other hand, It was not contemporaneous with enactment of the statute or long-standing. The agency's prior practice allowing podiatrists to treat ankles probably shouldn't count for much, since it wasn't formally articulated or, so far as we know, ever the subject of any real deliberation. Since the interpretation (at least in its formal sense) is new, there's been no reliance on it. Also, as mentioned above, the *Connecticut Medical* case plainly involved a turf battle between two economic interests--podiatry and medical. It was predictable that the podiatry agency would take a more expansive view of podiatrists' turf than the M.D.'s do.

3. *Application of law to fact.* Too many cases label application issues as "fact" or "law" in order to decide whether the agency or the court has primary responsibility for decision. Actually, application questions have elements of both fact and law, although they are not reducible to either. The term "mixed questions of law and fact" is revealing in that regard, although not particularly helpful to analysis.

As the text notes, the issue of how to classify application questions is not confined to administrative law. It comes up throughout the law—for example, in allocating issues between judge and jury and in determining the scope of an appellate court's review of trial court or jury decisions. Here's an interesting quote from Judge Posner discussing the problem in the context of negligence:

> Consider a finding of negligence in an ordinary tort suit. It is not a finding of fact in the sense that it could be made by someone uninstructed in the legal standard of negligence. Rather it is the application of the legal standard to the facts of the particular case. . . . [T]he application of law to fact is itself a question of fact for purposes of appellate review. The point is not that it is "really" a question of fact; that would be absurd. The point is that appellate review of the application of law to fact should be deferential, as it is in the case of rulings on questions of fact, and this for two reasons. The trier of fact, whether judge or jury, is closer to the facts than the appellate judges and is therefore better able, other things being equal, to assess their legal significance. And the dependence of the determination of negligence on the facts of the particular case, facts that will not recur exactly in any other case, would make quixotic an attempt to bring about uniformity of results by close appellate review.

United States v. McKinney, 919 F.2d 405, 419 (7th Cir.1990) (concurring opinion).

In at least one important respect, however, the problem is usually more complicated in the administrative law context than in a setting like negligence, in which the legal framework is often entirely settled. The "mixture" before the court often implicates both interpretation and application. The challenger will try to persuade the court that the agency erred "as a matter of law." If that argument fails, the court will go on to treat the remaining determinations the agency made en route to its result as though they were factual (although they aren't). *See* Levin, 74 Geo.L.J. at 27 ("What separates interpretation from application is simply a sequence of analytical steps. The province of the agency is defined *during* the process of construing the statute. . . . Therefore, the terms 'interpretation' and 'application' are, at best, after-the-fact labels and not guides to analysis.").

So, how *should* the court go about deciding whether the agency erred as a matter of law? One solution is to apply the *Yamaha* factors, as recommended in Asimow, 42 UCLA L.Rev. at 1216-20. As an operative matter, this largely obviates the need to draw a distinction between a legal issue and a law application issue. Another solution is to adopt a delegation analysis, as discussed in the next note.

4. *Delegation of authority.* Linde's analysis in *McPherson* is trenchant. His key observation is that "[j]udicial review of such evaluations [as "good cause"], though a 'question of law,' requires a court to determine how much the legislature has itself decided and how much it has left to be resolved by the agency." Note that the court's position that the Employment Division possesses delegated authority to define "good cause" does not rest on a presumption (à la *Chevron*). Rather the court finds (or purports to find) from the statutory language and legislative history that the Unemployment Compensation Act actually does delegate such authority. Having made that finding, the court has no trouble concluding that any judgments the agency makes within the scope of that delegation can be reviewed only for reasonableness. Substitution of judicial for administrative judgment would defeat the legislative purpose of entrusting the matter to the agency.

A court might well prefer to follow the *Yamaha* approach to resolving an application question in some circumstances and the *McPherson* approach in other circumstances. Justice Linde's reasoning will not work in a situation in which it is evident from the statutory scheme that the legislature withheld policymaking authority from the agency. The podiatry statute in *Connecticut Medical* is an example (or so the court says). The *Yamaha* weak deference model is clearly more apt in such a situation. Moreover, even where the legislature's intentions are more obscure, a court might decide that it can uphold or reject the agency's interpretation without considering the extent, if any, to which the legislature may have delegated such authority. In such a case an effort to identify the extent of the agency's sphere of discretion may be an unnecessary complication. *See* Asimow, 42 UCLA L.Rev. at 1220-22 (discouraging the delegation analysis as a default approach, on the grounds that it will often require construction of an artificial fiction and is confusing and difficult to explain to the novice).

On the other hand, the *McPherson* reasoning may well be preferable where the statute uses such broad language (such as "in the public interest" or "just and reasonable rates") that the legislature *must* have intended to delegate interpretive authority to the agency. *Id.* at 1222. "Good cause," the operative term in *McPherson*, may also fall into this category. Another reason why the court might want to use a delegation analysis in order to discourage appeals and give the agency some latitude to implement its mandate. There is, after all, nothing particularly unusual about the idea that the organic statute under which an agency adjudicates impliedly confers discretion upon the agency. After all, that is the premise of the commonplace assumption that an agency action is reviewable for *abuse* of discretion. A hard look case like *Salameda*, § 9.3, for example, would scarcely be intelligible if one did not assume that the BIA was using (or perhaps misusing) discretionary authority. (Conversely, however, the advantages of a delegation analysis are less pronounced in a relatively simple adjudicative situation, such as are involved in many administrative appeals in the state courts.)

Even where the court does approach an application question using a delegation analysis, it will normally draw some legal boundaries around the exercise of the agency's discretion. The text asks whether, if the Employment Division were to decide that a hostile work environment is not good cause, a court could overturn that conclusion. Linde's claim that there is an implied interpretive delegation would at first seem to militate against a court's invalidating such a finding. But consider the language in the opinion asserting that an employee is not required to be a one-dimensional "economic [wo]man" and that the statute does not require her to endure sexual slurs or personal abuse for fear that abandoning an oppressive situation will disqualify her from receiving benefits. That suggests that a rule excluding co-worker harassment from good cause would violate the underlying policy of the statute. Indeed, given developing trends in the law of sexual harassment, as well as in background principles in society at large, the court almost certainly *would* construe the statute that way if the hypothetical case were to arise today.

5. *State overview.* As the note observes, most states decline to follow *Chevron*, but the Iowa statutory provision takes a particularly restrictive approach to judicial deference to agency legal interpretations. Compare it, for example, with the California approach. *Yamaha* would permit appropriate deference, adjusted according to context, even in situations in which an agency is not wielding delegated lawmaking authority. The Iowa statute, however, provides that the agency "should not" defer in those circumstances. According to the reporter-draftsman's explanatory statement (which the Iowa courts have followed), the phrase "should not" is intended to discourage deference in most cases while also leaving room for a court to defer with respect to "highly technical [matters] requiring special expertness for adequate comprehension." *See Mosher v. Department of*

Inspections & Appeals, 671 N.W.2d 501, 510 (Iowa 2003) (quoting Professor Arthur Bonfield).

For example, if the podiatry board had been able in *Connecticut Medical* to demonstrate that its interpretation of "foot" was longstanding, consistently applied, and supported by thoughtful reasoning, it would have had a respectable claim to deference under *Yamaha*, but probably not under the Iowa statute.

The Iowa legislature's skepticism about deference is even more evident in subsection (10)(c) of the same provision, which empowers a court to set aside an erroneous interpretation of a statute unless a provision of law "clearly" vests its interpretation in the discretion of the agency. This is the opposite of the *Chevron* presumption, under which ambiguities are to be resolved in the agency's favor.

Note that the statute effectively mandates the use in all cases of a delegation-oriented analysis. One could wonder whether the statutory framework will prove overly cumbersome. So far, however, the Iowa courts seem to be taking it in stride.

6. *Implied authority*. The *Beam* case candidly acknowledges a policy in Pennsylvania of construing statutes with less liberality than other jurisdictions typically allow (although the full opinion also contains more equivocal language). The result in the *Insurance Federation* case seems to confirm that policy. Since the mandatory arbitration rule had been on the books for four decades, and the legislature must have known about it, the court's 5-2 decision striking it down looks audacious. A more indulgent court could surely have ruled the other way. Students should readily see that the issue of agencies' implied authority goes to the heart of the rationale for the administrative state—do we want administrative entities to be able to solve social problems effectively? Or are we more concerned about potential abuses of agency authority?

Conceptually speaking, of course, the cases discussed in this note do not purport to address standards of *judicial review*. As a practical matter, however, the idea that enabling statutes should be read broadly is roughly equivalent to the idea that a court should hesitate to overturn an agency's reading. Conversely, *Insurance Federation* and *Connecticut Medical* seem to follow slightly different conceptual paths leading to a common destination.

7. *Problem*. In *Sherman*, the court ordered the charges against Dr. Sherman dismissed. Its opinion struck a blow for the right of doctors to pursue unorthodox methods of treatment, despite a body of professional opinion that the method is a fraud. The court stated: "If the advancement

of medicine is to continue, the avenues of difference must be left open, and, under circumstances such as here, not be the basis of a charge of fraud and deceit . . . [A]n affirmance of the charges of fraud and deceit on the present record has the possibilities of reaching far beyond the present facts and having serious consequences upon the practice of medicine. . . ."

In addition to *Sherman*, see *Gentry v. Dept. of Prof. & Occup. Regs.*, 293 So.2d 95 (Fla.App.1974). There the issue was whether a method of diagnosis of gonorrhea was a reason to revoke a physician's license. The court likewise ruled against the agency. This time, however, the principal statutory basis for the charge against the doctor was "unprofessional conduct."

The New York and Florida decisions are critically evaluated in Frank Grad & Noelia Marti, PHYSICIANS' LICENSURE AND DISCIPLINE 179-82 (1979). The authors note, uncontroversially, that "[t]he court must first determine the meaning of the legislature's definitions of punishable conduct, and it must then decide whether the agency's interpretation and application of the law fell within the agency's authority and discretion as articulated by the legislature." In general, they say, courts should defer to reasonable interpretations of the medical licensing boards within the area delegated to them, because of the agencies' expertise and the need for flexibility as medical practice changes. However, they continue, the courts are expert in and responsible for statutory interpretation and the overall integrity of the legal system.

Grad and Marti reluctantly conclude that the New York court was probably correct in not allowing the phrase "fraud and deceit" to be expanded to reach claims of ineffective treatment. This interpretation is unsatisfactory from the standpoint of protection of the public, they say, but the legislature should rewrite the statute. As for *Gentry*, however, the authors argue that "unprofessional conduct" is so broad a term that the legislature must have intended a generous delegation of authority, and the Florida court probably erred in substituting its judgment for that of the medical board acting within the area of its professional expertise.

In our problem, the court might follow a variety of paths, none of which is exclusively "correct." (1) The court might decide "as a matter of law" that Dr. Sherman did not engage in "fraud and deceit" because he did not commit any misrepresentations. In reaching that conclusion, the court might rely on the commonly understood meaning of these words, much as the court in *Connecticut Medical* did. It might also decide, from a comparative qualifications perspective, that it is perfectly capable of interpreting the statutory words on its own, because fraud and deceit are terms with which courts have dealt for centuries. An additional factor in *Sherman* was that the case against the doctor was poorly prepared and presented. The court may have distrusted the agency, thinking that it represented only orthodox medical views and was out to repress innovation.

The *Yamaha* considerations can, however, cut two ways. The court in the problem might interpret the words "fraud and deceit" in a less confining fashion, so as to reach claims of ineffective treatment. Perhaps "fraud and deceit" should be construed differently in the context of prescription or diagnosis than in the context of negotiation of a contract. After all, the legislature surely intended that the board should be able to protect the public as well as the medical professional. Arguably Dr. Sherman deceived his patients by promising results that his treatments could not deliver. (This line of argument would implicate the policy of liberal interpretation identified but abjured in *Beam*.) If the court treats the words "fraud and deceit" as equivalent to "unprofessional conduct," the board's expertise in medicine and accountability for its regulatory choices would, as Grad and Marti suggest, provide good reasons for the court to give weight to the board's reading. Also relevant under *Yamaha*, although not illuminated by the facts given in the problem, would be whether the board's interpretation is longstanding, consistently applied, reasonably explained, etc.

(2) The court might decide to treat this case as involving an application of law to fact, or "mixed question of law and fact." The court might then decide to characterize the case as raising either an issue of law (which would largely track the analysis just outlined) or as an issue of fact. Calling the problem factual would be analytically shaky, as Judge Posner explained in *McKinney* (N.3 above), but in effect it would mean that the Board's findings would be reviewed for substantiality of evidence, i.e., reasonableness, and would probably survive.

(3) The court might also follow a more sophisticated line of reasoning by treating the disciplinary statute as making an implied delegation of policymaking authority to the Board. Indeed, it's not at all implausible to suppose that the legislature intended to protect the public by empowering a specialized and expert medical board to flesh out the law and apply it to the facts. On this hypothesis, the board would, under *McPherson*, have to decide "how much" authority has been left to the board. That inquiry would again turn on whether the court thinks that "fraud and deceit" can apply in the absence of intentional misrepresentation. If the court answers that question affirmatively, the board's exercise of its discretion will stand unless it is arbitrary and capricious. This is again a test of reasonableness, so it is largely equivalent to the "mixed question" approach. However, the delegation approach is somewhat more conducive to a potential argument by Dr. Sherman that the board abused its discretion (e.g., by applying the facially broad statutory standard inconsistently without explaining the discrepancy).

(4) Finally, the court might say that if the language of the statute is deemed ambiguous, the board should be allowed to adopt any reasonable interpretation of it. This is, of course, the *Chevron* approach, which is not directly addressed in § 9.2.1, but you might want to mention it along with the other options for the sake of completeness. Under *Chevron* the court might still be able to rule against the board by asserting that the language "fraud and deceit" clearly entails intentional misrepresentation, which is not supported by the record. Such a holding is not implausible, but it would require heavier lifting for the court than the other options under discussion.

§ 9.2.2 THE *CHEVRON* DOCTRINE

CHEVRON U.S.A. INC. v. NATURAL RESOURCES DEFENSE COUNCIL

Notes and Questions

1. *Chevron's impact.* This note attempts to demystify *Chevron* even while recognizing its dominance. Law students eternally crave a structure of analysis with which they can cope with a complex and conceptually challenging body of doctrine; and, whatever else you might say about it, at least *Chevron* provides a structured inquiry. Yet the case isn't universally applied, its terminology is somewhat perplexing, and it certainly doesn't always translate into "the agency wins." As Merrill's historical account should make clear, one can't make much progress in untangling these complexities by trying to figure out what the Court "really meant" in *Chevron*. The important thing is what the doctrine has come to mean, and this meaning has developed gradually over time and is still evolving at least at the margins.

2. *The Chevron two-step.* A well-known exposition of part of the theoretical justification for *Chevron* is found in Henry P. Monaghan, "*Marbury* and the Administrative State," 83 Colum.L.Rev. 1, 26-31 (1983). Monaghan's article was published the year before *Chevron* and focuses on the *Hearst* case discussed in this note. The issue it addresses is whether *Hearst*-like reasonableness review on issues of law is consistent with *Marbury v. Madison*.

Monaghan says yes. Courts must respect a statutory delegation of power to an agency to either make law (i.e. adopt legislative rules) or interpret law. In the face of a delegation to interpret, a court's only role is to assure that the law has been obeyed—that the agency's interpretation is within the bounds of the area delegated to it. If the court sticks to that role, it has not "abdicated" anything; it is faithful to congressional intent. On this score, Monaghan seems to us unimpeachably correct. (For a similar discussion, see Ronald M. Levin, "Identifying Questions of Law in

Administrative Law," 74 Geo.L.J. 1, 16-22 (1985).) As we note in the text, even the court in *Connecticut Medical* seemed to agree.

Chevron amplifies on this reasoning with a persuasive account of the legislative process, linking judicial review of questions of law with review of discretionary action. It recognizes that a legislature frequently leaves interpretive gaps in a statute, so that statutory interpretation is required. The issue may be left unsettled because Congress never considered it (i.e. the issue was too specific) or because it was so contentious that Congress could not compromise it and passed the buck to the agency. This is a familiar justification for judicial deference to agencies' exercises of *explicit* delegations of legislative rulemaking power. *Chevron* extends the analysis to *implicit* delegations of interpretive power. The Court indicates that the agency charged with responsibility for implementing a statute, in accordance with current presidential policy, should make the accommodation of conflicting statutory policies—not the less politically responsible judicial branch.

But Monaghan did not argue that a delegation to interpret was *automatically* present in the case of every ambiguous statute—nor did *Chevron* make a bulletproof argument in favor of finding an interpretive delegation in every such statute, regardless of context. The arguments for finding an implied delegation in *Chevron* itself were strong (a technical statute, a major policy dispute with high political saliency), but in many situations the arguments will be much weaker. For example, there are many legal issues concerning which an agency won't feel much political heat no matter what position it takes. Some interpretive issues aren't technically challenging, and many don't implicate a need for centralized managerial control as much as others do. In these situations, the assertion that interpretive authority should rest with administrators has only limited force.

A recurring problem with discussing the merits of *Chevron* deference is that writers don't always distinguish carefully between these two aspects of the doctrine. *Some* of what goes by the name of "*Chevron* deference" is simply the playing out of the *Hearst* logic. Complaints about judicial abdication in that context are, in our opinion, misdirected. But the presumption aspect of *Chevron* deference rests on much more controversial policy premises, and quite naturally many people reject those premises or at least would apply them less sweepingly than the Court does.

3. *Academic perspectives.* Goodness knows how many sins of omission we have committed by failing to cite more fully to the enormous law review literature on *Chevron*! We have kept this note short in the belief that, by now, *Chevron* is so well ensconced in federal law that the principal questions revolve around issues of *how* it will be applied, not *whether* it will.

But if you wanted to plunge more deeply into the theoretical debate at its most basic level, a couple of additional classic treatments that you wouldn't want to miss would include Stephen Breyer, "Judicial Review of Questions of Law and Policy," 38 Admin.L.Rev. 236 (1986); Antonin Scalia, "Judicial Deference to Administrative Interpretations of Law," 1989 Duke L.J. 511; Thomas W. Merrill, "Judicial Deference to Executive Precedent," 101 Yale L.J. 969 (1992); Michael Herz, "Deference Running Riot: Separating Interpretation and Lawmaking Under *Chevron*," 6 Admin.L.J.Am.U. 187 (1992).

The quotes in this note are all thoughtful, but if you care to raise questions about one or more of them, you certainly could. Pierce's emphasis on political accountability does have force, because it leaves to majoritarian institutions the resolution of disputes that the legislature did not resolve. But that rationale doesn't help when, as so often occurs, the very question at issue is whether a statute really *is* ambiguous. It also doesn't take account of the value of checks and balances in preventing executive authorities from accumulating too much power. Farina and Molot are attentive to this latter consideration. And yet, how powerful is the case for judicial independence if the best argument for it is a negative one, i.e., that judges are *not* part of the executive branch?

Molot's quote contains an interesting additional rationale for active judicial review. He suggests that one beneficial consequence of the courts' input into the interpretation of administrative statutes is that stare decisis renders judicial holdings "more stable and consistent over time." That can indeed be a virtue at times, but not always. *Chevron* itself draws attention to the need for agencies to be able to reassess policies on a continuing basis, and this theme gets reinforced in *Brown & Williamson*, § 9.2.3, and *Brand X*, § 9.2.4 N.7.

4. *Applying step one.* A goal of this note is to illustrate a range of ways in which courts approach statutory interpretation under *Chevron*. Sometimes an opinion reads as though the court thinks that the agency wins unless its reading of the statute is ridiculous (and you can't tell whether the court really is as deferential as it sounds, or instead just was unimpressed with the challenger's position but wants to put the responsibility on the agency). It's judicial decisions like these that provoke the outrage about *Chevron* that you hear from many lawyers. At other times, such as in the *MCI* and *Cardoza-Fonseca* cases discussed in the note, the court's review is so probing that the presumption of delegation seems to disappear. It's pointless to argue about which of these two types of responses represent the "real" *Chevron*. They both do (as do still other decisions that fall somewhere between those two poles).

The note focuses, however, on the relatively intrusive mood that courts sometimes display, so as to clarify for students how the deference argument can at times be overcome. *Cardoza-Fonseca* and *MCI* illustrate the proposition that a statute can be somewhat ambiguous yet not susceptible of supporting the agency's reading. The "precise question at issue," in *Chevron* terms, can frequently be framed in a variety of ways, as the challenger may desire, and if the court finds that "Congress has directly addressed" any of the premises of the agency's decision, it can construe the statute accordingly.

5. *Applying step two.* A recent case that fits the category of cases discussed in the second paragraph of this note is *Entergy Corp. v. Riverkeeper, Inc.*, 129 S.Ct. 1498, 1505 & n.4 (2009) (remarking that "if Congress has directly spoken to an issue then any agency interpretation contradicting what Congress has said would be unreasonable"). Like *Whitman* and *Iowa Utilities*, *Entergy* was written by Justice Scalia. In the abstract, one could infer from this language that, in his view (or in the Court's view when he writes the opinion), the agency wins unless its interpretation is "unreasonable" in the sense that we associate with *Universal Camera*, which turns on whether any reasonable person could agree with the agency's view.

Almost certainly, however, Scalia doesn't intend any such implication. These opinions read like other exercises in statutory construction. By virtue of the principle that the government wins unless the statute is "unambiguous," the agency does something of an edge, but nothing significant appears to turn on whether that edge is described in terms of "reasonableness" or "clear" meaning—nor whether it is labeled step one or step two. This is an object lesson in not taking the verbal formulas of judicial review overly seriously.

In deciding how to teach this section, you may find that the easiest way to present the material is to encourage students to interpret step two of *Chevron* exclusively in terms of the second of the two approaches discussed in the note, i.e., by associating step two "reasonableness" with arbitrary-capricious review. This simplifies judicial review of the normative premises of an agency action by reducing the scope of review to two questions, not three: (a) does the agency's position transgress any "unambiguous" limitation in the statute, and (b) is it the product of reasoned decisionmaking?

That suggestion comes close to the position of Stephenson and Vermeule in the essay cited at the end of this note. (Their essay has now been published at 95 Va.L.Rev. 597 (2009); the reply by Bamberger and Strauss is at 95 Va.L.Rev. 611 (2009).) We do not, however, advocate actually abolishing the second *Chevron* step, as those authors do. Now that thousands upon thousands of cases have driven home the notion that

Chevron requires a two-step inquiry, we can't envision the Supreme Court suddenly renouncing that notion. There is room for debate, however, about whether our doubts on that score bespeak salutary realism or mere defeatism. *See* Stephenson & Vermeule, 95 Va.L.Rev. at 604 n.28 (posing the issue in those terms); Levin, 72 Chi-Kent L.Rev. at 1296 (same).

6. *Summing up.* The *Chevron* doctrine poses unusual challenges from a teaching standpoint. It is a core topic in judicial review, yet the cases elaborating on it are confusing and elusive. Inconsistencies abound, in part because judges so often stretch or reinterpret deference principles in order to arrive at a desired substantive result. We have, therefore, quoted at length in this note from one ambitious effort to harmonize the case law.

The "Blackletter Statement" from which the excerpt is drawn was an effort by the ABA Administrative Law Section to summarize major doctrinal areas in federal administrative law. This was a consensus statement developed after prolonged consultation and debate among many Section members, including us. It does not account for every precedent, nor does it answer every uncertainty, but we think students will find it helpful.

7. *Chevron in the states.* The *National Lime & Stone* case is discussed and criticized in Jonathan A. Conte & Paul W. Casper, Jr.,"*State ex rel Celebrezze v. National Lime & Stone Co.*: Redefining Agency Deference in Ohio," 47 Admin.L.Rev. 97 (1995). The case is unusual in the degree to which it assumes responsibility for striking a policy balance between clean air and economic growth. This sort of policy decision is clearly delegated to the agency—as will be discussed further in § 9.4. The contrast with *Chevron,* which involves a similar issue of statutory interpretation, could not be more pronounced.

Note also that in *National Lime,* the agency was construing its own regulation—not a statute. As will be seen in a later unit, courts have, both before and after *Chevron,* accorded strong deference to an agency's interpretation of its own regulations. *See* § 9.2.4 N.9. Moreover, the idea that any ambiguities in a regulatory statute or rule should be construed in favor of the regulated party is quite an eye-opener. It could be referred to as reverse deference, and is similar to the rule of lenity in criminal cases (criminal statutes should be construed in favor of the defendant). But there will be students attracted to the reverse deference approach taken by the *National Lime* opinion.

The Schenkkan reading illustrates in bold strokes the idea that judicial review practices must be appraised in the context of the broader political environment in which they will operate. It also exemplifies the rather intense skepticism about *Chevron* that prevails in the bench and bar at the state level.

That said, however, Schenkkan's specific points are worth examining closely. His argument that the part-time Texas legislature has less of a checking influence on agencies than Congress does makes sense, but his other arguments look more debatable. First, although the plural executive in Texas may furnish a weaker check on agency abuses than the more unitary federal executive branch does, it is not clear why the direct accountability of various Texas agencies to the people does not furnish an equally good justification for deference. Second, it seems odd to argue that the Texas courts should engage in aggressive statutory interpretation because they take less of a "hard look" at agency discretion than the federal courts do. Presumably they could alter the latter practice if they chose.

Finally, the state courts' practice of giving *Chevron* deference to federal agencies, even when they don't give it to their own state's agencies, raises an interesting theoretical question: Is that practice mandatory? Possibly *Chevron* principles are an integral part of federal law, binding on the state courts through the Supremacy Clause, although we know of no authoritative discussion. Regardless, the state courts' practice is at least a sensible one in practical terms. It promotes the uniformity of federal administration and enables federal agencies to make judgments about the legality of their intended actions without having to wonder whether those actions will be reviewed in state court rather than federal court. Besides, the state court's application of federal law would ultimately be reviewable in the U.S. Supreme Court, which obviously would apply the appropriate federal test (*Chevron* or *Skidmore* as the case may be). A disparity between the review standards applied at these two levels of appeal would be confusing and disruptive.

8. *Problem.* In the *Ohio* case, the dispute arose under the Comprehensive Environmental Response, Compensation and Liability Act (CERCLA), better known as Superfund. The damage formula was in a regulation, and the court invalidated it as contrary to CERCLA under *Chevron* step one. It relied on legislative history and also on indications in the statutory text (similar to § 203 in our problem) that the legislature had a preference for damages calculated according to restoration cost.

Contracts teachers will recognize the problem from the old strip mining cases. The miner leases land to strip mine for coal and promises to restore the land after he's done. At that point, the land looks like the surface of the moon. The miner breaches the restoration promise; what are the damages? The decline in market value of the strip mined land is $500, because it is remote moose pasture; it has virtually no market value whether restored or unrestored. The cost of restoration is $10,000,000.

There is a split in the decisions about which sum is the measure of damages. The problem with giving $10,000,000 is that you know the owner isn't going to use it to restore the land; it's just a windfall. But the problem with giving $500 is that it's a windfall to the miner, who, no doubt, got the coal cheaper because of the costly promise to restore the land. The difference in our case is § 203, which requires MEQA to use the money to restore the resource; so there would be no windfall from awarding the $30,000,000.

In our problem, MEQA can easily frame an argument that the Act is so ambiguous that the agency's interpretation can withstand scrutiny under step one of *Chevron*. Section 201 provides for damage recoveries in oil spills, but obviously it is openended as to the measure of damages. Such statutory silence (which the drafters may have left deliberately vague in order to get the bill passed) is a strong indicator of delegation under *Chevron*. Section 203 isn't quite as vague, but neither does it specify any particular test for computation of damages. Overall, the choice of a measure of damages seems to be a matter of policy more than of law, and under *Chevron*, policy is the agency's bailiwick.

Here's how Judge Wald, writing for the court in the *Ohio* case, managed to find that the statute contained enough guidance to negate the interpretation adopted by the administering agency (the Department of the Interior):

> [T]he "precise question at issue" . . . is not what measure of damages should apply in any or all cases which are brought under the Act. As to that larger question, Interior is obviously correct in asserting that Congress delegated to it a considerable measure of discretion. . . . The precise question here is a far more discrete one: whether DOI is entitled to treat use value and restoration cost as having equal presumptive legitimacy as a measure of damages. . . . Thus, while we agree with DOI that CERCLA permits it to establish a rule exempting responsible parties in some cases from having to pay the full cost of restoration of natural resources, we also agree with Petitioners that it does not permit Interior to draw the line on an automatic "which costs less" basis.

According to the court, the provision in § 203 that damages may be spent only on restoration or acquisition of a substitute resource would not make sense unless the legislature assumed that damages should be normally be measured by the cost of restoration. The manifest purpose of the Act is to make polluters pay for cleaning up oil spills, but MEQA's decisional rule would usually mean that the resource would not be restored or replaced—or else that taxpayers would pick up the tab. Similarly, the court continued, the 'shall not be limited by" language of § 203 implies that restoration cost should usually be the basic measure of damages under the Act.

The legislative history quote adds further weight to Sierra Club's argument—or at least it does if the court is willing to take account of it. Even though we don't explicitly canvass the debate over legislative history until the next unit (§ 9.2.3 N.4), students probably will be aware that many courts mistrust committee reports. But even a textualist judge might agree that MEQA's interpretation tends to defeat the purpose of the legislation. If the agency is permitted to adopt the stingiest possible measure of damages for the spill, why would the legislature have felt it necessary to pass a law on that subject to improve on what the common law already allows?

In short, the court might see this case as analogous to *Cardoza-Fonseca*: The statute has a range of possible meanings, but it can't mean what MEQA says it means. If the court buys this proposition, it will presumably remand the case for further consideration. MEQA might well find in the end that a $30 million damage award would be excessive and inequitable, and it might even be able to justify the low $7500 figure it assessed earlier. But it will have to justify its conclusion on premises that display greater fidelity to the goals of the statute.

Assume now that, Judge Wald's arguments notwithstanding, the court in the *Petrol* case considers the statute ambiguous enough to get the agency past step one. Does Sierra Club have any hope of prevailing at step two? Possibly. It can argue that the *Petrol* rule is an unreasonable interpretation (i.e., arbitrary and capricious) because it does so little to advance the evident purpose of the Act. A comparison between *NRDC v. Daley*, N.5, and this case would not be entirely farfetched. But arbitrariness is a high threshold to meet, so the agency would have a good chance of winning on this score. And probably, if the court were disposed to rule for Sierra Club at all, it would have done so at step one, so that it could put the responsibility on Congress instead of its own judgment. (This is one reason why agencies usually lose, if at all, at step one rather than step two.)

If you've taught § 9.2.1 already, you might want to ask students how the case should be decided if the Madison courts follow a weak-deference model rather than *Chevron*. The *Yamaha* factors don't seem to weigh heavily in favor of deference here. In this first-impression case MEQA cannot claim to have experience with this statute, nor is the question of the measure of damages an inherently technical question calling for expertise. The ruling is not contemporaneous with passage of the statute (that was 6 years ago), and there is no showing that MEQA was involved in the legislative process. It is not a consistently held position. There has been no reliance on it, and the statute has not been reenacted so as to indicate legislative acquiescence in MEQA's view. On the other hand, MEQA did arrive at its damage formula in a contested case, with all of the inducements to careful consideration that such procedures can involve. Since the contextual factors do not give the agency much of a thumb on the scales, the court would probably have ample room to overturn the decision below. The results under *Chevron* and *Yamaha* may not differ, but the *Chevron* approach does impose a heavier burden of justification on the court, and not all judges will care to take on that burden.

§ 9.2.3 STATUTORY INTERPRETATION AND THE *CHEVRON* DOCTRINE

As we mentioned in our introductory comments to § 9.2 of this manual, you can easily skip this unit if you're running short of time in the course. The essential points about *Chevron* are all covered in § 9.2.2. At the same time, we invite you to give this unit a try, because the interplay between *Chevron* and other statutory interpretation principles gives rise to interesting issues, and *Brown & Williamson* in particular makes a fascinating test case regarding the limits of *Chevron* deference. An intermediate option would be to assign only Notes 5 and 6 of this unit, which take up elements of the "*Chevron* step zero" issue that are not otherwise addressed in § 9.2.4.

FDA v. BROWN & WILLIAMSON TOBACCO CORP.

Shortly before this manual went to press, Congress enacted the Family Smoking Prevention and Tobacco Control Act of 2009, Pub.L.No. 111-31 (June 22, 2009). This Act overrules *Brown & Williamson* by granting the FDA explicit jurisdiction over tobacco products. One can argue that the new Act validates the Court's decision to leave the tobacco problem to the elected legislature to frame a more democratically legitimate solution. A contrary argument would be that if the Court had upheld the FDA regulations, a decade's delay could have been avoided, or Congress could have responded if it were dissatisfied with the FDA's solution.

1. *Brown & Williamson.* *Chevron* suggests in footnote 9 that a court may consult all of the "traditional tools of statutory construction" in order to ascertain "clear congressional intent," and this case provides particularly striking confirmation of that proposition. Justice O'Connor doesn't rely on the language of the enabling provision of the Act. Moreover, she essentially concedes that the regulations would serve worthy public policy goals, and she nowhere suggests any policy factors favoring the result she reaches (unless one counts the hints in Part II.C. that the power claimed by the FDA may not belong in administrative hands). In the face of these obstacles, not to mention *Chevron* deference itself, she rules against the FDA by relying on statutory structure and on related enactments—which are not usually considered to be among the most powerful "tools" in the interpretive toolbox—and an innovative "common sense" argument.

493

(a) *Statutory context.* Consider first the majority's argument based on the structure of the FDCA as a whole. The Justices all appear to agree that a complete ban on tobacco products would be unacceptable. (Presumably some anti-tobacco activists would disagree, but their voice remains completely absent from this dialogue.) Initially, therefore, Justice O'Connor seems correct to argue that if the choice is between the status quo and a total ban on tobacco products, the former must prevail. But that way of framing the issue simply tees up the question of why the FDA's proposed intermediate solution is not viable.

The FDA's position that it can regulate rather than ban cigarettes rests on the theory that a total ban would be "dangerous" to addicts. This is at least an unnatural use of language, and the agency's regulations did entail a creative remedy that was not directly envisioned by the Act. Yet the conclusion that the FDA cannot effectively regulate tobacco seems at least equally anomalous, if not more so. The FDA regulates products that are a lot less dangerous than cigarettes, so why would one want to read the Act as effectively exempting tobacco when the statutory language does not require it? (Another irony: The tobacco companies spent decades insisting that cigarettes had not been definitively proved to be unsafe. *See United States v. Philip Morris USA, Inc.*, 449 F.Supp.2d 1 (D.D.C.2006), *aff'd in relevant part*, 566 F.3d 1095 (D.C.Cir.2009). Now they say that cigarettes are *so irredeemably unsafe* that the FDA cannot regulate them.)

Justice Breyer's major premise is that the remedial gap is the anomaly that must be avoided. In his words, it is "perverse" to read the Act to say that the FDA must either ban tobacco or leave it entirely unregulated. That conclusion is too much at odds with the reason we have an FDA. A sensible Congress would want the agency to be able to devise a middle-ground position. This is a classic "purposivist" argument, and Breyer very typically adopts such arguments.

The problem with his position in *Brown & Williamson* is that, although a sensible Congress wouldn't create such an anomaly, the Congress that we actually have—the legislature that adopts special interest legislation all the time, for logical or illogical reasons—might very well do so. And the Justices who anchored the majority are, indeed, the members of the Court who have been most receptive to the idea that a judge has to construe statutes by taking Congress as it is, starkly pluralistic though that view may be.

(b) *Related statutes.* The canon on which O'Connor relies in Part II.B. of her opinion—that a statute should be interpreted so as to "make sense" in relation to other statutes on the same subject—does have judicial support, but there are two difficulties. The first is that, as just argued, the preceding discussion in Part II.A. proceeds on the opposite premise: Congress has left the FDA with the dilemma of either ignoring tobacco or banning it, regardless of whether this "makes sense" or not.

Second, and more specifically, the evidence of ratification seems thin. It does seem clear that the members of Congress *believed* the FDA lacked jurisdiction over tobacco products, but this does not mean they intended to perpetuate that state of affairs. As Breyer argues, they may well have been willing to leave the FDA with whatever jurisdiction it may have possessed.

It seems not only possible but probable that the enactment of other tobacco-related statutes, such as the law that required warning labels on cigarette packs, resulted from hard-fought compromises reached by members with widely divergent views, ranging from strong defenders of the industry to strong advocates of public health protection. In all likelihood they agreed on what they enacted and not much more. They could have specifically barred the FDA from taking further action, but they did not. If they assumed that the agency would not seek to regulate tobacco on its own, their expectation was plausible based on the political environment when they acted. But the industry's supporters didn't "get it in writing," so they left themselves unprotected in the event the political winds changed. Or so one might have supposed, but the Court majority ascribes that protection to Congress anyway.

(c) *FDA's prior position.* Regardless of whether Congress relied on the FDA's prior assurances that it lacked jurisdiction over tobacco, the discrepancy between the agency's former and present position may weaken its credibility as a litigant. Even under weak deference, inconsistency in interpretation is a negative factor. On the other hand, agency interpretations are not "instantly carved in stone," according to *Chevron.* Decisions such as *Brand X*, § 9.2.4 N.7, and the very recent *Fox Television* case (discussed in § 9.4 of this manual) also attest to the Court's willingness, at least some of the time, to tolerate or even endorse agencies' changes of interpretation or policy over time.

With respect to the Court's final argument—that "common sense" shows that Congress would not have left so momentous a matter as tobacco regulation to the FDA's discretion, see N.5 below.

2. *Legislative purpose.* As we suggested in the preceding note, Justice Breyer's purposive argument in this case seems quite powerful. Even if the description of the FDCA as a "constitution" is somewhat hyperbolic, one would ordinarily think that an agency's organic statute should be read in a manner that promotes its basic purposes.

The *Rodriguez* case, discussed in this note, is an apt reminder that statutes usually embody compromises among multiple competing objectives.

That observation carries more weight in interpretation in some cases than in others. It works well in *Chevron*. Stevens makes clear that the Clean Air Act was intended to promote both cleaner air and economic growth, so an argument that the bubble policy is required because it would promote clean air would be, at best, incomplete. However, the *Rodriguez* reasoning is dubious as a rejoinder to Breyer's dissent in *Brown & Williamson*, because the majority opinion doesn't identify any secondary objectives of the FDCA that the agency's regulations would threaten to negate. You could reasonably assume that the economic interests of tobacco-growing states and the (unhealthy) tastes of citizens who smoke are implicated here, but Justice O'Connor doesn't explicitly bring these considerations into the discussion.

The broad question raised by the dissent's challenge is the extent to which an administrative agency's enabling statute should be read flexibly to solve social problems, even when its language does not readily lend itself to that end. We saw the Pennsylvania Supreme Court's restrictive (or at least cautious) response to that question in § 9.2.1 N.6.

The same question recurrently plays out at the federal level in various ways. Historically, for example, the FCC has been allowed to exercise "ancillary jurisdiction" over matters that were deemed reasonably necessary to the fulfillment of its responsibilities, even if it had no express authority over them. Thus, although Congress had not expressly empowered the Commission to regulate cable television, the Court allowed it to assert ancillary jurisdiction because of cable's impact on broadcasting, over which the Commission did have express jurisdiction. *United States v. Southwestern Cable Co.,* 392 U.S. 157 (1968). However, subsequent decisions on ancillary jurisdiction have gone both ways, and in *American Library Ass'n v. FCC,* 406 F.3d 689 (D.C.Cir.2005), the court thought it should be cautious about any further extensions. The FCC issued a rule to require that all digital television receivers must be capable of recognizing "broadcast flags"—digital codes that would be embedded in a broadcast and would prevent the equipment from redistributing the program. The Commission considered this step necessary to prevent unauthorized copying and redistribution of programs. The court set the rule aside. It said that the broadcast flag rule went too far, because the Commission had never before been thought to be able to regulate the use of reception equipment *after* the broadcast transmission was complete. That limitation sounds more than a little artificial, but the underlying lesson seems to be that courts are now less willing to accept openended interpretations of enabling legislation than they were in an earlier era.

3. *Canons.*

a. *Constitutional avoidance.* Nobody really doubts that constitutional avoidance is an important canon that can, in principle, overcome *Chevron* deference. Agencies themselves often invoke the principle of constitutional avoidance in their decisions, as does the Department of Justice through its Office of Legal Counsel. *See* Trevor Morrison, "Constitutional Avoidance in the Executive Branch," 106 Colum.L. Rev. 1189 (2006). At the same time, constitutional cases tend to involve deeply held ideological commitments that exert pressures that no scope of review principle can overcome. It would be naive to expect that a case on abortion rights, such as *Rust v. Sullivan,* is going to tell you much about how deference principles operate in routine cases.

b. *Retroactivity.* The quote here from *St. Cyr* approaches doubletalk, but Justice Stevens could have made his point in a less convoluted fashion: A statute that initially appears ambiguous may no longer be so after the canon against retroactivity is applied. Frequently, as we saw in § 5.2.2 N.3, the difficult question in such cases is whether the statute is retroactive at all.

c. *Lenity.* A premise of this note is that a statute must mean the same thing in all contexts, even when the rule of lenity would be relevant to only some of those contexts. The Court strongly reaffirmed the same basic idea in the context of constitutional avoidance in *Clark v. Martinez,* 543 U.S. 371, 380-82, 385 (2005) ("It is not at all unusual to give a statute's ambiguous language a limiting construction called for by one of the statute's applications, even though other of the statute's applications, standing alone, would not support the same limitation. The lowest common denominator, as it were, must govern.").

Siegel, however, argues that *Martinez's* "unitary" principle of construction is not always followed, and should not be. Courts sometimes do interpret a single phrase in a statute to apply differently to differing situations. Among the examples he cites are a few from administrative law, including the contrasting interpretations of the Medicare Act preclusion provision in *Erika* and *Michigan Academy,* § 10.4. *See* Jonathan R. Siegel, "The Polymorphic Principle and the Judicial Role in Statutory Interpretation," 84 Tex.L.Rev. 339, 357-58 (2005).

4. *Legislative history.* Justice Scalia did not necessarily abandon his principles regarding legislative history by joining the majority opinion in *Brown & Williamson.* He could argue that O'Connor's historical arguments are based primarily on actual enactments, a line of analysis that is entirely compatible with textualist methodology.

We do not, however, endorse the courts' occasional tendency to define *Chevron* step one in purely textualist terms. To the extent the tendency means that other "traditional tools of statutory construction" are simply postponed until step two, this fragmentation of the process of interpretation is pointless. On the other hand, to the extent that the tendency means adopting the jurisprudence of textualism itself, and thus *narrowing* the range of interpretive tools available in an administrative law case, it is subject to other objections.

We believe that a good solid legislative committee report can be excellent evidence of what a statute is supposed to mean. It's hard, at least for these authors, to imagine construing a complicated statute without being able to look at relatively authoritative sources of legislative history for assistance. Of course, some legislative history is bogus—inserted by staff which couldn't get its way in the statute. But we agree with Justice Breyer that "[t]he 'problem' of legislative history is its 'abuse,' not its 'use.' Care, not drastic change, is all that is warranted." Breyer, 65 S.Cal.L.Rev. at 874.

Moreover, we do not share Scalia's view that judges who rely on legislative history will become more willing to meddle in agencies' affairs because they will tend to discern congressional directives that the textualist would not acknowledge. *See* the above-cited lecture by Scalia, 1989 Duke L.J. at 521. Legislative history can either create doubts or dispel doubts, so the relationship that Scalia posits is questionable. Indeed, as Merrill argues in the article cited in this note, textualism is somewhat in tension with deference, because it encourages judges to look at interpretation as an abstract exercise that they themselves are presumably as well qualified as anyone to perform, and it devalues the notion that agencies should be faithful agents of the political branches (which would entail attention to what the legislature *intended* even if its words did not aptly capture that meaning). In short, we support independent judicial review of legal issues as a check on agency abuses, but a strong version of textualism is too crude an instrument for courts to use in pursuing that worthy function.

5. *Major questions.* The Court's suggestion that "extraordinary" cases with great "economic and political significance" do not warrant *Chevron* deference can be seen as either a threshold ("step zero") inquiry or as a principle of interpretation considered within the usual *Chevron* step one inquiry. *See* Sunstein, 92 Va.L.Rev. at 242-44. Regardless of which label may be more apt, we address the issue in this unit because *Brown & Williamson* makes a good vehicle for exploring it.

Sunstein offers several good reasons to doubt the soundness of this argument for withholding *Chevron* deference. *Id.* at 243-47. The line between major and interstitial questions is very fuzzy, and the typical rationales for *Chevron*, such as expertise and accountability, can be implicated just as fully when the issue is highly consequential as otherwise. In effect, what Justice O'Connor calls "common sense" seems to be an implicit bias against substantial departures from the status quo. Yet a statute like the FDCA is written to last indefinitely, with the understanding that it will be used in ways not initially foreseen. We would add that decisions with economic or political significance often produce gridlock at the legislative level, and the administrative process can serve to get things done (or at least induce a response from Congress). Dramatic changes sought by agencies can lead to abuses, for which the usual remedies exist, but at least we see no good reason to adopt a rule of construction *disfavoring* dramatic action as such.

In his *Brown & Williamson* dissent, Breyer says that the "major issues" limitation on *Chevron*, if it exists, does not apply to the tobacco case, because this particular high-profile action by the FDA will capture public attention, and the President and Congress will be held accountable. We fail to see how he can have it both ways. One could make the same argument about any regulation that has "enormous social consequences," and thus the "major issues" limitation would be swallowed by its own exception. A better response to this paradox, we think, would be to say that the political accountability rationale for *Chevron* resounds with particular clarity when a "major issue" is at stake, and therefore normal *Chevron* principles can apply to it. (Because judges are human, however, they may be especially prone to override deference principles in such cases, as illustrated by the abortion example mentioned above.)

An early question about *Chevron* was whether it applies to actions by which an agency seeks to expand its jurisdiction, as distinguished from seeking to alter a regulatory approach while acting within its admitted jurisdiction. *See Mississippi Power & Light Co. v. Mississippi ex rel. Moore*, 487 U.S. 354 (1987) (featuring separate opinions in which Justice Brennan questioned, and Justice Scalia endorsed, application of *Chevron* to such cases). The article by Gellhorn and Verkuil, cited in this note, makes as good a case for this proposition as is available. We have omitted this debate from the present edition because, after twenty-five years' experience with *Chevron*, this thesis has never gotten traction in the courts. *See Oklahoma Natural Gas Co. v. FERC*, 28 F.3d 1281 (D.C.Cir.1994) (rejecting the thesis). It was never going to be easy to articulate a broadly acceptable normative basis for treating jurisdictional issues differently on judicial review from other issues. Nevertheless, the "extraordinary cases" language of *Brown & Williamson* can plausibly be seen as a reworking of the *Mississippi Power* argument in a more functional, and to some minds more acceptable, fashion.

6. *Other questions that Congress is unlikely to have delegated.* We discussed the *Chevron* implications of *Dominion Energy* at length in § 3.1.1 N.3 of this manual and will refrain from repeating that entire discussion. Briefly, we think the First Circuit was too quick to assume that the statute being interpreted was the Clean Water Act rather than the APA. As Howarth has neatly argued, the case required the court to construe *both* statutes, and the court surely did not owe deference to the EPA on the issue

of what presumption, if any, is required by 5 U.S.C. § 554(a). Cooley R. Howarth, Jr., "Restoring the Applicability of the APA's Adjudicatory Procedures," 56 Admin.L.Rev. 1043, 1051-53 (2004).

Berry makes the broader argument that *all* procedural provisions in agency enabling statutes should be deemed to fall outside *Chevron*'s domain. She argues that independent judicial scrutiny of such provisions would better ensure fairness to litigants and that procedural issues are within the institutional competence of the judiciary. She also asserts that procedural provisions are generally imposed to circumscribe agency discretion, yet agencies will usually seek to construe them narrowly. The thesis has some intellectual appeal, particularly in its analysis of agency self-interest. Yet the courts have never entertained this thesis seriously. They regularly apply *Chevron* to procedural and substantive provisions alike. In addition to *Dominion Energy*, see *Envirocare*, § 4.1.1 N.5, and *Your Home Visiting Nurse Services, Inc. v. Shalala*, 525 U.S. 449, 453 (1999) (applying *Chevron* to the issue of whether a Medicare intermediary's refusal to reopen a determination is appealable to the Provider Reimbursement Review Board). This pattern in the decisions should not be surprising in light of cases such as *Vermont Yankee* and *PBGC v. LTV*, § 5.4.3. The Court strongly believes that agencies need procedural flexibility in order to carry out their mandates and that courts should not be quick to second-guess their procedural choices.

The gist of Pierce's criticism of *Adams Fruit* lies in the following passage in the cited article:

> Private right of action provisions in regulatory statutes usually interact with other provisions in myriad ways that make it desirable for a single institution to have authority to define all statutory terms relevant to the scope of the private rights of action. Moreover, Congress usually includes a provision in a regulatory statute that confers on the agency sufficiently broad rulemaking power to support a court holding that the agency has the authority to issue rules that courts must apply in resolving private disputes in which the construction of the statute is at issue.

48 Admin.L.Rev at 19. The accuracy of these generalizations is difficult to gauge, but Pierce makes a persuasive case that both statements were true in *Adams Fruit* itself, and he mentions a number of other cases in which the Court has reached conclusions on these issues that were more accommodating of administrative choices.

7. *Problem.* In *Sweet Home* the Court upheld the Interior Department's habitat modification regulation by a vote of 6-3, with a majority opinion by Stevens, a concurrence by O'Connor, and a dissent by Scalia. These opinions discuss most of the issues in the problem, and the

D.C. Circuit opinions below provide even more voluminous analysis. 1 F.3d 1 (D.C.Cir.1993), *rev'd on rehearing*, 17 F.3d 1463 (D.C.Cir.1994). Some of your students may already be aware of the case, but we do not think this possibility spoils the value of the problem as a teaching exercise. The main objective of the exercise is to get students to identify and think about a wide range of arguments that might be invoked on either side of the case. That can be a challenge even for a student who knows the "right" (Court-approved) answer.

We start from the premise that the *word* "harm" in the ESA is ambiguous. Thus, its interpretation will depend on the remaining language of the Act (whether deemed "plain" or not) and other contextual factors. Arguments that tend to favor the government include the following:

(a) *Chevron* itself. Said the Court, "The task of defining and listing endangered and threatened species requires an expertise and attention to detail that exceeds the normal province of Congress. . . . The proper interpretation of a term such as 'harm' involves a complex policy choice. When Congress has entrusted the Secretary with broad discretion, we are especially reluctant to substitute our views of wise policy for his. *See Chevron*." 515 U.S. at 708. Nevertheless, the opinion as a whole does not read as though the Court is simply checking to see that the Secretary's interpretation is within the realm of reason. As it has done in many other cases, the Court seems to treat the agency's views as just one factor to be considered along with others, rather than as furnishing a "standard of review." Interestingly, in addition to declaring that the Interior regulations passed muster under the *Chevron* two-step test, Stevens cited prominently to Breyer's 1986 essay on judicial review, observing that the breadth of the statute and the expertise needed to enforce it justifies "some deference" to the agency. *Id.* at 703-04. This adds a bit of a *Skidmore* flavor to the mix.

(b) Statutory purpose. Obviously the main purpose of the ESA is species protection, and DOI's broad construction of the Act promotes that purpose. In *Sweet Home*, Scalia relied on the *Rodriguez* case cited in N.2 to argue that the Act actually has multiple purposes, but to no avail. *Id.* at 735-36 (dissent). (He did persuade the Court to acknowledge those secondary purposes later, in the context of standing. *See Bennett v. Spear*, § 11.1.3 N.6.)

(c) Ratification. Students could argue, by analogy to *Brown & Williamson*, that Congress ratified the DOI habitat modification regulation, because it left that regulation in place in the course of authorizing "incidental take" permits. As a matter of environmental law, this point is complicated, because those permits *could* relate to the kinds of "takings" addressed by the regulation, but they might also be issued for unrelated activities, such as when a fisherman inadvertently catches a protected species of fish while actually seeking to catch a different, unprotected species.

Our own view is that, although the analogy to *Brown & Williamson* is valid enough, the ratification argument in both contexts is weak. The *absence* of a congressional consensus to alter the status quo should usually not be equated with the *presence* of a consensus to retain the status quo. Sometimes there simply is no consensus at all, except with respect to the precise issue that a fragile coalition of legislators managed to address through legislation.

Arguments tending to favor Sam include the following:

(d) Dictionary definition. The OED definition is helpful to Sam. But dictionary definitions can be overused. At best they are evidence of common usage, but Congress does not always legislate with the precise nuances of a dictionary definition in mind. The *MCI* case, § 9.2.2 N.4, has been criticized for placing more emphasis on dictionary meanings than the circumstances of that case warranted. *See generally* Note, "Looking It Up: Dictionaries and Statutory Interpretation," 107 Harv.L.Rev. 1437 (1994).

The argument gets weaker still when dictionaries disagree among themselves. In *Sweet Home* the majority found support for a broad reading of "harm" in one of the definitions of that word in Webster's Third New International Dictionary": "to cause hurt or damage to."

(e) *Noscitur a sociis.* The district court in the problem applied the maxim correctly, but canons of this kind are only weak indicators of legislative intent. Moreover, the language of § 9 does not perfectly fit the maxim, because some of the verbal "associates" of the word "take," including "harass," "collect," and even "kill," do not particularly connote violence. Note that DOI somewhat protected itself against challenge by limiting its regulation to prohibit only conduct that "actually kills or injures wildlife," as opposed to merely making habitat less hospitable to wildlife.

(f) Legislative history. Representative Sullivan's floor speech supports Sam's position that, in Congress's contemplation, injuries to property values should be rectified through purchases rather than restriction of primary conduct. But it stands to reason that the snippet of legislative debate quoted here is only one passage in a massive legislative record, and you can "prove" anything you want through selective quotation. These days, a court is going to hesitate to put much weight on this one passage. (The real case involved a typical full-scale battle of legislative history quotes, which we have omitted from the problem in the interest of simplicity.)

(g) Lenity. In *Sweet Home*, Stevens declined to read the ESA narrowly pursuant to the rule of lenity. He noted that criminal liability under the ESA requires a "knowing" violation, but in any event the proper occasion to consider scienter would be in an enforcement proceeding, not a preenforcement challenge to the regulation. Besides, it was not clear that the Secretary seeks criminal liability with any frequency. 515 U.S. at 696 n.9. Stevens also distinguished *Thompson/Center Arms* on the basis that one purpose of lenity is to give fair notice to potential defendants about their criminal exposure, and the Secretary's regulations served this purpose. *Id.* at 704 n.18. (No regulation was involved in *Thompson/Center Arms*, but the same cannot be said of the earlier *American Broadcasting* case cited in the note.) Another purpose of lenity, however, is to preserve legislative primacy in the definition of crimes. To that extent the tension between *Sweet Home* and cases like *Thompson/Center Arms* remains unresolved.

(h) Constitutional avoidance. The Due Process clause protects property rights under many circumstances, and Sam can argue that the court should read the Act narrowly to avoid having to decide whether the regulation could effect an unconstitutional "taking." Probably it is a valid "regulatory taking," but the point of the canon is to avoid having to adjudicate that issue in the first place.

(*I*) Major issue. Could the scope of "take" under the ESA be considered a decision with such "economic and political magnitude" that Congress could not reasonably be thought to have left it to an agency? Sunstein suggests that it might. 92 Va.L.Rev. at 239. But who knows? A telling criticism of this strand of the *Brown & Williamson* reasoning is the opinion's lack of any guidelines to indicate how "major" a rule has to be in order to negate *Chevron* deference.

§ 9.2.4 INFORMAL INTERPRETATIONS AND THE *SKIDMORE* ALTERNATIVE

Although *Mead* is the more prominent and widely discussed decision, our first principal case in this unit is *Christensen*. We made that choice for pedagogical reasons. *Mead* is a decidedly frustrating case to teach, due to the vagueness of the Court's holding (compounding the uncertainty as to how much difference the distinction between *Chevron* and *Skidmore* makes anyway). *Christensen*, on the other hand, sets forth a relatively concrete doctrinal rule. You can agree or disagree with that rule, but at least you know what it is, and in fact most case law adheres to it notwithstanding the qualifications introduced by subsequent cases. Although *Mead* has to be covered, we think that students will find *Christensen* a more accessible introduction to this topic.

CHRISTENSEN v. HARRIS COUNTY

UNITED STATES v. MEAD CORP.

Notes and Questions

1. *Christensen.* The holding of *Christensen* regarding the limited scope of *Chevron* was predictable. On its facts the case was quite similar to *Skidmore,* a venerable decision, and even after *Chevron* the Court had continued to use *Skidmore* as the basis for evaluating interpretive rules. *EEOC v. Arabian-American Oil Co.,* 499 U.S. 244 (1991). Moreover, the ACUS recommendation cited in this note signaled that there was significant support in the administrative law community for the direction in which the Court would go.

Yet the language of *Chevron* did not support the limitation that the Court placed on its scope, and the rationales that have generally been cited as justifying *Chevron* deference (expertise, political accountability, uniformity, etc.) do not, on their own terms, apply differently to formal and informal formats. Nevertheless, *Christensen* simply announced that informal pronouncements are subject to *Skidmore* rather than *Chevron.* It didn't explain why. Thus, the task of justifying the distinction had to await *Mead.*

The private cause of action authorized by the Fair Labor Standards Act suggests a limitation that the Court could have placed on the *Christensen* rule but did not. The structure of the FLSA demonstrates in a clearcut fashion that Congress delegated at least some interpretive authority to the judiciary. Indeed, in a private FLSA action a court can construe the statute even if the agency has said nothing about the issue in dispute. However, Justice Thomas stated the *Christensen* rule without referring to that aspect of the statute. He thus set the stage for *Mead,* in which the Court's unwillingness to follow *Chevron* had to rest more squarely on policy considerations. The manipulability of the ensuing analysis has probably contributed to the doctrinal instability that plagues this area. (One could reply, however, that *Chevron* was itself a judicial creation, and what the Court has given it can also take back.)

2. *Skidmore.* The distinction drawn by Hickman and Krueger between the "independent judgment" and "sliding scale" approaches to *Skidmore* review is useful. We think a close reading of the excerpt from the actual *Skidmore* case, as quoted at the beginning of this section, demonstrates that the sliding scale approach comes closer to what Justice Jackson had in mind originally. On the other hand, it's apparent from the information provided in the note that quite a few decisions seem to apply *Skidmore* using the independent judgment approach, even though it is a

minority approach. In the present state of the law, it can't be called "incorrect."

One implication of the sliding scale approach is that deference under *Skidmore* is not supposed to be left entirely to the inclinations of the individual judge. There is supposed to be a framework of analysis, albeit not the *Chevron* framework. In the casebook we call it "weak deference." Of course the *Skidmore* factors are ill-defined and still evolving. But a lower court faced with a particular case would not be well advised to ignore circuit precedents applying *Skidmore* to closely related situations.

The note also explores the challenging issue of whether and how far *Chevron* review is more agency-friendly than *Skidmore* review. Surely the usual assumption is that *Skidmore* entails less deference, but the data seem equivocal. Even though the Hickman and Krueger article is as rigorous a study as anybody is likely to devise, its comparison between *Chevron* and *Skidmore* is somewhat clouded by their having to rely on the findings of a separate study (Orin S. Kerr, "Shedding Light on *Chevron*: An Empirical Study of the *Chevron* Doctrine in the U.S. Courts of Appeals," 15 Yale J. on Reg. 1 (1998)) in which the methodological assumptions were not necessarily the same. Anyway, Hickman and Krueger themselves report (as the note says) that in a significant number of cases the court's *Skidmore* analysis sounds very much as though the court were applying *Chevron*.

The upshot seems to be that, although one can anticipate some difference in stringency between the two standards of review, that difference is nothing to count on. Thus, the nicknames "strong deference" (referring to *Chevron*) and "weak deference" (referring to *Skidmore*) should be used with care and not taken too literally. Perhaps the most important difference between the two standards is not how demanding they are, but instead the manner in which they are supposed to be applied. Under *Chevron* the reviewing court is supposed to analyze the merits using the structured two-step test that revolves around a presumption of delegation to the agency; but the *Skidmore* weak-deference approach permits a more free-form weighing of various prudential and contextual factors.

3. *Mead.* Justice Souter's emphasis on whether "Congress would expect the agency to be able to speak with the force of law" is confusing to say the least. He seems to mean that courts should accord *Chevron* deference when Congress would want them to do so. When Congress confers authority on agencies, however, it surely does not think about this esoteric judicial review issue with any frequency—if it ever does. And even if it does, a court would have little if any means of knowing it. As a practical matter, therefore, the congressional intent criterion is inescapably fictional.

Similarly, when Justice Breyer proposes to implement *Mead* by examining what a "reasonable member of Congress" would prefer, he doesn't have in mind a criterion that could be investigated in some objective sense. As we noted in discussing his dissent in *Brown & Williamson* (§ 9.2.3 N.1 of this manual), Breyer's concept of a reasonable legislator is a far cry from a *typical* member of Congress. All too obviously, he means a legislator who favors the same kind of pragmatic solutions to public policy problems that he himself does. Those solutions aren't necessarily bad ones, but we do not see how he can claim that there is anything "democratic" about his approach. Review of agency action by *real* legislators (as in a vigorously implemented scheme of congressional oversight) would confer democratic legitimacy, but review by Breyer-like *fictional* legislators seems very different.

Beneath the surface, *Mead* and *Barnhart* seem to indicate that the Court has developed second thoughts about the straightforward *Christensen* rule. The Justices apparently want to leave their options open. By manipulating the elastic criterion of imputed congressional intent, they can have *Chevron* deference whenever it seems like a good idea, and that seems to be the way they want it.

We question whether this much flexibility is really worthwhile. Merrill's article, cited in N.4, makes strong arguments for a more rule-like approach to Step Zero. A clearer approach would enable the Court to maintain better control over lower courts, and it would facilitate planning by agencies, Congress, and the private sector. 54 Admin.L.Rev. at 819-26. Also, in practice a good deal of flexibility is built into both the *Chevron* and *Skidmore* tests, and so the marginal benefit of injecting further flexibility to the choice *between* those standards may be low.

4. *Rules of thumb.* Anthony's 1990 article, cited in N.1, is a comprehensive exposition of the force of law approach. As we say in the note, we assume that in this context "force of law' should be equated with the procedurally binding effect that, for example, distinguishes legislative rules from guidance documents (or at least policy statements—the status of interpretive rules is less settled). *See* § 6.1.4. The suggestions in some passages in *Mead* that "force of law" is equivalent to strong deference are not very helpful, because they lead to the tautological assertion that only *Chevron*-eligible agency actions should be accorded *Chevron* deference.

Given that premise, a couple of arguments can be made in favor of the force of law test. First, *Chevron* is designed to accommodate congressional delegations of interpretive authority to agencies (and, indeed, to ascribe such delegations to Congress where the statute is merely ambiguous). In a guidance document or advice letter, however, the agency has *declined* to exercise its delegated power, even if it has any. Second, the force of law test rests on the policy argument that agency actions that have the force of law are *usually* accompanied by procedural safeguards that tend to promote thoughtful decisionmaking, so they generally deserve more deference than agency actions that can be issued without such safeguards. Third, although the correlation between legally binding action and procedural protections is imperfect, a small margin of over- and under-inclusiveness may be tolerable in the interest of maintaining a relatively clear, manageable standard of judicial review.

There are also reasonable arguments against the force of law test. First, the logical basis for this *Chevron* limitation is questionable. Congress imposes administrative procedures in order to constrain *agencies*, not in order to make a statement about judicial review. Only by a fiction can the former be equated with the latter. Second, although a guidance document is not an *actual* exercise of delegated authority, it is a statement about how the agency *intends* to use that authority, and a judicial review proceeding should not come out differently depending on whether the relevant interpretation happens to reach the court in review of a formal adjudication (*Chevron*-eligible) or a policy statement (not eligible). Third, many guidance documents are, in fact, written thoughtfully and in consultation with affected groups, and one might argue that such documents may be as deserving of *Chevron* deference as a more formally adopted one. This last point is apparently what lies behind *Barnhart* and similar cases.

As a potential alternative to the force of law test, the note suggests that eligibility for *Chevron* deference could be made to turn on a different single-factor criterion—the adequacy of the procedures employed. This method of simplifying *Mead* could be defended as an approach that, by definition, comes closest to implementing the functional reasoning articulated in that case. However, it would not solve the problem of indeterminacy, because the amount of procedure that an agency would need to employ in order to qualify for *Chevron* deference would be hard to predict across the broad spectrum of varieties of administrative action. Also, this solution would seem to mean that legislative rules that are exempt from notice and comment obligations, such as rules adopted under the good cause exemption because of their urgency, should be evaluated under *Skidmore*. This result would be counterintuitive, because such rules do have the force of law and would seem to warrant *Chevron* deference like other exercises of delegated authority.

5. *Informal adjudication.* The status of informal adjudication is unsettled and may remain so for some time. The *Nationsbank* and *PBGC* holdings would follow straightforwardly from the pure force of law test, but the Court wasn't thinking in *Mead* terms when it decided them. Over time they could well be limited to their facts.

Wilderness Society seems to say that an adjudicative order does not qualify as having the "force of law" for *Mead* purposes (i.e., as eligible for *Chevron* deference) unless it *makes* law in the sense of creating a citable precedent. *Mead* contains language that would support this reading: Souter emphasizes that the binding character of the Customs letter in that case "stops short of third parties." Moreover, this reading would carry forward the *Mead* project of narrowing *Chevron* to the most carefully considered of agency pronouncements.

On the other hand, this is a most unusual usage of "force of law." A judgment entered on a jury verdict is nonprecedential, but it does definitively resolve a dispute between litigants, and most lawyers would say that it has the force of law. In most circuits, the same could be said for an unpublished court of appeals decision. In the same way, a nonprecedential informal adjudication is surely an exercise of delegated adjudicatory power, and it may well be reached after a vigorous adversarial clash between the parties. For these reasons, the *Wilderness Society* construction of "force of law" may not be durable.

6. *The benefits of procedure.* Some had expected that *Long Island Care* would answer the question of whether an agency can bootstrap its way into *Chevron* deference by voluntarily resorting to notice and comment procedure as a basis for issuing a guidance document that, per *Christensen*, would otherwise have been judged under *Skidmore*. That would have been a good test of how far the Court is committed to the *Mead* approach of making *Chevron* depend on the presence or absence of deliberative procedures.

However, the Court avoided answering that question by deciding that what had pretty clearly seemed to be an interpretive rule was actually a legislative rule, thus obviously qualifying for *Chevron* deference. The idea that a pronouncement that is actually labeled a "statement of general policy and interpretation" could be a rule that has the force of law if the agency subjected it to notice and comment is startling, and it is not easy to reconcile with the recommendation by administrative law authorities that agencies should voluntarily solicit and respond to comments on statements that it intends to treat as guidance documents.

That point aside, *Long Island Care* resembles *Barnhart* in that the Court justifies its reliance on *Chevron* deference by referring to several different factors in combination. As a result, hardly any future cases will be squarely governed by either holding. Thus, notwithstanding the criticism that *Mead* has elicited for providing too little guidance to lower courts (*see* N.3), the Court doesn't seem to be responding to that criticism as of 2007.

7. *Stare decisis.* To judge from Justice Thomas's opinion in *Brand X*, the stare decisis principle of *Neal* has not merely been narrowed. It has

been abandoned entirely. According to *Brand X*, the only situation in which a prior judicial interpretation trumps a subsequent administrative interpretation is where the earlier court decision affirmatively stated that the statute was ambiguous. But that is the conclusion that one would have reached just from reading *Chevron* itself—the agency would lose at step one of the *Chevron* analysis. No special stare decisis doctrine is needed. This logic seems just as applicable to prior Supreme Court precedent as to prior court of appeals precedent. However, Justice Stevens's apparent disagreement with this reasoning keeps the *Neal* issue alive for the present.

Even with the relatively broad reading just discussed, we think *Brand X* reached a correct conclusion. Remember that the holding comes into play only if the court has previously deemed the statute ambiguous with respect to the point at issue. *Brand X is* concerned, therefore, only with agency interpretations that survive scrutiny under *Chevron* step one. At step two, however, what is loosely called "interpretation" of the statute is analytically equivalent to an exercise of administrative discretion, and the court's review resembles the inquiry that it might conduct in considering whether the agency action is arbitrary and capricious. *See* § 9.2.2 N.5. It's familiar law that an agency can revise its prior discretionary position, so long as it explains why it is making the change. *See* §§ 4.4.2, 9.3.

Moreover, *Brand X* ameliorates the "ossification" problem to which Justice Scalia referred in his *Mead* dissent. We've already mentioned in N.4 above that one disadvantage of the *Mead* rule is that a court may reach a different result on the exact same interpretive issue depending on whether it first encounters that issue in the context of a binding agency action or a nonbinding one. That situation looks bad, but it does not, standing alone, create practical problems. Had *Neal* remained good law, however, a more troublesome situation would have developed. If an agency took a position in an advice letter and the court reversed under *Skidmore*, that judicial interpretation would continue to bind the government even if the agency subsequently disagreed with the court's interpretation in a legislative rule that would be eligible for *Chevron* deference. *Brand X* avoids this path-dependency problem. It enables the agency to depart from judicial precedent as long as the agency's new position can survive *Chevron* scrutiny on its own terms. This seems to be exactly the scenario envisioned by Justice Souter in his brief concurrence in *Christensen*.

8. *Litigating positions.* That agency counsel may not speak for the agency itself is a familiar corollary of the *Chenery* doctrine. *See* § 4.3 N.5. But why did the D.C. Circuit say that even litigation statements approved by the agency head are suspect, because of the "special pressure" that may lie behind them? The court probably meant that once administrators have reached and announced a decision, bureaucratic incentives will often impel them to try to preserve it using any relevant legal arguments, even if they

would not otherwise have subscribed to those arguments. Naturally, they would like to win the case, move forward, and avoid a remand. This may be responsible behavior from a managerial perspective, but a reviewing court wouldn't want to put much confidence in it.

9. *Strong deference to agency interpretations of regulations.* We think that, in general, the *Seminole Rock* doctrine is sound. The usual *Chevron* policies of deferring to agency technical expertise, political accountability, and interests in uniformity apply just as fully to administrative interpretations of regulations as to administrative interpretations of statutes. In addition, an agency could often reasonably claim to know the actual intentions behind the regulation that it wrote itself. (Not always: the rule might have been on the books a long time.) There is, of course, the counterargument that *Seminole Rock* gives agencies an undue incentive to leave their regulations vague. *See* John F. Manning, "Constitutional Structure and Judicial Deference to Agency Interpretations of Agency Rules," 96 Colum.L.Rev. 612 (1996) (developing this argument). In our view, that critique gives too little weight to the *Bell Aerospace* principle that an agency is the best judge of how many of its policies should be codified in the form of regulations at a given time. *See* § 6.2.

We also think that *Auer*'s analysis of the post hoc rationalization doctrine makes sense. *Auer* was a suit between two private parties. The agency did not necessarily have a stake in who would win, so the "special pressure" that we discussed in N.8 above would not be present. Of course, the agency's reasons for favoring one interpretation over another may be deeply political, but that fact of life doesn't distinguish the *Auer* situation from the usual deference situation. So the *Auer* interpretation deserved at least *Skidmore* deference.

But why anything more than that? We see no justification for the discrepancy between the Court's use of *Skidmore* to review informal interpretations of statutes and its use of a *Chevron*-like standard for informal interpretations of rules. Yet the Court continues to adhere to it. Perhaps the Court simply doesn't think the inconsistency is important enough to demand a resolution, particularly since recent decisions have tended to blur rather than reinforce the teachings of the *Christensen* line of cases anyway.

For the most recent complication, see *Coeur Alaska, Inc. v. Southeast Alaska Conservation Council*, 129 S.Ct. 2180 (2009). The issue was whether discharges of "fill material," which the Army Corps of Engineers regulates under one provision of the Clean Water Act, must comply with performance standards prescribed by EPA under a different section of the Act. Regulations issued by the two agencies did not explicitly address this issue, but the Court answered the question in the negative by relying on a memorandum prepared by the two agencies. In an opinion by Justice Kennedy, the Court said that the memorandum, "though not subject to full *Chevron* deference, *see Mead*, is entitled to a measure of deference because it interprets the agencies' own regulatory scheme" and "is not 'plainly erroneous or inconsistent with the regulation[s].' *Auer*." The opinion seems deliberately vague as to whether this "measure of deference" is equivalent to *Skidmore* or to *Chevron* itself. It tends to reinforce the impression that the Court attaches little importance to that distinction.

10. *Problem.* In the real *Gonzalez* case the Eleventh Circuit handed down its initial opinion around the time of *Christensen*, and Lazaro moved for a rehearing in light of that case. The court responded by saying, in part, that *Christensen* didn't apply because this case involved a final, binding disposition of a concrete dispute, not a mere opinion letter.

In addition to reminding at least some students about the furor that the Elian Gonzalez affair ignited in 1999 and 2000, the incident makes an apt teaching problem for essentially two reasons. In the first place, the language of the appellate court's decision (which we have quoted from the real case) suggests that the court was reluctant to uphold the government and thus that the degree of deference might have made a difference to the outcome. During the class discussion some students may opine that the choice between *Skidmore* and *Chevron* review would not have mattered much as a practical matter. You should not necessarily discourage this notion. In fact the Eleventh Circuit's rehearing opinion does suggest that the court would have reached the same result under either test. You can, however, acknowledge that possibility and then ask the class to assume for the sake of discussion that Elian might have stood a better chance of winning if the court had applied *Skidmore* rather than *Chevron*. The court's grudging statement that the INS policy was "[not] totally unreasonable" makes this case about as strong an example of this potential divergence as one could find.

Second, the problem involves the unsettled area of informal adjudication. Indeed, on these facts the two readings of *Mead* discussed in N.4 seem to point in different directions. If the force of law test applies, the precondition for *Chevron* review seems to have been met, as the Eleventh Circuit concluded. This may not seem so clear to the students, because the INS not take any tangible action. Moreover, the rejection of Lazaro's and Elian's petitions would probably not have prevented as a matter of law from filing again. Still, the agency did dispose of an adversarial dispute, resulting in a final, appealable order. The decision certainly wasn't merely advisory.

On the other hand, the reading of *Mead* that focuses entirely on procedural safeguards would probably lead to an opposite conclusion. Here the agency's binding action was accompanied by minimal process—almost none. The policy in question was apparently devised on the spot, or at least had never been formally adopted. The issue took only a few days to resolve. True, this case did get personal attention from the Attorney General of the United States, which is not an everyday occurrence in immigration matters. But there was surely no "relatively formal administrative procedure tending to foster the fairness and deliberation that should underlie a pronouncement of [*Chevron*-eligible] force," in Souter's words.

Thus, the problem invites the students to try to pin down the most important basis of the *Mead* exception. Is that exception triggered by the immature nature of the exercise of discretion (not involved here), or the absence of deliberative procedure (very much involved)?

Of course the case might fall into the residual category in which, as in *Nationsbank*, the Court has "found [other] reasons" to accord *Chevron* deference. What would the "hypothetical reasonable member of Congress" do? Perhaps she would take account of the Attorney General's personal review of the case, which ensured an unusually high level of political accountability. Or she might consider the explosive foreign policy implications that surrounded this incident (in fact the Eleventh Circuit did cite them as a basis for deference). Or how about the risks that this divisive controversy was creating for Al Gore's upcoming presidential campaign? Nobody could have foreseen *how* pivotal Florida's electoral votes would turn out to be in the 2000 election, but all were aware that they could be important. Would a hypothetical reasonable member of Congress consider that factor relevant? Presumably not, although a *real* member of Congress would. The Court's incoherent jurisprudence on this Step Zero inquiry doesn't give us much help in answering these questions—which may be exactly the problem with that case law.

Indeed, might the circumstances be so "extraordinary" that "common sense" would suggest that Congress did not leave the issue to the INS? If you have taught *Brown & Williamson* you could raise that question. Of course the Elian problem does not involve issues of great economic significance, but O'Connor's language in the FDA case might be elastic enough to stretch this far.

§9.3 JUDICIAL REVIEW OF DISCRETIONARY DETERMINATIONS IN ADJUDICATION

CITIZENS TO PRESERVE OVERTON PARK, INC. v. VOLPE

An excellent review of *Overton Park*, including a detailed bureaucratic and political history of the events, is contained in Peter Strauss's "story" narrative cited in N.6. Strauss depicts the Court's opinion as clumsy judicial intervention into a political process that had worked well; the views of park users and environmentalists had been heeded during all phases of the dispute. In his view, there was no compelling need for judicial intervention into this polycentric dispute. The road was never built on any route, and the costs and delays resulting from the Court's decision were enormous.

SALAMEDA v. IMMIGRATION AND NATURALIZATION SERVICE

Notes and Questions

1. *Relevant factors.* There is a close connection between (I) the process of interpreting the meaning of the statute conferring discretion on the agency and (ii) the process of deciding whether the agency's discretionary action is arbitrary and capricious. We have suggested above that both *Chevron* step two and the "reasonableness" inquiry envisioned by *Hearst* are just alternative names for one aspect of the arbitrary and capricious test. *See* § 9.2.2 NN.2, 5. In other words, an allegation that an agency relied on the wrong statutory factors might be described as going either to legal interpretation or to the exercise of discretion. Neither description would be incorrect. This is spelled out in ¶ A in the ABA Administrative Law Section's checklist of components of the arbitrary and capricious test (N. 4 of this section).

Either way, the issue would be whether the agency's action is reasonable as an application of the legally required factors (as found by the court, or as sustained by the court under the appropriate deference methodology for issues of law, whether "weak" or "strong"). This sort of inquiry is perhaps the most easily defended aspect of arbitrary and capricious review. Without it, the guarantee of judicial review for compliance with law would be empty, because the agency could simply recite the legally correct test and then do something completely unrelated to it. The Court acknowledged this point a century ago: Judicial review must extend to "whether, even though the order be in form within the delegated power, nevertheless it must be treated as not embraced therein, because the exertion of authority which is questioned has been manifested in such an unreasonable manner as to cause it, in truth, to be within the elementary rule that the substance, and not the shadow, determines the validity of the exercise of the power." *ICC v. Illinois Central Railroad Co.*, 215 U.S. 433, 470 (1910).

Usually, however, the requirements of law are not necessarily the only "factors" that a court will consider "relevant" for purposes of arbitrary and capricious review. *Salameda*, for example, does not seem to turn very much on that conception of the "relevant factors" test. Indeed, Posner says outright that "[t]he issue we decide today is not one of statutory interpretation. It is whether the INS's judicial officers addressed in a rational manner the questions that the aliens tendered for consideration." He goes on to say that those questions concerned (I) the Salamedas' community service, and (ii) the impact of the proposed deportation on their son Lancelot.

To a small degree the former of these factors does implicate legal interpretation, because Posner says that other circuits have held that the Board must consider the aliens' community service and he is reluctant to create a circuit conflict. However, even if they have so held (which Easterbrook denies), Posner does not rest heavily on that case law. Indeed, he makes clear that he himself would not be inclined to read that requirement into the statute. His main point seems to be that the Board's precedents require consideration of community service, and that government counsel conceded (perhaps unwisely) that it must be considered. If the Board had so interpreted the statute in the past, but ignored the factor in this case, it violated the well recognized rule that it cannot change its position without an explanation. *See UAW v. NLRB*, § 4.4.2, also a Posner opinion. (Again, however, Easterbrook has some good arguments indicating that the Board's precedents had said no such thing.)

When Posner turns to the Board's failure to consider the impact of deporting the Salamedas on their son Lancelot, he makes essentially no effort to connect that factor to the statute. He thinks it's an important factor, and therefore the BIA should have considered it. Posner is not alone in seeming to claim the authority to identify, on his own initiative, factors that an agency should have discussed. *See State Farm*, § 9.4 (a rule is arbitrary if the agency "entirely failed to consider an important aspect of the problem"); *see also* ¶ E on the ABA checklist. Surely, however, such a subjective and unbounded approach to "relevant factors" analysis opens up risks of judicial overreaching.

At first reading, *PBGC v. LTV* would seem to cast doubt on the validity of such an approach. That case essentially says that a court may not force an agency to consider factors that have *some* statutory foundations but are not in the statute that the agency is charged with enforcing. One might think that it follows, a fortiori, that a court may not force the agency to consider a factor simply because the court deems it worthy of consideration. In practice, however, the courts do not seem to have interpreted the case as containing so strong a message of restraint. Thus, the outer boundaries of the "relevant factors" test (beyond statutory factors) remain very ill-defined at the present time.

2. *Clear error of judgment.* A variant on this component of the arbitrary and capricious test is the language of *State Farm*, § 9.4: a rule is arbitrary if the explanation for it is "so implausible that it could not be

ascribed to a difference in view or the product of agency expertise." However the inquiry may be phrased, relatively few cases actually reverse an agency by saying that the agency's result is inherently wrongheaded. One reason for this reluctance is, as the note suggests, that courts typically prefer to say that the agency's explanation is inadequate. The *Salameda* opinion is typical in this regard. Students should easily be able to understand this judicial preference. The "inadequate explanation" rationale is less overtly value-laden, not so easily characterized as "substituting judgment" for the agency's judgment. Besides, when a court remands on the basis of an inadequate explanation, its argument is not necessarily disingenuous. The court may really believe that the agency might be able to remedy the apparent weakness in its opinion; at least the court doesn't need to reach that question immediately.

Another reason why courts seldom state flatly that an agency has made a "clear error of judgment" is that it is usually easier to say that the agency has not reasonably implemented *the statute*. Note that ¶ B of the ABA checklist takes this approach. This latter formulation implies that the agency's quarrel is really with Congress, and the court is simply acting as the legislature's faithful agent. Again, this phrasing will not necessarily be insincere, and it certainly sounds more legitimate.

3. *Sanctions.* Judicial review of sanctions constitutes something of an exception to the generalizations in the preceding note. Although the court may not directly invoke the "clear error of judgment" test, a judicial finding that an agency's penalty is excessive is tantamount to a conclusion that the agency made an untenable discretionary decision. The meaning of the penalty statute is usually not at issue in a case of this sort, so a court would have trouble saying that the agency erred "as a matter of law." The court might, however, be able to soften the blow by asking the agency to *explain* its sanction more adequately. It might also try to justify its reversal by saying that the agency has acted inconsistently with its precedents—but that line of argument didn't work so well in *Butz v. Glover Livestock.*

As the note mentions, however, *Butz* has not entirely prevented the courts from considering whether sanctions are disproportionate. *See, e.g., Chrysler Corp. v. FTC*, 561 F.2d 357 (D.C.Cir.1977), in which Chrysler was found to have deceptively advertised its small cars' gas mileage. But the order which prohibited Chrysler from "misrepresenting in any manner, directly or by implication, the purpose, content, or conclusion of any test, report, study, research, demonstration, or analysis" was "potentially limitless" and had to be reconsidered.

In fact, review of the severity of remedies has lived on even in the very regulatory context from which *Butz v. Glover Livestock* arose. In *Ferguson v. USDA*, 911 F.2d 1273 (8th Cir.1990), the USDA's Judicial

Officer threw down the gauntlet to the Eighth Circuit (the court that had reversed him in the *Butz* case, only to be reversed itself by the Supremes). In an article, the Judicial Officer had argued that his sanction decisions were unreviewable under *Butz* and that a post-*Butz* Eighth Circuit decision had ignored the fact that he had 33 years of experience under the Act in deciding what constituted a serious violation. Needless to say, the court accepted the challenge and resoundingly overturned a penalty decision. It stated that in *Ferguson*, unlike *Butz*, the sanction had no "factual justification."

4. *Other abuses of discretion.* For extensive documentation and elaboration of the ABA checklist of theories that can lead to reversal under the arbitrary and capricious test, see Lisa Schultz Bressman, "Judicial Review of Agency Discretion," in ABA Section of Administrative Law and Regulatory Practice, A GUIDE TO JUDICIAL AND POLITICAL REVIEW OF FEDERAL AGENCIES 177 (John F. Duffy & Michael Herz eds.2005). The list is essentially a heuristic exercise. In practice, when judges write opinions in real cases, they do not normally draw fine distinctions among these discrete "tests" of arbitrariness. They tend to speak in much vaguer terms about the need for reasoned decisionmaking. *Salameda* basically adheres to this pattern, stating that the issue is whether "the INS's officers addressed [the aliens' contentions] in a rational manner." However, the agency's duty not to ignore its past precedents—which is one of the main props for the *Salameda* holding—is one of the most well established of the reasoned decisionmaking requirements. *See* § 4.4.2.

Your students will not fail to notice that disdain for the INS's substantive result pervades Posner's opinion in *Salameda*. In that respect the case furnishes a good illustration of the elasticity of the arbitrary/capricious standard in the hands of a court that wants to overturn an agency decision. And certainly there are equities favoring that disposition here. Clearly an important factor in the decision was the long delay (12 or 13 years) between the start and completion of the Salameda's deportation process. During those years, the Salamedas and their kids acquired substantial reliance interests in staying in the U.S. The greater the delay, the more "extreme" their hardship became.

On the other hand, Easterbrook's dissent leaves little doubt that the majority had to strain several points to justify overriding the INS in this case. Those who deplore this sort of intervention as unwarranted judicial activism may wish to reconsider their support for the arbitrary/capricious test. Note 1981 MSAPA § 5-116(c)(8)(iv), which brackets the language "otherwise unreasonable, arbitrary or capricious." According to the Comment, the reason for bracketing the language was "to discourage reviewing courts from substituting their judgment for that of the agency as to the wisdom or desirability of the agency action under review." For further discussion of the arbitrary/capricious test under state law, see § 9.4 N.6.

5. *Reasoned decisionmaking and the Chenery rule.* This note summarizes some of the implications of the *Chenery* doctrine. None is particularly controversial. Of particular importance is the principle that an agency action "cannot be sustained . . . where it is based not on the agency's own judgment but on an erroneous view of the law." *Prill*, 755 F.2d at 947. This is the basis on which *Chenery* itself was decided in its initial appearance in the Supreme Court. *SEC v. Chenery Corp.*, 318 U.S. 80 (1943). The Court held that the SEC had wrongly believed itself constrained by the common law of fiduciary duty, and thus its order could not stand. The Court added that the same order might be sustainable as an exercise of the agency's own discretion. When the SEC then reached the same result as before on a discretionary basis, it was upheld. *SEC v. Chenery Corp.*, 332 U.S. 194 (1947).

6. *Closed or open record?* A closed record is a natural complement to a system of judicial review that entails serious examination of the agency's exercise of discretion. If the record before the reviewing court is different from the one before the agency, the court cannot evaluate the agency's reasoning on its own terms and will be tempted to make the discretionary decision itself. Conversely, in a jurisdiction in which the court's scrutiny of the agency's exercise of discretion is concerned, at most, with evaluation of the bottom-line result, irrespective of the reasoning that underlies it, an open record system is easier to justify and has efficiency advantages.

Even within a basically closed record system, such as prevails in federal practice, private parties are allowed under limited circumstances to introduce evidence in the judicial review proceeding. The *Lands Council* case alludes generally to these circumstances, but the topic has many complexities that cannot be explored in the basic administrative law course. For example, the proposition that a court may examine extra-record evidence to determine "whether the agency has considered all relevant factors" has initial appeal, because the administrative record, by definition, will not show what the agency failed to consider. However, this way of expressing the exception is overbroad, because "relevant factors" can mean so many different things (as discussed in N.1 above). *See* Young, 10 Admin. L.J.Am.U. at 228-41.

The excellent student comment by Saul draws a helpful distinction between judicial *supplementation* of the record and *completion* of the record. "Supplementation" poses the most serious threat to agency discretion, as just explained. Courts will sometimes accept extra-record evidence for the purpose of clarifying technical issues, but they need to stop short of second-guessing the agency's substantive decision using evidence that the agency itself did not consider. *See Asarco, Inc. v. EPA*, 616 F.2d 1153, 1160 (9th Cir.1980). In practice, that line may not be easy to draw.

"Completion" of the record raises different issues. Courts will sometimes allow discovery or other evidentiary proceedings when a party makes a preliminary showing that the agency omitted some information from the record. This practice does, however, entail some tension with the *Morgan IV* presumption of regularity. The wide variety of informal agency action makes it difficult to generalize about this subject. Certainly, however, the agency will have a relatively strong claim to receive the benefit of the presumption if it has adopted a systematic approach to maintaining a decisional record as a matter of bureaucratic routine. If, on the other hand, it begins to compile the administrative record only when litigation begins, a court is likely to take a more active oversight role.

7. *Resource constraints.* Pierce's article, cited in text, is a thought-provoking argument in favor of modifying judicial review doctrines to take account of resource constraints. During tight budgetary times, he warns, hard look review will exacerbate delays and make the problem of inadequate resources even worse as excessive resources are allocated to judicially reviewed cases. Finally, Pierce contends, Congress will respond to these pressures in perhaps unattractive ways.

As the note points out, subsequent events in the immigration field were somewhat in line with Pierce's prediction: discretionary relief became harder to qualify for, and the courts were dealt completely out of the game. Moreover, the administration introduced streamlining "reforms" such as expanding the role of single-member BIA decisions and of decisions affirming the immigration judge with *no reason-giving allowed.* For fuller discussion of these pathologies, see §§ 3.3.5 N.4 and 4.2.2 of this manual. However, the developments in immigration law summarized here and in those notes have a number of causes, and one could debate the extent to which they are attributable either to hard look review or to resource pressures generated by it.

For a reply to Pierce on a more general level, see Patricia M. Wald, "Judicial Review in the Time of Cholera," 49 Admin.L.Rev. 659, 661-65 (1997). Judge Wald offered what she called a "'why us?' lament" and suggested that a better remedy for resource limitations would be better priority-setting at the administrative level. She suggested that courts would be sympathetic to managerial measures of that kind. (That solution would, however, probably be more relevant to rulemaking than to adjudication.)

8. *Problem—teacher dismissal.* In *Pell*, the Court upheld discharge of a number of teachers and other government employees for relatively trivial offenses under an arbitrary-capricious standard. Yet the New York

judicial review statute (CPLR § 7803(3)) explicitly permits review of "abuse of discretion as to the measure or mode of penalty or discipline imposed." *See* Patrick J. Borchers & David L. Markell, NEW YORK STATE ADMINISTRATIVE PROCEDURE AND PRACTICE §§ 8.6, 8.7 (1995). *Pell* bears a close relationship to *Butz*, N.3 of the text.

The offenses in *Pell* included I) a teacher who was absent and falsely certified that he was ill; ii) a bus driver who deliberately pocketed change amounting to $1.26 over 18 days ("nickeling"); iii) a policeman who worked a couple of days as a deliveryman while out on sick leave. In some of these cases, lower courts had reduced the penalty. In *Pell*, the court stated that the test in weighing whether a penalty is arbitrary is whether the discipline imposed "is so disproportionate to the offense, in the light of all the circumstances, as to be shocking to one's sense of fairness."

The *Pell* decision added that the application of this test requires consideration of the individual's misconduct and the harm to agency or public; the prospect of recurrence of the offense and of deterrence to others; and the standards of society. Consideration of the length of employment and effect on family play a role if there is absent grave moral turpitude. The court suggested that a different analysis might be in order for meting out discipline on a regulated person or entity outside of government. These nuances in the New York test seem to provide somewhat greater room for judicial interference than the test in *Butz*, although the court's actual disposition of the cases appealed in *Pell* would not be encouraging to a prospective plaintiff.

To *Pell*, compare *Skelly v. State Personnel Bd.*, 124 Cal.Rptr. 14, 31-32 (Cal.1975) (dismissal is excessive penalty for taking long lunch breaks). For similar California cases overturning agency remedial decisions as an abuse of discretion, see Michael Asimow, "The Scope of Judicial Review of the Decisions of California Administrative Agencies," 42 UCLA L.Rev. 1157, 1179 n.76 (1995). Some of the California decisions increase rather than decrease the penalty meted out by the agency. The ability of courts to overturn exercises of agency remedial discretion in extreme cases is an important part of the judicial checking power, although it should not be exercised very often (perhaps only in cases of "howlers," to use Easterbrook's term). After all, it is so very difficult ever to discharge an employee protected by civil service that the court should not make it even harder.

Pell and *Butz* suggest that a court would uphold Alice's dismissal, assuming that the Board furnished an adequate explanation, and assuming no reason to suspect that the stated reason for dismissal was not the true reason. As in case ii), involving "nickeling," one might suspect that the amounts taken were much greater but it is difficult or impossible to prove it. But *Skelly* leans the other way. *Salameda* could be useful to Alice too.

A big part of that decision is the court's outrage that the deportation proceeding had been dragged out for so many years, thus creating substantial reliance interests on the part of the Salamedas. The long tenure of these employees would similarly be relevant to the remedial discretion problem. At least the court might be persuaded to remand for a better explanation.

Bob's case is identical to *Harris* and shows that government entities don't get carte blanche to fire employees even in New York. Obviously the case has significant first amendment overtones (although the *Harris* decision denied this). The court reversed the discharge sanction and suggested that the sanction be as little as a letter of reprimand in the file, or at most a year's suspension. The court said that Bob's conduct involved neither moral delinquency or predatory motive; there was no suggestion that his acts were part of a pattern or that he was "persistently unwilling" to accept direction; no suggestion of lack of capacity in general or of a grave injury to the school district. In other words, parental outrage isn't sufficient reason to fire a teacher.

Along with *Salameda* and the post-*Butz* federal cases mentioned in N.3 and the accompanying manual discussion, *Harris* suggests that if you can persuade the court that a real injustice has occurred, it is likely to find some way to correct the injustice. And many state supreme courts might be far more tolerant than New York of judicial second-guessing of an agency's remedial jurisdiction.

Note that the agency action in these cases was formal adjudication (both due process and state civil service laws would require a formal hearing). Therefore the record on judicial review is closed. Only material considered by the agency (that which was introduced at the hearing plus material judicially noticed) can be part of the record for judicial review. If the case involved informal adjudication (for example, a decision refusing to hire a teacher for allegedly irrational reasons), the law of many states would contemplate an open record on judicial review. However, the federal rule would limit the record to whatever was in the agency's file; if this was insufficient to permit review, the case would be remanded to the agency.

9. *Problem—free drinks*. The problem is based directly on the *Labor Services* case, in which the First Circuit declined to enforce the Board's order to bargain. The court simply could not believe that the representation vote had reflected the uninhibited desires of the employees. The court also thought that the Board had too hastily treated this case as equivalent to an earlier decision (resembling the *Galvanics* case in our problem).

Circuit Judge Breyer dissented, arguing that the majority had substituted its judgment for the Board's: "Now that the majority has distinguished the 'tuna fish on rye with Pepsi' [as in *Galvanics*] from the 'double scotch,' what is next? Will we have to decide where beer and hamburgers fit on the spectrum? If the basic division of tasks between administrative agency and court continues to have meaning, the members of the NLRB, not the members of this court, should decide the content of the labor/management election day menu."

Breyer emphasized that this was the sort of "minor, detailed, interstitial, question of labor election policy that Congress asked the Labor Board, not the courts, to decide." He thought that the Board could reasonably regard the drinking incident as trivial. He also worried about where the majority's holding might lead: "Human nature being what it is, might not some drink-buying often prove inevitable and its presence offer a ready-made excuse to those seeking to delay or to prevent certification?"

The majority, however, seemed to regard the incident as almost self-evidently improper. It discounted the lack of direct evidence of inebriation, saying that if that consideration were given weight, "breathalyzers and similar apparatus would be standard gear for representation elections." Similarly the absence of coercive statements did not matter, because the gravamen of the offending conduct was "friendly cajolery rather than ugly intimidation."

Minor debating points aside, the basic issue posed by the problem is whether a judicial reversal can—or must—stand on any basis other than substitution of judgment. Perhaps that is enough. The Board's conclusion might be characterized as a "clear error of judgment." One distinctive feature of the problem is that it does not seem to implicate much if any administrative expertise. The deferential standard of review still applies, but in a situation that looks as self-explanatory as this one, it is unlikely to carry its usual force as a practical matter.

But if the court does not want to rest squarely on that rationale, it might instead argue that the Board's lack of discussion of the policy implications of encouraging bibulous entertainment by competing sides in an election contest constitutes a failure to consider a "relevant factor." That line of argument would raise the same issue as does *Salameda*: What, other than the court's say-so, makes this policy issue "relevant"? As for the Board's treatment of the *Galvanics* case, notice that the issue here is different from *Salameda* and other decisions in which an agency has departed from precedent without explanation. Here the objection is the reverse—an agency follows a precedent that (to the majority) looks easily distinguishable. The Board's decision can be characterized as lacking in reasoned decisionmaking (or, in the language of ¶ E on the ABA checklist, premised on "seriously flawed" reasoning).

One other notable feature of the *Labor Services* case is that the Board itself was split 3-2 on the key issue of whether the election had been valid. The situation is similar to the hearing examiner's disagreement with the Board in *Universal Camera*: Internal disagreements within the Board do not formally alter the APA standard of review, but in practice they may exert moral weight in opposition to the agency's decision.

§ 9.4 JUDICIAL REVIEW OF DISCRETIONARY DECISIONS IN RULEMAKING

MOTOR VEHICLE MANUFACTURERS ASS'N v. STATE FARM MUTUAL AUTOMOBILE INSURANCE CO.

For a detailed narrative and assessment of the passive restraints controversy, from origins to aftermath, see Jerry L. Mashaw, "The Story of *Motor Vehicle Mfrs. Ass'n v. State Farm Mutual Automobile Ins. Co.*: Law, Science and Politics in the Administrative State," in ADMINISTRATIVE LAW STORIES 334 (Peter L. Strauss ed.2006). Mashaw was one of the first scholars to warn about ossification as a possible side effect of hard look review, specifically in the context of NHTSA's auto safety regulations. He revisits some of that analysis in this essay.

One year after *State Farm*, NHTSA issued a new regulation requiring manufacturers to install passive restraints in all cars unless, by April 1989, states containing at least two-thirds of the total U.S. population passed laws requiring passengers to use seatbelts. These state "mandatory use laws" would also have to provide for various educational efforts plus seatbelt law enforcement. Some states did respond by passing mandatory use laws, but not enough of these laws satisfied the regulation's conditions, and so the NHTSA requirements did go into effect. Ultimately, the automobile manufacturers met the requirements by installing airbags, and in 1991 Congress made airbags mandatory. Thus the Supreme Court's action eventually pushed the industry into a new era of passive restraints.

BORDEN, INC. v. COMMISSIONER OF PUBLIC HEALTH

This case offers a good object lesson in contrasts between federal and state systems of judicial review. The most obvious contrast is in the standards of review. In Massachusetts the plaintiff has to prove "the absence of any conceivable ground upon which [the rule] may be upheld." The court explicitly equates this test with the one it would use if it were considering the constitutionality of a statute that contained similar provisions—like the *Pacific States* case cited in N.1. Obviously this is a far cry from the "reasoned analysis" that federal courts expect from agencies in the hard look era.

As with other contrasts among verbal formulas expressing the scope of judicial review, however, it's difficult to say whether the distinction makes much difference in actual practice. Note that, at the end of its opinion, the court actually does go over the evidence and tries to convince the reader that the facts reasonably justify the regulation.

But *Borden* also diverges from the federal model in more substantial ways. The court makes clear that the commissioner was not required to make findings in the record of the regulatory proceeding (footnote 8), nor even to provide a statement of reasons supporting the adoption of the regulation (footnote 9). Almost certainly, these operative differences from the federal scheme do make a practical difference. The Massachusetts system presumably imposes less discipline on the agency to analyze its position carefully. On the other hand, it doubtless make rules easier to issue.

Notes and Questions

1. *Hard look review.* For an excellent treatment of *State Farm, see* Merrick B. Garland, "Deregulation and Judicial Review," 98 Harv.L.Rev. 505 (1985).

The *State Farm* opinion relies on many of the elements of hard look review mentioned in Seidenfeld's synthesis. Before plunging into the policy debate about such review, you may want to spend a few minutes pinning down the precise bases of the *State Farm* holdings.

(a) *Airbags*: The Court is unanimous in holding that NHTSA erred in not giving adequate consideration to the option of requiring airbags. Is that because the Court itself considers airbags to be an important alternative? No, the last few lines of Part V.A. demonstrate that the opinion did not go so far. The Court's reason for saying the NHTSA had a duty to discuss airbags is that *the agency itself* had earlier deemed airbags to be effective and cost-justified. Thus, this part of the opinion is similar to "unexplained change of position" cases such as *UAW v. NLRB*, § 4.4.2 and *Salameda*. (The Court's analysis of non-detachable seatbelts at the end of Part V.B. draws upon similar reasoning.)

Notice, however, that the lower courts *have* pursued the notion that important alternatives, as such, must be considered, albeit with qualifiers that this obligation extends only to the most obvious and significant alternatives. *See* ¶ G of the ABA checklist in § 9.3 N.4. This line of authority can place agencies in a difficult position, because they will not necessarily be able to anticipate what alternatives a future reviewing court would consider important. The Supreme Court has not yet specifically weighed in on this broader component of the "reasoned decisionmaking" case law.

The Court has, however, recently modified, or at least fine-tuned, this aspect of the *State Farm* holding in a different way. In *FCC v. Fox Television Stations, Inc.*, 129 S.Ct. 1800 (2009), the Court reviewed the FCC's revision of its policies regarding enforcement of a statute that prohibits broadcasters from airing "indecent" speech. For about thirty years the FCC described its enforcement policy in this area as applicable only to broadcasts that involved repeated use of graphic language for shock value. Programs that contained fleeting, isolated expletives were uniformly tolerated. Beginning in 2004, however, the Commission began to follow a stricter approach, under which fleeting expletives would not necessarily be exempt. The Second Circuit held that an order in which the Commission applied its new policy was arbitrary and capricious. According to that court, *State Farm* requires an agency to make clear "'why the original reasons for adopting the [displaced] rule or policy are no longer dispositive'" as well as "'why the new rule effectuates the statute as well as or better than the old rule.'"

The Supreme Court, in an opinion by Justice Scalia, disagreed that a change in policy requires "heightened" scrutiny:

> To be sure, the requirement that an agency provide reasoned explanation for its action would ordinarily demand that it display awareness that it *is* changing position. . . . And of course the agency must show that there are good reasons for the new policy. But . . . the agency need not always provide a more detailed justification than what would suffice for a new policy created on a blank slate. Sometimes it must—when, for example, its new policy rests upon factual findings that contradict those which underlay its prior policy; or when its prior policy has engendered serious reliance interests that must be taken into account. It would be arbitrary or capricious to ignore such matters. In such cases it is not that further justification is demanded by the mere fact of policy change; but that a reasoned explanation is needed for disregarding facts and circumstances that underlay or were engendered by the prior policy.

Id. at 1811. Justice Breyer disagreed with this reading of *State Farm. Id.* at 1830-32 (dissent). The Court's clarified approach makes sense to us, although its language seems to be, at the least, a restrictive reading of the recitation in the *State Farm* opinion that "[a] settled course of behavior embodies the agency's informed judgment that, by pursuing that course, it will carry out the policies committed to it by Congress. There is, then, at least a presumption that those policies will be carried out best if the settled rule is adhered to." (This was quoted from *Atchison, Topeka & Santa Fe Railroad Do. v. Wichita Board of Trade*, 387 U.S. 397, 416 (1967).) The larger message of *Fox Television* may be that the Court is basically satisfied with the current hard look regime, because its analysis requires no more than a limited adjustment in current doctrine, rather than a wholesale reappraisal of it. For a complementary discussion of this case, see § 4.4.2 of this manual.

(b) *Detachable seatbelts*: The Court homed in on the question of whether the agency had record support for its conclusion that detachable belts flunked a cost-benefit analysis. True, the Court said that it had to defer to the agency concerning the reliability of its field tests (*see* N.3 below). And NHTSA had offered a detailed explanation on that point. But the majority found a number of danger signals that cast doubt on the agency's reasoning. It was concerned about the lack of direct evidence in support of the agency's counter-intuitive finding that detachable belts wouldn't increase usage. Of particular importance was the factor of inertia: The Court saw "grounds to believe" that detachable belts would lead to increased seatbelt usage, because they function automatically unless the consumers go out of their way to disconnect them. In effect the Court treated inertia as a "relevant factor" that the agency must take into account (and it tacitly claimed a broad power to determine what factors are relevant in this sense).

Obviously the Court was very skeptical about the agency's contention, after years of contrary pronouncements, that detachable belts would not contribute to safety. This skepticism energized the Court's declaration that, although an agency can find predictive facts in the face of uncertainty, it has to deal seriously with the record that it does have.

Similarly, the Court questioned the support in the record for the agency's conclusion concerning the costs of automatic seatbelts. The agency had rejected them because it feared adverse public reaction. But this projection of an adverse reaction rested on the same assumption (lack of safety benefits) that the Court had already questioned. In light of the clear congressional intention that safety be the preeminent factor in NHTSA's decision, the Court did not see how a reasonable administrator could have rejected automatic belts.

(c) *Vermont Yankee* implications. Technically speaking, the hard look doctrine can be reconciled with *Vermont Yankee*, because an agency has a choice about what procedures to use in order to generate a record that meets *State Farm*'s substantive standards of rational decisionmaking. We made this point briefly in § 5.4.3 N.4, and it is developed more fully in Jack M. Beermann & Gary Lawson, "Reprocessing *Vermont Yankee*," 75 Geo.Wash.L. Rev. 856, 880-82 (2007).

Looking through form to substance, however, one can easily discern a significant tension between *State Farm* and *Vermont Yankee*. The need to build a record that can withstand hard look review clearly induces agencies to make major adjustments in the methods by which they engage in rulemaking, even though the court may not specify what those methods will be. Thus, in a reply to the article just cited, Pierce argues strenuously that the Court should honor *Vermont Yankee*'s principles of agency autonomy by effecting a drastic curtailment of hard look review. Richard J. Pierce, Jr.,

"Waiting for *Vermont Yankee* III, IV, and V? A Response to Beermann and Lawson," 75 Geo.Wash.L.Rev. 902, 904-10, 919-20 (2007).

2. *Scholarly evaluations of hard look review.* The questions about the appropriateness of hard-look review are fundamental. Adequate treatment of this question brings up many questions covered earlier in the book about the propriety of broad delegations, the competence of courts to digest and understand massive and technical rulemaking records, the concern that judicial micro-management will disrupt the agency's policymaking process, whether agencies have all of the expertise they're supposed to have, about non-judicial political checks on agencies and about whether agencies are likely to be captured. Students who are steeped in common law subjects may have an exaggerated view of the ability of courts to solve every problem in society.

The academic and professional indictment of hard look review includes several charges in addition to the ossification critique. There are real concerns about its legitimacy. It can be argued that hard-look review results in substituting the judgment of unelected and inexpert judges for the more politically responsible agency. The legislature delegated to the agency, not the court, the power and responsibility for making the hard judgment calls in policymaking. Rehnquist's dissent in *State Farm* makes a valid point: a change in administration is a valid reason for a change in government policy, and judicial review must allow latitude for this to occur. Reagan made his deregulatory intentions clear during his presidential campaign, and the NHTSA decision was consonant with that platform. Moreover, the Miles & Sunstein study cited in this note supports the intuition that judges' decisions often reflect their own political views.

As against this indictment, you can address various affirmative justifications for hard look review. Sargentich emphasizes that executive decisionmaking has its own dysfunctional aspects, and judicial review of discretion serves as a check on these tendencies. It can serve a quality control function by counteracting careless or thoughtless decisions. (This is not a strong point in the specific context of *State Farm*, however. In this high profile case, NHTSA surely knew what it was doing.) It also can be defended for ensuring fidelity to statutory requirements. One of the most cogent arguments in *State Farm* was the Court's recognition that "Congress intended safety to be the preeminent factor under the Motor Vehicle Safety Act." The agency's rescission decision looks much weaker when juxtaposed with that premise.

A less obvious argument for hard look review is its capacity to puncture insupportable justifications for agency action and smoke out undisclosed motives. Here the Court is unwilling to allow NHTSA to abandon passive restraints with a facile claim that these devices do not really save lives. If the incoming administration wants to deregulate notwithstanding the safety benefits of passive restraints, it can, but it needs to defend that view forthrightly. The political accountability of the agency only works properly when the public understands the stakes that a new administration policy would entail.

As for ossification, the note makes clear that the empirical foundations of that critique are contested. That debate is still under way. *See* Jason Webb Yackee & Susan Webb Yackee, "Administrative Procedures and Bureaucratic performance: Is Federal Rulemaking 'Ossified'?," forthcoming in J.Pub.Admin.Res. & Theory (generally disputing the ossification thesis).

3. *Soft look and predictive facts.* Up to a point, *State Farm* is similar to *Baltimore Gas,* because the Court in the former case said that it would not "upset the agency's view of the facts," and indeed it deferred to NHTSA's conclusion that the field tests had little probative value. However, the broader message of *State Farm* cuts the other way, because of the Court's disapproval of the way in which NHTSA *used* the facts it had in reaching its overall prediction. *See* part V.B of the opinion. A court committed to hard look review will look behind agency predictions, even if they come armed with claims of agency expertise or backed by scientific studies, computer analyses, economic equations or whatever. The court will penetrate the technical details to ascertain whether the data really support the prediction, whether the agency arbitrarily failed to seek available further evidence, whether the assumptions underlying economic models hold water, etc.

We think, however, that *Baltimore Gas* makes a valid point. In the end, if there is a zone of irreducible uncertainty, the court must defer to what is much more than a "simple finding of fact." Instead, predictive facts frequently represent policy judgments about the acceptability of various levels of risk and of the costs of mitigating that risk. Thus they represent an exercise of discretion and must be reviewed accordingly--not so much because of agency expertise but because the agency has delegated power to strike the balance. *See Industrial Union Dep't v. Hodgson,* 499 F.2d 467, 474 (D.C.Cir.1974).

Citizens for Free Enterprise is, in our view, a soundly reasoned decision that vividly illustrates the predictive facts doctrine. The state liquor licensing authority adopted a prohibition on adult-oriented bars (no topless waitresses, lapdancing, adult videos, etc.), explaining that the ban would reduce crime. That conclusion rested primarily on impressionistic letters and testimony from law enforcement officers. Such a record might at first seem inadequate to satisfy a state APA that *expressly* provides that administrative rules must be "based on the record" and must rest on "substantial evidence." Indeed, one could easily suspect that the real impetus for the prohibition was moral disapproval rather than crime prevention as such.

As the court recognized, however, states pass restrictions of this kind all the time on the basis of hunches, value judgments, and "common sense." How could one expect the agency to do more than it did? A requirement that all rules must rest on the same kind of evidence that one might expect in the case of an environmental regulation would be unworkable. There are plenty of reasons to question the merit of restrictions of this kind, but the court could not accept that a lack of firm social science support for the premises of the rule was one of them.

Too late for inclusion in the casebook, the U.S. Supreme Court reached similar conclusions in *Fox Television, supra,* 129 S.Ct. at 1813. Said Justice Scalia:

> There are some propositions for which scant empirical evidence can be marshaled, and the harmful effect of broadcast profanity on children is one of them. One cannot demand a multiyear controlled study, in which some children are intentionally exposed to indecent broadcasts (and insulated from all other indecency), and others are shielded from all indecency. It is one thing to set aside agency action under the Administrative Procedure Act because of failure to adduce empirical data that can readily be obtained. *See, e.g., State Farm* (addressing the costs and benefits of mandatory passive restraints for automobiles). It is something else to insist upon obtaining the unobtainable.

4. *Judicial remedies.* The D.C. Circuit is the leader in using remand without vacation (RWV) in its decisions, although not all judges on the circuit support it. *See, e.g., North Carolina v. FERC,* 550 F.3d 1176 (D.C. Cir.2008); *NRDC v. EPA,* 489 F.3d 1250, 1262 (D.C.Cir.2007); *Chamber of Commerce v. SEC,* 443 F.3d 890 (D.C.Cir.2006).

Levin's article, cited in the note, is a comprehensive defense of RWV. It argues that APA § 706 should not be read literally, but rather in light of a longstanding canon of statutory construction that disfavors interpretations that would restrict the remedial discretion of the federal courts. *See* 53 Duke L.J. at 309-15. The article also contends that the option of remanding without vacation is a necessary tool by which judges can temper the disruptive consequences of hard look review. Judges recognize that some of the concerns that have led them to remand rules can border on nitpicking, but they don't want to simply ignore an irrationality in the agency's statement of basis and purpose. So they ask the agency for a better explanation, but in the meantime they can prevent chaos in the regulatory program by leaving the rule in place. *Id.* at 301-02.

Levin acknowledges that routine use of remand without vacation could unduly relieve agencies' incentives to do their work carefully and could discourage private persons from bringing suit to challenge unlawful agency actions. He thus urges that RWV should be used only if a careful weighing of interests favors that remedy. *Id.* at 373-77. In a similar vein, the ABA has endorsed the legality of RWV but has recommended that "a reviewing court should normally strike the balance in favor of vacating the agency's action, unless special circumstances exist." *Id.* at 387-88 (reprinting the ABA resolution).

A very different critique of RWV is that its availability makes courts too ready to reverse agencies through hard look review. *See* Daniel B. Rodriguez, "Of Gift Horses and Great Expectations: Remands without Vacatur in Administrative Law," 36 Ariz.St.L.J. 599 (2004). Ironically, however, this analysis, which favors broader judicial *deference* to agencies, is unlikely to appeal to the business interests that have been the strongest critics of RWV

The D.C. Circuit decides whether to allow RWV in a given case by using a balancing test that considers "the seriousness of the order's deficiencies (and thus the extent of doubt as to whether the agency chose correctly) and the disruptive consequences of an interim change that may itself be changed." *Allied-Signal, Inc. v. NRC*, 988 F.2d 146, 150-51 (D.C. Cir.1993). The court recognizes that when it remands a rule without vacating it, the agency has limited incentive to cure the problem with the rule expeditiously. Thus, the court will often put a strict time limit on the agency to ensure compliance with the judicial mandate. *See, e.g., In re Core Communications, Inc.*, 531 F.3d 849 (D.C.Cir.2008).

The remarkable Texas statute cited in the note is probably unique. Reportedly, the legislature passed it because it was upset about the disruptions that had followed in the wake of the *Texas Hospital Ass'n* case discussed in § 5.6 N.8. After the court vacated the medical fee reimbursement rule underlying that case, hospitals filed 20,000 claims for additional payments. *See* Pete Schenkkan, "Texas Administrative Law: Trials, Triumphs, and New Challenges," 7 Tex.Tech Admin.L.J. 287, 327 (2006). For reasons explained in the second paragraph of this note, we think the legislature probably went too far, but perhaps experience will prove otherwise.

5. *Substantial evidence v. arbitrary and capricious.* We think that both substantial evidence and arbitrary-capricious call for judgments about reasonableness as to both factual support and policy judgment. Not much, if anything, turns on what verbal formula the court says it is applying. Either way, the inquiry applied in rulemaking will look a lot different from the substantial evidence test as applied in review of formal adjudications,

where it applies mostly to credibility-based determinations or to inferences from circumstantial evidence.

In the context of agency discretionary activity, the reasonableness inquiry may be more or less intensive, depending on a number of factors. Among them are the comparative competence of agency and court, whether the facts are predictive or measurable, whether the court perceives the presence of danger signals, whether the court has confidence in the agency, and similar appropriate factors. In a case that turns on predictive facts, for example, courts do not necessarily assume that an agency must supply proof of unprovable propositions, even if the nominal standard of review is "substantial evidence." The *Industrial Union Dep't* and *Citizens for Free Enterprise* cases cited in N.3 contain very thoughtful expositions of this theme.

The substantial evidence provisions in the OSH Act and a few other rulemaking statutes passed in the 1970s now serve mainly to give a debating point to challengers and to activist courts, who can use it for rhetorical effect, proclaiming that Congress has called for unusually stringent review. *Corrosion Proof Fittings*, § 5.8, is a good example. We agree that these provisions were intended to convey a congressional signal (or "mood," to use the language of *Universal Camera*), but we disagree with the inference that these litigants and judges have drawn from it. At the time these statutes were passed, arbitrary-capricious review had a reputation (justified at that time in light of historical practice) for being a weak, empty standard. By inserting substantial evidence language, Congress intended to make sure that courts would review rules issued under these statutes conscientiously. Since that time, however, arbitrary-capricious review has itself become much more stringent than it had once been, so the distinction that Congress had in mind is obsolete. It simply doesn't make sense to imagine that Congress meant to say, "whatever degree of intrusiveness arbitrary and capricious review under the APA may entail at any given time in the future, we want review under this statute to be even more stringent than that." (And, as Scalia suggests in his *Data Processing* opinion, such a heightened standard might not be administrable anyway.)

6. *State court review of discretionary action.* William Funk, "Rationality Review of State Administrative Rulemaking," 43 Admin.L.Rev. 147, 161-79 (1991), contains an excellent review and critique of *Borden* and similar state-law extreme deference approaches. Funk explains that it is completely incorrect to analogize agencies and the legislature: Legislatures have plenary power, but agencies have only delegated power. He also challenges the argument that review for rationality will increase formality of rulemaking. Although review for rationality does require that agencies gather evidence and provide explanation for their rules, Funk argues that

these are not significant burdens and are well worth the cost. He argues that there is little danger of judicial substitution of judgment; he finds no examples of it in his study of state cases. And he refutes the idea that, because state agencies have less resources than federal ones, their rules should not be subjected to review for rationality. On the contrary, an external check is even more needed.

On the other hand, Edward A. Tomlinson argues that the Maryland court's refusal to engage in rationality review of regulations is hardly irrational, considering how serious the problem of ossification has become in the federal system. "The Maryland Administrative Procedure Act: Forty Years Old in 1997," 56 Md.L.Rev. 196, 237 (1997).

Borden offers a concrete illustration of these competing concerns. The stakes in many rulemaking proceedings are high, and the costs of a mistaken judgment would be considerable. It's far from clear that the commissioner should be able to ban UFFI with no serious check on the validity of his reasoning. Yet, consider *Gulf South Insulation v. CPSC,* 701 F.2d 1137 (5th Cir.1983), which involved a federal regulation banning UFFI in residences and schools. The rule was based both on increased risk of cancer and UFFI's irritant effects on asthma etc. The CPSC's rule failed under the substantial evidence test after the court criticized its reliance on various inconclusive studies. The case looks like a situation in which the court substituted its judgment for that of the agency, thus illustrating the perils of hard look review. *Borden* and *Gulf South* are at opposite deference poles. We would hope that both federal and state courts could find their way to resting points in between these poles. If they cannot, the *Borden* issue may come down to a choice between the lesser of two evils.

The Brodie & Linde article contains an excellent treatment of abuse of discretion review by state courts. It cautions that a court must not substitute its choices of goals or values, but that the rationality of the means chosen by an agency can often be judicially evaluated in light of the available facts and the presence or absence of expertise.

7. *Open or closed rulemaking record.* An open rulemaking record makes a certain amount of sense in a state in which the issue of arbitrariness turns solely on the objective reasonableness of the rule, as distinguished from the agency's reasons for adopting the rule. In such a system, nothing depends on whether the agency took account of a particular fact or not, and the court has little reason to refuse to consider as many facts as the parties choose to introduce in the judicial review proceeding. Also, the open rulemaking approach has the efficiency advantages mentioned in the rule. The agency doesn't need to build a record at all until such time as a judicial review proceeding is commenced. This is essentially the same procedural situation as exists when a regulatory statute is challenged as

unconstitutional. (As *Borden* points out, however, the freedom to introduce new evidence to challenge an agency rule won't do the plaintiff much good if the standard of review is as deferential as it is in Massachusetts.)

If the validity of the rule does depend on the agency's reasons for adopting it, a closed rulemaking record is essential for the reasons explained in *Western States.* Indeed, *Borden* looks greatly out of step with the modern trend. After all, all states now follow a systematic approach to rulemaking, which is conducive to the orderly creation of a record.

8. *Problem.* In *Public Interest Research Group (PIRG),* the court affirmed the 1 ppm standard and set aside the refusal to adopt a STEL. For an illuminating behind-the-scenes narrative of the EtO litigation, see David C. Vladeck, "Delay, Unreasonable Intervention: The Battle to Force Regulation of Ethylene Oxide," in ADMINISTRATIVE LAW STORIES, *supra,* at 191. Vladeck personally handled this case for the petitioners as a lawyer for the Nader-affiliated Public Interest Research Group. He provides a blow-by-blow description of seven years of struggle but, as he says, "make[s] no pretense of objectivity." *Id.* at 193.

The initial round of litigation forced a reluctant OSHA to propose the permissible exposure limit (PEL) of 1 ppm. Having won that much, Vladeck thereafter devoted his attention to trying to get the agency to adopt the STEL. In fact, he says that, in the judicial skirmishing that culminated in the *PIRG* decision involved in our problem, the STEL issue occupied most of the attention in the briefs. The long-term PEL was challenged by only one litigant, an association of hospitals (users of EtO), and most of the briefing related to the STEL. *Id.* at 213-14. Nevertheless, nearly all of the court's opinion related to the merits of the PEL, and our problem shares that emphasis.

a. *The 1 ppm PEL.* Of course, if the *Borden* approach were followed, this would be no contest; the rule obviously meets the minimum rationality test spelled out in that case. Under federal hard look, however, the appropriate result is less clear (at least in the problem).

The issues confronting OSHA were framed by its governing legislation. Under the OSH Act, health and safety regulations depend on what is technologically and economically feasible, regardless of what the agency might deem justified on the basis of a cost-benefit analysis. *American Textile Mfrs. Inst. v. Donovan,* 452 U.S. 490 (1981) (*Cotton Dust*). The Court has tempered that strict obligation, however, by also holding that OSHA may not regulate a substance unless it poses a significant risk. *Industrial Union Dept. v. American Petroleum Inst.,* 448 U.S. 607 (1980) (*Benzene*). (These holdings were briefly mentioned earlier in the casebook, in §§ 5.8 N.7 and 7.2.1, respectively.) Thus, the legality of the PEL in *PIRG* turned on whether substantial evidence supported OSHA's finding that EtO posed a significant risk.

As in the actual *PIRG* case, all of the studies relied on in the problem have arguable methodological flaws. Hogstedt, for example, failed to take account of exposure to other chemicals along with EtO; his sample is quite small, and his control group may not be comparable to the hospital workers. The rat study may have been spoiled by the viral infection that could have impaired the rats' immune system; also, the validity of extrapolation to human beings of rodent studies involving very intense exposure to a toxic chemical is highly debatable. The Hemminki study could be distorted by the fact that responding nurses knew the purpose of the study and might not have been truthful in reporting their experiences. Finally, none of the tests really supports a limit as low as 1 ppm; nobody really knows whether low dosage exposure to EtO is harmful.

The court upheld the 1 ppm rule, including the determination that there was a "significant" health hazard at any level above 1 ppm, based on extrapolations from the Bushy Run study to humans. OSHA admitted that the evidence was flawed, but these flaws did not invalidate the studies--just raised questions about them. Judge McGowan (also the author of *Industrial Union Dept. v. Hodgson*, N.3 above) relied squarely on "predictive facts" themes. A rule is reasonable when supported by many pieces of cumulative, yet individually inconclusive, bits of evidence. In drawing scientific conclusions at the frontiers of available knowledge, an agency must be given considerable leeway in interpreting studies. So long as it candidly states the assumptions on which it relies and presents its reasons for rejecting contrary arguments, the court should affirm. In comparing the case to *State Farm*, there was a lack of "danger signals" (such as a politically-oriented deregulation) that often trigger hard-look review.

The problem can be used to revisit nondelegation issues, because the OSH Act standard is notoriously vague. Recall that Rehnquist's concurrence in *Benzene*, excerpted in § 7.2.1, argued that the statute ran afoul of the nondelegation doctrine. Among his claims was that the statute was so broad that meaningful judicial review would be impossible. In a sense, this problem tests whether that warning had merit.

Another issue (discussed in N.5) is whether substantial evidence under the OSH Act means anything different from arbitrary/capricious. Despite academic commentary that the standards are identical, some courts have taken the substantial evidence test in the OSHA statute (and similar statutes) to mean that Congress was sending them a signal to exercise harder look review than they would exercise under arbitrary-capricious. Indeed, the court mentioned passingly that the arbitrary/capricious test is "more deferential," although it did not matter in this case because the agency survived even the supposedly less deferential substantial evidence scrutiny).

b. *The STEL*: Note that we are reviewing the failure to adopt a rule here. The standard should not be the highly deferential one used in cases where the agency refuses to initiate rulemaking or refuses to adopt any rule after going through a rulemaking proceeding. *See* §§ 6.3, 10.5 N.4. Here we aren't worried about disrupting the agency's allocation of resources, and we have a full record to review. In addition, the STEL issue is interwoven with the 1 ppm issue, which was the subject of a rule.

The statute requires adoption of all reasonably necessary and feasible health protections. OSHA admits there will still be 12-23 cancers even under the 1 ppm rule. A STEL could further reduce the risks of exposure to EtO, because it would protect workers from brief but intense exposures to EtO during sterilization operations. The PEL standing alone would not necessarily prevent such exposures, because a hospital could comply with the 1 ppm standard by maintaining a low background level of exposure to EtO, averaged over eight hours. Although, as OSHA said, the PEL would give hospitals an *incentive* to avoid intense short-term exposures, a flat prohibition on such exposures would be more protective.

The court acknowledged that substantial evidence supported OSHA's claim that it could not find that short-term exposures to EtO was more dangerous than the longterm exposure that the PEL did regulate. The predictive facts doctrine again worked in OSHA's favor on that score. But neither did OSHA have evidence that shortterm exposure was *not* more dangerous. Since a significant risk of cancer existed, the agency had to adopt additional safeguards.

It may sound draconian, but the conclusion can be traced back to *Cotton Dust*. If a workplace health risk is "significant" (as required by *Benzene*), OSHA must regulate it up to the level of feasibility, whether or not it would deem such regulation cost-justified. No one contended that the STEL was not feasible. (Thus the problem can be used as a springboard for reviewing cost-benefit analysis in regulation—more specifically whether a statute should prevent OSHA from balancing costs and benefits in setting standards relating to health, such as under the OSH Act. *See* § 5.8.) The court said that OSHA "entirely failed to consider an important aspect of the problem," which is grounds for reversal under *State Farm*. This part of the opinion reads more like *State Farm* than the part dealing with the 1 ppm issue.

Another factor that may support the court's holding is that there were danger signals with respect to the refusal to impose a STEL. The OMB intervention created doubts about OSHA's analysis. Also raising suspicion was OSHA's extreme delays in completing its EtO rulemaking; several lawsuits were necessary to prod it to take final action. 796 F.2d at 1483. The court did not reach the issues of the legality of OMB interference (since it overturned the decision on other grounds), but you might want to do so. Vladeck contends that OSHA's staff strongly supported the STEL, and the political appointees would have gone along had OMB not persisted in its objections (repeating industry arguments that the staff had already found to be mistaken). *See* Vladeck, *supra*, at 224 n.83.

Incidentally, the judges in *PIRG* (Robinson, Wright, McGowan) were all liberals. One might raise the question of whether conservative judges might have come out differently on the STEL issue, and, if so, whether that possibility undermines the legitimacy of hard look review.

c. *Remedy*. If the court were to decide to set the PEL rule aside, using hard look review to criticize the factual basis for the rule, and to question the agency's judgment about its impact, the issue would be--what remedy? Vacate the rule, making the agency start over? Or remand it for additional explanation and possible revision upward? Vacating is the normal remedy--otherwise you've given nothing to the successful plaintiffs and discourage others from litigating. However, when the court discerns a strong likelihood that the agency could cure the flaw the court has discovered, and the effect of vacating is to harm people who have already arranged their lives around the rule, remand without vacation should be considered.

Here, if the 1 ppm part of the rule were set aside, we think the rule should be vacated. This being a new rule, there probably hasn't been any significant reliance; and if the standard were to be later upped to 5 ppm, you wouldn't want to force people to install equipment that would bring it down to 1 ppm only to discover later that it was for naught. So this isn't a good case for remand without vacation. However, if only the part of the agency decision refusing to impose the STEL were set aside, there's a better argument for leaving the 1 ppm rule in place in the interests of protecting employees during the period of time the STEL is being reconsidered. That's apparently what happened, 796 F.2d at 1507, and it makes sense. Pro-worker groups shouldn't *lose* protective measures in the short run as a result of having *won* their case.

CHAPTER 10

REVIEWABILITY OF AGENCY DECISIONS

§ 10.1 PROCEDURAL ELEMENTS: JURISDICTION AND CAUSE OF ACTION

§ 10.1.1 Jurisdiction of Reviewing Court

a. *Statutory review.* For treatment of the question of whether review should be lodged in a trial or an appellate court, see ACUS Rec. 75-3, 40 Fed.Reg. 27,926 (1975); David P. Currie & Frank I. Goodman, "Judicial Review of Administrative Action: Quest for the Optimum Forum," 75 Colum.L.Rev. 1 (1975). *See generally* Richard J. Pierce, Jr. ADMINISTRATIVE LAW TREATISE § 18.2 (4th ed. 2002), arguing that courts of appeals should review actions that raise major issues of law and policy and that can be reviewed based on the agency record. District courts should review adjudications that are numerous and in which factual disputes predominate over issues of law and policy. Pierce has an extensive discussion of the problems involved in *Citizens Awareness* and *TRAC v. FCC*, 750 F.2d 70 (D.C.Cir.1984). *Citizens Awareness* holds that NRC rules should be reviewed in a court of appeals even though the statute refers only to "orders." *TRAC* holds that the court of appeals, not the district court, has jurisdiction over a petition to compel agency action that has been unreasonably delayed. *See* § 10.6 for further discussion of judicial review of agency inaction.

The doctrine of federal sovereign immunity still rears its head occasionally. For example, an action by an unpaid subcontractor on a federal construction project to impose an equitable lien on funds held by the government must be dismissed because of sovereign immunity. Although the action may be equitable in nature, it is really a suit against the government seeking money damages to which the government has not consented. Consequently, the APA's sovereign immunity waiver does not apply. *Dep't of the Army v. Blue Fox, Inc.*, 525 U.S. 255 (1999).

§ 10.1.2 Non-statutory Review: Forms of Action

For general treatment of common law remedies, see Louis L. Jaffe, JUDICIAL CONTROL OF ADMINISTRATIVE ACTION ch. 5 (1965). Chapter 6 contains an excellent (although now dated) treatment of sovereign immunity.

b. *Mandamus.* Instructors may wish to supplement the materials in the text by statutes or cases from their own jurisdiction. This material is so state-specific that generalities are misleading or worthless. For example, see Charles W. Rhodes, "Demystifying the Extraordinary Writ: Substantive and Procedural Requirements for the Issuance of Mandamus," 29 St. Mary's L.J. 525 (1998), a 70-page account of mandamus in Texas. In California, as discussed in § 9.1.2, mandamus (sometimes called "certiorarified mandamus") is used for the review of adjudicatory actions because early decisions held that certiorari was not available. *See* Michael Asimow, "The Scope of Judicial Review of Decisions of California Administrative Agencies," 42 UCLA L.Rev. 1157, 1164-67 (1995). Discussion of the ministerial/discretionary distinction follows Jaffe, *supra* at 176-192; Bernard Schwartz, ADMINISTRATIVE LAW §§ 9.10-14 (3d ed.1991).

Mandamus in the federal courts: *See generally* 4 Kenneth C. Davis, ADMINISTRATIVE LAW TREATISE §§ 23.8 to 23.14 (2d ed.1983) (not discussed in later editions) (denouncing mandamus tradition and calling for repeal of § 1361); Clark Byse & Joseph V. Fiocca, "Section 1361 of the Mandamus and Venue Act of 1962 and 'Nonstatutory' Judicial Review of Federal Administrative Action," 81 Harv.L.Rev. 308 (1967); Howard W. Brill, "Citizen Relief against Inactive Federal Officials: Case Studies in Mandamus," 16 Akron L.Rev. 339 (1983); Frederic P. Lee, "The Origins of Judicial Control of Federal Executive Action," 36 Geo.L.J. 287 (1948) (interesting treatment of *Kendall*); Note, "Mandamus in Administrative Actions: Current Approaches," 1973 Duke L.J. 207 (split in federal mandamus cases).

§ 10.2 DAMAGE ACTIONS AS A FORM OF JUDICIAL REVIEW

The subject of public torts can only be touched on in this course, so this subchapter is a once-over-lightly treatment. The subject encompasses damage actions to vindicate civil rights and to control "street level bureaucrats" such as police or social workers. The focus in the text is on damage actions as a remedy for illegal acts in the course of regulatory activity and as an alternative to trial-type hearings mandated by due process. The case law is confusing. Congress should address *Bivens*, § 1983, immunities, and the exceptions to the Federal Tort Claims Act (FTCA) in order to clear up the confusion.

§ 10.2.1 Tort Liability of Government

§ 10.2.1a The Federal Tort Claims Act

An interesting case that relates the FTCA to administrative law concerns is *Jayvee Brand, Inc. v. United States*, 721 F.2d 385 (D.C.Cir.1983). *Jayvee* involved an FTCA action for damages arising from a CPSC regulation that banned Tris-treated sleepwear but was adopted without following required procedure. Admittedly, adopting a rule is a discretionary function, but how about violation of mandatory procedural rules for rulemaking? Could violation of a mandatory procedural rule be a "discretionary function?" Judge Bork thought so but grounded his holding of non-liability on two additional ideas: government is not liable when it does something that private parties cannot do (engage in adjudication or rulemaking); and other remedies (i.e. invalidation of a rule) are provided for procedural errors. If the instructor prefers, *Jayvee* could be substituted for the complex problem at the end of this subchapter. The case also holds the Commissioners as rulemakers absolutely immune from personal liability.

Similarly, see *United States v. Agronics, Inc.*, 164 F.3d 1343 (10th Cir. 1999) (no FTCA claim where agency illegally ceded enforcement action against a particular mine to another agency); *C.P. Chemical Co. v. United States*, 810 F.2d 34 (2d Cir.1987) (FTCA is not a remedy for illegality of a rule or of procedures used to adopt it). This line of cases appears to create a non-statutory exception to FTCA for the sorts of governmental actions that have no private sector counterparts (and thus could not be the subject of tort action under state law), even though such action might not fit within the discretionary function exception. Thus these cases resemble the governmental/proprietary distinction historically applied to litigation against local governments.

§ 10.2.1b State and Local Government Liability.

You may wish to supplement this part with state-specific material. For summary of historical sources on municipal sovereign immunity, see Daniel R. Mandelker et al., STATE AND LOCAL GOVERNMENT IN A FEDERAL SYSTEM 523-33 (4th ed.1996). Rosenthal's article (cited in text) is an excellent survey and analysis.

Brown struggles with the problem of defining what governmental functions should not give rise to tort liability. The court was concerned that the state could be liable to thousands of bank depositors and other creditors from the negligent audit; as a result, the state would be deterred from exercising regulatory functions by the specter of tort liability. But that may be a false premise. When it creates a regulatory system, the state can provide by statute for tort liability or immunity for the particular function. A judgment holding the state liable in tort would stimulate legislative consideration of the immunity issue. That might be better than writing enigmatic opinions and creating mystical distinctions as in *Brown*.

Under a governmental/proprietary approach (such as is commonly used in connection with municipal tort liability), it is hard to see why auditing a bank's records is a governmental rather than a proprietary function. Auditing is routinely done in the private sector, and accounting firms are often subject to massive liabilities by reason of negligently prepared statements. On the other hand, many states preserve the rule of

Ultramares Corp. v. Touche, Niven & Co., 174 N.E. 441 (N.Y.1931), holding that accountants are under no duty to users of financial statements. That narrower approach would have taken the state off the hook in *Brown*.

Another approach would be judicial adoption of a discretionary function exception where the legislature has failed to write such an exception into the statute (several state courts have done so). As under FTCA, this exception would be difficult to apply. Thus, under *Gaubert*, it might be held that auditing involves choices but not application of policy and therefore is not a discretionary function. *See* Laura Robinson, Note, "Rebuilding the Walls of Sovereign Immunity: Municipal Liability for Negligent Building Inspection," 37 U.Fla.L.Rev. 343 (1985) (Florida—cities not liable for negligent building inspection). *But see Pendergrass v. Oregon*, 702 P.2d 444 (Ore.App.1985) (state liable for failing to adopt reasonable safeguards as to licensing of epileptic driver).

Many states have also adopted the distinction between the "planning" and "operational" levels, thus rendering the state liable for negligence in exercising discretion if it occurred at the operational level. *See Commercial Carrier Corp. v. Indian River County*, 371 So.2d 1010 (Fla.1979) (maintenance of road signs and traffic lights is at operational level—state liable). At one time that distinction prevailed at the federal level, as a construction of the discretionary function exception to the FTCA, but *Gaubert* disapproved it.

Some states have adopted special duty rules applicable to governmental torts. *Brown* holds that the state owes no duty to individual citizens to refrain from negligence in conducting a "self-imposed protective function." A number of states have held that government is not liable when it breaches a "public duty"—i.e. one owed to the public at large. It is liable only when it owes a special or specific duty to the plaintiff.

The Restatement 2d of Torts states only a narrow exception from the general rule of state and local responsibility: government is not liable for acts or omissions constituting the exercise of a judicial or legislative function or "the exercise of an administrative function involving the determination of fundamental governmental policy." §§ 895B (and comments d and e), 895C. Under this test, the state would be liable in *Brown*. The Appendix to the Restatement has a handy collection of immunity statutes for each state.

Here are some interesting recent state cases involving the discretionary function and similar exceptions to state governmental liability statutes. These could be used as class hypos.

The discretionary function exception to Oregon's Tort Claims Act precluded landowners from seeking monetary damages against the

Department of Fish and Wildlife on grounds that the Department failed to control public nudity and sexual activity in an adjacent wildlife area. The Department had discretion about whether to regulate nude recreation in the wildlife area and how to regulate it, absent a particular relationship to landowners that created a duty to take action to protect them. *Mark v. State Dept. of Fish and Wildlife*, 974 P.2d 716 (Or.App.1999).

A hiker slipped on loose gravel along the edge of a cliff in a state park. The hiker fell 40 feet into some trees below before coming to rest on a lower bluff. The hiker was paralyzed from the waist down. The hiker sued, claiming that the state was negligent in failing to maintain trails or erect guardrail and failing to protect park goers by ensuring the park was safe for visitors. The state's alleged tortious conduct fell within the discretionary function exception to Iowa's Tort Claims Act. *Shelton v. State*, 644 N.W.2d 27 (Iowa 2002).

A state traffic signal technician was performing maintenance on traffic signals and set a signal to manual flash mode, so that lights were flashing yellow in one direction and red in the other direction. An accident ensued when vehicle with flashing red tried making a turn and hit a vehicle with a flashing yellow. Plaintiff sued saying the State was negligent because the temporary control was inadequate for the amount of traffic at that time of day and had failed to provide adequate traffic control. The employee's choice of temporary traffic controls was a discretionary function shielding the state Agency of Transportation from liability. AOT manual stated that temporary traffic control was essential to maintenance operations but required state employees to decide appropriate temporary traffic control. *Johnson v. Agency of Transportation*, 904 A.2d 1060 (Vt. 2006).

Relatives of stranded travelers who perished in sub-zero temperatures after leaving their car in deep snow on a remote, unmaintained road brought a negligence action against the state and Department of Public Safety, claiming that state troopers had negligently failed to launch a search and rescue after hunters told troopers that they had found an unoccupied car, a "HELP" sign and arrow stamped in the snow, and footprints heading east. The initial decision of state trooper to delay launch of search and rescue effort for travelers was sufficiently based on resource allocation and public policy considerations that it was protected by the doctrine of discretionary function immunity. *Kiokun v. State, Department of Public Safety*, 74 P.3d 209 (Alaska 2003).

A state corrections agency was not liable to motorist killed in automobile collision with intoxicated probationer, on ground that parole officer had negligently failed to supervise probationer. Duties entailed by supervision of probationers were peculiar to government and had no equivalent in private sector. *Moore v. Commonwealth of Kentucky,* 846 S.W.2d 715 (Ky.App. 1992).

As to the Eleventh Amendment: The Court took a hard look at the *Ex Parte Young* exception to the Eleventh Amendment in *Idaho v. Coeur d'Alene Tribe,* 521 U.S. 261 (1997). The case involved an Indian tribe's attempt to assert property rights in submerged lands also claimed by Idaho. *Young* obviously represents a balancing act between giving federal courts enough power to enforce the Constitution and federal law (through the fiction that the individual officer is not the state) but not so much power that the Eleventh Amendment would be devitalized. Although the Justices in *Coeur d'Alene* wrote several opinions discussing *Young,* none of which commanded a Court majority, the bottom line was that the Eleventh Amendment immunizes the state from what was in effect (although not in form) a quiet title action over lands claimed by the state, because allowing such an action would be too invasive of state sovereignty. Thus application of the *Ex Parte Young* doctrine is often highly problematic.

Similarly, in *Seminole Tribe of Florida,* cited in the text, the Court decided that the relevant federal statute demonstrated an intent to foreclose application of *Ex Parte Young* to an injunctive action against state officials. Yet in *Verizon Maryland,* also cited in text, the Court was able say (with a straight face): "In determining whether the doctrine of *Ex Parte Young* avoids an Eleventh Amendment bar to suit, a court need only conduct a straightforward inquiry into whether [the] complaint alleges an ongoing violation of federal law and seeks relief properly characterized as prospective." 535 U.S. at 645.

The *South Carolina* case appears to invalidate federal whistle blower protections against state employers. One such scheme allows employees (including state employees) who claim they have been fired for reporting environmental violations to obtain relief in a proceeding before OSHA. *Rhode Island Dep't of Environmental Management v. United States,* 304 F.3d 31 (1st Cir.2002), involved four such employees. The First Circuit halted OSHA proceedings in mid-course on the authority of the *South Carolina* case. Like the FMC's proceedings in *South Carolina Ports,* the whistle-blower scheme was privately initiated, heard by an ALJ under the APA, and culminated in a decision that involves ordinary civil remedies. However, the court noted that if the Secretary of Labor chose to intervene in the employees' cases, the cases would be converted into federal government enforcement, rather than private enforcement, and state sovereign immunity would be inapplicable.

§ 10.2.2 Tort Liability of Officials

§ 10.2.2a Bases of Liability for Constitutional Torts

Bivens remains a controversial decision. The court has frequently undercut it, as in *Chilicky* and *Wilkie*. Similarly, see *Bush v. Lucas*, 462 U.S. 367 (1983), which held that a federal employee had no action under *Bivens* for violation of First Amendment rights, because Congress had already supplied an adequate remedy under the civil service system. However, *Carlson v. Green*, 446 U.S. 14 (1980), allowed a *Bivens* action against federal prison officials despite remedies under the FTCA (that remedy was considered not sufficiently comprehensive and specific). For withering criticism of the Court's post-*Bivens* decisions, see Gene R. Nichol, "*Bivens, Chilicky*, and Constitutional Damages Claims," 75 Va.L.Rev. 1117 (1989).

In *Wilkie*, Justice Thomas wrote a concurring opinion (joined by Scalia) arguing that "*Bivens* is a relic of the heady days in which this Court assumed common-law powers to create causes of action." These Justices would limit *Bivens* to its precise facts. Dissenting Justices Ginsburg and Stevens would have allowed a *Bivens* remedy in *Wilkie* because the government was administering "death by a thousand cuts," which could not be practically remedied in any other way, and because plaintiff alleged a vindictive scheme to "get him" for refusing to grant the easement, not just the usual bureaucratic arrogance.

Congress appears to have explicitly accepted the *Bivens* theory. The Westfall Act distinguishes actions "brought for a violation of the Constitution of the United States" from other tort actions. 28 U.S.C. § 2679(b)(2). For a proposal that the Court should routinely allow *Bivens* claims, rather than use the complex case-by-case approach that it now takes, see James E. Pfander & David Baltmanis, "Rethinking *Bivens*: Legitimacy and Constitutional Adjudication," 98 Georgetown L.J. __ (2009). Pfander & Baltmanis rely heavily on the guidance supplied by the Westfall Act.

Peter Schuck, SUING GOVERNMENT 43 (1983), speculates on why a plaintiff might sue law enforcement officials instead of the government under FTCA: FTCA contains immunities (discretionary function and limitations for some intentional torts) and defenses (e.g. scope of employment or absence of cause of action under relevant state law) different from those in actions against officials; plaintiff can get a jury and punitive damages; if defendant is not represented by a government attorney or isn't certain of indemnity, he may be more anxious to settle; attorney fee limits under FTCA (under § 2678 fees are limited to 25% of a judgment or 20% of a settlement) are not applicable to suits against officials.

§ 10.2.2b Immunity from Liability

At common law an official carrying out a statute was subject to strict liability if he made a mistake. *Miller v. Horton,* 26 N.E. 100 (Mass.1891) (official who mistakenly destroyed a horse suspected of disease is liable in tort without regard to good faith or reasonableness). This view has long been rejected in favor of a set of qualified and absolute immunities.

1. *Absolute immunity.* Judges and prosecutors are absolutely immune, but public defenders enjoy only qualified immunity. *Tower v. Glover,* 467 U.S. 914 (1984). Prosecutors are rather narrowly defined as persons who select cases for adjudication and try them. In contrast, persons engaged solely in investigation, law enforcement, and other aspects of regulation do not qualify for absolute immunity. See *Schlegel v. Bebout,* 841 F.2d 937 (9th Cir.1988), holding that harassment of a trucking company by state PUC officials was not part of the prosecutorial process, even though some of it was connected to a pending route authorization case. This seems an extraordinarily murky problem that calls out for additional Supreme Court clarification. For example, it is hard to say exactly why the Secretary and Assistant Secretary in *Butz* were not engaged in prosecution, since they apparently authorized the prosecution of Economou's firm.

An interesting case on legislative immunity holds that it applies to the governor and the chair of the New Jersey State Council for the Arts to the extent they recommended adoption of legislation abolishing the position of poet laureate. *Baraka v. McGreevy,* 481 F.3d 187, 195-202 (3d Cir. 2007) (2-1 decision). Allegedly, their action was retribution for an anti-Semitic poem Baraka wrote and read at a conference. The actions of the governor and the chair were "in the sphere of legitimate legislative activity" even though they were not legislators and even though the action was essentially directed at only a single person. The case contains a good discussion of the difference between legislative activities (entitled to absolute immunity) and political activities, such as constituent service or patronage activities (not so entitled), as well as the difference between legislative and administrative activities (the latter are also not entitled to absolute immunity).

2. *Qualified immunity.* Schuck presents withering criticisms of the distinctions in immunity defenses between absolute and qualified, and between common law and constitutional torts. He also asserts that qualified immunity gives relatively little protection to officials against long, costly, and highly distracting litigation. Moreover, immunity defenses deny many worthy plaintiffs any compensation for their injuries. Pp. 89-99.

3. *Who should be the defendant?* The Westfall Act wisely abolished personal actions against federal officials for common law torts within the scope of their employment. Unfortunately, it did not do the same for

constitutional torts of federal, state, or local officials. *See* Clark Byse, "Recent Developments—Damage Actions Against the Federal Government," 4 Admin.L.J. 275 (1990). Schuck (chapters 3-5) and Pierce, ADMINISTRATIVE LAW TREATISE § 19.2 (4th ed.2002) argue for a system that holds government, not officials, liable for officials' torts (constitutional or otherwise), and which significantly limits immunities. *See* ACUS Recommendation 82-6, 47 Fed.Reg. 58,208 (1982). Schuck argues that the private tort law systems of respondeat superior and enterprise liability should apply to public torts. Thus both federal and state governments should become directly liable for officials' torts to the same degree as private employers (and § 1983 should be amended to make states liable).

You might quote from *Respublica v. Sparhawk*, 1 Dall. 357 (Pa.1788): "The Lord Mayor of London, in 1666, when that city was on fire, would not give directions for, or consent to, the pulling down of 40 wooden houses, or to removing the furniture, etc., belonging to the Lawyers of Temple, then on the Circuit, for fear he should be answerable for a trespass; and in consequence of this conduct half that great city was burnt." And we've all seen excessively cautious behavior by doctors or lawyers who are panicked about being sued for malpractice.

Making government directly liable means that individuals can win judgments and actually collect them without impairing vigorous decisionmaking by officials. It would simplify public tort litigation. It should promote deterrence, because government would have a greater interest in preventing actions that render it liable (especially if the cost is reflected in an agency's budget) and can design the most effective disciplinary deterrent measures.

Problem. You can teach all of the tort material out of the problem. First spell out a tort claim based on intentional interference with prospective contractual relations. RESTATEMENT 2d OF TORTS § 766B; Dan B. Dobbs, THE LAW OF TORTS §450 (2000). Also spell out an arguable constitutional claim: government probably violates the First Amendment when it informally censors a seller of non-obscene materials by orchestrating a boycott. This appears to be a prohibited form of prior restraint on speech. *See* Rodney A. Smolla, SMOLLA AND NIMMER ON FREEDOM OF SPEECH §14.63 (2007); *Bantam Books, Inc. v. Sullivan*, 372 U.S. 58 (1963) (Commission enjoined from sending threatening notice implying possible prosecution to sellers of books "tending to corruption of youth"); *Playboy Enterprises* (President's Commission on Pornography preliminarily enjoined from conducting informal scheme of censorship of adult magazines); *Penthouse International* (government may criticize any publication even if that leads to retailers refusing to sell it—defendants at least entitled to qualified immunity). Students may respond that pornography that graphically displays the subordination of women can and should be constitutionally suppressed. *But see American Booksellers Ass'n v. Hudnut*, 771 F.2d 323 (7th Cir.1985), which held the contrary.

Another possible constitutional claim: did the Commission deny Mercury due process by failing to provide it with a hearing before listing it in the report? Mercury would argue that the listing deprived it of liberty by defaming its good name. However, *Paul v. Davis,* § 2.2.3 N.2, held that governmental defamation (absent some other deprivation or "stigma-plus") does not deprive plaintiff of liberty. *Roth* and *Perry* recognized that firing an untenured professor in retaliation for protected speech is a First Amendment violation, but the remedy was in court, not in a prior administrative hearing. *See* § 2.2.1 N.4. *See also Hannah v. Larche,* 363 U.S. 420 (1960) (Civil Rights Commission not obligated to grant confrontation to persons who might be accused of crime, because it was investigative, not adjudicative, body). Thus it seems unlikely that Mercury had a right to an administrative hearing before being included on a governmental blacklist, absent some other governmentally-imposed deprivation.

Even if there were a right to a hearing before blacklisting, what factual issues would be resolved at the hearing? Presumably Mercury admits selling Penthouse and admits that Penthouse contains erotic photos. The question is whether these are harmful to women and, if so, whether the Commission can blacklist anyone or call for a boycott. These are not issues involving adjudicative facts, but the Commission's action is individualized. Thus it depends how you read *Londoner,* § 2.5. This problem provides an opportunity to consider tort remedies as an alternative to procedural due process (see §2.4, especially N.2).

Now consider the prospects for a damage action based on these common law tort and constitutional law torts i) against government and ii) against officials. This assumes that Mercury can in fact prove its damages, (and lost profits are often difficult to prove).

a) Federal Pornography Commission:

i) Action against government. Under FTCA, the government agency is immune for several reasons. It is immune from most claims for intentional tort, including interference with contract rights. 26 U.S.C. § 2680(h). Its decision to call for boycotts is a discretionary function, because it represents a policy decision at the planning level. *Bivens* provides only for actions against individuals, not actions against government. The FTCA is the exclusive means of making the government liable in tort, even for constitutional violations. *FDIC v. Meyer,* 510 U.S. 471 (1994).

ii) Action against commissioners. Common law tort: If the commissioners are federal employees acting within the scope of their employment, under the Westfall Act the action against them must be dismissed and the case proceeds against the government. As already noted, since the action falls within FTCA exceptions, it would then be dismissed. *See Gutierrez de Martinez v. Lamagno,* 515 U.S. 417 (1995), which confirms that an action that falls under both the Westfall Act and an FTCA exception must be dismissed against both the employee and the government. However, *Gutierrez de Martinez* provides that courts can review the Attorney General's certification that the employee is within the scope of his employment (if the employee was outside the scope of employment, the Westfall Act would not apply, and the action could proceed against the employee).

Here it might be argued that blacklisting is outside the commissioners' scope of employment. In the common law immunity case of *Barr v. Matteo,* 360 U.S. 564 (1959), the issuance of a defamatory press release fell within the "outer perimeter" of an agency head's duties, thus rendering the head immune from tort action. Arguably, the Westfall Act determination of "scope of employment" would follow *Barr.* But perhaps the commission was supposed to study the problem and recommend legal means of containment—not initiate a blacklist or a boycott. Its authority, in other words, might be much narrower than that of the agency head in *Barr. Butz* makes clear that action outside scope of authority is not immunized. *See Playboy Enterprises* (questioning whether members of President's Commission on Pornography acted beyond its authority in threatening to include a blacklist in their report).

Bivens action for constitutional tort: *Butz* implies approval of damage action arising out of the First Amendment and out of a deprivation of Fifth Amendment due process. These officials enjoy only qualified, not absolute immunity. Rehnquist's dissent in *Butz* urged absolute immunity to avoid inhibiting official decision-making. Their qualified immunity depends on whether they violated a clearly established right of which a reasonable person should have been aware. You can discuss whether the commission members should reasonably have been aware of i) the First Amendment or ii) the Fifth Amendment violations. Or are these claims so arguable that they are not "clearly established?" See *Penthouse International,* holding that members of the Attorney General's Commission on Pornography were entitled to qualified immunity for sending letters to retailers offering them a chance to respond to charges that they were involved in the sale of pornography.

b) State Pornography Commission:

i) **Action against state.** Depends on state tort claims act, if any (otherwise state is immune). If this were a local government, it would also be immune, since this is a governmental, not a proprietary function. If there is a tort claims act but the state has no discretionary function exception, the court must decide what functions are immune. See foregoing discussion of *Brown*. Mercury can't sue the Commission for damages under § 1983 because it is a state instrumentality.

ii) **Action against commissioners.** State law generally immunizes officers from suit for discretionary functions (similar to *Barr v. Matteo*). Some states make exception for "malicious" or "corrupt" action, but we've no evidence of that here—commissioners appear to be acting out of honest conviction. A federal court § 1983 action against commissioners for constitutional violations raises the same immunity issues as under *Bivens*.

§ 10.3 RECOVERY OF FEES

Notes and Questions

1. *The American rule.* The D.C. Circuit reaffirmed the American rule in *Unbelievable, Inc. v. NLRB*, 118 F.3d 795 (D.C.Cir.1997). Since 1972, the NLRB had awarded litigation costs in cases where the losing party acted in egregious bad faith. This served as an effective disincentive to bad faith bargaining. However, the court of appeals held that the NLRB lacked the power to make such orders. The American rule means that NLRB lacks such authority absent clear support on the face of a statute or in the legislative history. The statute allowing the Board to issue an "order requiring [the losing party] to take such affirmative action . . . as will effectuate the policies of the Act" was not a sufficiently clear mandate to override the American rule. Judge Wald dissented.

2. *Statutes providing for fees.* In connection with material later in this unit on "prevailing parties," you might mention *Ruckelshaus v. Sierra Club*, 463 U.S. 680 (1983). This was a fee case under an "as appropriate" statute. It grew out of *Sierra Club v. Costle*, § 5.5.2. On the merits, the environmental public interest group plaintiffs lost hands down, but the D.C. Circuit awarded them fees anyway, on the theory that they had served the public interest by bringing their expertise to bear on an important case. The Supreme Court reversed in a 5-4 decision. The language of the Clean Air Act does not expressly limit fees to prevailing parties, only that the award must be "appropriate." But the Court reasoned that making a complete winner pay a complete loser is so contrary to tradition that the Act just couldn't be read to allow this result. A prevailing party limitation had to be implied.

3. *Reasonable attorney's fees.* The *Arbor Hill* decision contains a thorough discussion of the confusing case law about determination of the

reasonable hourly rate in calculating the lodestar. Although the Supreme Court has decided several cases in the area, it has failed to clear up the confusion. Under one line of authority (Third Circuit), there are two steps. First, a lodestar is calculated based on the number of hours times the attorney's usual hourly rate. In a second step, the resulting figure is adjusted for case-specific concerns. Under a second line (Fifth Circuit) there is only one rather than two steps; the court uses a balance of twelve factors to determine a reasonable fee. The Second Circuit *Arbor Hill* approach is an attempt to reconcile the two approaches with a one-step economic analysis—what would a reasonable client pay, based on case-specific and lawyer-specific factors.

The Arbor Hill suggests that the term "lodestar" be abandoned and that the inquiry focus on the determination of a "reasonable hourly rate," meaning "the rate a paying client would be willing to pay." This means consideration of all relevant factors but emphasizing that "a reasonable, paying client wishes to spend the minimum necessary to litigate the case effectively." The court should take into account that an "individual might be able to negotiate with his or her attorneys, using their desire to obtain the reputational benefits that might accrue from being associated with the case."

The narrow issue in *Arbor Hill* (which arose under the Voting Rights Act) was whether the plaintiffs, who were litigating in Albany, New York, could recover the normal hourly fee of a Manhattan firm that was brought in for its "muscle" (meaning its ability to prepare the appeal on an abbreviated briefing schedule). The court rejected a strict "forum" rule and indicated that a reasonable paying client might sometimes hire a non-local firm that charged higher rates, but that such circumstances would be exceptional.

The *Arbor Hill* opinion sweeps much more broadly than consideration of the "forum" rule. Its analysis requires consideration of various lawyer-specific factors that were not previously considered in setting a reasonable hourly rate. The court can consider not only such factors as the complexity and difficulty of the case and its timing demands, but also "whether the attorney had an interest (independent of that of his client) in achieving the ends of the litigation or initiated the representation himself, whether the attorney was initially acting *pro bono* (such that the client might be aware that the attorney expected low or non-existent remuneration), and other returns (such as reputation, etc.) that the attorney expected from the representation."

The court noted that a "reasonable, paying client would have known that law firms undertaking representation such as that of plaintiffs often obtain considerable non-monetary returns—in experience, reputation, or achievement of the attorneys' own interests and agendas—and would have insisted on paying his attorneys at [the Albany rather than Manhattan] rates." *Arbor Hill* suggests that governmental defendants will now try to persuade the court to lower the reasonable hourly rate to take account of reputational or psychic benefits that lawyers might enjoy from winning the case. Consequently, an attorney who is in the case strictly for the money might earn a higher fee than one who enjoyed psychic or reputational benefits from the case. Whether these lawyer-specific reputational or psychic benefits can really be considered in a principled way remains to be seen. However, the opinion has deeply offended public interest lawyers.

Of course, the determination of a reasonable fee includes a calculation of the hours reasonably spent on a matter as well as setting a reasonable hourly rate. The court's devastating critique of attorney over-billing in *Role Models America Inc. v. Brownlee*, 353 F.3d 962, 970-74 (D.C.Cir.2004) (involving a claim for 1058 hours of work on what the court thought was a relatively straightforward case) is a primer of what not to do when seeking fees. In the end, the court cut the number of hours in half. The time sheets should not lump together different tasks and must contain adequate detail. For example, the court criticized entries reflecting "research and writing for appellate brief" on eight consecutive weekdays. Such record keeping is inadequate to meet the applicant's "heavy obligation to present well-documented claims." The same is true for entries for "meetings" or "teleconferences" without explaining the purposes of the meetings or conferences. Similarly, entries for meeting with people whose relationship to the case is unclear will not pass muster.

Most serious, under *Role Models* and other cases, if the hours seem excessive given the difficulty of the case, the court will reduce them. "There is a point at which thorough and diligent litigation efforts become overkill." Thus the applicant failed to explain why a relatively straightforward case required the efforts of three senior attorneys, each billing at least $400 per hour. Such efforts are duplicative or redundant. Equally suspicious were entries where A claimed to meet with B but B's time sheets do not include any reference to a meeting with A. Finally, some chores don't warrant reimbursement at all, such as discussing the case with the press or revising the firm's engagement letter with the client or "applying for admission to the D. C. Bar."

4. *Equal Access to Justice Act.* The *Texas Food Industry Ass'n* case can be seen as a case pitting literal interpretation against statutory purpose. The majority said that the plaintiff was certainly an "association," which is one of the categories of entities that fit within the EAJA's definition of "party," and the association's budget fell below the statutory ceiling. The dissent called the result absurd because, given the wealth of its members,

the plaintiff could certainly have afforded to bring its challenge without government subsidy.

In a way, this case goes to the heart of the reasons why we have an EAJA. Is it basically to protect persons of modest means in their fight against big government—private Davids facing agency Goliaths? Probably that was the original idea. But perhaps EAJA is coming to be seen as a deterrent to agencies to engage in overreaching action. That perspective might make the Fifth Circuit's view seem more plausible.

The "substantial justification" issue is often difficult. The government's position might be "substantially justified" even if it lost the case because it failed to satisfy its burden of proof as in *Bricks*. It can even be substantially justified in cases where the reviewing court found that its action was not supported by substantial evidence or was arbitrary and capricious. In *Sotelo-Aquije v. Slattery*, 62 F.3d 54, 58 (2d Cir.1995), the court held that "substantial justification" and "substantial evidence" do not mean the same thing. As a result, a decision might be unsupported by substantial evidence, yet it could still be "substantially justified." However, a merits decision based on lack of substantial evidence or found to have been arbitrary and capricious places a high hurdle in front of the government when it seeks to show that its position was substantially justified.

5. *Fee awards when the agency settles.* *Buckhannon* has proved difficult to apply. In *Carbonell v. INS*, 429 F.3d 894 (9th Cir.2005), the court determined that a voluntary stipulation that allowed the subject of a deportation proceeding a stay of deportation made the fee-applicant a "prevailing party" who could recover fees. The reason was that the stipulation was incorporated into a judicial decree and thus became judicially enforceable. This provided the necessary "judicial imprimatur" and distinguished the stipulation from the normal private settlement that terminates ongoing litigation. The distinction seems thin, however, given that a purely private settlement can be judicially enforced in a breach of contract action. In any event, the court's reasoning in *Carbonell* makes it important for counsel to try to get a settlement agreement between the client and the government incorporated in a judicial decree in order to form the predicate for a subsequent EAJA fee application.

See generally Catherine R. Albiston & Laura B. Nielsen, "The Procedural Attack on Civil Rights: The Empirical Reality of *Buckhannon* for the Private Attorney General," 54 UCLA L.Rev. 1087 (2007), reporting results of an empirical survey suggesting that strategic capitulation is common under *Buckhannon*. The authors believe that the possibility that strategic capitulation will occur discourages attorneys from bringing lawsuits to which fee-shifting statutes apply. As a result, *Buckhannon* reduces the volume of civil rights litigation. California resoundingly rejected

Buckhannon and allows fees to be awarded under the catalyst theory rejected in *Buckhannon* (for example, for a settlement). *Graham v. DaimlerChrysler*, 101 P.3d 140 (Cal.2004). In addition, Congress overrode *Buckhannon* in an amendment to FOIA by providing that after a suit has been filed, the plaintiff can get attorneys' fees if the agency voluntarily relinquishes the records. P.L. 110-175, § 4(a)(2).

6. *Problem*. Mary, Bernice, and MGRAL (which paid the fees) are primarily interested in establishing the principle that the Civil Right Act applies to sexual orientation discrimination, not in forcing Ruth to rent to the couple. By the time judicial review ended, Mary and Bernice would long since have found another apartment. Monroe has adopted both EAJA and a "private attorney general" statute relating to attorneys' fees like Cal. Code of Civ. Proc. §1021.

i) EAJA: Since the plaintiff's victory came on judicial review rather than at the agency level, the cases is decided under 28 U.S.C. § 2412, and a court decides on reimbursement. If Mary and Bernice had won at the agency level, § 504 would require an ALJ to decide on reimbursement of fees. Assuming the APA applied to the agency hearing, they should be entitled to recover fees at both the agency and judicial levels.

Presumably the net worth of Mary and Bernice is less than $2 million. They should submit an affidavit to this effect. To the extent MGRAL was a party, if it qualifies as a tax exempt charitable organization, it meets the financial requirements. However, MGRAL might not be "charitable" under IRC § 501(c)(3), because it seeks to influence legislation. In that case, it would have to meet the net worth and number of employee tests set forth for corporate entities in EAJA, which it probably does.

Are Mary and Bernice "prevailing parties?" Note they won on one issue ("discrimination on the basis of sex" includes sexual orientation) but lost on the other (whether Ruth actually discriminated on the basis of sexual orientation). As a result, they did not secure the relief they wanted (an order requiring Ruth to rent to them). The Court discussed this situation in a case involving the civil rights fee-shifting statute, 42 U.S.C. § 1988:

> To qualify as a prevailing party, a civil rights plaintiff must obtain at least some relief on the merits of his claim. . . Whatever relief the plaintiff secures must directly benefit him at the time of the judgment or settlement. Otherwise the judgment or settlement cannot be said to "affect the behavior of the defendant toward the plaintiff. . . ." In short a plaintiff "prevails" when actual relief on the merits of his claim materially alters the legal relationship between the parties by modifying the defendant's behavior in a way that directly benefits the

plaintiff. . . . Of itself, "the moral satisfaction [that] results from any favorable statement of law" cannot bestow prevailing party status.

Farrar v. Hobby, 506 U.S. 103, 111-12 (1992). The plaintiff in *Farrar* asked for $17 million in damages and was awarded a dollar. Technically he "prevailed," the majority said, but, considering the low recovery, the district court's award of $280,000 in fees was far too generous. The majority implied that he should get no fees at all, although only Justice O'Connor was willing to come out and say so. "Prevailing party" cases decided under § 1988 are often cited as authoritative in EAJA cases.

Even if the plaintiffs are considered to be the "prevailing party," they must prove how much of your fee is attributable to the statutory interpretation issue, since they could recover only with respect to the issue on which they prevailed. *See Healey v. Leavitt*, 485 F.3d 63 (2d Cir.2007), holding that where plaintiff prevails on one theory (a procedural claim) while failing on a second distinct theory (a constitutional claim), it can recover fees incurred only on the successful rather than the unsuccessful claim. Therefore, it is imperative that your time sheets clearly reflect a defensible allocation of time between the issues.

Your firm can be reimbursed under EAJA for $125 per hour maximum, adjusted for inflation. The $125 figure was fixed by a 1996 statute, so cost of living increases after 1996 should be taken into account. Probably it should be adjusted upward by a multiplier based on increases in the Consumer Price Index to the year in which the services were rendered. Obviously, EAJA falls far short of reimbursing the fees. A court can further increase the $125 figure if it determines that a special factor (such as the limited availability of qualified attorneys for the proceedings involved) justifies a higher fee. *Pierce* makes clear that "limited availability" refers to attorneys having some distinctive knowledge or specialized skill needed for the litigation in question; you aren't going to meet that standard.

Can MCRC establish "that its position was substantially justified?" It must justify both the "position" taken by the agency in connection with the underlying dispute or the one taken in litigation. It is likely that MCRC's position on the statutory interpretation issue (arguing that discrimination on the basis of "sex" does not include discrimination on the basis of "sexual orientation") was substantially justified. A reasonable person could have taken that position which is the prevailing federal interpretation of Title VII. *See* Roberta Achtenberg, SEXUAL ORIENTATION AND THE LAW §5.03[2][b][i] (1985 & Curr.Supp.). The Monroe court's decision that discrimination on the basis of sex includes sexual orientation would be viewed as pioneering.

Assume now that the court found that MCRC's decision about Ruth's motivation for refusing to rent to the couple was not supported by substantial evidence. It is difficult to see how MCRC's position could be found unreasonable under the substantial evidence or arbitrary-capricious tests, yet be found reasonable under the substantial justification test as defined in *Pierce v. Underwood*. A finding of lack of substantial evidence or arbitrary-capricious places a high hurdle in front of the government on the EAJA issue, but the two tests are not synonymous. As *Bricks, Inc.* in the text, or *Sotelo-Aquije* in the manual show, the test under EAJA is whether the agency had a reasonable basis for taking the position it did—which it might have had even if a court later disagrees with it. If the case was a close call and agency counsel could not have predicted they would probably lose, for example because the credibility of their witness is successfully impeached, their position might be substantially justified.

ii) Private attorney general theory. This is a good place to discuss the private attorney general—someone who vindicates an important public right. A mechanism for payment of fees is essential to support public interest litigation. Otherwise, the free rider effect will doom most such litigation. Public interest litigation is too costly for most groups to sustain, absent volunteer lawyers (a scarce commodity, especially for lengthy and complex cases). The problem specifies that Monroe adopted a statute identical to Cal. Code Civ. Proc. § 1021.5, which rejects the "American Rule" and provides for fee-shifting in cases brought by private attorneys general.

Mary and Bernice must first establish that they were "successful." This is a difficult issue, similar to the "prevailing party" problem already discussed. If they get by that, it seems clear that the case "resulted in the enforcement of an important right affecting the public interest." In addition, the case conferred a "significant benefit" on a "large class of persons" (i.e., homosexuals who want to rent apartments). The necessity and financial burden of private enforcement make an award appropriate. Presumably, MCRC would have to pay only your fees allocated to the statutory interpretation issue, not to the factual issues.

Here one should address the lodestar issues. What is a reasonable hourly fee—$250 seems to be ballpark, but it must be within the range of fees charged by local attorneys. However, you should consider the *Arbor Hill* standard. That case questionably held that a reasonable fee might be less than market rates if the attorney is vindicating a personal or political agenda or might benefit by reputational enhancement. Here, you probably took this case because of your conviction about the legal and political issues relating to sexual orientation discrimination. Also, your big victory might bring you more cases of this kind. Also Mary and Bernice might have known that you would have taken the case pro bono (that is, even without any chance of recovering fees). Under *Arbor Hill,* all these factors are relevant in reducing your reasonable hourly rate for purposes of computing the lodestar. The issue is how low an hourly fee Mary and Bernice could have negotiated if they had negotiated fees with you.

This is also a good place to discuss the practical problems of keeping highly detailed time sheets. Being required to keep track of time in six-minute increments is one of the curses of private law practice, and having good time-keeping practices is essential to success in practice. You have to keep track as you go, of every phone call or interruption, or you'll lose time reconstructing it at the end of the day. Accurate time-keeping is equally vital if you are going to recover fees under fee-shifting statutes. Your time sheets will be scrutinized. As the *Role Models* case above shows, time sheets must be meticulously maintained and must contain adequate detail for every entry. You can't just say "worked on appellate brief" but must explain exactly what you were doing. If you seem to have been inefficient, or more lawyers worked on the case that seem necessary, your time will be cut. If you have a meeting with another lawyer, that lawyer's time sheets had better reflect the same meeting.

§ 10.4 PRECLUSION OF JUDICIAL REVIEW

Note that APA §§ 702-706 all hinge on § 701(a). Even though § 704 says that a person is entitled to judicial review, it may not be true: review is denied "to the extent" that (1) statutes preclude judicial review or (2) agency action is committed to agency discretion by law. Note that § 701(a) permits partial as well as total preclusion through the use of the phrase "to the extent that."

Preclusion under § 701(a) can be either express or implied (see *United States v. Erika, Inc.* and *Block v. Community Nutrition Inst.* both discussed below). However, the 1981 MSAPA takes the opposite tack. Under § 1-103(b), "to the extent that any other statute would diminish a right created or duty imposed by this Act, the other statute is superseded by this Act, unless the other statute expressly provides otherwise." And the Comment to § 1-103 requires that the Act prevails "unless there is a wholly unambiguous contrary legislative decision. . . . The burden should be on those seeking any exemption from the Act to demonstrate their entitlement thereto in unmistakable statutory language indicating that the legislature has actually considered the question of an exemption and determined that an exemption is warranted."

Notes and Questions

The Supreme Court distinguished *Michigan Academy* in its 5-4 decision in *Shalala v. Illinois Council on Long Term Care, Inc.,* 529 U.S. 1 (2000). In this case, nursing homes sought pre-enforcement judicial review of Medicare regulations relating to sanctions and remedies that might be imposed on them. The relevant statutes (which are the same as those relating to Social Security) channel all Medicare disputes into administrative hearings and judicial review of adverse determinations occurring in such hearings. They also provide that no action under § 1331 can be brought "to recover on any claim arising under" the Medicare laws. The Court held that this preclusion statute was applicable and it barred pre-enforcement review of the challenged regulations. The situation in *Illinois Council* was different from that in *Michigan Academy.* In the latter case, neither administrative nor judicial review would have been available if the preclusion statute were applied. In *Illinois Council,* the nursing homes could raise their objections to the regulations at a hearing after the government imposed sanctions and they could secure judicial review of adverse determinations.

1. *Implied preclusion. Abbott Labs* states that reviewability is presumed, and this presumption is often applied. Nevertheless, there are plenty of cases in which the Supreme Court and lower courts have found that judicial review has been impliedly precluded. An often-cited example is *Block v. Community Nutrition Institute,* 467 U.S. 340 (1984) (Congress impliedly precluded review by consumers—but not producers—of a USDA marketing order setting minimum prices for milk). Similarly, *Dalton v. Specter,* 512 U.S. 1247 (1994), concerned judicial review of the military base closing process. Four concurring Justices believed that the structure of the statute impliedly precluded judicial review of the actions of the military in recommending closures to the Base Closure Commission and the Commission's action in recommending closures to the President. Among the factors were a series of rigid time deadlines that would be disrupted by judicial review.

In *Erika,* the Court construed § 1395ff to deny review of a determination by Prudential (the designated insurance carrier) that a supplier of dialysis products was entitled to a much lower price than it had charged. The statute was not explicit on whether judicial review was precluded. It failed to provide for review of administrative denial of amount disputes under Medicare Part B while providing for review of denial of amount disputes under Part A. It also provided for judicial review of the denial of eligibility for benefits under Part B. Explicit legislative history indicated that amount determinations were not judicially reviewable. In

Michigan Academy, the Court could have followed *Erika* and held that §§ 1395ff and 1395ii also precluded review of *rules* that determine the amount of Part B benefits. However, the Court distinguished review of Part B individualized amount dispute *adjudications* which are precluded (*Erika*) from review of disputes concerning Part B *rules* relating to the amount of claims (*Michigan Academy*). Review of the latter are not precluded, since such rule challenges would otherwise receive *neither* administrative nor judicial review, as the insurance carriers were barred from considering the challenges at the administrative level.

Although Erika's claim was substantial in amount (it was the assignee of many purchasers of dialysis supplies), each of the aggregate claims was relatively small. There is merit to a construction that precludes federal court review of the vast number of relatively small, bureaucratically handled Medicare Part B claims (which have been subbed out to private insurance carriers) while permitting review (as in *Michigan Academy*) of the validity of regulations. The insurance carriers (who provide hearings on disputed Part B claims) are instructed not to consider the validity of regulations; it would have been illogical for claims relating to the validity of rules to receive *less* judicial attention than a small dollar claim.

There was no textual basis for the distinction between *Erika* and *Michigan Academy*. Instead, the distinction is driven by pragmatic considerations. *Erika* spares federal judges from having to spend a lot of time on "trivial matters;" but taking jurisdiction to determine the validity of a regulation (*Michigan Academy*) will consume relatively few judicial resources, while resolving in a single stroke a dispute that affects a broad class of providers. Obviously the court was impressed by the incongruous nature of the Government's argument in *Michigan Academy*—that the petitioner's claim was entitled neither to administrative nor judicial review.

Contrast *Michigan Academy* with *Thunder Basin Coal Co. v. Reich*, 510 U.S. 200 (1994). In *Thunder Basin,* the Court held that pre-enforcement review of regulations under the Mine Safety Act was impliedly precluded. The evidence for this conclusion was that the statute provided an elaborate post-enforcement administrative procedure that could address petitioner's claims of invalidity of the regulation (whereas in *Michigan Academy* the claims could not be presented at the administrative level). In addition, legislative history evidenced Congressional concern that delays in safety inspections put miners at risk. *Thunder Basin* may suggest that the Court is backing away from the approach exemplified by *Abbott Laboratories*, under which regulations typically can be challenged before they are enforced. Some scholars have cited pre-enforcement review of rules as a contributor to the problem of ossification of the rulemaking process. We consider this subject further in the material on ripeness, § 11.2.3.

Abbott Labs and its progeny found no preclusive force in the possibility that regulations could be challenged later, during administrative enforcement processes, but *Thunder Basin* thought this was quite significant. This may signal a re-evaluation of the *Abbott Laboratories* presumption against preclusion. The challenged regulation put mine owners in a bind: they could a) allow union officials to conduct safety inspections of their non-union mines (thus giving the union access to information and a toe-hold with the workers) or b) refuse to allow the union officials to participate in inspections and risk being subjected to severe penalties for flouting the regulations. This was just the sort of dilemma that *Abbott Labs* had focused on in its decision to allow pre-enforcement review.

In a questionable decision, the Fourth Circuit followed *Thunder Basin* and dismissed a pre-enforcement claim against Social Security, based on implied preclusion, because there was an administrative structure in place that could have adjudicated its claims. *National Taxpayers Union v. SSA*, 376 F.3d 239 (4th Cir.2004). *NTU* involved a "survey" (actually a fundraiser) circulated by NTU intended to plug its program of private investment accounts to replace Social Security. SSA believed that the survey conveyed the false impression that it was authorized by SSA. SSA threatened enforcement under § 1140 of the Social Security Act, which imposes civil money penalties in connection with ads that could be construed as suggesting that they are approved or authorized by SSA. Because there is an administrative enforcement procedure for considering such penalties, the Fourth Circuit held that *Thunder Basin* precludes immediate review of SSA's enforcement threats, which were chilling distribution of the survey. Because the claim in *NAU* relates to SSA's alleged suppression of free speech, administrative remedies seem peculiarly unsuitable for resolution of the claim.

You may wish to focus on a broader issue in *Michigan Academy* and *Erika*: the desirability of a system of non-adversary claims adjudication by insurance carriers, which is effectively dejudicialized and delawyered. Recall that the Court upheld the $10 limit on VA attorneys' fees in *Radiation Survivors* (§ 2.4). Students should consider whether it may not be better for a system that disposes of millions of small claims to be controlled only by bureaucratic checks rather than by attorneys and courts. Judicial review of the occasional claim can be quite destructive. *See* Jerry Mashaw, BUREAUCRATIC JUSTICE (1983), praising nonadversarial decisionmaking and questioning judicial review of Social Security disability claims.

2. *Interpreting preclusive statutes.* Preclusion is a difficult topic to teach, because each case is an idiosyncratic attempt to uncover legislative intent in a complex statute (and often to manipulate the statute so as to permit review in situations where it seems most needed). What the

legislature intended in one situation doesn't necessarily tell you what it intended in another. The *Abbott Labs* presumption in favor of review is some help, but experience has proven it fairly manipulable. Moreover, although preclusion statutes are often read narrowly, it would be wrong to suppose that the courts don't enforce them at all. The presumption does not, in itself, tell you whether a given case is a strong or weak candidate for preclusion.

The "hierarchy" suggested in the Levin article emphasizes the pragmatic considerations that have lurked in the background of many of these cases. Its generalizations will not hold true in every situation (for example, it would suggest a contrary result in *Thunder Basin*, discussed above). However, it provides an analytical perspective that allows for reasonable discussion of whether any particular claim would present a relatively strong case for finding preclusion.

We did not include detailed materials relating to preclusion of review in deportation cases (such as those under the REAL ID Act) or on the constitutionality of preclusion of habeas corpus (discussed in the next note) because of concerns about space and available instructional time. These issues get quite technical and are probably treated in other classes such as immigration law, federal courts, and constitutional law. Besides, they are in the process of rapid change and development, so that anything written for this edition would swiftly become obsolete. We will include coverage of these materials in our periodic supplements. Some instructors will wish to focus their class time on preclusion in deportation and war on terror cases rather than on the Social Security and Medicare materials. As of the time of publication, we recommend the Columbia note cited in text and Richard H. Fallon, Jr. & Daniel J. Meltzer, "Habeas Corpus Jurisdiction, Substantive Rights, and the War on Terror," 120 Harv.L.Rev. 2029 (2007).

3. *Preclusion of constitutional claims.* The citation in the final footnote of *Michigan Academy* to Hart's article supports the idea that Congress cannot preclude review of issues of law arising in an enforcement proceeding. Brandeis' concurring opinion in *St. Joseph Stockyards* said: "[T]he supremacy of law demands that there shall be an opportunity to have some court decide . . . whether an erroneous rule of law was applied, and whether the proceedings in which the facts were adjudicated were conducted regularly." If Brandeis is right, the constitutional right of review would extend to all issues of law and procedure. This would go far beyond the prevailing assumption that Congress can preclude review except of constitutional issues.

You might want to read Scalia's *Webster* dissent—it challenges the prevailing wisdom that there is something special about constitutional claims, so that Congress cannot preclude them, or even that courts should exercise heightened scrutiny over statutes that purport to preclude them. In addition to the Tribe and Chemerinsky treatises and the Fallon & Meltzer article cited in the preceding note, see Richard E. Levy & Sidney A. Shapiro, "Government Benefits and the Rule of Law: Toward a Standards-Based Theory of Judicial Review," 58 Admin.L.Rev. 499 (2006). As noted above, this area is subject to rapid change and will be updated in our periodic supplements as new developments occur. As this book is written, President Obama has promised to close Guantanamo, so the habeas issues resolved in *Boumediene* may become moot. Nevertheless, many issues remain about how to handle the detainees confined there and what sort of procedures would be appropriate to adjudicate their status. Similarly, the manner in which habeas petitions will be dealt with remains to be seen.

4. *Time limits.* Numerous environmental statutes preclude review of rules (including review during enforcement proceedings) after a short post-promulgation period. The statutes include the Federal Water Pollution Control Act, the Clean Air Act, and the Noise Control Act. *Yakus* is the prototype for these statutes. As in that case, the rationale for the statutes is to facilitate enforcement by getting a fast, fair, uniform and final resolution of the validity of a regulation of great national importance. The statutes are routinely enforced in the federal courts; they are a good demonstration that preclusion is an important element of administrative practice, notwithstanding *Abbott Labs. Yakus* has never been overruled and apparently is embodied in the last sentence of APA § 703. But § 703 leaves room for argument in individual situations about whether a prior, exclusive opportunity for judicial review was "adequate."

The Court recognized a due process constraint on the use of time limits to preclude review. In the context of a criminal enforcement action, Congress apparently cannot totally preclude judicial review of prior administrative action—even for non-constitutional errors. *United States v. Mendoza-Lopez,* 481 U.S. 828 (1987). That case involved prosecution of an alien for illegal entry into the country, following an earlier deportation for a prior illegal entry. A second illegal entry, after a prior deportation, is a felony; thus the earlier deportation was an element of the crime. The Court held that due process requires that the prior deportation be judicially reviewable, *either* at the time it occurred or in the criminal trial relating to the second illegal entry.

Verkuil argues that time-limit statutes should not preclude review in an enforcement proceeding of the issue of whether the rule has been properly applied to the defendant. Paul R. Verkuil, "Congressional Limitations on Judicial Review of Rules," 57 Tulane L.Rev. 733 (1983). That conclusion seems correct, because the question of whether the defendant violated the rule is not an issue that the agency could have decided when it promulgated the rule. If the defendant claims that the rule doesn't apply to its conduct, the court should entertain that contention either on direct appeal from the agency's determination that the rule does apply, or when the agency brings an enforcement proceeding. *Mendoza-Lopez* indicates that one option or the other must be available. But if the former opportunity is "adequate" (which was not the case in *Mendoza-Lopez*, because the government conceded that defendants' waiver of their right to appeal had been made without informed consent), the latter opportunity might properly be withheld.

5. *State law.* For a good discussion of the uncertain signal sent by the New York cases, see Patrick J. Borchers & David L. Markell, NEW YORK ADMINISTRATIVE PROCEDURE AND PRACTICE § 7.10 (1998).

6. *Problem.* *Lindahl* involved the preclusion statute quoted in the problem. Relying on legislative history and the general presumption of reviewability, the Supreme Court "construed" the statute to preclude review only of factual determinations, but not review of whether "there has been a substantial departure from important procedural rights, a misconstruction of the governing legislation, or some like error going to the heart of the administrative determination." The decision is 5-4, with the dissenters finding that all claims are precluded. The case is typical of those cited in N.2 of the text, in which preclusion statutes are narrowly interpreted to permit review of some issues (legal and constitutional) while precluding it for mere factual issues.

See also Lepre v. Dep't of Labor, 275 F.3d 59 (D.C.Cir.2001), also involving a disability claim. The court determined that a preclusion statute did not cut off a constitutional claim (that the "mailbox" rule violated due process). The agency refused to even consider the due process claim because it believed constitutional issues should be resolved by courts, not agencies—see §11.2 N.6. Consequently, if this claim were precluded, it could not be considered at either the judicial or administrative levels. This pattern is similar to *Michigan Academy* where application of the preclusion statute would knock out review at both the administrative and judicial levels.

Similarly, the *New York Dep't of Envir. Protec.* case cited in N.5 construed a statute that related to government personnel. It provided that the agency decision "shall be final and conclusive, and not subject to further review in any court." The New York Court of Appeals did not pretend that it was construing the language of the statute; it conceded that the legislature intended to cut off all judicial review. But it stated that the courts retain the power to set aside administrative decisions if the agency has acted unconstitutionally, illegally, or in excess of its jurisdiction. It is unclear whether this power is derived from the state constitution or is a rule of judicial superintendence of the agencies.

On the merits (if the reviewing court is permitted to reach them), MPA's decision might well flunk the substantial evidence test. Bruce is a GP, whereas Joan's two doctors are specialists. Joan's inability to cross-examine Bruce would, at a minimum, undercut the value of his written opinion. However, this is just the sort of factual determination that is subject to statutory preclusion under either *Lindahl* or *N.Y. Dept.* Dr. Bruce's report is hearsay, and it appears to be the only evidence in support of MPA's decision. If Monroe follows the residuum rule, the decision would appear to violate that rule.

You might discuss why the legislature chose to preclude review and whether this is good policy. Our view is that judicial review of agency factual determinations is of relatively little benefit in mass justice situations; judicial intervention occurs rarely, because of the small stakes involved, and is not likely to improve the agency's decisionmaking process. Review of such cases requires the court to make sophisticated medical judgments for which it is not well equipped, whereas the agency specializes in making them.

On the other hand, this case shows that judicial review could keep an agency honest; without judicial scrutiny, it is all too easy for an agency to reject marginal disability claims, thus minimizing state expenditures and satisfying the executive branch officials who appointed the MPA members and the legislature that must appropriate funds for the program. That's especially an issue with the sort of injury involved here, which could potentially mushroom into a giant cost item for the pension system. Ergonomic injuries are just starting to be recognized as a serious public health problem, and it is understandable that agencies like MPA would seek to discourage such claims.

There is an obvious procedural/constitutional issue here. Due process would seem to apply, since the right to disability retirement is a statutory entitlement (although there remains the lurking question of whether due process covers applications as well as terminations). The procedure employed here would seem to deny Joan her right to cross-examine the critical witness against her. In *Richardson v. Perales*, 402 U.S. 389 (1971), the Court upheld a decision based solely on written doctors' reports, but only because the disability applicant had waived his right to subpoena the doctors. We need further information on the state's subpoena provision. It might make issuance of subpoenas discretionary with the presiding officer. If the decision were reviewable, a court might find that the ALJ's decision not to issue a subpoena for a critical witness was an abuse of discretion. Also, reliance on Dr. Bruce's hearsay testimony could violate due process, since it denied Joan the right to confront the key and only witness against her.

The formulations in both *Lindahl, Lepre,* and *N.Y. Dept.* quoted above would indicate that review of these procedural-constitutional issues is not precluded, even if review of the factual issues is precluded. *Lindahl* and *Lepre* are based on "interpretation" of the preclusion statute; *N.Y. Dept.* apparently applies regardless of legislative intent. It can be argued that the rationale for precluding review of factual issues is inapplicable to serious procedural problems like the ones involved here, since the defective subpoena and confrontation problems will arise in many other cases. Moreover, courts have more expertise in deciding procedural/constitutional issues than in making medical decisions.

More broadly, it's worth discussing whether the legislature could preclude review of constitutional issues like the due process issue in the problem. It's unclear under federal law; the issue would probably split the Supreme Court. Note 12 in *Michigan Academy* hints that Congress could not do so; Scalia clearly believes the opposite. The New York decision at least implies that the legislature could not preclude review. And that leads you to a discussion of whether the legislature *should* be allowed to do so. Are constitutional claims really that different from the sort of claims that are subject to preclusion?

Czerkies, cited in text, is a Posner-Easterbrook debate that sheds some light on the preclusion question. The plaintiff was an injured federal worker who had been denied workers' compensation benefits under the Federal Employees Compensation Act. He claimed that the Labor Department had denied him substantive due process (apparently he thought that a wrongful denial of benefits is unconstitutional as such). Despite a seemingly absolute preclusion statute, not to mention the pitiful weakness of this constitutional argument, Posner wrote for the en banc court that constitutional claims were not precluded.

Easterbrook wrote a strong dissent, noting that Czerkies' constitutional grievance was not directed at any statute, regulation or systemic practice, as in *Michigan Academy*. It was directed solely at what the plaintiff considered unconstitutional treatment in his individual case. In that sense it was much like *Erika*. In such cases, Easterbrook said, the preclusion statute should be enforced as written. This would make practical sense, because hearing a systemic challenge settles many cases, but hearing individualized challenges opens the floodgates to weak administrative law claims dressed in constitutional language (and the majority agreed that this was a fair description of Czerkies' claim).

That the majority did not agree with Easterbrook is strong evidence of the special status, if not mystique, that surrounds the doctrine that courts will shun preclusion of review of constitutional contentions. It's not too hard to imagine Scalia putting together a majority to start paring back on that status, and a case like *Czerkies* might be a logical place for him to start. But doubtless the core of the special status will survive for some time to come, and Joan, whose constitutional grievances seem at least substantial (if not necessarily correct), will probably be able to get a court to look at them.

§ 10.5 COMMITMENT TO AGENCY DISCRETION

HECKLER v. CHANEY

Notes and Questions

1. *The expanding circle.* An agency's decision to fire an employee under a contract that the statute declares is an at-will relationship is not reviewable. *Steenholdt v. FAA*, 314 F.3d 633 (D.C. Cir.2003). This case could make a nice hypo because due process is inapplicable to a discharge under an at-will contract (*Roth* in § 2.2.1) and the decision is also judicially non-reviewable on the merits (*Steenholdt*), but might be reviewable on constitutional grounds (such as whether it was based on an illegal form of discrimination).

Webster v. Doe held that the discharge of an at-will CIA employee was non-reviewable under the commitment to agency discretion standard, but there were additional grounds for the decision arising out of foreign intelligence that were not present in *Steenholdt*. *Webster* did hold that constitutional review of the discharge could not be precluded and was possible. Thus a discharged at-will government employee gets no protection from an arbitrary merits decision at either the administrative or judicial level. Perhaps this is as it should be, to maximize agency management flexibility, but the subject is worth discussing.

2. *No law to apply.* Levin's article argues that even if there are no meaningful statutory standards (no "law to apply"), that eliminates only one part of abuse of discretion review—the part relating to consideration of correct factors. A court could still reverse if it found that the decision lacks factual support, is inconsistent with prior decisions without an explanation for the change, or is a "clear error of judgment." This is not to say that the court *should* engage in review in every case in which review would be feasible (which under this analysis would be virtually always). Rather, the point is that the reviewability question should turn on pragmatic considerations: on balance, is review undesirable? *See also* Kenneth C. Davis, "No Law to Apply," 25 U. San Diego L.Rev. 1 (1988).

Nevertheless, Levin does not maintain that the presence of "law to apply" is irrelevant. From a pragmatic viewpoint, judicial review of legal issues holds certain advantages over review of factual or discretionary issues. It allows courts to speak in the terrain where their comparative qualifications vis-à-vis the agencies are strongest. It is also a relatively efficient use of judicial resources, because it is likelier to result in a decision that will provide lasting guidance to agencies and the public, whereas a finding that the agency abused (or did not abuse) its discretion would generally have less precedential value. For all these reasons, the article maintains, the availability of "law to apply" should be regarded as relevant (though not controlling).

An interesting lower court decision on the "no law to apply" standard is *Center for Policy Analysis on Trade & Health v. Office of U.S. Trade Rep.*, 540 F.3d 940 (9th Cir.2008). The Center complained that an advisory committee appointed by the Trade Rep. failed to satisfy the "fairly balanced" requirement of FACA (and corresponding provisions of the Trade Act), because the committee had no representative of the public health community. *See* § 8.2.2. The court held that there were no standards by which it could decide whether the committee was fairly balanced and whether or not it should include a public health representative.

3. *Review of enforcement decisions.* Numerous lower court decisions have applied the *Chaney* analysis and declined to review agency non-enforcement decisions. For example, an agency's decision not to enforce its contract rights is unreviewable. *Oil, Chemical & Atomic Workers Int'l Union v. Richardson*, 214 F.3d 1379 (D.C.Cir.2000) (agency fails to enforce a contract with B to employ agency's former workers at a nuclear plant when B decommissions the plant). Where a statute requires an agency to investigate an employee's claim that he has been denied veterans' rights, a court cannot review the extent to which the agency investigated particular claims, since these involve resource-allocation decisions. *Greer v. Chao*, 492 F.3d 962 (8th Cir.2007).

Rehnquist listed a series of historical, functional and pragmatic reasons for a presumption of nonreviewability in non-enforcement cases. These obviously go far beyond the "no law to apply" approach.

i) An agency's decision not to enforce involves a complex balance of factors peculiarly within its expertise, such as prospects of success and sufficiency of resources. This is probably the strongest of the *Chaney* arguments. For a good discussion of the difficulties of judicial supervision of prosecutorial resource allocation, see *Board of Trade of Chicago v. SEC,* 883 F.2d 525, 530-31 (7th Cir.1989).

ii) When it refuses to act, an agency does not exercise coercive power over individual's liberty and property rights. But so what? Many non-coercive decisions are routinely reviewed in federal court, such as denials of Social Security benefits. If the non-enforcement decision injures someone—as it must if that person is to have standing to challenge the decision—why should disappointed beneficiaries be less entitled to review than persons coerced by the agency?

iii) An enforcement action provides a "focus" for review, which is lacking in non-enforcement cases. But there was a "focus" in *Chaney*—a clear, explained decision not to take enforcement action. Normally, there will be such a focus, such as a rejected petition to the agency.

iv) A refusal to enforce resembles the decision of a prosecutor not to indict—an exclusive responsibility of the executive under the "take care" clause. Arguably, however, refusal of an agency to enforce a statute is different from the typical situation in which a prosecutor passes on a particular case. *See* Ruth Colker, "Administrative Prosecutorial Indiscretion," 63 Tul.L.Rev. 877 (1989).

The majority opinion in *Chaney* set forth a lengthy list of possible exceptions to its presumption of non-reviewability.

i) Non-invocation of rulemaking (fn. 2). *Massachusetts v. EPA*, N.4, confirms that this is indeed an exception.

ii) Refusal to act based solely on belief that agency lacks jurisdiction (fn. 4).

iii) General policy that abdicates statutory responsibilities (fn. 4). *But cf. Riverkeeper, Inc. v. Collins*, 359 F.3d 156, 170 n.17 (2d Cir.2004) (entertaining an "abdication" argument, but rejecting it and adding: "No party has directed us to, nor can we locate, a decision by a court of appeals that has found, in performing the Chaney analysis, a federal agency to have abdicated its statutory duties.").

iv) Statutory guidelines to guide discretion. *Dunlop v. Bachowski*, discussed in *Chaney* (and also below), involved a statute that limited prosecutorial discretion. See 3 Richard J. Pierce, Jr., ADMINISTRATIVE LAW TREATISE § 17.7 (4th ed. 2002) for examples of cases that have reviewed non-enforcement decisions because of the presence of mandatory language and judicially manageable standards.

Compare FEC v. Akins, 524 U.S. 11 (1998). *Akins* involved a statute that expressly allowed aggrieved persons to seek judicial review of the Federal Election Commission's dismissal of a complaint. The case concerns standing to attack FEC inaction, but it illustrates a situation in which judicial review of agency refusal to enforce should be reviewable. Although this is not exactly the same as the *Dunlop* situation, it seems to fall squarely within the Court's emphasis on deference to Congress (as stated in the penultimate paragraph of the *Chaney* opinion).

v) Agency rules supply courts with adequate guidelines. See *McAlpine v. United States*, 112 F.3d 1429 (10th Cir.1997). In *McAlpine*, the court reviewed a decision by the Secretary of the Interior not to take Indian land into trust. The statute authorized the Secretary to do so "in his discretion." However, BIA regulations contain a list of factors to be employed in trust decisions. Even though the regulations do not indicate how the factors should be weighed and balanced, the regulations provide sufficient "law" to permit judicial review. *But see* Harold J. Krent, "Reviewing Agency Action for Inconsistency with Prior Rules and Regulations," 72 Chi.-Kent L.Rev. 1187, 1212-20 (1997) (arguing against this exception because it creates a disincentive to rulemaking).

vi) Violation of constitutional rights. The cite to *Yick Wo* is interesting. It suggests that enforcement against one group, selected for a constitutionally improper reason (such as race), combined with non-enforcement against everybody else, could be reviewable. *Webster v. Doe* emphasizes that courts can review constitutional arguments arising out of termination of CIA employees but not the merits of such decisions.

Rehnquist may have listed these possible exceptions to pick up votes; Brennan's concurrence suggests that the majority's dicta bought his vote. It seems doubtful that Rehnquist would necessarily vote to conduct review in all of these situations. For example, he dissented in *Dunlop*.

Brennan's concurring opinion in Chaney also listed nonenforcement for an entirely illegitimate reason (like taking a bribe) as an exception. He continued: "It may be presumed that Congress does not intend administrative agencies, agents of Congress' own creation, to ignore clear jurisdictional, regulatory, statutory or constitutional commands, and in some circumstances . . . the statutes or regulations at issue may well provide "law to apply."

See Cass R. Sunstein, "Reviewing Agency Inaction after *Heckler v. Chaney*," 52 U.Chi.L.Rev. 653, 675-82 (1985), which ranks the various possibilities left open in *Chaney* by their relative appropriateness for review.

Dunlop v. Bachowski, 421 U.S. 560 (1975), which is distinguished in *Chaney*, presents an alternative approach. The case concerned reviewability of the Secretary of Labor's decision not to challenge a union election. LMRDA provided that the Secretary "shall investigate" and if he finds probable cause "shall bring a civil action." This provided the congressional guidance needed to overcome the presumptive unreviewability of enforcement decisions. Nevertheless, all the *Dunlop* decision required was that the Secretary state reasons for not filing suit; a court could then evaluate whether the decision was arbitrary in light of those reasons.

Dunlop and *Chaney* seem at odds in their attitude toward reviewing enforcement discretion. True, *Dunlop* is a modest incursion on prosecutorial discretion; if the agency says that it investigated and failed to find evidence of law violations, review would be at an end. The *Dunlop* rule thus encourages an agency to be less than candid in its explanations. But one might argue that the Court should have required as least as much in the *Webster* situation as it did in *Dunlop*. If it had, the CIA would at least have been required to state reasons for a § 102(c) termination.

As to the seeming conflict between § 701(a)(2) and the nondelegation doctrine, Rehnquist might argue that a delegation of unfettered enforcement discretion is not an invalid delegation of power, because unlimited prosecutorial discretion has always been a feature of law enforcement (nobody expects that Congress has to "make the tough calls" about agency enforcement priorities). In contrast, standardless delegations of power to adopt rules that sweep widely throughout the national economy are a relatively recent and quite controversial development.

Chaney is an ironic illustration of the consequences of an unrestrained court of appeals decision. Clearly influenced by its opposition to capital punishment, the lower court argued unconvincingly that the FDA's decision was arbitrary. Actually, the FDA's decision that it would not get involved because there was no serious public health danger or a blatant scheme to defraud seems reasonable, as Justice Marshall observed. The lower court decision triggered a scathing dissent by Scalia (then on the D.C. Circuit), followed by a Supreme Court decision that rendered non-enforcement decisions almost completely unreviewable. Shades of *Vermont Yankee*!—in which anti-nuclear power manipulations by the D.C. Circuit led to a broad Supreme Court decision that erased judicial discretion to create procedural common law.

4. *Refusal to make a rule.* Is there a logical reason to distinguish an agency's rejection of a petition for rulemaking (reviewable) with its decision to refuse to take enforcement action (non-reviewable)? Compare the reasoning of *Michigan Academy,* § 10.4, allowing review of a rule even though review of individual claims was precluded. A refusal to commence rulemaking affects the interests of a class of people, and thus probably involves higher stakes than a refusal to bring enforcement action in an individual matter.

In *Massachusetts* and in *NRDC v. SEC,* §6.3 N.1, the court stated that the standard of review in such a case is exceptionally narrow. This makes sense: a decision not to regulate may be based on unavailability of budgetary and human resources (and competing claims on those resources), an agency's evaluation of its own competence, its decision about whether the time is right to make a rule (or whether the situation is changing too rapidly to do so), and similar concerns that are not susceptible to judicial second-guessing.

Yet despite the Court's protestations to the contrary, the decision in *Massachusetts* did not seem deferential at all. Primarily, the Court held that the agency committed a legal error in finding that it lacked jurisdiction to deal with greenhouse gases. But the Court also said that various prudential concerns cited by the agency could not be taken into account in refusing to adopt a rule, even though statute left rulemaking to EPA's "judgment." For example, the agency came forth with a "laundry list of reasons not to regulate," such as that other executive branch initiatives were responding to the threat of global warming, that a rule would impair the President's ability to negotiate with other nations, or that there was scientific uncertainty about the causes of climate change. The Court held that none of these were permissible reasons to refuse to regulate. The dissenting opinion urged strongly that these were wholly legitimate reasons for EPA not to adopt a greenhouse gas rule. For discussion of these competing positions, see § 6.3 NN.1-2 in this manual.

5. *Agency inaction and rights of initiation.* Whether the Court is serious about the various loopholes it seemed to open up in *Chaney* is open to doubt. These might have been written just to attract Justice Brennan's vote. Be that as it may, however, courts have by and large taken advantage of these loopholes to allow review despite *Chaney*.

An exception is *Crowley Caribbean*, which states that reviewing courts won't carve out a reviewable legal issue when it arises in the context of an agency decision not to enforce. That case is supported by *Brotherhood of Locomotive Engineers* to the extent that the latter makes clear that the presence of a legal issue does not necessarily render an otherwise unreviewable action reviewable. However, *Chaney* does say that a decision not to enforce is only presumptively unreviewable, and the availability of "law to apply" overcomes the presumption. It is unclear that this exception should not apply when the "law" in question relates to the substance of the agency's authority as opposed to the scope of its enforcement discretion. *Crowley* defended its limitation largely on the basis that a court may have trouble isolating a legal issue when it arises in the context of an ad hoc nonenforcement decision. That may be an obstacle in some instances, but not necessarily in all of them.

See also Ashutosh Bhagwat, "Three-Branch Monte," 72 Notre Dame L.Rev. 157 (1996). Bhagwat criticizes *Chaney* (or at least the post-*Chaney* case law) for encouraging agencies to make policy through exercising case-by-case enforcement discretion (unreviewable decisions) instead of rules (reviewable decisions). He also criticizes the enforcement/non-enforcement dichotomy of *Chaney* on legal realist grounds, because a non-enforcement policy is equivalent to a rule that the conduct involved should not be regulated.

Clients should not neglect political techniques for obtaining their goals, such as publicity of agency inaction, letter-writing campaigns, attempts to stimulate newspaper editorials, street demonstrations, campaign contributions, and attempts to find sympathetic legislators to prod the agency into action or to carry new legislation.

For discussion of private rights of initiation before the agency and private rights of action in court, see Richard Stewart & Cass Sunstein, "Public Programs and Private Rights," 95 Harv.L.Rev. 1195 (1982) and discussion in text and manual at § 11.2.4. Sunstein's article, 52 U.Chi.L.Rev. 653 (1985), observes that *Chaney* is consistent with *Chevron* and *Vermont Yankee* in reflecting mistrust by the Supreme Court of aggressive judicial review of discretionary decisions. (Yet *Massachusetts v. EPA, State Farm*, § 9.4, and *Industrial Union*, § 7.2.1, point the opposite way.) Sunstein argues that judicial review of agency inaction reflects our awareness that beneficiaries of statutes should be entitled to protection as much as regulated parties. He contends that an agency should be allowed to allocate scarce resources but not refuse to carry out a law. He argues that there are few alternative remedies for beneficiaries of statutes if the agency will not enforce the law, and that sophisticated courts can review inaction without unduly interfering with agency resource allocations.

6. *State law.* The Illinois decisions provide apt illustrations of the cross-currents here: concern with embroiling the courts in review of standardless individualized decisions (denying parole) while wanting to retain judicial controls over decisions that involve significant public policy and a lot of people (financing large low-income housing projects that could turn into urban ghettos). In the housing case, the court ignored the fact that the statute had used language evidencing commitment to discretion: "undue" income homogeneity and "judgment of the Authority." Perhaps in the parole case the court could have followed *Dunlop* and required the Board to state reasons for denying parole—and then reviewed the decision to assure that the reasons were appropriate (for example, a statement that the Board will never parole women convicted of killing abusive partners might be improper).

The 1981 MSAPA entitled a person who meets standing and timing requirements to judicial review of final agency action or inaction. §§ 1-102(2), 5-102. There is no exception for action committed to agency discretion. However, this omission could be explained by the fact that the Act did not provide for review of the merits of discretionary decisions. Instead, it bracketed a provision for arbitrary and capricious review, meaning that adoption of that provision is merely optional with the states. § 5-116(c)(8).

1981 MSAPA § 1-102(2)—especially clause (iii)—is explicit that various forms of inaction are reviewable. The comment explains that the broad definition of agency action is to assure that all such action is reviewable—but a narrow scope of review is relied on to discourage frivolous litigation rather than preclusion of whole classes of potential cases. Thus a court can review legal and procedural issues, but probably not the actual balancing of factors. The comment states that a provision for arbitrary/capricious review is bracketed to discourage courts from substituting their judgment for that of the agency as to wisdom or desirability of the agency action under review.

7. *Problem.* This problem asks whether beneficiaries of a statutory program have a right of initiation to compel the government to implement the program. In addition to *Markgraf*, see *Iowa v. Block*, 771 F.2d 347 (8th Cir.1985); *Allison v. Block*, 723 F.2d 631 (8th Cir.1983); *Shick v. FmHA*, 748 F.2d 35 (1st Cir. 1984). These cases held that the Secretary's refusal to implement § 19 is not committed to agency discretion. The legislative history shows that Congress wanted the Secretary to exercise this authority to help farmers in distress (otherwise how could the Secretary be "of greater service to farmers and the rural community?"). The use of the verb "may" was not addressed to the question of whether to implement the program—only to the question of whether to grant relief in individual cases. The fact that the borrower must request relief indicates only that Congress wanted the Secretary to act on a case-by-case basis.

How does this reasoning fit with *Chaney*? *Iowa v. Block* (which post-dates *Chaney*) emphasized the distinction between individualized failure to act and a generalized failure to implement the program. Indeed, FmHA's inaction could be an example of a general policy that abdicates statutory responsibilities—one of the exceptions articulated in note 4 of *Chaney*. *Cf. Roman v. Korson*, 918 F.Supp. 1108, 1112 (W.D.Mich.1995) (FmHA abdicated responsibility to enforce regulations restricting borrowers' ability to charge rent). Moreover, these courts thought that the legislative history showing that Congress intended that there be a program provided the "law to apply" that was lacking in *Chaney*. But see *Lincoln v. Vigil*, 508 U.S. 182, 192-93 (1993) (indicating that legislative history is not "law" in this sense).

Markgraf considered whether the court should defer to FmHA's interpretation of § 19 (that the program was purely permissive). The court brushed aside FmHA's legal interpretation, saying that an agency is entitled to little deference when it has never implemented its authority. This reasoning harmonizes with *Mead;* FmHA's interpretation does not merit

Chevron strong deference since it wasn't arrived at in the course of rulemaking or adjudication. *See* § 9.2.4.

Another issue here is whether FmHA's failure to implement § 19 is "agency action." Under *SUWA* (*see* § 10.6), this may be a necessary step in the analysis, since §706(1) provides for review of "agency action unlawfully withheld." *SUWA* held that the action in question must be one of the discrete items listed in § 551(13)—rule, order, license, sanction, relief or the equivalent or denial thereof. Presumably, Mary could petition for FmHA to adopt a rule about implementing § 19, which would bring the case under *Massachusetts v. EPA.* Or perhaps the failure is in connection with an agency "order" (that is, the foreclosure of the property). But the court might say that this is basically an agency management decision that *SUWA* renders unreviewable.

Assuming the decision not to implement § 19 is reviewable, and found to be unlawful, what relief should the court grant? *Markgraf* shied away from requiring FmHA to adopt regulations structuring its discretion. While FmHA should adopt standards to prevent arbitrary action, it could adopt them either in the course of rulemaking or case-by-case adjudication. *Allison* agreed with *Markgraf* on this point.

Markgraf upheld the judgment of foreclosure because Mary had not applied for relief. Cases in other circuits (*Shick, Allison*) disagreed. In *Markgraf,* Posner's dissent argued that the court should impose an obligation to notify the borrower about the availability of relief. Since FmHA has to notify the borrower that it is foreclosing the loan, there would be no additional burden from adding a sentence giving notice of the right to request relief. Without notice, it is unlikely the average farmer would know to ask for relief and thus Congressional purpose for § 19 would be frustrated. And the idea that everybody is presumed to know the law is an absurd legal fiction that breeds popular disrespect for law.

Suppose that Mary had requested relief and that FmHA had turned her down without giving an explanation. Note that § 19 does contain some standards (circumstances beyond control, temporary inability to make payments, payments would unduly impair standard of living). Thus there is law to apply. Alternatively, you might apply *Dunlop* and require a statement of reasons that the court could review. Or you might go further and require factual support for the reasons, as in *Overton Park.* (Note that this is not an enforcement decision but a decision to deny a benefit, which makes it distinguishable from *Chaney.*)

Another hypothetical variation: suppose the Secretary had written back to Mary refusing her relief on the ground that, in his view, the loan forgiveness program may be extended only to victims of natural disasters other than drought. Nothing on the face of the statute supports this. Even if there is no "law to apply" in reviewing individual denials of deferral, it might be possible to decide the legal issue. This raises the issue (dealt with in *Brotherhood of Locomotive Engineers* (text, N.1) and *Crowley*) of whether the court can decide a legal question embedded within an otherwise unreviewable exercise of individual discretion. But *Crowley* is not controlling, because this is not a "nonenforcement" case and there is "law to apply."

§10.6 AGENCY INACTION AND DELAY

NORTON v. SOUTHERN UTAH WILDERNESS ALLIANCE

SUWA should be set in context. It is part of a line of cases (including those cited in N.3 of the text) in which a majority of the Supreme Court relies on various justiciability rationales (particularly standing and timing doctrines) to keep federal courts from becoming entangled in essentially political disputes, particularly where the beneficiaries of a statutory scheme attempt to enforce it in court. *SUWA* relies on a narrow construction of the term "agency action" in the APA to achieve the same result.

SUWA and *Chaney* should be viewed as disputes over how an agency should allocate its highly limited human and budgetary resources. Even institutions as large as federal government agencies cannot do everything they might like to. They cannot investigate or prosecute every wrongdoer or enforce every command of every statute or regulation or spend the money needed to solve all of the problems they are supposed to be solving. Given that unavoidable reality, it is understandable that courts would be reluctant to compel an agency to reorder its priorities and allocate resources in a way differently than the agency heads have determined.

Adherents of the unitary executive theory believe that the politically accountable president, not the unaccountable courts, should manage the government and resolve resource allocation disputes like those involved in *Chaney* and *SUWA*. As Bressman points out, *SUWA* is about the struggle between the off-road user community and the environmental and wilderness community. The administration has come down on the side of the much more numerous ORV users and the Court does not wish to second-guess this essentially political call, despite the "non-impairment" mandate in the statute. Of course, the sharply split decision in *Massachusetts v. EPA* runs in the opposite direction and indicates that the law in this area remains unstable.

Notes and Questions

1. *Reviewability of an agency's failure to act.* The Court fails to give a persuasive reason for saying that "failure to act" means failure to take one of the five types of action listed in § 551(13). The only rationale is *ejusdem generis*—colloquially meaning "birds of a feather fly together." That is not a very persuasive reason for a construction that so sharply narrows judicial powers.

Araiza's article (cited in N.3 of the text) argues that this rather formalistic approach ignores the modern evolution of government regulation which often centers on supervision of ongoing relationships (such as management of public lands or supervision of capital markets) rather than taking discrete action such as rulemaking or adjudication. 56 Admin.L.Rev. at 983-85. He points out that the definition of "agency action" in APA § 551(13) "includes" the five types of discrete action, but it does not say "means" (as do several of the other definitional subsection of § 551) or "is limited to." The APA's use of the term "includes" implies that the named items are illustrative, not exclusive. The legislative history of § 551(13) states that the broad definition of "agency action" is designed to "Assure the complete coverage of every form of agency power, proceeding, action, or inaction." S. Rep. 752, p. 198, quoted in Araiza at 985 n.29. This legislative history seems to conflict with the limitation of "failure to act" to the five listed types of discrete agency action.

SUWA was applied to a subsequent case challenging NSA warrantless wiretapping of overseas communications. The court noted that this was not agency action as defined in *SUWA*, since it was agency conduct, but not one of the five discrete actions listed in § 551(13). *ACLU v. National Security Agency*, 493 F.3d 644, 678-79 (6th Cir.2007).

Araiza points out that if the BLM's non-regulation of ORVs were treated as agency action, it would be unclear whether the action was "final" as required by APA § 704, given that it was part of an ongoing scheme of regulatory decisionmaking. However, if BLM declined to take action against the ORVs over a lengthy period, its inaction might violate the "unreasonably delayed" prong of §706(1), discussed in N.2, which gets around the final agency action rule. 55 Admin.L.Rev. at 985-90. For discussion of finality, see § 11.2.2.

SUWA could also have been decided on a "commitment to agency discretion" rationale. The Court could have extended *Chaney* to treat the non-regulation of ORVs as discretionary enforcement decisions. Biber (also cited in N.3 of the text) discusses this possibility at length, pointing out that the boundaries of the *Chaney* doctrine are highly indeterminate. *Chaney* suggests that courts are primarily in the business of reviewing agency decisions that exercise coercive power over an individual's liberty or property rights, not those that decline to take action and thus disappoint beneficiaries of the statutory scheme. That approach could pretty well cancel out all review of agency inaction.

The text asks whether the result would change if SUWA had petitioned BLM to adopt a rule banning ORVs, and the BLM rejected the petition. That rejection would be "discrete," and it would also seem like "action" rather than "inaction." The distinction between "action" and "inaction" is less clear than it may seem. Indeed, BLM's actions in *SUWA* could be viewed as either action (allowing ORV use or rejecting a petition to prohibit such use) or inaction (failure to prohibit ORV use). The same is true of *Chaney*—FDA's decision could be seen as action (rejection of a petition) or inaction (refusal to get involved with capital punishment disputes). Since "action" is reviewed under §706(2), rather than 706(1), plaintiffs might be better off framing their case in action rather than inaction terms. Biber points out that the mandamus tradition never distinguished action from inaction; if a statute imposed a non-discretionary duty, the court would order the official to perform it whether this involved action or inaction.

2. *Administrative delay.* One problem in judicial review of administrative delay is that the APA restricts judicial review to "final agency action." APA § 704. Finality is discussed in § 11.2.2. Since "agency action" includes "agency inaction," review is available only for final agency inaction. But what is the significance of finality when the agency hasn't done anything but says it will get around to acting sometime? Perhaps the key is the determination required under APA §706(1) and *TRAC* that the delay is "unreasonable." Once delay passes from reasonable to unreasonable, it should be treated as "final" for judicial review purposes.

Delay cases can be divided into those that involve statutory deadlines (which are much more likely to trigger judicial relief) and those that don't. In the latter category, the decisions reflect great concern about protecting the agency's decisions about priorities and resource allocation. *See, e.g., Sierra Club v. Thomas*, 828 F.3d 783 (D.C.Cir.1987), refusing to require EPA to finalize a rulemaking relating to pollution caused by strip mining. The rulemaking had gone on for three years and only one year had passed since the comment period closed. The court thought it was better to give the agency enough time to get the rule right.

Similarly, *Oil, Chemical, & Atomic Workers Union v. OSHA*, 145 F.3d 120 (3d Cir.1998), refused to order OSHA to commence a rulemaking about lowering exposure limits to hexavalent chromium. The agency had repeatedly delayed the date of proposing a rule but the court respected its conflicting resource demands and credited the agency with at least working on the problem. In contrast, in *In re American Rivers and Idaho Rivers United*, 372 F.3d 412 (D.C.Cir.2004), FERC had delayed for six years in responding to a petition that it consult with the National Marine Fisheries Service about declining populations of anadromous fish caused by hydro projects. Stating that the agency claimed no excuses, and that a reasonable time to respond to a petition was measured in weeks or months, not years, the court ordered the agency to respond within 45 days.

For more on judicial review of administrative delay, see § 6.3 N.8.

3. *Judicial review of resource allocation disputes.* A court could probably design a remedy for BLM's apparent failure to enforce the non-impairment standard without entangling itself in the day-to-day management of public lands. It could retain jurisdiction to supervise the agency's progress or set a general timetable for action. Nevertheless, it is understandable that courts would not wish to take on the job of becoming permanent managers of the public lands with the responsibility for settling a maze of disputes between the many BLM constituencies in a multiple-use environment. Moreover, a precedent allowing courts to do so could soon be applied to all public lands disputes everywhere in the country.

Obviously, all judicial review decisions have resource allocation dimensions. A decision rejecting an agency rule requires the agency to start over at considerable opportunity cost and out-of-pocket expenditure of money and manpower, but courts don't hesitate to invalidate rules when otherwise appropriate. Here the agency has already committed resources to the rulemaking project, a fact that may alleviate a court's concern that the agency would have to allocate more of them to rectifying the problem. Yet it is instructive to distinguish between judicial action that interferes with an agency's choice of priorities and resource allocations, on the one hand, and judicial action to uphold congressional mandates, on the other.

Biber sets out a grid of the four possible relationships between resource allocations and statutory supremacy. 1) important questions both of resource allocation and statutory supremacy, 2) important questions of resource allocation but minimal questions of statutory supremacy, 3) minimal questions of resource allocation but important questions of statutory supremacy, 4) minimal questions of both resource allocation and statutory supremacy. Courts would be highly deferential in sector 2, highly non-deferential in sector 3. Categories 1 and 4 present difficult issues. Biber thinks courts will likely allow statutory supremacy to trump resource allocation in sector 1. Sector 4 will turn on other questions such as deference to expertise or accuracy of agency fact-finding.

This analytical framework may be useful in analyzing particular instances in which the resource allocation issue is presented. For example, since rules affect a large number of people, and there are relatively few rulemaking proceedings, courts should be willing to uphold statutory supremacy, despite resource implications, as in *Massachusetts v. EPA*. This is a category 3 case. The opposite is true in the situation of review of individual decisions whether to investigate a complaint or enforce the law. These are category 2 cases, like *Chaney*. In such cases, a great many matters could be investigated or prosecuted, each of them is highly case-specific, they are non-precedential, each affects only a particular individual, courts have difficulty assessing the reasonableness of the agency decision, and judicial interference could have a very large and negative impact on agency priorities.

One could defend the result in *SUWA* by saying that it is in category 2; the resource allocation and judicial management issues are very substantial. While there is a statutory mandate for non-impairment of WSAs, the same issue is presented in many different WSAs and the individual decisions by BLM are highly fact-based and non-precedential. Thus, even if SUWA had gotten around the discrete action and legally required hurdles, the refusal to regulate might have been treated as committed to agency discretion.

4. *Problem.* Following *SUWA*, this lawsuit would seek judicial review of agency inaction. The study is "legally required" under the Council's ordinance but there is an issue of whether the failure to start or complete the study is "agency action." The study is neither a rule, order, license, sanction, or relief, the types of discrete action mentioned in APA § 551(13). *SUWA* holds that the failure to take action that is not one of those forms of discrete action is not "agency action." Consequently, the APA judicial review provisions do not apply to it. As noted above, this holding is disputable, since § 551(13) uses the word "include," which might mean that the five types of action listed are not the only types of agency action. Similarly, it can be argued that the term "failure to act" in §551(13) is not intended to be limited to the five kinds of discrete action.

The problem might also be framed as a question of unreasonable delay under § 706(1) rather than inaction. It looks like the study is basically going to be deferred forever. However, the Council didn't set a date for the study to commence or be completed, so the court would have to deal with the *TRAC* factors, particularly the fact that human health is not involved. In addition, the case would encounter the same problem of agency action as if framed as a problem of inaction.

The problem brackets the issue of standing, which would indeed be a problem if federal standing law were applied, particularly the question of whether the failure to conduct the study is a cause of Gloria's economic difficulty (as opposed to basic trends in demography and real estate economics that are driving working class people out of the neighborhood). Moreover, an order to conduct the study is unlikely to remediate Gloria's injury in fact (*see* § 11.1.2). Who knows what the study will recommend? Perhaps nothing (especially since that would, no doubt, be what the mayor wants it to recommend). Even if the study recommended some form of mitigation, such as rent control or subsidies, such measures would be extremely controversial and might well not be enacted. If they were, they might not be enacted in time to do Gloria's family any good. Also there are substantial difficulties here with the final agency action rule (*see* § 11.2.2).

More fundamentally, the problem raises issues of priority setting and resource allocation which *SUWA, Chaney*, and numerous other cases caution the courts to stay away from. How the City spends its money and human resources is a highly political problem. Realistically, the ordinance calling for a study might have been intended to be meaningless; it's a traditional way for politicians to avoid dealing with a problem by sweeping it under the rug. There might be many studies ordered by the Council over the years that were never actually initiated or completed. The Department no doubt has many other ways to spend its scarce resources, and an order to conduct the study will pull resources away from those other uses.

On the other hand, the case seems distinguishable from *SUWA*, and more like *Massachusetts v. EPA.* Only a single discrete piece of government action is called for (conducting a study) as opposed to the ongoing management of public lands subject to multiple-use constraints (as in *SUWA*) or engaging in individualized enforcement action (as in *Chaney*). *SUWA* mentions the mandamus tradition; here the ordinance called for a study, and the court could easily mandate that one occur. The City Council has already made a judgment that the study is worth the resources that would be required to complete it. The court wouldn't have to worry about the outcome of the study, and it wouldn't have to compel the political elites in City to implement the results of the study.

This is a good chance to discuss some intensely practical law office management issues. Whether you should accept this piece of legal business depends largely on economic concerns. The chances of a favorable outcome are not too good, as discussed above, but the lawsuit would probably get a lot of media publicity. You would probably have to assume that your work will be pro bono. Do you want to work for free? You might, particularly if you're interested in the publicity that would accompany a victory or even fighting back against city hall. A lot depends on how busy you are; if you have nothing to do, working for free is better than not working at all. But there are a lot of possibilities if you want to work pro bono; is this the most attractive one? After all, if you win, all you get is a study. On the other hand, if the state has a private attorney general legal fee statute (as California does, see § 10.3), you could get paid if you win. You might get the case certified as a class action on behalf of all Kenwood low income renters, but this would only complicate the litigation and probably wouldn't help get you paid, since the lawsuit doesn't seek money damages and thus won't create a pot of money from which a fee could be paid.

CHAPTER 11

STANDING TO SEEK JUDICIAL REVIEW AND THE TIMING OF JUDICIAL REVIEW

§ 11.1 STANDING TO SEEK REVIEW

§ 11.1.1 Background and History of Standing Law

For an excellent history of American standing law, particularly the question of whether the injury in fact test is rooted in Article III, see Cass R. Sunstein, "What's Standing After *Lujan*?: Of Citizen Suits, 'Injuries,' and Article III," 91 Mich.L.Rev. 163 (1992). Another interesting historical and analytical article is William A. Fletcher, "The Structure of Standing," 98 Yale L.J. 221 (1988).

The "legal interest" or "legal wrong" test reflected a pre-New Deal philosophy of limited government. Absent legislative authorization that met all constitutional constraints, government could not infringe the liberty or the contract and property rights of citizens. When government did so, the aggrieved individual could seek judicial review, and the government could defend only by proving valid legislative authorization for its actions. The legal interest test worked fine in these situations. Richard B. Stewart, "The Reformation of American Administrative Law," 88 Harv.L.Rev. 1667, 1724 (1975). The test also served the purpose of the New Deal Court to keep conservative lower courts away from regulatory action taken by New Deal agencies.

The legal interest test was a poor way to decide who could challenge agency action. The test resolved one difficult question (who should have access to the courts?) by referring to an unrelated but often equally difficult one: could you spell out a right to sue at common law if the defendant had been a private party rather than the government? This forced courts to consider obscure tort or contract issues that had little to do with the actual issue in the case-the legality of government conduct. It also tended to limit standing to the objects of regulation as opposed to the beneficiaries of regulation.

An example of the contorted reasoning required by the legal interest test is *Joint Anti-Fascist Refugee Committee v. McGrath*, 341 U.S. 123, 140-41 (1951). This was a challenge to the Attorney General's blacklist of subversive organizations. Inclusion on the blacklist entailed no sanction for an organization, only for government employees who belonged to it. Thus standing of the organization was problematic. The court found that a charitable organization whose ability to carry on its work was detrimentally affected by a defendant's defamatory statements had a common law tort action. It followed that the organization could then sue the government—but not for defamation, only to claim that the blacklisting program was legally unauthorized or that its inclusion on the blacklist without notice or hearing violated due process. These issues had nothing to do with the common law defamation question.

The pre-1970 cases reflect judicial disinclination to resolve broad administrative and constitutional questions on the merits, as well as a genuine fear that a liberalization of standing would open the floodgates. After the trauma of the early 1930's, the Court was understandably reluctant to deal with constitutionality of the TVA. The result, however, was that nobody had standing to challenge the legality of the government's conduct in many cases. The legal interest test was ill-equipped to serve as a screen for cases that the Court wished to avoid on prudential grounds. Issues of whether someone should be able to obtain judicial review of government action are radically different from the merits of common law tort, property, or contract actions. A standing test that resolves the former by reference to the latter could never work, especially as the nation moved into an administrative state in which indirect harms from government action became common.

The pre-1970 standing cases frequently turned on statutory interpretation. When a statute indicated congressional intention to protect the plaintiff against a particular harm, the plaintiff had standing, notwithstanding the lack of a common law legal right. *Hardin v. Kentucky Utilities* (cited in the text); *Chicago Junction Case*, 264 U.S. 258 (1924). One problem with such cases is that the standing issue shades into the merits: was the government action illegal? However, standing and merits were not completely synonymous. In *Hardin*, after finding that Congress intended to protect competitors harmed by TVA expansion, the Court held that plaintiff was not protected against the particular competition in question. In *ADPSO*, § 11.1.3, Douglas rightly criticized the legal interest test (and by implication cases like *Hardin*) as going to the merits, without really resolving the merits.

The *Sanders Bros.* case was a critical breakthrough. It held that Congress has power to deputize a person to seek judicial review, even though that person's legal rights were not invaded and even though no statute conferred substantive protection on that person (because economic harm to a competitor, in itself, is not the basis for denial of a license). *Sanders* is thus distinguishable from *Hardin*, where Congress did intend to protect private utilities from a particular form of competition. An important Second Circuit case provides the generally accepted explanation of *Sanders*. *Associated Industries of N.Y. v. Ickes*, 134 F.2d 694 (2d Cir.), vacated as moot, 320 U.S. 707 (1943) (statute permitted consumers to challenge ratemaking decision as private attorneys general). Since the Attorney

General historically could sue to protect the public interest from illegal government action, Congress could deputize anyone else to function as a "private attorney general" to do the same thing.

§ 11.1.2 Constitutional Standing Doctrines

LUJAN v. DEFENDERS OF WILDLIFE

Notes and Questions

1. *Injury in fact.* Nichol points out that "injury in fact" is a question-begging judicial construct. As presently administered, the injury requirement reads the judge's value scheme into the Constitution. Outrage about possible extinction of a species can be an "injury in fact" if we want it to be. Gene R. Nichol, Jr., "Justice Scalia, Standing, and Public Law Litigation," 42 Duke L.J. 1141, 1154-60 (1993). Similarly, see Sunstein, cited in the preceding section, 91 Mich.L.Rev. at 186-93.

Skilbred and Kelly wanted to observe animals, and their loss of the ability to do so could potentially satisfy Article III's injury in fact test. The Court had previously so held in *Japan Whaling Society v. American Cetacean Society*, 478 U.S. 221 (1986): "whale watching and studying of their members would be adversely affected by continued whale harvesting." The Court makes clear at the beginning of Part III.A. of the *Defenders* opinion that it accepts this premise. So the problem in *Defenders* is not that the loss of opportunity to observe the creatures isn't injury in fact; the problem is "imminence" of that injury.

Defenders suggests that Skilbred and Kelly need definite plans for their trip to observe the endangered species to satisfy the "imminence" requirement. It's hard to believe this degree of definiteness of plans is really required as a matter of constitutional law. In *ADPSO,* § 11.1.3, which launched the modern standing era, Douglas seemed to contemplate a simple, fact-based analysis of injury in fact—not a minefield like the one the Court has constructed. Indeed, the plaintiff's injury in *Data Processing* seems no less conjectural than the one in *Defenders.* For criticism, see Sunstein, 91 Mich.L.Rev. at 202-06.

The requirement of "imminence" as applied in *Defenders* embroils courts in a difficult and seemingly tangential issue and requires the expenditure of substantial litigation and judicial resources. Thus it's hard to reconcile *Baur* (cited in this note) with *Defenders*, given the court's premise that mad-cow disease had never entered the United States.

In *Laidlaw*, discussed below at N.4, the injury and imminence tests were applied more leniently to persons who refrained from using a polluted river (and who were backed by a citizen suit statute); Scalia dissented strongly. Similarly, see *Animal Legal Def. Fund v. Espy*, 23 F.3d 496 (D.C.Cir.1994), in which there's a 2-1 split on the question of whether the injury to an animal researcher arising out of the government's failure to include rats in its rule requiring humane experimental treatment of animals is sufficiently "imminent." To Judge Williams, who dissented, the allegation that an established researcher plans to return to research (lest she sacrifice the human capital accumulated in the past) meets the imminence requirement, but the majority sees it as "speculative," since she can't say when she will return to doing such research. It is difficult to believe that this kind of hair-splitting could really be determinative of whether the plaintiff presents a case or controversy under Article III.

Refreshingly different is *Students for the Ethical Treatment of Animals v. Institutional Animal Care & Use Committee*, 833 P.2d 337 (Ore.App.1992), which holds that persons interested in preventing cruelty to animals have standing as "persons affected" to challenge a meeting approving animal experimentation under the Oregon Open Meeting Act. The court said: "Defendants argue that plaintiffs must show a 'palpable' impact by a governmental decision and that plaintiffs here have shown only an 'enthusiastic' and 'political' interest. . . . It is often precisely because a person's interest is 'enthusiastic' and 'political' that access is most important."

Article III standing issues continue to generate 5-4 splits on the Supreme Court. In *Sprint Communications Co. v. APCC Services,* Inc., 128 S.Ct. 2531 (2008), the issue was whether an assignee for collection of claims by payphone operators against long distance carriers could sue to collect the claims. The payphone operators assigned 100% of their claims to APCC. APCC was contractually required to pay over all recoveries to the pay phone operators and was compensated by a fee for its services. The problem was that the assignees had no injury in fact and would keep none of the amounts recovered. Breyer's majority opinion documented that assignees for collection have long been entitled to bring suit, and he could find no reason to depart from that historic practice. Four Justices dissented, arguing that the assignees could not meet the Article III injury in fact requirement, because they had nothing to gain from their lawsuit and thus no personal stake in the litigation. A reader can be pardoned for marveling at the ferocity of this dispute, given that the contract between assignors and assignees could be easily modified to give the assignees a small percentage of the recovery.

2. *Associations as plaintiffs.* The free rider and transaction cost phenomena provide an urgent reason to allow standing to ideological associations. It does not pay for a single aggrieved person (like a single

animal lover) to incur the financial and emotional costs and risks of bringing a lawsuit. Few persons voluntarily contribute to the cost of someone else's lawsuit, because they stand to benefit from a victory whether they have contributed or not (the free rider effect). Finally, the transaction costs of organizing a group of persons to bring the lawsuit could be prohibitive.

Thus the best plaintiffs in both private and public actions are pre-existing associations composed of persons who are interested in the problem, such as a trade association (as in *ADPSO*) or an existing environmental pressure group (like Defenders of Wildlife). Since the group is already in place, there are no transaction costs of organizing it. The free rider effect is overcome; the members feel that it is worthwhile to pay dues—which cover a variety of activities, not just bringing lawsuits—since they get a psychic or pecuniary benefit from membership which exceeds the cost.

Equally important, an association with a track record of dealing with a problem acquires a skilled and experienced staff or can attract skilled pro bono lawyers. Such organizations have expertise and staying power. In short, there is a better chance that it will litigate skillfully and tenaciously than in the case of a solo plaintiff who may run out of resources or feel great pressure to settle.

The first and possibly the second prongs of *Washington Apple* are constitutional in nature, but the third prong is prudential and can be overridden by statute. *United Food & Commercial Workers Union v. Brown Group, Inc.*, 517 U.S. 544 (1996).

Oregon rejected organizational standing in *Local 290 v. Oregon Dep't of Environmental Quality*, 919 P.2d 1168 (Or. 1996). The Oregon APA allows standing to persons who are "aggrieved" or "adversely affected" but says nothing about associational standing. The court did not look beyond the language of the statute or refer to policy considerations, federal cases, or the law of other states. The large number of amicus briefs filed in the case could not have failed to alert the court to federal and state authority supporting associational standing under statutes like the Oregon APA, but for whatever reason the court studiously ignored the issue. This seems surprising, considering the fact that Oregon has often been a leader in the development of state administrative law. *See, e.g., Students for the Ethical Treatment of Animals*, cited just above; *Megdal* (and other Oregon cases), § 6.2 N.7; and *McPherson*, § 9.2.1 N.4.

3. *Public actions. Sierra Club v. Morton* raises a fundamental policy question that underlies the entire debate about constitutional standing requirements. The policy issue is why ideologically motivated plaintiffs should be precluded from bringing public actions against allegedly illegal government action unless they also make a showing of a concrete "case or

controversy." If they are outraged by the government action, why isn't that enough?. The answer cannot be that they are less likely than other plaintiffs to provide a well financed, highly adversary presentation. These cases are typically brought by sophisticated associations with excellent legal talent and plenty of staying power. In *Flast*, discussed in N.8, the Court stated that the injury in fact test would weed out unsuitable plaintiffs, but this fallacious theory has been abandoned.

Nor is the floodgates argument persuasive. It is so expensive to carry this sort of litigation to the final appeal that only a few highly determined and solidly financed plaintiffs can attempt it (especially if there is no provision for recovery of attorneys' fees). State courts are not flooded with taxpayer actions (see below), and when Congress has expanded the right of persons to bring public actions, there has been no sign of open floodgates.

It's true that public actions can create difficult remedial problems, but it seems wrong to avoid them through the use of a broadly preclusive set of standing rules that knocks out cases in which there are no remedial difficulties. In *Defenders,* for example, there would be no great remedial problem in invalidating the regulation and telling Interior that the consultation requirement applies to funding actions outside the United States.

The result of the rule barring ideological plaintiffs is that many constitutional and legal issues cannot be brought to court by anyone, because nobody has the requisite concrete and particularized injury (or nobody can meet the causation and redressability requirements discussed below). Such issues have to be resolved within the legislative and executive branches—if they are addressed at all. The use of standing doctrine to vindicate other concerns, such as separation of powers, has seriously overloaded the doctrine and produced confusing, disordered law. *See* Gene R. Nichol, Jr., "Rethinking Standing," 72 Cal.L.Rev. 68, 87-88, 98-101 (1984).

The separation of powers argument in favor of turning away ideological plaintiffs is often based on a historical analogy. The framers rejected a role for the courts as a Council of Revision that would take part in the legislative enactment process. Would the federal courts become a council of revision if outraged plaintiffs can make them decide public actions? Nichol, *id.* at 93-94, criticizes this analogy. The Council was to take part in the enactment process rather than review already-enacted laws, was to be concerned with wisdom as well as constitutionality, and was rejected in order to protect the later judicial review function from potential conflict by the judges who had approved the law before enactment.

Sometimes, the separation of powers argument is based on the idea that wide-ranging judicial intervention interferes with the President's responsibility "to take care that the laws be faithfully executed." Const. Art. II, § 3, cl.4. Yet this seems circular; if agency action is illegal, the laws are not being faithfully executed. Carried to the extreme, this argument would undermine all judicial review of executive action.

Another separation of powers argument is based on the undemocratic nature of courts. Judicial review is needed, on this account, to protect individual rights or minorities victimized by illegal action, whereas it is not needed for protection of groups who can resort to political approaches to vindicate their interests. Judicial protection of large or even majority interests is both more anti-democratic and less necessary than judicial protection of minority interests. Antonin Scalia, "The Doctrine of Standing as an Essential Element of the Separation of Power," 17 Suffolk U.L.Rev. 881, 894 (1983).

In his dissent in *Akins*, discussed in N. 8, Scalia reiterated these themes. He concluded: "If today's decision is correct, it is within the power of Congress to authorize any interested person to manage (through the courts) the Executive's enforcement of any law that includes a requirement for the filing and public availability of a piece of paper. This is not the system we have had, and it is not the system we should desire."

As the text notes, many states (in addition to California) permit public actions either because of the importance of the issue or because the plaintiff is an appropriate choice to litigate them. *See* John DiManno, Note, "Beyond Taxpayers' Suits: Public Interest Standing in the States, 41 Conn.L.Rev. 639 (2008) (discussing law in New Mexico, Ohio, Utah, and Alaska). On the other hand, some states, including Texas, follow the Florida approach that applies federal law banning public interest litigation. William V. Dorsaneo, "The Enigma of Standing Doctrine in Texas Courts," 28 Rev.Litig. 35 (2008).

For a comparative slant, see Matt Handley, Comment, "Why Crocodiles, Elephants, and American Citizens Should Prefer Foreign Courts: A Comparative Analysis of Standing to Sue," 21 Rev.Litig. 97 (2002) (environmental standing in Italian and Brazilian law); James H. Wilson III, Comment, "Opening the Door, Not the Floodgates: An Adaptation of Canadian Standing Criteria to Citizen or Taxpayer Suits in the United States," 26 Emory L.J. 185 (1977) (Canadian decisions allow citizen standing in constitutional cases).

Incidently, none of the other Justices accepted Douglas's argument in *Sierra Club* that trees should have standing, despite a famous article so urging. Christopher Stone, "Do Trees Have Standing?—Toward Legal Rights for Natural Objects," 45 S.Cal.L.Rev. 450 (1972). Surprisingly, however, the Ninth Circuit has held that animals *could* have standing to sue if a statute provided for it. (Of course, they'd need a human guardian ad litem to do the legal work for them, as would the trees.) Unfortunately for them, however, the word "person" in the Endangered Species Act and in APA § 702 refers only to human beings. *Cetacean Community v. Bush*, 386 F.3d 1169 (9th Cir.2004). This decision points the way for Congress get around *Defenders* by opening the courts to endangered creatures. All it needs to do is to pass a statute granting them the right to sue. This would certainly lead to an interesting Supreme Court decision.

4. *Causation and redressability*. In *Defenders*, four Justices saw a problem with redressability; three did not; two did not address the issue. So *Defenders* really isn't a precedent on causation and redressability. Still, it is typical of a large number of similar decisions, so it can be used to analyze those doctrines. *Defenders* and *Wrestling* make a nice contrast with *Massachusetts,* discussed in text N.5. The causation/redressability cases frequently involve choices by third parties who are not before the court; the decisions often say that the plaintiff's injury isn't "fairly traceable" to the government's action; the third party caused the problem. And a change in the government's position wouldn't be likely to solve plaintiff's problem either—the third party might not cooperate.

In *Friends of the Earth, Inc. v. Laidlaw Environmental Services, Inc.,* 528 U.S. 167, 180-88 (2000), the Court applied the redressability requirement in a decidedly relaxed fashion. Members of FOE suffered injury in fact from river pollution (although those allegations seemed weak and speculative; as Scalia argued in dissent, they seem to fall short of what is required by the imminence discussion in *Defenders*).

FOE sued a polluter for civil penalties that would be paid to the government. How could such penalties remedy the plaintiffs' injury from pollution? Plaintiff survived the redressability hurdle by arguing that the prospect of paying civil penalties deters dischargers from violating their NPDES permits, thereby making it likely that the river-users' injury will be remedied. The decision is by a 7-2 vote. One possible explanation for the liberality of this decision is that the Court, although using the language of standing, was addressing a problem that has traditionally been analyzed in terms of mootness, which has often been applied flexibly and leniently (think, for example, of the "capable of repetition but evading review" exception). Unsurprisingly, however, Justices Scalia and Thomas dissented.

If the Court were to decide to extrapolate from *Laidlaw*, however, it could allow a public interest plaintiff to satisfy the causation requirement by demonstrating that the illegal conduct *could well be* the cause of the injury in fact (or is at least one cause among others). Similarly, plaintiff could meet the redressability requirement if removing the illegal government conduct would reduce the risk that the injury in fact would occur. (In other words, "betters the odds," to use the language in the *Wrestling* case). If the model of the procedural injury cases were followed (see N.6), it would be easy to get around the causation and redressability problems, because in those cases the mere likelihood that compliance with procedural requirements might help the injured plaintiff is sufficient to secure standing. Procedural and substantive injuries would be treated the same for this purpose.

5. *The global warming case—Massachusetts v. EPA.* The resolution of the standing issues in the *Massachusetts* case is surprising. This is just the sort of case that the conservative Justices abhor. In this case, environmentalists are forcing government to regulate what it doesn't want to regulate. The decision interferes with the political process and with international relations. It is far from clear whether the benefits from regulating greenhouse gas emissions from American cars will outweigh the costs of doing so. Yet Justice Kennedy swung over to the majority and joined the four liberal Justices.

It is unclear why, or even whether, Massachusetts had a better standing case than (say) a private coastal landowner. Some speculate that Justice Stevens emphasized this approach to attract the vote of Justice Kennedy, who is a strong believer in state sovereignty. The dictum in the majority opinion suggests a parens patriae theory. "It is of considerable relevance that the party seeking review here is a sovereign State and not . . .a private individual." The Court relied on the ancient case of *Georgia v. Tennessee Copper Co.*, cited in the text, which in rather poetical language seems to give states a quasi-sovereign status in protecting natural resources on behalf of its citizens.

Yet, when the Court turned to the specific facts of the Massachusetts case, it didn't rely squarely on the theory the state had the ability to sue to protect its citizens from ills such as global warming. It said that Massachusetts had standing because of injury from rising sea waters to coastal properties that the state itself owns. A private landowner, it would seem, could have made the same argument. Nevertheless, the dicta in the Court's opinion probably insure that many future environmental cases attacking federal inaction will be brought by states. *See generally* Bradford Mank, "Should States Have Greater Standing Rights than Ordinary Citizens?" 49 Wm.& Mary L.Rev. 1701 (2008) (arguing that standing rules should be relaxed for state plaintiffs); Daniel A. Farber, "A Place-Based Theory of Standing," 55 UCLA L.Rev. 1505 (2008) (arguing that a plaintiff should have standing to contest environmental violations involving specific geographical areas with which the plaintiff has an appropriate personal connection— and a state would have the strongest possible connection). The Administrative & Regulatory Law News (published by the ABA Administrative Law Section) has a set of articles about the *Massachusetts* case in its Spring 2009 issue.

On the issues of injury in fact, imminence, particularized harm, causation, and redressability, *Massachusetts* strikes many observers as out of line with *Defenders* and numerous other Supreme Court cases, as well as lower court cases like *Wrestling*. Many suspect that the majority Justices were annoyed by actions of the Bush administration in avoiding action on the climate change issue (effectively publicized in Al Gore's documentary "An Inconvenient Truth"). Others speculate that the Court was disturbed by the Bush administration's rather cavalier attitudes toward science. Whether cases like *Massachusetts* and *Laidlaw* really portend a sharp change in direction on standing issues simply cannot be predicted at this time, given the closeness of the Court's decision on these issues and the unpredictability of Justice Kennedy's vote.

6. *Procedural injuries.* The Court pretty much had to make the concession it did in footnote 7, since there is never any guarantee that a procedural right will achieve the required substantive result. For example, most people who have been deprived of liberty or property without a hearing cannot show that they would "likely" have done better if they had been heard more fully; yet they have standing to complain that the hearing should have been granted. Same thing for someone complaining that a rule has been adopted without the required advance notice and comment. Thus a contrary ruling on this point would have abolished a good part of administrative law.

The Court distinguished the *Defenders* case from other procedural injury situations, because the plaintiffs' claim that they had a right to have the Secretary consult with AID is "an abstract, self-contained, noninstrumental 'right' to have the Executive observe the procedures required by law." Thus their claim is unlike that of the person who will be injured by having a dam constructed next door. In other words, a procedural injury claim can avoid strict causation and redressability requirements with respect to the effect of the procedure, but it does not dispense with the need to prove injury in fact. *Summers*, discussed in N.8 below, strongly reaffirms these teachings. However, that injury might be one that is defined by the statute creating the procedural obligation on government—not necessarily one that would have existed in the absence of the statute.

The procedural injury doctrine is well illustrated by cases involving plaintiffs who complain about the failure of agencies to file environmental impact statements. *See City of Dania Beach v. FAA*, 485 F.3d 1181 (D.C.Cir.2007); *Florida Audubon Society v. Bentsen*, 94 F.3d 658 (D.C.Cir.1996). These cases require plaintiffs to establish that the agency's failure to follow the procedure will cause a distinct risk to a particularized interest of the plaintiff, such as the risk that an aircraft runway built near their homes will cause harmful noise and air pollution. The imminence, causation and redressability requirements are satisfied by a showing of the connection between the agency action and the alleged injury (but plaintiff does not have to show that if the procedure had been provided, the substantive result would have been altered).

7. *Citizen suit provisions.* On the separation of powers issue, *see* Cass R. Sunstein, "What's Standing After *Lujan?* Of Citizen Suits, 'Injuries,' and Article III," 91 Mich.L.Rev. 163 (1992). Sunstein indicates that, aside from *Chadha, Defenders of Wildlife* may have invalidated more Congressional statutes than any other Supreme Court decision, so common are citizen suit provisions. He critiques a 1983 Scalia article that set forth the principle eventually adopted in *Defenders. Id.* at 165, 193, 209-23.

The ban on citizen suit provisions is not supported by the array of cases holding that no person has standing to enforce generally applicable constitutional provisions (such as the requirement that the CIA publish a budget or that members of the military not be members of Congress). In effect, these cases simply refuse to spell out private rights of action from the constitutional provisions in issue.

We believe that citizen suit provisions are different. When it enacts a citizen suit provision, Congress has demonstrated a desire to delegate enforcement of environmental statutes to citizens generally. The separation of powers is strengthened, not weakened, by allowing Congress to create its own enforcement mechanism. The "Take Care" clause of the Constitution surely implies that the executive has to be faithful to statutes. The majoritarian process is frustrated when the executive deliberately underenforces a statute, and the Court invalidates the enforcement mechanism Congress itself put in place.

For a contrary view, see Marshall Breger, "Defending *Defenders*: Remarks on Nichol & Pierce," 42 Duke L.J. 1202 (1993). Breger argues that Congress can confer standing only on persons injured in fact in order to prevent a large amount of judicial policymaking and, potentially, limitations on the rights of individuals. For example, he hypothesizes, Congress could enact a national set of rules for notification and consent before getting an abortion and give any person the right to sue to vindicate the statute. That would allow anti-abortion groups to litigate any abortion in the country. *Id.* at 1208.

Another article questioning citizen suit statutes rests on separation of powers themes. *See* Harold J. Krent & Ethan G. Shenkman, "Of Citizen Suits and Citizen Sunstein," 91 Mich.L.Rev. 1793 (1993). The authors view these provisions as illegitimate vehicles by which Congress teams up with private interest groups to usurp the executive branch's authority to enforce the laws. This detracts from coordination, discretion, and especially accountability in the implementation of the laws. Thus private citizens should be able to sue only if they can show individuated harm to themselves (i.e., injury in fact).

By way of contrast, California upheld a citizen suit provision that had been enacted by the voters in an initiative measure. The court held that the requirements of causation and redressability do not apply under state law. The citizen suit provision allowed any person to sue any business that exposed the public to toxic chemicals without furnishing the public with a clear warning. *National Paint & Coatings Ass'n v. State*, 68 Cal.Rptr.2d 360 (Ct.App.1997). The Attorney General can also sue under this provision, Businesses complain they have been harassed by citizen suits when the Attorney General decides not to sue. The decision is unsurprising in light of the fact that California is quite tolerant of both public interest citizen suits and taxpayer suits.

8. *Legislatively created interests.* In light of the Kennedy-Souter concurrence in *Defenders,* the real issue is what Congress has to do to create a legal interest that could be vindicated by a citizen suit. *See, e.g,, Trafficante v. Metropolitan Life*, 409 U.S. 205 (recognizing that whites have standing to vindicate an interest created by statute in interracial association). *Akins* can also be placed in this category—Congress creates a legal interest to information that can be vindicated by any citizen who claims he needs that information.

Why should it be essential for Congress, in Kennedy's words, to "identify the injury it seeks to vindicate and relate the injury to the class of persons entitled to bring suit?" *See* Richard J. Pierce, Jr., "*Lujan v. Defenders of Wildlife*: Standing as a Judicially Imposed Limit on Legislative Power," 42 Duke L.J. 1170, 1181 (1993). Pierce argues that the Kennedy-Souter opinion employs a peculiar form of strict scrutiny. Normally in constitutional adjudication (aside from cases involving fundamental rights or suspect classes), Congress is not required to spell out findings and reasons. If it is possible to spell out a theory on which Congress could have justified the citizen suit provision (such as "ecosystem nexus"), Pierce contends, that should be sufficient.

Kennedy might respond that Congress has to spell this out so that the court will have a more precise sense of what the suit is about. If the court knows that the basis for Ms. Skilbred's suit is her congressionally recognized interest in viewing leopards in Sri Lanka, it can weigh that interest against whatever grounds the agency may cite for its action. Framing the issue in that light may, in Kennedy's mind, be more meaningful than merely knowing that the suit is brought to protect endangered species in foreign lands. Of course, the concurrence's perspective rests on the controversial premise that the role of judicial review as part of the checks and balances system of government is basically incidental to its role in resolving narrowly defined disputes between an individual and the government.

Here's a query that you might use to test the limits of the Kennedy-Souter theory. If, under *Akins, Public Citizen*, and like cases, Congress can confer on everyone a right to receive government information (as under FOIA) and to attend government meetings (as under FACA or the Sunshine Act), and thereby create standing to enforce these rights, can it also confer an individualized right to submit comments in a rulemaking proceeding and have those comments seriously considered—and then make that right enforceable even by people who have no other concrete interest in the subject matter of the rule? The ABA Administrative Law Section suggested a few years ago that this was at least an open issue, but its viability would depend in the first instance on whether Congress decided to take that step, or on whether statutes like APA § 553 were construed as having already done so. The Section said that such a statutory provision would be distinguishable from the consultation provision that *Defenders* said was insufficient for standing (i.e., the provision requiring the Secretary of the Interior to consult with other officials), because the latter provision did not even purport to confer on citizens any individualized right of participation in or access to government functions. ABA Section of Administrative Law and Regulatory Practice, "A Blackletter Statement of Federal Administrative Law," 54 Admin.L.Rev. 1, 54-55 (2002).

This is an interesting theory, but *Summers*, summarized in N.2, has subsequently come very close to rejecting it. The Court treated the plaintiffs' claim to standing based on an asserted right to file comments on Forest Service actions as squarely controlled by *Defenders*: "deprivation of a procedural right without some concrete interest that is affected by the deprivation—a procedural right *in vacuo*—is insufficient to create Article III standing [even if] the procedural right has been conferred by Congress." 129 S.Ct. at 1151. Kennedy wrote a concurrence to say specifically that he agreed. *Summers* does not technically dispose of the Section's argument, because it arose under Forest Service regulations, not the APA. It seems reasonable to assume, however, that any future for that argument will require a substantial turnover in the composition of the Court.

9. *Taxpayer actions.* You might wonder how the Court in *Hein* could possibly have justified saying that a taxpayer has standing to challenge religiously-motivated expenditures if they are authorized by Congress (*Flast*), but not if they are authorized by the executive branch. The answer is—it didn't even try. Justice Alito's opinion basically said that this case involved the latter situation, and he did not need to go any further. The implication was that the Court might well overrule *Flast* if it were to

encounter a case that squarely presented that issue. Of course, whether this would actually happen would depend on the composition of the Court at the time of such a case.

10. *Problem.* ET is injured in fact—its application for a grant has been turned down. The company could certainly put the money to good use, regardless of whether it will be able to stimulate a successful development drive. ET also easily meets the zone of interest test discussed in § 11.1.3 (surely potential grantees are within the zone of interests the agency is supposed to be protecting). Its injury is particularized, concrete and imminent. But how about causation and redressability?

As far as causation goes, ET's injury may not be "fairly traceable" to MFA's decision. On the merits, ET's argument presumably is not that it was itself entitled to a grant, but rather that the award to Dinner was impermissible. (That is, the award was not only tainted by favoritism, but also a misapplication of the regulations, because Dinner is far from being a start-up organization.) ET can also argue that if Dinner had been denied a grant, ET would have been likely to receive one, because of the regulation requiring equitable geographic distribution. However, this is speculative at best. ET's application might have been denied anyway, because of MAF's doubts about the company's financial viability.

Similarly, ET's injury may not be redressable by the court. Even if Dinner were knocked out of contention for the future, ET would not necessarily be better off. Dinner seems well established and will probably continue to exist even without additional grants. MAF staff has stated that Elm cannot support another theater company (particularly one presenting unknown plays, as opposed to the fluff that Dinner is presenting). So it seems unlikely that ET will get a grant, no matter what happens to Dinner's grant. There are no doubt many competing applicants for theatrical grants. The money might instead go to another theater fifteen miles away. However, it is possible that the region has no other theaters, and that if Dinner were excluded from the competition MFA would feel compelled to fund ET in order to comply with its mandate to spread grants across the state. If this is the case, ET should allege it with particularity.

Under the Supreme Court's rulings, the pleadings must set forth a plausible, non-conjectural causation chain and present substantial assurances of redressability. At the summary judgment stage, ET must be prepared to support the factual assertions of the complaint with solid affidavits.

You might want to spin this problem further if you've covered zone of interest—the subject of the next subchapter. Or you can return to the problem after teaching zone of interest if you like this problem better than the one in § 11.1.3. This possibility is particularly relevant to the case of Nate, the lawyer, if he were serving as the plaintiff.

Nate's injury is that he is deprived of a product (avant garde theater) that he wants to purchase. This might well be an injury of the sort accepted in *United Church of Christ* (exposure to racist TV programming, denial of racially balanced programming), or an environmental or a consumer one. Does it meet the test of concreteness? Yes. He personally is denied avant garde theater, which he personally would patronize. Does it meet the test of particularity? Yes, the injury is limited to residents of Elm who like avant garde theater and who plan to purchase tickets for it.

But Nate has the same causation and redressability problems that ET has. And he has a zone of interests problem. The statutory provisions in question (which are not quoted in the problem and are probably just sketchy provisions setting up MAF and appropriating funds for it) might require the agency to consider only organizations seeking funds, not the needs of ticket buyers.

According to *Clarke*, the zone test denies a right of review if the plaintiff's interests are "so marginally related to or inconsistent with the purposes implicit in the statute that it cannot reasonably be assumed that Congress intended to permit the suit." It would seem that a cultural consumer should be able to satisfy this test fairly easily. Yet other cases, like *Air Courier,* seem to demand affirmative evidence that the legislature wanted to benefit the class in question. To a contracts teacher, this sounds like the test for whether someone is an intended (as opposed to a merely incidental) third party beneficiary of a contract and thus entitled to enforce the contract. Nate would have to consult the legislative history to see whether the legislature displayed concern for consumers of the arts.

Another possibility is a taxpayer action, which is permitted under the law of many states (though not federal law). This case seems to involve abuse of discretion more than an illegal appropriation (as in *Rudder v. Pataki,* text N.9). Other states might accept the argument that the use of money to offset Dinner's operating deficits violates regulations and thus is an illegal use of taxpayer funding. So Nate might consider suing as a taxpayer in addition to suing in his personal capacity.

§ 11.1.3 Standing under the APA: The Zone of Interest Test

ASSOCIATION OF DATA PROCESSING SERVICE ORGS. (ADPSO) v. CAMP

The Association would have been denied standing under pre-APA law. Under cases like *Tennessee Electric Power,* the members of the Association have no right to be free of unwanted competition. Consequently they don't have standing to challenge government action permitting such competition even if the government action was illegal. Nor would plaintiffs have statutory standing under cases like *Hardin,* since there is no clear statutory support for their action. Therefore, the standing language in the APA, now § 702, definitely changed the law.

APA § 10(a), now § 702, preserves the legal interest (or legal wrong) test discussed in § 11.1.1, if anybody needs to use it ("A person suffering legal wrong because of agency action . . . is entitled to judicial review thereof). *ADPSO* construes the "adversely aggrieved or affected" language in § 10(a) to mean "injury in fact"—the constitutional minimum for standing in a federal court. Both economic and non-economic injuries can meet that standard. The language "within the meaning of a relevant statute" seems to be the basis for the "zone of interest" test.

Notes and Questions

2. *Applying the zone of interests test.* The zone test has ebbed and flowed, and the Court's opinions applying it are generally weak. Siegel's article, cited in text, provides an excellent and critical summary and history. He points out that the cases are in hopeless conflict over three issues (92 Geo.L.J. at 327-37):

a. The source of the zone test— is it APA § 702 or a general prudential standing requirement;

b. Whether plaintiff has to establish congressional intent to benefit it (*NCUA* and *Clarke* say no, *Air Courier* says yes);

c. Whether the "relevant statute" means

> i) the particular provision of the statute plaintiff relies on to show illegality of action (*Air Courier, Bennett v. Spear*),

> ii) or any provision of that statute (*Lujan v. National Wildlife*);

> iii) or any statute that might be helpful in revealing

Siegel presents a menu of policy options for how courts or legislators might deal with the zone test. *Id.* at 350-65. These range from an "intended beneficiary" approach (granting standing only to those who can show congressional intention to benefit their class) to an "open" approach (basically scrapping the zone of interest test altogether). Siegel also evaluates some intermediate standards, such as allowing parties to sue only if their interests are congruent (that is, they systematically parallel) those whom Congress intended to protect (a test that would require different results in both *Air Courier* and *NCUA*); or allowing parties to sue only if this would not disrupt the statutory scheme. In the end, he suggests the "open approach."

Siegel observes that the lower court decisions (as of 2004) are a muddle. *Id.* at 337-41. They haven't improved since that time. For example, compare *TAP Pharmaceuticals v. HHS*, 163 F.3d 199 (4th Cir.1998), and *Amgen, Inc. v. Scully*, 357 F.3d 103 (D.C.Cir.2004). In these cases, pharmaceutical companies challenge actions by Medicare that limit the amount it will pay for particular drugs, making it less likely that plaintiffs' high-cost drugs will be purchased by hospitals. Do the companies have standing? *TAP* said no—they are not in the zone of interests protected by Medicare, since that statute is intended to lower the costs of treatment. *Amgen* says yes—one of the purposes of Medicare is to make sure that beneficiaries have access to new bio-engineered drugs, so the purposes of Medicare are "congruent" with the interests of the drug companies.

The authors of this casebook disagree about the merits of the zone test. Asimow thinks the test makes little sense. In accord with the *ADPSO* dissent, Asimow believes that the zone test embroils courts in a difficult but irrelevant search for hints that the plaintiff is in a protected class. The outcomes seem often to depend on whether a majority of the Court wants to reach the merits. As Siegel points out, *id.* at 347-50, businessmen challenging agency action that allows new competition for established business are always within the zone, but environmentalists and other do-gooders have to establish congressional intent to protect them. In short, Asimow thinks the zone test was tossed off by Douglas in *ADPSO* and *Barlow*, treated summarily in subsequent banking cases, considered "undemanding" in *Clarke*, applied very leniently in *NCUA*, but treated as quite demanding in *Air Courier*. He believes that *NCUA* and *Air Courier* can't be reconciled.

Asimow would scrap the test entirely. It contributes little by way of screening out lawsuits that shouldn't be brought, but contributes a great deal of confusion and delay to an area that is already confusing enough. Let's dispense with these costly hassles over standing, Asimow urges, and get to the merits. Thus he would favor an amendment to the APA that would jettison the zone test. He fought hard and successfully to keep the zone test out of a pending judicial review statutory revision in California (a revision which, sadly, died in committee). He finds it inexplicable that 1981 MSAPA includes a variation of that test.

Levin's view of the zone test is more sympathetic. He would agree that the "arguably within the zone" language of *Data Processing* is awkward. In *Clarke*, however, the Court restated the test in more elegant language (quoted in N.1 of the text) that appears to express what the Court has been trying to say in all of these cases: the zone test denies standing where "the plaintiff's interests are so marginally related to or inconsistent with the purposes implicit in the statute that it cannot reasonably be assumed that Congress intended to permit the suit." That, he thinks, is a more defensible formula.

Levin acknowledges that the banking regulation cases are unsatisfying. He agrees with the dissent in *NCUA* that the Court's holding rested on precious little evidence of congressional concern for the interests of the plaintiffs, but he also agrees with the majority that this case didn't go very far beyond previous opinions in that regard. Behind the obscure language in *NCUA* asserting that there was a "link" between the plaintiffs' interests and the purposes of the statute, the Court seems to be applying a tacit rule that if Congress passes a statute in order to "limit a market" in any way, all competitors who would benefit from such limitation are within the zone of interests. That proposition seems to carry the zone test beyond the limits of its logic, so the dissent was probably right in saying that the plaintiffs in *NCUA* should have flunked the test.

On the other hand, Levin finds *Air Courier* readily distinguishable on its facts from the zone test cases that have ruled in favor of standing. In that case the unions apparently didn't even argue that the PES would support their standing. Rather they argued that separate legislation, the labor-management provisions of the Postal Reorganization Act, showed congressional concern for their interests. The Court decided that the relationship between these two statutes was too attenuated, even though they were codified in close proximity in the U.S. Code. The Court's argument seems legitimate enough, Levin thinks. (Consider one possible extension of the employees' argument: If you want to challenge the Treasury Department's application of a specific provision of the Internal Revenue Code, can you satisfy the zone test by merely showing that some provision in the Code was intended to benefit you—a showing that everybody could make? See *Tax Analysts and Advocates v. Blumenthal*, 566 F.2d 130, 140-41 (D.C.Cir.1977) (no, you have to satisfy the test with reference to the particular tax legislation in question).

Levin does not disagree with Asimow's general attitude that standing rules should be applied leniently. By and large, when there are good reasons to limit judicial review, those reasons militate in favor of foreclosing review across the board, not merely in relation to certain potential challengers. Thus, the doctrine of reviewability generally offers a more appropriate vehicle for rationing judicial review than the doctrine of standing does. Nevertheless, Levin thinks that our legal system will continue to impose some standing restrictions, in order to shield agency actions from disruption at the instigation of intermeddlers; and as between the zone test and the injury in fact test, he much prefers the former.

In the first place, Levin thinks, the zone test is a more rational means of sorting out who deserves judicial review. The theory behind the test is that people whose interests have absolutely nothing to do with the objectives that led Congress to pass the substantive statute are less likely to bring suits that will promote those objectives. Consequently, they have a relatively weak claim on the court's attention. Sure, some of the case law is unpersuasive, but the core idea is a logical one. The constitutional tests show up poorly by comparison: the questions of concrete and redressable injury are not intended, even in theory, to have anything to do with whether the plaintiff's suit would serve to promote the objectives of the substantive legislation.

Second, as to the difficulty of administering the zone test, Levin would again ask: compared with what? With the constitutional tests, which for over three decades have forced litigants to engage in elaborate and exhausting discovery proceedings to iron out complex and imponderable inquiries into imminent harm, causation, and redressability? The zone test doesn't require a lot of affidavits and depositions—it only requires briefing a legal issue, the kind of inquiry that appellate courts are best equipped to handle.

Moreover, although some zone test issues are hard to resolve, a judicial opinion that speaks to the relationship between a litigant's interests and the purposes of the regulatory scheme can have precedential effect. It can settle the issue of that litigant's zone test standing thereafter, or at least can narrow the boundaries of argument among the parties to future cases. Precedent has less force in the administration of the injury in fact test. A court's fact findings on imminence, causation, and redressability concerning a particular agency action are usually not very pertinent to a subsequent appeal, so the parties have to return to square one.

Finally, Levin doubts that the concurrence in *ADPSO* should be read as a strong repudiation of the zone test. To his eye the concurrence endorses practically the same test—but calls it reviewability. Some of Brennan's language suggests a presumption in plaintiffs' favor, but other language suggests that the reviewing court has to make an affirmative finding that Congress intended members of the plaintiff's class to be beneficiaries of the statute—although "slight indicia" of such an intention will do. That would appear to be essentially identical to the zone test. Thus, Levin thinks, the disagreement between Douglas and Brennan is largely a semantic quibble over whether this inquiry should be called reviewability or standing. And on that point, Douglas may well have the edge, because in common usage "reviewability" generally refers to the question of whether an agency action can be examined in court at all, and "standing" refers to the question of who can sue.

3. *Zone of interests in the states.* Section 7 of 1961 MSAPA seems to adopt the old legal interest test for challenges of rules. It provides: "The validity or applicability of a rule may be determined in an action for declaratory judgment in the [District Court of . . . County] if it is alleged that the rule, or its threatened application, interferes with or impairs, or threatens to interfere with or impair, the legal rights or privileges of the plaintiff. . ." Under that provision, the Association in *ADPSO* would probably have lacked standing, because unwanted competition does not impair a legal right or privilege.

1981 MSAPA § 5-106(a)(5) seems to adopt the reasoning of *ADPSO* with respect to injury in fact, since it grants standing to persons "otherwise aggrieved or adversely affected by the agency action." That test in turn means "the agency action has prejudiced or is likely to prejudice that person." MSAPA goes on to embody the zone of interest test, because it requires a plaintiff to show that its interests "are among those the agency was required to consider when it engaged in the agency action challenged. . . ." Washington enacted this provision. At the time this Manual is written, the proposed new MSAPA also contains, as an option, a variation of the zone test based on language in *Clarke*, but its status is in flux.

1981 MSAPA also includes causation and redressability requirements (discussed in § 11.1.2). Plaintiff has to show that "a judgment in favor of that person would substantially eliminate or redress the prejudice to that person caused or likely to be caused by the agency action." It is not clear why the drafters of the MSAPA decided to adhere so closely to U.S. Supreme Court decisions, given their difficulty of application. After all, the states are not bound by Article III.

4. *Third party standing.* For an interesting application of jus tertii, *see Kowalski v. Tesmer*, 543 U.S. 125 (2004), holding that attorneys, whose only relationship with indigent criminal defendants is a prospective attorney-client relationship with as yet unknown clients, lack standing to challenge the practice of refusing to appoint appellate counsel for indigent defendants who plead guilty. There is no hindrance to the clients from

making the same arguments themselves (even though without attorneys).

5. *Standing of agencies.* In *Newport News,* cited in text, the Supreme Court expressed strong disapproval of agencies suing other agencies. The Director of Workers Compensation sought review of a decision of the Benefits Review Board that she believed insufficiently compensated a claimant. The claimant did not appeal.

The Director contended that the BRB decision frustrated her administrative and enforcement responsibilities. The Court observed that Congress could and often does confer standing in this situation, but had failed to do so in this instance. "To acknowledge the general adequacy of such an interest would put the federal courts into the regular business of deciding intra-branch and intra-agency policy disputes— a role that would be most inappropriate."

California generally allows public interest standing. *See* § 11.1.2 N.3. However, in *Carsten,* also cited in text, the California Supreme Court denied standing to a member of an agency to sue that agency over a policy dispute, arguing that it would immobilize agencies if policy disputes among their members were aired in court. However, the decision was 4-3. The dissenters argued that an agency member is particularly well situated to bring public interest litigation, since she is well informed and motivated.

It may be worth rethinking the rule that prevents subordinate agencies from appealing decisions of their superiors. As § 11.1.2 showed, agency decisions that are favorable to regulated parties are difficult to appeal, because ideological plaintiffs often lack standing. Therefore, many agency decisions are wholly insulated from judicial review. Allowing staff members (or sub-agencies) that are more regulation-minded than their superiors to have access to court might be a useful countermeasure against agency capture or regulatory lethargy.

6. *Problem.* In the *Bennett* case, some of Ted's claims were brought under the citizen suit provision of the Endangered Species Act (ESA) discussed in *Defenders of Wildlife,* §11.1.2. The Court held that the zone test does not apply when plaintiff sues under a citizen suit provision rather than the APA, since Congress can abolish the prudential zone test. However, other claims were brought under the APA rather than the ESA citizen suit provision, so the Court had to deal with the zone of interest test.

Ted suffered injury in fact by alleging that he would suffer a cut in his personal allocation of water. However, at the summary judgment or trial stages, he might be required to show that this would really happen; just because the aggregate amount of water would be cut, it doesn't necessarily follow that every farmer's allocation would be cut. Some might have priority. This illustrates the discussion in *Defenders of Wildlife*, § 11.1.2, about the increasing requirements of specificity in establishing injury in fact at the pleading, summary judgment, and trial stages. Also, Ted's showing of imminence might be questionable in light of the very strict treatment of that issue in *Defenders of Wildlife* (which invalidated claims of injury because plaintiffs could not say exactly when they would return to the habitat of the endangered species).

The lower court in *Bennett* held that persons suffering economic harm by reason of a species designation or of measures to protect the species' habitat were not within the zone of interest protected by the ESA, since that statute's overriding purpose was species preservation.

The Supreme Court said this was the wrong approach. The zone test depends not on the overall purpose of the Act but on the *particular provision* of law upon which the plaintiff relies. If read literally, this approach seems consistent with *Air Courier* but not with numerous other zone of interest cases dating back to *APDSO*. It also seems inconsistent with the test in *Clarke* about whether the plaintiff's efforts are "more likely to frustrate than to further" the objectives of the ESA or whether "the plaintiff's interests are so marginally related to or inconsistent with the purposes implicit in the statute that it cannot reasonably be assumed that Congress intended to permit the suit." Under the latter approach, one might easily argue that Ted's interest is inconsistent with the purposes of the ESA.

The Court seems to be making a legitimate point in an overstated way. What it probably meant to say (or should have meant to say) is that a plaintiff can satisfy the zone test by relying *either* on the purposes of a specific provision *or* on the overall purposes of the relevant legislation. So interpreted, the *Bennett* gloss on the zone test makes a certain amount of sense, as discussed below.

Here the narrow provision on which plaintiff relies is that the Secretary must "use the best scientific and commercial data available." Plaintiffs claimed that the Secretary had failed to do this.

> The obvious purpose of the requirement that each agency "use the best scientific and commercial data available" is to insure that the ESA not be implemented haphazardly, on the basis of speculation or surmise. While this no doubt serves to advance the ESA's overall goal of species preservation, we think it readily apparent that another objective (if not indeed the primary one) is to avoid needless economic dislocation produced by agency officials zealously but unintelligently pursuing their environmental objectives.

This problem illustrates that regulatory schemes normally have multiple purposes. Legislators with a wide variety of constituencies have to forge compromises in order to get the statute through Congress; regulated interests as well as beneficiaries have to be accommodated. All sides to the deal should be considered to fall within the zone of interests. This insight harmonizes with the teaching of *APDSO* that persons whose interests are "arguably . . . to be protected or regulated by the statute" have standing.

We don't disagree with the Court's finding that the zone test was satisfied in *Bennett*. The bigger question is whether the game is worth the candle. Why bother with the zone test, engaging in speculation about what interests Congress really cared about and which ones it didn't really care about? See the debate between Asimow and Levin in N.2 above.

To raise this issue in class, one might return to the statutory mandate that the Secretary must base a rule on "the best . . . scientific data available." Suppose the Secretary relied on scientific data published by Irwin, and Judy is a rival scientist whose data was not used. Judy believes her data is indeed the best, and that her career will be impaired because of the Secretary's unfavorable comments about her research studies as compared with Irwin's. These circumstances might show an "injury in fact," at least at the motion to dismiss stage, but obviously Congress wasn't motivated in any way by concern about the reputations of scientists when it passed the ESA.

Judy's situation, therefore, is somewhat like that of the court reporters in Scalia's hypothetical about "on the record" hearings (see N.1 in text). She could never satisfy the zone test, but should it matter? The question of whether Judy would have standing to challenge the rule may allow you to explore the policy arguments bearing on whether injury in fact should be enough for standing.

§ 11.2 TIMING OF JUDICIAL REVIEW

For a good treatment of the way that New York courts confuse the four timing doctrines, see Patrick J. Borchers & David L. Markell, NEW YORK STATE ADMINISTRATIVE PROCEDURE AND PRACTICE § 7.6 to 7.9 (2d ed. 1998).

FEDERAL TRADE COMMISSION v. STANDARD
OIL CO. OF CALIFORNIA

Notes and Questions

Apparently the folks at Standard Oil Co. of California (Socal) hated to be associated in the public's mind with a famous administrative law case. So, soon after the Supreme Court decision came down, they changed the company's name. Now it is known as "Chevron."

1. *Final agency action.* Current finality cases generally rely on the *Bennett v. Spear* two-part definition. 520 U.S. 154, 177-78 (1997). *Bennett* involved issuance of a "Biological Opinion" by the Fish and Wildlife Service advising the Bureau of Reclamation that it could minimize harm to an endangered fish species by maintaining minimum depth in a lake. The Court held this was "final" agency action because 1) it marked the consummation of the Service's decisionmaking and 2) the Opinion altered the legal regime to which the Bureau's action is subject, because it authorized the Bureau to take the endangered species if it complied with the prescribed minimum-depth condition. For a critique of *Bennett's* second prong, see Gwendolyn McKee, "Judicial Review of Agency Guidance Documents: Rethinking the Finality Doctrine," 60 Admin.L.Rev. 371 (2008) (second prong confuses finality with ripeness).

The *Bennett* approach has been followed in other recent cases. Permissions granted by an agency are treated as final action even if it is not certain that the permittee will take advantage of the permission. Cases of this kind also raise standing issues and thus are good for class discussion or exam purposes. For example, *see Oregon Natural Desert Ass'n v. U. S. Forest Service*, 465 F.3d 977, 983 (9th Cir.2006). This case held (by a 2-1 vote) that "annual operating instructions" (AOIs) issued by the Forest Service to holders of national forest grazing permits are "final agency action," because they are the agency's last word (at least for the moment) and because they have a direct and immediate legal and practical effect on the day to day business of the permittees. The AOIs involve periodic adjustments such as changes in the grazing season arising out of changes on the ground such as drought or insect infestations. Disregard of the AOIs could trigger sanctions against permittees; following the AOIs assures the permittees that they will stay out of trouble. Thus "legal consequences will flow" from the instructions, in the language of *Bennett v. Spear*. The dissenting judge argued that the instructions were not final because they had no legal consequences; they were mere resource management tools that implemented the terms of the permits. Otherwise, the dissent feared, every bit of guidance issued by the Forest Service to permittees could be considered reviewable final agency action.

City of Dania Beach v. FAA, 485 F.3d 1181 (D.C.Cir.2007), provides another example. A prior agreement between FAA and County provided that only one of airport's three runways would be in regular use. The FAA then announced that it planned to use all the runways, thus furnishing permission to airlines and air traffic controllers to use the other runways on a regular basis. City (objecting to airport noise) challenged the announcement because of failure to file an environmental impact statement. The court held that the announcement was final agency action under Bennett because it was FAA's last word on the subject and provided "new marching orders" to air traffic controllers. Exactly why these new orders should be treated as "legal" rather than "practical" consequences is unclear, however.

If the Bennett test were applied to the FTC's "reason to believe" determination in Socal, the court would say that the determination was not "the consummation of the agency's decisionmaking process" but instead was "interlocutory" in character. However, the determination might satisfy the second prong of the Bennett test. Although the "reason to believe" determination is not one "by which rights or obligations have been determined," it could be one "from which legal consequences will flow," if Socal's obligation to respond and face an administrative hearing can be regarded as "legal consequences."

2. *Can a non-final order be reviewed along with the final decision?* Of course, Socal (which believes it is the subject of a witchhunt) is unwilling to accept delayed review of the "reason to believe" determination—it wants to abort the proceeding right now. As a practical matter, it's hard to imagine a court that reviews a final FTC cease and desist order (which by definition would find that Socal had violated the law) deciding to reverse that order on the basis that the agency initially had not found that it had "reason to believe" that Socal was committing the violation. Nevertheless, dictum in Socal says that the "reason to believe" determination is reviewable in connection with review of a final cease and desist order. It even states that, if necessary, a reviewing court could order the FTC to take additional evidence on this point if the record is otherwise inadequate.

If a reviewing court were called upon to review the "reason to believe" determination, it might hold that the decision is unreviewable because it is "committed to agency discretion by law" under § 701(a)(2) and Heckler v. Chaney. See § 10.5. Note that the statute requires that the FTC not only find "reason to believe that any . . . corporation . . . is using an unfair method of competition," but also that "it shall appear to the Commission that a proceeding by it in respect thereof would be to the interest of the public . . ." The latter standard reeks with discretion, but the reviewing court could, in theory, separate the two clauses and hold that the former determination is not committed to agency discretion.

In *Socal* the Ninth Circuit held that the determination was committed to agency discretion, but it nevertheless remanded to the District Court to ascertain whether the FTC had in fact made a bona fide reasonable cause determination (as opposed to not having made one but deciding to prosecute anyway for political reasons). The Supreme Court majority did not address that issue. 449 U.S. at 238 nn.7, 13. Concurring in the judgment, Justice Stevens said that there was a strong presumption against finding action committed to agency discretion. *Id.* at 249 n.5.

Socal was decided prior to the Court's holding in *Heckler v. Chaney* (§ 10.5) that prosecutorial decisions are committed to agency discretion. Yet one might argue that *this* particular prosecutorial decision hinged on a legal determination ("reason to believe"). In *Chaney,* the Court suggested that prosecutorial decisions could be reviewed if "the substantive statute has provided guidelines for the agency to follow in exercising its enforcement powers. . . Congress may limit an agency's exercise of enforcement powers if it wishes, either by setting substantive priorities, or by otherwise circumscribing an agency's power to discriminate among issues or cases it will pursue." The *Chaney* opinion seemed to approve *Dunlop v. Bachowski,* which granted limited review to a decision not to prosecute where the statute required prosecution if the agency found "probable cause to believe a violation has occurred."

In material omitted from the text, Justice Stevens argued that the FTC's determination that it had "reason to believe" is not reviewable even at the time of review of the final order, because it is not "agency action." 449 U.S. at 247-49. Under the APA definitions, "agency action includes the whole or a part of an agency . . . order, sanction. . . or the equivalent or denial thereof." APA § 551(13). In turn, "order" means "the whole or a part of a final disposition, whether affirmative, negative, injunctive, or declaratory in form, of an agency in a matter other than rulemaking but including licensing. . ." APA § 551(6). Given that the determination is obviously not "final," as the majority held, that means it isn't an "order" either. Also, note that in *SUWA* (§10.6), the Court emphasized that the various categories of "agency action" all meant "circumscribed, discrete" actions, which sounds like they don't include such preliminary determinations as probable cause determinations. Stevens thought that review of such preliminary determinations, along with the final order, would produce mischief.

The majority opinion in *Socal* disagreed with Stevens on this point. The majority says that the "reason to believe" determination is "agency action" since it will be a "part" of a "final disposition" (that is, part of the final decision on the merits). 449 U.S. at 238 n.7. It quoted legislative history of the APA: "the term [agency action] includes the supporting procedures, findings, conclusions, or statements or reasons or basis for the action or inaction." But that language seems to refer to the various parts of the final disposition, not to preliminary decisions.

3. *When is a non-final order treated as final?* *Socal* indicates that an otherwise non-final order may be treated as final if there is sufficient practical impact on petitioner's business (but litigation costs don't qualify as a sufficient practical burden). The 1981 Model State APA explicitly made an exception to the finality rule for non-final action that imposed irreparable harm disproportionate to the public benefit derived from postponing review. §5-103(2). It is unclear whether this aspect of *Socal* would be followed.

The *Bennett v. Spear* formulation does not overtly invite exceptions to the finality rule on practical grounds or even irreparable harm in the absence of "legal consequences." However, *Bennett* stated its formulation as "a general matter," so perhaps that language allows for exceptions in particularly compelling cases. Whether cases like the DDT cases would be reviewable after *Bennett* remains to be seen. The refusal to suspend DDT registration seems to flunk the first part of the *Bennett* test, because the decision to take no action on the suspension petition is not the "consummation" of the decisionmaking process with respect to DDT. But it is the only decision the agency will make on the short-run availability of DDT, so perhaps it is definitive enough, as discussed below. This decision also arguably meets the second prong ("legal consequences will flow"), since non-suspension allows continued sale of the pesticide. It is a form of agency permission, like *Bennett* and the other cases discussed in Manual N.1.

Socal would be a very weak case for making an exception to finality on practical grounds:

i) Judicial intervention into an ongoing process denies the agency an opportunity to correct its own mistakes and to apply its expertise. (But this argument seems dubious when Socal has, as the Court admits, exhausted its remedy before the FTC on the point in issue).

ii) Intervention leads to piecemeal review, which is inefficient and might be unnecessary (because, as note 11 makes clear, Socal might prevail on the merits—especially if the complaint is really trumped up).

iii) Intervention would delay resolution of the ultimate question of whether the Act was violated.

iv) Every FTC respondent could make the same claim (i.e. that the FTC had no "reason to believe") and harass the FTC with immediate review, thus turning "prosecutor into defendant before adjudication concludes."

It is necessary to weigh the harm from delayed review against these obvious benefits of deferring review. But Socal suffered no irreparable legal or practical harm, only the burden of litigating the case. Absent unusual circumstances, that kind of harm is insufficient. However, if the burden of costs were truly crippling (which, of course, they would not be to a big company like Socal), the cost factor, in conjunction with a showing of irreparable harm or clear error, might push a close case over the line and justify a court in making an exception to the final agency action rule.

In material omitted from the text, *Socal* discussed the "collateral order" doctrine of *Cohen v. Beneficial Loan Co.*, 337 U.S. 541 (1949). *Cohen* granted immediate review of a trial court decision that a plaintiff need not post security for the defendant's litigation expenses. That seems right: a decision on posting security may be dispositive of the case, because most plaintiffs will not proceed if they must post security. Yet the posting issue has nothing to do with the merits. Unlike *Cohen*, however, the "reason to believe" determination in *Socal* does concern the merits and so is not a collateral order. (This issue of collateral-ness arises again when we discuss exhaustion of remedies.) That an issue is collateral is certainly relevant in making a pragmatic analysis of "finality" as well as "exhaustion."

The DDT cases provide a good illustration of review of non-final orders when the effect of deferring review is a serious danger to public health. The court stated that finality is designed to prevent premature judicial intervention in an administrative process before agency action is fully considered and the dispute focused. However, no further action would sharpen the dispute arising from a refusal to suspend in the face of a strong prima facie showing of imminent health hazard. Inaction on the request for suspension is equivalent to a denial of that request, threatens to impose irreparable injury on a massive scale, and thus qualifies as a "final order" under the statute. Of course, the agency had not literally entered an order, final or otherwise, rejecting the plaintiffs' request, but it is treated as if it had, in order to make the controversy immediately reviewable. Note that the court did not order a suspension, which would have reached too far into the agency's domain. Instead, it gave EPA 30 days to either suspend DDT or clearly explain the basis for its refusal so as to permit prompt and effective review. The dissenting opinion in *EDF II* argued that suspension was a matter committed to EPA's discretion and thus not reviewable. It asserted that the majority had gone too far in managing EPA. This provides a good opportunity for a reprise of the commitment to discretion problem.

The question of whether the manufacturer could appeal immediately from an order granting interim suspension is closer, because in this situation the court could not justify intervention by pointing to a perceived danger to public health. In *Nor-Am* the Seventh Circuit refused immediate review of a suspension order, noting that the "primary interests threatened in this case are not public but private. They are interests of property rather than of life or liberty." The court also wanted to avoid interference with ongoing agency proceedings, which should not be "interrupted before issues have been crystalized and narrowed and without affording opportunity for application of technical expertise and informed judgment."

In *EDF II*, however, the D.C. Circuit responded that the threat of economic injury can create finality. The difference between a grant and a denial of suspension could be relevant to the merits of the controversy but not to the availability of judicial review. Moreover, the court said, during the forthcoming cancellation proceedings, the agency would not necessarily revisit the issue of whether the product should remain on the market during the pendency of the case.

Although that last observation sounds like Socal's unsuccessful argument that the FTC would never revisit the "reason to believe" issue, the case for interlocutory judicial review on these facts is stronger than in *Socal*. The interim determination from which the manufacturer seeks relief is not merely a decision that it must incur litigation cost, but a substantive agency action that directly restrains its primary conduct. Immediate judicial review of an EPA order of suspension is the only tool the courts can wield to protect a manufacturer from irreparable injury resulting from a possibly arbitrary or groundless agency decision. The D.C. Circuit's position is supported by a civil procedure analogy: the federal courts take a pretty strict line against interlocutory appeals from district court judgments, but one well-defined exception to the "final judgment" rule is that orders granting or denying a preliminary injunction are reviewable immediately. *See* 28 U.S.C. § 1292(a)(1).

Another example of a final order exception might be a serious procedural infirmity or violation of some clear statutory mandate. A famous example is *Leedom v. Kyne*, 358 U.S. 184 (1958), allowing review of a non-final NLRB order that violated an express statutory prohibition that was intended to protect this particular class of plaintiff.

Judge Leventhal stated that an ongoing proceeding can be interrupted by judicial review only in case of an outright violation of a clear statutory provision or a violation of basic rights from a structural flaw that can be reviewed without involvement with the merits. *Ass'n of Nat'l Advertisers v. FTC*, 627 F.2d 1151, 1156, 1177 (D.C.Cir.1979) (concurring opinion), a case earlier considered (§ 5.5.3). Leventhal thought that immediate review of Pertschuk's refusal to recuse himself drew the court too far into the merits to justify an exception from the final order rule.

4. *Catch 22.* *Franklin* involved actions by one decisionmaker that affected but did not bind actions taken by a second. Similarly, *Dalton v. Specter,* 532 U.S. 462 (1994), refused to review action by the Secretary of Defense and the President under the Base Closing Act. The Secretary recommends which bases to close; the President has discretion to accept or reject the Secretary's report. Once more, the Court held that the Secretary's report was not "final" and the President is not an "agency."

The Court distinguished these cases in *Bennett v. Spear, supra,* text and manual N.1. *Bennett* involved issuance of a Biological Opinion by Agency A to Agency B recommending that B take certain steps to preserve an endangered species. The Court held that the Opinion was final as it authorized B to take action without concern for the penalties that might otherwise apply.

Theoretically one can distinguish the "final order" analysis in *Franklin* and *Dalton* from that in *Bennett* because of the President's absolute discretion to reject the recommendations in the former two cases. But the distinction is thin, because, realistically speaking, the President is very unlikely to exercise that discretion. In *Franklin,* the dissent argued that the President's role in census matters was intended by Congress to be purely ministerial. In *Dalton* if the President rejected the recommendation he had to do so in toto, not base by base. The reality is that the Court apparently wished to avoid review in *Franklin* and *Dalton,* both of which were politically sensitive cases; in *Bennett* the Court seemed anxious to allow review on behalf of a farmer who was protesting a decision that protected an endangered species.

5. *Exhaustion, finality and ripeness.* *Socal* is useful in drawing a distinction between exhaustion and finality. Socal exhausted its remedy on the "reason to believe" issue, because the FTC had ruled definitively that it had reason to believe a violation had occurred. Thus there was no further remedy to exhaust on that issue. Nevertheless, the determination of "reason to believe" was not "final" because it was a preliminary step in the adjudicatory process.

6. *Witchhunts and judicial review.* The problem of witchhunts is real, and there are plenty of examples of politically motivated agency prosecutions (coming from both left and right). The solution, however, is not obvious. How can you tell whether one is occurring? Unless a decision maker foolishly admits political motivation or personal animus, it is hard to distinguish a witchhunt from an appropriate prosecution of someone who is justifiably despised by everyone. It's not likely that *Socal's* precatory footnote 14 will help much.

As *Socal* points out, anyone can claim political motivation, thereby temporarily derailing an administrative process and turning the prosecutor into the defendant. Case law under the finality rule has persistently refused to stop an ongoing process because of potential bias of decision-makers, and this seems like the right result. For the same reasons, and because of concern about judicial review of prosecutorial discretion, one should be dubious about whether courts can or should do much to abort politically motivated prosecutions.

Yet courts are not oblivious to the political tides of the day and should be able to sense a possible witchhunt when the final decision is judicially reviewed. This would be a good time to be a little distrustful of the agency and to demand a greater quantum of evidence under the substantial evidence test than would otherwise be required.

7. *Problem.* This problem provides an opportunity to review the material on issue and claim preclusion in § 4.4.1 (or to cover it now if you skipped it the first time). Issue preclusion (or collateral estoppel if you prefer the traditional term) applies in the administrative arena, although in somewhat weakened form compared to its judicial version. Here it would appear that both sides had ample opportunity to submit evidence in the court case. Assuming the burdens of proof and legal standards are the same in both proceedings, collateral estoppel should apply, thus precluding the administrative case. But does the finality rule prevent immediate judicial review that would stop the administrative proceeding?

Top Choice is similar to the problem except that it involves claim preclusion rather than issue preclusion. The equities are weaker, however, since Top Choice lost on most of the issues below in the first case and is arguing that the issues raised in the second case should have been raised in the first one. The court relied on the lack of finality to dismiss the appeal. Both the first and second cases were administrative hearings.

Top Choice relies on *R.R. Donnelley & Sons v. FTC,* 931 F.2d 430 (7th Cir.1991) which involved a disputed merger. Like the problem, *Donnelley* involved a court case followed by an administrative case. The court applied the final action rule under APA § 704 and dismissed the appeal, although Judge Easterbrook directed some hard words toward the FTC:

> There is very little to be said as a matter of prudence—or of decency—for letting an ALJ inflict millions of dollars in pointless loss without supervision by the Commissioners. . . . We sympathize with Donnelley's frustration at its inability to get the Commissioners' attention, and we regret the high costs of litigation—especially if the outcome is foredoomed. Members of the public lose along with Donnelley if a protracted case raises the costs of its product. But in the long run judges serve best by enforcing the laws on the books,

and not the rules litigants (even judges) wish were there.

The problem seems much like *Socal*—it's an attempt to abort a complaint when first issued. The only harm to Security is the expense and bother of litigation—exactly the harms that didn't impress the Court in *Socal*. Yet courts have made exceptions to the finality rule in cases of qualified immunity and double jeopardy. Both of these doctrines are thwarted if a second trial occurs that should never have occurred, because the defendant was immune or had been placed twice in jeopardy. The whole point of these doctrines is to save the defendant the cost and bother of submitting to a second trial with respect to issues that had been or should have been resolved in an earlier trial. Review of these non-final orders has been available either under an exception to the final agency action rule or under the collateral order rule (see Manual N.3).

However, *Donnelley* held that issue preclusion is not in the same league as qualified immunity or double jeopardy, partly because the latter doctrines are constitutionally based. Issue preclusion is not constitutional and the doctrine is more nuanced, especially in its administrative law incarnation. It depends on whether there was an adequate opportunity to put on evidence in the first case. Sometimes legal errors in the first case or changes in the law permit a second trial despite the issue preclusion principle.

Convalescent Center of Bloomfield v. Dep't of Income Maintenance, 544 A.2d 604, 608 (Conn.1988), contains dictum suggesting that an agency order that an earlier case is not collateral estoppel should be an appealable final order, since it is the civil law analogue to double jeopardy—both involve a right to avoid a second trial on the merits.

Town of Huntington, the New York case cited in text, involved multiple administrative cases claiming that the town had discriminated against an employee. The first hearing was under the civil service law; the city won on all issues, including the issue of whether the discharge was tainted by racial discrimination. The town then sought to abort the second case before the state human rights commission. The court refused to review this non-final order despite claims that the second hearing was barred by collateral estoppel.

In New York, judicial review of non-final orders is considered by means of the writ of prohibition and is subject to historic limitations on that writ. The writ lies only to prevent a body from acting beyond its jurisdiction and only when a clear legal right to relief appears and in the court's discretion the remedy is warranted. The court also considers the gravity of harm to the appellant and whether there is some other remedy. The concept of "jurisdiction" here is foggy, but the court just didn't think the claim for extraordinary relief was strong enough. Patrick J. Borchers & David L. Markell, NEW YORK STATE ADMINISTRATIVE PRACTICE AND PROCEDURE § 7.7 (1995).

§ 11.2.3 Exhaustion of Administrative Remedies

PORTELA-GONZALEZ v. SECRETARY OF THE NAVY

In our second edition, we used *McCarthy v. Madigan* as the lead case in this section, but we changed to *Portela-Gonzalez* because *McCarthy* seemed unrepresentative of federal exhaustion cases. It suggested to students that it is easier to get out of the exhaustion rule than it really is. In addition, *McCarthy* was overruled by *Booth v. Churner* with respect to the need to exhaust prison remedies in a case seeking money damages. *See* N.2 of the text. *Portela-Gonzalez* is a good case for classroom use since it involves a situation students can easily relate to. Some instructors may prefer to use *McCarthy* instead of Portela-Gonzalez.

One notable feature of the *Portela-Gonzalez* opinion is Judge Selya's characteristically hyperactive vocabulary. In case students ask for definitions, we provide a few here (in the order in which they appear in the opinion) in order to save you the trouble of looking them up. From Webster's New Collegiate Dictionary:

Purlieu: "a frequently visited place" or "an outlying or adjacent district." Here it simply seems to mean "situation"
Modicum: "a limited quantity"
Limned: (pronounced to rhyme with "trimmed"): "to outline in clear sharp detail"
Resupinate: "appearing by a twist of the axis to be upside down"
Celeritously: "rapidity of action" (from celerity)
Pavane: "a stately court dance"
Perlustration: (had to go on-line for this one): "The act of viewing all over"

Notes and Questions

1. *Exhaustion of remedies or exhaustion of litigants?* It seems pretty obvious that her supervisors had it in for Ms. Portela-Gonzalez, since her infraction of the rules seemed trivial and borderline. It would seem to call more naturally for some kind of rebuke, or a disciplinary letter in her personnel file, or at most a brief suspension, not discharge of a long-term employee. Perhaps she had enemies in the wrong places, and her superiors had been looking for a long time for a way to get rid of her. Perhaps she had a history of fudging the rules, or perhaps the Exchange was trying to send a message to other employees that the rules would be strictly enforced. In

short, the decision seems pretextual, but it is very difficult for an employee to establish this if the employer jumps through all the hoops. Thus the system of due process hearings does an employee little good in this situation. Had she been allowed to reach the merits, Ms. Portela-Gonzalez could have argued that even if she violated the regulations, the sanction of discharge for this trivial infraction was arbitrary and capricious (in fact the district court apparently rejected this argument). See § 9.3 N.3.

2. *Exceptions to the exhaustion requirement.* To determine whether to excuse a failure to exhaust remedies in a case involving discretionary rather than jurisdictional exhaustion, courts employ a balancing test. Although the various potential exceptions are well established (irreparable harm, inability to grant remedy, futility, etc.), the court is free to mix and match when it evaluates the exhaustion issue. In that evaluation, the strength of the merits of the legal claim that the petitioner seeks to advance is quite relevant. If it seems like a strong claim, the court is more likely to excuse a failure to exhaust. Whether the petitioner is seeking to manipulate the system by avoiding an agency rejection of its legal claim is also a factor. Similarly, courts obviously consider the degree of injury that will befall the party if they delay review (or preclude it entirely by saying that it is too late to exhaust remedies). Finally, the courts consider whether they would get anything useful out of the unexhausted remedy (for example, by clarifying the factual record or taking advantage of agency expertise). *Portela-Gonzalez* seems like a case in which the court would get nothing useful out of the final appeal to the Deputy Secretary of the Navy.

Courts strongly prefer a construction of statute by which exhaustion is not a jurisdictional prerequisite, because, if it isn't, they can apply the exhaustion exceptions in a proper case. In addition to *Avocados, see Munsell v. USDA,* 509 F.3d 572, 579-91 (D.C.Cir.2007) (the language "Notwithstanding any provision of law, a person shall exhaust all administrative appeal procedures" before suing does not make exhaustion a jurisdictional prerequisite).

In case of jurisdictional exhaustion, it is much more difficult to establish an excuse for failing to exhaust. Yet it is possible. In Social Security cases there is a jurisdictional exhaustion requirement, but *Mathews v. Eldridge,* § 2.3, excused exhaustion where the procedural dues process claim was collateral to the merits and also couldn't be reviewed at the time of the final decision.

The policies behind the exhaustion requirement are embodied in the quoted material from *McCarthy* about protecting agency authority and promoting judicial efficiency. On the "agency authority" prong, if petitioners can circumvent agency remedies and get to court quickly, the agency cannot correct its own mistakes, and its processes are disrespected. Indeed, litigants would be encouraged to attempt an end-run around the agency process. On the judicial efficiency prong, courts can avoid reviewing the case altogether if the petitioner prevails by taking advantage of the agency remedy. Even if that doesn't occur, the judicial review function is improved if the courts have the benefit of a full factual exploration and careful consideration of the claim at the agency level.

The various exceptions arise when these basic purposes for exhaustion don't seem to be persuasive in a particular case. For example, the futility exception presupposes that it is virtually certain that the petitioner will lose at the agency level. If the agency is not going to change its mind, there seems little to gain from forcing the petitioner to exhaust a useless remedy.

Subsequent cases under the post-*McCarthy* amendment concerning prisoner claims: Failure to exhaust is an affirmative defense; a prisoner need not plead that he has exhausted remedies. Nor does he have to name every possible defendant in his prison complaint. If he has exhausted remedies with respect to some claims but not others, he can proceed to seek review with respect to the claims on which exhaustion occurred. *Jones v. Bock*, 549 U.S. 199 (2007). If a petitioner failed to exhaust remedies because he missed a short time deadline established by state rules, he cannot seek federal court review even though the remedy is no longer available. *Woodford v. Ngo*, 548 U.S. 81 (2006). For a critique of the prisoner exhaustion cases, particularly the apparent abolition of the futility exception, see Eugene Novikov, Comment, "Stacking the Deck: Futility and the Exhaustion Provision of the Prison Litigation Reform Act," 156 U.Pa.L Rev. 817 (2008).

3. *Exhaustion of remedies and issues of law or jurisdiction.* The law of many states (New Jersey being the most prominent) challenges the federal rule that exhaustion applies to legal and jurisdictional questions. In *Ward v. Keenan*, cited in text, the New Jersey court severely criticized *Myers*. *Ward* construed the New Jersey rule of court that required exhaustion "except where it is manifest that the interests of justice require otherwise." The case held that exhaustion was not required when the jurisdiction of a tribunal was "questioned on persuasive grounds" or when the charges before it were so "palpably defective" that its jurisdiction was merely colorable. Numerous later New Jersey cases have applied the same rules.

However, we believe that the federal rule is right, even in cases where the facts are undisputed or irrelevant to the legal issue. The ultimate decision is likely to be more informed if litigants have first aired the facts, law, and policy at the agency level. Courts do not have a monopoly on wisdom or on skills of jurisdiction-determination. Moreover, "jurisdiction" is a term that is expansive enough to cover many legal questions that arise before the agency; therefore an exception for "jurisdiction" threatens to eat up the exhaustion requirement. Nor is it helpful to waive exhaustion only where jurisdiction is "doubtful." To find out if it is "doubtful," you have to take a hard look at the merits before the agency has. Avoiding this is the purpose of the exhaustion principle.

Agencies should have first crack at issues of law. If a court is to defer to an agency's legal interpretation (whether the court is engaged in strong or weak deference— *see* § 9.2), it needs a high-level agency decision to defer to. If you excuse exhaustion in these cases, you invite the litigants to "sandbag"—meaning that they will manipulate the system to bring the legal question before a court and avoid having to give any deference to the agency's legal interpretation.

4. *Exhaustion of remedies under the APA.* The *Darby* decision seems to make little policy sense. The rationales for exhaustion spelled out in *McCarthy* suggest that Darby should be required to appeal to the Secretary before going to court. *See* Bernard Schwartz, "Administrative Law Cases During 1993," 46 Admin.L.Rev. 307, 317 (1994). This poor result could have been avoided if the Court had chosen to read the last sentence in § 704 to relate only to the final agency action rule, not to exhaustion. After all, the language refers explicitly to finality, not to exhaustion, and the Court in *Darby* recognizes that they are two separate doctrines.

The holding in *Darby* is consistent with the Supreme Court's preference for literalist statutory construction over judicial common law. Here, Congress apparently gave a direct answer to the question before the Court—for, as *Darby* said, "If courts were able to impose additional exhaustion requirements beyond those provided by Congress or the agency, the last sentence of [§ 704] would make no sense." 509 U.S. at 146-47. It was predictable, therefore, that the Court would take Congress at its word, particularly inasmuch as any agency that wanted to require parties to exhaust the agency appeal remedy could readily achieve that result by adopting the appropriate regulation.

If an agency exempts itself from the last sentence of § 704 by adopting a rule requiring exhaustion, as HUD did following its loss in the Supreme Court, *Darby* may be read to make § 704 into a jurisdictional exhaustion requirement. In that case, courts would be precluded from engaging in *McCarthy*-type balancing in APA judicial review cases. *Volvo GM,* cited in text, holds that exhaustion of all agency remedies is mandatory in cases brought under the APA. *Volvo GM* involved Exec. Order 11246, the federal government's scheme prohibiting race or sex discrimination by government contractors. Volvo-GM attempted to circumvent administrative remedies on the ground that OFCCP had delayed for 7 years in filing its complaint. The court held that after *Darby* it lacked power to exercise discretion to excuse exhaustion, for example on the basis of futility or because the claim was brought after a relevant statute of limitations expired.

Darby does contains language that would support the Fourth Circuit's thesis: "Section [704] explicitly requires exhaustion of all intra-agency appeals mandated either by statute or by agency rule." 509 U.S. at 147. However, even if it does so require, this probably does not meet the standard for jurisdictional exhaustion. As the *Avocados* case (N.2) indicates, a statute must be quite explicit to make exhaustion jurisdictional rather than discretionary.

Moreover, this language appears to misread § 704, which does not require exhaustion but merely prohibits the application of normal exhaustion principles unless procedural regulations require an intra-agency appeal. Furthermore, the agency proceedings in *Volvo GM* were not "otherwise final" when the company sought judicial review; in fact they had barely begun. So the concluding sentence of § 704 wasn't really applicable in the first place. Finally, the whole discussion of the court's power to require exhaustion was unnecessary to the decision in *Volvo GM*, because the Fourth Circuit seemed to say that none of the discretionary exceptions to exhaustion would have been applicable even if the court had power to apply them. The court dealt separately with Volvo GM's claim that the administrative delay violated due process; as discussed in N.6, discretionary exhaustion applies to this sort of constitutional claim, and the court declined to exercise its discretion in Volvo GM's favor.

The law on this point is just beginning to develop. *Volvo GM* will surely not be the last word on the subject.

5. *Exhaustion and constitutional issues.* The interface between exhaustion of remedies and constitutional issues is confusing. Much depends on whether we're talking about jurisdictional or discretionary exhaustion; whether it's an on-the-face as opposed to as-applied challenge; and whether there are non-constitutional issues that might moot the constitutional issue. Of course, states that excuse exhaustion for questions of law or jurisdiction (see N. 3) would be more likely to tackle constitutional questions without exhaustion. For an interesting variation on these themes, see *Hettinga v. United States,* 560 F.3d 498 (D.C.Cir.2009), permitting an on-the-face constitutional challenge to a statute that required a particular milk producer to be subject to regulation. The court held that it need not decide whether a statute creating an administrative remedy that would exempt the plaintiff from regulation was jurisdictional. Because the agency lacked power to hold its own statute unconstitutional, and the agency could not grant the relief requested, exhaustion was not required.

8. *Actions under section 1983.* *Patsy* might have been more properly treated as a primary jurisdiction case. Section 1983 is an explicit statutory basis for trial court jurisdiction. A trial under § 1983 isn't judicial review of a prior agency decision, it is the initial decision as to whether state officials denied plaintiff constitutional or statutory rights. Therefore, the case seems to present a primary jurisdiction issue rather than an exhaustion issue. And the rationales for primary jurisdiction seem quite weak in § 1983 cases (it would not really promote uniformity and the agencies have little expertise or technical knowledge). See §11.2.5.

In *Patsy,* two Justices dissented, two more urged Congress to consider the matter and require exhaustion, and a fifth (Justice White) seemed ambivalent. The majority based its holding largely on stare decisis, on the difficulties of judicially designing an exhaustion requirement for the vast array of § 1983 cases, and on rather unpersuasive arguments drawn from apparent congressional approval of the Court's prior no-exhaustion decisions. Thus the decision is not based on a strong policy argument.

If *Patsy* really involves exhaustion rather than primary jurisdiction, it seems to us that it would make sense to require exhaustion of adequate state administrative remedies. Section 1983 actions are a copious source of cases for the highly overburdened federal courts. A requirement that plaintiffs exhaust adequate, timely, non-burdensome state administrative remedies before suing under § 1983 seems fair and reasonable for the usual reasons—plus additional reasons arising from federalism and respect for the states. As the query about complaining to the boss suggests, the *Patsy* rule can produce an absurd result.

Patsy might want to avoid state remedies because of the delay involved, and also because of concern about their res judicata effect. In *University of Tenn. v. Elliott,* 478 U.S. 788 (1986), the Court held that a state proceeding in an employment discrimination case is issue preclusive in a race discrimination case under § 1983 but not under Title VII.

10. *Problem.* i) Request a hearing. Even if Ann's case in court is dismissed because of failure to exhaust, she could still go the hearing route and get judicial review later. But if she fails to ask for a hearing and the date for requesting a hearing passes, she could be precluded from ever seeking judicial review. And if the hearing date comes up while you're waiting for a court date or for the court to decide, absolutely attend the hearing and make your best case, lest you lose both judicial and administrative remedies.

ii) If Ann loses at the hearing, you should appeal the result to the Welfare Board. Under APA § 704, however, *Darby* holds that she does not have to pursue the appeal before going to court unless a regulation makes such appeal mandatory. In this problem, it isn't clear whether the APA is applicable (it just says "federal law applies"); if the APA does apply, you could probably skip the Welfare Board appeal. If federal law applies but not the APA, *Darby* would probably not be followed and exhaustion of the appellate remedy would be required. Regardless, the safest thing to do is to appeal to the Welfare Board.

iii) Will the court enforce the exhaustion rule in this case, given that you're raising questions of law concerning whether receipt of IHSS amounts disqualifies Ann for ATD? You're challenging whether IHSS payments are "compensation"; if so, whether that rule is consistent with state statute; and if so, whether it is constitutional to penalize someone for caring for her own child. Under the New Jersey formulation, these issues can be decided in court without exhausting remedies. Under the federal rule, however, exhaustion is required with respect to legal issues. It is also required with respect to constitutional issues when there are other issues in the case that might enable the court to avoid the constitutional issue. Moreover, this appears to be an as-applied constitutional challenge, as to which exhaustion is required under federal law.

This is a good opportunity to discuss the policy in favor of and against the New Jersey approach. Using the *McCarthy* calculus quoted in *Portela-Gonzalez,* balance the litigant's interest in immediate judicial review against the governments interests in efficiency or administrative autonomy that the exhaustion doctrine is designed to further. Obviously, Ann has a serious irreparable injury argument, given the fact that she desperately needs the money now and exhausting the administrative remedies will entail substantial delays. (This assumes that her payments will stop pending judicial review—but she might be able to get a stay pending review). However, on the other side of the equation, it is necessary to get the agency's legal interpretation in order to grant it appropriate deference. If the court preempts the legal issue, it has no opportunity to grant deference.

iv) Waiver. Assuming the Board has power to waive its normal rules, this case presents a good case for doing so. The money received under IHSS is hardly a typical form of compensation, and it is consistent with Ann's being totally disabled and unable to work in the private sector. Really, it's just another form of welfare, which shouldn't disqualify her from receiving ATD.

Issues involving agency discretion are the ones most suitable for requiring exhaustion of remedies. The difference between reviewing an agency discretionary determination under the arbitrary/capricious standard, and deciding the issue de novo, is huge. Having the court decide this issue now would be a serious incursion on agency autonomy. Acceding to this kind of strategy would strongly encourage litigants to do an end run around the agency in order to get to court first, and would be very burdensome to courts, because it would require a detailed factual trial instead of a decision based on submissions in briefs.

11.2.4 Ripeness

ABBOTT LABORATORIES v. GARDNER

The story of *Abbott Labs* and *Toilet Goods* is told in detail in Ronald M. Levin, "The Story of the *Abbott Labs* Trilogy: The Seeds of the Ripeness Doctrine," in ADMINISTRATIVE LAW STORIES 430 (Peter L. Strauss ed. 2006). Note that there were two *Toilet Goods* cases. The case discussed in the text involved inspection of the facilities of cosmetics manufacturers. The other case, not discussed in the text, involved statutory interpretation. The Act provided that "color additives" could be marketed only with prior approval from the FDA. The issue was whether this term included an entire cosmetics product, such as lipstick, or only the ingredient that actually imparted color.

Levin's account begins with the Kefauver hearings on the drug industry and the resulting legislation on labeling. *Id.* at 432-38. He then turns to the labeling rulemaking proceeding, the doctrinal background of the ripeness controversy, and the lower court decisions. *Id.* at 438-47. Levin then covers the *Toilet Goods* disputes concerning oversight of color additives. *Id.* at 447-59.

Levin's treatment of the Supreme Court's consideration of the three cases, *id.* at 459-67, reveals interesting new information about the cases. Four Justices favored deferral of review in all of the cases (Fortas, Warren, White, Clark), while four Justices favored pre-enforcement review in all of them (Harlan, Stewart, Black, and Douglas). Brennan disqualified himself, because his son worked for one of the law firms involved. Affirmance by an equally divided Court would be unacceptable, because the Second and Third Circuit decisions under review conflicted. Harlan then switched sides on *Toilet Goods* and was assigned the opinion. White later switched sides in *Abbott Labs*, voting for immediate review. Stewart and Black then switched sides and joined Harlan's opinion. Levin points out that Harlan's opinion was based directly on Henry Friendly's pragmatic Second Circuit opinion, which in turn was influenced by Louis Jaffe's work.

Although it lost on the ripeness issues, the FDA was thrilled with the result, because Harlan's opinion stated that the regulations had the force of law. Prior to the decision, the general consensus was that FDA regulations adopted through informal rulemaking under § 701(a) were merely interpretive. To adopt legislative rules, the FDA had assumed it was required to engage in formal rulemaking under § 701(e).

The regulatory aftermath of the *Abbott Labs* case was anticlimactic. The parties settled. In return for plaintiffs' dropping the case, the FDA replaced the "every time" reg with a much narrower requirement. It is still in effect and has not been controversial. The *Toilet Goods* dispute continued, with decisions rejecting the FDA's views on the definition of the term "color additive." Meanwhile, the rules on access to facilities were never challenged and supposedly work smoothly, perhaps vindicating the Court's refusal to hear that challenge. *Id.* at 467-74. Levin concludes with an overview of ripeness law after the trilogy. *Id.* at 474-79.

Notes and Questions

1. *The Abbott Labs equation*. Generally ripeness cases are prudential determinations that review is or is not presently appropriate. In extreme cases the ripeness doctrine has constitutional dimensions; a sufficiently unripe case is a request for an advisory opinion, contrary to the Article III case or controversy requirement. Lack of ripeness reaches constitutional dimensions when injury to plaintiff's legal rights is highly uncertain or speculative. Gene R. Nichol, Jr., "Ripeness and the Constitution," 54 U.Chi.L.Rev. 153 (1987).

The *Abbott Labs* equation requires a balance of several factors. The magnitude of hardship to the plaintiff from delay of review is balanced against the suitability of the issues for immediate review. The suitability issue requires a determination of the extent to which a court would benefit from further delay. Further delay might allow the agency to enforce the rule under consideration, thus clarifying the question of its effects on the plaintiff and, often, its legal status.

Generally, when the petition presents solely legal rather than factual issues, the issues are fit for immediate review. In unusual cases, however, a pragmatic judge might be interested in knowing how the government's interpretation works out in practice. In *Toilet Goods* the Court contemplated just this possibility. One issue was whether the inspection regulation was authorized by a statute empowering the FDA to issue rules "for the efficient enforcement" of the FDC Act. A judicial decision as to whether the regulation was a permissible use of this authority could well turn in part on facts clarifying how often the inspections are conducted, how useful those inspections are to the FDA, and so forth.

On the other hand, a case can be "fit" for review even if it turns on non-legal issues, such as whether the rule in question was supported by the factual record before the agency or whether it is arbitrary and capricious. Because agency action is almost always reviewed on a closed record (*see* § 9.4 N.7), the information base is fixed at the time the agency action is completed, and postponement of review will not bring further data to the court's attention. (Notice how confusingly the *Cement Kiln* case cited in the note handles this point. The court realized that *Abbott Labs* is often described as holding that a rule must be "purely legal" in order to be fit for immediate review, although the Supreme Court opinion doesn't actually say that. But then, instead of acknowledging that this rule of thumb is an overgeneralization, the court reaffirms it and then defines "purely legal" so broadly as to include arbitrariness and procedural issues.)

But again, it's hard to generalize. Information about how a regulation is working out might prove to be pertinent to the issue of whether a rule is arbitrary. A court that wants to await such developments might pronounce the case unripe if immediate review were sought.

As *Abbott* recognizes, ripeness and finality issues are often intertwined. Judicial review under the APA and under most review statutes requires that the agency action in question be "final." Under the *Bennett v. Spear* test, legislative rules are final agency action, since they mark the consummation of the agency's decisionmaking process (and are not tentative or interlocutory). And they are legally binding, so they meet *Bennett's* second prong. As we'll see below, it is more difficult to generalize about finality when discussing non-legislative rules.

Sometimes the question of public interest also enters the balance—the public interest may be served or disserved by immediate review. Often the public and agency may benefit from a prompt court decision clearing away legal doubts about a particular rule or program, but immediate review might lead to significant delays in implementation of vitally needed regulatory programs.

On its face, the analysis in *Toilet Goods* does not look entirely convincing—especially the belittling treatment of the color manufacturers' hardship from deferral of review. The Court suggests that a suspension of certification service following a refusal to allow inspection would not constitute serious hardship. Yet, if destroying labels and printing new ones ranked as hardship for Abbott, a shutdown of manufacturing (as the result of a suspension of certification) would likewise seem to be serious.

But then again, the Court in *Toilet Goods* indicated that, for all it knew, there might not be many inspections, and the FDA might not often make use of its power to suspend certifications. Why not wait and find out? In short, the Court may have heeded Fortas' recommendation of "healthy skepticism" and concluded that the manufacturers' worst-case scenarios were greatly exaggerated (as indeed they were, according to Levin's retrospective account of the impact of the regulation). In addition, as the Court noted, if a shutdown did occur, the manufacturer could apply for injunctive relief at that time.

The court of appeals cases cited at the end of the note are persuasive modern illustrations of how a legislative rule can be unripe for review. The petitioner in *North Am. Aviation* didn't have a pending case, so there was no urgency about its desire to challenge the NTSB's new rules of practice. Similarly, the channel assignment decision in *Mount Wilson* seems to pose no great immediate hardship. Yes, the market value of the incumbent stations might be affected, but they didn't allege that they wanted to sell their stations, so this injury was basically abstract. Furthermore, as the court said, the issue of signal interference should be decided in the context of a specific license award, because the extent of interference could depend on exactly where the new station would be located, how powerful it would be, etc. In contrast, the ex parte contacts issue in *Sangamon* was much more "fit" for immediate review, because it was already clear that the contacts had tainted the FCC's proceedings, and a subsequent licensing decision would not further clarify that issue.

2. *Justice Fortas and predictions of doom.* The note sets forth the arguments on both sides of the debate over pre-enforcement review of (legislative) rules, but on the whole we take Seidenfeld's side. Mashaw is probably correct to predict that if regulated parties did not have the option of direct review, they would in many cases simply decide to comply with a newly issued regulation. Whatever benefits the rule was intended to confer would then reach the public more quickly. But what this reasoning leaves out of the equation is the possibility that the rule may have been unlawful. People who are faced with a new legal requirement deserve a fair and timely opportunity to test its legality, and Mashaw's approach seems to cut too far into that opportunity.

When the legislature enacts a new statute, people who are subject to it will often seek declaratory relief immediately. They can't get it in every case, but they don't have to contend with a presumption *against* immediate review (analogous to what Fortas and Mashaw advocated for administrative rules). *Abbott Labs* basically made the ripeness determination turn on standard declaratory judgment criteria, and we don't think this is excessive.

There is also force to Seidenfeld's argument that the preenforcement stage is really the only time when beneficiaries of regulation can sue to challenge a rule. If courts are going to allow that (a proposition that we think uncontroversial), it would be hard to justify denying the same opportunity to regulated persons. And this also means that if both sides sue, the court can conveniently consider both petitions at the same time.

Levin's historical account highlights the irony of Fortas's warnings about the propensity of counsel for regulated interests to engage in obstruction and exaggeration—he wrote this dissent just two years after his departure from Arnold, Fortas & Porter. (As Levin notes, however, the really curious dissent in these cases was the largely forgotten opinion of Justice Clark. It included such unusual material as a complaint that he had personally purchased a brand name drug for labyrinthitis for $12 when he could have bought the generic for $1.)

3. *Ripeness and guidance documents.* Traditionally, non-legislative rules and other forms of informal agency action were not ripe for review. See *Helco Products v. McNutt*, 137 F.2d 681 (D.C.Cir. 1943), denying review of an advisory letter from FDA asserting that the poppy seeds Helco planned to sell were adulterated.

Although the *Abbott Laboratories* analysis opened the way for *some* review of guidance documents that cause immediate practical harm to persons regulated by them, the matter remains confusing. The leading case allowing review of an interpretive rule is *National Automatic Laundry and Cleaning Council v. Shultz*, 443 F.2d 689 (D.C.Cir.1971). There the D.C. Circuit allowed review of a letter in which the Administrator of the Wage and Hour Division of the Department of Labor had declared that employees at coin-operated laundries were protected by the Fair Labor Standards Act. The court recognized that the threat of judicial review might deter agencies from dispensing advice. This case, however, involved the relatively rare situation of an interpretive ruling signed by the Administrator himself, which indicated more strongly than usual that the decision was authoritative.

There are a number of reasons why guidance documents (a term that includes interpretive rules, policy statements, and other informal agency pronouncements) are less likely to be ripe for review than legislative rules:

a. Since no notice and comment procedure will usually not have been utilized, there may be a less adequate record for review.

b. Guidance documents may receive less careful consideration. They are more likely to be revised or changed. They are usually issued by staff members below the level of agency heads, whereas legislative rules are always issued by the head of the agency or someone who can legally act for the agency.

c. Policy statements by definition are tentative expressions of how the agency might act in subsequent proceedings; regulated parties must have an opportunity to challenge them before the agency. This *may* suggest that they are not final, and it also indicates that a reviewing court might well benefit from finding out how the statement is applied (if at all) in practice. Similarly, the agency might benefit from a deferral of review, so that it can refine guidance documents through subsequent application.

d. Guidance documents are not law. Private parties need not follow them, and thus the rules may produce less hardship than binding rules. Moreover, the lack of binding legal effect suggests a lack of finality.

e. Pre-enforcement review might discourage agencies from adopting some guidance documents, which would be an unfortunate outcome, as the public needs as much guidance from the agency as it can possibly furnish.

These are rough generalizations that will apply more forcefully to some guidance documents than to others. The pragmatic approach of *Abbott Labs* contemplates that the strength of these arguments should be weighed on a case by case basis against the hardship of withholding review. *Aviators* is a good example of a guidance document that was (mostly) ripe for review under the *Abbott* criteria. Sometimes, however, the factors just listed can, in combination, add up to a powerful case in favor of withholding review. An example is the Court's unanimous decision in *Ohio Forestry*, which strikes us as an easy case for lack of ripeness.

At still other times, the arguments for and against review will be more evenly balanced, and the issue of ripeness will be a close call. The 6-3 decision in *National Park Hospitality* may have been such a case. It turned squarely on ripeness. The Court did not question the finality of § 51.3, because it was embedded in a legislative rule, and legislative rules are normally final agency action. (Had § 51.3 stood on its own, however, its finality could have been questioned, as cases in the next note show. Since § 51.3 was not itself a legislative rule, it had no binding legal effect on anyone, only practical effect. If one takes *Bennett v. Spear* seriously, the lack of legal effect might have rendered § 51.3 non-final, even though it appeared to be the agency's last word on the subject.)

The dissents by Breyer and Stevens seem to have the better of the dispute about ripeness. The agency's position about the CDA does influence potential bidders for national park concession contracts. They might decide not to bid at all, or will bid lower, on the grounds that future dispute settlement will be slower and more costly if they can't use the administrative remedy and must litigate in court. Thus § 51.3 has a definite real world consequence and affects private behavior and decisionmaking.

With respect to fitness for review, Stevens' dissent says: "Even if there may be a few marginal cases in which the application of the CDA may depend on unique facts, the regulation's blanket exclusion of concession contracts is either a correct or an incorrect interpretation of the statute. The issue has been fully briefed and argued and, in my judgment, is ripe for decision."

The weak spot in the majority's opinion is that it does not explain clearly why it disagrees with Stevens's assertion. Thomas mentions that the Act might apply differently to some concessionaires than to others, but he doesn't elaborate. That doesn't mean the majority is mistaken. It is certainly *possible* that deferring review would shed further light on the range of problems that can arise under the CDA. Perhaps the majority would then be able to fashion an intermediate position that would differ from the all-or-nothing solutions tendered by the parties. That the dissenters don't see a need for a fuller record doesn't prove otherwise, because different judges often read statutes differently. What you *can* say, however, is that Thomas did not do a good job of explaining to the concessionaires *why* they should have to continue to live with the hardship of uncertainty about the applicability of the CDA, which may be less of a burden than the hardships found in prior cases but surely isn't nonexistent.

The majority thought § 51.3 was a policy statement, whereas Breyer thought it was an interpretive rule, but little seems to turn on the distinction.

4. *Guidance documents and finality.* As the text points out, there are two lines of conflicting authority on how to determine whether non-legislative rules are "final" for purposes of pre-enforcement review. Neither pays much attention to the criterion stressed by *National Automatic Laundry*—whether it was signed by the agency head. *See Appalachian Power Co. v. EPA*, 208 F.3d 1015, 1020 n.10 (D.C.Cir.1999) (guidance document final even though signed by officials of EPA below level of administrator). For a critique of the conflicting case law relating to finality, ripeness, and judicial review of guidance documents, see the McKee article cited in this note.

In *Aviators*, the association launched an attack on the "notice," which seems more like an interpretive rule than a policy statement. It challenged both the procedure by which the notice was adopted (no notice and comment) and its substantive correctness. The First Circuit determined that the notice was final agency action because it did not appear subject to reconsideration. The court then moved on to a ripeness analysis, which was similar to that in *Abbott Labs*. Air taxi companies had to either disregard the notice and face the risk of serious sanctions or follow it and disrupt their business model and incur additional costs by not being able to call pilots during rest periods. Thus finality is not used as a filter. The practical effect of the notice is sufficient. But whether finality can be established by practical effect, as opposed to legal effect, remains a serious issue under *Bennett v. Spear's* definition of finality.

The text omits part of the *Aviators* decision. There was a second variation of the on-call procedure (the "duty to be available"). The company could call a pilot during the rest period and the pilot had to be available by phone, but the pilot was not required to accept the assignment. The notice was unclear about whether it covered the "duty to be available" situation. The court held this issue was not ripe for review. Future developments would provide clarity about whether the FAA believed that the "duty to be available" scenario violated the "rest" rule. This part of the *Aviators* opinion makes it clear that the determination of finality is not co-terminous with the merits of the case. A guidance document can be "final" yet unripe.

In contrast to *Aviators, Center for Auto Safety* and various other cases use finality as a filter to weed out cases of attempted judicial review of guidance documents. For example, in *Cement Kiln Recycling v. Coalition v. EPA*, 493 F.3d 207 (D.C.Cir.2007), the industry leveled a procedural attack on the guidance document in question (which could have been a policy statement or a procedural rule). The court decided finality by merging that issue with the merits. If a policy statement is binding on agency personnel, rather than tentative, it is a legislative rule, not a policy statement. *See* § 6.1.4. All of the language in the document in question indicated that it was tentative, not binding on agency personnel. Therefore it was a policy statement and, by the same token, it was not final because it lacked legal effect. This approach ignores the practical impact of the document and concentrates on whether it has a legal impact.

In *Cement Kiln,* the plaintiffs made no attempt to show that EPA was applying the document in a binding rather than a tentative way. In fact, they could not make such a showing, since the document hadn't yet been applied. If they had attempted to establish the invalidity of the document by proving agency practice, they would have further weakened their case, because those particular issues would not have been fit for immediate review.

Similarly, in *Flue-Cured Tobacco Cooperative Stabilization Corp. v. EPA*, 313 F.3d 852 (4th Cir.2002) the court held that the EPA's report that classified second hand tobacco smoke as a known carcinogen was not final agency action despite its powerful practical effect on third parties. Under the *Bennett v. Spear* test, it had no legal effect (indeed a statute specifically provided that EPA could not give any regulatory effect to the report other than research, development, or information dissemination).

The idea that a guidance document is, by definition, nonfinal for purposes of judicial review seems deeply problematic, particularly in cases involving interpretive rules, which have frequently been found to be ripe for review. It seems to us that cases of this kind should be decided by applying the *Abbott Labs* ripeness criteria, not the less flexible doctrine of finality. Although the practical impact of a document on private persons is relevant both to its readiness for review and to its status as a guidance document (as opposed to a legislative rule), different policies are involved in the two situations. A court could very plausibly decide that the practical impact of a document on private persons is *sufficient* to justify immediate judicial review (because we want to facilitate people's ability to obtain judicial relief from unlawful pronouncements, assuming the issues are "fit" for immediate consideration), yet *insufficient* to cause the document to lose its rulemaking exemption (because we want to encourage agencies to issue guidance documents so that the public will obtain insight into the agency's views).

5. *Judicial stays. See generally* L. Harold Levinson, "Interim Relief in Administrative Procedure," 42 Am.J.Comp.L. (Supp.) 639 (1994). There are relatively few current cases under § 705. The subject of judicial stays of agency action has been subsumed into the law of preliminary injunctions.

In a case handed down after the casebook went to press, the Supreme Court distinguished judicial stays from injunctions and reaffirmed the traditional four-part test for granting a stay (from *Virginia Petroleum Jobbers* discussed in text). *Nken v. Holder*, 129 S.Ct. 1749 (2009). The case involved review of a BIA decision denying Nken's claim for asylum & ordering deportation. Nken sought a stay pending appeal. A statute (IIRIRA, passed in 1996) specifically provided: "Notwithstanding any other provision of law, no court shall enjoin the removal of any alien pursuant to a final order under this section unless the alien shows by clear and convincing evidence that the entry or execution of such order is prohibited as a matter of law." The Court had to decide whether this provision supplanted the usual four-part test for a stay. The Court distinguished injunctions from stays and held that the traditional test continued to apply.

However, the Court seemed to toughen the traditional four-part test. It is the same as the normal standard for granting a preliminary injunction (as distinguished from the special injunction standard stated in IIRIRA). The second factor, dealing with irreparable injury, is not satisfied simply by reason of the fact that the individual will be deported, because the appeal can be continued even after deportation occurs. When the Government is the opposing party, the third and fourth factors merge; "courts must be mindful that the Government's role as the respondent in every removal proceeding does not make the public interest in each individual one negligible. . . ." Instead, "there is always a public interest in prompt execution of removal orders."

Kennedy's concurring opinion (joined by Scalia) emphasized that a "stay of removal is an extraordinary remedy that should not be granted in the ordinary case." An alien "must show both irreparable injury and a likelihood of success on the merits, in addition to establishing that the interests of the parties and the public weigh in his or her favor. . . When considering success on the merits and irreparable harm, courts cannot dispense with the required showing of one simply because there is a strong likelihood of the other." However, this tough language about balancing the factors appears limited to stays of removal in deportation cases, not to other sorts of cases that are on appeal.

In *Cuomo* the issue on appeal was whether NRC had to file a supplementary environmental impact statement to license low power testing, in light of the fact that Suffolk County had not adopted an emergency evacuation plan, thus apparently preventing the issuance of a full-power license. The court remarked that the first two factors in the analysis had an inverse relationship: a high probability of success on the merits suggests that a stay should be granted even if the degree of irreparable injury is low, while a strong showing of irreparable injury would justify a stay even if the probability of success were low. However, the plaintiff in *Cuomo* demonstrated neither a high probability of success nor irreparable injury from low-power testing.

Posner's opinion in *Cronin* addresses the problem of requiring the reviewing court to take a "peek" at the merits to resolve the stay order. Recall Douglas' concern about a similar problem in *Data Processing*—that the "legal interest" version of standing requires a peek at the merits. Posner says that whenever the reviewing court is deciding the case based on a closed record, which it normally does, why not just decide the merits rather than doing so in a half-baked fashion while deciding the stay motion? But this seems unrealistic, given crowded dockets and huge records. Somebody has to decide immediately if the agency decision is going into effect, assuming the agency refused to grant a stay.

Cronin involved the question of whether an EIS had to be filed before trees in a national forest were cut—the classic situation of the stay motion being equivalent to the merits. No stay means the trees are gone, leaving nothing to litigate. If the stay and the merits are separated, there's a strong case for granting the stay—the plaintiff's harm is irreparable, the defendant's loss (delay in getting the money from loggers) is trivial (and can be rectified by making plaintiff post a bond). But if the two issues are not separated, the plaintiff might lose both the stay and the case if its case on the merits is weak. Thus the settlement value of the plaintiff's case is vastly less if the two issues are decided together. If plaintiff can get a stay, that might delay the tree cutting for several years and force the defendant to settle.

It is difficult to say whether a stay should be granted in the *Abbott Labs* situation, assuming the FDA opposed one, unless you have information about the strength of the plaintiff's case on the merits. (In fact, their case on the merits was fairly strong. They had already won in district court. See Levin's account, cited in N.1 of this section of the manual, at 436-37, 445-46,

468.) If you believe that the destruction of labels etc. is a persuasive showing of irreparable harm, you might go along with a stay on the theory that otherwise the damage to plaintiff which justified pre-enforcement review would inevitably occur during the pendency of the appeal. The damage to the public from deferral of the "every time" rule does not seem too severe. Thus it is quite possible a stay would be granted. However, if you agree with Fortas that the plaintiff's claim of harm is vastly overblown, you might refuse a stay.

6. *Problem.* HRS was not adopted with notice and comment, which means that the record will be skimpy, but under *Overton Park,* the record will consist of the agency's file, so it should be possible to bring before the court everything it needs to make a decision.

Obviously, Zolt Chemicals can only attack the policy statement on its face, not as applied in practice, since there is no practice yet. It will not, for example, be able to argue that the policy statement has been applied rigidly rather than tentatively in practice. That means the attack will be based strictly on issues of law. Thus Zolt might be arguing that HRS is a legislative rule that should have been adopted with notice and comment (for example, because its language shows that it is binding on agency staff and won't be reconsidered, regardless of what Zolt might argue after its site is shortlisted). Or it might be arguing that in some way HRS is incompatible with the statutory scheme. Or it might be arguing that it employs a defective methodology.

There are two issues: i) is HRS "final" and, if so, ii) is it ripe for immediate review?

i) On the finality issue, cases like *Aviators* seem concerned only with whether the policy is definitive, not under continued consideration. Notwithstanding *Bennett v. Spear*, the court does not ask whether the policy statement has "legal consequences," but apparently believes the finality requirement is satisfied by practical effect (a determination that resembles the issue of hardship under the first *Abbott* prong). The problem does not say whether the head of EPA signed off on the policy statement, which is a relevant factor under *National Automatic Laundry,* but later cases have not insisted that the document issue from the agency heads.

Cases like *Center for Auto Safety* treat finality as a serious filter in cases seeking review of guidance documents. They merge finality with the procedural merits. If the petitioner can't show that the policy statement is really a legislative rule (because it's binding on the staff), it follows that it is not final. Thus the court would not reach the further issues of whether HRS violates the statute or whether its methodology is arbitrary.

ii) If the petitioner gets by finality, the court must apply the two-prong *Abbott Labs* test. The chances don't look good. The agency has many steps left to take before Zolt has to actually do anything. In that respect, the case resembles *Ohio Forestry*.

Zolt encounters no serious hardship until its site is actually placed on the list—and even then, it is unclear just what sort of cleanup orders will be made. It might be very costly, or not too bad. What is Zolt going to do differently right now? Nothing—just hope that it will luck out somehow on the priority list, or that the cleanup process will not be too expensive. But it is not placed in a serious dilemma as in *Abbott* or *Aviators*. It needs to make no immediate decisions. But then again, it may in fact encounter serious hardship if the uncertainty about a very costly toxic waste cleanup means that it can't borrow money, sell stock, or hire top executives.

The court may rely on *National Park Hospitality* and deprecate the degree of Zolt's hardship resulting from issuance of HRS. One can imagine a quotation from the case, to the effect that it isn't the court's business to reduce legal uncertainty so as to permit more precise pricing of a product.

Similarly, the *Abbott* "fitness" prong poses difficulties for Zolt. The court may well be able to render a more informed decision when it is informed by actual practice, such as the methodology that in fact is used to put Zolt's toxic waste dump high on the cleanup list. Of course, practice is particularly pertinent to the question of whether HRS was validly adopted (if it is applied bindingly in practice it won't be a policy statement).

Nevertheless, if the only issue is whether HRS was legally adopted under the APA, the case is probably ripe for review (although difficult to win in the absence of any information about how HRS will be applied in practice). The court will probably rule that questions of ultra vires and arbitrariness of methodology are not ripe for review now.

In addition, judicial review at this stage might result in protracted delay of agency action in tackling this vital national problem. And that may be Zolt's intention. Public interest should always be weighed as a factor in applying the *Abbott* equation.

In light of this analysis, a stay should not be granted. Balancing the factors discussed in N.5: Even if there is a strong likelihood Zolt will prevail on the merits, the showing of harm from deferral of review is weak. However, the damage to EPA and to the public is substantial. EPA should be permitted to move forward with the necessary research and data collection for HRS pending the litigation. If Zolt ultimately wins on judicial review, the agency would have to make changes in HRS or would have to go through notice and comment; but eventually it will come up with some sort of ranking system, and the research it wants to get started on now will be useful. So let it go ahead with compiling the list.

§ 11.2.5 Primary Jurisdiction

FARMERS INSURANCE EXCHANGE v. SUPERIOR COURT

Notes and Questions

1. *Primary jurisdiction and exclusive jurisdiction.* It's important to spell out the distinctions drawn in this note. If the agency has *exclusive* jurisdiction (as it did for the first issue in *Farmers*), the adjudication in court is precluded. If the court has *exclusive* jurisdiction, as in *SUWA* (text N.1), adjudication by the agency is precluded. But if jurisdiction is *concurrent*, meaning under the applicable statute *both* the court and the agency have trial jurisdiction, then the court must decide whether to apply the primary jurisdiction doctrine (and kick the case to the agency) or refuse to apply that doctrine and keep the case itself. In other words, the court has to decide whether it or the agency should go first.

Differentiate the two kinds of primary jurisdiction: dismissal of an entire case is far more drastic than retaining jurisdiction and staying a case while the agency handles one or more issues. Once a court dismisses the action, it has lost control over the case; it will confront it again (if ever) only when the matter is judicially reviewed. Judicial review proceeds under the constraints of the substantial evidence rule, deference to agency legal interpretations, the arbitrary-capricious rule, etc.—so the ultimate result might be much less favorable to plaintiff than if the court had kept the case. Dismissal also means that the statute of limitations might run on further court action, and it means that the plaintiff cannot make use of judicial remedies.

Farmers involved primary jurisdiction of issues. Because the Insurance Commissioner can't grant the remedy that the People are seeking, the court stays the action under § 17000 until the Commissioner has decided whether Farmers violated the law by failing to offer the good-driver discounts.

In some cases, it might be more efficient to request an agency to file an amicus brief than to stay the case and remand it. See *Distrigas Corp. v. Boston Gas Co.*, 693 F.2d 1113 (1st Cir.1982). This works only if the agency could furnish input without holding a full fledged hearing. Another option (which was discussed in *SUWA*) is that the court might remand a private v. private case to the agency in order to allow the agency to consider the issues and come up with its own position on them, but not actually adjudicate them. These tactics leave the court much more latitude to decide the case while still having the benefit of the agency's views.

2. *Rationale for primary jurisdiction.* Prior to *Farmers*, California courts didn't recognize the difference between exhaustion and primary jurisdiction. But there is a big difference. Courts are supposed to exercise their statutory jurisdiction, not duck cases properly before them. Courts need a persuasive reason to kick the parties out of court and down to the agency. That course of action entails additional expense, delay and complication. In contrast, in *exhaustion* cases, it's presumed that you have to exhaust remedies; it's the exceptional case when you can get to court without exhausting them.

i) *Uniformity*: The doctrine was invented in *Texas & Pacific*, discussed in *Farmers*. The Court dismissed an action for refund of an unreasonable freight charge (despite a statute which protected existing common law judicial remedies) in favor of ICC jurisdiction. The problem was uniformity. District courts might render conflicting decisions concerning the reasonableness of a particular rate, so that shippers in some states would pay more than others.

Today that rationale may be less persuasive, in light of the availability of class actions and other judicial devices to consolidate multi-district litigation. It also may be unpersuasive in state cases, where judicial decisions will presumably have statewide application, although it is easy to imagine disparate decisions from trial courts around the state until the appellate courts can clear up the confusion.

Was there a risk of disuniformity in *Farmers*? Sure. The court might come up with an entirely different approach than the agency, especially because the agency has exclusive jurisdiction over the good driver discount issue under § 1861.02. The unfair business practices approach for getting the case into court and seeking penalties seems like an end run around the Commission's power to handle these cases under § 1861.02. As a result, the decision seems correct.

ii) *Expertise*: As *Farmers* explains, many cases (particularly those involving common carrier issues in the fields of transportation and communication) have been remanded to the agency because the issues involve technical questions of fact uniquely within the expertise and experience of a specialized agency. For example, the reasonableness of the rate charged by a carrier, or the economics of whether a pipeline should be extended to a new customer, is an issue better suited to administrative than judicial consideration.

Farmers explains that the cases on railway tariff construction split. If the issue is like a conventional problem of construing a contract, as in

631

Merchants, the court retains jurisdiction. If the issue seems to require expertise, as in *Western Pacific*, it's remanded. In the latter case, a court couldn't construe the tariff without understanding the possible reasons for the higher rate—the extra costs and dangers of transporting bombs. In *Farmers*, complex problems of insurance ratemaking were involved. The court thought the Commissioner could do a better job of resolving these issues. In fact, that argument seems somewhat strained in *Farmers*. The issue doesn't really seem all that complex.

iii) Immunity: If a statute allows an agency to immunize the conduct in question, it would be wasteful for the court to decide its legality first. This seems to be an important aspect of *Farmers*, because if the Commission decides that Farmers didn't have to provide the discounts in the § 1861.02 case, it would be absurd to penalize the company under § 17000. In effect, the Commission does have immunity power.

The remedy problem is solved through the device of primary jurisdiction over issues. The court sends the case to the Commissioner, who decides whether Farmers violated the law by not providing good driver discounts. If the Commissioner decides Farmers did violate the law, the case returns to court, which assesses the penalties called for by § 17000. But some cases, like *Nader*, have found the lack of an administrative remedy to be a good reason not to send the case to the agency at all. This is similar to a factor often applied in exhaustion of remedy cases like *McCarthy*: the lack of an administrative remedy is a reason not to require exhaustion.

3. *Primary jurisdiction and the administration of justice.* The Attorney General resisted remand of the issues concerning good driver discounts to the Insurance Commissioner, because primary jurisdiction vastly complicates and slows down the case. Additional delay is inevitable (you have to wait for a hearing at the agency, followed by another proceeding in court on the retained issues).

By the time the case wends its way through the Insurance Commissioner's process, what looks like a hot political issue will probably be ancient history. Referral is certain to increase litigation expense; for these reasons, primary jurisdiction favors well-heeled defendants (like AT&T or big insurance companies) over less well-financed plaintiffs (even the Attorney General doesn't have nearly the resources to devote to this case that Farmers has). Which is why the insurance company wanted the case shipped to the Commissioner.

At a more fundamental level, regulatory agencies are more likely to favor the interests of regulated defendants than courts are. The agency deals with regulated companies all the time, and may be more concerned with stability in the industry and solvency of the regulated companies than a trial court, which might be more oriented to consumer protection.

4. *Private rights of action.* A case may present i) a private right of action issue, ii) an exclusive agency jurisdiction issue, and iii) a primary jurisdiction issue. First you must decide whether a court has jurisdiction over the case at all (the private right of action issue). If it does, and if the regulatory statute does not give exclusive jurisdiction to the agency, then you reach the primary jurisdiction issue of which body goes first.

Richard Fallon, et. al. HART AND WECHSLER'S THE FEDERAL COURTS AND THE FEDERAL SYSTEM 775-89 (5th ed.2003) has a good treatment of the private right of action issue. Whether to imply a right of action tends to sharply split the liberal and conservative wings of the Supreme Court, as *Alexander v. Sandoval* illustrates.

In the 1960's, the Court often construed statutes to provide a private right. *See e.g., J. I. Case Co. v. Borak,* cited in the text (implying a private action for violation of SEC's proxy rules). A private right of action supplements agency enforcement of regulatory statutes without consuming agency resources and helps assure compensation for victims. *Cannon v. University of Chicago* (cited in the *Alexander v. Sandoval* discussion) was a fairly typical example of such implication. Justice Powell's dissent in *Cannon* attacked *Cort v. Ash,* arguing that the Court should never imply a right of action when Congress has failed to provide one.

Powell lost the battle but he won the war. Federal courts seldom imply private rights any more, absent some indication in legislative history that one was intended. However, they haven't overruled earlier cases that did imply them. Note that if the inquiry requires resort to legislative history, the insistence by several Justices that legislative history should never be consulted would further restrict courts' ability to imply private rights of action.

An important reason for this change in attitude (aside from philosophical shifts in the makeup of the Court) is concern for the swollen dockets of federal courts. Some of the previously recognized private rights have been prolific litigation breeders, such as Rule 10b-5 of the Securities Exchange Act of 1934. In addition, courts now tend to think that agencies are more competent than courts to enforce complex or vague regulatory statutes. There is also concern that judicial plus administrative enforcement might result in over-enforcement. *See, e.g., California v. Sierra Club,* 451 U.S. 287 (1981) (statutory ban on improvements to navigable waters without approval of Corps of Engineers—no private right of action recognized).

5. *Problem.* First, does Leonard have a common law cause of action?

Campione (cited in the problem) held that casino patrons can maintain common law claims (in that case for discrimination against card-counters), subject to the CCC's primary jurisdiction to interpret its regulations (see below). *Smerling v. Harrah's Entertainment, Inc.*, 912 A.2d 168 (N.J.App. Div.2006), held that patrons can maintain statutory and common law actions for advertising fraud against casinos based on phony vouchers.

However, it is debatable whether the Madison courts would recognize a common law contract or tort claim in Leonard's case. He could seek to rescind the contract (i.e. the various losing bets) with Dusty's on the basis of intoxication. *See* RESTATEMENT OF CONTRACTS 2d § 16, which permits avoidance of a contract where the defendant knows or has reason to know of the plaintiff's intoxication. Avoidance is permitted where the intoxicated party is unable to act in a reasonable manner in relation to the transaction. Prompt action is required to avoid the contract. Note that in contract cases you normally can't get punitive damages. Here the contract theory is probably rescission and restitution—Leonard gets his money back.

The Restatement comment observes that a court is more likely to decree avoidance of the contract where the defendant is the one who plied plaintiff with booze. But it also observes that if the contract is one that a reasonably competent person would have made, the intoxicated party cannot avoid it. That could cover the gambling situation, since sober people make similar bets. Basically, the court would be required to go through a policy-oriented exercise in deciding whether to apply an intoxication defense. It might decide to furnish a contract remedy as a way of deterring casinos from getting people drunk and letting them gamble. The presence of the regulation banning casinos from allowing drunk patrons to gamble could help the court in this determination, in the same way that safety regulations can provide evidence in a tort case of the standard of care.

Leonard might also pursue a tort theory, along the lines of dram shop liability (holding providers of alcohol liable for traffic accidents caused by drunk patrons). That might open the door to punitive damages. In *Hakimoglu v. Trump Taj Mahal Assoc.*, 70 F.3d 291 (3d Cir.1995), the court in a 2-1 decision written by Judge (now Justice) Alito predicted that the New Jersey Supreme Court would not recognize that a casino is liable in tort to a drunk patron. The court stressed the proximate cause issues (drunk gamblers can win and sober gamblers can lose and often will) and proof problems (actions can be brought up to two years after the losses, and how can the casino show that the patron wasn't visibly drunk?). But a dissenting opinion by Judge Becker argued that New Jersey would recognize both the tort and contract causes of action.

If the contract or tort theories don't work, Leonard might argue that the statute plus the regulation give rise to a private right of action.

Although intoxicated gamblers are probably members of the class for whose special benefit the regulation was passed, and it might be consistent with the regulatory scheme to imply a remedy for intoxicated gamblers (two of the *Cort v. Ash* factors), we have no evidence that the legislature contemplated judicial enforcement of CCC regulations. Thus *Alexander v. Sandoval* would indicate that no private right should be implied.

Of course, Madison isn't bound by *Alexander* or similar cases. Still, courts might be cautious before opening up a theory that could cause a huge rash of cases. Moreover, a court would be concerned that judicial enforcement might result in over-enforcement of the regulatory norm. If every drunk gambler (or person who successfully claims he was drunk) could get punitive damages, or even get his money back, wouldn't that threaten the economic viability of the casino industry (on which the state is counting for a lot of tax revenue)? Following earlier cases, *Campione* held that casino patrons had no private right of action for damages implied from CCC regulations.

Assuming there is a judicial remedy (either common-law or implied from the regulation), the next question is whether the statute precludes it by giving the CCC exclusive jurisdiction over this kind of claim. The use of the word "exclusive" in the statute would be evidence of that. *Campione* and *Greate Bay Hotel* hold that the word "exclusive" in the state's gambling regulatory statute is not intended to be preclusive. In *Campione,* the New Jersey Supreme Court held that casino patrons can pursue common law theories in court (in that case, discrimination against card-counters). The primary reason was that the CCC does not provide a money remedy for patrons' complaints. While the CCC can order restitution (but not other forms of compensatory damages), customers lack the ability to initiate an action before the CCC to obtain restitution. Therefore, the legislature did not intend to preclude judicial consideration of patron's claims for money damages.

Campione held that the CCC has primary jurisdiction over the issue of how to interpret its own regulations involving card counting. It indicated that the traditional criteria for primary jurisdiction applied: concern with uniform results and invocation of the special competence of the agency, especially given the pervasiveness of regulation of the casino industry. The court retains jurisdiction until receipt of the agency's views. It was highly unclear whether the counter-measures adopted by the casino against Campione were authorized by the regulations. Thus if the CCC were to rule that the counter-measures were permitted by its regulations (lowering the betting limit for a single patron or prohibiting that patron from playing multiple hands), that would snuff out Campione's discrimination claim in court (assuming the CCC decision survived judicial review). But if the CCC ruled that the the regulations did not authorize the counter-measures, the common-law discrimination suit could proceed.

Campione held that the CCC does not have primary jurisdiction over the claim for damages under common law, given the lack of a clear remedy in the agency. This is similar to the *Nader* case decided by the Supreme Court (holding no primary jurisdiction for FAA in case of common law fraud). In addition, the pragmatic arguments here against primary jurisdiction of the common law claim are that Dusty's has vastly greater resources than Leonard. Therefore, Dusty's welcomes the additional delays and complications inherent in remanding the case to the CCC. Maybe a remand to the Commission will discourage Leonard and make him settle his claim for a low amount. Moreover, there may be reason to suspect that CCC is under the domination of the casino industry and wouldn't be sympathetic to claims like this one. The Director might bury the case, or the CCC might well refuse to grant any relief, perhaps on the theory that Leonard was as responsible for the loss as Dusty's. So one can see why Dusty's would favor primary jurisdiction while private plaintiffs would try to avoid it, and why the court might want to hang onto the case.

In Leonard's case, it does not appear that the CCC has primary jurisdiction over the issue of construing the regulation (thus distinguishing *Campione*). The regulation seems to clearly prohibit the casinos from allowing persons to gamble while intoxicated, so there is no need to remand to consider that issue. The only question is whether to allow a common law tort or contract claim and, if one is allowed, whether Leonard can meet his burden of proof to recover and, if so, the amount of damages to be awarded.